# Your Guide to High-Paying Careers

# Your Guide to High-Paying Careers

LAURENCE SHATKIN, PHD

Meyer & Meyer Media

British Library Cataloguing in Publication Data

A catalogue record for this book is available from the British Library.

Your Guide to High Paying Careers
Maidenhead: Meyer & Meyer Media (UK) Ltd.,
ISBN: 978-1-78255-040-2

© 2014 by Meyer & Meyer Media (UK) ltd.
Aachen, Auckland, Beirut, Budapest, Cairo, Cape Town, Dubai, Hägendorf, Indianapolis,
Singapore, Sydney, Tehran, Wien.

Printed in the United States of America
ISBN: 978-1-78255-040-2

Email: info@m-m-sports.com
www.m-m-sports.com

Dedicated to the memory of Sidney Shatkin, my father, who showed me that the key to good earnings is finding work that demands diverse skills.

**Credits and Acknowledgments:** I am extremely grateful to the economists, data analysts, and editors at the U.S. Department of Labor and the U.S. Census Bureau. These authoritative sources provided the economic information that appears in this book. Other occupational information is derived from the O*NET database, which was developed by researchers and developers under the direction of the U.S. Department of Labor. I used release 18 of the O*NET database, the most recent version available. The U.S. Department of Education developed the taxonomy of college majors and other educational and training programs (the Classification of Instructional Programs) that is used here. We are very fortunate to be living in a nation that makes available such rich sources of information.

# WHY YOU'RE GOING TO LOVE THIS BOOK

This book is aimed at you if you meet this description: **You want to plan for a future career.** You may be a young person planning for a first occupation in your career. You may be in the middle of life and planning for a career shift. You may even be thinking about a retirement job coming at the end of a career.

No matter where you are in your career, you'll want to find work that will satisfy you. And, let's face it, the paycheck is a big part of the satisfaction you expect to get from work. So I'm using this book to get you interested in some **high-paying** occupations. One of these may be just what you're looking for.

The book is crammed with facts from the U.S. Bureau of Labor Statistics (BLS), but I've written the information in an easy-to-read style, and I've organized the book so you can dive right into it:

- You can start by looking at the lists of high-paying occupations in part I, finding some you're curious about, and then browsing the detailed descriptions in part II.

- Or you can start by leafing through part II to find intriguing career options and then see how they stack up against other alternatives using the lists in part I.

Either way, you're bound to find new career ideas. Just be sure to keep an open mind. You'll get inspired!

## How This Book Is Organized

**Introduction.** This overview explains how I selected information for the book and how you can best use this information to plan a rewarding career. *Starts on page ix.*

**Part I: Lists of High-Paying Occupations.** These 46 lists help you look at 173 high-paying occupations from many perspectives. In addition to the basic list of career options with outstanding paychecks, you can see lists of occupations that are growing fast, that suit various personality types, that pay six figures in certain parts of the country, and that have other interesting characteristics. *Starts on page 1.*

**Part II: Descriptions of High-Paying Occupations.** This section is a gold mine of facts about the careers that are included in the part I lists. It covers 173 major occupations and 182 job specializations. For each occupation, read about the earnings, projected growth, work tasks, skills, entry requirements, work environment, and many other details. *Starts on page 139.*

**Appendix: Definitions of Key Terms in the Part II Descriptions.** Here you'll find explanations of some terms used in the job descriptions in part II. *Starts on page 469.*

# TABLE OF CONTENTS

INTRODUCTION — XIII

FINDING HAPPINESS IN A
HIGH-PAYING JOB — XII

HOW I CHOSE THE OCCUPATIONS
FOR THIS BOOK — XV

SOURCES OF THE INFORMATION — XV

THE LISTS IN PART I — XVII

THE INFORMATION IN THE PART II
JOB DESCRIPTIONS — XIX

YOUR NEXT STEPS — XX

## Part I: List of High-Paying Occupations — 1

THE HIGHEST-PAYING OCCUPATIONS — 1

THE 173 HIGHEST-PAYING
OCCUPATIONS — 2

THE 50 HIGH-PAYING OCCUPATIONS
WITH THE FASTEST GROWTH — 13

THE 50 HIGH-PAYING OCCUPATIONS
WITH THE MOST JOB OPENINGS — 16

LISTS OF HIGH-PAYING OCCUPATIONS BASED ON
EDUCATION, TRAINING, AND
EXPERIENCE REQUIRED — 20

LISTS OF HIGH-PAYING OCCUPATIONS
BASED ON THE EARNINGS-PREPARATION
BALANCE — 34

LISTS OF HIGH-PAYING OCCUPATIONS
BASED ON PERSONALITY TYPES — 38

LISTS OF HIGH-PAYING OCCUPATIONS
BASED ON CAREER CLUSTERS — 53

INDUSTRIES FOR EARNING SIX FIGURES — 74

SIX-FIGURE OCCUPATION-
INDUSTRY COMBINATIONS — 75

METROPOLITAN AREAS FOR EARNING
SIX FIGURES — 100

SIX-FIGURE OCCUPATION-METRO
COMBINATIONS — 101

HIGH-PAYING OCCUPATIONS CONCENTRATED
IN URBAN AND RURAL AREAS — 118

HIGH-PAYING OCCUPATIONS
CONCENTRATED IN URBAN AREAS — 119

HIGH-PAYING OCCUPATIONS
CONCENTRATED IN RURAL AREAS — 123

HIGH-PAYING OCCUPATIONS WITH
MANY SELF-EMPLOYED WORKERS — 126

HIGH-PAYING OCCUPATIONS WITH
UNSTABLE EARNINGS — 129

HIGH-PAYING OCCUPATIONS WITH
A FEW SUPERSTARS — 133

## Part II: Descriptions of High-Paying Occupations — 137

ACCOUNTANTS AND AUDITORS — 137

ACTUARIES — 140

ADMINISTRATIVE SERVICES MANAGERS — 141

ADVERTISING AND PROMOTIONS MANAGERS — 143

AEROSPACE ENGINEERS — 145

AGENTS AND BUSINESS MANAGERS OF
ARTISTS, PERFORMERS, AND ATHLETES — 146

AIRLINE PILOTS, COPILOTS, AND
FLIGHT ENGINEERS — 148

ANTHROPOLOGY AND ARCHEOLOGY
TEACHERS, POSTSECONDARY — 149

ARCHITECTS, EXCEPT LANDSCAPE AND
NAVAL — 149

ARCHITECTURAL AND ENGINEERING
MANAGERS — 151

ARCHITECTURE TEACHERS,
POSTSECONDARY — 153

AREA, ETHNIC, AND CULTURAL STUDIES
TEACHERS, POSTSECONDARY — 153

ART DIRECTORS — 153

## Your Guide to High-Paying Careers

ART, DRAMA, AND MUSIC TEACHERS, POSTSECONDARY 155

ATMOSPHERIC, EARTH, MARINE, AND SPACE SCIENCES TEACHERS, POSTSECONDARY 155

AUDIOLOGISTS 155

BIOCHEMISTS AND BIOPHYSICISTS 156

BIOLOGICAL SCIENCE TEACHERS, POSTSECONDARY 158

BIOLOGICAL SCIENTISTS, ALL OTHER 158

BIOMEDICAL ENGINEERS 161

BOILERMAKERS 163

BUDGET ANALYSTS 165

BUSINESS OPERATIONS SPECIALISTS, ALL OTHER 166

BUSINESS TEACHERS, POSTSECONDARY 171

CAPTAINS, MATES, AND PILOTS OF WATER VESSELS 171

CARTOGRAPHERS AND PHOTO-GRAMMETRISTS 174

CHEMICAL ENGINEERS 176

CHEMISTRY TEACHERS, POSTSECONDARY 177

CHEMISTS 177

CHIEF EXECUTIVES 178

CHIROPRACTORS 181

CIVIL ENGINEERS 182

CLAIMS ADJUSTORS, EXAMINERS, AND INVESTIGATORS 184

CLINICAL, COUNSELING, AND SCHOOL PSYCHOLOGISTS 186

COMMERCIAL AND INDUSTRIAL DESIGNERS 189

COMMERCIAL PILOTS 191

COMMUNICATIONS TEACHERS, POSTSECONDARY 192

COMPENSATION AND BENEFITS MANAGERS 192

COMPENSATION, BENEFITS, AND JOB ANALYSIS SPECIALISTS 194

COMPLIANCE OFFICERS 196

COMPUTER AND INFORMATION RESEARCH SCIENTISTS 201

COMPUTER AND INFORMATION SYSTEMS MANAGERS 202

COMPUTER HARDWARE ENGINEERS 203

COMPUTER PROGRAMMERS 205

COMPUTER SCIENCE TEACHERS, POSTSECONDARY 207

COMPUTER SYSTEMS ANALYSTS 207

CONSTRUCTION MANAGERS 209

COST ESTIMATORS 211

CREDIT ANALYSTS 212

CRIMINAL JUSTICE AND LAW ENFORCEMENT TEACHERS, POSTSECONDARY 213

DATABASE ADMINISTRATORS 213

DENTAL HYGIENISTS 215

DENTISTS 216

DETECTIVES AND CRIMINAL INVESTIGATORS 221

DIAGNOSTIC MEDICAL SONOGRAPHERS 225

ECONOMICS TEACHERS, POSTSECONDARY 226

ECONOMISTS 226

EDUCATION ADMINISTRATORS, ALL OTHER 229

EDUCATION ADMINISTRATORS, ELEMENTARY AND SECONDARY SCHOOL 231

EDUCATION ADMINISTRATORS, POSTSECONDARY 234

EDUCATION TEACHERS, POSTSECONDARY 233

ELECTRICAL AND ELECTRONIC ENGINEERING TECHNICIANS 234

ELECTRICAL AND ELECTRONICS REPAIRS, POWERHOUSE, SUBSTATION, AND RELAY 237

ELECTRICAL ENGINEERS 238

ELECTRICAL POWER-LINE INSTALLERS AND REPAIRERS 240

ELECTRONICS ENGINEERS, EXCEPT COMPUTER 241

ELEVATOR INSTALLERS AND REPAIRERS 243

ENGINEERING TEACHERS, POSTSECONDARY 245

ENGINEERING TECHNICIANS, EXCEPT DRAFTERS, ALL OTHER 245

ENGINEERS, ALL OTHER 255

ENVIRONMENTAL ENGINEERS 264

ENVIRONMENTAL SCIENCE TEACHERS, POSTSECONDARY 267

ENVIRONMENTAL SCIENTISTS AND SPECIALISTS, INCLUDING HEALTH 267

FINANCIAL ANALYSTS 270

FINANCIAL EXAMINERS 272

FINANCIAL MANAGERS 274

FINANCIAL SPECIALISTS, ALL OTHER 276

FIRST-LINE SUPERVISORS OF CORRECTIONAL OFFICERS 280

FIRST-LINE SUPERVISORS OF FIRE FIGHTING AND PREVENTION WORKERS 281

FIRST-LINE SUPERVISORS OF MECHANICS, INSTALLERS, AND REPAIRERS 284

FIRST-LINE SUPERVISORS OF NON-RETAIL SALES WORKERS 285

FIRST-LINE SUPERVISORS OF POLICE AND DETECTIVES 286

FOOD SCIENTISTS AND TECHNOLOGISTS 288

FOREIGN LANGUAGE AND LITERATURE TEACHERS, POSTSECONDARY 289

FORESTRY AND CONSERVATION SCIENCE TEACHERS, POSTSECONDARY 289

GENERAL AND OPERATIONS MANAGER 289

GEOGRAPHY TEACHERS, POSTSECONDARY 291

GEOSCIENTISTS, EXCEPT HYDROLOGISTS AND GEOGRAPHERS 291

HEALTH AND SAFETY ENGINEERS, EXCEPT MINING SAFETY ENGINEERS AND INSPECTORS 292

HEALTH DIAGNOSING AND TREATING PRACTITIONERS, ALL OTHER 295

HEALTH SPECIALTIES TEACHERS, POSTSECONDARY 298

HISTORY TEACHERS, POSTSECONDARY 298

HOME ECONOMICS TEACHERS, POSTSECONDARY 298

HUMAN RESOURCES MANAGERS 298

INDUSTRIAL ENGINEERS 300

INDUSTRIAL PRODUCTION MANAGERS 303

INSTRUCTIONAL COORDINATORS 308

INSURANCE UNDERWRITERS 311

JUDGES, MAGISTRATE JUDGES, AND MAGISTRATES 312

LANDSCAPE ARCHITECTS 313

LANGUAGE AND LITERATURE TEACHERS, POSTSECONDARY 315

LAW TEACHERS, POSTSECONDARY 315

LAWYERS 315

LIBRARY SCIENCE TEACHERS, POSTSECONDARY 317

LOAN OFFICERS 317

LOGISTICIANS 318

MANAGEMENT ANALYSTS 321

MANAGERS, ALL OTHER 323

MARKET RESEARCH ANALYSTS AND MARKETING SPECIALISTS 330

MARKETING MANAGERS 332

MATERIALS ENGINEERS 333

MATHEMATICAL SCIENCE TEACHERS, POSTSECONDARY 335

MECHANICAL ENGINEERS 335

MEDICAL AND CLINICAL LABORATORY TECHNOLOGISTS 338

MEDICAL AND HEALTH SERVICES MANAGERS 341

MEDICAL SCIENTISTS, EXCEPT EPIDEMIOLOGISTS 343

MICROBIOLOGISTS 345

MULTIMEDIA ARTISTS AND ANIMATORS 346

NATURAL SCIENCES MANAGERS 348

NETWORK AND COMPUTER SYSTEMS ADMINISTRATORS 351

NUCLEAR ENGINEERS 352

NUCLEAR MEDICINE TECHNOLOGISTS 354

NURSING INSTRUCTORS AND TEACHERS, POSTSECONDARY 355

OCCUPATIONAL HEALTH AND SAFETY SPECIALISTS 355

OCCUPATIONAL THERAPISTS 357

OPERATIONS RESEARCH ANALYSTS 359

OPTOMETRISTS 361

PERSONAL FINANCIAL ADVISORS 362

PETROLEUM ENGINEERS 363

PHARMACISTS 365

PHILOSOPHY AND RELIGION
TEACHERS, POSTSECONDARY 366

PHYSICAL SCIENTISTS, ALL OTHER 366

PHYSICAL THERAPISTS 368

PHYSICIAN ASSISTANTS 369

PHYSICIANS AND SURGEONS 371

PHYSICISTS 379

PHYSICS TEACHERS, POSTSECONDARY 380

PODIATRISTS 380

POLITICAL SCIENCE TEACHERS,
POSTSECONDARY 382

PRODUCERS AND DIRECTORS 382

PSYCHOLOGISTS, ALL OTHER 386

PSYCHOLOGY TEACHERS, POSTSECONDARY 388

PUBLIC RELATIONS AND FUNDRAISING
MANAGERS 388

PURCHASING AGENTS, EXCEPT WHOLESALE,
RETAIL, AND FARM PRODUCTS 390

PURCHASING MANAGERS 391

RADIATION THERAPISTS 393

REAL ESTATE BROKERS 394

RECREATION AND FITNESS STUDIES
TEACHERS, POSTSECONDARY 395

REGISTERED NURSES 395

SALES ENGINEERS 400

SALES MANAGERS 402

SALES REPRESENTATIVES, WHOLESALE AND
MANUFACTURING, TECHNICAL AND
SCIENTIFIC PRODUCTS 404

SECURITIES, COMMODITIES, AND FINANCIAL
SERVICES SALES AGENTS 406

SHIP ENGINEERS 409

SOCIAL AND COMMUNITY SERVICE
MANAGERS 410

SOCIAL SCIENTISTS AND RELATED
WORKERS, ALL OTHER 412

SOCIAL WORK TEACHERS, POSTSECONDARY 413

SOCIOLOGY TEACHERS, POSTSECONDARY 413

SOFTWARE DEVELOPERS, APPLICATIONS 413

SOFTWARE DEVELOPERS, SYSTEMS
SOFTWARE 415

SOIL AND PLANT SCIENTISTS 416

SPECIAL EDUCATION TEACHERS,
SECONDARY SCHOOL 418

SPEECH-LANGUAGE PATHOLOGISTS 419

STATISTICIANS 420

SUPERVISORS OF CONSTRUCTION AND
EXTRACTION WORKERS 424

SURVEYORS 425

TEACHERS, POSTSECONDARY 428

TECHNICAL WRITERS 454

TRAINING AND DEVELOPMENT MANAGERS 455

TRANSPORTATION INSPECTORS 457

TRANSPORTATION, STORAGE, AND
DISTRIBUTION MANAGERS 460

URBAN AND REGIONAL PLANNERS 463

VETERINARIANS 465

ZOOLOGISTS AND WILDLIFE BIOLOGISTS 467

Appendix: Definitions of Key Terms
in the Part II Descriptions 469

SKILLS 469

KNOWLEDGE/COURSES 470

CREDITS 473

# Introduction

This book is designed to help you discover and plan for a high-paying career goal.

If your dream career has always been to perform street theater or to stock the shelves in a big-box store, this is not the book for you. Jobs like that pay little or no money, so you won't find them here. This book focuses on the occupations that pay enough to let you to live with more than the basics. Wouldn't it be nice to be able to afford living in a good neighborhood, vacationing in fine places, and enjoying some of the extras?

Many occupations here require a college or graduate degree, but they pay well enough that you should be able to pay off reasonably sized college loans without making huge sacrifices. Some occupations in this book require less than four years of college but still pay well.

Job opportunities in the U.S. economy have been changing in recent years. Many of the occupations that have plenty of job openings are low-skill, low-paid service jobs. And although the occupations that used to pay well still do pay well, many of those have far fewer job openings than they used to. But I designed this book to help you avoid these two dead ends: low pay and limited opportunities. The occupations included here all pay a national average of at least $56,200, and all are projected to grow over this decade.

## Finding Happiness in a High-Paying Job

You have certainly heard that money can't buy happiness, and it's also true that the best-paying jobs are not carefree. Every day on the job is not payday, so you have to consider other characteristics of the job that are likely to accompany the high pay. As part of the research I did for this book, I looked to see which features of occupations are most closely related to high pay.

I used a statistical procedure called *correlation*. If *a* and *b* are highly correlated, it means that when you find *a*, the odds are strong that you'll also find *b*. I applied this analysis to the O*NET database, which has a wealth of information about 1,000 or so occupations and is maintained for the U.S. Department of Labor. I looked at how the occupations are rated for various features of the day-to-day situations that the work involves. Here are the 15 work context features most highly correlated with high pay for the same occupation:

1. Electronic mail
2. Letters and memos
3. Freedom to make decisions
4. Structured versus unstructured work
5. Duration of typical work week
6. Telephone
7. Impact of decisions on co-workers or company results
8. Level of competition
9. Coordinate or lead others
10. Spend time sitting

11.   Public speaking

12.   Indoors, environmentally controlled

13.   Face-to-face discussions

14.   Responsibility for outcomes and results

15.   Importance of being exact or accurate

Some of these are features you might actually enjoy, like freedom to make decisions (3) or working indoors in a place with heat and air conditioning (12). Maybe you don't mind having to answer lots of e-mail, letters, and phone calls (1, 2, and 6). But how do you feel about working long hours (5) or having lots of competition (8)? Do you think you might feel stressed if a lot were riding on your decisions (7), if you had to shoulder lots of responsibility (14), or if it were important for you to be exact (15)? Are you nervous about public speaking (11)?

Of course, every job has its good points and bad points. And, in truth, the correlations here are not very high. The two highest features have correlations close to 0.5, which means that a high level of e-mail and letters is linked to high-paying jobs only about half of the time. So these work context features, some good and some bad, are present in some high-paying jobs but absent in many others. The tricky part is figuring out *which* occupations have the features (besides good pay) that you really want and which have the drawbacks that bother you the most.

That's one way this book can be helpful: When you read the description of an occupation, you learn a lot more than just what it pays. You also learn the work tasks, work environment, skills used, and other facts that will help you decide whether this job is a good choice for you.

I can't tell you which occupation is right for you, because I don't know whether you enjoy public speaking or fear it; whether you want to be sitting most of the time or be physically active; whether you like telephone calls and face-to-face discussion; or whether you prefer

quiet time to think. These are personal issues that you're going to have to decide for yourself. But with this book, you'll have the important facts about occupations to help you decide which career options are most likely to make you happy.

You'll notice that I give a lot of prominence in this book to projected job growth and job openings. These two factors indicate the employment outlook for the occupation. You may be thinking that these are just two ways of saying the same thing, but there is a difference. Some occupations that are growing very fast are still tiny specializations, like a grain of rice that doubles in size. Even at the end of the decade, they still will have a small workforce that will create few job openings. On the other hand, some very large occupations may be growing very slowly, but because their workforce is so large, many job openings appear regularly from turnover: people who retire, die, or move on. That's why you need to look at both of these outlook figures to judge your job opportunities in an occupation.

Another consideration is how much formal education you'll need to get the job. I calculated the correlation between high pay and the level of education typically required. The correlation score came to 0.7, which means it's much stronger than any of the connections in the previous list of features. In other words, high pay usually means a high level of education. The Department of Labor reports that, on average, people with a bachelor's degree earn 63 percent more weekly than people with only a high school diploma.

Keep in mind that higher education can be expensive, and some college students take out large tuition loans that they struggle to pay off later. Some students fail to graduate and have little to show for their debts. So be prudent about what you commit yourself to. Get some advice from an academic advisor about ways to gauge your chances of achieving the necessary grades in the major you're considering. Ask questions about the college's record of graduation and job placement, especially if it is a for-profit institution. By doing the research, you should be able to find a program that suits your interests and abilities.

On the other hand, not everyone needs to go to college to earn the big bucks. Industrial Production Managers and Gaming Managers, for example, are two high-paying occupations that require only work experience in a related occupation. Again, the facts in this book can help you with your choices: You can find high-paying career options that let you avoid long years of schooling, if that's something that is very important to you. One set of lists in part I focuses on this particular issue.

One more thing to keep in mind is that not everybody in a high-paying occupation earns top wages. For this book, I chose occupations that pay most workers a good salary, but every collection of people includes a few under-achievers. On the other hand, the reverse is also true: Even in low-paying occupations, some people earn decent wages, and in the occupations I include in this book, some people earn spectacular sums. The last list in part I identifies the occupations where this is most achievable.

## How I Chose the Occupations for This Book

I started with 725 occupations for which I could obtain a full set of information from government databases (the BLS and O*NET). Some occupations did not make this cut because they do not have reliable annual salary information (for example, Actors) and others because they lack ratings in the O*NET database. I sorted these occupations by their average annual earnings and eliminated 510 because their salaries were less than $56,200. This figure seemed like a reasonable cutoff point because people above this level are in the *upper one-quarter* of wage-earners.

I did not want to get you interested in occupations that have a bad outlook, so I eliminated 15 occupations that are not projected to grow at all and another 27 that are projected to have an average of fewer than 500 job openings per year. This produced a list of 173 occupations.

I should point out that some of the postsecondary teaching occupations included here may actually have fewer than 500 annual job openings, but there is no way to tell because the Bureau of Labor Statistics (BLS) projects only one figure, 58,610 jobs, for all 36 postsecondary teaching occupations *taken together*. The BLS also reports only one figure for the projected growth of these 36 specializations, 17.4 percent, even though they probably will grow at different rates. I examined their growth patterns over the preceding decade and found that the number of postsecondary Agricultural Sciences Teachers actually shrank, as did the number of Graduate Teaching Assistants. I expect these trends to continue, so these two occupations are among the 15 that I eliminated because of projected lack of growth.

## Sources of the Information

Information about salaries, which is at the heart of this book, is based on the Occupational Employment Statistics (OES) program of the BLS. This program collects survey data from state workforce agencies and covers both full-time and part-time workers. It does not cover self-employed workers or business owners, who can be a significant fraction of some occupations. Wages for the OES survey are straight-time, gross pay, exclusive of premium pay. The wage figures include base rate, cost-of-living allowances, guaranteed pay, hazardous-duty pay, incentive pay, including commissions and production bonuses, and tips. They exclude back pay, jury duty pay, overtime pay, severance pay, shift differentials, nonproduction bonuses, and tuition reimbursements.

When I refer to *average* salary in this book, I'm talking about the *median* salary: half earn more, half earn less. Understand that this figure is useful but does not tell the whole story about earnings in the occupation. The average that I use for the part I lists applies to the nation as a whole, but wages in your area may be higher or lower. Some of the regional factors that can affect salaries are industry clusters (think of Silicon Valley for high tech or Nashville for music), proximity to research universities, presence of natural resources, access to shipping, and amount of unionization. Before you make a decision based on salary, try to find what employers in your area are paying. In part II, I identify the top-paying metropolitan areas for each occupation.

Pay also may differ based on which industry you're working in. For example, Industrial Production Managers who work where computers and electronic products are manufactured earn an average of $100,500 per year, but those working in food manufacturing average only $80,430. Here again, part II can help you, because I identify the best-paying industries for each occupation.

In many occupations, men and women earn different levels of pay. The pay differences are often for unfair reasons, and they have been shrinking, but this is a reality you should be aware of.

The salary figures in the book are estimates for May 2012, the most recent figures available as this book goes to press. The nation is now experiencing only slow inflation, so these figures will remain useful for several years.

In some places, you may notice the salary figure "$187,200+." The highest salary that the BLS reports is $187,200, but workers in a few highly lucrative professions earn more, so this is the only way I could represent those earnings.

For all workers in *all* occupations, the median earnings figure is $34,750. For the 173 occupations in this book, the average annual earnings range from a high of $187,200+ to a low of $56,230. The middle 50 percent of the occupations earn a high of $89,190 and a low of $64,180. The median is $73,660.

In some occupations, most people earn close to the median. Other occupations have a much bigger spread. That's why, in part II, I include figures that show the range of the *middle 50 percent* of the workers. The low end of that range should give you a rough idea of the earnings of workers with less experience, less formal education, or lower skills. And the size of the gap between that low-end figure and the median should help you understand your potential for salary growth as you gain professionalism in the occupation.

To make this even clearer, I also include a phrase and percentage figure I call the *earnings growth potential*. This information helps you understand, for each occupation, whether beginners have a lot of room for wage growth or whether they are unlikely to see much improvement. To determine this potential, I looked at the wage figure that the BLS reports for the 10th percentile of the workforce—in other words, the figure that is exceeded by 90 percent of the workers. This figure is a rough stand-in for a beginner's wages. I subtracted this figure from the median and computed the percentage that this difference represents. To give the number some context, I provide a verbal phrase. For figures lower than 25.0 percent, I use "Very low"; from 25.0 to 31.9 percent, "Low"; from 32.0 to 43.9 percent, "Medium"; from 44.0 to 49.9 percent, "High"; and for 50.0 percent and higher, "Very high."

The figures about projected job growth and job openings are derived from the Employment Projections office of the BLS and apply to the years 2010 to 2020. These projections are the BLS's best estimates of how the labor market will respond to future demands for goods and services. In formulating the projections, the labor economists at the BLS consider demographic trends, changes in the laws, technological advances, changing business practices, and foreign competition, among other factors. The projections are an average over this ten-year period; growth will be slower during recessions and faster during boom years.

If you're unsure what to make of the growth projections in the book, understand that the average growth projected for all occupations is 14.3 percent. For the 173 occupations included here for which I could obtain growth projections, growth ranges from a high of 61.8 percent to a low of 1.9 percent. The middle 50 percent of the occupations have growth projections that range from a high of 22.0 percent to a low of 8.5 percent. The median for the occupations in the book is exactly the same as it is for all occupations: 14.3 percent.

Keep in mind that the figure for the average annual job openings does not tell you how many people will be competing with you for those openings. In some fields, and for many high-paying occupations, the competition can be intense. In the part II job descriptions, I include a brief statement of "Outlook Considerations," and this sometimes mentions the level of competition or what specializations offer the best opportunities. Location usually has a large impact on the level of competition, however, just as it does for salary. Follow my suggestions in the "Your Next Steps" section at the end of this introduction to learn what the job market is like where you live.

## The Lists in Part I

### THE HIGHEST-PAYING OCCUPATIONS

The first list in this section is the basis of all the other lists in this book. It features 173 occupations with high pay and an employment outlook that is fair or better. I explain how I created this list earlier in this introduction.

The other two lists in this section each identify 50 occupations with the best job opportunities, measured in terms of projected workforce growth and job openings.

### LISTS OF HIGH-PAYING OCCUPATIONS BASED ON EDUCATION, TRAINING, AND EXPERIENCE REQUIRED

This set of lists groups the 173 occupations based on how much education, training, and work experience is typically needed for career entry. If you want to pursue a high-paying occupation without spending years of time and tens of thousands of dollars on college classes, you may want to see the career options that are open to people with only on-the-job training or work experience in a related occupation. Or you may look for occupations that require only a couple of years of formal postsecondary education.

### LISTS OF HIGH-PAYING OCCUPATIONS BASED ON THE EARNINGS-PREPARATION BALANCE

Many people want to enter a high-paying career with a minimal investment in education, training, or work experience. I devised a formula for comparing the 173 occupations in terms of their balance between the amount of required preparation and the dollar payoff. Using this formula, I created one list of occupations for which the balance tilts heavily toward earnings and another list of occupations for which the balance tilts heavily toward amount of preparation. As you scan these lists, think about what trade-off between preparation and income works best for you.

### LISTS OF HIGH-PAYING OCCUPATIONS BASED ON PERSONALITY TYPES

These six lists are based on a popular framework for describing personalities in career-related terms. Many people find this framework a useful way to narrow down the career goals they are considering. Read the definitions of the personality types, decide which type or types fit you best, and then look at the high-paying occupations that are considered good matches for those types.

## LISTS OF HIGH-PAYING OCCUPATIONS BASED ON CAREER CLUSTERS

These lists are based on 16 career clusters that many school districts use to categorize their curriculums. If you have been enrolled in a curriculum based on a career cluster, or if you are considering enrolling in one, you probably want to see what high-paying occupations are associated with that cluster. If you are not familiar with the career clustering scheme, you may choose to regard these as the names of major industries in the U.S. economy, and you may scan these lists to see what high-paying occupations are associated with each industry.

## INDUSTRIES FOR EARNING SIX FIGURES

The preceding set of lists is based on clusters that may be regarded as *major* industries (such as one that combines agriculture, food, and natural resources), but this list is based on somewhat more *detailed* industry categories (such as Oil and Gas Extraction). To create this list, I identified the industries where the high-paying occupations earn an average of more than $100,000 per year. Actually, only 61 of the 173 occupations from the basic list made the cut. Some of these occupations earn six figures in only one industry, but many of them bring in the big bucks in multiple industries. This list may give you ideas about specializations that can put you among the highest-earning workers in the high-earning occupations.

## METROPOLITAN AREAS FOR EARNING SIX FIGURES

Sometimes you can boost your pay by moving to a geographic area where the salaries are higher. This list identifies the metropolitan areas where some of the high-paying occupations earn an average of more than $100,000 per year. If you are not tied down to one location, this list may inspire you to investigate other places for starting your career.

## HIGH-PAYING OCCUPATIONS CONCENTRATED IN URBAN AND RURAL AREAS

For some people, geographical preferences are not a matter of east, west, north, or south, but rather urban or rural. If you have a strong preference for one lifestyle or the other, look at the occupations on one of these two lists. They are selected because they have a higher-than-average concentration of workers in either metropolitan or non-metropolitan areas of the country.

## HIGH-PAYING OCCUPATIONS WITH MANY SELF-EMPLOYED WORKERS

Many people dream of being their own boss. If self-employment appeals to you, consider this list of high-paying occupations in which at least 10 percent of the workers are self-employed.

## HIGH-PAYING OCCUPATIONS WITH UNSTABLE EARNINGS

Not all workers can count on a steady, reliable paycheck. In some of the high-paying occupations, earnings have occasionally diminished from one year to the next. In this section, using graphs instead of lists, I show 18 of the high-paying occupations that have seen their average income experience year-to-year declines twice or more over a nine-year period. Despite these dips, these occupations still pay considerably better than the average, so you may not want to write them off.

## HIGH-PAYING OCCUPATIONS WITH A FEW SUPERSTARS

Some occupations offer the chance for a few workers to earn really outstanding sums, but you can't tell which these are by looking at the *average* income figures. I used a little statistical trick to identify 21 of them for you. You'll face a lot of competition to be one of the superstar earners, but it's nice to know which occupations offer this opportunity.

# The Information in the Part II Job Descriptions

The occupations that appear in the part I lists in this book are based on a classification scheme called the Standard Occupational Classification (SOC), which is the taxonomy that the government uses to report wage and outlook information about occupations. The O*NET database, however, recognizes that some of the occupations in the SOC taxonomy are so diverse in terms of skills, interests, work conditions, and other factors that they need to be broken up into specializations. For example, the SOC classification has one occupation named Accountants and Auditors, and the BLS provides salary and outlook information only for this two-part title. The O*NET database, however, has separate information about skills, work tasks, and other issues for Accountants and for Auditors.

I decided that you would want to see the more-detailed O*NET information in cases where it is available, so you will find that some occupational descriptions in part II have subheadings such as "Job Specialization: Accountants" and "Job Specialization: Auditors."

The occupations in part II are ordered alphabetically by their SOC titles. Here are some explanations of the topics that are covered in the job descriptions:

- **Definition:** This brief statement, in bold type, explains the basic function of the occupation or job specialization.

- **Average Annual Earnings:** This is the median, based on the BLS national estimates for May 2012, the most recent figure available.

- **Middle 50 Percent of Earners:** The odds are very small that you'll be earning exactly the median in this occupation, but half of the workers fall within the range bracketed by these two figures.

- **Earnings Growth Potential:** This indicates how much room there is for salary growth in the occupation, as explained earlier in this introduction.

- **Growth:** This is the percentage that the workforce is projected to grow from 2010 to 2020, according to the economists at the BLS.

- **Annual Job Openings:** This is the average number of job openings that are projected for the occupation. The figure includes openings from both occupational growth and employee turnover.

- **Self-Employed:** This is the percentage of workers that the BLS estimates own a small business, work as consultants, or have some other self-employment arrangement.

- **Best-Paying Industries:** This tabulation shows the top-paying industries for the occupation and includes industry-specific figures for both the average earnings and the workforce size. Industries included must employ more than 100 workers and more than 5 percent of the total workforce of the occupation.

- **Best-Paying Metropolitan Areas:** This tabulation shows the top-paying metropolitan areas for the occupation and includes geographically-specific figures for both the average earnings and the workforce size. Metro areas included must employ more than 2 percent of the nationwide workforce of the occupation.

- **Considerations for Job Outlook:** This information explains the major economic forces that are affecting future job opportunities in the occupation. It is derived from the *Occupational Outlook Handbook,* a publication (now Web-based) of the BLS.

- **Major Work Tasks:** These are the most important work tasks identified in the O*NET database. Some entries have been edited to avoid exceeding 2,200 characters.

- **Usual Educational Requirement:** This is the degree or other type of postsecondary educational program that is most commonly required of new entrants to the occupation, according to the BLS.

- **Relevant Educational Programs:** This listing of educational and training programs was created jointly by the BLS and the National Center for Education Statistics. Some entries have been edited to avoid exceeding 1,000 characters.

- **Related Knowledge/Courses:** This list itemizes and orders the most important areas of knowledge that are used on the job. Often these are similar or identical to the names of courses that are taken as preparation for the career. For every occupation, I identified the highest-rated field of knowledge in the O*NET database, so every occupation has at least one knowledge listed. I also listed all fields of knowledge that were rated higher than the average rating for all occupations. All of the knowledge/courses are defined in the appendix.

- **Work Experience Needed** and **On-the-Job Training Needed:** These ratings are derived from the BLS and indicate what level of preparation is most commonly required.

- **Certification/Licensure:** This entry indicates what kind(s) of formal certification or government licensure is normally required or is an option that many workers pursue. The information is derived from the BLS and is national in scope. Understand that there are local exceptions, so be sure to investigate the requirements or expectations of your community.

- **Personality Types:** This information is based on ratings in the O*NET database and describes the occupation in terms of the six personality types developed by John Holland.

- **Key Career Cluster** and **Key Career Pathway:** These entries connect the occupation to a career cluster and pathway, based on a crosswalk developed by the Center for Technical Education. I simplified the crosswalk by narrowing it down to one connection per occupation.

- **Skills:** This list itemizes and orders the most important skills that are used on the job. Using ratings from the O*NET database, I ordered the occupations by how much their rating (for level required on the job) exceeds the average rating for all occupations. All of the skill names are defined in the appendix.

- **Physical Environment:** This list includes any feature of the physical work environment that is rated higher than the midpoint of the scale in the O*NET database. The order does not indicate the importance on the job. If there are hazards present, workers are given protective equipment and training in safety procedures.

- **Structural Environment:** These features from the O*NET database indicate some of the performance expectations that workers need to meet. Some of these features may be stressful, but consider that high-paying jobs generally are demanding. Like the skills, these are ordered by how much their rating exceeds the average rating for all occupations.

## Your Next Steps

I don't expect you to make a final decision about your career plans right after you put down this book. Even with all the facts that I put into it, this book is just the first step toward a careful career decision. When you have identified an occupation that you think might be a good choice, take the following steps:

1. Investigate what the occupation is like from the inside.
   - Visit a place where the work goes on. Find out what it looks like, sounds like, and smells like.
   - Talk to people at work. Ask what a good day is like, what a bad day is like. Ask what job opportunities will be like in this field. Ask how the work is likely to change.
   - Talk to people who do hiring. Explain that you're not looking for a job now, but you want to know what they look for in new employees. Ask what skills the field will need a few years from now.
2. Investigate your options for getting the education, training, or work experience you'll need for entry.
   - Again, talk to people in the occupation. Ask them how they got started and what they would recommend to a newcomer.
   - Also talk to people who are currently preparing for entry. Ask why they chose the entry route they did and what they find to be the hardest part of the process.
   - Finally, if there is an educational institution involved, talk to admissions staff, but understand that they are probably trying to recruit you. Use your critical thinking in evaluating what you hear. Compare it to what the workers and current students have told you.
3. Get feedback.
   - Talk to people who know you well: family, friends, former teachers, co-workers. Ask whether your plans sound realistic. Again, use your critical thinking. Although they wish you well, they may have their own agendas.
   - Try to get family and friends to buy into your plans. Their support can help when the going gets rough.

You may want to formulate a "plan B" that can be an option if you don't reach your intended goal. Ideally, it might be a career path that can salvage some of the effort that you put into your main goal. Most important of all, always think of your career plan as a work in progress. Be ready to modify it in response to unforeseen opportunities.

# PART I

# Lists of High-Paying Occupations

Everybody loves lists: They are easy to read and allow you to make comparisons readily. I designed the lists in this section so that you can easily browse them and compare occupations on many different criteria. The lists have self-explanatory titles, and I provide brief introductions to help you understand how I put each list together. Use these lists to get ideas for occupations that you might want to explore in greater depth in part II.

I have ordered the occupations on the lists so that the occupations closest to the top have the most of some feature, but none of the career options here are "losers." *Every* occupation in this book has high earnings, plus an outlook that is at least reasonably good. Even an occupation that appears low on a list may have some features that appeal to you. Occupations on the lists often have similar amounts of income, projected growth, or job openings. When two or more occupations are exactly tied on a criterion (for example, two with the same earnings), I list them in alphabetical order. Even a difference of four or five positions on a list is not very significant. Keep an open mind as you browse the lists and don't rule out a career option just because it's not familiar to you. Instead, read the description in part II; it may be just what you're looking for.

All the lists in part I are based on the 173 high-paying occupations in the first list. (The introduction to this book explains how I created that list.) Because the BLS does not provide data on the outlook for the 33 specialized postsecondary teaching occupations, I was unable to include these occupations in the two lists that are based on employment outlook. In lists where these occupations appear, you will find a dash (–) instead of a number for their projected job growth and job openings. Understand that their *average* projected growth, taken as a group, is 17.4 percent, and each specialization will offer some fraction of the 58,610 job openings that the entire group will provide each year.

Now, dive in and see what new career ideas you'll get.

## The Highest-Paying Occupations

If high pay matters a lot to you, the lists in this section are good places to begin your browsing. The first one is the master list for this whole book and is based on average earnings. The two lists that follow focus on other important rewards: job growth and job openings.

These economic facts are not the only rewards and features that you should consider when making a career choice. But they are very popular. Everybody expects to get paid—the more, the better. And job growth and job openings matter because to enjoy the other rewards of work (such as creativity, prestige, and variety), you must get hired. Finally, these economic rewards are factors for which good-quality information is available, thanks to the BLS. If you wanted to choose occupations where people have, for example, the best sense of humor, I would not be able to create a list to help you decide.

**Your Guide to High-Paying Careers**

## THE 173 HIGHEST-PAYING OCCUPATIONS

This first list is ordered on the basis of the average (median) earnings for the occupations. Remember that the earnings figures here are national averages. In each occupation, many people earn more or less than this average.

| The 173 Highest-Paying Occupations | | | |
|---|---|---|---|
| Title | Annual Earnings | Percent Growth | Annual Openings |
| 1. Physicians and Surgeons | $187,200+ | 24.4% | 30,510 |
| 2. Chief Executives | $168,140 | 4.2% | 11,150 |
| 3. Dentists | $149,310 | 20.7% | 6,640 |
| 4. Petroleum Engineers | $130,280 | 17.0% | 1,180 |
| 5. Architectural and Engineering Managers | $124,870 | 8.6% | 4,970 |
| 6. Computer and Information Systems Managers | $120,950 | 18.1% | 10,280 |
| 7. Marketing Managers | $119,480 | 13.6% | 7,600 |
| 8. Pharmacists | $116,670 | 25.4% | 13,960 |
| 9. Podiatrists | $116,440 | 20.0% | 510 |
| 10. Judges, Magistrate Judges, and Magistrates | $115,760 | 9.2% | 960 |
| 11. Natural Sciences Managers | $115,730 | 7.7% | 3,350 |
| 12. Airline Pilots, Copilots, and Flight Engineers | $114,200 | 6.4% | 3,130 |
| 13. Lawyers | $113,530 | 10.1% | 21,200 |
| 14. Financial Managers | $109,740 | 8.8% | 14,280 |

| The 173 Highest-Paying Occupations | | | |
|---|---|---|---|
| **Title** | **Annual Earnings** | **Percent Growth** | **Annual Openings** |
| 15. Physicists | $106,840 | 14.2% | 800 |
| 16. Sales Managers | $105,260 | 11.7% | 13,970 |
| 17. Nuclear Engineers | $104,270 | 10.2% | 620 |
| 18. Aerospace Engineers | $103,720 | 4.9% | 2,180 |
| 19. Computer and Information Research Scientists | $102,190 | 18.7% | 1,060 |
| 20. Computer Hardware Engineers | $100,920 | 9.0% | 2,290 |
| 21. Managers, All Other | $100,890 | 7.9% | 24,940 |
| 22. Purchasing Managers | $100,170 | 7.2% | 2,560 |
| 23. Law Teachers, Postsecondary | $99,950 | — | — |
| 24. Human Resources Managers | $99,720 | 12.9% | 2,690 |
| 25. Software Developers, Systems Software | $99,000 | 32.4% | 16,800 |
| 26. Optometrists | $97,820 | 33.1% | 2,340 |
| 27. Public Relations and Fundraising Managers | $95,450 | 16.4% | 2,790 |
| 28. General and Operations Managers | $95,440 | 4.6% | 41,010 |
| 29. Training and Development Managers | $95,400 | 14.6% | 1,160 |
| 30. Compensation and Benefits Managers | $95,250 | 2.8% | 870 |
| 31. Chemical Engineers | $94,350 | 5.9% | 1,140 |
| 32. Actuaries | $93,680 | 26.7% | 1,890 |

3

## The 173 Highest-Paying Occupations

| Title | Annual Earnings | Percent Growth | Annual Openings |
|---|---|---|---|
| 33. Engineering Teachers, Postsecondary | $92,670 | — | — |
| 34. Engineers, All Other | $92,030 | 6.6% | 4,480 |
| 35. Economists | $91,860 | 6.1% | 580 |
| 36. Sales Engineers | $91,830 | 14.4% | 3,210 |
| 37. Electronics Engineers, Except Computer | $91,820 | 4.9% | 4,060 |
| 38. Physical Scientists, All Other | $91,640 | 8.5% | 1,330 |
| 39. Physician Assistants | $90,930 | 29.5% | 4,060 |
| 40. Geoscientists Except Hydrologists and Geographers | $90,890 | 21.2% | 1,710 |
| 41. Software Developers, Applications | $90,060 | 27.6% | 19,790 |
| 42. Psychologists, All Other | $90,020 | 18.2% | 870 |
| 43. Industrial Production Managers | $89,190 | 9.1% | 4,900 |
| 44. Advertising and Promotions Managers | $88,590 | 13.3% | 1,620 |
| 45. Medical and Health Services Managers | $88,580 | 22.4% | 14,190 |
| 46. Economics Teachers, Postsecondary | $87,950 | — | — |
| 47. Electrical Engineers | $87,920 | 7.0% | 4,780 |
| 48. Education Administrators, Elementary and Secondary School | $87,760 | 9.8% | 8,970 |
| 49. Biomedical Engineers | $86,960 | 61.7% | 1,310 |
| 50. Education Administrators, Postsecondary | $86,490 | 19.0% | 6,910 |

4

| The 173 Highest-Paying Occupations | | | |
|---|---|---|---|
| Title | Annual Earnings | Percent Growth | Annual Openings |
| 51. Materials Engineers | $85,150 | 8.7% | 810 |
| 52. Veterinarians | $84,460 | 35.9% | 3,420 |
| 53. Construction Managers | $82,790 | 16.6% | 12,040 |
| 54. Atmospheric, Earth, Marine, and Space Sciences Teachers, Postsecondary | $82,180 | — | — |
| 55. Forestry and Conservation Science Teachers, Postsecondary | $81,930 | — | — |
| 56. Transportation, Storage, and Distribution Managers | $81,830 | 10.0% | 3,370 |
| 57. Biochemists and Biophysicists | $81,480 | 30.8% | 1,340 |
| 58. Health Specialties Teachers, Postsecondary | $81,140 | — | — |
| 59. Administrative Services Managers | $81,080 | 14.5% | 9,980 |
| 60. Environmental Engineers | $80,890 | 21.9% | 2,260 |
| 61. Art Directors | $80,880 | 9.0% | 2,430 |
| 62. Mechanical Engineers | $80,580 | 8.8% | 9,960 |
| 63. Physical Therapists | $79,860 | 39.0% | 10,060 |
| 64. Computer Systems Analysts | $79,680 | 22.1% | 22,250 |
| 65. Civil Engineers | $79,340 | 19.4% | 10,440 |
| 66. Industrial Engineers | $78,860 | 6.4% | 5,750 |
| 67. Management Analysts | $78,600 | 21.9% | 27,430 |

5

| The 173 Highest-Paying Occupations | | | |
| --- | --- | --- | --- |
| **Title** | **Annual Earnings** | **Percent Growth** | **Annual Openings** |
| 68. Physics Teachers, Postsecondary | $78,540 | — | — |
| 69. First-Line Supervisors of Police and Detectives | $78,270 | 2.1% | 3,870 |
| 70. Radiation Therapists | $77,560 | 20.3% | 670 |
| 71. Environmental Science Teachers, Postsecondary | $77,320 | — | — |
| 72. Database Administrators | $77,080 | 30.6% | 5,270 |
| 73. Medical Scientists, Except Epidemiologists | $76,980 | 36.4% | 4,260 |
| 74. Financial Analysts | $76,950 | 23.0% | 10,420 |
| 75. Education Administrators, All Other | $76,860 | 13.6% | 1,360 |
| 76. Health and Safety Engineers, Except Mining Safety Engineers and Inspectors | $76,830 | 13.1% | 820 |
| 77. Elevator Installers and Repairers | $76,650 | 11.3% | 820 |
| 78. Social Scientists and Related Workers, All Other | $76,540 | 8.1% | 1,760 |
| 79. Anthropology and Archeology Teachers, Postsecondary | $76,020 | — | — |
| 80. Financial Examiners | $75,800 | 27.0% | 1,410 |
| 81. Statisticians | $75,560 | 14.1% | 1,870 |
| 82. Occupational Therapists | $75,400 | 33.5% | 5,710 |
| 83. Sales Representatives, Wholesale and Manufacturing, Technical and Scientific Products | $74,970 | 16.4% | 15,970 |

## The 173 Highest-Paying Occupations

| Title | Annual Earnings | Percent Growth | Annual Openings |
|---|---|---|---|
| 84. Detectives and Criminal Investigators | $74,300 | 2.9% | 3,010 |
| 85. Computer Programmers | $74,280 | 12.0% | 12,800 |
| 86. Biological Science Teachers, Postsecondary | $74,180 | — | — |
| 87. Business Teachers, Postsecondary | $73,660 | — | — |
| 88. Commercial Pilots | $73,280 | 21.2% | 1,930 |
| 89. Architects, Except Landscape and Naval | $73,090 | 24.5% | 5,090 |
| 90. Logisticians | $72,780 | 25.5% | 4,870 |
| 91. Health Diagnosing and Treating Practitioners, All Other | $72,710 | 19.0% | 2,120 |
| 92. Biological Scientists, All Other | $72,700 | 6.3% | 1,030 |
| 93. Network and Computer Systems Administrators | $72,560 | 27.8% | 15,530 |
| 94. Computer Science Teachers, Postsecondary | $72,200 | — | — |
| 95. Political Science Teachers, Postsecondary | $72,170 | — | — |
| 96. Operations Research Analysts | $72,100 | 14.6% | 3,000 |
| 97. Chemists | $71,770 | 3.8% | 2,990 |
| 98. Securities, Commodities, and Financial Services Sales Agents | $71,720 | 15.2% | 13,370 |
| 99. Architecture Teachers, Postsecondary | $71,610 | — | — |

| The 173 Highest-Paying Occupations | | | |
|---|---|---|---|
| Title | Annual Earnings | Percent Growth | Annual Openings |
| 100. Producers and Directors | $71,350 | 11.0% | 4,970 |
| 101. Chemistry Teachers, Postsecondary | $71,140 | — | — |
| 102. Ship Engineers | $70,890 | 18.0% | 620 |
| 103. Dental Hygienists | $70,210 | 37.7% | 10,490 |
| 104. Nuclear Medicine Technologists | $70,180 | 18.9% | 750 |
| 105. First-Line Supervisors of Non-Retail Sales Workers | $70,060 | 4.0% | 12,350 |
| 106. Speech-Language Pathologists | $69,870 | 23.4% | 5,230 |
| 107. Audiologists | $69,720 | 36.8% | 560 |
| 108. Budget Analysts | $69,280 | 10.4% | 1,960 |
| 109. Electrical and Electronics Repairers, Powerhouse, Substation, and Relay | $68,810 | 4.9% | 690 |
| 110. First-Line Supervisors of Fire Fighting and Prevention Workers | $68,210 | 8.2% | 3,310 |
| 111. Psychology Teachers, Postsecondary | $68,020 | — | — |
| 112. Geography Teachers, Postsecondary | $67,820 | — | — |
| 113. Clinical, Counseling, and School Psychologists | $67,650 | 21.9% | 8,230 |
| 114. Personal Financial Advisors | $67,520 | 32.1% | 9,020 |
| 115. Area, Ethnic, and Cultural Studies Teachers, Postsecondary | $67,360 | — | — |
| 116. Occupational Health and Safety Specialists | $66,790 | 8.5% | 2,570 |

| The 173 Highest-Paying Occupations | | | |
|---|---|---|---|
| Title | Annual Earnings | Percent Growth | Annual Openings |
| 117. Microbiologists | $66,260 | 13.3% | 720 |
| 118. Chiropractors | $66,160 | 28.3% | 2,530 |
| 119. Captains, Mates, and Pilots of Water Vessels | $66,150 | 20.4% | 2,070 |
| 120. Sociology Teachers, Postsecondary | $66,150 | — | — |
| 121. History Teachers, Postsecondary | $65,870 | — | — |
| 122. Diagnostic Medical Sonographers | $65,860 | 43.5% | 3,170 |
| 123. Library Science Teachers, Postsecondary | $65,780 | — | — |
| 124. Technical Writers | $65,500 | 17.2% | 1,830 |
| 125. Registered Nurses | $65,470 | 26.0% | 120,740 |
| 126. Urban and Regional Planners | $65,230 | 16.2% | 1,680 |
| 127. Business Operations Specialists, All Other | $65,120 | 11.6% | 32,720 |
| 128. Mathematical Science Teachers, Postsecondary | $64,990 | — | — |
| 129. Philosophy and Religion Teachers, Postsecondary | $64,990 | — | — |
| 130. Nursing Instructors and Teachers, Postsecondary | $64,850 | — | — |
| 131. Landscape Architects | $64,180 | 16.0% | 780 |
| 132. Home Economics Teachers, Postsecondary | $64,040 | — | — |

| The 173 Highest-Paying Occupations | | | |
|---|---|---|---|
| **Title** | **Annual Earnings** | **Percent Growth** | **Annual Openings** |
| 133. Transportation Inspectors | $63,680 | — | — |
| 134. Environmental Scientists and Specialists, Including Health | $63,570 | 18.7% | 4,320 |
| 135. Accountants and Auditors | $63,550 | 15.7% | 45,210 |
| 136. Agents and Business Managers of Artists, Performers, and Athletes | $63,370 | 14.0% | 800 |
| 137. Electrical Power-Line Installers and Repairers | $63,250 | 13.2% | 5,270 |
| 138. Social Work Teachers, Postsecondary | $63,250 | — | — |
| 139. Insurance Underwriters | $62,870 | 5.9% | 3,910 |
| 140. Communications Teachers, Postsecondary | $62,180 | — | — |
| 141. Art, Drama, and Music Teachers, Postsecondary | $62,160 | — | — |
| 142. Compliance Officers | $62,020 | 15.0% | 5,860 |
| 143. Multimedia Artists and Animators | $61,370 | 8.3% | 2,140 |
| 144. Financial Specialists, All Other | $61,160 | 6.1% | 4,490 |
| 145. Credit Analysts | $61,080 | 19.7% | 2,590 |
| 146. Market Research Analysts and Marketing Specialists | $60,300 | 41.2% | 19,180 |
| 147. First-Line Supervisors of Mechanics, Installers, and Repairers | $60,250 | 11.9% | 16,490 |
| 148. Instructional Coordinators | $60,050 | 19.5% | 5,810 |

| The 173 Highest-Paying Occupations | | | |
|---|---|---|---|
| **Title** | **Annual Earnings** | **Percent Growth** | **Annual Openings** |
| 149. English Language and Literature Teachers, Postsecondary | $60,040 | — | — |
| 150. Social and Community Service Managers | $59,970 | 26.7% | 6,480 |
| 151. Claims Adjusters, Examiners, and Investigators | $59,960 | 3.0% | 7,990 |
| 152. Loan Officers | $59,820 | 14.2% | 11,520 |
| 153. Supervisors of Construction and Extraction Workers | $59,700 | 23.5% | 25,970 |
| 154. Commercial and Industrial Designers | $59,610 | 10.5% | 1,690 |
| 155. Engineering Technicians, Except Drafters, All Other | $59,440 | 4.7% | 1,680 |
| 156. Education Teachers, Postsecondary | $59,350 | — | — |
| 157. Compensation, Benefits, and Job Analysis Specialists | $59,090 | 5.0% | 2,400 |
| 158. Cost Estimators | $58,860 | 36.4% | 10,300 |
| 159. Purchasing Agents, Except Wholesale, Retail, and Farm Products | $58,760 | 5.3% | 9,120 |
| 160. Soil and Plant Scientists | $58,740 | 12.1% | 860 |
| 161. Foreign Language and Literature Teachers, Postsecondary | $58,670 | — | — |
| 162. Real Estate Brokers | $58,350 | 7.6% | 2,970 |
| 163. Food Scientists and Technologists | $58,070 | 8.0% | 680 |

| The 173 Highest-Paying Occupations | | | |
|---|---|---|---|
| Title | Annual Earnings | Percent Growth | Annual Openings |
| 164. Criminal Justice and Law Enforcement Teachers, Postsecondary | $58,040 | — | — |
| 165. Recreation and Fitness Studies Teachers, Postsecondary | $57,920 | — | — |
| 166. Electrical and Electronic Engineering Technicians | $57,850 | 1.9% | 3,180 |
| 167. First-Line Supervisors of Correctional Officers | $57,840 | 5.6% | 1,650 |
| 168. Zoologists and Wildlife Biologists | $57,710 | 7.4% | 590 |
| 169. Medical and Clinical Laboratory Technologists | $57,580 | 11.3% | 5,210 |
| 170. Cartographers and Photogrammetrists | $57,440 | 22.2% | 610 |
| 171. Special Education Teachers, Secondary School | $56,830 | 7.3% | 5,110 |
| 172. Boilermakers | $56,560 | 21.3% | 1,180 |
| 173. Surveyors | $56,230 | 25.4% | 2,420 |

## THE 50 HIGH-PAYING OCCUPATIONS WITH THE FASTEST GROWTH

As I noted in the introduction, fast-growing occupations do not always offer lots of job opportunities. Occupations that are very small, such as the first two on the following list, will not create many job openings. On the other hand, some of the larger occupations, such as the third- and fourth-ranked titles, will do lots of hiring. Another advantage of fast-growing occupations is that they are often fast-changing as well, shifting to new technologies, new business practices, or new locations. You can play a part in their growth and evolution, with many opportunities to do innovative work.

| The 50 High-Paying Occupations with the Fastest Growth | | | |
|---|---|---|---|
| Title | Annual Earnings | Percent Growth | Annual Openings |
| 1. Biomedical Engineers | $86,960 | 61.7% | 1,310 |
| 2. Diagnostic Medical Sonographers | $65,860 | 43.5% | 3,170 |
| 3. Market Research Analysts and Marketing Specialists | $60,300 | 41.2% | 19,180 |
| 4. Physical Therapists | $79,860 | 39.0% | 10,060 |
| 5. Dental Hygienists | $70,210 | 37.7% | 10,490 |
| 6. Audiologists | $69,720 | 36.8% | 560 |
| 7. Cost Estimators | $58,860 | 36.4% | 10,300 |
| 8. Medical Scientists, Except Epidemiologists | $76,980 | 36.4% | 4,260 |
| 9. Veterinarians | $84,460 | 35.9% | 3,420 |
| 10. Occupational Therapists | $75,400 | 33.5% | 5,710 |
| 11. Optometrists | $97,820 | 33.1% | 2,340 |
| 12. Software Developers, Systems Software | $99,000 | 32.4% | 16,800 |
| 13. Personal Financial Advisors | $67,520 | 32.1% | 9,020 |
| 14. Biochemists and Biophysicists | $81,480 | 30.8% | 1,340 |

| The 50 High-Paying Occupations with the Fastest Growth | | | |
|---|---|---|---|
| Title | Annual Earnings | Percent Growth | Annual Openings |
| 15. Database Administrators | $77,080 | 30.6% | 5,270 |
| 16. Physician Assistants | $90,930 | 29.5% | 4,060 |
| 17. Chiropractors | $66,160 | 28.3% | 2,530 |
| 18. Network and Computer Systems Administrators | $72,560 | 27.8% | 15,530 |
| 19. Software Developers, Applications | $90,060 | 27.6% | 19,790 |
| 20. Financial Examiners | $75,800 | 27.0% | 1,410 |
| 21. Actuaries | $93,680 | 26.7% | 1,890 |
| 22. Social and Community Service Managers | $59,970 | 26.7% | 6,480 |
| 23. Registered Nurses | $65,470 | 26.0% | 120,740 |
| 24. Logisticians | $72,780 | 25.5% | 4,870 |
| 25. Pharmacists | $116,670 | 25.4% | 13,960 |
| 26. Surveyors | $56,230 | 25.4% | 2,420 |
| 27. Architects, Except Landscape and Naval | $73,090 | 24.5% | 5,090 |
| 28. Physicians and Surgeons | $187,200+ | 24.4% | 30,510 |
| 29. Supervisors of Construction and Extraction Workers | $59,700 | 23.5% | 25,970 |
| 30. Speech-Language Pathologists | $69,870 | 23.4% | 5,230 |
| 31. Financial Analysts | $76,950 | 23.0% | 10,420 |
| 32. Medical and Health Services Managers | $88,580 | 22.4% | 14,190 |

## The 50 High-Paying Occupations with the Fastest Growth

| Title | Annual Earnings | Percent Growth | Annual Openings |
|---|---|---|---|
| 33. Cartographers and Photogrammetrists | $57,440 | 22.2% | 610 |
| 34. Computer Systems Analysts | $79,680 | 22.1% | 22,250 |
| 35. Clinical, Counseling, and School Psychologists | $67,650 | 21.9% | 8,230 |
| 36. Environmental Engineers | $80,890 | 21.9% | 2,260 |
| 37. Management Analysts | $78,600 | 21.9% | 27,430 |
| 38. Boilermakers | $56,560 | 21.3% | 1,180 |
| 39. Commercial Pilots | $73,280 | 21.2% | 1,930 |
| 40. Geoscientists, Except Hydrologists and Geographers | $90,890 | 21.2% | 1,710 |
| 41. Dentists | $149,310 | 20.7% | 6,640 |
| 42. Captains, Mates, and Pilots of Water Vessels | $66,150 | 20.4% | 2,070 |
| 43. Radiation Therapists | $77,560 | 20.3% | 670 |
| 44. Podiatrists | $116,440 | 20.0% | 510 |
| 45. Credit Analysts | $61,080 | 19.7% | 2,590 |
| 46. Instructional Coordinators | $60,050 | 19.5% | 5,810 |
| 47. Civil Engineers | $79,340 | 19.4% | 10,440 |
| 48. Education Administrators, Postsecondary | $86,490 | 19.0% | 6,910 |
| 49. Health Diagnosing and Treating Practitioners, All Other | $72,710 | 19.0% | 2,120 |
| 50. Nuclear Medicine Technologists | $70,180 | 18.9% | 750 |

## THE 50 HIGH-PAYING OCCUPATIONS WITH THE MOST JOB OPENINGS

The figures for job openings in this book reflect both newly-created jobs and jobs that come open to replace workers who retire, die, or move on. Occupations with a lot of openings are attractive because they can provide many opportunities for you to land your first job or move to a better position after you have gained some experience.

Remember that the number of job openings is only a rough indicator of your chances of finding work. Almost every job opening will have several candidates competing to be hired, and in some occupations the competition can be intense. As part of your research into any career option, you need to learn about the level of competition that you can expect. If you plan to look for a local job, you need to investigate conditions in the local job market.

| The 50 High-Paying Occupations with the Most Job Openings | | | |
|---|---|---|---|
| **Title** | **Annual Earnings** | **Percent Growth** | **Annual Openings** |
| 1. Registered Nurses | $65,470 | 26.0% | 120,740 |
| 2. Accountants and Auditors | $63,550 | 15.7% | 45,210 |
| 3. General and Operations Managers | $95,440 | 4.6% | 41,010 |
| 4. Business Operations Specialists, All Other | $65,120 | 11.6% | 32,720 |
| 5. Physicians and Surgeons | $187,200+ | 24.4% | 30,510 |
| 6. Management Analysts | $78,600 | 21.9% | 27,430 |
| 7. Supervisors of Construction and Extraction Workers | $59,700 | 23.5% | 25,970 |
| 8. Managers, All Other | $100,890 | 7.9% | 24,940 |
| 9. Computer Systems Analysts | $79,680 | 22.1% | 22,250 |
| 10. Lawyers | $113,530 | 10.1% | 21,200 |
| 11. Software Developers, Applications | $90,060 | 27.6% | 19,790 |
| 12. Market Research Analysts and Marketing Specialists | $60,300 | 41.2% | 19,180 |

| The 50 High-Paying Occupations with the Most Job Openings | | | |
|---|---|---|---|
| **Title** | **Annual Earnings** | **Percent Growth** | **Annual Openings** |
| 13. Software Developers, Systems Software | $99,000 | 32.4% | 16,800 |
| 14. First-Line Supervisors of Mechanics, Installers, and Repairers | $60,250 | 11.9% | 16,490 |
| 15. Sales Representatives, Wholesale and Manufacturing, Technical and Scientific Products | $74,970 | 16.4% | 15,970 |
| 16. Network and Computer Systems Administrators | $72,560 | 27.8% | 15,530 |
| 17. Financial Managers | $109,740 | 8.8% | 14,280 |
| 18. Medical and Health Services Managers | $88,580 | 22.4% | 14,190 |
| 19. Sales Managers | $105,260 | 11.7% | 13,970 |
| 20. Pharmacists | $116,670 | 25.4% | 13,960 |
| 21. Securities, Commodities, and Financial Services Sales Agents | $71,720 | 15.2% | 13,370 |
| 22. Computer Programmers | $74,280 | 12.0% | 12,800 |
| 23. First-Line Supervisors of Non-Retail Sales Workers | $70,060 | 4.0% | 12,350 |
| 24. Construction Managers | $82,790 | 16.6% | 12,040 |
| 25. Loan Officers | $59,820 | 14.2% | 11,520 |
| 26. Chief Executives | $168,140 | 4.2% | 11,150 |
| 27. Dental Hygienists | $70,210 | 37.7% | 10,490 |
| 28. Civil Engineers | $79,340 | 19.4% | 10,440 |

| The 50 High-Paying Occupations with the Most Job Openings | | | |
|---|---|---|---|
| **Title** | **Annual Earnings** | **Percent Growth** | **Annual Openings** |
| 29. Financial Analysts | $76,950 | 23.0% | 10,420 |
| 30. Cost Estimators | $58,860 | 36.4% | 10,300 |
| 31. Computer and Information Systems Managers | $120,950 | 18.1% | 10,280 |
| 32. Physical Therapists | $79,860 | 39.0% | 10,060 |
| 33. Administrative Services Managers | $81,080 | 14.5% | 9,980 |
| 34. Mechanical Engineers | $80,580 | 8.8% | 9,960 |
| 35. Purchasing Agents, Except Wholesale, Retail, and Farm Products | $58,760 | 5.3% | 9,120 |
| 36. Personal Financial Advisors | $67,520 | 32.1% | 9,020 |
| 37. Education Administrators, Elementary and Secondary School | $87,760 | 9.8% | 8,970 |
| 38. Clinical, Counseling, and School Psychologists | $67,650 | 21.9% | 8,230 |
| 39. Claims Adjusters, Examiners, and Investigators | $59,960 | 3.0% | 7,990 |
| 40. Marketing Managers | $119,480 | 13.6% | 7,600 |
| 41. Education Administrators, Postsecondary | $86,490 | 19.0% | 6,910 |
| 42. Dentists | $149,310 | 20.7% | 6,640 |
| 43. Social and Community Service Managers | $59,970 | 26.7% | 6,480 |
| 44. Compliance Officers | $62,020 | 15.0% | 5,860 |

| The 50 High-Paying Occupations with the Most Job Openings | | | |
|---|---|---|---|
| Title | Annual Earnings | Percent Growth | Annual Openings |
| 45. Instructional Coordinators | $60,050 | 19.5% | 5,810 |
| 46. Industrial Engineers | $78,860 | 6.4% | 5,750 |
| 47. Occupational Therapists | $75,400 | 33.5% | 5,710 |
| 48. Database Administrators | $77,080 | 30.6% | 5,270 |
| 49. Electrical Power-Line Installers and Repairers | $63,250 | 13.2% | 5,270 |
| 50. Speech-Language Pathologists | $69,870 | 23.4% | 5,230 |

## Lists of High-Paying Occupations Based on Education, Training, and Experience Required

For most people, the choice of a career goal depends heavily on the entry requirements. All things being equal, an occupation with a faster entry route is usually more appealing than one that requires spending long years and lots of dollars for college classes. Of course, all things rarely are equal, and more education usually opens the door to better-paying jobs. Nevertheless, you should take a look at the occupations that require only on-the-job training or work experience in a related occupation. You may be surprised at how many high-paying choices do not require a degree, or at least not an advanced degree.

I organized the 173 occupations for this book into lists based on how much education, training, or work experience they typically require. Within each list, I ordered the occupations by their average earnings.

Some of the following lists are based purely on an educational level that is required, and any additional training or experience needed is identified in a footnote at the bottom of the list. However, so many occupations require a bachelor's degree that I found it useful to break out several separate bachelor's-degree lists according to *additional* entry requirements, such as on-the-job training or work experience.

*Short-term on-the-job training* takes one month or less to complete. *Moderate-term on-the-job training* takes from one month to a year. *Long-term on-the-job training* takes more than one year. An *apprenticeship* is a formal long-term on-the-job training arrangement that typically takes from three to five years and includes night classes.

Sometimes the entry requirements identified here are ironclad; for example, you can't become a physician without an appropriate degree and clinical training. However, many other occupations listed here are more flexible. Some job applicants who lack formal credentials may be hired because of the skills and knowledge that they have acquired through work experience and informal study.

| High-Paying Occupations that Require Moderate-Term On-the-Job Training | | | |
|---|---|---|---|
| **Title** | **Annual Earnings** | **Percent Growth** | **Annual Openings** |
| 1. First-Line Supervisors of Police and Detectives | $78,270 | 2.1% | 3,870 |
| 2. Detectives and Criminal Investigators | $74,300 | 2.9% | 3,010 |
| 3. Loan Officers | $59,820 | 14.2% | 11,520 |
| 4. First-Line Supervisors of Correctional Officers | $57,840 | 5.6% | 1,650 |
| *All of these occupations except #3 require an additional one to five years of work experience.* | | | |

## High-Paying Occupations that Require Long-Term On-the-Job Training

| Title | Annual Earnings | Percent Growth | Annual Openings |
|---|---|---|---|
| 1. Elevator Installers and Repairers | $76,650 | 11.3% | 820 |
| 2. Business Operations Specialists, All Other | $65,120 | 11.6% | 32,720 |
| 3. Transportation Inspectors | $63,680 | 14.4% | 1,070 |
| 4. Electrical Power-Line Installers and Repairers | $63,250 | 13.2% | 5,270 |
| 5. Claims Adjusters, Examiners, and Investigators | $59,960 | 3.0% | 7,990 |
| 6. Purchasing Agents, Except Wholesale, Retail, and Farm Products | $58,760 | 5.3% | 9,120 |
| 7. Boilermakers | $56,560 | 21.3% | 1,180 |

*For occupations #1 and #7, the training is usually part of an apprenticeship. For occupation #3, workers usually need some college but no degree before getting training.*

## High-Paying Occupations that Require One to Five Years of Work Experience

| Title | Annual Earnings | Percent Growth | Annual Openings |
|---|---|---|---|
| 1. Managers, All Other | $100,890 | 7.9% | 24,940 |
| 2. Administrative Services Managers | $81,080 | 14.5% | 9,980 |
| 3. First-Line Supervisors of Mechanics, Installers, and Repairers | $60,250 | 11.9% | 16,490 |
| 4. Real Estate Brokers | $58,350 | 7.6% | 2,970 |

| High-Paying Occupations that Require More than Five Years of Work Experience | | | |
|---|---|---|---|
| **Title** | **Annual Earnings** | **Percent Growth** | **Annual Openings** |
| 1. Transportation, Storage, and Distribution Managers | $81,830 | 10.0% | 3,370 |
| 2. First-Line Supervisors of Non-Retail Sales Workers | $70,060 | 4.0% | 12,350 |
| 3. Supervisors of Construction and Extraction Workers | $59,700 | 23.5% | 25,970 |

| High-Paying Occupations that Require Postsecondary Vocational Training | | | |
|---|---|---|---|
| **Title** | **Annual Earnings** | **Percent Growth** | **Annual Openings** |
| 1. Commercial Pilots | $73,280 | 21.2% | 1,930 |
| 2. Electrical and Electronics Repairers, Powerhouse, Substation, and Relay | $68,810 | 4.9% | 690 |
| 3. First-Line Supervisors of Fire Fighting and Prevention Workers | $68,210 | 8.2% | 3,310 |
| *Occupation #2 requires additional long-term on-the-job training. Occupation #3 requires an additional one to five years of work experience.* | | | |

| High-Paying Occupations that Require Only an Associate Degree | | | |
|---|---|---|---|
| **Title** | **Annual Earnings** | **Percent Growth** | **Annual Openings** |
| 1. General and Operations Managers | $95,440 | 4.6% | 41,010 |
| 2. Construction Managers | $82,790 | 16.6% | 12,040 |
| 3. Radiation Therapists | $77,560 | 20.3% | 670 |
| 4. Dental Hygienists | $70,210 | 37.7% | 10,490 |
| 5. Nuclear Medicine Technologists | $70,180 | 18.9% | 750 |
| 6. Diagnostic Medical Sonographers | $65,860 | 43.5% | 3,170 |
| 7. Registered Nurses | $65,470 | 26.0% | 120,740 |
| 8. Engineering Technicians, Except Drafters, All Other | $59,440 | 4.7% | 1,680 |
| 9. Electrical and Electronic Engineering Technicians | $57,850 | 1.9% | 3,180 |

*Occupation #1 requires one to five years of work experience in addition to the degree. Occupation #2 requires more than five years of work experience in addition to the degree.*

| High-Paying Occupations that Require Only a Bachelor's Degree | | | |
|---|---|---|---|
| **Title** | **Annual Earnings** | **Percent Growth** | **Annual Openings** |
| 1. Petroleum Engineers | $130,280 | 17.0% | 1,180 |
| 2. Nuclear Engineers | $104,270 | 10.2% | 620 |
| 3. Aerospace Engineers | $103,720 | 4.9% | 2,180 |
| 4. Computer Hardware Engineers | $100,920 | 9.0% | 2,290 |
| 5. Software Developers, Systems Software | $99,000 | 32.4% | 16,800 |
| 6. Chemical Engineers | $94,350 | 5.9% | 1,140 |
| 7. Engineers, All Other | $92,030 | 6.6% | 4,480 |
| 8. Economists | $91,860 | 6.1% | 580 |
| 9. Electronics Engineers, Except Computer | $91,820 | 4.9% | 4,060 |
| 10. Physical Scientists, All Other | $91,640 | 8.5% | 1,330 |
| 11. Geoscientists, Except Hydrologists and Geographers | $90,890 | 21.2% | 1,710 |
| 12. Software Developers, Applications | $90,060 | 27.6% | 19,790 |
| 13. Medical and Health Services Managers | $88,580 | 22.4% | 14,190 |
| 14. Electrical Engineers | $87,920 | 7.0% | 4,780 |
| 15. Biomedical Engineers | $86,960 | 61.7% | 1,310 |
| 16. Materials Engineers | $85,150 | 8.7% | 810 |
| 17. Environmental Engineers | $80,890 | 21.9% | 2,260 |
| 18. Mechanical Engineers | $80,580 | 8.8% | 9,960 |
| 19. Computer Systems Analysts | $79,680 | 22.1% | 22,250 |

| High-Paying Occupations that Require Only a Bachelor's Degree (cont.) | | | |
|---|---|---|---|
| **Title** | **Annual Earnings** | **Percent Growth** | **Annual Openings** |
| 20. Civil Engineers | $79,340 | 19.4% | 10,440 |
| 21. Industrial Engineers | $78,860 | 6.4% | 5,750 |
| 22. Financial Analysts | $76,950 | 23.0% | 10,420 |
| 23. Health and Safety Engineers, Except Mining Safety Engineers and Inspectors | $76,830 | 13.1% | 820 |
| 24. Social Scientists and Related Workers, All Other | $76,540 | 8.1% | 1,760 |
| 25. Computer Programmers | $74,280 | 12.0% | 12,800 |
| 26. Network and Computer Systems Administrators | $72,560 | 27.8% | 15,530 |
| 27. Operations Research Analysts | $72,100 | 14.6% | 3,000 |
| 28. Chemists | $71,770 | 3.8% | 2,990 |
| 29. Ship Engineers | $70,890 | 18.0% | 620 |
| 30. Budget Analysts | $69,280 | 10.4% | 1,960 |
| 31. Personal Financial Advisors | $67,520 | 32.1% | 9,020 |
| 32. Microbiologists | $66,260 | 13.3% | 720 |
| 33. Captains, Mates, and Pilots of Water Vessels | $66,150 | 20.4% | 2,070 |
| 34. Environmental Scientists and Specialists, Including Health | $63,570 | 18.7% | 4,320 |
| 35. Accountants and Auditors | $63,550 | 15.7% | 45,210 |
| 36. Credit Analysts | $61,080 | 19.7% | 2,590 |

| High-Paying Occupations that Require Only a Bachelor's Degree (cont.) | | | |
|---|---|---|---|
| Title | Annual Earnings | Percent Growth | Annual Openings |
| 37. Market Research Analysts and Marketing Specialists | $60,300 | 41.2% | 19,180 |
| 38. Commercial and Industrial Designers | $59,610 | 10.5% | 1,690 |
| 39. Compensation, Benefits, and Job Analysis Specialists | $59,090 | 5.0% | 2,400 |
| 40. Cost Estimators | $58,860 | 36.4% | 10,300 |
| 41. Soil and Plant Scientists | $58,740 | 12.1% | 860 |
| 42. Food Scientists and Technologists | $58,070 | 8.0% | 680 |
| 43. Zoologists and Wildlife Biologists | $57,710 | 7.4% | 590 |
| 44. Medical and Clinical Laboratory Technologists | $57,580 | 11.3% | 5,210 |
| 45. Cartographers and Photogrammetrists | $57,440 | 22.2% | 610 |
| 46. Surveyors | $56,230 | 25.4% | 2,420 |

| High-Paying Occupations that Require a Bachelor's Degree Plus On-the-Job Training | | | |
|---|---|---|---|
| **Title** | **Annual Earnings** | **Percent Growth** | **Annual Openings** |
| 1. Airline Pilots, Copilots, and Flight Engineers | $114,200 | 6.4% | 3,130 |
| 2. Actuaries | $93,680 | 26.7% | 1,890 |
| 3. Sales Engineers | $91,830 | 14.4% | 3,210 |
| 4. Financial Examiners | $75,800 | 27.0% | 1,410 |
| 5. Sales Representatives, Wholesale and Manufacturing, Technical and Scientific Products | $74,970 | 16.4% | 15,970 |
| 6. Architects, Except Landscape and Naval | $73,090 | 24.5% | 5,090 |
| 7. Securities, Commodities, and Financial Services Sales Agents | $71,720 | 15.2% | 13,370 |
| 8. Occupational Health and Safety Specialists | $66,790 | 8.5% | 2,570 |
| 9. Technical Writers | $65,500 | 17.2% | 1,830 |
| 10. Landscape Architects | $64,180 | 16.0% | 780 |
| 11. Insurance Underwriters | $62,870 | 5.9% | 3,910 |
| 12. Compliance Officers | $62,020 | 15.0% | 5,860 |
| 13. Multimedia Artists and Animators | $61,370 | 8.3% | 2,140 |
| 14. Financial Specialists, All Other | $61,160 | 6.1% | 4,490 |
| 15. Special Education Teachers, Secondary School | $56,830 | 7.3% | 5,110 |

*For occupation #9, the training is short-term. For occupations #1, #3, #5, #11, #12, and #14, the training is moderate-term. For occupations #6, #10, and #15, the training is in an internship program. Occupations #1 and #9 require an additional one to five years of work experience.*

27

| High-Paying Occupations that Require a Bachelor's Degree Plus One to Five Years of Work Experience | | | |
|---|---|---|---|
| **Title** | **Annual Earnings** | **Percent Growth** | **Annual Openings** |
| 1.  Marketing Managers | $119,480 | 13.6% | 7,600 |
| 2.  Sales Managers | $105,260 | 11.7% | 13,970 |
| 3.  Human Resources Managers | $99,720 | 12.9% | 2,690 |
| 4.  Public Relations and Fundraising Managers | $95,450 | 16.4% | 2,790 |
| 5.  Training and Development Managers | $95,400 | 14.6% | 1,160 |
| 6.  Compensation and Benefits Managers | $95,250 | 2.8% | 870 |
| 7.  Industrial Production Managers | $89,190 | 9.1% | 4,900 |
| 8.  Advertising and Promotions Managers | $88,590 | 13.3% | 1,620 |
| 9.  Art Directors | $80,880 | 9.0% | 2,430 |
| 10. Management Analysts | $78,600 | 21.9% | 27,430 |
| 11. Database Administrators | $77,080 | 30.6% | 5,270 |
| 12. Education Administrators, All Other | $76,860 | 13.6% | 1,360 |
| 13. Logisticians | $72,780 | 25.5% | 4,870 |
| 14. Producers and Directors | $71,350 | 11.0% | 4,970 |
| 15. Agents and Business Managers of Artists, Performers, and Athletes School | $63,370 | 14.0% | 800 |
| 16. Social and Community Service Managers | $59,970 | 26.7% | 6,480 |

| High-Paying Occupations that Require a Bachelor's Degree Plus More than Five Years of Work Experience | | | |
|---|---|---|---|
| **Title** | **Annual Earnings** | **Percent Growth** | **Annual Openings** |
| 1. Chief Executives | $168,140 | 4.2% | 11,150 |
| 2. Architectural and Engineering Managers | $124,870 | 8.6% | 4,970 |
| 3. Computer and Information Systems Managers | $120,950 | 18.1% | 10,280 |
| 4. Natural Sciences Managers | $115,730 | 7.7% | 3,350 |
| 5. Financial Managers | $109,740 | 8.8% | 14,280 |
| 6. Purchasing Managers | $100,170 | 7.2% | 2,560 |

| High-Paying Occupations that Require a Master's Degree | | | |
|---|---|---|---|
| **Title** | **Annual Earnings** | **Percent Growth** | **Annual Openings** |
| 1. Physician Assistants | $90,930 | 29.5% | 4,060 |
| 2. Psychologists, All Other | $90,020 | 18.2% | 870 |
| 3. Education Administrators, Elementary and Secondary School | $87,760 | 9.8% | 8,970 |
| 4. Education Administrators, Postsecondary | $86,490 | 19.0% | 6,910 |
| 5. Statisticians | $75,560 | 14.1% | 1,870 |
| 6. Occupational Therapists | $75,400 | 33.5% | 5,710 |
| 7. Health Diagnosing and Treating Practitioners, All Other | $72,710 | 19.0% | 2,120 |
| 8. Speech-Language Pathologists | $69,870 | 23.4% | 5,230 |
| 9. Urban and Regional Planners | $65,230 | 16.2% | 1,680 |
| 10. Instructional Coordinators | $60,050 | 19.5% | 5,810 |

*Occupation #2 requires additional training in an internship or residency program. Occupations #3 and #4 require an additional one to five years of work experience.*

30

## High-Paying Occupations that Require a Doctoral or Professional Degree

| Title | Annual Earnings | Percent Growth | Annual Openings |
|---|---|---|---|
| 1. Physicians and Surgeons | $187,200+ | 24.4% | 30,510 |
| 2. Dentists | $149,310 | 20.7% | 6,640 |
| 3. Pharmacists | $116,670 | 25.4% | 13,960 |
| 4. Podiatrists | $116,440 | 20.0% | 510 |
| 5. Judges, Magistrate Judges, and Magistrates | $115,760 | 9.2% | 960 |
| 6. Lawyers | $113,530 | 10.1% | 21,200 |
| 7. Physicists | $106,840 | 14.2% | 800 |
| 8. Computer and Information Research Scientists | $102,190 | 18.7% | 1,060 |
| 9. Law Teachers, Postsecondary | $99,950 | — | — |
| 10. Optometrists | $97,820 | 33.1% | 2,340 |
| 11. Engineering Teachers, Postsecondary | $92,670 | — | — |
| 12. Economics Teachers, Postsecondary | $87,950 | — | — |
| 13. Veterinarians | $84,460 | 35.9% | 3,420 |
| 14. Atmospheric, Earth, Marine, and Space Sciences Teachers, Postsecondary | $82,180 | — | — |
| 15. Forestry and Conservation Science Teachers, Postsecondary | $81,930 | — | — |
| 16. Biochemists and Biophysicists | $81,480 | 30.8% | 1,340 |
| 17. Health Specialties Teachers, Postsecondary | $81,140 | — | — |

31

| High-Paying Occupations that Require a Doctoral or Professional Degree (cont.) | | | |
|---|---|---|---|
| **Title** | **Annual Earnings** | **Percent Growth** | **Annual Openings** |
| 18. Physical Therapists | $79,860 | 39.0% | 10,060 |
| 19. Physics Teachers, Postsecondary | $78,540 | — | — |
| 20. Environmental Science Teachers, Postsecondary | $77,320 | — | — |
| 21. Medical Scientists, Except Epidemiologists | $76,980 | 36.4% | 4,260 |
| 22. Anthropology and Archeology Teachers, Postsecondary | $76,020 | — | — |
| 23. Biological Science Teachers, Postsecondary | $74,180 | — | — |
| 24. Business Teachers, Postsecondary | $73,660 | — | — |
| 25. Biological Scientists, All Other | $72,700 | 6.3% | 1,030 |
| 26. Computer Science Teachers, Postsecondary | $72,200 | — | — |
| 27. Political Science Teachers, Postsecondary | $72,170 | — | — |
| 28. Architecture Teachers, Postsecondary | $71,610 | — | — |
| 29. Chemistry Teachers, Postsecondary | $71,140 | — | — |
| 30. Audiologists | $69,720 | 36.8% | 560 |
| 31. Psychology Teachers, Postsecondary | $68,020 | — | — |
| 32. Geography Teachers, Postsecondary | $67,820 | — | — |
| 33. Clinical, Counseling, and School Psychologists | $67,650 | 21.9% | 8,230 |

| High-Paying Occupations that Require a Doctoral or Professional Degree (cont.) | | | |
|---|---|---|---|
| Title | Annual Earnings | Percent Growth | Annual Openings |
| 34. Area, Ethnic, and Cultural Studies Teachers, Postsecondary | $67,360 | — | — |
| 35. Chiropractors | $66,160 | 28.3% | 2,530 |
| 36. Sociology Teachers, Postsecondary | $66,150 | — | — |
| 37. History Teachers, Postsecondary | $65,870 | — | — |
| 38. Library Science Teachers, Postsecondary | $65,780 | — | — |
| 39. Mathematical Science Teachers, Postsecondary | $64,990 | — | — |
| 40. Philosophy and Religion Teachers, Postsecondary | $64,990 | — | — |
| 41. Nursing Instructors and Teachers, Postsecondary | $64,850 | — | — |
| 42. Home Economics Teachers, Postsecondary | $64,040 | — | — |
| 43. Social Work Teachers, Postsecondary | $63,250 | — | — |
| 44. Communications Teachers, Postsecondary | $62,180 | — | — |
| 45. Art, Drama, and Music Teachers, Postsecondary | $62,160 | — | — |
| 46. English Language and Literature Teachers, Postsecondary | $60,040 | — | — |
| 47. Education Teachers, Postsecondary | $59,350 | — | — |
| 48. Foreign Language and Literature Teachers, Postsecondary | $58,670 | — | — |

| High-Paying Occupations that Require a Doctoral or Professional Degree (cont.) | | | |
|---|---|---|---|
| **Title** | **Annual Earnings** | **Percent Growth** | **Annual Openings** |
| 49. Criminal Justice and Law Enforcement Teachers, Postsecondary | $58,040 | — | — |
| 50. Recreation and Fitness Studies Teachers, Postsecondary | $57,920 | — | — |
| *Occupations #1, #2, #4, and #35 require additional training in an internship or residency program. Occupation #5 requires an additional one to five years of work experience plus short-term on-the-job training.* | | | |

## Lists of High-Paying Occupations Based on the Earnings-Preparation Balance

The previous set of lists shows that entering a high-paying occupation sometimes—but not always—requires several years of education, training, or work experience. Your career decision depends partly on what *balance* you want to strike between the years of preparation and the rewards you expect to reap from work. That is, you want to find a comfortable balance between something that most people want to minimize (the time, expense, and effort of preparation) and something that most people want to maximize (high income).

I thought it would be interesting to see which high-paying occupations tilt very far in one direction or the other: which occupations have comparatively high wages but require only a few years of preparation; and which have comparatively low wages despite many years of preparation.

To find out, I quantified the amount of preparation that the BLS assigns to each occupation. For education, I assigned points on a scale that ranged from 0 for *less than a high school diploma* to 14 for *doctoral or professional degree*. The scale actually has only seven levels above zero, but I doubled the points for education because postsecondary education is something you usually have to pay for, whereas you actually get paid while gaining work experience or being trained on the job. For work experience, I assigned zero points for *none* and three points for *more than five years*. For on-the-job training, my scale ran from zero points for *none* to four points for *internship/ residency*. Then I divided the median earnings of each occupation by the sum of these three scores. The resulting figure gives a rough idea of how much dollar payoff you can expect for each unit of preparation: the *earnings-preparation balance*.

The following two lists show the 20 occupations with an earnings-preparation balance that tilts most heavily in each direction.

The occupations in the first list provide an excellent dollar payoff for the investment you'll make in preparing for entry.

34

| High-Paying Occupations with an Earnings-Preparation Balance that Tilts Heavily Toward Earnings | | | | |
|---|---|---|---|---|
| Title | Education Points | Experience Points | Training Points | Earnings-Prep Balance |
| 1. Elevator Installers and Repairers | 0 | 3 | 0 | $25,550 |
| 2. Managers, All Other | 2 | 0 | 2 | $25,223 |
| 3. Administrative Services Managers | 2 | 0 | 2 | $20,270 |
| 4. Boilermakers | 0 | 3 | 0 | $18,853 |
| 5. Commercial Pilots | 4 | 0 | 0 | $18,320 |
| 6. Transportation, Storage, and Distribution Managers | 2 | 0 | 3 | $16,366 |
| 7. First-Line Supervisors of Mechanics, Installers, and Repairers | 2 | 0 | 2 | $15,068 |
| 8. Loan Officers | 2 | 2 | 0 | $14,955 |
| 9. Real Estate Brokers | 2 | 0 | 2 | $14,588 |
| 10. First-Line Supervisors of Non-Retail Sales Workers | 2 | 0 | 3 | $14,012 |
| 11. First-Line Supervisors of Police and Detectives | 2 | 2 | 2 | $13,045 |
| 12. Petroleum Engineers | 10 | 0 | 0 | $13,028 |
| 13. Chief Executives | 10 | 0 | 3 | $12,934 |
| 14. Electrical Power-Line Installers and Repairers | 2 | 3 | 0 | $12,650 |

| High-Paying Occupations with an Earnings-Preparation Balance that Tilts Heavily Toward Earnings (cont.) | | | | |
|---|---|---|---|---|
| Title | Education Points | Experience Points | Training Points | Earnings-Prep Balance |
| 15. Detectives and Criminal Investigators | 2 | 2 | 2 | $12,383 |
| 16. Claims Adjusters, Examiners, and Investigators | 2 | 3 | 0 | $11,992 |
| 17. First-Line Supervisors of Construction Trades and Extraction Workers | 2 | 0 | 3 | $11,940 |
| 18. Purchasing Agents, Except Wholesale, Retail, and Farm Products | 2 | 3 | 0 | $11,752 |
| 19. First-Line Supervisors of Fire Fighting and Prevention Workers | 4 | 0 | 2 | $11,368 |
| 20. Business Operations Specialists, All Other | 2 | 3 | 1 | $10,853 |

The occupations on the following list pay relatively low wages for the amount of preparation that they require. But please understand that I'm not necessarily trying to discourage you from pursuing these careers. It's true that most people want to minimize the time, expense, and effort of preparation and want to maximize their earnings. However, some people get great enjoyment from the learning that they experience during the preparation process, and the following occupations have many rewards beyond the paycheck. If you're the kind of person who gets satisfaction from helping other people or from working in an educational setting, one of these career goals might be perfect for you.

| High-Paying Occupations with an Earnings-Preparation Balance that Tilts Heavily Toward Preparation | | | | |
|---|---|---|---|---|
| **Title** | **Education Points** | **Experience Points** | **Training Points** | **Earnings-Prep Balance** |
| 1. Clinical, Counseling, and School Psychologists | 14 | 4 | 0 | $3,758 |
| 2. Instructional Coordinators | 12 | 0 | 3 | $4,003 |
| 3. Special Education Teachers, Secondary School | 10 | 4 | 0 | $4,059 |
| 4. Recreation and Fitness Studies Teachers, Postsecondary | 14 | 0 | 0 | $4,137 |
| 5. Criminal Justice and Law Enforcement Teachers, Postsecondary | 14 | 0 | 0 | $4,146 |
| 6. Foreign Language and Literature Teachers, Postsecondary | 14 | 0 | 0 | $4,191 |
| 7. Education Teachers, Postsecondary | 14 | 0 | 0 | $4,239 |
| 8. English Language and Literature Teachers, Postsecondary | 14 | 0 | 0 | $4,289 |
| 9. Art, Drama, and Music Teachers, Postsecondary | 14 | 0 | 0 | $4,440 |
| 10. Communications Teachers, Postsecondary | 14 | 0 | 0 | $4,441 |
| 11. Social Work Teachers, Postsecondary | 14 | 0 | 0 | $4,518 |

| High-Paying Occupations with an Earnings-Preparation Balance that Tilts Heavily Toward Preparation (cont.) | | | | |
|---|---|---|---|---|
| **Title** | **Education Points** | **Experience Points** | **Training Points** | **Earnings-Prep Balance** |
| 12. Home Economics Teachers, Postsecondary | 14 | 0 | 0 | $4,574 |
| 13. Landscape Architects | 10 | 4 | 0 | $4,584 |
| 14. Nursing Instructors and Teachers, Postsecondary | 14 | 0 | 0 | $4,632 |
| 15. Mathematical Science Teachers, Postsecondary | 14 | 0 | 0 | $4,642 |
| 16. Philosophy and Religion Teachers, Postsecondary | 14 | 0 | 0 | $4,642 |
| 17. Library Science Teachers, Postsecondary | 14 | 0 | 0 | $4,699 |
| 18. History Teachers, Postsecondary | 14 | 0 | 0 | $4,705 |
| 19. Sociology Teachers, Postsecondary | 14 | 0 | 0 | $4,725 |
| 20. Chiropractors | 14 | 0 | 0 | $4,726 |

## Lists of High-Paying Occupations Based on Personality Types

Many people find it useful to think in terms of personality types when exploring careers. This approach is based on the theory that certain interests, skills, and other work-related preferences tend to cluster together in ways that can be summarized as a small set of personality types. According to this theory, if you can identify which type best matches you and which occupations are good work environments for this type, you should be able to find work where you will fit in well. The concept of *fit* (technically called *congruence*) means that you will be comfortable with the work tasks and settings and also that your co-workers will tend to share your personality type.

John L. Holland developed one of the most widely used sets of personality types in the 1950s. It is sometimes called RIASEC after the initials of the six types that he described. Here are the six types, defined in terms of people who match them:

- **Realistic** personalities prefer work activities that include practical, hands-on problems and solutions. They enjoy dealing with plants, animals, or real-world materials like wood, tools, and machinery. They often prefer working outside and avoiding a lot of paperwork or working closely with others.

- **Investigative** personalities prefer working with ideas and doing work that requires an extensive amount of thinking. They enjoy searching for facts and figuring out problems mentally.

- **Artistic** personalities prefer working with forms, designs, and patterns. They enjoy self-expression and work that can be done without following a clear set of rules.

- **Social** personalities prefer working with, communicating with, and teaching people. They enjoy helping or providing service to others.

- **Enterprising** personalities prefer starting up and carrying out projects. They enjoy leading people and making many decisions. The work they prefer sometimes requires risk taking and often deals with business.

- **Conventional** personalities prefer following set procedures and routines. They enjoy working with data and details more than with ideas. They prefer work in which there is a clear line of authority to follow.

John Holland recognized that personality theory is not an exact science and that the world of work does not divide cleanly into easy-to-categorize work environments. To accommodate this fuzziness, he suggested that people (and occupations) often fit not only a primary personality type but also one or two secondary types. For example, Electrical Engineers are considered to be primarily Investigative, because their work is mainly about finding mental solutions to problems, but Realistic is a secondary type for this occupation because the work involves hands-on tasks and equipment. So the Holland code for Electrical Engineers is IR.

If you have ever taken an assessment to determine your Holland type or if you have simply read the six definitions and given the matter some thought, you will probably want to look at one of the lists that follow to see which high-paying occupations are consistent with your primary personality type.

If one or two secondary types also describe your personality, you may want to look at all of these six lists and examine the Holland codes in the rightmost column so you can detect secondary personality types. For example, if you consider yourself a Conventional personality, you should be careful not to overlook Sales Managers. Although it appears in the Enterprising list, its EC code indicates that Conventional is its secondary type, so it may suit you.

I assigned occupations to the lists by applying ratings from the O*NET database to the 173 occupations in this book, using the O*NET developers' formula for determining primary and secondary RIASEC types. I sorted each list as I did many others: from highest- to lowest-paying.

If you compare the lists, you may notice that some personality types are associated with better pay than others. The occupations on the Investigative list have average earnings of $93,466, compared to $64,010 for those on the Conventional list. This difference happens largely because the Investigative occupations tend to require more education and involve high-level skills that computers are unlikely to master. On the other hand, the Social list also has a low average level of pay ($67,702), even though most of the occupations on this list involve college teaching and require a doctoral degree. This situation reflects the fact that much college teaching is now done by comparatively low-paid adjunct faculty, whose earnings fall short of what you might expect for people who are so well-educated. Still, they earn a good paycheck compared to the U.S. workforce as a whole, which is why they are included in this book.

| High-Paying Occupations for the Realistic Personality Type | | | | |
|---|---|---|---|---|
| Title | Annual Earnings | Percent Growth | Annual Openings | Personality Type |
| 1. Airline Pilots, Copilots, and Flight Engineers | $114,200 | 6.4% | 3,130 | RCI |
| 2. Physical Scientists, All Other | $91,640 | 8.5% | 1,330 | RI |
| 3. Mechanical Engineers | $80,580 | 8.8% | 9,960 | RI |
| 4. Civil Engineers | $79,340 | 19.4% | 10,440 | RIC |
| 5. Elevator Installers and Repairers | $76,650 | 11.3% | 820 | RIC |
| 6. Commercial Pilots | $73,280 | 21.2% | 1,930 | REI |
| 7. Ship Engineers | $70,890 | 18.0% | 620 | RCE |
| 8. Electrical and Electronics Repairers, Powerhouse, Substation, and Relay | $68,810 | 4.9% | 690 | RC |
| 9. Captains, Mates, and Pilots of Water Vessels | $66,150 | 20.4% | 2,070 | REC |
| 10. Transportation Inspectors | $63,680 | 14.4% | 1,070 | RCI |
| 11. Electrical Power-Line Installers and Repairers | $63,250 | 13.2% | 5,270 | RIC |
| 12. Engineering Technicians, Except Drafters, All Other Managers | $59,440 | 4.7% | 1,680 | RIC |

## High-Paying Occupations for the Realistic Personality Type (cont.)

| Title | Annual Earnings | Percent Growth | Annual Openings | Personality Type |
|---|---|---|---|---|
| 13. Electrical and Electronic Engineering Technicians | $57,850 | 1.9% | 3,180 | RIC |
| 14. Cartographers and Photogrammetrists | $57,440 | 22.2% | 610 | RCI |
| 15. Boilermakers | $56,560 | 21.3% | 1,180 | RC |
| 16. Surveyors | $56,230 | 25.4% | 2,420 | RCI |

## High-Paying Occupations for the Investigative Personality Type

| Title | Annual Earnings | Percent Growth | Annual Openings | Personality Type |
|---|---|---|---|---|
| 1. Physicians and Surgeons | $187,200+ | 24.4% | 30,510 | ISR |
| 2. Dentists | $149,310 | 20.7% | 6,640 | IRS |
| 3. Petroleum Engineers | $130,280 | 17.0% | 1,180 | IRC |
| 4. Pharmacists | $116,670 | 25.4% | 13,960 | ICS |
| 5. Podiatrists | $116,440 | 20.0% | 510 | ISR |
| 6. Physicists | $106,840 | 14.2% | 800 | IR |
| 7. Nuclear Engineers | $104,270 | 10.2% | 620 | IRC |
| 8. Aerospace Engineers | $103,720 | 4.9% | 2,180 | IR |
| 9. Computer and Information Research Scientists | $102,190 | 18.7% | 1,060 | IRA |
| 10. Computer Hardware Engineers | $100,920 | 9.0% | 2,290 | IRC |

| High-Paying Occupations for the Investigative Personality Type (cont.) | | | | |
|---|---|---|---|---|
| Title | Annual Earnings | Percent Growth | Annual Openings | Personality Type |
| 11. Software Developers, Systems Software | $99,000 | 32.4% | 16,800 | ICR |
| 12. Optometrists | $97,820 | 33.1% | 2,340 | ISR |
| 13. Chemical Engineers | $94,350 | 5.9% | 1,140 | IR |
| 14. Engineers, All Other | $92,030 | 6.6% | 4,480 | IR |
| 15. Economists | $91,860 | 6.1% | 510 | ISR |
| 16. Electronics Engineers, Except Computer | $91,820 | 4.9% | 4,060 | IR |
| 17. Geoscientists, Except Hydrologists and Geographers | $90,890 | 21.2% | 1,710 | IR |
| 18. Software Developers, Applications | $90,060 | 27.6% | 19,790 | IRC |
| 19. Psychologists, All Other | $90,020 | 18.2% | 870 | ISA |
| 20. Electrical Engineers | $87,920 | 7.0% | 4,780 | IR |
| 21. Biomedical Engineers | $86,960 | 61.7% | 1,310 | IR |
| 22. Materials Engineers | $85,150 | 8.7% | 810 | IRE |
| 23. Veterinarians | $84,460 | 35.9% | 3,420 | IR |
| 24. Biochemists and Biophysicists | $81,480 | 30.8% | 1,340 | IAR |
| 25. Environmental Engineers | $80,890 | 21.9% | 2,260 | IR |

| High-Paying Occupations for the Investigative Personality Type (cont.) | | | | |
|---|---|---|---|---|
| Title | Annual Earnings | Percent Growth | Annual Openings | Personality Type |
| 26. Computer Systems Analysts | $79,680 | 22.1% | 22,2500 | IC |
| 27. Industrial Engineers | $78,860 | 6.4% | 5,750 | IR |
| 28. Management Analysts | $78,600 | 21.9% | 27,430 | IEC |
| 29. Medical Scientists, Except Epidemiologists | $76,980 | 36.4% | 4,260 | IAR |
| 30. Health and Safety Engineers, Except Mining Safety Engineers and Inspectors | $76,830 | 13.1% | 820 | IRC |
| 31. Social Scientists and Related Workers, All Other | $76,540 | 8.1% | 1,760 | ICR |
| 32. Computer Programmers | $74,280 | 12.0% | 12,800 | IC |
| 33. Health Diagnosing and Treating Practitioners, All Other | $72,710 | 19.0% | 2,120 | ISR |
| 34. Biological Scientists, All Other | $72,700 | 6.3% | 1,030 | IRA |
| 35. Network and Computer Systems Administrators | $72,560 | 27.8% | 15,530 | IRC |
| 36. Operations Research Analysts | $72,100 | 14.6% | 3,000 | ICE |
| 37. Chemists | $71,770 | 3.8% | 2,990 | IRC |

| High-Paying Occupations for the Investigative Personality Type (cont.) | | | | |
|---|---|---|---|---|
| **Title** | **Annual Earnings** | **Percent Growth** | **Annual Openings** | **Personality Type** |
| 38. Nuclear Medicine Technologists | $70,180 | 18.9% | 750 | IRS |
| 39. Audiologists | $69,720 | 36.8% | 560 | IS |
| 40. Clinical, Counseling, and School Psychologists | $67,650 | 21.9% | 8,230 | ISA |
| 41. Occupational Health and Safety Specialists | $66,790 | 8.5% | 2,570 | IC |
| 42. Microbiologists | $66,260 | 13.3% | 720 | IR |
| 43. Diagnostic Medical Sonographers | $65,860 | 43.5% | 3,170 | ISR |
| 44. Urban and Regional Planners | $65,230 | 16.2% | 1,680 | IEA |
| 45. Environmental Scientists and Specialists, Including Health | $63,570 | 18.7% | 4,320 | IER |
| 46. Market Research Analysts and Marketing Specialists | $60,300 | 41.2% | 19,180 | IEC |
| 47. Soil and Plant Scientists | $58,740 | 12.1% | 860 | IR |
| 48. Food Scientists and Technologists | $58,070 | 8.0% | 680 | IRC |
| 49. Zoologists and Wildlife Biologists | $57,710 | 7.4% | 590 | IR |
| 50. Medical and Clinical Laboratory Technologists | $57,580 | 11.3% | 5,210 | IRC |

## High-Paying Occupations for the Artistic Personality Type

| Title | Annual Earnings | Percent Growth | Annual Openings | Personality Type |
|---|---|---|---|---|
| 1. Art Directors | $80,880 | 9.0% | 2,430 | AE |
| 2. Architects, Except Landscape and Naval | $73,090 | 24.5% | 5,090 | AI |
| 3. Technical Writers | $65,500 | 17.2% | 1,830 | AIC |
| 4. Landscape Architects | $64,180 | 16.0% | 780 | AIR |
| 5. Multimedia Artists and Animators | $61,370 | 8.3% | 2,140 | AI |
| 6. Commercial and Industrial Designers | $59,610 | 10.5% | 1,690 | AER |

## High-Paying Occupations for the Social Personality Type

| Title | Annual Earnings | Percent Growth | Annual Openings | Personality Type |
|---|---|---|---|---|
| 1. Law Teachers, Postsecondary | $99,950 | — | — | SIE |
| 2. Engineering Teachers, Postsecondary | $92,670 | — | — | SIR |
| 3. Physician Assistants | $90,930 | 29.5% | 4,060 | SIR |
| 4. Economics Teachers, Postsecondary | $87,950 | — | — | SI |
| 5. Atmospheric, Earth, Marine, and Space Sciences Teachers, Postsecondary | $82,180 | — | — | SI |

| High-Paying Occupations for the Social Personality Type (cont.) | | | | |
|---|---|---|---|---|
| **Title** | **Annual Earnings** | **Percent Growth** | **Annual Openings** | **Personality Type** |
| 6. Forestry and Conservation Science Teachers, Postsecondary | $81,930 | — | — | SIR |
| 7. Health Specialties Teachers, Postsecondary | $81,140 | — | — | SI |
| 8. Physical Therapists | $79,860 | 39.0% | 10,060 | SIR |
| 9. Physics Teachers, Postsecondary | $78,540 | — | — | SI |
| 10. Radiation Therapists | $77,560 | 20.3% | 670 | SRC |
| 11. Environmental Science Teachers, Postsecondary | $77,320 | — | — | SIA |
| 12. Anthropology and Archeology Teachers, Postsecondary | $76,020 | — | — | SI |
| 13. Occupational Therapists | $75,400 | 33.5% | 5,710 | SI |
| 14. Biological Science Teachers, Postsecondary | $74,180 | — | — | SI |
| 15. Business Teachers, Postsecondary | $73,660 | — | — | SEI |
| 16. Computer Science Teachers, Postsecondary | $72,200 | — | — | SIC |
| 17. Political Science Teachers, Postsecondary | $72,170 | — | — | SEA |
| 18. Architecture Teachers, Postsecondary | $71,610 | — | — | SA |

| High-Paying Occupations for the Social Personality Type (cont.) | | | | |
|---|---|---|---|---|
| **Title** | **Annual Earnings** | **Percent Growth** | **Annual Openings** | **Personality Type** |
| 19. Chemistry Teachers, Postsecondary | $71,140 | — | — | SIR |
| 20. Dental Hygienists | $70,210 | 37.7% | 10,490 | SRC |
| 21. Speech-Language Pathologists | $69,870 | 23.4% | 5,230 | SIA |
| 22. Psychology Teachers, Postsecondary | $68,020 | — | — | SIA |
| 23. Geography Teachers, Postsecondary | $67,820 | — | — | SI |
| 24. Area, Ethnic, and Cultural Studies Teachers, Postsecondary | $67,360 | — | — | SIA |
| 25. Chiropractors | $66,160 | 28.3% | 2,530 | SIR |
| 26. Sociology Teachers, Postsecondary | $66,150 | — | — | SIA |
| 27. History Teachers, Postsecondary | $65,870 | — | — | SIA |
| 28. Library Science Teachers, Postsecondary | $65,780 | — | — | SIC |
| 29. Registered Nurses | $65,470 | 26.0% | 120,740 | SI |
| 30. Mathematical Science Teachers, Postsecondary | $64,990 | — | — | SIA |
| 31. Philosophy and Religion Teachers, Postsecondary | $64,990 | — | — | SAI |

| High-Paying Occupations for the Social Personality Type (cont.) | | | | |
|---|---|---|---|---|
| **Title** | **Annual Earnings** | **Percent Growth** | **Annual Openings** | **Personality Type** |
| 32. Nursing Instructors and Teachers, Postsecondary | $64,850 | — | — | SI |
| 33. Home Economics Teachers, Postsecondary | $64,040 | — | — | SIA |
| 34. Social Work Teachers, Postsecondary | $63,250 | — | — | SI |
| 35. Communications Teachers, Postsecondary | $62,180 | — | — | SA |
| 36. Art, Drama, and Music Teachers, Postsecondary | $62,160 | — | — | SA |
| 37. Instructional Coordinators | $60,050 | 19.5% | 5,810 | SEI |
| 38. English Language and Literature Teachers, Postsecondary | $60,040 | — | — | SAI |
| 39. Education Teachers, Postsecondary | $59,350 | — | — | SAI |
| 40. Foreign Language and Literature Teachers, Postsecondary | $58,670 | — | — | SAI |
| 41. Criminal Justice and Law Enforcement Teachers, Postsecondary | $58,040 | — | — | SI |
| 42. Recreation and Fitness Studies Teachers, Postsecondary | $57,920 | — | — | S |
| 43. Special Education Teachers, Secondary School | $56,830 | 7.3% | 5,110 | SI |

| High-Paying Occupations for the Enterprising Personality Type | | | | |
|---|---|---|---|---|
| Title | Annual Earnings | Percent Growth | Annual Openings | Personality Type |
| 1. Chief Executives | $168,140 | 4.2% | 11,150 | EC |
| 2. Architectural and Engineering Managers | $124,870 | 8.6% | 4,970 | EI |
| 3. Computer and Information Systems Managers | $120,950 | 18.1% | 10,280 | ECI |
| 4. Marketing Managers | $119,480 | 13.6% | 7,600 | EC |
| 5. Judges, Magistrate Judges, and Magistrates | $115,760 | 9.2% | 960 | ES |
| 6. Natural Sciences Managers | $115,730 | 7.7% | 3,350 | EIC |
| 7. Lawyers | $113,530 | 10.1% | 21,200 | EI |
| 8. Financial Managers | $109,740 | 8.8% | 14,280 | EC |
| 9. Sales Managers | $105,260 | 11.7% | 13,970 | EC |
| 10. Managers, All Other | $100,890 | 7.9% | 24,940 | EC |
| 11. Purchasing Managers | $100,170 | 7.2% | 2,560 | EC |
| 12. Human Resources Managers | $99,720 | 12.9% | 2,690 | ESC |
| 13. Public Relations and Fundraising Managers | $95,450 | 16.4% | 2,790 | EA |
| 14. General and Operations Managers | $95,440 | 4.6% | 41,010 | ECS |
| 15. Training and Development Managers | $95,400 | 14.6% | 1,160 | ES |

| High-Paying Occupations for the Enterprising Personality Type (cont.) | | | | |
|---|---|---|---|---|
| **Title** | **Annual Earnings** | **Percent Growth** | **Annual Openings** | **Personality Type** |
| 16. Compensation and Benefits Managers | $95,250 | 2.8% | 870 | ECS |
| 17. Sales Engineers | $91,830 | 14.4% | 3,210 | ERI |
| 18. Industrial Production Managers | $89,190 | 9.1% | 4,900 | ECR |
| 19. Advertising and Promotions Managers | $88,590 | 13.3% | 1,620 | EAC |
| 20. Medical and Health Services Managers | $88,580 | 22.4% | 14,190 | ECS |
| 21. Education Administrators, Elementary and Secondary School | $87,760 | 9.8% | 8,970 | ESC |
| 22. Education Administrators, Postsecondary | $86,490 | 19.0% | 6,910 | ECS |
| 23. Construction Managers | $82,790 | 16.6% | 12,040 | ERC |
| 24. Transportation, Storage, and Distribution Managers | $81,830 | 10.0% | 3,370 | EC |
| 25. Administrative Services Managers | $81,080 | 14.5% | 9,980 | EC |
| 26. First-Line Supervisors of Police and Detectives | $78,270 | 2.1% | 3,870 | ESC |
| 27. Education Administrators, All Other | $76,860 | 13.6% | 1,360 | EC |
| 28. Financial Examiners | $75,800 | 27.0% | 1,410 | EC |

| High-Paying Occupations for the Enterprising Personality Type (cont.) | | | | |
|---|---|---|---|---|
| Title | Annual Earnings | Percent Growth | Annual Openings | Personality Type |
| 29. Sales Representatives, Wholesale and Manufacturing, Technical and Scientific Products | $74,970 | 16.4% | 15,970 | EC |
| 30. Detectives and Criminal Investigators | $74,300 | 2.9% | 3,010 | ECI |
| 31. Securities, Commodities, and Financial Services Sales Agents | $71,720 | 15.2% | 13,370 | EC |
| 32. Producers and Directors | $71,350 | 11.0% | 4,970 | EAC |
| 33. First-Line Supervisors of Non-Retail Sales Workers | $70,060 | 4.0% | 12,350 | ECS |
| 34. First-Line Supervisors of Fire Fighting and Prevention Workers | $68,210 | 8.2% | 3,310 | ER |
| 35. Personal Financial Advisors | $67,520 | 32.1% | 9,020 | ECS |
| 36. Business Operations Specialists, All Other | $65,120 | 11.6% | 32,720 | EC |
| 37. Agents and Business Managers of Artists, Performers, and Athletes | $63,370 | 14.0% | 800 | ECS |
| 38. First-Line Supervisors of Mechanics, Installers, and Repairers | $60,250 | 11.9% | 16,490 | ECR |
| 39. Social and Community Service Managers | $59,970 | 26.7% | 6,480 | ES |

| High-Paying Occupations for the Enterprising Personality Type (cont.) | | | | |
|---|---|---|---|---|
| **Title** | **Annual Earnings** | **Percent Growth** | **Annual Openings** | **Personality Type** |
| 40. Supervisors of Construction and Extraction Workers | $59,700 | 23.5% | 25,970 | ERC |
| 41. Real Estate Brokers | $58,350 | 7.6% | 2,970 | EC |
| 42. First-Line Supervisors of Correctional Officers | $57,840 | 5.6% | 1,650 | ECR |

| High-Paying Occupations for the Conventional Personality Type | | | | |
|---|---|---|---|---|
| **Title** | **Annual Earnings** | **Percent Growth** | **Annual Openings** | **Personality Type** |
| 1. Actuaries | $93,680 | 26.7% | 1,890 | CIE |
| 2. Database Administrators | $77,080 | 30.6% | 5,270 | CI |
| 3. Financial Analysts | $76,950 | 23.0% | 10,420 | CIE |
| 4. Statisticians | $75,560 | 14.1% | 1,870 | CI |
| 5. Logisticians | $72,780 | 25.5% | 4,870 | CEI |
| 6. Budget Analysts | $69,280 | 10.4% | 1,960 | CEI |
| 7. Accountants and Auditors | $63,550 | 15.7% | 45,210 | CEI |
| 8. Insurance Underwriters | $62,870 | 5.9% | 3,910 | CEI |
| 9. Compliance Officers | $62,020 | 15.0% | 5,860 | CEI |
| 10. Financial Specialists, All Other | $61,160 | 6.1% | 4,490 | CEI |

| High-Paying Occupations for the Conventional Personality Type (cont.) | | | | |
|---|---|---|---|---|
| Title | Annual Earnings | Percent Growth | Annual Openings | Personality Type |
| 11. Credit Analysts | $61,080 | 19.7% | 2,590 | CE |
| 12. Claims Adjusters, Examiners, and Investigators | $59,960 | 3.0% | 7,990 | CE |
| 13. Loan Officers | $59,820 | 14.2% | 11,520 | CES |
| 14. Compensation, Benefits, and Job Analysis Specialists | $59,090 | 5.0% | 2,400 | CE |
| 15. Cost Estimators | $58,860 | 36.4% | 10,300 | CE |
| 16. Purchasing Agents, Except Wholesale, Retail, and Farm Products | $58,760 | 5.3% | 9,120 | CE |

## Lists of High-Paying Occupations Based on Career Clusters

Like the Holland personality types, career clusters are a useful way to break down the sprawling world of work into manageable sectors based on preferences that many people share. The 16 career clusters were developed in 1999 by a collaborative effort of the U.S. Department of Education, the Office of Vocational and Adult Education, the National School-to-Work Office, and the National Skill Standards Board. The purpose is to categorize similar programs of vocational education together so that educators can focus on teaching the transferable skills that are most relevant within each cluster. K–12 students can choose the educational program for the cluster that interests them, learn the relevant skills shared across the occupations in their chosen cluster, and postpone the decision about a specific occupational goal until later in the educational process.

This clustering scheme was never intended to be rigid and has allowed individual states to create their own variations to reflect their differing economies. Some states have fewer than 16 or use slightly different titles for the clusters. I found it useful to employ the 16 cluster titles that the O*NET database uses.

I also followed O*NET in assigning occupations to clusters, including the instances where O*NET links a single occupation to more than one cluster. An extreme example is Chief Executives, which is linked to four clusters: Business, Management, and Administration; Govern-

53

ment and Public Administration; Human Services; and Transportation, Distribution, and Logistics.

If you are not yet ready to choose a specific occupational goal, you might browse the following lists and make a note of which career cluster includes several of the occupations that look most interesting to you. Then you may want to work on developing the skills that are shared across occupations within that cluster. (You can find skills information in part II.) For example, if you are interested in a "STEM" career, you'll want to look at the occupations in the Science, Technology, Engineering, and Mathematics cluster. Or if you're more artistic, the Arts, Audio/ Video Technology, and Communications cluster may appeal to you.

If you are thinking about a mid-career change and want to utilize the skills you have learned in your present job, find an occupation like yours in these lists and consider entry into another occupation in the same cluster. Of course, there's no law that says you can't jump from one cluster to another if an occupation attracts you so strongly that you want to make that jump. Understand, however, that this career change will probably require you to learn a new set of skills.

On the following lists, the occupations are sorted by their median earnings, with the best-paying occupations at the top of each cluster's list.

| High-Paying Occupations in the Agriculture, Food, and Natural Resources Cluster | | | |
| --- | --- | --- | --- |
| Title | Annual Earnings | Percent Growth | Annual Openings |
| 1. Economists | $91,860 | 6.1% | 580 |
| 2. Veterinarians | $84,460 | 35.9% | 3,420 |
| 3. Forestry and Conservation Science Teachers, Postsecondary | $81,930 | — | — |
| 4. Biochemists and Biophysicists | $81,480 | 30.8% | 1,340 |
| 5. Environmental Science Teachers, Postsecondary | $77,320 | — | — |
| 6. Biological Science Teachers, Postsecondary | $74,180 | — | — |
| 7. Biological Scientists, All Other | $72,700 | 6.3% | 1,030 |
| 8. Occupational Health and Safety Specialists | $66,790 | 8.5% | 2,570 |

| High-Paying Occupations in the Agriculture, Food & Natural Resources Cluster (cont.) | | | |
|---|---|---|---|
| Title | Annual Earnings | Percent Growth | Annual Openings |
| 9. Environmental Scientists and Specialists, Including Health | $63,570 | 18.7% | 4,320 |
| 10. Engineering Technicians, Except Drafters, All Other | $59,440 | 4.7% | 1,680 |
| 11. Soil and Plant Scientists | $58,740 | 12.1% | 860 |
| 12. Food Scientists and Technologists | $58,070 | 8.0% | 680 |
| 13. Recreation and Fitness Studies Teachers, Postsecondary | $57,920 | — | — |
| 14. Zoologists and Wildlife Biologists | $57,710 | 7.4% | 590 |

| High-Paying Occupations in the Architecture and Construction Cluster | | | |
|---|---|---|---|
| Title | Annual Earnings | Percent Growth | Annual Openings |
| 1. Architectural and Engineering Managers | $124,870 | 8.6% | 4,970 |
| 2. Engineering Teachers, Postsecondary | $92,670 | — | — |
| 3. Engineers, All Other | $92,030 | 6.6% | 4,480 |
| 4. Construction Managers | $82,790 | 16.6% | 12,040 |
| 5. Architects, Except Landscape and Naval | $73,090 | 24.5% | 5,090 |
| 6. Architecture Teachers, Postsecondary | $71,610 | — | — |
| 7. Landscape Architects | $64,180 | 16.0% | 780 |
| 8. Electrical Power-Line Installers and Repairers | $63,250 | 13.2% | 5,270 |

| High-Paying Occupations in the Architecture and Construction Cluster (cont.) | | | |
|---|---|---|---|
| **Title** | **Annual Earnings** | **Percent Growth** | **Annual Openings** |
| 9.  Supervisors of Construction and Extraction Workers | $59,700 | 23.5% | 25,970 |
| 10. Engineering Technicians, Except Drafters, All Other | $59,440 | 4.7% | 1,680 |
| 11. Cost Estimators | $58,860 | 36.4% | 10,300 |
| 12. Cartographers and Photogrammetrists | $57,440 | 22.2% | 610 |
| 13. Boilermakers | $56,560 | 21.3% | 1,180 |
| 14. Surveyors | $56,230 | 25.4% | 2,420 |

| High-Paying Occupations in the Arts, Audio/ Video Technology, and Communications Cluster | | | |
|---|---|---|---|
| **Title** | **Annual Earnings** | **Percent Growth** | **Annual Openings** |
| 1.  Managers, All Other | $100,890 | 7.9% | 24,940 |
| 2.  Art Directors | $80,880 | 9.0% | 2,430 |
| 3.  Producers and Directors | $71,350 | 11.0% | 4,970 |
| 4.  Technical Writers | $65,500 | 17.2% | 1,830 |
| 5.  Agents and Business Managers of Artists, Performers, and Athletes | $63,370 | 14.0% | 800 |
| 6.  Communications Teachers, Postsecondary | $62,180 | — | — |
| 7.  Art, Drama, and Music Teachers, Postsecondary | $62,160 | — | — |

| High-Paying Occupations in the Arts, Audio/ Video Technology, and Communications Cluster (cont.) | | | |
|---|---|---|---|
| **Title** | **Annual Earnings** | **Percent Growth** | **Annual Openings** |
| 8. Multimedia Artists and Animators | $61,370 | 8.3% | 2,140 |
| 9. English Language and Literature Teachers, Postsecondary | $60,040 | — | — |
| 10. Commercial and Industrial Designers | $59,610 | 10.5% | 1,690 |

| High-Paying Occupations in the Business, Management, and Administration Cluster | | | |
|---|---|---|---|
| **Title** | **Annual Earnings** | **Percent Growth** | **Annual Openings** |
| 1. Chief Executives | $168,140 | 4.2% | 11,150 |
| 2. Computer and Information Systems Managers | $120,950 | 18.1% | 10,280 |
| 3. Natural Sciences Managers | $115,730 | 7.7% | 3,350 |
| 4. Financial Managers | $109,740 | 8.8% | 14,280 |
| 5. Sales Managers | $105,260 | 11.7% | 13,970 |
| 6. Managers, All Other | $100,890 | 7.9% | 24,940 |
| 7. Purchasing Managers | $100,170 | 7.2% | 2,560 |
| 8. Human Resources Managers | $99,720 | 12.9% | 2,690 |
| 9. Public Relations and Fundraising Managers | $95,450 | 16.4% | 2,790 |
| 10. General and Operations Managers | $95,440 | 4.6% | 41,010 |
| 11. Training and Development Managers | $95,400 | 14.6% | 1,160 |

| High-Paying Occupations in the Business, Management, and Administration Cluster (cont.) | | | |
|---|---|---|---|
| Title | Annual Earnings | Percent Growth | Annual Openings |
| 12. Compensation and Benefits Managers | $95,250 | 2.8% | 870 |
| 13. Economists | $91,860 | 6.1% | 580 |
| 14. Industrial Production Managers | $89,190 | 9.1% | 4,900 |
| 15. Advertising and Promotions Managers | $88,590 | 13.3% | 1,620 |
| 16. Economics Teachers, Postsecondary | $87,950 | — | — |
| 17. Construction Managers | $82,790 | 16.6% | 12,040 |
| 18. Transportation, Storage, and Distribution Managers | $81,830 | 10.0% | 3,370 |
| 19. Administrative Services Managers | $81,080 | 14.5% | 9,980 |
| 20. Management Analysts | $78,600 | 21.9% | 27,430 |
| 21. Financial Analysts | $76,950 | 23.0% | 10,420 |
| 22. Financial Examiners | $75,800 | 27.0% | 1,410 |
| 23. Statisticians | $75,560 | 14.1% | 1,870 |
| 24. Business Teachers, Postsecondary | $73,660 | — | — |
| 25. Logisticians | $72,780 | 25.5% | 4,870 |
| 26. Operations Research Analysts | $72,100 | 14.6% | 3,000 |
| 27. Budget Analysts | $69,280 | 10.4% | 1,960 |
| 28. Technical Writers | $65,500 | 17.2% | 1,830 |
| 29. Business Operations Specialists, All Other | $65,120 | 11.6% | 32,720 |

| High-Paying Occupations in the Business, Management, and Administration Cluster (cont.) | | | |
|---|---|---|---|
| **Title** | **Annual Earnings** | **Percent Growth** | **Annual Openings** |
| 30. Accountants and Auditors | $63,550 | 15.7% | 45,210 |
| 31. Agents and Business Managers of Artists, Performers, and Athletes | $63,370 | 14.0% | 800 |
| 32. Communications Teachers, Postsecondary | $62,180 | — | — |
| 33. Credit Analysts | $61,080 | 19.7% | 2,590 |
| 34. Market Research Analysts and Marketing Specialists | $60,300 | 41.2% | 19,180 |
| 35. Social and Community Service Managers | $59,970 | 26.7% | 6,480 |
| 36. Compensation, Benefits, and Job Analysis Specialists | $59,090 | 5.0% | 2,400 |
| 37. Cost Estimators | $58,860 | 36.4% | 10,300 |

| High-Paying Occupations in the Education and Training Cluster | | | |
|---|---|---|---|
| **Title** | **Annual Earnings** | **Percent Growth** | **Annual Openings** |
| 1. Physicists | $106,840 | 14.2% | 800 |
| 2. Law Teachers, Postsecondary | $99,950 | — | — |
| 3. Training and Development Managers | $95,400 | 14.6% | 1,160 |
| 4. Engineering Teachers, Postsecondary | $92,670 | — | — |
| 5. Education Administrators, Elementary and Secondary School | $87,760 | 9.8% | 8,970 |

| High-Paying Occupations in the Education and Training Cluster (cont.) | | | |
|---|---|---|---|
| **Title** | **Annual Earnings** | **Percent Growth** | **Annual Openings** |
| 6. Education Administrators, Postsecondary | $86,490 | 19.0% | 6,910 |
| 7. Atmospheric, Earth, Marine, and Space Sciences Teachers, Postsecondary | $82,180 | — | — |
| 8. Forestry and Conservation Science Teachers, Postsecondary | $81,930 | — | — |
| 9. Health Specialties Teachers, Postsecondary | $81,140 | — | — |
| 10. Environmental Science Teachers, Postsecondary | $77,320 | — | — |
| 11. Education Administrators, All Other | $76,860 | 13.6% | 1,360 |
| 12. Anthropology and Archeology Teachers, Postsecondary | $76,020 | — | — |
| 13. Biological Science Teachers, Postsecondary | $74,180 | — | — |
| 14. Business Teachers, Postsecondary | $73,660 | — | — |
| 15. Computer Science Teachers, Postsecondary | $72,200 | — | — |
| 16. Political Science Teachers, Postsecondary | $72,170 | — | — |
| 17. Chemists | $71,770 | 3.8% | 2,990 |
| 18. Architecture Teachers, Postsecondary | $71,610 | — | — |
| 19. Psychology Teachers, Postsecondary | $68,020 | — | — |
| 20. Geography Teachers, Postsecondary | $67,820 | — | — |

| High-Paying Occupations in the Education and Training Cluster (cont.) | | | |
|---|---|---|---|
| Title | Annual Earnings | Percent Growth | Annual Openings |
| 21. Area, Ethnic, and Cultural Studies Teachers, Postsecondary | $67,360 | — | — |
| 22. Sociology Teachers, Postsecondary | $66,150 | — | — |
| 23. History Teachers, Postsecondary | $65,870 | — | — |
| 24. Library Science Teachers, Postsecondary | $65,780 | — | — |
| 25. Philosophy and Religion Teachers, Postsecondary | $64,990 | — | — |
| 26. Nursing Instructors and Teachers, Postsecondary | $64,850 | — | — |
| 27. Home Economics Teachers, Postsecondary | $64,040 | — | — |
| 28. Social Work Teachers, Postsecondary | $63,250 | — | — |
| 29. Communications Teachers, Postsecondary | $62,180 | — | — |
| 30. Art, Drama, and Music Teachers, Postsecondary | $62,160 | — | — |
| 31. Instructional Coordinators | $60,050 | 19.5% | 5,810 |
| 32. English Language and Literature Teachers, Postsecondary | $60,040 | — | — |
| 33. Education Teachers, Postsecondary | $59,350 | — | — |
| 34. Foreign Language and Literature Teachers, Postsecondary | $58,670 | — | — |
| 35. Criminal Justice and Law Enforcement Teachers, Postsecondary | $58,040 | — | — |

| High-Paying Occupations in the Education and Training Cluster (cont.) | | | |
|---|---|---|---|
| Title | Annual Earnings | Percent Growth | Annual Openings |
| 36. Recreation and Fitness Studies Teachers, Postsecondary | $57,920 | — | — |
| 37. Special Education Teachers, Secondary School | $56,830 | 7.3% | 5,110 |

| High-Paying Occupations in the Finance Cluster | | | |
|---|---|---|---|
| Title | Annual Earnings | Percent Growth | Annual Openings |
| 1. Financial Managers | $109,74 0 | 8.8% | 14,280 |
| 2. Actuaries | $93,680 | 26.7% | 1,890 |
| 3. Financial Analysts | $76,950 | 23.0% | 10,420 |
| 4. Business Teachers, Postsecondary | $73,660 | — | — |
| 5. Securities, Commodities, and Financial Services Sales Agents | $71,720 | 15.2% | 13,370 |
| 6. Budget Analysts | $69,280 | 10.4% | 1,960 |
| 7. Personal Financial Advisors | $67,520 | 32.1% | 9,020 |
| 8. Insurance Underwriters | $62,870 | 5.9% | 3,910 |
| 9. Financial Specialists, All Other | $61,160 | 6.1% | 4,490 |
| 10. Credit Analysts | $61,080 | 19.7% | 2,590 |
| 11. Claims Adjusters, Examiners, and Investigators | $59,960 | 3.0% | 7,990 |
| 12. Loan Officers | $59,820 | 14.2% | 11,820 |

## High-Paying Occupations in the Government and Public Administration Cluster

| Title | Annual Earnings | Percent Growth | Annual Openings |
|---|---|---|---|
| 1. Chief Executives | $168,140 | 4.2% | 11,150 |
| 2. Managers, All Other | $100,890 | 7.9% | 24,940 |
| 3. General and Operations Managers | $95,440 | 4.6% | 41,010 |
| 4. Transportation, Storage, and Distribution Managers | $81,830 | 10.0% | 3,370 |
| 5. Administrative Services Managers | $81,080 | 14.5% | 9,980 |
| 6. Financial Examiners | $75,800 | 27.0% | 1,410 |
| 7. Political Science Teachers, Postsecondary | $72,170 | — | — |
| 8. Urban and Regional Planners | $65,230 | 16.2% | 1,680 |
| 9. Accountants and Auditors | $63,550 | 15.7% | 45,210 |
| 10. Compliance Officers | $62,020 | 15.0% | 5,860 |
| 11. Social and Community Service Managers | $59,970 | 26.7% | 6,480 |

## High-Paying Occupations in the Health Science Cluster

| Title | Annual Earnings | Percent Growth | Annual Openings |
|---|---|---|---|
| 1. Physicians and Surgeons | $187,200+ | 24.4% | 30,510 |
| 2. Dentists | $149,310 | 20.7% | 6,640 |
| 3. Pharmacists | $116,670 | 25.4% | 13,960 |
| 4. Podiatrists | $116,440 | 20.0% | 510 |

| High-Paying Occupations in the Health Science Cluster (cont.) | | | |
|---|---|---|---|
| **Title** | **Annual Earnings** | **Percent Growth** | **Annual Openings** |
| 5.  Optometrists | $97,820 | 33.1% | 2,340 |
| 6.  Engineers, All Other | $92,030 | 6.6% | 4,480 |
| 7.  Physical Scientists, All Other | $91,640 | 8.5% | 1,330 |
| 8.  Physician Assistants | $90,930 | 29.5% | 4,060 |
| 9.  Psychologists, All Other | $90,020 | 18.2% | 870 |
| 10. Medical and Health Services Managers | $88,580 | 22.4% | 14,190 |
| 11. Veterinarians | $84,460 | 35.9% | 3,420 |
| 12. Health Specialties Teachers, Postsecondary | $81,140 | — | — |
| 13. Physical Therapists | $79,860 | 39.0% | 10,060 |
| 14. Computer Systems Analysts | $79,680 | 22.1% | 22,250 |
| 15. Radiation Therapists | $77,560 | 20.3% | 670 |
| 16. Medical Scientists, Except Epidemiologists | $76,980 | 36.4% | 4,260 |
| 17. Occupational Therapists | $75,400 | 33.5% | 5,710 |
| 18. Health Diagnosing and Treating Practitioners, All Other | $72,710 | 19.0% | 2,120 |
| 19. Biological Scientists, All Other | $72,700 | 6.3% | 1,030 |
| 20. Dental Hygienists | $70,210 | 37.7% | 10,490 |
| 21. Nuclear Medicine Technologists | $70,180 | 18.9% | 750 |

## High-Paying Occupations in the Health Science Cluster (cont.)

| Title | Annual Earnings | Percent Growth | Annual Openings |
|---|---|---|---|
| 22. Speech-Language Pathologists | $69,870 | 23.4% | 5,230 |
| 23. Audiologists | $69,720 | 36.8% | 560 |
| 24. Psychology Teachers, Postsecondary | $68,020 | — | — |
| 25. Clinical, Counseling, and School Psychologists | $67,650 | 21.9% | 8,230 |
| 26. Occupational Health and Safety Specialists | $66,790 | 8.5% | 2,570 |
| 27. Chiropractors | $66,160 | 28.3% | 2,530 |
| 28. Diagnostic Medical Sonographers | $65,860 | 43.5% | 3,170 |
| 29. Registered Nurses | $65,470 | 26.0% | 120,740 |
| 30. Nursing Instructors and Teachers, Postsecondary | $64,850 | — | — |
| 31. Home Economics Teachers, Postsecondary | $64,040 | — | — |
| 32. Communications Teachers, Postsecondary | $62,180 | — | — |
| 33. Medical and Clinical Laboratory Technologists | $57,580 | 11.3% | 5,210 |

## High-Paying Occupations in the Hospitality and Tourism Cluster

| Title | Annual Earnings | Percent Growth | Annual Openings |
|---|---|---|---|
| 1. Managers, All Other | $100,890 | 7.9% | 24,940 |

65

| High-Paying Occupations in the Human Services Cluster | | | |
|---|---|---|---|
| Title | Annual Earnings | Percent Growth | Annual Openings |
| 1. Chief Executives | $168,140 | 4.2% | 11,150 |
| 2. Sales Managers | $105,260 | 11.7% | 13,970 |
| 3. Managers, All Other | $100,890 | 7.9% | 24,940 |
| 4. Psychologists, All Other | $90,020 | 18.2% | 870 |
| 5. Social Scientists and Related Workers, All Other | $76,540 | 8.1% | 1,760 |
| 6. Psychology Teachers, Postsecondary | $68,020 | — | — |
| 7. Clinical, Counseling, and School Psychologists | $67,650 | 21.9% | 8,230 |
| 8. Area, Ethnic, and Cultural Studies Teachers, Postsecondary | $67,360 | — | — |
| 9. Philosophy and Religion Teachers, Postsecondary | $64,990 | — | — |
| 10. Home Economics Teachers, Postsecondary | $64,040 | — | — |
| 11. Social Work Teachers, Postsecondary | $63,250 | — | — |
| 12. Social and Community Service Managers | $59,970 | 26.7% | 6,480 |

| High-Paying Occupations in the Information Technology Cluster | | | |
|---|---|---|---|
| Title | Annual Earnings | Percent Growth | Annual Openings |
| 1. Architectural and Engineering Managers | $124,870 | 8.6% | 4,970 |
| 2. Computer and Information Systems Managers | $120,950 | 18.1% | 10,280 |
| 3. Computer and Information Research Scientists | $102,190 | 18.7% | 1,060 |
| 4. Computer Hardware Engineers | $100,920 | 9.0% | 2,290 |
| 5. Software Developers, Systems Software | $99,000 | 32.4% | 16,800 |
| 6. Engineering Teachers, Postsecondary | $92,670 | — | — |
| 7. Physical Scientists, All Other | $91,640 | 8.5% | 1,330 |
| 8. Software Developers, Applications | $90,060 | 27.6% | 19,790 |
| 9. Computer Systems Analysts | $79,680 | 22.1% | 22,250 |
| 10. Database Administrators | $77,080 | 30.6% | 5,270 |
| 11. Computer Programmers | $74,280 | 12.0% | 12,800 |
| 12. Biological Scientists, All Other | $72,700 | 6.3% | 1,030 |
| 13. Network and Computer Systems Administrators | $72,560 | 27.8% | 15,530 |
| 14. Computer Science Teachers, Postsecondary | $72,200 | — | — |
| 15. Multimedia Artists and Animators | $61,370 | 8.3% | 2,140 |

| High-Paying Occupations in the Law, Public Safety, Corrections, and Security Cluster | | | |
|---|---|---|---|
| Title | Annual Earnings | Percent Growth | Annual Openings |
| 1.  Judges, Magistrate Judges, and Magistrates | $115,760 | 9.2% | 960 |
| 2.  Lawyers | $113,530 | 10.1% | 21,200 |
| 3.  Law Teachers, Postsecondary | $99,950 | — | — |
| 4.  Physical Scientists, All Other | $91,640 | 8.5% | 1,330 |
| 5.  First-Line Supervisors of Police and Detectives | $78,270 | 2.1% | 3,870 |
| 6.  Anthropology and Archeology Teachers, Postsecondary | $76,020 | — | — |
| 7.  Detectives and Criminal Investigators | $74,300 | 2.9% | 3,010 |
| 8.  First-Line Supervisors of Fire Fighting and Prevention Workers | $68,210 | 8.2% | 3,310 |
| 9.  Psychology Teachers, Postsecondary | $68,020 | — | — |
| 10. Compliance Officers | $62,020 | 15.0% | 5,860 |
| 11. Criminal Justice and Law Enforcement Teachers, Postsecondary | $58,040 | — | — |
| 12. First-Line Supervisors of Correctional Officers | $57,840 | 5.6% | 1,650 |

| High-Paying Occupations in the Manufacturing Cluster | | | |
|---|---|---|---|
| **Title** | **Annual Earnings** | **Percent Growth** | **Annual Openings** |
| 1. Elevator Installers and Repairers | $76,650 | 11.3% | 820 |
| 2. Electrical and Electronics Repairers, Powerhouse, Substation, and Relay | $68,810 | 4.9% | 690 |
| 3. Occupational Health and Safety Specialists | $66,790 | 8.5% | 2,570 |
| 4. First-Line Supervisors of Mechanics, Installers, and Repairers | $60,250 | 11.9% | 16,490 |
| 5. Engineering Technicians, Except Drafters, All Other | $59,440 | 4.7% | 1,680 |
| 6. Cost Estimators | $58,860 | 36.4% | 10,300 |
| 7. Electrical and Electronic Engineering Technicians | $57,850 | 1.9% | 3,180 |

| High-Paying Occupations in the Marketing, Sales, and Service Cluster | | | |
|---|---|---|---|
| **Title** | **Annual Earnings** | **Percent Growth** | **Annual Openings** |
| 1. Marketing Managers | $119,480 | 13.6% | 7,600 |
| 2. Sales Managers | $105,260 | 11.7% | 13,970 |
| 3. Sales Engineers | $91,830 | 14.4% | 3,210 |
| 4. Advertising and Promotions Managers | $88,590 | 13.3% | 1,620 |
| 5. Sales Representatives, Wholesale and Manufacturing, Technical and Scientific Products | $74,970 | 16.4% | 15,970 |

## High-Paying Occupations in the Marketing, Sales, and Service Cluster (cont.)

| Title | Annual Earnings | Percent Growth | Annual Openings |
|---|---|---|---|
| 6. Business Teachers, Postsecondary | $73,660 | — | — |
| 7. First-Line Supervisors of Non-Retail Sales Workers | $70,060 | 4.0% | 12,350 |
| 8. Business Operations Specialists, All Other | $65,120 | 11.6% | 32,720 |
| 9. Purchasing Agents, Except Wholesale, Retail, and Farm Products | $58,760 | 5.3% | 9,120 |
| 10. Real Estate Brokers | $58,350 | 7.6% | 2,970 |

## High-Paying Occupations in the Science, Technology, Engineering, and Mathematics Cluster

| Title | Annual Earnings | Percent Growth | Annual Openings |
|---|---|---|---|
| 1. Petroleum Engineers | $130,280 | 17.0% | 1,180 |
| 2. Architectural and Engineering Managers | $124,870 | 8.6% | 4,970 |
| 3. Natural Sciences Managers | $115,730 | 7.7% | 3,350 |
| 4. Physicists | $106,840 | 14.2% | 800 |
| 5. Nuclear Engineers | $104,270 | 10.2% | 620 |
| 6. Aerospace Engineers | $103,720 | 4.9% | 2,180 |
| 7. Computer Hardware Engineers | $100,920 | 9.0% | 2,290 |
| 8. Chemical Engineers | $94,350 | 5.9% | 1,140 |

| High-Paying Occupations in the Science, Technology, Engineering, and Mathematics Cluster (cont.) | | | |
|---|---|---|---|
| **Title** | **Annual Earnings** | **Percent Growth** | **Annual Openings** |
| 9. Engineering Teachers, Postsecondary | $92,670 | — | — |
| 10. Engineers, All Other | $92,030 | 6.6% | 4,480 |
| 11. Economists | $91,860 | 6.1% | 580 |
| 12. Electronics Engineers, Except Computer | $91,820 | 4.9% | 4,060 |
| 13. Physical Scientists, All Other | $91,640 | 8.5% | 1,330 |
| 14. Geoscientists, Except Hydrologists and Geographers | $90,890 | 21.2% | 1,710 |
| 15. Psychologists, All Other | $90,020 | 18.2% | 870 |
| 16. Economics Teachers, Postsecondary | $87,950 | — | — |
| 17. Electrical Engineers | $87,920 | 7.0% | 4,780 |
| 18. Biomedical Engineers | $86,960 | 61.7% | 1,310 |
| 19. Materials Engineers | $85,150 | 8.7% | 810 |
| 20. Atmospheric, Earth, Marine, and Space Sciences Teachers, Postsecondary | $82,180 | — | — |
| 21. Biochemists and Biophysicists | $81,480 | 30.8% | 1,340 |
| 22. Health Specialties Teachers, Postsecondary | $81,140 | — | — |
| 23. Environmental Engineers | $80,890 | 21.9% | 2,260 |
| 24. Mechanical Engineers | $80,580 | 8.8% | 9,960 |
| 25. Civil Engineers | $79,340 | 19.4% | 10,440 |

| High-Paying Occupations in the Science, Technology, Engineering, and Mathematics Cluster (cont.) | | | |
|---|---|---|---|
| Title | Annual Earnings | Percent Growth | Annual Openings |
| 26. Industrial Engineers | $78,860 | 6.4% | 5,750 |
| 27. Physics Teachers, Postsecondary | $78,540 | — | — |
| 28. Medical Scientists, Except Epidemiologists | $76,980 | 36.4% | 4,260 |
| 29. Health and Safety Engineers, Except Mining Safety Engineers and Inspectors | $76,830 | 13.1% | 820 |
| 30. Social Scientists and Related Workers, All Other | $76,540 | 8.1% | 1,760 |
| 31. Anthropology and Archeology Teachers, Postsecondary | $76,020 | — | — |
| 32. Statisticians | $75,560 | 14.1% | 1,870 |
| 33. Biological Science Teachers, Postsecondary | $74,180 | — | — |
| 34. Biological Scientists, All Other | $72,700 | 6.3% | 1,030 |
| 35. Political Science Teachers, Postsecondary | $72,170 | — | — |
| 36. Operations Research Analysts | $72,100 | 14.6% | 3,000 |
| 37. Chemists | $71,770 | 3.8% | 2,990 |
| 38. Architecture Teachers, Postsecondary | $71,610 | — | — |
| 39. Chemistry Teachers, Postsecondary | $71,140 | — | — |
| 40. Geography Teachers, Postsecondary | $67,820 | — | — |

| High-Paying Occupations in the Science, Technology, Engineering, and Mathematics Cluster (cont.) | | | |
|---|---|---|---|
| **Title** | **Annual Earnings** | **Percent Growth** | **Annual Openings** |
| 41. Microbiologists | $66,260 | 13.3% | 720 |
| 42. Sociology Teachers, Postsecondary | $66,150 | — | — |
| 43. History Teachers, Postsecondary | $65,870 | — | — |
| 44. Mathematical Science Teachers, Postsecondary | $64,990 | — | — |
| 45. Cost Estimators | $58,860 | 36.4% | 10,300 |
| 46. Zoologists and Wildlife Biologists | $57,710 | 7.4% | 590 |
| 47. Cartographers and Photogrammetrists | $57,440 | 22.2% | 610 |

| High-Paying Occupations in the Transportation, Distribution, and Logistics Cluster | | | |
|---|---|---|---|
| **Title** | **Annual Earnings** | **Percent Growth** | **Annual Openings** |
| 1. Chief Executives | $168,140 | 4.2% | 11,150 |
| 2. Airline Pilots, Copilots, and Flight Engineers | $114,200 | 6.4% | 3,130 |
| 3. Managers, All Other | $100,890 | 7.9% | 24,940 |
| 4. Transportation, Storage, and Distribution Managers | $81,830 | 10.0% | 3,370 |
| 5. Environmental Engineers | $80,890 | 21.9% | 2,260 |
| 6. Health and Safety Engineers, Except Mining Safety Engineers and Inspectors | $76,830 | 13.1% | 820 |
| 7. Commercial Pilots | $73,280 | 21.2% | 1,930 |

| High-Paying Occupations in the Transportation, Distribution, and Logistics Cluster (cont.) | | | |
|---|---|---|---|
| **Title** | **Annual Earnings** | **Percent Growth** | **Annual Openings** |
| 8. Logisticians | $72,780 | 25.5% | 4,870 |
| 9. Ship Engineers | $70,890 | 18.0% | 620 |
| 10. Captains, Mates, and Pilots of Water Vessels | $66,150 | 20.4% | 2,070 |
| 11. Transportation Inspectors | $63,680 | 14.4% | 1,070 |
| 12. Environmental Scientists and Specialists, Including Health | $63,570 | 18.7% | 4,320 |
| 13. Compliance Officers | $62,020 | 15.0% | 5,860 |

## Industries for Earning Six Figures

One way to earn high wages compared to other people in your occupation is to get a job in a high-paying industry. Sometimes the difference in pay can be dramatic. For example, Chemists who are employed in the Oil and Gas Extraction industry average twice the earnings of those in the Educational Services industry. But try to be realistic about your ambitions. The Oil and Gas Extraction industry employed only 40 Chemists nationwide in 2012. That number is expanding with the recent growth of this industry, but the high pay means that competition for these jobs is probably intense. You're not likely to get the job unless you have highly specialized knowledge and skills, such as how to compound fracking fluids. By contrast, the Educational Services industry (schools, colleges, and universities) employed more than 3,600 Chemists in 2012, so you can expect many more job openings in this less-specialized industry.

Specialization is why it sometimes is difficult to move from one industry to another. People working in one industry learn to "speak the language" of that industry and may be unfamiliar with how other industries operate. Even when the job title on the business card is the same in two industries, the context of the work tasks may be very different. In addition, the network of contacts you develop as you work in an industry may be of little use when you start looking for work in another industry.

Probably the best time for you to target a high-paying industry is when you search for your first job or, even better, while you are preparing for career entry. You may even consider choosing one college over another because one has better contacts in a high-paying industry or more relevant course offerings.

## SIX-FIGURE OCCUPATION-INDUSTRY COMBINATIONS

I thought it would be interesting to assemble lists of the industries where the high-paying occupations bring in the highest earnings. Because many of us are dazzled by the idea of earning six figures, I decided to restrict the list to occupation-industry combinations where the workers average more than $100,000 per year. To keep this a realistic set of career options, I included only those occupation-industry combinations for which the specialized workforce equals more than 100 workers *and* equals more than one-tenth of one percent of the total workforce of the occupation. In addition, to avoid giving too much room to a few occupations that earn high pay in numerous industries (such as Chief Executives), I included only the 10 best-paying industries for any one occupation.

Of the 173 high-paying occupations, 61 met the criteria for inclusion in this list. I ordered the occupations alphabetically. Within each occupation, the industries are listed in descending order of their median earnings. For each occupation-industry combination, I also include a figure showing the workforce size to give you an idea of how much competition you'll be facing. (In part II, you can see the top-paying industries for each occupation, not limited to those paying six figures.)

75

| Six-Figure Occupation-Industry Combinations | | | |
|---|---|---|---|
| **Title** | **Industry** | **Annual Earnings** | **Workforce Size** |
| 1. Adminstrative Services Managers | Monetary Authorities-Central Bank | $116,100 | 310 |
| | Securities, Commodity Contracts, and Other Financial Investments and Related Activities | $114,260 | 3,470 |
| | Other Information Services | $105,550 | 500 |
| | Transportation Equipment Manufacturing | $100,810 | 1,240 |
| | Computer and Electronic Product Manufacturing | $100,300 | 3,280 |
| 2. Advertising and Promotions Managers | Professional, Scientific, and Technical Services | $114,560 | 9,590 |
| | Telecommunications | $104,480 | 270 |
| | Merchant Wholesalers, Durable Goods | $102,720 | 130 |
| 3. Aerospace Engineers | Federal, State, and Local Government (excluding state and local schools and hospitals) | $110,750 | 9,070 |
| | Computer and Electronic Product Manufacturing | $109,860 | 8,080 |
| | Administrative and Support Services | $108,760 | 1,070 |
| | Professional, Scientific, and Technical Services | $108,300 | 26,980 |

| Six-Figure Occupation-Industry Combinations (cont.) | | | |
|---|---|---|---|
| **Title** | **Industry** | **Annual Earnings** | **Workforce Size** |
| 4. Airline Pilots, Copilots, and Flight Engineers | Air Transportation | $117,180 | 57,930 |
| 5. Architectural and Engineering Managers | Oil and Gas Extraction | $152,500 | 6,960 |
| | Petroleum and Coal Products Manufacturing | $147,860 | 890 |
| | Support Activities for Mining | $138,610 | 1,320 |
| | Computer and Electronic Product Manufacturing | $138,150 | 26,810 |
| | Repair and Maintenance | $137,760 | 310 |
| | Pipeline Transportation | $136,600 | 460 |
| | Publishing Industries (except Internet) | $135,470 | 370 |
| | Merchant Wholesalers, Nondurable Goods | $132,070 | 320 |
| | Telecommunications | $131,840 | 3,120 |
| | Wholesale Electronic Markets and Agents and Brokers | $131,730 | 440 |
| 6. Art Directors | Merchant Wholesalers, Nondurable Goods | $111,760 | 340 |
| | Motion Picture and Sound Recording Industries | $104,310 | 2,440 |

| | Six-Figure Occupation-Industry Combinations (cont.) | | |
|---|---|---|---|
| **Title** | **Industry** | **Annual Earnings** | **Workforce Size** |
| 7. Biochemists and Biophysicists | Merchant Wholesalers, Nondurable Goods | $103,290 | 530 |
| 8. Biological Science Teachers, Postsecondary | Professional, Scientific, and Technical Services | $129,480 | 180 |
| 9. Chemical Engineers | Management of Companies and Enterprises | $126,050 | 1,250 |
| | Oil and Gas Extraction | $118,590 | 580 |
| | Support Activities for Mining | $111,530 | 190 |
| | Utilities | $105,790 | 550 |
| | Petroleum and Coal Products Manufacturing | $105,310 | 1,890 |
| | Waste Management and Remediation Services | $104,290 | 160 |
| 10. Chief Executives | Utilities | $186,610 | 1,260 |
| | Nonstore Retailers | $186,460 | 990 |
| | Performing Arts, Spectator Sports, and Related Industries | $183,890 | 1,460 |
| | Primary Metal Manufacturing | $181,160 | 990 |
| | Food Manufacturing | $180,200 | 2,340 |
| | Machinery Manufacturing | $179,620 | 3,800 |

| Six-Figure Occupation-Industry Combinations (cont.) | | | |
|---|---|---|---|
| **Title** | **Industry** | **Annual Earnings** | **Workforce Size** |
| 10. Chief Executives (continued) | Plastics and Rubber Products Manufacturing | $178,540 | 1,800 |
| | Construction of Buildings | $178,410 | 3,540 |
| | Transportation Equipment Manufacturing | $178,320 | 2,450 |
| | Real Estate | $177,550 | 2,940 |
| 11. Compensation and Benefits Managers | Transportation Equipment Manufacturing | $114,760 | 110 |
| | Funds, Trusts, and Other Financial Vehicles | $114,240 | 160 |
| | Securities, Commodity Contracts, and Other Financial Investments and Related Activities | $114,080 | 350 |
| | Publishing Industries (except Internet) | $113,330 | 320 |
| | Chemical Manufacturing | $110,800 | 140 |
| | Computer and Electronic Product Manufacturing | $109,950 | 400 |
| | Merchant Wholesalers, Durable Goods | $109,230 | 190 |
| | Telecommunications | $108,730 | 130 |
| | Air Transportation | $108,270 | 120 |
| | Insurance Carriers and Related Activities | $107,390 | 1,280 |

| Six-Figure Occupation-Industry Combinations (cont.) | | | |
|---|---|---|---|
| **Title** | **Industry** | **Annual Earnings** | **Workforce Size** |
| 12. Computer and Information Research Scientists | Management of Companies and Enterprises | $119,370 | 220 |
| | Insurance Carriers and Related Activities | $111,790 | 280 |
| | Chemical Manufacturing | $110,820 | 330 |
| | Publishing Industries (except Internet) | $109,520 | 2,230 |
| | Wholesale Electronic Markets and Agents and Brokers | $106,480 | 200 |
| | Computer and Electronic Product Manufacturing | $105,560 | 950 |
| | Professional, Scientific, and Technical Services | $104,090 | 9,340 |
| | Federal, State, and Local Government (excluding state and local schools and hospitals) | $101,420 | 6,560 |
| | Administrative and Support Services | $100,200 | 130 |
| 13. Computer and Information Systems Managers | Other Information Services | $149,130 | 4,350 |
| | Motion Picture and Sound Recording Industries | $147,690 | 1,010 |
| | Securities, Commodity Contracts, and Other Financial Investments and Related Activities | $143,510 | 8,330 |

| Six-Figure Occupation-Industry Combinations (cont.) | | | |
|---|---|---|---|
| **Title** | **Industry** | **Annual Earnings** | **Workforce Size** |
| 13. Computer and Information Systems Managers (continued) | Computer and Electronic Product Manufacturing | $137,020 | 14,210 |
| | Transportation Equipment Manufacturing | $136,980 | 3,220 |
| | Publishing Industries (except Internet) | $134,220 | 13,330 |
| | Oil and Gas Extraction | $129,310 | 560 |
| | Monetary Authorities-Central Bank | $129,020 | 580 |
| | Broadcasting (except Internet) | $128,910 | 1,040 |
| | Telecommunications | $128,460 | 7,950 |
| 14. Computer Hardware Engineers | Securities, Commodity Contracts, and Other Financial Investments and Related Activities | $118,100 | 130 |
| | Publishing Industries (except Internet) | $113,250 | 900 |
| | Other Information Services | $108,740 | 250 |
| | Wholesale Electronic Markets and Agents and Brokers | $106,030 | 430 |
| | State, and Local Government (excluding state and local schools and hospitals) | $103,640 | 4,630 |

| Six-Figure Occupation-Industry Combinations (cont.) | | | |
|---|---|---|---|
| **Title** | **Industry** | **Annual Earnings** | **Workforce Size** |
| 14. Computer Hardware Engineers (continued) | Computer and Electronic Product Manufacturing | $103,560 | 31,280 |
| | Merchant Wholesalers, Durable Goods | $103,330 | 3,270 |
| | Management of Companies and Enterprises | $102,030 | 1,500 |
| | Electronics and Appliance Stores | $101,760 | 280 |
| 15. Computer Systems Analysts | Support Activities for Mining | $100,910 | 530 |
| 16. Construction Managers | Oil and Gas Extraction | $102,550 | 290 |
| | Telecommunications | $101,660 | 460 |
| 17. Dentists | Ambulatory Health Care Services | $102,550 | 290 |
| | Telecommunications | $146,990 | 89,150 |
| | Administrative and Support Services | $146,140 | 280 |
| | Federal, State, and Local Government (excluding state and local schools and hospitals) | $126,040 | 1,980 |
| | Hospitals | $118,570 | 1,440 |

| Six-Figure Occupation-Industry Combinations (cont.) | | | |
|---|---|---|---|
| Title | Industry | Annual Earnings | Workforce Size |
| 18. Economists | Monetary Authorities-Central Bank | $126,920 | 360 |
| | Credit Intermediation and Related Activities | $122,400 | 230 |
| 19. Education Administrators, Postsecondary | Hospitals | $105,740 | 320 |
| 20. Electrical Engineers | Oil and Gas Extraction | $100,770 | 230 |
| 21. Electronics Engineers, Except Computer | Other Information Services | $116,310 | 180 |
| | Publishing Industries (except Internet) | $102,450 | 150 |
| | Federal, State, and Local Government (excluding state and local schools and hospitals) | $102,410 | 17,760 |
| | Transportation Equipment Manufacturing | $102,070 | 3,150 |
| 22. Engineers, All Other | Oil and Gas Extraction | $108,280 | 1,170 |
| | Federal, State, and Local Government (excluding state and local schools and hospitals) | $108,100 | 31,780 |
| | Support Activities for Mining | $104,800 | 210 |
| | Pipeline Transportation | $103,740 | 360 |
| | Motion Picture and Sound Recording Industries | $102,300 | 220 |

| Six-Figure Occupation-Industry Combinations (cont.) | | | |
|---|---|---|---|
| **Title** | **Industry** | **Annual Earnings** | **Workforce Size** |
| 23. Environmental Engineers | Oil and Gas Extraction | $114,470 | 580 |
| 24. Financial Managers | Securities, Commodity Contracts, and Other Financial Investments and Related Activities | $156,510 | 24,200 |
| | Oil and Gas Extraction | $139,270 | 2,510 |
| | Funds, Trusts, and Other Financial Vehicles | $138,410 | 1,850 |
| | Publishing Industries (except Internet) | $132,170 | 4,930 |
| | Motion Picture and Sound Recording Industries | $131,040 | 1,040 |
| | Professional, Scientific, and Technical Services | $130,120 | 50,280 |
| | Other Information Services | $127,910 | 1,260 |
| | Management of Companies and Enterprises | $124,840 | 54,450 |
| | Computer and Electronic Product Manufacturing | $123,740 | 8,290 |
| | Insurance Carriers and Related Activities | $122,410 | 26,230 |
| 25. First-Line Supervisors of Non-Retail Sales Workers | Securities, Commodity Contracts, and Other Financial Investments and Related Activities | $109,620 | 7,070 |

84

| Six-Figure Occupation-Industry Combinations (cont.) | | | |
|---|---|---|---|
| **Title** | **Industry** | **Annual Earnings** | **Workforce Size** |
| 26. General and Operations Managers | Securities, Commodity Contracts, and Other Financial Investments and Related Activities | $177,260 | 17,750 |
| | Funds, Trusts, and Other Financial Vehicles | $138,180 | 1,930 |
| | Computer and Electronic Product Manufacturing | $136,420 | 22,260 |
| | Oil and Gas Extraction | $136,370 | 5,400 |
| | Other Information Services | $135,040 | 4,650 |
| | Professional, Scientific, and Technical Services | $132,490 | 197,130 |
| | Insurance Carriers and Related Activities | $126,840 | 38,630 |
| | Management of Companies and Enterprises | $123,200 | 79,070 |
| | Electrical Equipment, Appliance, and Component Manufacturing | $120,850 | 5,750 |
| | Publishing Industries (except Internet) | $120,740 | 16,200 |
| 27. Geoscientists, Except Hydrologists and Geographers | Petroleum and Coal Products Manufacturing | $142,310 | 320 |
| | Oil and Gas Extraction | $137,750 | 9,640 |
| | Support Activities for Mining | $127,030 | 1,710 |

| Six-Figure Occupation-Industry Combinations (cont.) | | | |
|---|---|---|---|
| **Title** | **Industry** | **Annual Earnings** | **Workforce Size** |
| 27. Geoscientists, Except Hydrologists and Geographers (continued) | Machinery Manufacturing | $119,480 | 330 |
| | Data Processing, Hosting, and Related Services | $105,720 | 110 |
| 28. Health and Safety Engineers, Except Mining Safety Engineers and Inspectors | Oil and Gas Extraction | $104,250 | 220 |
| 29. Health Diagnosing and Treating Practitioners, All Other | Professional, Scientific, and Technical Services | $124,350 | 420 |
| 30. Health Specialties Teachers, Postsecondary | Hospitals | $119,370 | 6,410 |
| 31. Human Resources Managers | Motion Picture and Sound Recording Industries | $139,420 | 270 |
| | Other Information Services | $131,900 | 300 |
| | Securities, Commodity Contracts, and Other Financial Investments and Related Activities | $129,780 | 960 |
| | Broadcasting (except Internet) | $124,460 | 210 |
| | Computer and Electronic Product Manufacturing | $121,900 | 2,460 |
| | Telecommunications | $118,800 | 960 |
| | Publishing Industries (except Internet) | $118,700 | 1,270 |

| | Six-Figure Occupation-Industry Combinations (cont.) | | |
|---|---|---|---|
| **Title** | **Industry** | **Annual Earnings** | **Workforce Size** |
| 31. Human Resources Managers (continued) | Funds, Trusts, and Other Financial Vehicles | $117,300 | 180 |
| | Nonstore Retailers | $117,130 | 300 |
| | Credit Intermediation and Related Activities | $115,740 | 2,460 |
| 32. Industrial Engineers | Oil and Gas Extraction | $115,890 | 2,950 |
| | Petroleum and Coal Products Manufacturing | $102,180 | 1,400 |
| 33. Industrial Production Managers | Telecommunications | $116,950 | 170 |
| | Oil and Gas Extraction | $114,140 | 1,440 |
| | Utilities | $108,880 | 2,530 |
| | Management of Companies and Enterprises | $105,700 | 7,990 |
| | Professional, Scientific, and Technical Services | $105,290 | 3,710 |
| | Petroleum and Coal Products Manufacturing | $103,570 | 1,390 |
| | Computer and Electronic Product Manufacturing | $100,500 | 11,160 |
| 34. Judges, Magistrate Judges, and Magistrates | Federal, State, and Local Government (excluding state and local schools and hospitals) | $115,760 | 27,220 |

| Six-Figure Occupation-Industry Combinations (cont.) | | | |
|---|---|---|---|
| **Title** | **Industry** | **Annual Earnings** | **Workforce Size** |
| 35. Lawyers | Securities, Commodity Contracts, and Other Financial Investments and Related Activities | $174,420 | 3,910 |
| | Oil and Gas Extraction | $171,310 | 1,270 |
| | Telecommunications | $162,070 | 1,490 |
| | Computer and Electronic Product Manufacturing | $160,710 | 1,310 |
| | Publishing Industries (except Internet) | $160,400 | 1,660 |
| | Credit Intermediation and Related Activities | $160,300 | 3,750 |
| | Utilities | $157,050 | 650 |
| | Management of Companies and Enterprises | $155,060 | 14,560 |
| | Real Estate | $149,140 | 1,880 |
| | Merchant Wholesalers, Durable Goods | $146,690 | 1,010 |
| 36. Logisticians | Publishing Industries (except Internet) | $102,400 | 1,310 |
| 37. Managers, All Other | Oil and Gas Extraction | $141,960 | 1,030 |
| | Pipeline Transportation | $138,140 | 350 |
| | Petroleum and Coal Products Manufacturing | $134,210 | 1,000 |

| | Six-Figure Occupation-Industry Combinations (cont.) | | |
|---|---|---|---|
| **Title** | **Industry** | **Annual Earnings** | **Workforce Size** |
| 37. Managers, All Other (continued) | Securities, Commodity Contracts, and Other Financial Investments and Related Activities | $126,300 | 2,670 |
| | Computer and Electronic Product Manufacturing | $116,800 | 3,270 |
| | Funds, Trusts, and Other Financial Vehicles | $116,690 | 510 |
| | Miscellaneous Manufacturing | $116,440 | 1,840 |
| | Utilities | $115,400 | 3,180 |
| | Telecommunications | $113,430 | 3,690 |
| | Other Information Services | $111,770 | 1,560 |
| 38. Marketing Managers | Oil and Gas Extraction | $160,570 | 540 |
| | Securities, Commodity Contracts, and Other Financial Investments and Related Activities | $155,700 | 4,440 |
| | Other Information Services | $144,220 | 1,720 |
| | Funds, Trusts, and Other Financial Vehicles | $137,040 | 310 |
| | Computer and Electronic Product Manufacturing | $133,620 | 7,300 |
| | Transportation Equipment Manufacturing | $133,100 | 1,500 |

| | Six-Figure Occupation-Industry Combinations (cont.) | | |
|---|---|---|---|
| **Title** | **Industry** | **Annual Earnings** | **Workforce Size** |
| 38. Marketing Managers (continued) | Publishing Industries (except Internet) | $132,800 | 8,370 |
| | Motion Picture and Sound Recording Industries | $132,100 | 1,170 |
| | Broadcasting (except Internet) | $129,760 | 900 |
| | Professional, Scientific, and Technical Services | $129,640 | 34,190 |
| 39. Materials Engineers | Federal, State, and Local Government (excluding state and local schools and hospitals) | $104,190 | 1,640 |
| 40. Mechanical Engineers | Oil and Gas Extraction | $114,380 | 420 |
| | Merchant Wholesalers, Nondurable Goods | $101,240 | 300 |
| 41. Medical and Health Services Managers | Chemical Manufacturing | $117,070 | 320 |
| | Health and Personal Care Stores | $107,860 | 380 |
| | Insurance Carriers and Related Activities | $103,700 | 5,050 |
| 42. Medical Scientists, Except Epidemiologists | Wholesale Electronic Markets and Agents and Brokers | $118,750 | 110 |
| | Merchant Wholesalers, Nondurable Goods | $105,250 | 1,400 |

| Six-Figure Occupation-Industry Combinations (cont.) | | | |
|---|---|---|---|
| **Title** | **Industry** | **Annual Earnings** | **Workforce Size** |
| 42. Medical Scientists, Except Epidemiologists (continued) | Federal, State, and Local Government (excluding state and local schools and hospitals) | $104,350 | 1,860 |
| 43. Natural Sciences Managers | Oil and Gas Extraction | $180,400 | 250 |
| | Insurance Carriers and Related Activities | $178,740 | 180 |
| | Merchant Wholesalers, Nondurable Goods | $162,900 | 860 |
| | Miscellaneous Manufacturing | $153,190 | 240 |
| | Professional, Scientific, and Technical Services | $143,690 | 17,390 |
| | Management of Companies and Enterprises | $140,090 | 2,840 |
| | Food Manufacturing | $128,070 | 160 |
| | Computer and Electronic Product Manufacturing | $127,510 | 250 |
| | Chemical Manufacturing | $116,300 | 5,480 |
| | Religious, Grantmaking, Civic, Professional, and Similar Organizations | $111,830 | 330 |
| 44. Network and Computer Systems Administrators | Oil and Gas Extraction | $101,300 | 2,060 |
| | Petroleum and Coal Products Manufacturing | $101,010 | 590 |

| | Six-Figure Occupation-Industry Combinations (cont.) | | |
|---|---|---|---|
| **Title** | **Industry** | **Annual Earnings** | **Workforce Size** |
| 45. Nuclear Engineers | Professional, Scientific, and Technical Services | $115,530 | 8,050 |
| | Management of Companies and Enterprises | $113,050 | 160 |
| | Waste Management and Remediation Services | $106,280 | 500 |
| 46. Optometrists | General Merchandise Stores | $103,050 | 150 |
| | Health and Personal Care Stores | $102,890 | 3,550 |
| 47. Petroleum Engineers | Oil and Gas Extraction | $144,810 | 19,880 |
| | Management of Companies and Enterprises | $143,240 | 2,120 |
| | Chemical Manufacturing | $133,880 | 270 |
| | Merchant Wholesalers, Nondurable Goods | $129,580 | 320 |
| | Petroleum and Coal Products Manufacturing | $120,440 | 2,120 |
| | Professional, Scientific, and Technical Services | $119,550 | 4,360 |
| | Machinery Manufacturing | $113,320 | 310 |
| | Pipeline Transportation | $108,700 | 430 |
| | Support Activities for Mining | $101,800 | 5,120 |
| | Utilities | $101,380 | 640 |

| | Six-Figure Occupation-Industry Combinations (cont.) | | |
|---|---|---|---|
| **Title** | **Industry** | **Annual Earnings** | **Workforce Size** |
| 48. Pharmacists | General Merchandise Stores | $125,100 | 31,870 |
| | Ambulatory Health Care Services | $118,690 | 9,310 |
| | Health and Personal Care Stores | $117,840 | 123,020 |
| | General Merchandise Stores | $103,050 | 150 |
| | Management of Companies and Enterprises | $117,550 | 2,610 |
| | Food and Beverage Stores | $116,000 | 22,590 |
| | Merchant Wholesalers, Nondurable Goods | $114,150 | 4,610 |
| | Insurance Carriers and Related Activities | $114,110 | 1,200 |
| | Hospitals | $114,100 | 65,200 |
| | Wholesale Electronic Markets and Agents and Brokers | $113,890 | 460 |
| | Administrative and Support Services | $113,420 | 2,690 |
| 49. Physical Scientists, All Other | Computer and Electronic Product Manufacturing | $124,580 | 400 |
| | Management of Companies and Enterprises | $122,880 | 950 |
| | Professional, Scientific, and Technical Services | $107,590 | 6,490 |

| Six-Figure Occupation-Industry Combinations (cont.) | | | |
|---|---|---|---|
| **Title** | **Industry** | **Annual Earnings** | **Workforce Size** |
| 49. Physical Scientists, All Other (continued) | Federal, State, and Local Government (excluding state and local schools and hospitals) | $100,850 | 10,350 |
| 50. Physicians and Surgeons | Nursing and Residential Care Facilities | $182,280 | 1,160 |
| | Federal, State, and Local Government (excluding state and local schools and hospitals) | $179,760 | 39,900 |
| | Social Assistance | $175,760 | 1,140 |
| | Hospitals | $154,430 | 145,960 |
| 51. Physicists | Hospitals | $152,280 | 1,080 |
| | Ambulatory Health Care Services | $150,510 | 470 |
| | Oil and Gas Extraction | $142,630 | 330 |
| | Professional, Scientific, and Technical Services | $108,950 | 8,210 |
| | Federal, State, and Local Government (excluding state and local schools and hospitals) | $106,370 | 3,550 |
| 52. Podiatrists | Ambulatory Health Care Services | $117,000 | 7,930 |

| Six-Figure Occupation-Industry Combinations (cont.) | | | |
|---|---|---|---|
| **Title** | **Industry** | **Annual Earnings** | **Workforce Size** |
| 52. Podiatrists (continued) | Federal, State, and Local Government (excluding state and local schools and hospitals) | $112,820 | 720 |
| | Hospitals | $108,910 | 390 |
| 53. Public Relations and Fundraising Managers | Publishing Industries (except Internet) | $134,100 | 630 |
| | Oil and Gas Extraction | $132,850 | 160 |
| | Securities, Commodity Contracts, and Other Financial Investments and Related Activities | $125,370 | 540 |
| | Telecommunications | $124,850 | 510 |
| | Professional, Scientific, and Technical Services | $120,610 | 7,860 |
| | Transportation Equipment Manufacturing | $120,520 | 210 |
| | Chemical Manufacturing | $113,710 | 110 |
| | Credit Intermediation and Related Activities | $111,540 | 1,200 |
| | Management of Companies and Enterprises | $111,030 | 5,120 |
| | Air Transportation | $109,520 | 140 |

| Six-Figure Occupation-Industry Combinations (cont.) | | | |
|---|---|---|---|
| **Title** | **Industry** | **Annual Earnings** | **Workforce Size** |
| 54. Purchasing Managers | Oil and Gas Extraction | $127,080 | 470 |
| | Telecommunications | $126,730 | 340 |
| | Professional, Scientific, and Technical Services | $117,770 | 4,920 |
| | Federal, State, and Local Government (excluding state and local schools and hospitals) | $115,710 | 7,630 |
| | Publishing Industries (except Internet) | $113,920 | 370 |
| | Management of Companies and Enterprises | $112,430 | 11,420 |
| | Insurance Carriers and Related Activities | $110,330 | 480 |
| | Data Processing, Hosting, and Related Services | $108,760 | 190 |
| | Support Activities for Mining | $106,620 | 140 |
| | Computer and Electronic Product Manufacturing | $105,970 | 4,280 |
| 55. Sales Engineers | Educational Services | $127,970 | 190 |
| | Publishing Industries (except Internet) | $110,790 | 1,560 |
| | Professional, Scientific, and Technical Services | $105,760 | 14,460 |

| Six-Figure Occupation-Industry Combinations (cont.) | | | |
|---|---|---|---|
| **Title** | **Industry** | **Annual Earnings** | **Workforce Size** |
| 55. Sales Engineers (continued) | Heavy and Civil Engineering Construction | $105,100 | 110 |
| | Electronics and Appliance Stores | $102,540 | 690 |
| | Chemical Manufacturing | $101,100 | 220 |
| 56. Sales Managers | Securities, Commodity Contracts, and Other Financial Investments and Related Activities | $182,530 | 6,390 |
| | Other Information Services | $146,590 | 2,080 |
| | Oil and Gas Extraction | $138,330 | 470 |
| | Professional, Scientific, and Technical Services | $132,780 | 25,540 |
| | Motion Picture and Sound Recording Industries | $129,510 | 1,140 |
| | Data Processing, Hosting, and Related Services | $128,800 | 1,600 |
| | Computer and Electronic Product Manufacturing | $127,730 | 7,610 |
| | Publishing Industries (except Internet) | $127,290 | 7,680 |
| | Telecommunications | $125,120 | 6,310 |
| | Broadcasting (except Internet) | $123,660 | 3,460 |

| Six-Figure Occupation-Industry Combinations (cont.) | | | |
|---|---|---|---|
| **Title** | **Industry** | **Annual Earnings** | **Workforce Size** |
| 57. Securities, Commodities, and Financial Services Sales Agents | Securities, Commodity Contracts, and Other Financial Investments and Related Activities | $101,590 | 178,410 |
| 58. Software Developers, Applications | Nonstore Retailers | $105,360 | 5,850 |
| | Transportation Equipment Manufacturing | $103,160 | 9,180 |
| | Other Information Services | $102,920 | 12,390 |
| | Motion Picture and Sound Recording Industries | $102,330 | 2,990 |
| | Securities, Commodity Contracts, and Other Financial Investments and Related Activities | $100,740 | 12,560 |
| 59. Software Developers, Systems Software | Other Information Services | $112,340 | 3,410 |
| | Transportation Equipment Manufacturing | $105,810 | 13,740 |
| | Computer and Electronic Product Manufacturing | $105,030 | 58,410 |
| | Securities, Commodity Contracts, and Other Financial Investments and Related Activities | $102,850 | 4,690 |
| | Credit Intermediation and Related Activities | $102,690 | 10,200 |

| | Six-Figure Occupation-Industry Combinations (cont.) | | |
|---|---|---|---|
| **Title** | **Industry** | **Annual Earnings** | **Workforce Size** |
| 60. Training and Development Managers | Data Processing, Hosting, and Related Services | $122,260 | 160 |
| | Computer and Electronic Product Manufacturing | $116,340 | 350 |
| | Other Information Services | $116,180 | 150 |
| | Publishing Industries (except Internet) | $114,760 | 320 |
| | Securities, Commodity Contracts, and Other Financial Investments and Related Activities | $114,670 | 540 |
| | Wholesale Electronic Markets and Agents and Brokers | $112,340 | 210 |
| | Utilities | $112,080 | 360 |
| | Miscellaneous Manufacturing | $111,820 | 220 |
| | Professional, Scientific, and Technical Services | $109,090 | 2,760 |
| | Chemical Manufacturing | $107,240 | 310 |
| 61. Transportation, Storage, and Distribution Managers | Oil and Gas Extraction | $129,640 | 370 |
| | Computer and Electronic Product Manufacturing | $106,840 | 780 |
| | Telecommunications | $106,340 | 170 |

| Six-Figure Occupation-Industry Combinations (cont.) | | | |
|---|---|---|---|
| **Title** | **Industry** | **Annual Earnings** | **Workforce Size** |
| 61. Transportation, Storage, and Distribution Managers (continued) | Transportation Equipment Manufacturing | $105,460 | 1,010 |
| | Pipeline Transportation | $103,300 | 310 |
| | Miscellaneous Manufacturing | $101,550 | 370 |

## Metropolitan Areas for Earning Six Figures

Geographical regions usually differ by how much they pay people working in the same occupation, just as industries do. For example, Economists employed in the metropolitan area called Houston–Sugar Land–Baytown, TX, earn more than twice as much as Economists in Austin–Round Rock, TX.

The following list may give you ideas about where you might move to if you want to earn more than $100,000 per year. Keep in mind that your wage dollar will buy you more in some regions of the country than in others, so a six-figure salary in a high-rent region may not afford you as comfortable a lifestyle as an $80,000 salary in a region with a lower cost of living. In fact, high wages and a high cost of living often go together geographically. On the following list, you'll notice several metropolitan areas that appear numerous times because they are areas with generally high wages. In such areas, the good pay that many workers receive gets built into the prices of many of the things you buy, especially services. In addition, real estate prices are often higher in the high-wage areas. So remember that the dollar figure is only a rough indication of the lifestyle you would enjoy.

One suggestion that I made about choosing an industry also applies somewhat to choosing a location: It's probably easiest to do this very early in your career. Later in life, more complications are likely to arise, such as having a family with roots in a community. Selling one house and buying another long-distance, which is never easy, can be especially frustrating if you want to move from a low-wage region to a high-wage region, where the trade-in value of your starter home will buy you much less fancy living quarters. Regional differences in workplace culture, though not as great as the differences between industries, may also add to the difficulty of a mid-career change, and your network of contacts may have less clout in a distant city. This is not to say you should not try to relocate mid-career; a great many people have done so successfully.

Although the following two lists are based on metropolitan areas, understand that a metro area consists of a core city (or cluster of cities) and also the surrounding counties that have strong social and economic ties to the core. The figures I report here are the medians for entire metro areas, not just their core cities. That means that if urban life does not appeal to you, you may be able to enjoy the high wages of a metro area without living in the core city and maybe without even needing to commute to the core city.

## SIX-FIGURE OCCUPATION-METRO COMBINATIONS

The following list covers 61 of the 173 high-paying occupations and identifies the metropolitan areas where the average earnings are above $100,000. The occupations are ordered alphabetically. When I assembled this list, I didn't want you to get excited about metro areas where the workforce is tiny, so for each occupation I limited the metros to those with more than 2,500 workers in the occupation and more than 1 percent of the nationwide workforce. (The rightmost column shows the workforce size.) And to prevent the list from being dominated by occupations that are high-paid almost everywhere, I limited the list to a maximum of 10 six-figure metros for any one occupation. (In part II, you can see the top-paying metro areas for each occupation, not limited to those paying six figures.)

| Six-Figure Occupation-Metro Combinations | | | |
|---|---|---|---|
| **Title** | **Metro Area** | **Annual Earnings** | **Workforce Size** |
| 1. Actuaries | New York–Northern New Jersey–Long Island, NY-NJ-PA | $110,330 | 3,330 |
| 2. Administrative Services Managers | New York–Northern New Jersey–Long Island, NY-NJ-PA | $108,830 | 19,170 |
| | Philadelphia-Camden-Wilmington, PA-NJ-DE-MD | $102,320 | 5,330 |
| | San Francisco–Oakland–Fremont, CA | $101,200 | 5,190 |
| | Miami–Fort Lauderdale–Pompano Beach, FL | $100,630 | 2,740 |
| 3. Advertising and Promotions Managers | New York–Northern New Jersey–Long Island, NY-NJ-PA | $129,590 | 4,610 |
| 4. Aerospace Engineers | Washington-Arlington-Alexandria, DC-VA-MD-WV | $131,740 | 4,310 |
| | Los Angeles–Long Beach–Santa Ana, CA | $117,250 | 10,190 |
| | Huntsville, AL | $112,150 | 3,000 |

**101**

| Six-Figure Occupation-Metro Combinations (cont.) | | | |
|---|---|---|---|
| **Title** | **Metro Area** | **Annual Earnings** | **Workforce Size** |
| 4. Aerospace Engineers (continued) | Dallas–Fort Worth–Arlington, TX | $103,560 | 4,040 |
| | Seattle-Tacoma-Bellevue, WA | $100,160 | 7,680 |
| 5. Agents and Business Managers of Artists, Performers, and Athletes | Los Angeles–Long Beach–Santa Ana, CA | $103,380 | 3,340 |
| 6. Airline Pilots, Copilots, and Flight Engineers | New York–Northern New Jersey–Long Island, NY-NJ-PA | $148,290 | 4,750 |
| | Miami–Fort Lauderdale–Pompano Beach, FL | $118,690 | 2,590 |
| | Chicago-Naperville-Joliet, IL-IN-WI | $117,380 | 5,540 |
| 7. Architectural and Engineering Managers | San Jose–Sunnyvale–Santa Clara, CA | $168,350 | 6,790 |
| | Houston–Sugar Land–Baytown, TX | $167,240 | 8,210 |
| | San Francisco–Oakland–Fremont, CA | $153,610 | 5,090 |
| | Los Angeles–Long Beach–Santa Ana, CA | $144,370 | 10,320 |
| | Philadelphia-Camden-Wilmington, PA-NJ-DE-MD | $139,840 | 3,010 |
| | Boston-Cambridge-Quincy, MA-NH | $139,550 | 6,030 |

| Six-Figure Occupation-Metro Combinations (cont.) | | | |
|---|---|---|---|
| **Title** | **Metro Area** | **Annual Earnings** | **Workforce Size** |
| 7. Architectural and Engineering Managers (continued) | Washington-Arlington-Alexandria, DC-VA-MD-WV | $136,770 | 7,020 |
| | New York–Northern New Jersey–Long Island, NY-NJ-PA | $136,320 | 7,060 |
| | Dallas–Fort Worth–Arlington, TX | $133,860 | 5,130 |
| 8. Art Directors | New York–Northern New Jersey–Long Island, NY-NJ-PA | $117,220 | 6,730 |
| 9. Chemical Engineers | Houston–Sugar Land–Baytown, TX | $118,000 | 3,740 |
| 10. Chemists | Washington-Arlington-Alexandria, DC-VA-MD-WV | $114,710 | 2,820 |
| 11. Chief Executives | Minneapolis–St. Paul–Bloomington, MN-WI | $175,160 | 6,370 |
| | Chicago-Naperville-Joliet, IL-IN-WI | $167,350 | 15,600 |
| | Detroit-Warren-Livonia, MI | $165,850 | 4,840 |
| | Kansas City, MO-KS | $159,730 | 3,370 |
| | St. Louis, MO-IL | $149,210 | 3,890 |
| | Phoenix-Mesa-Scottsdale, AZ | $149,050 | 3,220 |
| | Nashville-Davidson–Murfreesboro, TN | $145,590 | 3,600 |

| Six-Figure Occupation-Metro Combinations (cont.) | | | |
|---|---|---|---|
| **Title** | **Metro Area** | **Annual Earnings** | **Workforce Size** |
| 12. Civil Engineers | Sacramento–Arden-Arcade–Roseville, CA | $101,680 | 3,860 |
| | San Francisco–Oakland–Fremont, CA | $101,670 | 7,260 |
| 13. Computer and Information Research Scientists | Washington-Arlington-Alexandria, DC-VA-MD-WV | $115,960 | 2,740 |
| 14. Computer and Information Systems Managers | San Jose–Sunnyvale–Santa Clara, CA | $169,770 | 9,320 |
| | San Francisco–Oakland–Fremont, CA | $152,060 | 9,190 |
| | New York–Northern New Jersey–Long Island, NY-NJ-PA | $143,800 | 31,130 |
| | Washington-Arlington-Alexandria, DC-VA-MD-WV | $141,010 | 19,390 |
| | Seattle-Tacoma-Bellevue, WA | $136,010 | 6,060 |
| | Philadelphia-Camden-Wilmington, PA-NJ-DE-MD | $165,850 | 4,840 |
| | Boston-Cambridge-Quincy, MA-NH | $133,890 | 14,740 |
| | Los Angeles–Long Beach–Santa Ana, CA | $133,180 | 13,290 |
| | Houston–Sugar Land–Baytown, TX | $132,450 | 4,970 |

| | Six-Figure Occupation-Metro Combinations (cont.) | | |
|---|---|---|---|
| **Title** | **Metro Area** | **Annual Earnings** | **Workforce Size** |
| 15. Computer Hardware Engineers | San Jose–Sunnyvale–Santa Clara, CA | $129,640 | 8,840 |
| | San Francisco–Oakland–Fremont, CA | $119,400 | 3,030 |
| | Los Angeles–Long Beach–Santa Ana, CA | $109,830 | 4,320 |
| | Boston-Cambridge-Quincy, MA-NH | $109,200 | 3,690 |
| | Washington-Arlington-Alexandria, DC-VA-MD-WV | $106,680 | 5,560 |
| 16. Construction Managers | New York–Northern New Jersey–Long Island, NY-NJ-PA | $111,160 | 12,180 |
| | Philadelphia-Camden-Wilmington, PA-NJ-DE-MD | $110,490 | 2,670 |
| | San Francisco–Oakland–Fremont, CA | $108,540 | 3,880 |
| 17. Dental Hygienists | San Francisco–Oakland–Fremont, CA | $103,340 | 3,100 |
| | Los Angeles–Long Beach–Santa Ana, CA | $103,070 | 7,050 |
| 18. Dentists | Boston-Cambridge-Quincy, MA-NH | $161,380 | 2,960 |
| | Washington-Arlington-Alexandria, DC-VA-MD-WV | $144,570 | 2,790 |
| | New York–Northern New Jersey–Long Island, NY-NJ-PA | $133,360 | 7,690 |

| Six-Figure Occupation-Metro Combinations (cont.) | | | |
|---|---|---|---|
| **Title** | **Metro Area** | **Annual Earnings** | **Workforce Size** |
| 18. Dentists (continued) | Los Angeles–Long Beach–Santa Ana, CA | $114,720 | 4,640 |
| 19. Detectives and Criminal Investigators | Los Angeles–Long Beach–Santa Ana, CA | $102,600 | 3,840 |
| 20. Economists | Washington-Arlington-Alexandria, DC-VA-MD-WV | $112,230 | 5,110 |
| 21. Education Administrators, Elementary and Secondary School | New York–Northern New Jersey–Long Island, NY-NJ-PA | $129,120 | 17,600 |
| | Philadelphia-Camden-Wilmington, PA-NJ-DE-MD | $109,110 | 4,350 |
| | Washington-Arlington-Alexandria, DC-VA-MD-WV | $106,580 | 5,050 |
| | Chicago-Naperville-Joliet, IL-IN-WI | $106,310 | 10,840 |
| | Los Angeles–Long Beach–Santa Ana, CA | $106,290 | 6,820 |
| 22. Education Administrators, Postsecondary | Philadelphia-Camden-Wilmington, PA-NJ-DE-MD | $107,450 | 2,690 |
| | New York–Northern New Jersey–Long Island, NY-NJ-PA | $102,790 | 7,270 |
| 23. Electrical Engineers | San Jose–Sunnyvale–Santa Clara, CA | $113,730 | 6,920 |
| | San Francisco–Oakland–Fremont, CA | $103,460 | 2,940 |

| Six-Figure Occupation-Metro Combinations (cont.) | | | |
|---|---|---|---|
| **Title** | **Metro Area** | **Annual Earnings** | **Workforce Size** |
| 23. Electrical Engineers (continued) | Los Angeles–Long Beach–Santa Ana, CA | $103,090 | 7,610 |
| | Boston-Cambridge-Quincy, MA-NH | $100,080 | 7,150 |
| 24. Electronics Engineers, Except Computer | San Jose–Sunnyvale–Santa Clara, CA | $124,130 | 8,040 |
| | Washington-Arlington-Alexandria, DC-VA-MD-WV | $107,960 | 4,880 |
| | Boston-Cambridge-Quincy, MA-NH | $106,380 | 4,800 |
| | San Diego–Carlsbad–San Marcos, CA | $103,990 | 3,420 |
| | San Francisco–Oakland–Fremont, CA | $100,190 | 3,300 |
| | New York–Northern New Jersey–Long Island, NY-NJ-PA | $100,130 | 4,390 |
| 25. Engineers, All Other | Washington-Arlington-Alexandria, DC-VA-MD-WV | $126,240 | 7,400 |
| | Houston–Sugar Land–Baytown, TX | $114,450 | 3,810 |
| | Huntsville, AL | $110,790 | 3,070 |
| | San Francisco–Oakland–Fremont, CA | $103,160 | 3,060 |

| Six-Figure Occupation-Metro Combinations (cont.) | | | |
|---|---|---|---|
| **Title** | **Metro Area** | **Annual Earnings** | **Workforce Size** |
| 25. Engineers, All Other (continued) | New York–Northern New Jersey–Long Island, NY-NJ-PA | $100,590 | 4,270 |
| 26. Financial Managers | New York–Northern New Jersey–Long Island, NY-NJ-PA | $155,870 | 44,060 |
| | San Francisco–Oakland–Fremont, CA | $142,080 | 12,750 |
| | San Jose–Sunnyvale–Santa Clara, CA | $141,180 | 5,690 |
| | Washington-Arlington-Alexandria, DC-VA-MD-WV | $131,040 | 17,700 |
| | Philadelphia-Camden-Wilmington, PA-NJ-DE-MD | $128,930 | 10,930 |
| | Los Angeles–Long Beach–Santa Ana, CA | $127,800 | 26,810 |
| | Charlotte-Gastonia-Concord, NC-SC | $122,590 | 6,160 |
| | Houston–Sugar Land–Baytown, TX | $120,780 | 8,980 |
| | Miami–Fort Lauderdale–Pompano Beach, FL | $119,160 | 5,680 |
| 27. First-Line Supervisors of Fire Fighting and Prevention Workers | New York–Northern New Jersey–Long Island, NY-NJ-PA | $107,630 | 3,570 |
| 28. First-Line Supervisors of Non-Retail Sales Workers | New York–Northern New Jersey–Long Island, NY-NJ-PA | $101,070 | 20,610 |

| | Six-Figure Occupation-Metro Combinations (cont.) | | |
|---|---|---|---|
| **Title** | **Metro Area** | **Annual Earnings** | **Workforce Size** |
| 29. First-Line Supervisors of Police and Detectives | New York–Northern New Jersey–Long Island, NY-NJ-PA | $110,440 | 11,210 |
| | Chicago-Naperville-Joliet, IL-IN-WI | $101,300 | 4,140 |
| 30. General and Operations Managers | New York–Northern New Jersey–Long Island, NY-NJ-PA | $138,980 | 115,450 |
| | Washington-Arlington-Alexandria, DC-VA-MD-WV | $129,760 | 68,140 |
| | Philadelphia-Camden-Wilmington, PA-NJ-DE-MD | $122,350 | 29,410 |
| | San Francisco–Oakland–Fremont, CA | $121,620 | 36,730 |
| | Boston-Cambridge-Quincy, MA-NH | $112,880 | 44,600 |
| | Denver-Aurora, CO | $112,400 | 23,040 |
| | Los Angeles–Long Beach–Santa Ana, CA | $111,120 | 92,890 |
| | Baltimore-Towson, MD | $110,650 | 23,580 |
| | San Diego–Carlsbad–San Marcos, CA | $105,240 | 21,410 |
| 31. Geoscientists, Except Hydrologists and Geographers | Houston–Sugar Land–Baytown, TX | $143,710 | 7,720 |

| Six-Figure Occupation-Metro Combinations (cont.) | | | |
|---|---|---|---|
| **Title** | **Metro Area** | **Annual Earnings** | **Workforce Size** |
| 32. Health Diagnosing and Treating Practitioners, All Other | Washington-Arlington-Alexandria, DC-VA-MD-WV | $122,740 | 4,520 |
| 33. Health Specialties Teachers, Postsecondary | Denver-Aurora, CO | $123,110 | 3,090 |
| | Seattle-Tacoma-Bellevue, WA | $118,950 | 2,850 |
| | Gainesville, FL | $117,730 | 2,600 |
| | New York–Northern New Jersey–Long Island, NY-NJ-PA | $113,090 | 8,250 |
| | San Francisco–Oakland–Fremont, CA | $100,480 | 4,410 |
| 34. Human Resources Managers | Washington-Arlington-Alexandria, DC-VA-MD-WV | $132,020 | 3,800 |
| | New York–Northern New Jersey–Long Island, NY-NJ-PA | $120,880 | 8,790 |
| | Boston-Cambridge-Quincy, MA-NH | $114,440 | 2,800 |
| | Los Angeles–Long Beach–Santa Ana, CA | $110,070 | 4,650 |
| | Minneapolis–St. Paul–Bloomington, MN-WI | $103,360 | 2,620 |
| 35. Industrial Engineers | San Jose–Sunnyvale–Santa Clara, CA | $104,880 | 4,240 |
| | Houston–Sugar Land–Baytown, TX | $104,660 | 5,910 |

| | Six-Figure Occupation-Metro Combinations (cont.) | | |
|---|---|---|---|
| **Title** | **Metro Area** | **Annual Earnings** | **Workforce Size** |
| 36. Industrial Production Managers | New York–Northern New Jersey–Long Island, NY-NJ-PA | $109,860 | 5,690 |
| | Houston–Sugar Land–Baytown, TX | $109,620 | 3,930 |
| | Detroit-Warren-Livonia, MI | $106,750 | 5,450 |
| | Boston-Cambridge-Quincy, MA-NH | $101,640 | 2,970 |
| 37. Lawyers | Houston–Sugar Land–Baytown, TX | $156,490 | 10,910 |
| | San Francisco–Oakland–Fremont, CA | $155,280 | 14,520 |
| | Washington-Arlington-Alexandria, DC-VA-MD-WV | $148,510 | 43,200 |
| | Los Angeles–Long Beach–Santa Ana, CA | $145,700 | 29,040 |
| | New York–Northern New Jersey–Long Island, NY-NJ-PA | $140,470 | 69,200 |
| | Chicago-Naperville-Joliet, IL-IN-WI | $132,380 | 25,440 |
| | Atlanta–Sandy Springs–Marietta, GA | $131,350 | 12,130 |
| | Denver-Aurora, CO | $127,720 | 8,450 |
| | Philadelphia-Camden-Wilmington, PA-NJ-DE-MD | $126,810 | 18,510 |

| Six-Figure Occupation-Metro Combinations (cont.) | | | |
|---|---|---|---|
| **Title** | **Metro Area** | **Annual Earnings** | **Workforce Size** |
| 38. Loan Officers | New York–Northern New Jersey–Long Island, NY-NJ-PA | $102,030 | 17,140 |
| 39. Managers, All Other | Washington-Arlington-Alexandria, DC-VA-MD-WV | $126,240 | 33,210 |
| | San Francisco–Oakland–Fremont, CA | $125,940 | 6,740 |
| | Houston–Sugar Land–Baytown, TX | $119,930 | 4,510 |
| | New York–Northern New Jersey–Long Island, NY-NJ-PA | $115,470 | 25,920 |
| | San Diego–Carlsbad–San Marcos, CA | $114,970 | 3,830 |
| | Los Angeles–Long Beach–Santa Ana, CA | $113,700 | 12,050 |
| | Denver-Aurora, CO | $109,730 | 3,890 |
| | Boston-Cambridge-Quincy, MA-NH | $109,550 | 4,460 |
| | Philadelphia-Camden-Wilmington, PA-NJ-DE-MD | $109,350 | 5,720 |
| | Dallas–Fort Worth–Arlington, TX | $109,010 | 5,400 |
| 40. Market Research Analysts and Marketing Specialists | San Jose–Sunnyvale–Santa Clara, CA | $103,760 | 7,640 |

| | Six-Figure Occupation-Metro Combinations (cont.) | | |
|---|---|---|---|
| **Title** | **Metro Area** | **Annual Earnings** | **Workforce Size** |
| 41. Marketing Managers | San Jose–Sunnyvale–Santa Clara, CA | $166,840 | 4,330 |
| | San Francisco–Oakland–Fremont, CA | $152,370 | 6,100 |
| | New York–Northern New Jersey–Long Island, NY-NJ-PA | $151,930 | 16,420 |
| | Washington-Arlington-Alexandria, DC-VA-MD-WV | $143,810 | 5,850 |
| | Philadelphia-Camden-Wilmington, PA-NJ-DE-MD | $140,220 | 3,990 |
| | Bridgeport-Stamford-Norwalk, CT | $133,950 | 2,510 |
| | Boston-Cambridge-Quincy, MA-NH | $132,590 | 6,900 |
| | Houston–Sugar Land–Baytown, TX | $132,500 | 2,920 |
| | Los Angeles–Long Beach–Santa Ana, CA | $129,600 | 11,010 |
| 42. Mechanical Engineers | San Jose–Sunnyvale–Santa Clara, CA | $103,890 | 3,840 |
| 43. Medical and Health Services Managers | San Francisco–Oakland–Fremont, CA | $109,510 | 4,250 |
| | New York–Northern New Jersey–Long Island, NY-NJ-PA | $108,150 | 24,510 |

| Six-Figure Occupation-Metro Combinations (cont.) | | | |
|---|---|---|---|
| **Title** | **Metro Area** | **Annual Earnings** | **Workforce Size** |
| 43. Medical and Health Services Managers (continued) | Los Angeles–Long Beach–Santa Ana, CA | $104,570 | 9,300 |
| | Houston–Sugar Land–Baytown, TX | $102,120 | 3,990 |
| 44. Medical Scientists, Except Epidemiologists | Washington-Arlington-Alexandria, DC-VA-MD-WV | $100,130 | 3,020 |
| 45. Natural Sciences Managers | New York–Northern New Jersey–Long Island, NY-NJ-PA | $151,640 | 3,510 |
| | Washington-Arlington-Alexandria, DC-VA-MD-WV | $129,540 | 3,570 |
| 46. Operations Research Analysts | New York–Northern New Jersey–Long Island, NY-NJ-PA | $110,840 | 4,580 |
| 47. Petroleum Engineers | Houston–Sugar Land–Baytown, TX | $140,730 | 14,160 |
| 48. Pharmacists | San Francisco–Oakland–Fremont, CA | $134,600 | 3,310 |
| | Los Angeles–Long Beach–Santa Ana, CA | $129,810 | 8,880 |
| | Phoenix-Mesa-Scottsdale, AZ | $126,500 | 3,570 |
| | Minneapolis–St. Paul–Bloomington, MN-WI | $122,550 | 3,200 |
| | Dallas–Fort Worth–Arlington, TX | $118,270 | 5,500 |
| | Washington-Arlington-Alexandria, DC-VA-MD-WV | $115,540 | 4,740 |

| | Six-Figure Occupation-Metro Combinations (cont.) | | |
|---|---|---|---|
| **Title** | **Metro Area** | **Annual Earnings** | **Workforce Size** |
| 48. Pharmacists (continued) | Seattle-Tacoma-Bellevue, WA | $115,030 | 3,300 |
| | Tampa–St. Petersburg–Clearwater, FL | $113,530 | 3,270 |
| | St. Louis, MO-IL | $113,480 | 3,120 |
| | Miami–Fort Lauderdale–Pompano Beach, FL | $113,440 | 5,670 |
| 49. Physical Scientists, All Other | Washington-Arlington-Alexandria, DC-VA-MD-WV | $115,730 | 3,220 |
| 50. Producers and Directors | Los Angeles–Long Beach–Santa Ana, CA | $113,940 | 20,110 |
| 51. Public Relations and Fundraising Managers | New York–Northern New Jersey–Long Island, NY-NJ-PA | $134,340 | 5,920 |
| | Washington-Arlington-Alexandria, DC-VA-MD-WV | $126,310 | 3,970 |
| 52. Purchasing Managers | New York–Northern New Jersey–Long Island, NY-NJ-PA | $127,430 | 4,450 |
| | Washington-Arlington-Alexandria, DC-VA-MD-WV | $126,250 | 4,040 |
| | Los Angeles–Long Beach–Santa Ana, CA | $106,210 | 3,090 |
| 53. Registered Nurses | San Francisco–Oakland–Fremont, CA | $119,580 | 35,340 |

| Six-Figure Occupation-Metro Combinations (cont.) | | | |
|---|---|---|---|
| **Title** | **Metro Area** | **Annual Earnings** | **Workforce Size** |
| 54. Sales Engineers | San Jose–Sunnyvale–Santa Clara, CA | $125,340 | 3,480 |
| | San Francisco–Oakland–Fremont, CA | $108,690 | 2,760 |
| | New York–Northern New Jersey–Long Island, NY-NJ-PA | $105,850 | 3,720 |
| 55. Sales Managers | San Jose–Sunnyvale–Santa Clara, CA | $164,470 | 4,870 |
| | New York–Northern New Jersey–Long Island, NY-NJ-PA | $153,770 | 23,570 |
| | San Francisco–Oakland–Fremont, CA | $131,480 | 9,010 |
| | Boston-Cambridge-Quincy, MA-NH | $131,050 | 10,230 |
| | Washington-Arlington-Alexandria, DC-VA-MD-WV | $126,410 | 5,660 |
| | Philadelphia-Camden-Wilmington, PA-NJ-DE-MD | $122,650 | 6,450 |
| | Seattle-Tacoma-Bellevue, WA | $119,190 | 6,130 |
| | Miami–Fort Lauderdale–Pompano Beach, FL | $118,980 | 4,730 |
| | Dallas–Fort Worth–Arlington, TX | $118,430 | 9,260 |

| | Six-Figure Occupation-Metro Combinations (cont.) | | |
|---|---|---|---|
| **Title** | **Metro Area** | **Annual Earnings** | **Workforce Size** |
| 56. Sales Representatives, Wholesale and Manufacturing, Technical and Scientific Products | San Jose–Sunnyvale–Santa Clara, CA | $101,860 | 8,130 |
| 57. Securities, Commodities, and Financial Services Sales Agents | Bridgeport-Stamford-Norwalk, CT | $168,300 | 5,560 |
| | New York–Northern New Jersey–Long Island, NY-NJ-PA | $126,680 | 66,580 |
| | Boston-Cambridge-Quincy, MA-NH | $103,870 | 8,050 |
| 58. Software Developers, Applications | San Jose–Sunnyvale–Santa Clara, CA | $116,070 | 24,160 |
| | San Francisco–Oakland–Fremont, CA | $106,250 | 21,670 |
| | Washington-Arlington-Alexandria, DC-VA-MD-WV | $104,840 | 32,150 |
| | Seattle-Tacoma-Bellevue, WA | $102,020 | 36,300 |
| 59. Software Developers, Systems Software | San Jose–Sunnyvale–Santa Clara, CA | $127,660 | 24,790 |
| | Baltimore-Towson, MD | $113,680 | 6,500 |
| | Washington-Arlington-Alexandria, DC-VA-MD-WV | $111,450 | 32,710 |
| | Los Angeles–Long Beach–Santa Ana, CA | $110,040 | 21,330 |

| Six-Figure Occupation-Metro Combinations (cont.) | | | |
|---|---|---|---|
| Title | Metro Area | Annual Earnings | Workforce Size |
| 59. Software Developers, Systems Software (continued) | San Francisco–Oakland–Fremont, CA | $109,890 | 15,440 |
| | Boston-Cambridge-Quincy, MA-NH | $108,910 | 27,890 |
| | San Diego–Carlsbad–San Marcos, CA | $105,580 | 7,150 |
| | New York–Northern New Jersey–Long Island, NY-NJ-PA | $101,930 | 18,540 |
| 60. Training and Development Managers | New York–Northern New Jersey–Long Island, NY-NJ-PA | $122,390 | 2,610 |
| 60. Transportation Storage, and Distribution Managers | New York–Northern New Jersey–Long Island, NY-NJ-PA | $100,150 | 5,630 |

## High-Paying Occupations Concentrated in Urban and Rural Areas

You may have concluded from the previous list that some of the best earning opportunities are in cities. It's also true that large population centers have more workers and therefore tend to offer more job openings.

But there's another factor at work: Many occupations need a critical mass of both customers and workers to be sustainable. For an extreme example, think of careers in the theater. You won't find a theater district (and the jobs it creates) in a rural small town because there simply are not enough theatergoers and professionally trained actors in that setting to make the industry financially viable. Several other industries tend to cluster in urban areas for the same reason. By contrast, even small towns need school teachers. And a few occupations, such as many involved in agriculture or mining, are viable only where open land is available, and therefore these occupations create few jobs in cities.

So when you consider a career goal, one issue you should think about is whether or not the occupation tends to cluster in urban areas and whether this matters to you. Some people prefer the diversity, lively cultural scene, public transportation, really good restaurants, and fast pace of city life. Others would rather enjoy the big horizons, closeness to nature, traditional values, quiet, and slow pace of rural life.

I wanted to give you a chance to consider this issue, so I created two lists of high-paying occupations, one showing occupations with the highest density of workers in cities and the other showing occupations with the highest density in rural areas.

## HIGH-PAYING OCCUPATIONS CONCENTRATED IN URBAN AREAS

To calculate the *urban percentage* for each occupation, I identified the 38 largest metropolitan areas out of all 380 metro areas for which the BLS reports workforce size. For each occupation, I summed the number of workers employed in these 38 metro areas and then divided it by the total number of workers in that same occupation throughout the United States.

For the following list, I set the cutoff for this urban percentage at 60. In other words, from the original 173 occupations covered in this book, this list shows those for which at least 60 percent of the workers are employed in the largest cities. The occupations are ordered to put those with the highest urban percentage at the top of the list.

Note that this list features *two* earnings figures: the annual *urban* earnings and the annual *nationwide* earnings. To furnish the average urban earnings, I computed the weighted average of the median earnings in the 38 largest metropolitan areas. (In a weighted average, the pay in each city is given a weight proportionate to the number of workers in that city.)

The figure for urban earnings is a useful summary, but this single figure conceals the variation that may often be found among different regions. For example, look at the first occupation on the list: Agents and Business Managers of Artists, Performers, and Athletes. You'll note that for this occupation (as for all 53 others on this list), the figure for average urban earnings is higher than the figure for the national average. No surprise here: Pay tends to be higher in big cities. But for the best pay, you may want to look for work in a *particular* city where your targeted industry has a large presence. This occupation earns an average of $103,380 in Los Angeles-Long Beach-Santa Ana, CA, the urban area that includes Hollywood, whereas it averages only $28,460 in Tampa-St. Petersburg-Clearwater, FL.

So if this list gets you thinking about seeking an urban setting for your career, I suggest you look at the description in part II of your occupational goal to see the metro areas where earnings are highest.

| High-Paying Occupations Concentrated in Urban Areas | | | |
|---|---|---|---|
| Title | Urban Percentage | Urban Earnings | Nationwide Earnings |
| 1. Agents and Business Managers of Artists, Performers, and Athletes | 82% | $75,594 | $63,370 |
| 2. Art Directors | 78% | $89,900 | $80,880 |
| 3. Multimedia Artists and Animators | 74% | $66,461 | $61,370 |
| 4. Producers and Directors | 74% | $86,836 | $71,350 |
| 5. Software Developers, Applications | 74% | $94,920 | $90,060 |
| 6. Economists | 73% | $100,180 | $91,860 |
| 7. Financial Analysts | 72% | $81,811 | $76,950 |
| 8. Medical Scientists, Except Epidemiologists | 72% | $82,022 | $76,980 |
| 9. Sales Engineers | 72% | $96,456 | $91,830 |
| 10. Securities, Commodities, and Financial Services Sales Agents | 72% | $84,581 | $71,720 |
| 11. Marketing Managers | 71% | $127,157 | $119,480 |
| 12. Software Developers, Systems Software | 71% | $103,343 | $99,000 |
| 13. Computer and Information Systems Managers | 70% | $129,958 | $120,950 |
| 14. Market Research Analysts and Marketing Specialists | 70% | $65,052 | $60,300 |
| 15. Architects, Except Landscape and Naval | 69% | $74,934 | $73,090 |
| 16. Computer Systems Analysts | 69% | $83,513 | $79,680 |

| High-Paying Occupations Concentrated in Urban Areas (cont.) | | | |
|---|---|---|---|
| Title | Urban Percentage | Urban Earnings | Nationwide Earnings |
| 17. Lawyers | 69% | $127,110 | $113,530 |
| 18. Advertising and Promotions Managers | 68% | $102,357 | $88,590 |
| 19. Financial Examiners | 68% | $81,367 | $75,800 |
| 20. Operations Research Analysts | 67% | $78,870 | $72,100 |
| 21. Computer Hardware Engineers | 66% | $105,364 | $100,920 |
| 22. Computer Programmers | 66% | $78,392 | $74,280 |
| 23. Database Administrators | 66% | $82,482 | $77,080 |
| 24. Management Analysts | 66% | $83,827 | $78,600 |
| 25. Public Relations and Fundraising Managers | 66% | $108,020 | $95,450 |
| 26. Statisticians | 66% | $82,112 | $75,560 |
| 27. Actuaries | 65% | $99,430 | $93,680 |
| 28. Managers, All Other | 65% | $105,544 | $100,890 |
| 29. Personal Financial Advisors | 65% | $74,620 | $67,520 |
| 30. Sales Representatives, Wholesale and Manufacturing, Technical and Scientific Products | 65% | $78,403 | $74,970 |
| 31. Technical Writers | 65% | $70,413 | $65,500 |
| 32. Business Operations Specialists, All Other | 64% | $68,426 | $65,120 |
| 33. Compensation, Benefits, and Job Analysis Specialists | 64% | $62,845 | $59,090 |

| High-Paying Occupations Concentrated in Urban Areas (cont.) | | | |
|---|---|---|---|
| **Title** | **Urban Percentage** | **Urban Earnings** | **Nationwide Earnings** |
| 34. Elevator Installers and Repairers | 64% | $78,090 | $76,650 |
| 35. Health Diagnosing and Treating Practitioners, All Other | 64% | $84,660 | $72,710 |
| 36. Sales Managers | 64% | $116,704 | $105,260 |
| 37. Chemists | 63% | $75,141 | $71,770 |
| 38. Electronics Engineers, Except Computer | 63% | $96,015 | $91,820 |
| 39. Financial Managers | 63% | $121,590 | $109,740 |
| 40. Human Resources Managers | 63% | $108,812 | $99,720 |
| 41. Network and Computer Systems Administrators | 63% | $78,562 | $72,560 |
| 42. Accountants and Auditors | 62% | $67,596 | $63,550 |
| 43. Compensation and Benefits Managers | 62% | $105,216 | $95,250 |
| 44. Physicists | 62% | $113,678 | $106,840 |
| 45. Architectural and Engineering Managers | 61% | $134,496 | $124,870 |
| 46. Claims Adjusters, Examiners, and Investigators | 61% | $61,654 | $59,960 |
| 47. Financial Specialists, All Other | 61% | $62,829 | $61,160 |
| 48. Insurance Underwriters | 61% | $66,648 | $62,870 |
| 49. Training and Development Managers | 61% | $104,570 | $95,400 |
| 50. Administrative Services Managers | 60% | $88,064 | $81,080 |

| High-Paying Occupations Concentrated in Urban Areas (cont.) | | | |
|---|---|---|---|
| Title | Urban Percentage | Urban Earnings | Nationwide Earnings |
| 51. Credit Analysts | 60% | $66,001 | $61,080 |
| 52. Engineers, All Other | 60% | $96,697 | $92,030 |
| 53. Purchasing Managers | 60% | $108,566 | $100,170 |

## HIGH-PAYING OCCUPATIONS CONCENTRATED IN RURAL AREAS

To calculate the *rural percentage* for the 173 high-paying occupations, I used a procedure similar to what I used for the urban percentage. However, instead of using workforce figures that applied to metropolitan areas, I used figures for the 172 non-metropolitan areas for which the BLS reports occupational earnings. These non-metro areas are regions such as east central Pennsylvania, the Low Country of South Carolina, coastal Oregon, and the Upper Peninsula of Michigan.

In the following list, the cutoff percentage is 10, which means that at least 10 percent of the workforce of each occupation is employed in the 172 non-metropolitan areas. The occupations with the highest rural percentages are at the top of the list. Like the previous list, this list shows not only the earnings figures for the nation as a whole but also the weighted average earnings for workers in the 172 non-metro areas. You should not be surprised to find that almost all of these average rural earnings are lower than the nationwide averages for the same occupations. However, as with figures for average urban earnings, be aware that the rural average conceals a lot of variation. Some rural jobs pay as well as or better than urban jobs. In addition, the cost of living tends to be lower in rural areas.

| High-Paying Occupations Concentrated in Rural Areas | | | |
|---|---|---|---|
| Title | Rural Percentage | Rural Earnings | Nationwide Earnings |
| 1. Electrical Power-Line Installers and Repairers | 27% | $59,284 | $63,250 |
| 2. First-Line Supervisors of Correctional Officers | 23% | $52,682 | $57,840 |
| 3. Education Administrators, Elementary and Secondary School | 18% | $76,617 | $87,760 |
| 4. Industrial Production Managers | 17% | $78,765 | $89,190 |
| 5. Zoologists and Wildlife Biologists | 17% | $58,742 | $57,710 |
| 6. First-Line Supervisors of Mechanics, Installers, and Repairers | 16% | $54,444 | $60,250 |
| 7. Judges, Magistrate Judges, and Magistrates | 16% | $82,152 | $115,760 |
| 8. Special Education Teachers, Secondary School | 15% | $49,441 | $56,830 |
| 9. Detectives and Criminal Investigators | 14% | $67,504 | $74,300 |
| 10. First-Line Supervisors of Police and Detectives | 14% | $58,501 | $78,270 |
| 11. Social and Community Service Managers | 14% | $50,254 | $59,970 |
| 12. Veterinarians | 14% | $74,712 | $84,460 |
| 13. Loan Officers | 13% | $53,368 | $59,820 |
| 14. Medical and Health Services Managers | 13% | $74,698 | $88,580 |
| 15. Occupational Health and Safety Specialists | 13% | $62,351 | $66,790 |

| High-Paying Occupations Concentrated in Rural Areas (cont.) | | | |
|---|---|---|---|
| **Title** | **Rural Percentage** | **Rural Earnings** | **Nationwide Earnings** |
| 16. Pharmacists | 13% | $118,012 | $116,670 |
| 17. Soil and Plant Scientists | 13% | $53,187 | $58,740 |
| 18. Chief Executives | 12% | $112,521 | $168,140 |
| 19. General and Operations Managers | 12% | $75,343 | $95,440 |
| 20. Physical Therapists | 12% | $77,866 | $79,860 |
| 21. Registered Nurses | 12% | $56,202 | $65,470 |
| 22. Speech-Language Pathologists | 12% | $60,811 | $69,870 |
| 23. Surveyors | 12% | $49,202 | $56,230 |
| 24. Captains, Mates, and Pilots of Water Vessels | 11% | $72,219 | $66,150 |
| 25. Compliance Officers | 11% | $53,290 | $62,020 |
| 26. Dental Hygienists | 11% | $64,053 | $70,210 |
| 27. Industrial Engineers | 11% | $69,115 | $78,860 |
| 28. Clinical, Counseling, and School Psychologists | 10% | $57,774 | $67,650 |
| 29. Cost Estimators | 10% | $50,842 | $58,860 |
| 30. Education Administrators, Postsecondary | 10% | $74,912 | $86,490 |
| 31. Instructional Coordinators | 10% | $55,542 | $60,050 |
| 32. Medical and Clinical Laboratory Technologists | 10% | $52,504 | $57,580 |

| High-Paying Occupations Concentrated in Rural Areas (cont.) | | | |
|---|---|---|---|
| **Title** | **Rural Percentage** | **Rural Earnings** | **Nationwide Earnings** |
| 33. Occupational Therapists | 10% | $69,801 | $75,400 |
| 34. Physician Assistants | 10% | $89,615 | $90,930 |
| 53. Purchasing Managers, Except Whole-sale, Retail, and Farm Products | 10% | $49,605 | $58,760 |

## High-Paying Occupations With Many Self-Employed Workers

Have you ever thought about being your own boss? You may find this arrangement appealing because you want to be in full control of all decisions about your work and collect all the profits from your work. Of course, there will be limits to your independence, because you will always have to please your customers or clients. You also will take on all the financial risks of your business and all the responsibilities of advertising, bookkeeping, insurance, finance, office management, and sometimes personnel management. But many people enjoy dealing with all these business issues and laying the groundwork for a successful enterprise.

Several kinds of work arrangements are possible for self-employed people. For example, many Construction Managers run a small business and do projects for clients using several employees and equipment that the business owns or leases. Many health-care professionals, such as Chiropractors, Podiatrists, or Optometrists, own a practice in which they treat patients, usually with the support of an office staff and perhaps some aides. Self-employed Lawyers usually work in a similar situation. Some self-employed workers are consultants who use their expertise to advise other businesses or individuals; Management Analysts and Personal Financial Advisors do this kind of work. Still others are freelancers who team up with other freelancers to work on a project and then move on when the collaborative project is done; this is the arrangement for many Producers and Directors, as well as Multimedia Artists and Animators.

One of these situations might be right for you, but understand that the type of work arrangement will depend greatly on the nature of the occupation. For example, Chiropractors rarely are able to create a business that lets them work as freelancers or consultants. And 21 of the high-paying occupations in this book, such as Compliance Officers, Financial Examiners, and Budget Analysts, offer essentially no opportunities for self-employment.

If you enter an occupation that does allow self-employment, and if you have an independent spirit, you may choose to start your career in a self-employed arrangement, but another strategy is to start as someone else's employee and try to learn all aspects of the business before establishing an organization of your own.

The occupations on the following list are the high-paying occupations with the most opportunities for self-employment. I created it by eliminating all of the high-paying occupations in which less than 10 percent of the workers are self-employed. I then ordered the remaining 34 occupations from highest percentage of self-employment to lowest.

Unlike most other lists in part I, this list does not include any earnings figures, because the BLS does not collect data on earnings from self-employment. (The earnings figures you'll see elsewhere for these occupations are the averages for those who are wage-earners.) However, I thought you'd be interested in the amount of employment growth from 2010 to 2020 that the BLS projects for the self-employed sector of each occupation, so I include that percentage figure in the rightmost column of the table.

| High-Paying Occupations With Many Self-Employed Workers | | |
|---|---|---|
| **Title** | **Percent Self-Employed** | **Projected Growth of Self-Employed** |
| 1. Construction Managers | 63.8% | 8.0% |
| 2. Art Directors | 59.1% | 2.8% |
| 3. Multimedia Artists and Animators | 58.8% | 2.8% |
| 4. Real Estate Brokers | 57.3% | 2.9% |
| 5. Managers, All Other | 55.8% | 8.0% |
| 6. Chiropractors | 50.1% | 25.8% |
| 7. Agents and Business Managers of Artists, Performers, and Athletes | 49.9% | 1.8% |
| 8. First-Line Supervisors of Non-Retail Sales Workers | 41.8% | -2.3% |
| 9. Health Diagnosing and Treating Practitioners, All Other | 40.0% | 25.6% |
| 10. Clinical, Counseling, and School Psychologists | 34.2% | 25.2% |
| 11. Dentists | 32.3% | 25.8% |
| 12. Psychologists, All Other | 32.1% | 25.2% |
| 13. Commercial and Industrial Designers | 30.0% | 12.0% |

| High-Paying Occupations With Many Self-Employed Workers (cont.) | | |
|---|---|---|
| Title | Percent Self-Employed | Projected Growth of Self-Employed |
| 14. Producers and Directors | 28.7% | 16.3% |
| 15. Podiatrists | 26.1% | 25.7% |
| 16. Landscape Architects | 23.9% | 9.4% |
| 17. Architects, Except Landscape and Naval | 23.9% | 17.3% |
| 18. Personal Financial Advisors | 23.9% | 23.0% |
| 19. Management Analysts | 22.6% | 17.5% |
| 20. Lawyers | 21.6% | 18.6% |
| 21. Optometrists | 21.6% | 25.7% |
| 22. Judges, Magistrate Judges, and Magistrates | 21.3% | 18.6% |
| 23. Chief Executives | 20.4% | 6.9% |
| 24. Supervisors of Construction and Extraction Workers | 15.9% | 7.7% |
| 25. Surveyors | 13.8% | 19.0% |
| 26. Cartographers and Photogrammetrists | 13.6% | 31.8% |
| 27. Physicians and Surgeons | 12.4% | 25.3% |
| 28. Captains, Mates, and Pilots of Water Vessels | 12.4% | 12.1% |
| 29. Advertising and Promotions Managers | 12.3% | 17.4% |
| 30. Physical Scientists, All Other | 11.9% | 13.4% |

| High-Paying Occupations With Many Self-Employed Workers (cont.) | | |
|---|---|---|
| Title | Percent Self-Employed | Projected Growth of Self-Employed |
| 31. Social Scientists and Related Workers, All Other | 11.5% | 21.4% |
| 32. Securities, Commodities, and Financial Services Sales Agents | 10.8% | 24.2% |
| 33. Food Scientists and Technologists | 10.8% | 14.0% |
| 34. Soil and Plant Scientists | 10.5% | 14.0% |

## High-Paying Occupations With Unstable Earnings

You're reading this book because you're interested in occupations that have high earnings, but maybe you should also give some thought to the *stability* of earnings. In some occupations, earnings can vary widely from one year to the next. These income variations can make it difficult for you to budget for recurring expenses such as mortgage payments, car loan payments, and your kids' college tuition bills.

I looked at the earnings reported each year from 2003 through 2012 for each occupation in this book. In the great majority of instances, earnings went up steadily from one year to the next. Sometimes, however, earnings for an occupation went down from one year to another. For example, the earnings of Statisticians declined from $64,320 in 2003 to $58,620 in 2004, although not at any other time over the nine years I examined. I would not consider Statisticians, with just one earnings dip, an occupation with unstable earnings.

To identify the occupations with truly unstable earnings, I tallied the number of times the earnings figures declined from one year to the next. I identified 18 occupations that had two or more instances of income declines. I decided that graphs would illustrate these ups and downs of income better than tables of figures, so I created six graphs. On each of the following graphs, you can see three lines that represent the changing earnings of three occupations from this book, plus a fourth (lower) line that represents the average earnings of all workers in all occupations.

The most noticeable trend in all of the charts is the contrast between the three upper lines and the lower line: roller-coaster profiles versus a steady upward progress. This contrast shows that income in the individual occupations, although considerably higher than average, is also more unstable than average.

Another interesting thing to note in these graphs is that the dips in earnings often do not occur during the recession years that began at the end of 2007. For many of these occupations, the effect of this recession on earnings was either minimal or was delayed by a few years. (Hiring, however, is another issue.)

# High-Paying Occupations With Unstable Earnings

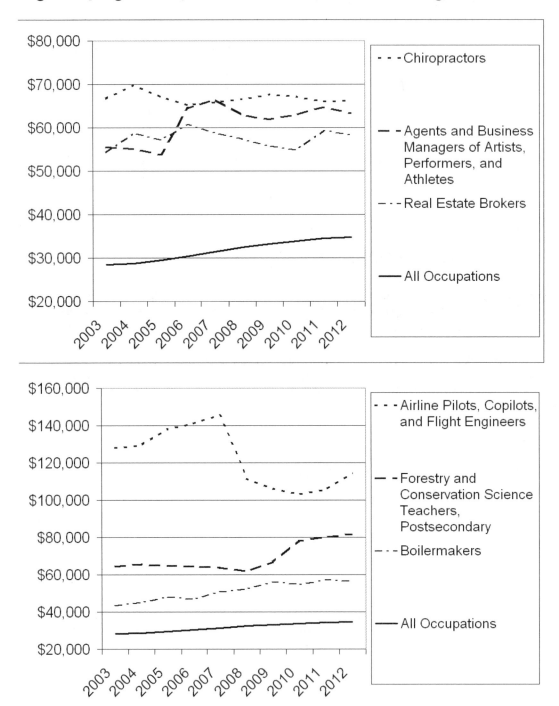

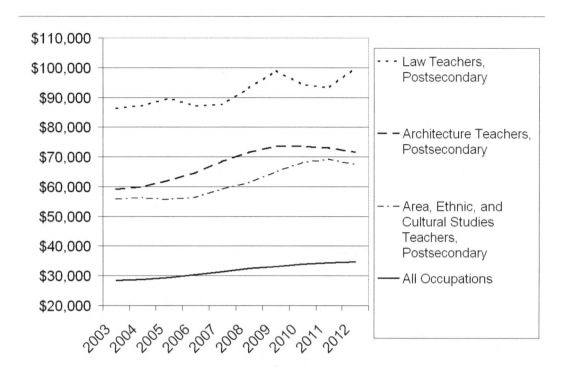

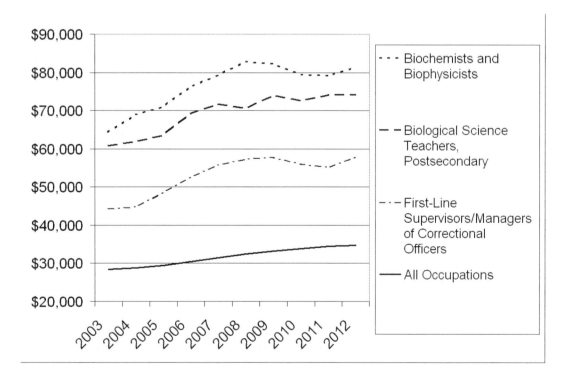

131

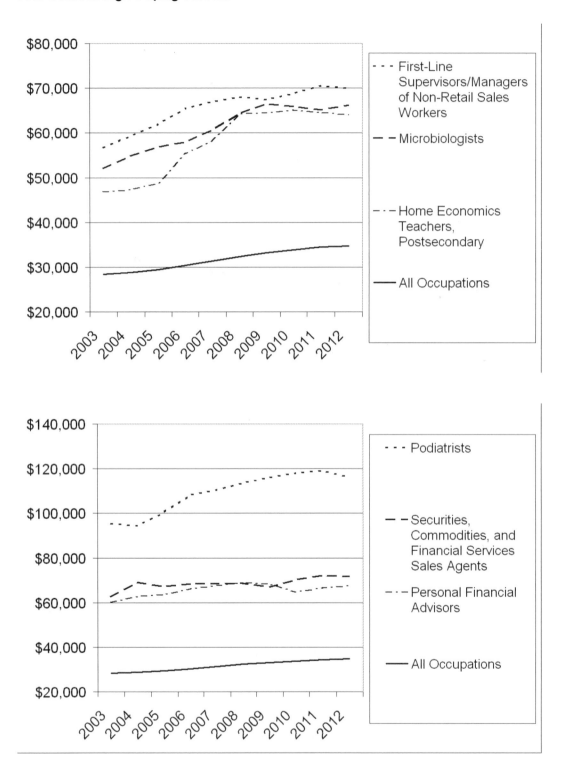

# High-Paying Occupations With a Few Superstars

Have you ever fantasized about winning the lottery jackpot? Some occupations have a few jackpot positions that pay extremely well. You're certainly familiar with movie stars who earn the millions that most struggling actors can only dream about. The radio plays songs by musical superstars who bring home more than the combined earnings of 100 bar bands.

Among the occupations included in this book, some offer extremely high earning opportunities for a relatively small subset of workers. You can't tell which occupations these are by looking at the median wage figure or even at the range of the middle 50 percent of earners. But I have a way of identifying these occupations for you.

Imagine this situation: Five friends are sitting around a restaurant table having lunch. They all earn roughly the same amount:

| PERSON | EARNINGS |
|---|---|
| Joe | $50,000 |
| Lydia | $51,000 |
| Mateo | $52,000 |
| Isabella | $53,000 |
| Mike | $54,000 |

For the group, the median earnings figure is $52,000 (half earn more, half earn less). If you calculate the *mean* earnings (add them all up and divide by 5), you'll get the same figure, $52,000. But let's say Mike gets a phone call telling him that he was just promoted to vice president and is now earning $150,000. Note that the median for the group *has not changed,* but the mean has jumped to $71,200. Because there is now one superstar earner in the group, the mean is now 37 percent higher than the median.

For the 173 occupations in this book, I calculated the difference between the median earnings and the mean earnings. (The BLS reports both figures.) The following list includes those occupations in which the mean is at least 15 percent higher than the median. They are ordered by how much the mean exceeds the median. For each occupation, I list both earnings figures.

What might cause you to be among the highest of the high-paid workers? Here are some possible reasons:

- You have an outstanding talent. Maybe you were born with some ability that few other people have.

- Through hard work or study, you have developed outstanding skills. Whether these are physical or mental skills, they can put you ahead of the pack.

- You use mass media to reach a very large paying audience. Think about how much more a TV chef can earn compared to a one-restaurant chef.

- You find a specialization or a geographic location that causes you to be in high demand but have no competition. This advantage may be only temporary, but you may be able to command high earnings as long as you are the go-to person for your narrow field or community.

## Your Guide to High-Paying Careers

- You go into management. The list of work context features in the book's introduction pretty much describes a managerial job.

Whether you look at the following list as a collection of nice fantasies or as possible roadmaps to your future, the list makes for interesting reading.

| High-Paying Occupations with a Few Superstars | | |
|---|---|---|
| **Title** | **Median Earnings** | **Mean Earnings** |
| 1. Securities, Commodities, and Financial Services Sales Agents | $71,720 | $100,910 |
| 2. Agents and Business Managers of Artists, Performers, and Athletes | $63,370 | $88,620 |
| 3. Real Estate Brokers | $58,350 | $80,220 |
| 4. Personal Financial Advisors | $67,520 | $90,820 |
| 5. Producers and Directors | $71,350 | $92,390 |
| 6. Health Specialties Teachers, Postsecondary | $81,140 | $100,370 |
| 7. Advertising and Promotions Managers | $88,590 | $107,060 |
| 8. General and Operations Managers | $95,440 | $114,850 |
| 9. Chiropractors | $66,160 | $79,550 |
| 10. Art, Drama, and Music Teachers, Postsecondary | $62,160 | $73,340 |
| 11. Health Diagnosing and Treating Practitioners, All Other | $72,710 | $85,740 |
| 12. Loan Officers | $59,820 | $70,350 |
| 13. First-Line Supervisors of Non-Retail Sales Workers | $70,060 | $82,320 |

| High-Paying Occupations with a Few Superstars (cont.) | | |
|---|---|---|
| **Title** | **Median Earnings** | **Mean Earnings** |
| 14. Geoscientists, Except Hydrologists and Geographers | $90,890 | $106,780 |
| 15. Biological Science Teachers, Postsecondary | $74,180 | $87,060 |
| 16. Art Directors | $80,880 | $94,260 |
| 17. Business Teachers, Postsecondary | $73,660 | $85,730 |
| 18. Financial Analysts | $76,950 | $89,410 |
| 19. Law Teachers, Postsecondary | $99,950 | $115,550 |
| 20. Area, Ethnic, and Cultural Studies Teachers, Postsecondary | $67,360 | $77,690 |
| 21. Lawyers | $113,530 | $130,880 |

Now that you have browsed the lists, turn to part II and read the descriptions of the occupations that interest you most. Also be sure to investigate a few occupations that are unfamiliar to you. You may be surprised at what you discover.

# PART II

# Descriptions of High-Paying Occupations

In this part of the book you'll find many detailed facts about the 173 occupations in the part I lists. Most of the information is derived from the Bureau of Labor Statistics. You can find full explanations of these descriptions and their sources in the introduction to this book.

Understand that the information here describes average tendencies for each occupation, and an occupation is a collection of individual jobs that have a lot in common but are never completely identical. Each local job that comes open may pay more, require less education, require higher skills, or have a different work environment than the average that is described here. You can find out about the specific nature of the jobs in your community by following the tips in the last section of the book's introduction, "Your Next Steps." So think of part II as a first step in career exploration, not as a final answer.

The occupations appear in alphabetical order, but many of the entries include descriptions of *job specializations*. For example, the entry for Physicians and Surgeons includes Anesthesiologists, Psychiatrists, and six other job specializations. The titles of all 182 job specializations are listed in the book's index.

## Accountants and Auditors

**Examine, analyze, and interpret accounting records to prepare financial statements, give advice, or audit and evaluate statements prepared by others.**

- Average annual earnings: $63,550
- Middle 50% of earners: $49,540–$84,220
- Earnings growth potential: Medium (37.2%)
- Growth: 15.7%
- Annual job openings: 45,210
- Self-employed: 7.6%

### BEST-PAYING INDUSTRIES

| Industry | Median Earnings | Workforce |
|---|---|---|
| Professional, Scientific, and Technical Services | $65,100 | 394,010 |
| Management of Companies and Enterprises | $64,670 | 82,790 |
| Federal, State, and Local Government | $61,270 | 101,750 |

## Your Guide to High-Paying Careers

**BEST-PAYING METROPOLITAN AREAS**

| Metro Area | Median Earnings | Workforce |
|---|---|---|
| New York–Northern New Jersey–Long Island, NY-NJ-PA | $78,810 | 95,960 |
| Washington-Arlington-Alexandria, DC-VA-MD-WV | $75,340 | 39,060 |
| Boston-Cambridge-Quincy, MA-NH | $70,500 | 29,560 |
| Philadelphia-Camden-Wilmington, PA-NJ-DE-MD | $69,800 | 29,210 |
| Los Angeles–Long Beach–Santa Ana, CA | $68,460 | 56,440 |
| Houston–Sugar Land–Baytown, TX | $67,730 | 28,240 |
| Chicago-Naperville-Joliet, IL-IN-WI | $67,380 | 33,750 |
| Dallas–Fort Worth–Arlington, TX | $66,760 | 29,050 |
| Atlanta–Sandy Springs–Marietta, GA | $66,190 | 26,870 |
| Miami–Fort Lauderdale–Pompano Beach, FL | $61,350 | 25,860 |

**Considerations for Job Outlook:** Accountants and auditors who have earned professional recognition, especially as a Certified Public Accountants (CPA), should have the best prospects. Job applicants who have a master's degree in accounting or a master's degree in business with a concentration in accounting also may have an advantage. However, competition should be strong for jobs with the most prestigious accounting and business firms.

**Major Work Tasks:** For tasks, see the job specializations.

**Usual Educational Requirement:** Bachelor's degree. **Relevant Educational Programs**: Accounting; Accounting and Business/Management; Accounting and Computer Science; Accounting and Finance; Auditing; Financial Forensics and Fraud Investigation; Taxation. **Work Experience Needed:** None. **On-the-Job Training Needed:** None. **Certification/Licensure:** Licensure for most specializations; voluntary certification by association.

**Key Career Cluster:** 04 Business, Management, and Administration. **Key Career Pathway:** 4.2 Business Financial Management and Accounting.

**JOB SPECIALIZATION: ACCOUNTANTS**

**Analyze financial information and prepare financial reports to determine or maintain record of assets, liabilities, profit and loss, tax liability, or other financial activities within an organization.**

**Major Work Tasks:** Prepare, examine, or analyze accounting records, financial statements, or other financial reports to assess accuracy, completeness, and conformance to reporting and procedural standards. Report to management regarding the finances of establishment. Establish tables of accounts and assign entries to proper accounts. Develop, implement, modify, and document recordkeeping and accounting systems, making use of current computer technology. Compute taxes owed and prepare tax returns, ensuring compliance with payment, reporting or other tax requirements. Analyze business operations, trends, costs, revenues, financial commitments, and obligations, to project future revenues and expenses or to provide advice. Develop, maintain, and analyze budgets, preparing periodic reports that compare budgeted costs to actual costs. Prepare forms and manuals for accounting and bookkeeping personnel, and direct their work activities. Survey operations to ascertain accounting needs and to recommend, develop, or maintain solutions to business and financial problems. Advise management about issues such as resource utilization, tax strategies, and the assumptions underlying budget fore-

138

casts. Provide internal and external auditing services for businesses or individuals. Advise clients in areas such as compensation, employee health-care benefits, the design of accounting or data processing systems, or long-range tax or estate plans. Represent clients before taxing authorities and provide support during litigation involving financial issues. Appraise, evaluate, and inventory real property and equipment, recording information such as the description, value, and location of property. Maintain or examine the records of government agencies. Serve as bankruptcy trustees or business valuators.

**Related Knowledge/Courses:** Economics and Accounting; Clerical Practices; Mathematics; Computers and Electronics; Personnel and Human Resources; Administration and Management.

**Personality Types:** Conventional–Enterprising.

**Skills:** Operations analysis; mathematics; systems analysis; management of financial resources; systems evaluation; critical thinking; judgment and decision making; negotiation.

**Physical Environment:** Indoors; sitting; repetitive motions. **Structural Environment:** Importance of being exact or accurate; importance of repeating same tasks; structured versus unstructured work; freedom to make decisions; frequency of decision making; impact of decisions on co-workers or company results.

### JOB SPECIALIZATION: AUDITORS

**Examine and analyze accounting records to determine financial status of establishment and prepare financial reports concerning operating procedures.**

**Major Work Tasks:** Collect and analyze data to detect deficient controls, duplicated effort, extravagance, fraud, or non-compliance with laws, regulations, and management policies. Report to management about asset utilization and audit results and to recommend changes in operations and financial activities. Prepare detailed reports on audit findings. Review data about material assets, net worth, liabilities, capital stock, surplus, income, and expenditures. Inspect account books and accounting systems for efficiency, effectiveness, and use of accepted accounting procedures to record transactions. Examine and evaluate financial and information systems, recommending controls to ensure system reliability and data integrity. Supervise auditing of establishments and determine scope of investigation required. Prepare, analyze, and verify annual reports, financial statements, and other records, using accepted accounting and statistical procedures to assess financial condition and facilitate financial planning. Confer with company officials about financial and regulatory matters. Inspect cash on hand, notes receivable and payable, negotiable securities, and canceled checks to confirm records are accurate. Examine inventory to verify journal and ledger entries. Examine whether the organization's objectives are reflected in its management activities and whether employees understand the objectives. Examine records and interview workers to ensure recording of transactions and compliance with laws and regulations. Direct activities of personnel engaged in filing, recording, compiling, and transmitting financial records. Produce up-to-the-minute information, using internal computer systems, to allow management to base decisions on actual, not historical, data. Conduct pre-implementation audits to determine if systems and programs under development will work as planned. Review taxpayer accounts and conduct audits on-site, by correspondence or by summoning taxpayer to office. Evaluate taxpayer finances to determine tax liability, using knowledge of interest and discount rates, annuities, valuation of stocks and bonds, and amortization valuation of depletable assets.

**Related Knowledge/Courses:** Economics and Accounting; Administration and Management;

Personnel and Human Resources; Law and Government; Computers and Electronics; Mathematics.

**Personality Types:** Conventional–Enterprising–Investigative.

**Skills:** Systems evaluation; systems analysis; management of financial resources; mathematics; programming; operations analysis; writing; management of personnel resources.

**Physical Environment:** Indoors; sitting. **Structural Environment:** Importance of being exact or accurate; freedom to make decisions; time pressure; structured versus unstructured work; importance of repeating same tasks; frequency of decision making.

## Actuaries

**Analyze statistical data to forecast risk and liability for payment of future benefits.**

- Average annual earnings: $93,680
- Middle 50% of earners: $69,780–$132,340
- Earnings growth potential: Medium (40.5%)
- Growth: 26.7%
- Annual job openings: 1,890
- Self-employed: 5.6%

### BEST-PAYING INDUSTRIES

| Industry | Median | Workforce |
|---|---|---|
| Insurance Carriers and Related Activities | $94,810 | 14,140 |
| Professional, Scientific, and Technical Services | $93,890 | 3,930 |
| Management of Companies and Enterprises | $86,710 | 1,480 |

### BEST-PAYING METROPOLITAN AREAS

| Metro Area | Median Earnings | Workforce |
|---|---|---|
| Kansas City, MO-KS | $124,120 | 500 |
| New York–Northern New Jersey–Long Island, NY-NJ-PA | $110,330 | 3,330 |
| Hartford–West Hartford–East Hartford, CT | $105,810 | 910 |
| Boston-Cambridge-Quincy, MA-NH | $103,650 | 800 |
| Los Angeles–Long Beach–Santa Ana, CA | $101,640 | 1,000 |
| Minneapolis–St. Paul–Bloomington, MN-WI | $91,860 | 800 |
| Chicago-Naperville-Joliet, IL-IN-WI | $89,750 | 600 |
| San Francisco–Oakland–Fremont, CA | $87,180 | 440 |

**Considerations for Job Outlook:** Actuaries should expect strong competition for most jobs. Actuaries are a small field, and the relatively high pay and comfortable working conditions make being an actuary a desirable career. Students who have passed at least one actuarial exam and have had an internship while in college should have the best job prospects for entry-level positions.

**Major Work Tasks:** Ascertain premium rates required and cash reserves and liabilities necessary to ensure payment of future benefits. Analyze statistical information to estimate mortality, accident, sickness, disability, and retirement rates. Design, review, and help administer insurance, annuity, and pension plans, determining financial soundness and calculating premiums. Collaborate with programmers, underwriters, accounts, claims experts, and senior management to help companies develop plans for new lines of business or improving existing business. Determine or help determine company policy and explain complex technical matters to company executives, government officials, shareholders, policyholders, or the public. Testify before public agencies on proposed legislation affecting businesses. Provide advice to clients on a contract basis, working as a consultant. Testify in court as expert witness or to provide legal evidence on matters such as the value of potential lifetime earnings of a person who is disabled or killed in an accident. Construct probability tables for events such as fires, natural disasters, and unemployment, based on analysis of statistical data and other pertinent information. Determine policy contract provisions for each type of insurance. Provide expertise to help financial institutions manage risks and maximize returns associated with investment products or credit offerings. Determine equitable basis for distributing surplus earnings under participating insurance and annuity contracts in mutual companies. Manage credit and help price corporate security offerings. Explain changes in contract provisions to customers.

**Usual Educational Requirement:** Bachelor's degree. **Relevant Educational Programs**: Actuarial Science; Applied Mathematics, General; Computational and Applied Mathematics; Mathematical Statistics and Probability; Mathematics and Statistics; Statistics, General; Statistics, Other. **Related Knowledge/Courses:** Economics and Accounting; Mathematics; Computers and Electronics; Administration and Management; Personnel and Human Resources; Sales and Marketing. **Work Experience Needed:** None. **On-the-Job Training Needed:** Long-term on-the-job training. **Certification/Licensure:** None.

**Personality Types:** Conventional–Investigative–Enterprising. **Key Career Cluster:** 06 Finance. **Key Career Pathway:** 6.4 Insurance Services.

**Skills:** Mathematics; management of financial resources; systems evaluation; systems analysis; programming; operations analysis; judgment and decision making; complex problem solving.

**Physical Environment:** Indoors; sitting. **Structural Environment:** Importance of being exact or accurate; impact of decisions on co-workers or company results; freedom to make decisions; structured versus unstructured Work; frequency of decision making; level of competition.

## Administrative Services Managers

**Plan, direct, or coordinate one or more administrative services of an organization.**

- Average annual earnings: $81,080
- Middle 50% of earners: $60,250–$108,660
- Earnings growth potential: High (45.3%)
- Growth: 14.5%
- Annual job openings: 9,980
- Self-employed: 0.3%

### BEST-PAYING INDUSTRIES

| Industry | Median Earnings | Workforce |
|---|---|---|
| Management of Companies and Enterprises | $90,600 | 15,800 |
| Professional, Scientific, and Technical Services | $88,620 | 24,340 |
| Hospitals | $84,930 | 15,970 |
| Federal, State, and Local Government | $81,030 | 35,680 |
| Educational Services | $76,830 | 37,430 |
| Administrative and Support Services | $72,440 | 15,080 |

141

## Your Guide to High-Paying Careers

### BEST-PAYING METROPOLITAN AREAS

| Metro Area | Median Earnings | Workforce |
|---|---|---|
| New York–Northern New Jersey–Long Island, NY-NJ-PA | $108,830 | 19,170 |
| Philadelphia-Camden-Wilmington, PA-NJ-DE-MD | $102,320 | 5,330 |
| Washington-Arlington-Alexandria, DC-VA-MD-WV | $92,440 | 7,370 |
| Boston-Cambridge-Quincy, MA-NH | $91,930 | 8,800 |
| Los Angeles–Long Beach–Santa Ana, CA | $90,680 | 13,340 |
| Houston–Sugar Land–Baytown, TX | $88,090 | 6,620 |
| Dallas–Fort Worth–Arlington, TX | $85,990 | 7,360 |
| Atlanta–Sandy Springs–Marietta, GA | $83,060 | 8,250 |
| Minneapolis–St. Paul–Bloomington, MN-WI | $78,570 | 5,900 |
| Chicago-Naperville-Joliet, IL-IN-WI | $72,340 | 11,360 |

**Considerations for Job Outlook:** Applicants will likely face strong competition for the limited number of higher-level administrative services management jobs. Competition should be less severe for lower-level management jobs. Job prospects also are expected to be better for those who can manage a wide range of responsibilities than for those who specialize in particular functions.

**Major Work Tasks:** Direct or coordinate the supportive services department of a business, agency, or organization. Set goals and deadlines for the department. Prepare and review operational reports and schedules to ensure accuracy and efficiency. Analyze internal processes and recommend and implement procedural or policy changes to improve operations, such as supply changes or the disposal of records. Acquire, distribute, and store supplies. Monitor the facility to ensure that it remains safe, secure, and well-maintained. Plan, administer, and control budgets for contracts, equipment, and supplies. Oversee construction and renovation projects to improve efficiency and to ensure that facilities meet environmental, health, and security standards and comply with government regulations. Hire and terminate clerical and administrative personnel. Oversee the maintenance and repair of machinery, equipment, and electrical and mechanical systems. Manage leasing of facility space. Participate in architectural and engineering planning and design, including space and installation management. Conduct classes to teach procedures to staff. Dispose of, or oversee the disposal of, surplus or unclaimed property.

**Usual Educational Requirement:** High school diploma or equivalent. **Relevant Educational Programs**: Business Administration and Management, General; Business/Commerce, General; Medical/Health Management and Clinical Assistant/Specialist Training; Purchasing, Procurement/Acquisitions and Contracts Management. **Related Knowledge/ Courses:** Clerical Practices; Economics and Accounting; Personnel and Human Resources; Customer and Personal Service; Sales and Marketing; Administration and Management. **Work Experience Needed:** 1 to 5 years. **On-the-Job Training Needed:** None. **Certification/ Licensure:** Licensure for some specializations.

**Personality Types:** Enterprising–Conventional. **Key Career Cluster:** 04 Business, Management, and Administration. **Key Career Pathway:** 4.1 Management.

**Skills:** Management of financial resources; management of material resources; management of personnel resources; negotiation; coordination; time management; social perceptiveness; service orientation.

**Physical Environment:** Indoors; sitting. **Structural Environment:** Structured versus unstructured work; freedom to make decisions; frequency of decision making; time pressure; importance of being exact or accurate; impact of decisions on co-workers or company results.

## Advertising and Promotions Managers

**Plan, direct, or coordinate advertising policies and programs or produce collateral materials to create extra interest in the purchase of a product or service.**

- Average annual earnings: $88,590
- Middle 50% of earners: $60,820–$135,930
- Earnings growth potential: Very high (51.2%)
- Growth: 13.3%
- Annual job openings: 1,620
- Self-employed: 12.3%

### BEST-PAYING INDUSTRIES

| Industry | Median Earnings | Workforce |
|---|---|---|
| Professional, Scientific, and Technical Services | $114,560 | 9,590 |
| Management of Companies and Enterprises | $92,930 | 2,670 |
| Merchant Wholesalers, Nondurable Goods | $84,140 | 1,770 |
| Publishing Industries (except Internet) | $79,770 | 1,860 |
| Religious, Grantmaking, Civic, Professional, and Similar Organizations | $75,870 | 1,490 |
| Broadcasting (except Internet) | $74,130 | 1,490 |

### BEST-PAYING METROPOLITAN AREAS

| Metro Area | Median Earnings | Workforce |
|---|---|---|
| New York–Northern New Jersey–Long Island, NY-NJ-PA | $129,590 | 4,610 |
| Los Angeles–Long Beach–Santa Ana, CA | $118,870 | 1,880 |
| Minneapolis–St. Paul–Bloomington, MN-WI | $104,710 | 720 |
| San Francisco–Oakland–Fremont, CA | $101,710 | 790 |
| Boston-Cambridge-Quincy, MA-NH | $99,870 | 710 |
| Washington-Arlington-Alexandria, DC-VA-MD-WV | $92,900 | 660 |
| Chicago-Naperville-Joliet, IL-IN-WI | $84,570 | 2,440 |

**Considerations for Job Outlook:** Advertising, promotions, and marketing manager positions are highly desirable and are often sought by other managers and experienced professionals. As a result, strong competition is expected. With Internet-based advertising becoming more important, advertising managers who can navigate the digital world should have the best prospects.

**Major Work Tasks:** Prepare budgets and submit estimates for program costs as part of campaign plan development. Plan and prepare advertising and promotional material to increase sales of products or services, working with customers, company officials, sales departments, and advertising agencies. Assist with annual budget development. Inspect layouts and advertising copy and edit scripts, audio and video tapes, and other promotional material for adherence to specifications. Prepare and negotiate advertising and sales contracts. Identify and develop contacts for promotional campaigns and industry pro-

**143**

grams that meet identified buyer targets such as dealers, distributors, or consumers. Gather and organize information to plan advertising campaigns. Confer with department heads or staff to discuss topics such as contracts, selection of advertising media, or product to be advertised. Confer with clients to provide marketing or technical advice. Read trade journals and professional literature to stay informed on trends, innovations, and changes that affect media planning. Formulate plans to extend business with established accounts and to transact business as agent for advertising accounts. Provide presentation and product demonstration support during the introduction of new products and services to field staff and customers. Direct, motivate, and monitor the mobilization of a campaign team to advance campaign goals. Plan and execute advertising policies and strategies for organizations. Direct and coordinate product research and development. Represent company at trade association meetings to promote products. Consult publications to learn about conventions and social functions and to organize prospect files for promotional purposes. Coordinate activities of departments, such as sales, graphic arts, media, finance, and research. Monitor and analyze sales promotion results to determine cost effectiveness of promotion campaigns. Track program budgets and expenses and campaign response rates to evaluate each campaign based on program objectives and industry norms.

**Usual Educational Requirement:** Bachelor's degree. **Relevant Educational Programs**: Advertising; Marketing/Marketing Management, General; Public Relations, Advertising, and Applied Communication; Public Relations/Image Management. **Related Knowledge/Courses:** Communications and media; fine arts; sales and marketing; telecommunications; English language; design. **Work Experience Needed:** 1 to 5 years. **On-the-Job Training Needed:** None. **Certification/Licensure:** None.

**Personality Types:** Enterprising–Artistic–Conventional. **Key Career Cluster:** 07 Government and Public Administration. **Key Career Pathway:** 7.1 Governance.

**Skills:** Management of financial resources; operations analysis; management of personnel resources; coordination; systems evaluation; negotiation; management of material resources; speaking.

**Physical Environment:** Indoors; sitting. **Structural Environment:** Time pressure; structured versus unstructured Work; Freedom to make decisions; impact of decisions on co-workers or company results; frequency of decision making; importance of being exact or accurate.

## JOB SPECIALIZATION: GREEN MARKETERS

**Create and implement methods to market green products and services.**

**Major Work Tasks:** Maintain portfolios of marketing campaigns, strategies, and other marketing products or ideas. Devise or evaluate methods and procedures for collecting data, such as surveys, opinion polls, and questionnaires. Analyze the effectiveness of marketing tactics or channels. Analyze regional energy markets, including energy pricing, market structures, energy generation competition, and energy transmission constraints. Monitor green-related industry statistics or literature to identify trends. Generate or identify sales leads for green products and technologies. Write marketing content for green product web sites, brochures, or other communication media. Revise existing marketing plans or campaigns for green products, technologies, or services. Identify marketing channels for green products or services. Develop communications materials, advertisements, presentations, or public relations initiatives to promote awareness of green products and technologies. Conduct research on consumer opinions and buying habits and identify target audiences for green products, services, or technologies. Attend or participate in conferences, community events, and promotional events related to green products or technologies. Analyze green product marketing or sales trends to forecast future conditions. Develop branding or sales initiatives for green products, such as solar energy systems, green cleaning products, or products using renewable or recycled materials. Develop comprehensive marketing strategies, using knowledge of green products and technologies, markets, and regulations. Coordinate with other marketing team members and workers such as graphic artists to develop and implement marketing programs.

**Related Knowledge/Courses:** No data available.

**Personality Types:** Enterprising–Artistic–Investigative.

**Skills:** No data available.

**Physical Environment:** No data available.
**Structural Environment:** No data available.

## Aerospace Engineers

**Perform engineering duties in designing, constructing, and testing aircraft, missiles, and spacecraft.**

- Average annual earnings: $103,720
- Middle 50% of earners: $81,890–$127,570
- Earnings growth potential: Medium (36.9%)
- Growth: 4.9%
- Annual job openings: 2,180
- Self-employed: 1.1%

**Considerations for Job Outlook:** Aerospace engineers who know how to use collaborative engineering tools and processes and who know about modeling, simulation, and robotics should have good opportunities. Opportunities also should be favorable for those trained in Computational Fluid Dynamics software, which has enabled companies to test designs in a digital environment, thereby lowering testing costs.

### BEST-PAYING INDUSTRIES

| Industry | Median Earnings | Workforce |
|---|---|---|
| Federal, State, and Local Government | $110,750 | 9,070 |
| Computer and Electronic Product Manufacturing | $109,860 | 8,080 |
| Professional, Scientific, and Technical Services | $108,300 | 26,980 |
| Transportation Equipment Manufacturing | $97,510 | 31,410 |

### BEST-PAYING METROPOLITAN AREAS

| Metro Area | Median Earnings | Workforce |
|---|---|---|
| Washington-Arlington-Alexandria, DC-VA-MD-WV | $131,740 | 4,310 |
| San Jose–Sunnyvale–Santa Clara, CA | $125,910 | 2,400 |
| Los Angeles–Long Beach–Santa Ana, CA | $117,250 | 10,190 |
| Houston–Sugar Land–Baytown, TX | $116,840 | 2,420 |
| Huntsville, AL | $112,150 | 3,000 |
| Denver-Aurora, CO | $105,000 | 2,010 |
| Dallas–Fort Worth–Arlington, TX | $103,560 | 4,040 |
| Seattle-Tacoma-Bellevue, WA | $100,160 | 7,680 |
| Wichita, KS | $94,910 | 3,100 |
| Hartford–West Hartford–East Hartford, CT | $90,620 | 2,130 |

145

**Major Work Tasks:** Formulate conceptual design of aeronautical or aerospace products or systems to meet customer requirements. Direct or coordinate activities of engineering or technical personnel involved in designing, fabricating, modifying, or testing of aircraft or aerospace products. Develop design criteria for aeronautical or aerospace products or systems, including testing methods, production costs, quality standards, and completion dates. Plan or conduct experimental, environmental, operational, or stress tests on models or prototypes of aircraft or aerospace systems or equipment. Evaluate product data and design from inspections and reports for conformance to engineering principles, customer requirements, and quality standards. Write technical reports or other documentation, such as handbooks or bulletins, for use by engineering staff, management, or customers. Analyze project requests, proposals, or engineering data to determine feasibility, productibility, cost, or production time of aerospace or aeronautical products. Review performance reports and documentation from customers and field engineers and inspect malfunctioning or damaged products to determine problem. Plan or coordinate activities concerned with investigating and resolving customers' reports of technical problems with aircraft or aerospace vehicles. Maintain records of performance reports for future reference. Formulate mathematical models or other methods of computer analysis to develop, evaluate, or modify design, according to customer engineering requirements. Direct research and development programs. Evaluate and approve selection of vendors by studying past performance or new advertisements. Design new or modify existing aerospace systems to reduce polluting emissions, such as nitrogen oxide, carbon monoxide, or smoke emissions. Design or engineer filtration systems that reduce harmful emissions. Evaluate biofuel performance specifications to determine feasibility for aerospace applications. Research new materials to determine quality or conformance to environmental standards. Review aerospace engineering designs to determine how to reduce negative environmental impacts.

**Usual Educational Requirement:** Bachelor's degree. **Relevant Educational Programs:** Aerospace, Aeronautical and Astronautical/Space Engineering; Electrical and Electronics Engineering; Mechanical Engineering. **Related Knowledge/Courses:** Engineering and Technology; Physics; Design; Mechanical Devices; Mathematics; Production and Processing. **Work Experience Needed:** None. **On-the-Job Training Needed:** None. **Certification/Licensure:** Licensure beyond entry level.

**Personality Types:** Investigative–Realistic. **Key Career Cluster:** 15 Science, Technology, Engineering, and Mathematics. **Key Career Pathway:** 15.1 Engineering and Technology.

**Skills:** Science; operations analysis; technology design; mathematics; quality control analysis; reading comprehension; systems analysis; writing.

**Physical Environment:** Indoors; sitting. **Structural Environment:** Importance of being exact or accurate; structured versus unstructured work; freedom to make decisions; time pressure; impact of decisions on co-workers or company results; importance of repeating same tasks.

## Agents and Business Managers of Artists, Performers, and Athletes

**Represent and promote artists, performers, and athletes in dealings with current or prospective employers.**

- Average annual earnings: $63,370
- Middle 50% of earners: $41,410–$110,550
- Earnings growth potential: Very high (56.6%)
- Growth: 14.0%
- Annual job openings: 800
- Self-employed: 49.9%

BEST-PAYING INDUSTRIES

| Industry | Median Earnings | Workforce |
|---|---|---|
| Performing Arts, Spectator Sports, and Related Industries | $63,600 | 10,300 |
| Motion Picture and Sound Recording Industries | $61,430 | 590 |

BEST-PAYING METROPOLITAN AREAS

| Metro Area | Median Earnings | Workforce |
|---|---|---|
| Los Angeles–Long Beach–Santa Ana, CA | $103,380 | 3,340 |
| New York–Northern New Jersey–Long Island, NY-NJ-PA | $75,400 | 2,480 |
| Chicago-Naperville-Joliet, IL-IN-WI | $64,930 | 450 |
| Nashville-Davidson–Murfreesboro, TN | $38,830 | 540 |
| Atlanta–Sandy Springs–Marietta, GA | $38,320 | 290 |
| Miami–Fort Lauderdale–Pompano Beach, FL | $36,080 | 390 |

**Considerations for Job Outlook:** Much-faster-than-average employment growth is projected.

**Major Work Tasks:** Collect fees, commissions, or other payments, according to contract terms. Confer with clients to develop strategies for their careers and to explain actions taken on their behalf. Develop contacts with individuals and organizations and apply effective strategies and techniques to ensure their clients' success. Schedule promotional or performance engagements for clients. Negotiate with managers, promoters, union officials, and other persons regarding clients' contractual rights and obligations. Keep informed of industry trends and deals. Manage business and financial affairs for clients, such as arranging travel and lodging, selling tickets, and directing marketing and advertising activities. Conduct auditions or interviews to evaluate potential clients. Arrange meetings concerning issues involving their clients. Prepare periodic accounting statements for clients. Advise clients on financial and legal matters such as investments and taxes. Obtain information about or inspect performance facilities, equipment, and accommodations to ensure that they meet specifications. Hire trainers or coaches to advise clients on performance matters such as training techniques or performance presentations.

**Usual Educational Requirement:** Bachelor's degree. **Relevant Educational Programs**: Arts, Entertainment, and Media Management, Other; Arts, Entertainment, and Media Management, General; Fine and Studio Arts Management; Purchasing, Procurement/Acquisitions and Contracts Management; Sports Communication. **Related Knowledge/Courses:** Fine Arts; Sales and Marketing; Communications and Media; Clerical Practices; Customer and Personal Service; Economics and Accounting. **Work Experience Needed:** 1 to 5 years. **On-the-Job Training Needed:** None. **Certification/ Licensure:** None.

**Personality Types:** Enterprising–Social. **Key Career Cluster:** 04 Business, Management, and Administration. **Key Career Pathway:** 4.1 Management.

**Skills:** Negotiation; persuasion; management of financial resources; service orientation; judgment and decision making; speaking; management of personnel resources; time management.

**Physical Environment:** Indoors; sitting. **Structural Environment:** Impact of decisions on coworkers or company results; freedom to make decisions; structured versus unstructured work; frequency of decision making; level of competition; importance of being exact or accurate.

**147**

## Airline Pilots, Copilots, and Flight Engineers

**Pilot and navigate the flight of fixed-wing, multi-engine aircraft, usually on scheduled air carrier routes, for the transport of passengers and cargo.**

- Average annual earnings: $114,200
- Middle 50% of earners: $87,240–$154,100
- Earnings growth potential: Medium (41.4%)
- Growth: 6.4%
- Annual job openings: 3,130
- Self-employed: 0.0%

### BEST-PAYING INDUSTRIES

| Industry | Median Earnings | Workforce |
|---|---|---|
| Air Transportation | $117,180 | 57,930 |
| Federal, State, and Local Government | $96,280 | 3,440 |

### BEST-PAYING METROPOLITAN AREAS

| Metro Area | Median Earnings | Workforce |
|---|---|---|
| New York–Northern New Jersey–Long Island, NY-NJ-PA | $148,290 | 4,750 |
| Dallas–Fort Worth–Arlington, TX | $143,400 | 1,580 |
| Miami–Fort Lauderdale–Pompano Beach, FL | $118,690 | 2,590 |
| Los Angeles–Long Beach–Santa Ana, CA | $117,710 | 2,460 |
| Chicago-Naperville-Joliet, IL-IN-WI | $117,380 | 5,540 |
| Washington-Arlington-Alexandria, DC-VA-MD-WV | $102,170 | 2,370 |
| Denver-Aurora, CO | $95,780 | 2,340 |

**Considerations for Job Outlook:** As older pilots retire and younger pilots advance, entry-level positions may open up. And the demand for flight instructors may increase as they are needed to train a greater number of student pilots. Job prospects should be best with regional airlines, on low-cost carriers, or in general aviation, because these segments are anticipated to grow faster than the major airlines. In addition, entry-level requirements are lower for regional and commercial jobs. However, pilots with less than 500 flight hours will probably need to accumulate hours as flight instructors or commercial pilots before qualifying for regional airline jobs. Pilots seeking jobs at the major airlines will face strong competition because those firms tend to attract many more applicants than the number of job openings.

**Major Work Tasks:** Use instrumentation to guide flights when visibility is poor. Respond to and report in-flight emergencies and malfunctions. Work as part of a flight team with other crew members, especially during take-offs and landings. Contact control towers for takeoff clearances, arrival instructions, and other information, using radio equipment. Steer aircraft along planned routes, using autopilot and flight management computers. Monitor gauges, warning devices, and control panels to verify aircraft performance and to regulate engine speed. Start engines, operate controls, and pilot airplanes to transport passengers, mail, or freight, adhering to flight plans, regulations, and procedures. Inspect aircraft for defects and malfunctions, according to pre-flight checklists. Check passenger and cargo distributions and fuel amounts to ensure that weight and balance specifications are met. Monitor engine operation, fuel consumption, and functioning of aircraft systems during flights. Confer with flight dispatchers and weather forecasters to keep abreast of flight conditions. Order changes in fuel supplies, loads, routes, or schedules to ensure safety of

**148**

flights. Choose routes, altitudes, and speeds that will provide the fastest, safest, and smoothest flights. Direct activities of aircraft crews during flights. Brief crews about flight details, such as destinations, duties, and responsibilities. Record in log books information such as flight times, distances flown, and fuel consumption. Make announcements regarding flights, using public address systems. Coordinate flight activities with ground crews and air traffic control and inform crew members of flight and test procedures. File instrument flight plans with air traffic control to ensure that flights are coordinated with other air traffic. Perform minor maintenance work, or arrange for major maintenance. Instruct other pilots and student pilots in aircraft operations and the principles of flight. Conduct in-flight tests and evaluations at specified altitudes and in all types of weather to determine the receptivity and other characteristics of equipment and systems. Evaluate other pilots or pilot-license applicants for proficiency.

**Usual Educational Requirement:** Bachelor's degree. **Relevant Educational Programs**: Airline/Commercial/Professional Pilot and Flight Crew Training; Flight Instructor Training. **Related Knowledge/Courses:** Transportation; Geography; Physics; Psychology; Telecommunications; Public Safety and Security. **Work Experience Needed:** 1 to 5 years. **On-the-Job Training Needed:** Moderate-term on-the-job training. **Certification/Licensure:** Federal licensure.

**Personality Types:** Realistic–Conventional–Investigative. **Key Career Cluster:** 16 Transportation, Distribution, and Logistics. **Key Career Pathway:** 16.1 Transportation Operations.

**Skills:** Operation and control; operation monitoring; troubleshooting; science; mathematics; instructing; judgment and decision making; time management.

**Physical Environment:** Outdoors; indoors; sitting; using hands; repetitive motions; noise. **Structural Environment:** Importance of being exact or accurate; frequency of decision making; impact of decisions on co-workers or company results; importance of repeating same tasks; freedom to make decisions; time pressure.

## Anthropology and Archeology Teachers, Postsecondary

*See Teachers, Postsecondary.*

## Architects, Except Landscape and Naval

**Plan and design structures, such as private residences, office buildings, theaters, factories, and other structural property.**

- Average annual earnings: $73,090
- Middle 50% of earners: $56,090–$93,010
- Earnings growth potential: Medium (39.0%)
- Growth: 24.5%
- Annual job openings: 5,090
- Self-employed: 23.9%

**Considerations for Job Outlook:** With a growing number of students graduating with architectural degrees, applicants will experience competition for jobs. Competition for jobs will be especially strong at the most prestigious architectural firms. Although those who have completed internships will have an advantage, the best job opportunities will be for candidates

### BEST-PAYING INDUSTRIES

| Industry | Median Earnings | Workforce |
| --- | --- | --- |
| Professional, Scientific, and Technical Services | $72,220 | 72,730 |

**149**

**BEST-PAYING METROPOLITAN AREAS**

| Metro Area | Median Earnings | Workforce |
|---|---|---|
| San Francisco–Oakland–Fremont, CA | $88,670 | 2,710 |
| Washington-Arlington-Alexandria, DC-VA-MD-WV | $85,400 | 3,610 |
| Los Angeles–Long Beach–Santa Ana, CA | $81,490 | 4,360 |
| New York–Northern New Jersey–Long Island, NY-NJ-PA | $78,260 | 8,780 |
| Boston-Cambridge-Quincy, MA-NH | $76,550 | 3,070 |
| Atlanta–Sandy Springs–Marietta, GA | $76,450 | 1,680 |
| Philadelphia-Camden-Wilmington, PA-NJ-DE-MD | $76,030 | 1,700 |
| Houston–Sugar Land–Baytown, TX | $74,880 | 2,250 |
| Chicago-Naperville-Joliet, IL-IN-WI | $69,740 | 3,050 |
| Dallas–Fort Worth–Arlington, TX | $68,730 | 2,420 |
| Seattle-Tacoma-Bellevue, WA | $64,100 | 2,700 |

who can distinguish themselves with their creativity. Employment of architects is strongly tied to the activity of the construction industry. Therefore, these workers, especially the self-employed, may experience periods of unemployment when the overall level of construction falls.

**Major Work Tasks:** Prepare information regarding design, structure specifications, materials, color, equipment, estimated costs, or construction time. Consult with clients to determine functional or spatial requirements of structures. Direct activities of workers engaged in preparing drawings and specification documents. Plan layout of project. Prepare contract documents for building contractors. Prepare scale drawings. Integrate engineering elements into unified architectural designs. Conduct periodic on-site observation of work during construction to monitor compliance with plans. Administer construction contracts. Represent clients in obtaining bids or awarding construction contracts. Seek new work opportunities through marketing, writing proposals, or giving presentations. Prepare operating and maintenance manuals, studies, or reports. Calculate potential energy savings by comparing estimated energy consumption of proposed design to baseline standards. Design environmentally sound structural upgrades to existing buildings, such as natural lighting systems, green roofs, or rainwater collection systems. Design or plan construction of green building projects to minimize adverse environmental impact or conserve energy. Design structures that incorporate environmentally friendly building practices or concepts, such as Leadership in Energy and Environmental Design (LEED) standards. Gather information related to projects' environmental sustainability. Perform predesign services, such as feasibility or environmental impact studies. Plan or design structures such as residences, office buildings, theatres, factories, or other structural properties in accordance with environmental, safety, or other regulations.

**Usual Educational Requirement:** Bachelor's degree. **Relevant Educational Programs**: Architectural History and Criticism, General; Architecture (BArch, BA/BS, MArch, MA/MS, PhD); Environmental Design/Architecture. **Related Knowledge/Courses:** Design; Building and Construction; Engineering and Technology; Fine Arts; Sales and Marketing; Law and Government. **Work Experience Needed:** None. **On-the-Job Training Needed:** Internship/residency. **Certification/Licensure:** Licensure.

150

**Personality Types:** Artistic–Investigative. **Key Career Cluster:** 02 Architecture and Construction. **Key Career Pathway:** 2.1 Design/Pre-construction.

**Skills:** Operations analysis; management of financial resources; management of material resources; mathematics; science; judgment and decision making; negotiation; quality control analysis.

**Physical Environment:** Indoors; sitting; using hands; repetitive motions. **Structural Environment:** Freedom to make decisions; importance of being exact or accurate; structured versus unstructured work; frequency of decision making; time pressure; impact of decisions on co-workers or company results.

## Architectural and Engineering Managers

**Plan, direct, or coordinate activities in such fields as architecture and engineering or research and development in these fields.**

- Average annual earnings: $124,870
- Middle 50% of earners: $100,040–$154,990
- Earnings growth potential: Medium (35.7%)
- Growth: 8.6%
- Annual job openings: 4,970
- Self-employed: 0.0%

**Considerations for Job Outlook:** Job opportunities should be better in rapidly growing disciplines, such as environmental and biomedical engineering, than in more slowly growing areas, such as electrical and mechanical engineering. Those with advanced technical knowledge and strong communication skills will likely be in the best position to become managers. Because architectural and engineering managers are involved in the financial, production, and marketing activities of their firm, business management skills are a plus for those seeking management positions.

### BEST-PAYING INDUSTRIES

| Industry | Median Earnings | Workforce |
|---|---|---|
| Computer and Electronic Product Manufacturing | $138,150 | 26,810 |
| Professional, Scientific, and Technical Services | $128,180 | 61,630 |
| Transportation Equipment Manufacturing | $125,150 | 13,130 |
| Federal, State, and Local Government | $119,240 | 16,970 |

### BEST-PAYING METROPOLITAN AREAS

| Metro Area | Median Earnings | Workforce |
|---|---|---|
| San Jose–Sunnyvale–Santa Clara, CA | $168,350 | 6,790 |
| Houston–Sugar Land–Baytown, TX | $167,240 | 8,210 |
| San Francisco–Oakland–Fremont, CA | $153,610 | 5,090 |
| Los Angeles–Long Beach–Santa Ana, CA | $144,370 | 10,320 |
| Boston-Cambridge-Quincy, MA-NH | $139,550 | 6,030 |
| Washington-Arlington-Alexandria, DC-VA-MD-WV | $136,770 | 7,020 |
| New York–Northern New Jersey–Long Island, NY-NJ-PA | $136,320 | 7,060 |
| Dallas–Fort Worth–Arlington, TX | $133,860 | 5,130 |
| Seattle-Tacoma-Bellevue, WA | $133,790 | 4,020 |
| Minneapolis–St. Paul–Bloomington, MN-WI | $125,350 | 3,960 |
| Detroit-Warren-Livonia, MI | $114,960 | 5,360 |
| Chicago-Naperville-Joliet, IL-IN-WI | $110,870 | 5,050 |

In addition to the openings resulting from employment growth, job openings will result from the need to replace managers who retire or move into other occupations.

**Major Work Tasks:** Confer with management, production, or marketing staff to discuss project specifications or procedures. Plan or direct the installation, testing, operation, maintenance, or repair of facilities or equipment. Present and explain proposals, reports, or findings to clients. Consult or negotiate with clients to prepare project specifications. Manage the coordination and overall integration of technical activities in architecture or engineering projects. Direct, review, or approve project design changes. Prepare budgets, bids, or contracts. Assess project feasibility by analyzing technology, resource needs, and market demand. Direct recruitment, placement, and evaluation of architecture or engineering project staff. Review, recommend, or approve contracts or cost estimates. Develop or implement policies, standards, or procedures for engineering and technical work. Perform administrative functions, such as reviewing or writing reports, approving expenditures, enforcing rules, or purchasing of materials or services. Administer highway planning, construction, or maintenance. Direct the engineering of water control, treatment, or distribution projects. Develop or implement programs to improve sustainability or reduce the environmental impacts of engineering or architecture activities or operations. Evaluate environmental regulations or social pressures related to environmental issues to inform strategic or operational decision-making. Evaluate the environmental impacts of engineering, architecture, or research and development activities. Identify environmental threats or opportunities associated with the development and launch of new technologies. Establish scientific or technical goals within broad outlines provided by top management. Solicit project support by conferring with officials or providing information to the public. Plan, direct, or coordinate survey work with other project activities.

**Usual Educational Requirement:** Bachelor's degree. **Relevant Educational Programs**: Aerospace, Aeronautical and Astronautical/Space Engineering; Agricultural Engineering; Architectural and Building Sciences/Technology; Architectural Engineering; Architecture (BArch, BA/BS, MArch, MA/MS, PhD); Biochemical Engineering; Bioengineering and Biomedical Engineering; Biological/Biosystems Engineering; Ceramic Sciences and Engineering; Chemical and Biomolecular Engineering; Chemical Engineering; Chemical Engineering, Other; City/Urban, Community and Regional Planning; Civil Engineering, General; Civil Engineering, Other; Computer Engineering, General; Computer Engineering, Other; Computer Hardware Engineering; Computer Software Engineering; Construction Engineering; Electrical and Electronics Engineering; Electrical, Electronics and Communications Engineering, Other; Electromechanical Engineering; Engineering Chemistry; Engineering Design; Engineering Mechanics; Engineering Physics/Applied Physics; Engineering Science; Engineering, General; Engineering, Other; others. **Related Knowledge/Courses:** Engineering and Technology; Design; Physics; Building and Construction; Geography; Mechanical. **Work Experience Needed:** More than 5 years. **On-the-Job Training Needed:** None. **Certification/Licensure:** Voluntary certification by association.

**Personality Types:** Enterprising–Realistic–Investigative. **Key Career Cluster:** 15 Science, Technology, Engineering, and Mathematics. **Key Career Pathway:** 15.1 Engineering and Technology.

**Skills:** Management of financial resources; management of material resources; negotiation; management of personnel resources; mathematics; active learning; persuasion; judgment and decision making.

**Physical Environment:** Indoors; sitting. **Structural Environment:** Structured versus unstructured work; freedom to make decisions; time pressure; importance of being exact or accurate; frequency of decision making; impact of decisions on co-workers or company results.

## JOB SPECIALIZATION: BIOFUELS/ BIODIESEL TECHNOLOGY AND PRODUCT DEVELOPMENT MANAGERS

**Define, plan, or execute biofuel/biodiesel research programs that evaluate alternative feedstock and process technologies with near-term commercial potential.**

**Major Work Tasks:** Develop lab scale models of industrial scale processes, such as fermentation. Develop computational tools or approaches to improve biofuels research and development activities. Develop carbohydrates arrays and associated methods for screening enzymes involved in biomass conversion. Provide technical or scientific guidance to technical staff in the conduct of biofuels research or development. Prepare, or oversee the preparation of, experimental plans for biofuels research or development. Prepare biofuels research and development reports for senior management or technical professionals. Perform protein functional analysis and engineering for processing of feedstock and creation of biofuels. Develop separation processes to recover biofuels. Develop methods to recover ethanol or other fuels from complex bioreactor liquid and gas streams. Develop methods to estimate the efficiency of biomass pretreatments. Design or execute solvent or product recovery experiments in laboratory or field settings. Design or conduct applied biodiesel or biofuels research projects on topics such as transport, thermodynamics, mixing, filtration, distillation, fermentation, extraction, and separation. Design chemical conversion processes, such as etherification, esterification, interesterification, transesterification, distillation, hydrogenation, oxidation or reduction of fats and oils, and vegetable oil refining. Conduct experiments on biomass or pretreatment technologies. Conduct experiments to test new or alternate feedstock fermentation processes. Analyze data from biofuels studies, such as fluid dynamics, water treatments, or solvent extraction and recovery processes. Oversee biodiesel/biofuels prototyping or development projects. Propose new biofuels products, processes, technologies, or applications based on findings from applied biofuels or biomass research projects. Conduct research to breed or develop energy crops with improved biomass yield, environmental adaptability, pest resistance, production efficiency, bioprocessing characteristics, or reduced environmental impacts.

**Related Knowledge/Courses:** No data available.

**Personality Types:** Enterprising–Investigative.

**Skills:** No data available.

**Physical Environment:** No data available. **Structural Environment:** No data available.

## Architecture Teachers, Postsecondary

*See Teachers, Postsecondary.*

## Area, Ethnic, and Cultural Studies Teachers, Postsecondary

*See Teachers, Postsecondary.*

## Art Directors

**Formulate design concepts and presentation approaches for visual communications media, such as print, broadcasting, and advertising.**

- Average annual earnings: $80,880
- Middle 50% of earners: $57,830–$117,090
- Earnings growth potential: High (45.8%)
- Growth: 9.0%
- Annual job openings: 2,430
- Self-employed: 59.1%

153

## Your Guide to High-Paying Careers

### BEST-PAYING INDUSTRIES

| Industry | Median Earnings | Workforce |
|---|---|---|
| Motion Picture and Sound Recording Industries | $104,310 | 2,440 |
| Professional, Scientific, and Technical Services | $86,220 | 16,390 |
| Publishing Industries (except Internet) | $70,400 | 4,560 |

### BEST-PAYING METROPOLITAN AREAS

| Metro Area | Median Earnings | Workforce |
|---|---|---|
| New York–Northern New Jersey–Long Island, NY-NJ-PA | $117,220 | 6,730 |
| San Francisco–Oakland–Fremont, CA | $110,140 | 1,210 |
| Los Angeles–Long Beach–Santa Ana, CA | $99,940 | 3,360 |
| Seattle-Tacoma-Bellevue, WA | $92,770 | 660 |
| Boston-Cambridge-Quincy, MA-NH | $86,680 | 1,110 |
| Washington-Arlington-Alexandria, DC-VA-MD-WV | $81,210 | 720 |
| Hartford–West Hartford–East Hartford, CT | $90,620 | 2,130 |
| Minneapolis–St. Paul–Bloomington, MN-WI | $71,600 | 730 |
| Dallas–Fort Worth–Arlington, TX | $68,470 | 710 |
| Chicago-Naperville-Joliet, IL-IN-WI | $61,280 | 1,720 |

**Considerations for Job Outlook:** Strong competition for jobs is expected as many talented designers and artists seek to move into these positions.

**Major Work Tasks:** Formulate basic layout design or presentation approach and specify material details, such as style and size of type, photographs, graphics, animation, video, and sound. Review and approve art materials, copy materials, and proofs of printed copy developed by staff members. Manage own accounts and projects, working within budget and scheduling requirements. Confer with creative, art, copywriting, or production department heads to discuss client requirements and presentation concepts and to coordinate creative activities. Present final layouts to clients for approval. Confer with clients to determine objectives, budget, background information, and presentation approaches, styles, and techniques. Hire, train, and direct staff members who develop design concepts into art layouts or who prepare layouts for printing. Work with creative directors to develop design solutions. Review illustrative material to determine if it conforms to standards and specifications. Attend photo shoots and printing sessions to ensure that the products needed are obtained. Create custom illustrations or other graphic elements. Negotiate with printers and estimators to determine what services will be performed. Research current trends and new technology, such as printing production techniques, computer software, and design trends. Mark up, paste, and complete layouts and write typography instructions to prepare materials for typesetting or printing. Conceptualize and help design interfaces for multimedia games, products, and devices. Prepare detailed storyboards showing sequence and timing of story development for television production.

**Usual Educational Requirement:** Bachelor's degree. **Relevant Educational Programs**: Digital Arts; Graphic Design; Intermedia/Multimedia. **Related Knowledge/Courses:** Fine Arts;

Communications and Media; Sales and Marketing; Sociology and Anthropology; Design; Computers and Electronics. **Work Experience Needed:** 1 to 5 years. **On-the-Job Training Needed:** None. **Certification/Licensure:** None.

**Personality Types:** Artistic–Enterprising. **Key Career Cluster:** 04 Business, Management, and Administration. **Key Career Pathway:** 4.5 Marketing.

**Skills:** Management of financial resources; operations analysis; management of material resources; coordination; systems evaluation; negotiation; management of personnel resources; time management.

**Physical Environment:** Indoors; sitting; using hands; repetitive motions. **Structural Environment:** Time pressure; importance of being exact or accurate; structured versus unstructured work; freedom to make decisions; impact of decisions on co-workers or company results; frequency of decision making.

## Art, Drama, and Music Teachers, Postsecondary

*See Teachers, Postsecondary.*

## Atmospheric, Earth, Marine, and Space Sciences Teachers, Postsecondary

*See Teachers, Postsecondary.*

## Audiologists

**Assess and treat people with hearing and related disorders.**

- Average annual earnings: $69,720
- Middle 50% of earners: $56,330–$85,040
- Earnings growth potential: Medium (37.1%)
- Growth: 36.8%
- Annual job openings: 560
- Self-employed: 0.0%

### BEST-PAYING INDUSTRIES

| Industry | Median Earnings | Workforce |
|---|---|---|
| Hospitals | $74,930 | 1,510 |
| Ambulatory Health-Care Services | $70,270 | 6,250 |
| Educational Services | $66,550 | 1,590 |
| Health and Personal Care Stores | $64,160 | 2,230 |

### BEST-PAYING METROPOLITAN AREAS

| Metro Area | Median Earnings | Workforce |
|---|---|---|
| New York–Northern New Jersey–Long Island, NY–NJ–PA | $85,940 | 590 |
| Denver-Aurora, CO | $84,670 | 290 |
| Chicago-Naperville-Joliet, IL–IN–WI | $81,440 | 470 |
| Dallas–Fort Worth–Arlington, TX | $76,780 | 280 |
| Los Angeles–Long Beach–Santa Ana, CA | $72,710 | 900 |

**Considerations for Job Outlook:** Job prospects are expected to be favorable for audiologists with a doctoral degree. Demand may be greater in areas with large numbers of retirees, so audiologists who are willing to relocate may have the best job prospects.

**Major Work Tasks:** Examine and clean patients' ear canals. Educate and supervise audiology students and health-care personnel. Develop and supervise hearing screening programs. Counsel and instruct patients and their families in techniques to improve hearing and communication related to hearing loss. Evaluate hearing and balance disorders to determine diagnoses and courses of treatment. Program and monitor cochlear implants to fit the needs of patients. Participate in conferences or training to update or share knowledge of new hear-

155

ing or balance disorder treatment methods or technologies. Conduct or direct research on hearing or balance topics and report findings to help in the development of procedures, technology, or treatments. Plan and conduct treatment programs for patients' hearing or balance problems, consulting with educators, physicians, nurses, psychologists, speech-language pathologists, and other health-care personnel as necessary. Administer hearing tests and examine patients to collect information on type and degree of impairment, using specialized instruments and electronic equipment. Engage in marketing activities, such as developing marketing plans, to promote business for private practices. Recommend assistive devices according to patients' needs or nature of impairments. Fit, dispense, and repair assistive devices, such as hearing aids. Advise educators or other medical staff on hearing or balance topics. Provide information to the public on hearing or balance topics. Instruct patients, parents, teachers, or employers in communication strategies to maximize effective receptive communication. Work with multidisciplinary teams to assess and rehabilitate recipients of implanted hearing devices through auditory training and counseling. Monitor patients' progress and provide ongoing observation of hearing or balance status. Measure noise levels in workplaces and conduct hearing conservation programs in industry, military, schools, and communities. Refer patients to additional medical or educational services if needed. Perform administrative tasks, such as managing office functions and finances.

**Usual Educational Requirement:** Doctoral or professional degree. **Relevant Educational Programs**: Audiology/Audiologist; Audiology/Audiologist and Speech-Language Pathology/Pathologist; Communication Disorders Sciences and Services, Other; Communication Disorders, General; Communication Sciences and Disorders, General. **Related Knowledge/**

**Courses:** Therapy and Counseling; Medicine and Dentistry; Sales and Marketing; Psychology; Sociology and Anthropology; Biology. **Work Experience Needed:** None. **On-the-Job Training Needed:** None. **Certification/Licensure:** Licensure; also voluntary certification by association.

**Personality Types:** Investigative–Social. **Key Career Cluster:** 08 Health Science. **Key Career Pathway:** 8.1 Therapeutic Services.

**Skills:** Science; repairing; equipment selection; reading comprehension; troubleshooting; technology design; active learning; learning strategies.

**Physical Environment:** Indoors; sitting; using hands; exposed to disease or infections. **Structural Environment:** Freedom to make decisions; importance of being exact or accurate; frequency of decision making; structured versus unstructured work; impact of decisions on coworkers or company results; time pressure.

## Biochemists and Biophysicists

**Study the chemical composition or physical principles of living cells and organisms, their electrical and mechanical energy, and related phenomena.**

- Average annual earnings: $81,480
- Middle 50% of earners: $55,360–$112,200
- Earnings growth potential: High (49.2%)
- Growth: 30.8%
- Annual job openings: 1,340

**Considerations for Job Outlook:** Biochemists and biophysicists involved in basic research should expect strong competition for permanent research and faculty positions at colleges and universities. Biochemists and biophysicists with postdoctoral experience who have had research articles published in scientific journals should have the best prospects for these positions. Many biochemists and biophysicists work through multiple postdoctoral appointments before getting a permanent po-

## BEST-PAYING INDUSTRIES

| Industry | Median Earnings | Workforce |
|---|---|---|
| Professional, Scientific, and Technical Services | $85,820 | 14,770 |
| Chemical Manufacturing | $81,220 | 4,290 |
| Educational Services | $53,010 | 3,940 |

## BEST-PAYING METROPOLITAN AREAS

| Metro Area | Median Earnings | Workforce |
|---|---|---|
| Boston-Cambridge-Quincy, MA-NH | $98,650 | 2,860 |
| San Jose–Sunnyvale–Santa Clara, CA | $96,040 | 850 |
| San Diego–Carlsbad–San Marcos, CA | $91,940 | 1,560 |
| San Francisco–Oakland–Fremont, CA | $84,570 | 1,290 |
| Los Angeles–Long Beach–Santa Ana, CA | $81,060 | 1,220 |
| Washington-Arlington-Alexandria, DC-VA-MD-WV | $66,060 | 1,070 |
| Minneapolis–St. Paul–Bloomington, MN-WI | $64,410 | 560 |

sition in academia. A large portion of basic research in biochemistry and biophysics is dependent on funding from the federal government through the National Institutes of Health and the National Science Foundation. Therefore, federal budgetary decisions will have a large impact on job prospects in basic research from year to year. Biochemists and biophysicists who have a broad understanding of biochemistry and its relationship to other disciplines should have the best opportunities. For entry-level biochemist positions, strong competition is expected because of the grow-

ing interest in biochemistry and other biological sciences at the undergraduate level. Applicants who have previous laboratory experience, either through coursework or prior work experience, should have the best opportunities.

**Major Work Tasks:** Prepare reports or recommendations, based upon research outcomes. Develop new methods to study the mechanisms of biological processes. Manage laboratory teams or monitor the quality of a team's work. Share research findings by writing scientific articles or by making presentations at scientific conferences. Develop or execute tests to detect diseases, genetic disorders, or other abnormalities. Study the mutations in organisms that lead to cancer or other diseases. Study spatial configurations of submicroscopic molecules, such as proteins, using X-rays or electron microscopes. Study the chemistry of living processes, such as cell development, breathing and digestion, or living energy changes, such as growth, aging, or death. Determine the three-dimensional structure of biological macromolecules. Investigate the nature, composition, or expression of genes or research how genetic engineering can impact these processes. Study physical principles of living cells or organisms and their electrical or mechanical energy, applying methods and knowledge of mathematics, physics, chemistry, or biology. Isolate, analyze, or synthesize vitamins, hormones, allergens, minerals, or enzymes and determine their effects on body functions. Design or perform experiments with equipment such as lasers, accelerators, or mass spectrometers. Teach or advise undergraduate or graduate students or supervise their research. Develop or test new drugs or medications intended for commercial distribution. Prepare pharmaceutical compounds for commercial distribution. Research the chemical effects of substances, such as drugs, serums, hormones, or food, on tissues or vital processes. Research how characteristics of plants or animals are

**157**

carried through successive generations. Develop methods to process, store, or use foods, drugs, or chemical compounds. Produce pharmaceutically or industrially useful proteins, using recombinant DNA technology. Research transformations of substances in cells, using atomic isotopes. Examine the molecular or chemical aspects of immune system functioning. Design or build laboratory equipment needed for special research projects.

**Usual Educational Requirement:** Doctoral or professional degree. **Relevant Educational Programs**: Biochemistry; Biochemistry and Molecular Biology; Biophysics; Cell/Cellular Biology and Anatomical Sciences, Other; Molecular Biochemistry; Molecular Biophysics. **Related Knowledge/Courses:** Biology; Chemistry; Physics; Mathematics; Engineering and Technology; Medicine and Dentistry. **Work Experience Needed:** None. **On-the-Job Training Needed:** None. **Certification/Licensure:** None.

**Personality Types:** Investigative–Artistic–Realistic. **Key Career Cluster:** 15 Science, Technology, Engineering, and Mathematics. **Key Career Pathway:** 15.2 Science and Mathematics.

**Skills:** Science; mathematics; programming; active learning; technology design; writing; operations analysis; reading comprehension.

**Physical Environment:** Indoors; sitting; using hands; hazardous conditions. **Structural Environment:** Structured versus unstructured work; freedom to make decisions; importance of being exact or accurate; level of competition; consequence of error; impact of decisions on co-workers or company results.

## Biological Science Teachers, Postsecondary

*See Teachers, Postsecondary.*

## Biological Scientists, All Other

**All biological scientists not listed separately.**

- Average annual earnings: $72,700
- Middle 50% of earners: $57,310–$87,350
- Earnings growth potential: Medium (42.4%)
- Growth: 6.3%
- Annual job openings: 1,030
- Self-employed: 4.4%

### BEST-PAYING INDUSTRIES

| Industry | Median Earnings | Workforce |
|---|---|---|
| Professional, Scientific, and Technical Services | $75,510 | 5,540 |
| Federal, State, and Local Government | $73,390 | 17,740 |
| Educational Services | $61,410 | 4,830 |

### BEST-PAYING METROPOLITAN AREAS

| Metro Area | Median Earnings | Workforce |
|---|---|---|
| Boston-Cambridge-Quincy, MA-NH | $97,800 | 990 |
| Washington-Arlington-Alexandria, DC-VA-MD-WV | $89,020 | 3,630 |
| San Francisco–Oakland–Fremont, CA | $81,540 | 840 |
| Los Angeles–Long Beach–Santa Ana, CA | $78,870 | 1,360 |
| Seattle-Tacoma-Bellevue, WA | $68,820 | 820 |
| San Diego–Carlsbad–San Marcos, CA | $67,930 | 1,390 |

**Considerations for Job Outlook:** In federal government, a small increase is expected as funding for scientific research programs is expected to fare better than other areas of government in future budgets.

**Major Work Tasks:** No task data available.

**Usual Educational Requirement:** Doctoral or professional degree. **Relevant Educational Programs**: Anatomy; Animal Genetics; Animal Physiology; Aquatic Biology/Limnology; Biochemistry and Molecular Biology; Biological and Biomedical Sciences, Other; Biology/Biological Sciences, General; Biomathematics, Bioinformatics, and Computational Biology, Other; Biometry/Biometrics; Biostatistics; Biotechnology; Botany/Plant Biology; Botany/Plant Biology, Other; Cell Biology and Anatomy; Cell/Cellular and Molecular Biology; Cell/Cellular Biology and Anatomical Sciences, Other; Cell/Cellular Biology and Histology; Computational Biology; Conservation Biology; Developmental Biology and Embryology; Ecology; Ecology and Evolutionary Biology; Ecology, Evolution, Systematics and Population Biology, Other; Entomology; Environmental Biology; Evolutionary Biology; Genetics, General; Genetics, Other; Genome Sciences/Genomics; Human Biology; Immunology; Marine Biology and Biological Oceanography; Marine Sciences; Mathematical Biology; Medical Microbiology and Bacteriology; others. **Work Experience Needed:** None. **On-the-Job Training Needed:** None. **Certification/Licensure:** None.

**Key Career Cluster:** 15 Science, Technology, Engineering, and Mathematics. **Key Career Pathway:** 15.2 Science and Mathematics.

### JOB SPECIALIZATION: BIOINFORMATICS SCIENTISTS

**Conduct research using bioinformatics theory and methods in areas such as pharmaceuticals, medical technology, biotechnology, computational biology, proteomics, computer information science, biology, and medical informatics. May design databases and develop algorithms for processing and analyzing genomic information or other biological information.**

**Major Work Tasks:** Keep abreast of new biochemistries, instrumentation, or software by reading scientific literature and attending professional conferences. Provide statistical and computational tools for biologically based activities, such as genetic analysis, measurement of gene expression, and gene function determination. Direct the work of technicians and information technology staff applying bioinformatics tools or applications in areas such as proteomics, transcriptomics, metabolomics, and clinical bioinformatics. Develop new software applications or customize existing applications to meet specific scientific project needs. Develop data models and databases. Create or modify web-based bioinformatics tools. Design and apply bioinformatics algorithms, including unsupervised and supervised machine learning, dynamic programming, or graphic algorithms. Create novel computational approaches and analytical tools as required by research goals. Compile data for use in activities, such as gene expression profiling, genome annotation, and structural bioinformatics. Communicate research results through conference presentations, scientific publications, or project reports. Manipulate publicly accessible, commercial, or proprietary genomic, proteomic, or post-genomic databases. Consult with researchers to analyze problems, recommend technology-based solutions, or determine computational strategies. Analyze large molecular datasets such as raw microarray data, genomic sequence data, and proteomics data for clinical or basic research purposes. Recommend new systems and processes to improve operations. Confer with departments such as marketing, business development, and operations to coordinate product development or improvement. Collaborate with software developers in the development and modification of commercial bioinformatics software. Test new and updated bioinformatics tools and software. Prepare summary statistics of information regarding human genomes. Instruct others in the selection and use of bioinformatics tools. Improve user interfaces to bioinformatics software and databases.

**Related Knowledge/Courses:** Biology; Chemistry; Computers and Electronics; Mathematics; Physics; Engineering and Technology.

**Personality Types:** Investigative–Conventional–Realistic.

**Skills:** Science; mathematics; writing; reading comprehension; systems evaluation; technology design; complex problem solving; active learning.

**Physical Environment:** Indoors; sitting. **Structural Environment:** Freedom to make decisions; structured versus unstructured work; importance of being exact or accurate; level of competition; time pressure; impact of decisions on co-workers or company results.

### JOB SPECIALIZATION: GENETICISTS

**Research and study the inheritance of traits at the molecular, organism, or population level. May evaluate or treat patients with genetic disorders.**

**Major Work Tasks:** Write grants and papers or attend fundraising events to seek research funds. Verify that cytogenetic, molecular genetic, and related equipment and instrumentation is maintained in working condition to ensure accuracy and quality of experimental results. Maintain laboratory safety programs and train personnel in laboratory safety techniques. Design and maintain genetics computer databases. Confer with information technology specialists to develop computer applications for genetic data analysis. Collaborate with biologists and other professionals to conduct appropriate genetic and biochemical analyses. Attend clinical and research conferences and read scientific literature to keep abreast of technological advances and current genetic research findings. Supervise or direct the work of other geneticists, biologists, technicians, or biometricians working on genetics research projects. Review, approve, or interpret genetic laboratory results. Search scientific literature to select and modify methods and procedures most appropriate for genetic research goals. Prepare results of experimental findings for presentation at professional conferences or in scientific journals. Maintain laboratory notebooks that record research methods, procedures, and results. Extract deoxyribonucleic acid (DNA) or perform diagnostic tests involving processes such as gel electrophoresis, Southern blot analysis, and polymerase chain reaction analysis. Evaluate genetic data by performing appropriate mathematical or statistical calculations and analyses. Develop protocols to improve existing genetic techniques or to incorporate new diagnostic procedures. Design sampling plans or coordinate the field collection of samples such as tissue specimens. Create or use statistical models for the analysis of genetic data. Plan or conduct basic genomic and biological research related to areas such as regulation of gene expression, protein interactions, metabolic networks, and nucleic acid or protein complexes. Analyze determinants responsible for specific inherited traits and devise methods for altering traits or producing new traits.

**Related Knowledge/Courses:** Biology; Chemistry; Medicine and Dentistry; Education and Training; English Language; Mathematics.

**Personality Types:** Investigative–Artistic–Realistic.

**Skills:** Science; mathematics; writing; reading comprehension; instructing; learning strategies; systems analysis; management of material resources.

**Physical Environment:** Indoors; sitting; using hands. **Structural Environment:** Importance of

**160**

being exact or accurate; freedom to make decisions; structured versus unstructured work; level of competition; impact of decisions on co-workers or company results; importance of repeating same tasks.

## JOB SPECIALIZATION: MOLECULAR AND CELLULAR BIOLOGISTS

**Research and study cellular molecules and organelles to understand cell function and organization.**

**Major Work Tasks:** Verify all financial, physical, and human resources assigned to research or development projects are used as planned. Develop guidelines for procedures such as the management of viruses. Coordinate molecular or cellular research activities with scientists specializing in other fields. Supervise technical personnel and postdoctoral research fellows. Prepare reports, manuscripts, and meeting presentations. Provide scientific direction for project teams regarding the evaluation or handling of devices, drugs, or cells for in vitro and in vivo disease models. Perform laboratory procedures following protocols including deoxyribonucleic acid (DNA) sequencing, cloning and extraction, ribonucleic acid (RNA) purification, or gel electrophoresis. Monitor or operate specialized equipment such as gas chromatographs and high pressure liquid chromatographs, electrophoresis units, thermocyclers, fluorescence activated cell sorters, and phosphoimagers. Maintain accurate laboratory records and data. Instruct undergraduate and graduate students within the areas of cellular or molecular biology. Evaluate new technologies to enhance or complement current research. Direct, coordinate, organize, or prioritize biological laboratory activities. Develop assays that monitor cell characteristics. Design molecular or cellular laboratory experiments, oversee their execution, and interpret results. Compile and analyze molecular or cellular experimental data and adjust experimental designs as necessary. Conduct

research on cell organization and function including mechanisms of gene expression, cellular bioinformatics, cell signaling, or cell differentiation. Conduct applied research aimed at improvements in areas such as disease testing, crop quality, pharmaceuticals, and the harnessing of microbes to recycle waste. Participate in all levels of bio-product development including proposing new products, performing market analyses, designing and performing experiments, and collaborating with operations and quality control teams during product launches. Evaluate new supplies and equipment to ensure operability in specific laboratory settings.

**Related Knowledge/Courses:** Biology; Chemistry; English Language; Medicine and Dentistry; Computers and Electronics; Mathematics.

**Personality Types:** Investigative–Realistic–Artistic.

**Skills:** Science; programming; reading comprehension; active learning; mathematics; management of financial resources; writing; operations analysis.

**Physical Environment:** Indoors; sitting; using hands; hazardous conditions. **Structural Environment:** Importance of being exact or accurate; freedom to make decisions; structured versus unstructured work; level of competition; impact of decisions on co-workers or company results; time pressure.

## Biomedical Engineers

**Apply knowledge of engineering, biology, and biomechanical principles to the design, development, and evaluation of biological and health systems and products.**

- Average annual earnings: $86,960
- Middle 50% of earners: $67,440–$111,610
- Earnings growth potential: Medium (39.5%)
- Growth: 61.7%

161

## Your Guide to High-Paying Careers

- Annual job openings: 1,310
- Self-employed: 0.0%

### BEST-PAYING INDUSTRIES

| Industry | Median Earnings | Workforce |
|---|---|---|
| Miscellaneous Manufacturing | $88,820 | 4,840 |
| Chemical Manufacturing | $87,310 | 2,940 |
| Hospitals | $70,190 | 1,300 |
| Educational Services | $63,440 | 1,360 |

### BEST-PAYING METROPOLITAN AREAS

| Metro Area | Median Earnings | Workforce |
|---|---|---|
| San Jose–Sunnyvale–Santa Clara, CA | $110,420 | 930 |
| Minneapolis–St. Paul–Bloomington, MN-WI | $105,170 | 920 |
| San Francisco–Oakland–Fremont, CA | $102,900 | 1,010 |
| Los Angeles–Long Beach–Santa Ana, CA | $92,650 | 1,640 |
| San Diego–Carlsbad–San Marcos, CA | $92,540 | 440 |
| Washington-Arlington-Alexandria, DC-VA-MD-WV | $92,010 | 660 |
| Boston-Cambridge-Quincy, MA-NH | $91,360 | 1,550 |
| New York–Northern New Jersey–Long Island, NY-NJ-PA | $84,730 | 510 |
| Philadelphia-Camden-Wilmington, PA-NJ-DE-MD | $83,350 | 870 |
| Houston–Sugar Land–Baytown, TX | $81,300 | 450 |

**Considerations for Job Outlook:** Rapid advances in technology will continue to change what biomedical engineers do and continue to create new areas for them to work in. Thus, the expanding range of activities in which biomedical engineers are engaged should translate into very favorable job prospects.

**Major Work Tasks:** Evaluate the safety, efficiency, and effectiveness of biomedical equipment. Advise and assist in the application of instrumentation in clinical environments. Research new materials to be used for products, such as implanted artificial organs. Develop models or computer simulations of human biobehavioral systems to obtain data for measuring or controlling life processes. Design and develop medical diagnostic and clinical instrumentation, equipment, and procedures, using the principles of engineering and biobehavioral sciences. Conduct research, along with life scientists, chemists, and medical scientists, on the engineering aspects of the biological systems of humans and animals. Teach biomedical engineering or disseminate knowledge about field through writing or consulting. Design and deliver technology to assist people with disabilities. Diagnose and interpret bioelectric data, using signal processing techniques. Adapt or design computer hardware or software for medical science uses. Write documents describing protocols, policies, standards for use, maintenance, and repair of medical equipment. Manage team of engineers by creating schedules, tracking inventory, creating and using budgets, and overseeing contract obligations and deadlines. Advise hospital administrators on the planning, acquisition, and use of medical equipment. Analyze new medical procedures to forecast likely outcomes. Develop new applications for energy sources, such as using nuclear power for biomedical implants. Install, adjust, maintain, repair, or provide technical support for biomedical equipment. Keep documentation of service histories on all biomedical equipment.

Conduct training or in-services to educate clinicians and other personnel on proper use of equipment. Conduct preventative maintenance on equipment.

**Usual Educational Requirement:** Bachelor's degree. **Relevant Educational Programs**: Bioengineering and Biomedical Engineering; Biological/Biosystems Engineering. **Related Knowledge/Courses:** Biology; Engineering and Technology; Physics; Design; Medicine and Dentistry; Chemistry. **Work Experience Needed:** None. **On-the-Job Training Needed:** None. **Certification/Licensure:** None.

**Personality Types:** Investigative–Realistic. **Key Career Cluster:** 08 Health Science. **Key Career Pathway:** 8.5 Biotechnology Research and Development.

**Skills:** Science; technology design; programming; operations analysis; installation; mathematics; troubleshooting; equipment selection.

**Physical Environment:** Indoors; sitting. **Structural Environment:** Freedom to make decisions; importance of being exact or accurate; structured versus unstructured work; level of competition; impact of decisions on co-workers or company results; frequency of decision making.

## Boilermakers

**Construct, assemble, maintain, and repair stationary steam boilers and boiler house auxiliaries.**

- Average annual earnings: $56,560
- Middle 50% of earners: $42,370–$69,610
- Earnings growth potential: Medium (42.7%)
- Growth: 21.3%
- Annual job openings: 1,180
- Self-employed: 4.0%

**Considerations for Job Outlook:** Overall job prospects should be favorable because the work of a boilermaker remains hazardous and

### BEST-PAYING INDUSTRIES

| Industry | Median Earnings | Workforce |
|---|---|---|
| Specialty Trade Contractors | $64,530 | 5,910 |
| Repair and Maintenance | $61,680 | 1,270 |
| Heavy and Civil Engineering Construction | $57,790 | 2,200 |
| Fabricated Metal Product Manufacturing | $42,290 | 3,080 |

### BEST-PAYING METROPOLITAN AREAS

| Metro Area | Median Earnings | Workforce |
|---|---|---|
| Indianapolis-Carmel, IN | $66,560 | 1,130 |
| Chicago-Naperville-Joliet, IL-IN-WI | $66,190 | 970 |
| Albany-Schenectady-Troy, NY | $65,860 | 360 |
| Beaumont–Port Arthur, TX | $65,330 | 470 |
| Houston–Sugar Land–Baytown, TX | $47,040 | 1,480 |
| Cincinnati-Middletown, OH-KY-IN | $46,460 | 440 |
| Detroit-Warren-Livonia, MI | $44,810 | 400 |
| Dallas–Fort Worth–Arlington, TX | $34,570 | 700 |

physically demanding, leading some qualified applicants to seek other types of work. Although employment growth will generate some job openings, the majority of positions will arise from the need to replace the large number of boilermakers expected to retire in the coming decade. People who have welding training or a welding certificate should have the best opportunities to be selected for boilermaker apprenticeship programs. As with many other construction workers, employment of boilermakers is sensitive to fluctuations of the economy. On the one hand, workers may experience periods of unemployment when the overall level of construction falls. On the other hand, shortages of workers may occur in some areas during peak periods of building activity. However, maintenance and repair of boilers must continue even during economic downturns, so boilermaker mechanics in manufacturing and other industries generally have more stable employment than those in construction.

**Major Work Tasks:** Examine boilers, pressure vessels, tanks, or vats to locate defects, such as leaks, weak spots, or defective sections, so that they can be repaired. Bolt or arc weld pressure vessel structures and parts together, using wrenches or welding equipment. Inspect assembled vessels or individual components, such as tubes, fittings, valves, controls, or auxiliary mechanisms, to locate any defects. Repair or replace defective pressure vessel parts, such as safety valves or regulators, using torches, jacks, caulking hammers, power saws, threading dies, welding equipment, or metalworking machinery. Attach rigging and signal crane or hoist operators to lift heavy frame and plate sections or other parts into place. Bell, bead with power hammers, or weld pressure vessel tube ends to ensure leakproof joints. Lay out plate, sheet steel, or other heavy metal and locate and mark bending and cutting lines, using protractors, compasses, and drawing instruments or templates. Install manholes, handholes, taps, tubes, valves, gauges, or feedwater connections in drums of water tube boilers, using hand tools. Study blueprints to determine locations, relationships, or dimensions of parts. Straighten or reshape bent pressure vessel plates or structure parts, using hammers, jacks, or torches. Shape seams, joints, or irregular edges of pressure vessel sections or structural parts to attain specified fit of parts, using cutting torches, hammers, files, or metalworking machines. Position, align, and secure structural parts or related assemblies to boiler frames, tanks, or vats of pressure vessels, following blueprints. Locate and mark reference points for columns or plates on boiler foundations, following blueprints and using straightedges, squares, transits, or measuring instruments. Shape or fabricate parts, such as stacks, uptakes, or chutes, to adapt pressure vessels, heat exchangers, or piping to premises, using heavy-metalworking machines such as brakes, rolls, or drill presses. Clean pressure vessel equipment, using scrapers, wire brushes, and cleaning solvents. Install refractory bricks or other heat-resistant materials in fireboxes of pressure vessels.

**Usual Educational Requirement:** High school diploma or equivalent. **Relevant Educational Program**: Boilermaking/Boilermaker. **Related Knowledge/Courses:** Building and Construction; Mechanical Devices; Engineering and Technology; Design; Physics; Transportation. **Work Experience Needed:** None. **On-the-Job Training Needed:** Apprenticeship. **Certification/Licensure:** Licensure in some states.

**Personality Types:** Realistic–Conventional. **Key Career Cluster:** 13 Manufacturing. **Key Career Pathway:** 13.1 Production.

**Skills:** Repairing; equipment maintenance; operation and control; troubleshooting; equipment selection; quality control analysis; operation monitoring; installation.

**Physical Environment:** Outdoors; standing; using hands; noise; very hot or cold; bright or inadequate lighting. **Structural Environment:** Freedom to make decisions; structured versus unstructured work; frequency of decision making; impact of decisions on co-workers or company results; time pressure; importance of being exact or accurate.

## Budget Analysts

**Examine budget estimates for completeness, accuracy, and conformance with procedures and regulations.**

- Average annual earnings: $69,280
- Middle 50% of earners: $55,800–$87,160
- Earnings growth potential: Medium (34.0%)
- Growth: 10.4%
- Annual job openings: 1,960
- Self-employed: 0.0%

**Considerations for Job Outlook:** The greater complexity of the job and its expanding job duties are expected to create a need for more budget analysts. Efficient use of public funds is increasingly expected.

**Major Work Tasks:** Analyze monthly department budgeting and accounting reports to maintain expenditure controls. Direct the preparation of regular and special budget reports. Consult with managers to ensure that budget adjustments are made in accordance with program changes. Provide advice and technical assistance with cost analysis, fiscal allocation, and budget preparation. Summarize budgets and submit recommendations for the approval or disapproval of funds requests. Seek new ways to improve efficiency and increase profits. Review operating budgets to analyze trends affecting budget needs. Examine budget estimates for completeness, accuracy, and conformance with procedures and regulations. Perform cost-benefit analyses to compare operating programs, review financial requests, or explore alternative financing methods. Interpret budget directives and establish policies for carrying out directives. Compile and analyze accounting records and other data to determine the financial resources required to implement a program. Match appropriations for specific programs with appropriations for broader programs, including items for emergency funds. Testify before examining and

### BEST-PAYING INDUSTRIES

| Industry | Median Earnings | Workforce |
|---|---|---|
| Professional, Scientific, and Technical Services | $78,550 | 6,120 |
| Transportation Equipment Manufacturing | $75,520 | 4,290 |
| Management of Companies and Enterprises | $72,640 | 4,470 |
| Federal, State, and Local Government | $67,070 | 24,020 |
| Educational Services | $60,940 | 7,570 |

### BEST-PAYING METROPOLITAN AREAS

| Metro Area | Median Earnings | Workforce |
|---|---|---|
| Washington-Arlington-Alexandria, DC-VA-MD-WV | $89,030 | 4,830 |
| San Francisco–Oakland–Fremont, CA | $84,120 | 2,150 |
| Los Angeles–Long Beach–Santa Ana, CA | $76,750 | 3,580 |
| Boston-Cambridge-Quincy, MA-NH | $74,780 | 1,610 |
| New York–Northern New Jersey–Long Island, NY-NJ-PA | $73,880 | 2,590 |
| Philadelphia-Camden-Wilmington, PA-NJ-DE-MD | $71,450 | 1,180 |
| Atlanta–Sandy Springs–Marietta, GA | $70,380 | 1,220 |
| Dallas–Fort Worth–Arlington, TX | $68,360 | 1,340 |

fund-granting authorities, clarifying and promoting the proposed budgets.

**Usual Educational Requirement:** Bachelor's degree. **Relevant Educational Programs**: Accounting; Accounting and Finance; Finance, General; Public Finance. **Related Knowledge/ Courses:** Economics and Accounting; Clerical Practices; Administration and Management; Mathematics; Personnel and Human Resources; Law and Government. **Work Experience Needed:** None. **On-the-Job Training Needed:** None. **Certification/Licensure:** None.

**Personality Types:** Conventional–Enterprising–Investigative. **Key Career Cluster:** 04 Business, Management, and Administration. **Key Career Pathway:** 4.4 Business Analysis.

**Skills:** Management of financial resources; operations analysis; systems analysis; mathematics; management of material resources; systems evaluation; judgment and decision making; active learning.

**Physical Environment:** Indoors; sitting; repetitive motions. **Structural Environment:** Importance of being exact or accurate; structured versus unstructured work; importance of repeating same tasks; freedom to make decisions; impact of decisions on co-workers or company results; time pressure.

## Business Operations Specialists, All Other

**All business operations specialists not listed separately.**

- Average annual earnings: $65,120
- Middle 50% of earners: $47,990–$86,950
- Earnings growth potential: High (46.0%)
- Growth: 11.6%
- Annual job openings: 32,720

**Considerations for Job Outlook:** In federal government, a small increase is expected as positions with specialized titles in areas such as defense and energy increase.

### BEST-PAYING INDUSTRIES

| Industry | Median Earnings | Workforce |
|---|---|---|
| Professional, Scientific, and Technical Services | $71,100 | 116,460 |
| Management of Companies and Enterprises | $68,800 | 54,320 |
| Federal, State, and Local Government | $68,590 | 258,910 |
| Educational Services | $56,420 | 80,610 |
| Religious, Grantmaking, Civic, Professional, and Similar Organizations | $52,980 | 49,530 |

### BEST-PAYING METROPOLITAN AREAS

| Metro Area | Median Earnings | Workforce |
|---|---|---|
| Washington-Arlington-Alexandria, DC-VA-MD-WV | $84,060 | 63,480 |
| San Francisco–Oakland–Fremont, CA | $78,320 | 23,630 |
| Dallas–Fort Worth–Arlington, TX | $71,570 | 24,580 |
| Los Angeles–Long Beach–Santa Ana, CA | $69,510 | 41,940 |
| New York–Northern New Jersey–Long Island, NY-NJ-PA | $69,090 | 52,840 |
| Denver-Aurora, CO | $67,680 | 24,550 |
| Atlanta–Sandy Springs–Marietta, GA | $67,660 | 21,470 |
| Minneapolis–St. Paul–Bloomington, MN-WI | $60,880 | 20,170 |
| Chicago-Naperville-Joliet, IL-IN-WI | $59,900 | 52,350 |
| Miami–Fort Lauderdale–Pompano Beach, FL | $58,440 | 18,980 |

**Major Work Tasks:** For tasks, see the job specializations.

**Usual Educational Requirement:** High school diploma or equivalent. **Relevant Educational Program**: Business Administration and Management, General. **Work Experience Needed:** Less than 1 year. **On-the-Job Training Needed:** Long-term on-the-job training. **Certification/Licensure:** Licensure for some specializations; voluntary certification by association.

**Key Career Cluster:** 04 Business, Management, and Administration. **Key Career Pathway:** 4.1 Management.

### JOB SPECIALIZATIONS: BUSINESS CONTINUITY PLANNERS

**Develop, maintain, and implement business continuity and disaster recovery strategies and solutions. Perform risk analyses. Act as a coordinator for recovery efforts in emergency situations.**

**Major Work Tasks:** Write reports to summarize testing activities, including descriptions of goals, planning, scheduling, execution, results, analysis, conclusions, and recommendations. Maintain and update organization information technology applications and network systems blueprints. Interpret government regulations and applicable codes to ensure compliance. Identify individual or transaction targets to direct intelligence collection. Establish, maintain, or test call trees to ensure appropriate communication during disaster. Design or implement products and services to mitigate risk or facilitate use of technology-based tools and methods. Create business continuity and disaster recovery budgets. Create or administer training and awareness presentations or materials. Attend professional meetings, read literature, and participate in training or other educational offerings to keep abreast of new developments and technologies related to disaster recovery and business continuity. Test documented disaster recovery strategies and plans. Review existing disaster recovery, crisis management, or business continuity plans. Recommend or implement methods to monitor, evaluate, or enable resolution of safety, operations, or compliance interruptions. Prepare reports summarizing operational results, financial performance, or accomplishments of specified objectives, goals, or plans. Analyze impact on, and risk to, essential business functions or information systems to identify acceptable recovery time periods and resource requirements. Identify opportunities for strategic improvement or mitigation of business interruption and other risks caused by business, regulatory, or industry-specific change initiatives. Develop disaster recovery plans for physical locations with critical assets such as data centers. Create scenarios to re-establish operations from various types of business disruptions. Conduct or oversee contingency plan integration and operation. Develop emergency management plans for recovery decision making and communications, continuity of critical departmental processes, or temporary shutdown of non-critical departments to ensure continuity of operation and governance.

**Related Knowledge/Courses:** Public Safety and Security; Telecommunications; Administration and Management; Geography; Communications and Media; Economics and Accounting.

**Personality Types:** Enterprising–Investigative–Conventional.

**Skills:** Management of financial resources; management of material resources; complex problem solving; systems analysis; systems evaluation; judgment and decision making; operations analysis; persuasion.

**Physical Environment:** Indoors; sitting. **Structural Environment:** Structured versus unstructured work; freedom to make decisions; impact of decisions on co-workers or company results; importance of being exact or accurate; frequency of decision making; time pressure.

167

## JOB SPECIALIZATION: CUSTOMS BROKERS

**Prepare customs documentation and ensure that shipments meet all applicable laws to facilitate the import and export of goods. Determine and track duties and taxes payable and process payments on behalf of client. Sign documents under a power of attorney. Represent clients in meetings with customs officials and apply for duty refunds and tariff reclassifications. Coordinate transportation and storage of imported goods.**

**Major Work Tasks:** Sign documents on behalf of clients, using powers of attorney. Provide advice on transportation options, types of carriers, or shipping routes. Post bonds for the products being imported or assist clients in obtaining bonds. Insure cargo against loss, damage, or pilferage. Obtain line releases for frequent shippers of low-risk commodities, high-volume entries, or multiple-container loads. Contract with freight forwarders for destination services. Arrange for transportation, warehousing, or product distribution of imported or exported products. Suggest best methods of packaging or labeling products. Request or compile necessary import documentation, such as customs invoices, certificates of origin, and cargo-control documents. Stay abreast of changes in import or export laws or regulations by reading current literature, attending meetings or conferences, or conferring with colleagues. Quote duty and tax rates on goods to be imported, based on federal tariffs and excise taxes. Prepare papers for shippers to appeal duty charges. Pay, or arrange for payment of, taxes and duties on shipments. Monitor or trace the location of goods. Maintain relationships with customs brokers in other ports to expedite clearing of cargo. Inform importers and exporters of steps to reduce duties and taxes. Confer with officials in various agencies to facilitate clearance of goods through customs and quarantine. Classify goods according to tariff coding system. Calculate duty and tariff payments owed on shipments. Apply for tariff concessions or for duty drawbacks and other refunds. Advise customers on import and export restrictions, tariff systems, insurance requirements, quotas, or other customs-related matters. Prepare and process import and export documentation according to customs regulations, laws, or procedures. Clear goods through customs and to their destinations for clients.

**Related Knowledge/Courses:** Clerical Practices; Geography; Transportation; Sales and Marketing; Law and Government; Economics and Accounting.

**Personality Types:** Enterprising–Conventional.

**Skills:** Management of financial resources; management of material resources; negotiation; programming; mathematics; management of personnel resources; writing; systems analysis.

**Physical Environment:** Indoors; sitting. **Structural Environment:** Importance of being exact or accurate; time pressure; frequency of decision making; importance of repeating same tasks; impact of decisions on co-workers or company results; freedom to make decisions.

## JOB SPECIALIZATION: ENERGY AUDITORS

**Conduct energy audits of buildings, building systems, and process systems. May also conduct investment grade audits of buildings or systems.**

**Major Work Tasks:** Measure energy usage with devices such as data loggers, universal data recorders, light meters, sling psychrometers, psychrometric charts, flue gas analyzers, amp probes, watt meters, volt meters, thermometers, or utility meters. Perform tests such as blower-door tests to locate air leaks. Inspect or evaluate building envelopes, mechanical systems, electrical systems, or process systems to determine the energy consumption of each system. Prepare audit reports containing energy analysis results or recommendations for energy cost savings. Analyze energy bills including utility rates or tariffs to gather historical energy usage data. Analyze technical feasibility of energy saving measures using knowledge of engineering, energy production, energy use, construction, maintenance, system operation, or process systems. Calculate potential for energy savings. Collect and analyze field data related to energy usage. Compare existing energy consumption levels to normative data. Determine patterns of building use to show annual or monthly needs for heating, cooling, lighting, or other energy needs. Educate customers on energy efficiency or answer questions on topics such as the costs of running household appliances or the selection of energy efficient appliances. Identify and prioritize energy saving measures. Identify opportunities to improve the operation, maintenance, or energy efficiency of building or process systems. Quantify energy consumption to establish baselines for energy use or need. Oversee installation of equipment such as water heater wraps, pipe insulation, weather-stripping, door sweeps, or low flow showerheads to improve energy efficiency. Prepare job specification sheets for home energy improvements, such as attic insulation, window retrofits, or heating system upgrades. Recommend energy efficient technologies or alternate energy sources. Examine commercial sites to determine the feasibility of installing equipment that allows building management systems to reduce electricity consumption during peak demand periods. Identify any health or safety issues related to planned weatherization projects.

**Related Knowledge/Courses:** Building and Construction; Physics; Sales and Marketing; Design; Mechanical Devices; Clerical.

**Personality Types:** Conventional–Enterprising.

**Skills:** Operations analysis; science; systems evaluation; systems analysis; mathematics;

operation and control; management of financial resources; writing.

**Physical Environment:** Outdoors; indoors; standing; using hands; very hot or cold; bright or inadequate lighting. **Structural Environment:** Freedom to make decisions; structured versus unstructured work; time pressure; frequency of decision making; impact of decisions on co-workers or company results; importance of being exact or accurate.

## JOB SPECIALIZATION: ONLINE MERCHANTS

**Plan, direct, or coordinate retail activities of businesses operating online. May perform duties such as preparing business strategies, buying merchandise, managing inventory, implementing marketing activities, fulfilling and shipping online orders, and balancing financial records.**

**Major Work Tasks:** Participate in online forums or conferences to stay abreast of online retailing trends, techniques, or security threats. Upload digital media, such as photos, video, or scanned images to online storefront, auction sites, or other shopping websites. Order or purchase merchandise to maintain optimal inventory levels. Maintain inventory of shipping supplies, such as boxes, labels, tape, bubble wrap, loose packing materials, or tape guns. Integrate online retailing strategy with physical or catalogue retailing operations. Determine and set product prices. Disclose merchant information and terms and policies of transactions in online or offline materials. Deliver e-mail confirmation of completed transactions and shipment. Create, manage, or automate orders or invoices, using order management or invoicing software. Create or maintain database of customer accounts. Create or distribute offline promotional material, such as brochures, pamphlets, business cards, stationary, or signage. Collaborate with search engine shopping specialists to place marketing content in desired online locations. Cancel orders based on customer requests or inventory or delivery problems. Transfer digital media, such as music, video, or software, to customers via the Internet. Select and purchase technical web services, such as web hosting services, online merchant accounts, shopping cart software, payment gateway software, or spyware. Promote products in online communities through weblog or discussion-forum postings, e-mail marketing programs, or online advertising. Fill customer orders by packaging sold items and documentation for direct shipping or by transferring orders to manufacturers or third-party distributors. Measure and analyze website usage data to maximize search engine returns or refine customer interfaces. Investigate sources, such as auctions, estate sales, liquidators, wholesalers, or trade shows for new items, used items, or collectibles. Investigate products or markets to determine areas for opportunity or viability for merchandising specific products, using online or offline sources. Initiate online auctions through auction hosting sites or auction management software.

**Related Knowledge/Courses:** No data available.

**Personality Types:** Enterprising–Conventional–Realistic.

**Skills:** No data available.

**Physical Environment:** No data available.
**Structural Environment:** No data available.

### JOB SPECIALIZATION: SECURITY MANAGEMENT SPECIALISTS

**Conduct security assessments for organizations and design security systems and processes. May specialize in areas, such as physical security, personnel security, or information security. May work in fields, such as health care, banking, gaming, security engineering, or manufacturing.**

**Major Work Tasks:** Prepare documentation for case reports or court proceedings. Review design drawings or technical documents for completeness, correctness, or appropriateness. Budget and schedule security design work. Develop conceptual designs of security systems. Respond to emergency situations on an on-call basis. Train personnel in security procedures or use of security equipment. Prepare, maintain, or update security procedures, security system drawings, or related documentation. Monitor the work of contractors in the design, construction, and start-up phases of security systems. Inspect security design features, installations, or programs to ensure compliance with applicable standards or regulations. Inspect fire, intruder detection, or other security systems. Engineer, install, maintain, or repair security systems, programmable logic controls, or other security-related electronic systems. Recommend improvements in security systems or procedures. Develop or review specifications for design or construction of security systems. Design security policies, programs, or practices to ensure adequate security relating to issues such as protection of assets, alarm response, and access card use. Perform risk analyses so that appropriate countermeasures can be developed. Conduct security audits to identify potential vulnerabilities related to physical security, staff safety, or asset protection. Provide system design and integration recommendations. Assess the nature and level of threats so that the scope of the problem can be determined. Design or implement or establish requirements for security systems, video surveillance, motion detection, or closed-circuit television systems to ensure proper installation and operation. Determine the value loss impact and criticality of assets. Outline system security criteria for pre-bid meetings with clients and companies to ensure comprehensiveness and appropriateness for implementation. Test security measures for final acceptance and implement or provide procedures for ongoing monitoring and evaluation of the measures. Monitor tapes or digital recordings to identify the source of losses.

**Related Knowledge/Courses:** Building and Construction; Design; Engineering and Technology; Public Safety and Security; Telecommunications; Personnel and Human Resources.

**Personality Types:** Realistic–Investigative–Conventional.

**Skills:** Installation; technology design; operations analysis; management of material resources; programming; management of financial resources; equipment selection; systems evaluation.

**Physical Environment:** Indoors; sitting. **Structural Environment:** Structured versus unstructured work; freedom to make decisions; impact of decisions on co-workers or company results; frequency of decision making; time pressure; importance of being exact or accurate.

### JOB SPECIALIZATION: SUSTAINABILITY SPECIALISTS

**Address organizational sustainability issues, such as waste stream management, green building practices, and green procurement plans.**

**Major Work Tasks:** Review and revise sustainability proposals or policies. Research or review regulatory, technical, or market issues related to sustainability. Identify or create new sustainability indicators. Write grant applications, rebate applications, or project proposals to secure funding for sustainability projects. Provide technical or administrative support for sustainability programs or issues. Identify or procure needed resources to implement sustainability programs or projects. Create or maintain plans or other documents related to sustainability projects. Develop reports or presentations to communicate the effectiveness of sustainability initiatives. Create marketing or outreach media, such as brochures or websites, to communicate sustainability issues, procedures, or objectives. Collect information about waste stream management or green building practices to inform decision-makers. Assess or propose sustainability initiatives, considering factors such as cost effectiveness, technical feasibility, and acceptance. Monitor or track sustainability indicators, such as energy usage, natural resource usage, waste generation, and recycling. Develop sustainability project goals, objectives, initiatives, or strategies in collaboration with other sustainability professionals. Identify or investigate violations of natural resources, waste management, recycling, or other environmental policies.

**Related Knowledge/Courses:** Building and Construction; Design; Geography; Engineering and Technology; Sociology and Anthropology; Sales and Marketing.

**Personality Types:** Enterprising–Investigative–Artistic.

**Skills:** Systems evaluation; systems analysis; management of financial resources; management of material resources; management of personnel resources; writing; programming; installation.

**Physical Environment:** Indoors; sitting. **Structural Environment:** Structured versus unstructured work; freedom to make decisions; impact of decisions on co-workers or company results; frequency of decision making; importance of being exact or accurate; time pressure.

## Business Teachers, Postsecondary

*See Teachers, Postsecondary.*

## Captains, Mates, and Pilots of Water Vessels

**Command or supervise operations of ships and water vessels, such as tugboats and ferryboats.**

- Average annual earnings: $66,150
- Middle 50% of earners: $44,460–$93,790
- Earnings growth potential: Very high (52.2%)
- Growth: 20.4%

## Your Guide to High-Paying Careers

- Annual job openings: 2,070
- Self-employed: 12.4%

### BEST-PAYING INDUSTRIES

| Industry | Median Earnings | Workforce |
|---|---|---|
| Support Activities for Transportation | $76,010 | 7,680 |
| Water Transportation | $66,480 | 13,550 |
| Federal, State, and Local Government | $66,340 | 2,370 |
| Scenic and Sightseeing Transportation | $42,580 | 2,320 |

### BEST-PAYING METROPOLITAN AREAS

| Metro Area | Median Earnings | Workforce |
|---|---|---|
| Houston–Sugar Land–Baytown, TX | $79,980 | 1,640 |
| Baltimore-Towson, MD | $76,890 | 670 |
| New Orleans–Metairie-Kenner, LA | $73,530 | 2,400 |
| Seattle-Tacoma-Bellevue, WA | $71,800 | 1,410 |
| Houma–Bayou Cane–Thibodaux, LA | $71,200 | 3,610 |
| New York–Northern New Jersey–Long Island, NY-NJ-PA | $68,560 | 1,920 |
| Virginia Beach–Norfolk–Newport News, VA-NC | $67,680 | 1,530 |
| Los Angeles–Long Beach–Santa Ana, CA | $64,600 | 1,240 |
| Lafayette, LA | $61,060 | 800 |
| Miami–Fort Lauderdale–Pompano Beach, FL | $34,960 | 1,370 |

**Considerations for Job Outlook:** Job prospects should be favorable. Many workers leave water transportation occupations, especially sailors and marine oilers, because recently hired workers often decide they do not enjoy spending a lot of time away at sea. In addition, a number of officers and engineers are approaching retirement, creating job openings. The number of applicants for all types of jobs may be limited by high regulatory and security requirements.

**Major Work Tasks:** For tasks, see the job specializations.

**Usual Educational Requirement:** Bachelor's degree. **Relevant Educational Programs**: Commercial Fishing; Marine Science/Merchant Marine Officer. **Work Experience Needed:** None. **On-the-Job Training Needed:** None. **Certification/Licensure:** Licensure.

**Key Career Cluster:** 16 Transportation, Distribution, and Logistics. **Key Career Pathway:** 16.1 Transportation Operations.

### JOB SPECIALIZATION: MATES—SHIP, BOAT, AND BARGE

**Supervise and coordinate activities of crew aboard ships, boats, barges, or dredges.**

**Major Work Tasks:** Steer vessels, using navigational devices, such as compasses or sextants, or navigational aids, such as lighthouses or buoys. Stand watches on vessels during specified periods while vessels are under way. Determine geographical positions of ships, using lorans, azimuths of celestial bodies, or computers, and use this information to determine the course and speed of a ship. Assume command of vessels in the event that ships' masters become incapacitated. Inspect equipment, such as cargo-handling gear, lifesaving equipment, visual-signaling equipment, or fishing, towing, or dredging gear, to detect problems. Participate in activities related to maintenance of vessel security. Arrange for ships to be stocked, fueled, or repaired. Observe loading or unloading of cargo or equipment to ensure

**172**

that handling and storage are performed according to specifications. Supervise crew members in the repair or replacement of defective gear or equipment. Supervise crews in cleaning or maintaining decks, superstructures, or bridges. Observe water from ships' mastheads to advise on navigational direction.

**Related Knowledge/Courses:** Transportation; Geography; Public Safety and Security; Telecommunications; Mechanical Devices; Personnel and Human Resources.

**Personality Types:** Enterprising–Realistic–Conventional.

**Skills:** Repairing; equipment maintenance; operation and control; troubleshooting; operation monitoring; equipment selection; quality control analysis; management of personnel resources.

**Physical Environment:** Outdoors; indoors; standing; balancing; using hands; noise. **Structural Environment:** Frequency of decision making; impact of decisions on co-workers or company results; time pressure; consequence of error; freedom to make decisions; importance of being exact or accurate.

### JOB SPECIALIZATION: PILOTS, SHIP

**Command ships to steer them into and out of harbors, estuaries, straits, and sounds and on rivers, lakes, and bays. Must be licensed by U.S. Coast Guard with limitations indicating class and tonnage of vessels for which licenses are valid and routes and waters that may be piloted.**

**Major Work Tasks:** Set ships' courses that avoid reefs, outlying shoals, or other hazards, using navigational aids, such as lighthouses or buoys. Direct courses and speeds of ships, based on specialized knowledge of local winds, weather, water depths, tides, currents, and hazards. Steer ships into or out of berths or signal tugboat captains to berth or unberth ships. Prevent ships under their navigational control from engaging in unsafe operations.

Consult maps, charts, weather reports, or navigation equipment to determine and direct ship movements. Give directions to crew members who are steering ships. Maintain ship logs. Serve as a vessel's docking master upon arrival at a port or when at a berth. Operate ship-to-shore radios to exchange information needed for ship operations. Provide assistance in maritime rescue operations. Provide assistance to vessels approaching or leaving seacoasts, navigating harbors, or docking and undocking. Report to appropriate authorities any violations of federal or state pilotage laws. Learn to operate new technology systems and procedures, through the use of instruction, simulators, or models. Advise ships' masters on harbor rules and customs procedures. Oversee cargo storage on or below decks. Relieve crew members on tugs or launches. Maintain or repair boats or equipment. Make nautical maps.

**Related Knowledge/Courses:** Transportation; Geography; Public Safety and Security; Telecommunications; Mechanical Devices; Law and Government.

**Personality Types:** Realistic–Conventional–Investigative.

**Skills:** Operation and control; operation monitoring; troubleshooting; equipment maintenance; management of personnel resources; repairing; quality control analysis; complex problem solving.

**Physical Environment:** Outdoors; indoors; standing; using hands; noise; very hot or cold. **Structural Environment:** Impact of decisions on co-workers or company results; frequency of decision making; freedom to make decisions; importance of being exact or accurate; consequence of error; structured versus unstructured work.

### JOB SPECIALIZATION: SHIP AND BOAT CAPTAINS

**Command vessels in oceans, bays, lakes, rivers, and coastal waters.**

**Major Work Tasks:** Steer and operate vessels, using radios, depth finders, radars, lights, buoys, or lighthouses. Compute positions, set courses, and determine speeds, using charts, area plotting sheets, compasses, sextants, and knowledge of local conditions. Inspect vessels to ensure efficient and safe operation of vessels and equipment and conformance to regulations. Measure depths of water, using depth-measuring equipment. Direct or coordinate crew members or workers performing activities such as loading or unloading cargo, steering vessels, operating engines, or operating, maintaining, or repairing ship equipment. Monitor the loading or discharging of cargo or passengers. Calculate sightings of land, using electronic sounding devices and following contour lines on charts. Signal passing vessels, using whistles, flashing lights, flags, or radios. Maintain boats or equipment on board, such as engines, winches, navigational systems, fire extinguishers, or life preservers. Signal crew members or deckhands to rig tow lines, open or close gates or ramps, or pull guard chains across entries. Read gauges to verify sufficient levels of hydraulic fluid, air pressure, or oxygen. Maintain records of daily activities, personnel reports, ship positions and movements, ports of call, weather and sea conditions, pollution control efforts, or cargo or passenger status. Arrange for ships to be fueled, restocked with supplies, or repaired. Assign watches or living quarters to crew members. Purchase supplies or equipment. Tow and maneuver barges or signal tugboats to tow barges to destinations. Perform various marine duties, such as checking for oil spills or other pollutants around ports or harbors or patrolling beaches. Collect fares from customers or signal ferryboat helpers to collect fares. Sort logs, form log booms, or salvage lost logs. Resolve questions or problems with customs officials. Interview and hire crew members.

**Related Knowledge/Courses:** Transportation; Public Safety and Security; Geography; Tele-communications; Mechanical Devices; Psychology.

**Personality Types:** Enterprising–Realistic.

**Skills:** Operation and control; repairing; management of material resources; equipment maintenance; management of financial resources; troubleshooting; operation monitoring; equipment selection.

**Physical Environment:** Outdoors; indoors; standing; using hands; repetitive motions; noise. **Structural Environment:** Impact of decisions on co-workers or company results; frequency of decision making; structured versus unstructured work; freedom to make decisions; consequence of error; importance of being exact or accurate.

## Cartographers and Photogrammetrists

**Collect, analyze, and interpret geographic information provided by geodetic surveys, aerial photographs, and satellite data.**

- Average annual earnings: $57,440
- Middle 50% of earners: $44,330–$75,310
- Earnings growth potential: Medium (39.3%)
- Growth: 22.2%
- Annual job openings: 610
- Self-employed: 13.6%

**Considerations for Job Outlook:** Photogrammetrists should have excellent opportunities, because of the limited number of college graduates receiving degrees in this field.

### BEST-PAYING INDUSTRIES

| Industry | Median Earnings | Workforce |
|---|---|---|
| Federal, State, and Local Government | $60,380 | 3,910 |
| Professional, Scientific, and Technical Services | $55,470 | 5,820 |

## BEST-PAYING METROPOLITAN AREAS

| Metro Area | Median Earnings | Workforce |
|---|---|---|
| Washington-Arlington-Alexandria, DC-VA-MD-WV | $80,840 | 640 |
| Los Angeles–Long Beach–Santa Ana, CA | $73,210 | 300 |
| Denver-Aurora, CO | $72,930 | 460 |
| Sacramento–Arden-Arcade–Roseville, CA | $69,630 | 250 |
| Houston–Sugar Land–Baytown, TX | $68,470 | 250 |
| Portland-Vancouver-Beaverton, OR-WA | $60,390 | 450 |
| San Diego–Carlsbad–San Marcos, CA | $57,770 | 230 |
| Phoenix-Mesa-Scottsdale, AZ | $57,070 | 230 |
| Huntsville, AL | $40,770 | 390 |
| Austin–Round Rock, TX | $39,320 | 240 |

**Major Work Tasks:** Identify, scale, and orient geodetic points, elevations, and other planimetric or topographic features, applying standard mathematical formulas. Collect information about specific features of the Earth using aerial photography and other digital remote sensing techniques. Revise existing maps and charts, making all necessary corrections and adjustments. Compile data required for map preparation, including aerial photographs, survey notes, records, reports, and original maps. Inspect final compositions to ensure completeness and accuracy. Determine map content and layout, as well as production specifications such as scale, size, projection, and colors, and direct production to ensure that specifications are followed. Examine and analyze data from ground surveys, reports, aerial photographs, and satellite images to prepare topographic maps, aerial-photograph mosaics, and related charts. Delineate aerial photographic detail such as control points, hydrography, topography, and cultural features using precision stereoplotting apparatus or drafting instruments. Build and update digital databases. Prepare and alter trace maps, charts, tables, detailed drawings, and three-dimensional optical models of terrain using stereoscopic plotting and computer graphics equipment. Determine guidelines that specify which source material is acceptable for use. Select aerial photographic and remote sensing techniques and plotting equipment needed to meet required standards of accuracy. Study legal records to establish boundaries of local, national, and international properties. Travel over photographed areas to observe, identify, record, and verify all relevant features.

**Usual Educational Requirement:** Bachelor's degree. **Relevant Educational Programs**: Geographic Information Science and Cartography; Surveying Technology/Surveying. **Related Knowledge/Courses:** Geography; Design; Computers and Electronics; Mathematics; Production and Processing. **Work Experience Needed:** None. **On-the-Job Training Needed:** None. **Certification/Licensure:** Voluntary certification by association.

**Personality Types:** Realistic–Investigative–Conventional. **Key Career Cluster:** 01 Agriculture, Food, and Natural Resources. **Key Career Pathway:** 1.5 Natural Resources Systems.

**Skills:** Mathematics; systems analysis; writing; programming; reading comprehension; instructing; learning strategies; technology design.

**Physical Environment:** Indoors; sitting; using hands; repetitive motions. **Structural Environment:** Importance of being exact or accurate; importance of repeating same tasks; time pressure; structured versus unstructured work; freedom to make decisions; frequency of decision making.

## Chemical Engineers

**Design chemical plant equipment and devise processes for manufacturing chemicals and products.**

- Average annual earnings: $94,350
- Middle 50% of earners: $73,810–$119,100
- Earnings growth potential: Medium (37.6%)
- Growth: 5.9%
- Annual job openings: 1,140
- Self-employed: 2.6%

### BEST-PAYING INDUSTRIES

| Industry | Median Earnings | Workforce |
|---|---|---|
| Petroleum and Coal Products Manufacturing | $105,310 | 1,890 |
| Chemical Manufacturing | $94,580 | 9,850 |
| Professional, Scientific, and Technical Services | $93,840 | 10,170 |

### BEST-PAYING METROPOLITAN AREAS

| Metro Area | Median Earnings | Workforce |
|---|---|---|
| Houston–Sugar Land–Baytown, TX | $118,000 | 3,740 |
| Baton Rouge, LA | $108,240 | 1,340 |
| Philadelphia-Camden-Wilmington, PA-NJ-DE-MD | $107,140 | 1,580 |
| New York–Northern New Jersey–Long Island, NY-NJ-PA | $101,290 | 1,530 |
| Boston-Cambridge-Quincy, MA-NH | $93,750 | 1,110 |
| Chicago-Naperville-Joliet, IL-IN-WI | $93,680 | 820 |
| Los Angeles–Long Beach–Santa Ana, CA | $92,550 | 850 |

**Considerations for Job Outlook:** Chemical engineers should have favorable job prospects as many workers in the occupation reach retirement age from 2010 to 2020.

**Major Work Tasks:** Develop safety procedures to be employed by workers operating equipment or working in close proximity to on-going chemical reactions. Determine most effective arrangement of operations such as mixing, crushing, heat transfer, distillation, and drying. Prepare estimate of production costs and production progress reports for management. Direct activities of workers who operate or who are engaged in constructing and improving absorption, evaporation, or electromagnetic equipment. Perform laboratory studies of steps in manufacture of new product and test proposed process in small scale operation such as a pilot plant. Develop processes to separate components of liquids or gases or generate electrical currents using controlled chemical processes. Conduct research to develop new and improved chemical manufacturing processes. Design measurement and control systems for chemical plants based on data collected in laboratory experiments and in pilot plant operations. Design and plan layout of equipment. Troubleshoot problems with chemical manufacturing processes. Evaluate chemical equipment and processes to identify ways to optimize performance or to ensure compliance with safety and environmental regulations. Perform tests and monitor performance of processes throughout stages of production to determine degree of control over variables such as temperature, density, specific gravity, and pressure.

**Usual Educational Requirement:** Bachelor's degree. **Relevant Educational Programs**: Biochemical Engineering; Chemical and Biomolecular Engineering; Chemical Engineering; Chemical Engineering, Other; Engineering Chemistry; Paper Science and Engineering. **Related Knowledge/Courses:** Engineering and Technology; Chemistry; Physics; Design;

**176**

Production and Processing; Biology. **Work Experience Needed:** None. **On-the-Job Training Needed:** None. **Certification/Licensure:** Licensure beyond entry level.

**Personality Types:** Investigative–Realistic. **Key Career Cluster:** 15 Science, Technology, Engineering, and Mathematics. **Key Career Pathway:** 15.1 Engineering and Technology.

**Skills:** Science; operations analysis; technology design; mathematics; troubleshooting; systems evaluation; management of financial resources; programming.

**Physical Environment:** Indoors; sitting. **Structural Environment:** Freedom to make decisions; structured versus unstructured work; importance of being exact or accurate; impact of decisions on co-workers or company results; consequence of error; time pressure.

## Chemistry Teachers, Postsecondary

*See Teachers, Postsecondary.*

## Chemists

**Conduct qualitative and quantitative chemical analyses or experiments in laboratories for quality or process control or to develop new products or knowledge.**

- Average annual earnings: $71,770
- Middle 50% of earners: $52,630–$96,150
- Earnings growth potential: Medium (42.8%)
- Growth: 3.8%
- Annual job openings: 2,990
- Self-employed: 0.3%

**Considerations for Job Outlook:** In addition to job openings resulting from employment growth, some job openings will result from the need to replace chemists and materials scientists who retire or otherwise leave the occupation. Chemists and materials scientists with

### BEST-PAYING INDUSTRIES

| Industry | Median Earnings | Workforce |
|---|---|---|
| Federal, State, and Local Government | $80,670 | 10,400 |
| Chemical Manufacturing | $72,100 | 25,700 |
| Professional, Scientific, and Technical Services | $70,090 | 28,640 |

### BEST-PAYING METROPOLITAN AREAS

| Metro Area | Median Earnings | Workforce |
|---|---|---|
| Washington-Arlington-Alexandria, DC-VA-MD-WV | $114,710 | 2,820 |
| San Francisco–Oakland–Fremont, CA | $85,320 | 2,660 |
| San Diego–Carlsbad–San Marcos, CA | $82,340 | 1,890 |
| Boston-Cambridge-Quincy, MA-NH | $81,080 | 3,320 |
| Philadelphia-Camden-Wilmington, PA-NJ-DE-MD | $80,490 | 6,630 |
| New York–Northern New Jersey–Long Island, NY-NJ-PA | $77,310 | 7,490 |
| Chicago-Naperville-Joliet, IL-IN-WI | $73,500 | 3,080 |
| Los Angeles–Long Beach–Santa Ana, CA | $65,390 | 3,000 |

advanced degrees, particularly those with a PhD, are expected to experience better opportunities. Large pharmaceutical and biotechnology firms provide openings for these workers at research laboratories, and many others work in colleges and universities. Furthermore, chemists with advanced degrees will continue to fill most senior research and upper management positions.

**177**

**Major Work Tasks:** Analyze organic or inorganic compounds to determine chemical or physical properties, composition, structure, relationships, or reactions, using chromatography, spectroscopy, or spectrophotometry techniques. Develop, improve, or customize products, equipment, formulas, processes, or analytical methods. Compile and analyze test information to determine process or equipment operating efficiency or to diagnose malfunctions. Confer with scientists or engineers to conduct analyses of research projects, interpret test results, or develop nonstandard tests. Direct, coordinate, or advise personnel in test procedures for analyzing components or physical properties of materials. Induce changes in composition of substances by introducing heat, light, energy, or chemical catalysts for quantitative or qualitative analysis. Write technical papers or reports or prepare standards and specifications for processes, facilities, products, or tests. Prepare test solutions, compounds, or reagents for laboratory personnel to conduct tests. Maintain laboratory instruments to ensure proper working order and troubleshoot malfunctions when needed. Conduct quality control tests. Evaluate laboratory safety procedures to ensure compliance with standards or to make improvements as needed. Purchase laboratory supplies, such as chemicals, when supplies are low or near their expiration date. Study effects of various methods of processing, preserving, or packaging on composition or properties of foods.

**Usual Educational Requirement:** Bachelor's degree. **Relevant Educational Programs**: Analytical Chemistry; Chemical Physics; Chemistry, General; Chemistry, Other; Environmental Chemistry; Forensic Chemistry; Inorganic Chemistry; Materials Chemistry; Organic Chemistry; Physical Chemistry; Polymer Chemistry; Theoretical Chemistry. **Related Knowledge/Courses:** Chemistry; Engineering and Technology; Production and Processing; Mathematics; Biology; Mechanical. **Work Experience Needed:** None. **On-the-Job Training Needed:** None. **Certification/Licensure:** None.

**Personality Types:** Investigative–Realistic–Conventional. **Key Career Cluster:** 15 Science, Technology, Engineering, and Mathematics. **Key Career Pathway:** 15.2 Science and Mathematics.

**Skills:** Science; mathematics; equipment maintenance; equipment selection; writing; repairing; reading comprehension; quality control analysis.

**Physical Environment:** Indoors; sitting; using hands; noise; contaminants; hazardous conditions. **Structural Environment:** Importance of being exact or accurate; structured versus unstructured work; freedom to make decisions; time pressure; frequency of decision making; impact of decisions on co-workers or company results.

## Chief Executives

**Determine and formulate policies and provide overall direction of companies or private and public sector organizations within guidelines set up by a board of directors or similar governing body.**

- Average annual earnings: $168,140
- Middle 50% of earners: $109,940–$187,200+
- Earnings growth potential: Very high (54.7%)
- Growth: 4.2%
- Annual job openings: 11,150
- Self-employed: 20.4%

**Considerations for Job Outlook:** Those with an advanced degree and extensive managerial experience will have the best job prospects.

**Major Work Tasks:** Direct or coordinate an organization's financial or budget activities to fund operations, maximize investments, or increase efficiency. Confer with board members, organization officials, or staff members to dis-

## BEST-PAYING INDUSTRIES

| Industry | Median Earnings | Workforce |
|---|---|---|
| Management of Companies and Enterprises | $187,199+ | 21,600 |
| Professional, Scientific, and Technical Services | $187,199+ | 25,580 |
| Educational Services | $137,580 | 22,340 |
| Federal, State, and Local Government | $105,040 | 24,530 |

## BEST-PAYING METROPOLITAN AREAS

| Metro Area | Median Earnings | Workforce |
|---|---|---|
| Los Angeles–Long Beach–Santa Ana, CA | $187,199 | 10,900 |
| Washington-Arlington-Alexandria, DC-VA-MD-WV | $187,199 | 9,350 |
| Boston-Cambridge-Quincy, MA-NH | $187,199 | 10,510 |
| New York–Northern New Jersey–Long Island, NY-NJ-PA | $187,199 | 12,420 |
| Minneapolis–St. Paul–Bloomington, MN-WI | $175,160 | 6,370 |
| Chicago-Naperville-Joliet, IL-IN-WI | $167,350 | 15,600 |

cuss issues, coordinate activities, or resolve problems. Analyze operations to evaluate performance of a company or its staff in meeting objectives or to determine areas of potential cost reduction, program improvement, or policy change. Direct, plan, or implement policies, objectives, or activities of organizations or businesses to ensure continuing operations, to maximize returns on investments, or to increase productivity. Prepare budgets for approval, including those for funding or implementation of programs. Direct or coordinate activities of businesses or departments concerned with production, pricing, sales, or distribution of products. Negotiate or approve contracts or agreements with suppliers, distributors, federal or state agencies, or other organizational entities. Review reports submitted by staff members to recommend approval or to suggest changes. Appoint department heads or managers and assign or delegate responsibilities to them. Direct human resources activities, including the approval of human resource plans or activities, the selection of directors or other high-level staff, or establishment or organization of major departments. Preside over or serve on boards of directors, management committees, or other governing boards. Prepare or present reports concerning activities, expenses, budgets, government statutes or rulings, or other items affecting businesses or program services. Establish departmental responsibilities and coordinate functions among departments and sites. Implement corrective action plans to solve organizational or departmental problems. Coordinate the development or implementation of budgetary control systems, recordkeeping systems, or other administrative control processes. Direct non-merchandising departments, such as advertising, purchasing, credit, or accounting. Deliver speeches, write articles, or present information at meetings or conventions to promote services, exchange ideas, or accomplish objectives.

**Usual Educational Requirement:** Bachelor's degree. **Relevant Educational Programs**: Business Administration and Management, General; Business/Commerce, General; Entrepreneurship/Entrepreneurial Studies; Finance, General; International Business/ Trade/Commerce; Management Science; Public Administration. **Related Knowledge/ Courses:** Economics and Accounting; Administration and Management; Sales and Marketing; Personnel and Human Resources; Law and Government; Medicine and Dentistry. **Work**

**179**

**Experience Needed:** More than 5 years. **On-the-Job Training Needed:** None. **Certification/Licensure:** Voluntary certification for some specializations.

**Personality Types:** Enterprising–Conventional. **Key Career Cluster:** 04 Business, Management, and Administration. **Key Career Pathway:** 4.2 Business Financial Management and Accounting.

**Skills:** Management of financial resources; management of material resources; management of personnel resources; systems evaluation; systems analysis; judgment and decision making; persuasion; operations analysis.

**Physical Environment:** Indoors; sitting. **Structural Environment:** Impact of decisions on co-workers or company results; frequency of decision making; importance of being exact or accurate; freedom to make decisions; structured versus unstructured work; time pressure.

### JOB SPECIALIZATION: CHIEF SUSTAINABILITY OFFICERS

**Communicate and coordinate with management, shareholders, customers, and employees to address sustainability issues. Enact or oversee a corporate sustainability strategy.**

**Major Work Tasks:** Identify educational, training, or other development opportunities for sustainability employees or volunteers. Identify and evaluate pilot projects or programs to enhance the sustainability research agenda. Conduct sustainability- or environment-related risk assessments. Create and maintain sustainability program documents, such as schedules and budgets. Write project proposals, grant applications, or other documents to pursue funding for environmental initiatives. Supervise employees or volunteers working on sustainability projects. Write and distribute financial or environmental impact reports. Review sustainability program objectives, progress, or status to ensure compliance with policies, standards, regulations, or laws. For-

mulate or implement sustainability campaign or marketing strategies. Research environmental sustainability issues, concerns, or stakeholder interests. Evaluate and approve proposals for sustainability projects, considering factors such as cost effectiveness, technical feasibility, and integration with other initiatives. Develop sustainability reports, presentations, or proposals for supplier, employee, academia, media, government, public interest, or other groups. Develop, or oversee the development of, sustainability evaluation or monitoring systems. Develop, or oversee the development of, marketing or outreach media for sustainability projects or events. Develop methodologies to assess the viability or success of sustainability initiatives. Monitor and evaluate effectiveness of sustainability programs. Direct sustainability program operations to ensure compliance with environmental or governmental regulations. Develop or execute strategies to address issues such as energy use, resource conservation, recycling, pollution reduction, waste elimination, transportation, education, and building design.

**Related Knowledge/Courses:** Building and Construction; Sales and Marketing; Design; Geography; Engineering and Technology; Economics and Accounting.

**Personality Types:** Enterprising–Conventional–Investigative.

**Skills:** Management of financial resources; operations analysis; systems analysis; systems evaluation; management of material resources; management of personnel resources; complex problem solving; writing.

**Physical Environment:** Indoors; sitting. **Structural Environment:** Freedom to make decisions; structured versus unstructured work; impact of decisions on co-workers or company results; time pressure; frequency of decision making; level of competition.

## Chiropractors

**Assess, treat, and care for patients by manipulation of spine and musculoskeletal system.**

- Average annual earnings: $66,160
- Middle 50% of earners: $46,060–$96,170
- Earnings growth potential: Very high (53.1%)
- Growth: 28.3%
- Annual job openings: 2,530
- Self-employed: 50.1%

### BEST-PAYING INDUSTRIES

| Industry | Median Earnings | Workforce |
|---|---|---|
| Ambulatory Health-Care Services | $66,290 | 27,300 |

### BEST-PAYING METROPOLITAN AREAS

| Metro Area | Median Earnings | Workforce |
|---|---|---|
| New York–Northern New Jersey–Long Island, NY-NJ-PA | $82,450 | 1,360 |
| Chicago-Naperville-Joliet, IL-IN-WI | $76,240 | 1,150 |
| Los Angeles–Long Beach–Santa Ana, CA | $70,470 | 940 |
| Detroit-Warren-Livonia, MI | $58,890 | 870 |
| Miami–Fort Lauderdale–Pompano Beach, FL | $54,520 | 600 |
| Atlanta–Sandy Springs–Marietta, GA | $49,260 | 630 |
| Dallas–Fort Worth–Arlington, TX | $41,290 | 650 |

**Considerations for Job Outlook:** People across all age groups are increasingly seeking chiropractic care, because most chiropractors treat patients without performing surgery or prescribing drugs. Chiropractic treatment of the back, neck, limbs, and joints has become more accepted as a result of research and changing attitudes about alternative health care. The aging of the large baby-boom generation will lead to new opportunities for chiropractors, because older adults are more likely to experience musculoskeletal and joint problems. Demand for chiropractic treatment is related to the ability of patients to pay, either directly or through health insurance. Although more insurance plans now cover chiropractic services, the extent of such coverage varies among plans.

**Major Work Tasks:** Perform a series of manual adjustments to the spine or other articulations of the body to correct the musculoskeletal system. Evaluate the functioning of the neuromuscularskeletal system and the spine using systems of chiropractic diagnosis. Diagnose health problems by reviewing patients' health and medical histories, questioning, observing, and examining patients and interpreting X-rays. Maintain accurate case histories of patients. Advise patients about recommended courses of treatment. Obtain and record patients' medical histories. Analyze X-rays to locate the sources of patients' difficulties and to rule out fractures or diseases as sources of problems. Counsel patients about nutrition, exercise, sleeping habits, stress management, or other matters. Consult with or refer patients to appropriate health practitioners when necessary. Suggest and apply the use of supports such as straps, tapes, bandages, or braces if necessary. Recommend and arrange for diagnostic procedures, such as blood chemistry tests, saliva tests, X-rays, or other imaging procedures.

**Usual Educational Requirement:** Doctoral or professional degree. **Relevant Educational Program**: Chiropractic (DC). **Related Knowledge/Courses:** Medicine and Dentistry; Biology; Therapy and Counseling; Psychology; Sales and Marketing; Sociology and Anthropology. **Work Experience Needed:** None. **On-the-Job Training Needed:** None. **Certification/Licensure:** Licensure.

**Personality Types:** Social–Investigative–Realistic. **Key Career Cluster:** 08 Health Science. **Key Career Pathway:** 8.1 Therapeutic Services.

**Skills:** Science; service orientation; reading comprehension; social perceptiveness; active learning; systems evaluation; active listening; writing.

**Physical Environment:** Indoors; standing; using hands; bending or twisting the body; repetitive motions; exposed to disease or infections. **Structural Environment:** Freedom to make decisions; structured versus unstructured work; importance of being exact or accurate; impact of decisions on co-workers or company results; frequency of decision making; importance of repeating same tasks.

## Civil Engineers

**Perform engineering duties in planning, designing, and overseeing construction and maintenance of building structures and facilities.**

- Average annual earnings: $79,340
- Middle 50% of earners: $63,030–$100,330
- Earnings growth potential: Medium (35.4%)
- Growth: 19.4%
- Annual job openings: 10,440
- Self-employed: 3.8%

**Considerations for Job Outlook:** As infrastructure continues to age, civil engineers will be needed to manage projects to rebuild bridges, repair roads, and upgrade levees and dams.

**Major Work Tasks:** Analyze survey reports, maps, drawings, blueprints, aerial photography, and other topographical or geologic data to plan projects. Plan and design transportation or hydraulic systems and structures, fol-

### BEST-PAYING INDUSTRIES

| Industry | Median Earnings | Workforce |
|---|---|---|
| Federal, State, and Local Government | $80,680 | 73,170 |
| Professional, Scientific, and Technical Services | $79,620 | 139,230 |
| Construction of Buildings | $73,530 | 14,890 |

### BEST-PAYING METROPOLITAN AREAS

| Metro Area | Median Earnings | Workforce |
|---|---|---|
| San Francisco–Oakland–Fremont, CA | $101,670 | 7,260 |
| Houston–Sugar Land–Baytown, TX | $96,560 | 10,050 |
| Los Angeles–Long Beach–Santa Ana, CA | $91,870 | 10,390 |
| New York–Northern New Jersey–Long Island, NY-NJ-PA | $85,350 | 12,810 |
| Seattle-Tacoma-Bellevue, WA | $84,260 | 6,570 |
| Washington-Arlington-Alexandria, DC-VA-MD-WV | $82,400 | 8,130 |
| Chicago-Naperville-Joliet, IL-IN-WI | $80,280 | 6,080 |
| Philadelphia-Camden-Wilmington, PA-NJ-DE-MD | $80,170 | 5,250 |

lowing construction and government standards, using design software and drawing tools. Compute load and grade requirements, water flow rates, or material stress factors to determine design specifications. Inspect project sites to monitor progress and ensure conformance to design specifications and safety or sanitation standards. Direct or participate in surveying to lay out installations or establish reference points, grades, or elevations to guide construction. Estimate quantities and cost of materials, equipment, or labor to determine project feasibility. Prepare or present public reports on topics such as bid proposals, deeds, environmental impact statements, or property and right-of-way descriptions. Test soils or materials to determine the adequacy and strength of foundations, concrete, asphalt, or steel. Provide technical advice regarding design, construction, or program modifications and structural repairs to industrial and managerial personnel. Conduct studies of traffic patterns or environmental conditions to identify engineering problems and assess potential project impact. Manage and direct staff members and the construction, operations, or maintenance activities at project site. Analyze manufacturing processes or byproducts to identify engineering solutions to minimize the output of carbon or other pollutants. Design energy efficient or environmentally sound civil structures. Design or engineer systems to efficiently dispose of chemical, biological, or other toxic wastes. Develop or implement engineering solutions to clean up industrial accidents or other contaminated sites. Direct engineering activities ensuring compliance with environmental, safety, or other governmental regulations. Identify environmental risks and develop risk management strategies for civil engineering projects.

**Usual Educational Requirement:** Bachelor's degree. **Relevant Educational Programs**: Civil Engineering, General; Civil Engineering, Other; Construction Engineering; Geotechnical and Geoenvironmental Engineering; Structural Engineering; Transportation and Highway Engineering; Water Resources Engineering. **Related Knowledge/Courses:** Engineering and Technology; Building and Construction; Design; Physics; Transportation; Geography. **Work Experience Needed:** None. **On-the-Job Training Needed:** None. **Certification/Licensure:** Licensure for offering services to public.

**Personality Types:** Realistic–Investigative–Conventional. **Key Career Cluster:** 02 Architecture and Construction. **Key Career Pathway:** 2.1 Design/Pre-construction.

**Skills:** Operations analysis; science; mathematics; management of financial resources; management of material resources; programming; systems evaluation; systems analysis.

**Physical Environment:** Indoors; sitting. **Structural Environment:** Importance of being exact or accurate; freedom to make decisions; structured versus unstructured work; impact of decisions on co-workers or company results; frequency of decision making; time pressure.

## JOB SPECIALIZATION: TRANSPORTATION ENGINEERS

**Develop plans for surface transportation projects according to established engineering standards and state or federal construction policy. Prepare plans, estimates, or specifications to design transportation facilities. Plan alterations and modifications of existing streets, highways, or freeways to improve traffic flow.**

**Major Work Tasks:** Present data, maps, or other information at construction-related public hearings or meetings. Review development plans to determine potential traffic impact. Prepare administrative, technical, or statistical reports on traffic-operation matters, such as accidents, safety measures, or pedestrian volume or practices. Evaluate transportation systems or traffic control devices or lighting systems to determine need for modification or expansion. Evaluate traffic control devices or lighting systems to determine need for modification or expansion. Prepare project budgets, schedules, or specifications for labor or materials. Plan alteration or modification of existing transportation structures to improve safety or function. Participate in contract bidding, negotiation, or administration. Model transportation scenarios to evaluate the impacts of activities such as new development or to identify possible solutions to transportation problems. Investigate traffic problems and recommend methods to improve traffic flow or safety. Inspect completed transportation projects to ensure safety or compliance with applicable standards or regulations. Estimate transportation project costs. Confer with contractors, utility companies, or government agencies to discuss plans, specifications, or work schedules. Check construction plans, design calculations, or cost estimations to ensure completeness, accuracy, or conformity to engineering standards or practices. Analyze environmental impact statements for transportation projects. Design or prepare plans for new transportation systems or parts of systems, such as airports, commuter trains, highways, streets, bridges, drainage structures, or roadway lighting. Develop or assist in the development of transportation-related computer software or computer processes. Prepare final project layout drawings that include details such as stress calculations. Investigate or test specific construction project materials to determine compliance to specifications or standards. Direct the surveying, staking, or laying-out of construction projects. Supervise the maintenance or repair of transportation systems or system components.

**Related Knowledge/Courses:** Engineering and Technology; Design; Transportation; Building and Construction; Physics; Geography.

**Personality Types:** Realistic–Investigative.

**Skills:** Management of financial resources; operations analysis; management of material resources; mathematics; programming; technology design; systems analysis; science.

**Physical Environment:** Indoors; sitting. **Structural Environment:** Importance of being exact or accurate; impact of decisions on co-workers or company results; freedom to make decisions; structured versus unstructured work; time pressure; frequency of decision making.

## Claims Adjusters, Examiners, and Investigators

**Review settled claims to determine that payments and settlements are made in accordance with company practices and procedures.**

- Average annual earnings: $59,960
- Middle 50% of earners: $46,080–$74,620
- Earnings growth potential: Medium (38.4%)
- Growth: 3.0%
- Annual job openings: 7,990
- Self-employed: 0.9%

### BEST-PAYING INDUSTRIES

| Industry | Median Earnings | Workforce |
|---|---|---|
| Federal, State, and Local Government | $66,530 | 54,790 |
| Insurance Carriers and Related Activities | $57,920 | 185,120 |

### BEST-PAYING METROPOLITAN AREAS

| Metro Area | Median Earnings | Workforce |
|---|---|---|
| New York–Northern New Jersey–Long Island, NY-NJ-PA | $68,240 | 19,800 |
| Philadelphia-Camden-Wilmington, PA-NJ-DE-MD | $63,110 | 8,130 |
| Chicago-Naperville-Joliet, IL-IN-WI | $62,680 | 10,390 |
| Los Angeles–Long Beach–Santa Ana, CA | $62,350 | 12,340 |
| Dallas–Fort Worth–Arlington, TX | $59,030 | 8,270 |
| Tampa–St. Petersburg–Clearwater, FL | $53,560 | 6,160 |

**Considerations for Job Outlook:** Job opportunities for claims adjusters and examiners should be best in the health insurance industry as the number of health insurance customers expands. Additionally, prospects for claims adjusters in property and casualty insurance will likely be best in areas susceptible to natural disasters.

**Major Work Tasks:** For tasks, see the job specializations.

**Usual Educational Requirement:** High school diploma or equivalent. **Relevant Educational Programs**: Health/Medical Claims Examiner Training; Insurance. **Work Experience Needed:** None. **On-the-Job Training Needed:** Long-term on-the-job training. **Certification/ Licensure:** Licensure in some states for some specializations.

**Key Career Cluster:** 06 Finance. **Key Career Pathway:** 6.4 Insurance Services.

### JOB SPECIALIZATION: CLAIMS EXAMINERS, PROPERTY AND CASUALTY INSURANCE

**Review settled insurance claims to determine that payments and settlements have been made in accordance with company practices and procedures. Report overpayments, underpayments, and other irregularities. Confer with legal counsel on claims requiring litigation.**

**Major Work Tasks:** Investigate, evaluate, and settle claims, applying technical knowledge and human relations skills to effect fair and prompt disposal of cases and to contribute to a reduced loss ratio. Pay and process claims within designated authority level. Adjust reserves or provide reserve recommendations to ensure that reserve activities are consistent with corporate policies. Enter claim payments, reserves, and new claims in computer system, inputting concise yet sufficient file documentation. Resolve complex, severe exposure claims, using high service-oriented file handling. Maintain claim files such as records of settled claims and an inventory of claims requiring detailed analysis. Verify and analyze data used in settling claims to ensure that claims are valid and that settlements are made according to company practices and procedures. Examine claims investigated by insurance adjusters, further investigating questionable claims to determine whether to authorize payments. Present cases and participate in their discussion at claim committee meetings. Contact or interview claimants, doctors, medical specialists, or employers to get additional information. Confer with legal counsel on claims requiring litigation. Report overpayments, underpayments, and other irregularities. Communicate with reinsurance brokers to obtain information necessary for processing claims. Supervise claims adjusters to ensure that adjusters have followed proper methods. Conduct detailed bill reviews to implement sound litigation management and expense control. Prepare reports to be submitted to company's data processing department.

**Related Knowledge/Courses:** Customer and Personal Service; Law and Government; Building and Construction; Administration and Management; Clerical Practices; English Language.

**Personality Types:** Conventional–Enterprising.

**Skills:** Negotiation; persuasion; service orientation; reading comprehension; writing; critical thinking; management of financial resources; active listening.

**Physical Environment:** Indoors; sitting; repetitive motions; noise. **Structural Environment:** Importance of being exact or accurate; frequency of decision making; impact of decisions on co-workers or company results; freedom to make decisions; importance of repeating same tasks; time pressure.

## JOB SPECIALIZATION: INSURANCE ADJUSTERS, EXAMINERS, AND INVESTIGATORS

**Investigate, analyze, and determine the extent of insurance company's liability concerning personal, casualty, or property loss or damages and attempt to effect settlement with claimants. Correspond with or interview medical specialists, agents, witnesses, or claimants to compile information. Calculate benefit payments and approve payment of claims within a certain monetary limit.**

**Major Work Tasks:** Examine claims forms and other records to determine insurance coverage. Analyze information gathered by investigation, and report findings and recommendations. Negotiate claim settlements and recommend litigation when settlement cannot be negotiated. Prepare report of findings of investigation. Collect evidence to support contested claims in court. Interview or correspond with agents and claimants to correct errors or omissions and to investigate questionable claims. Refer questionable claims to investigator or claims adjuster for investigation or settlement. Investigate and assess damage to property and create or review property damage estimates. Interview or correspond with claimants, witnesses, police, physicians, or other relevant parties to determine claim settlement, denial, or review. Review police reports, medical treatment records, medical bills, or physical property damage to determine the extent of liability. Examine titles to property to determine validity and act as company agent in transactions with property owners. Obtain credit information from banks and other credit services. Communicate with former associates to verify employment record and to obtain background information regarding persons or businesses applying for credit.

**Related Knowledge/Courses:** Customer and Personal Service; Clerical Practices; Building and Construction; English Language; Law and Government.

**Personality Types:** Conventional–Enterprising.

**Skills:** Management of financial resources; negotiation; mathematics; critical thinking; active listening; speaking; reading comprehension; writing.

**Physical Environment:** Indoors; sitting; repetitive motions. **Structural Environment:** Frequency of decision making; importance of being exact or accurate; time pressure; impact of decisions on co-workers or company results; freedom to make decisions; structured versus unstructured work.

## Clinical, Counseling, and School Psychologists

Diagnose and treat mental disorders; learning disabilities; and cognitive, behavioral, and emotional problems, using individual, child, family, and group therapies.

- Average annual earnings: $67,650
- Middle 50% of earners: $50,480–$87,910
- Earnings growth potential: Medium (43.2%)
- Growth: 21.9%
- Annual job openings: 8,230
- Self-employed: 34.2%

### BEST-PAYING INDUSTRIES

| Industry | Median Earnings | Workforce |
|---|---|---|
| Hospitals | $74,920 | 8,680 |
| Federal, State, and Local Government | $74,720 | 8,620 |
| Educational Services | $68,490 | 48,510 |
| Ambulatory Health-Care Services | $66,770 | 22,140 |
| Social Assistance | $55,270 | 8,130 |

BEST-PAYING METROPOLITAN AREAS

| Metro Area | Median Earnings | Workforce |
|---|---|---|
| New York–Northern New Jersey–Long Island, NY-NJ-PA | $84,650 | 9,050 |
| San Francisco–Oakland–Fremont, CA | $79,290 | 2,570 |
| Boston-Cambridge-Quincy, MA-NH | $77,510 | 2,960 |
| Los Angeles–Long Beach–Santa Ana, CA | $76,560 | 7,190 |
| Philadelphia-Camden-Wilmington, PA-NJ-DE-MD | $74,250 | 2,640 |
| Chicago-Naperville-Joliet, IL-IN-WI | $68,680 | 4,180 |

**Considerations for Job Outlook:** Job prospects should be best for those who have a doctoral degree in an applied specialty and those with a specialist or doctoral degree in school psychology. Because admission to psychology graduate programs is so selective, job opportunities for doctoral graduates are expected to be fair. Employment of school psychologists will grow to accommodate the increasing number of children in schools, and many will also be needed to replace workers who retire. Because of the limited number of graduates in this specialty, school psychologists are expected to have good job opportunities. Candidates with a master's degree will face competition for positions, and many master's degree holders will find jobs in a related field outside of psychology.

**Major Work Tasks:** For tasks, see the job specializations.

**Usual Educational Requirement:** Doctoral or professional degree. **Relevant Educational Programs**: Applied Behavior Analysis; Clinical Child Psychology; Clinical Psychology; Counseling Psychology; Developmental and Child Psychology; Geropsychology; Health/Medical Psychology; Psychoanalysis and Psychotherapy; Psychology, General; School Psychology. **Work Experience Needed:** None. **On-the-Job Training Needed:** Internship/residency. **Certification/Licensure:** Licensure.

**Key Career Cluster:** 05 Education and Training. **Key Career Pathway:** 5.2 Support Services.

JOB SPECIALIZATION: CLINICAL PSYCHOLOGISTS

**Diagnose or evaluate mental and emotional disorders of individuals through observation, interview, and psychological tests and formulate and administer programs of treatment.**

**Major Work Tasks:** Identify psychological, emotional, or behavioral issues and diagnose disorders, using information obtained from interviews, tests, records, and reference materials. Develop and implement individual treatment plans, specifying type, frequency, intensity, and duration of therapy. Interact with clients to assist them in gaining insight, defining goals, and planning action to achieve effective personal, social, educational, and vocational development and adjustment. Discuss the treatment of problems with clients. Use a variety of treatment methods, such as psychotherapy, hypnosis, behavior modification, stress reduction therapy, psychodrama, and play therapy. Counsel individuals and groups regarding problems, such as stress, substance abuse, and family situations, to modify behavior or to improve personal, social, and vocational adjustment. Write reports on clients and maintain required paperwork. Evaluate the effectiveness of counseling or treatments and the accuracy and completeness of diagnoses, modifying plans and diagnoses as necessary. Obtain and study medical, psychological, social, and family histories by interviewing individuals, couples, or families and by reviewing records. Consult reference material, such as textbooks, manuals, and journals, to identify symptoms, make diagnoses, and develop ap-

**187**

proaches to treatment. Maintain current knowledge of relevant research. Observe individuals at play, in group interactions, or in other contexts to detect indications of mental deficiency, abnormal behavior, or maladjustment. Select, administer, score, and interpret psychological tests to obtain information on individuals' intelligence, achievements, interests, and personalities. Refer clients to other specialists, institutions, or support services as necessary. Provide occupational, educational, and other information to individuals so that they can make educational and vocational plans. Consult with or provide consultation to other doctors, therapists, or clinicians regarding patient care. Provide psychological or administrative services and advice to private firms and community agencies regarding mental health programs or individual cases.

**Related Knowledge/Courses:** Therapy and Counseling; Psychology; Philosophy and Theology; Sociology and Anthropology; Personnel and Human Resources; Customer and Personal Service.

**Personality Types:** Investigative–Social–Artistic.

**Skills:** Social perceptiveness; science; service orientation; active listening; persuasion; reading comprehension; speaking; active learning.

**Physical Environment:** Indoors; sitting; exposed to disease or infections. **Structural Environment:** Freedom to make decisions; structured versus unstructured work; frequency of decision making; impact of decisions on co-workers or company results; importance of being exact or accurate; consequence of error.

### JOB SPECIALIZATION: COUNSELING PSYCHOLOGISTS

Assess and evaluate individuals' problems through the use of case history, interview, and observation and provide individual or group counseling services to assist individuals in achieving more effective personal, social, educational, and vocational development and adjustment.

**Major Work Tasks:** Collect information about individuals or clients, using interviews, case histories, observational techniques, and other assessment methods. Develop therapeutic and treatment plans based on clients' interests, abilities, and needs. Analyze data such as interview notes, test results, and reference manuals to identify symptoms and to diagnose the nature of clients' problems. Advise clients on how they could be helped by counseling. Evaluate the results of counseling methods to determine the reliability and validity of treatments. Refer clients to specialists or to other institutions for non-counseling treatment of problems. Select, administer, and interpret psychological tests to assess intelligence, aptitudes, abilities, or interests. Document patient information including session notes, progress notes, recommendations, and treatment plans. Counsel individuals, groups, or families to help them understand problems, deal with crisis situations, define goals, and develop realistic action plans. Supervise interns, clinicians in training, and other counselors. Consult with other professionals, agencies, or universities to discuss therapies, treatments, counseling resources or techniques, and to share occupational information. Provide consulting services, including educational programs, outreach programs, and prevention talks to schools, social service agencies, businesses, and the general public. Conduct research to develop or improve diagnostic or therapeutic counseling techniques.

**Related Knowledge/Courses:** Therapy and Counseling; Psychology; Sociology and Anthropology; Philosophy and Theology; Customer and Personal Service; Clerical.

**Personality Types:** Social–Investigative–Artistic.

**Skills:** Social perceptiveness; science; negotiation; service orientation; operations analysis; active listening; persuasion; reading comprehension.

**Physical Environment:** Indoors; sitting. **Structural Environment:** Freedom to make decisions; structured versus unstructured work; frequency of decision making; impact of decisions on co-workers or company results; time pressure; consequence of error.

### JOB SPECIALIZATION: SCHOOL PSYCHOLOGISTS

**Investigate processes of learning and teaching and develop psychological principles and techniques applicable to educational problems.**

**Major Work Tasks:** Compile and interpret students' test results, along with information from teachers and parents, to diagnose conditions and to help assess eligibility for special services. Report any pertinent information to the proper authorities in cases of child endangerment, neglect, or abuse. Assess an individual child's needs, limitations, and potential, using observation, review of school records, and consultation with parents and school personnel. Select, administer, and score psychological tests. Provide consultation to parents, teachers, administrators, and others on topics such as learning styles and behavior modification techniques. Promote an understanding of child development and its relationship to learning and behavior. Collaborate with other educational professionals to develop teaching strategies and school programs. Counsel children and families to help solve conflicts and problems in learning and adjustment. Develop individualized educational plans in collaboration with teachers and other staff members. Maintain student records, including special education reports, confidential records, records of services provided, and behavioral data. Serve as a resource to help families and schools deal with crises, such as separation and loss. Attend workshops, seminars, or professional meetings to remain informed of new developments in school psychology. Design classes and programs to meet the needs of special students. Refer students and their families to appropriate community agencies for medical, vocational, or social services. Initiate and direct efforts to foster tolerance, understanding, and appreciation of diversity in school communities. Collect and analyze data to evaluate the effectiveness of academic programs and other services, such as behavioral management systems. Provide educational programs on topics such as classroom management, teaching strategies, or parenting skills. Conduct research to generate new knowledge that can be used to address learning and behavior issues. Interpret test results and prepare psychological reports for teachers, administrators, and parents.

**Related Knowledge/Courses:** Therapy and Counseling; Psychology; Sociology and Anthropology; Education and Training; Foreign Language; Mathematics.

**Personality Types:** Investigative–Social.

**Skills:** Social perceptiveness; learning strategies; writing; judgment and decision making; negotiation; active listening; reading comprehension; time management.

**Physical Environment:** Indoors; sitting. **Structural Environment:** Importance of being exact or accurate; impact of decisions on co-workers or company results; frequency of decision making; freedom to make decisions; time pressure; structured versus unstructured work.

## Commercial and Industrial Designers

**Develop and design manufactured products, such as cars, home appliances, and children's toys.**

- Average annual earnings: $59,610
- Middle 50% of earners: $44,430–$76,930
- Earnings growth potential: Medium (41.9%)
- Growth: 10.5%
- Annual job openings: 1,690
- Self-employed: 30.0%

**189**

## Your Guide to High-Paying Careers

| Industry | Median Earnings | Workforce |
|---|---|---|
| Transportation Equipment Manufacturing | $64,470 | 2,430 |
| Professional, Scientific, and Technical Services | $63,580 | 7,570 |
| Miscellaneous Manufacturing | $53,590 | 1,870 |
| Machinery Manufacturing | $53,140 | 1,820 |
| Merchant Wholesalers, Durable Goods | $52,920 | 2,330 |

| Metro Area | Median Earnings | Workforce |
|---|---|---|
| Detroit-Warren-Livonia, MI | $72,330 | 2,310 |
| Boston-Cambridge-Quincy, MA-NH | $67,480 | 680 |
| New York–Northern New Jersey–Long Island, NY-NJ-PA | $67,090 | 1,840 |
| Philadelphia-Camden-Wilmington, PA-NJ-DE-MD | $59,130 | 680 |
| Chicago-Naperville-Joliet, IL-IN-WI | $58,560 | 770 |
| Los Angeles–Long Beach–Santa Ana, CA | $54,300 | 1,640 |
| Dallas–Fort Worth–Arlington, TX | $48,140 | 820 |

**Considerations for Job Outlook:** Prospects are best for job applicants with a strong background in computer-aided design (CAD) and computer-aided industrial design (CAID).

**Major Work Tasks:** Prepare sketches of ideas, detailed drawings, illustrations, artwork, or blueprints, using drafting instruments, paints and brushes, or computer-aided design equipment. Direct and coordinate the fabrication of models or samples and the drafting of working drawings and specification sheets from sketches. Modify and refine designs, using working models, to conform with customer specifications, production limitations, or changes in design trends. Coordinate the look and function of product lines. Confer with engineering, marketing, production, or sales departments, or with customers, to establish and evaluate design concepts for manufactured products. Present designs and reports to customers or design committees for approval, and discuss need for modification. Evaluate feasibility of design ideas, based on factors such as appearance, safety, function, serviceability, budget, production costs/methods, and market characteristics. Research production specifications, costs, production materials, and manufacturing methods and provide cost estimates and itemized production requirements. Design graphic material for use as ornamentation, illustration, or advertising on manufactured materials and packaging or containers. Develop manufacturing procedures and monitor the manufacture of their designs in a factory to improve operations and product quality. Fabricate models or samples in paper, wood, glass, fabric, plastic, metal, or other materials, using hand or power tools. Investigate product characteristics such as the product's safety and handling qualities, its market appeal, how efficiently it can be produced, and ways of distributing, using, and maintaining it. Participate in new product planning or market research, including studying the potential need for new products. Read publications, attend showings, and study competing products and design styles and motifs to obtain perspective and generate design concepts. Supervise assistants' work throughout the design process. Develop industrial standards and regulatory guidelines. Advise corporations on issues involving corporate image projects or problems.

**Usual Educational Requirement:** Bachelor's degree. **Relevant Educational Programs**: Commercial and Advertising Art; Design and Visual Communications, General; Energy Management and Systems Technology/Technician; Industrial and Product Design; Packaging Science. **Related Knowledge/Courses:** Design; Engineering and Technology; Mechanical Devices; Production and Processing; Physics; Fine Arts. **Work Experience Needed:** None. **On-the-Job Training Needed:** None. **Certification/Licensure:** None.

**Personality Types:** Artistic–Enterprising–Realistic. **Key Career Cluster:** 03 Arts, Audiovisual Technology, and Communications. **Key Career Pathway:** 3.3 Visual Arts.

**Skills:** Technology design; operations analysis; systems evaluation; science; mathematics; active learning; systems analysis; quality control analysis.

**Physical Environment:** Indoors; sitting; using hands; noise. **Structural Environment:** Importance of being exact or accurate; freedom to make decisions; impact of decisions on coworkers or company results; frequency of decision making; time pressure; structured versus unstructured work.

## Commercial Pilots

**Pilot and navigate the flight of fixed-wing aircraft on nonscheduled air carrier routes or helicopters.**

- Average annual earnings: $73,280
- Middle 50% of earners: $53,050–$96,810
- Earnings growth potential: High (47.4%)
- Growth: 21.2%
- Annual job openings: 1,930
- Self-employed: 9.0%

**Considerations for Job Outlook:** As older pilots retire and younger pilots advance, entry-level positions may open up. And the demand for flight instructors may increase as they are

**BEST-PAYING INDUSTRIES**

| Industry | Median Earnings | Workforce |
|---|---|---|
| Air Transportation | $74,610 | 14,750 |
| Ambulatory Health-Care Services | $69,810 | 2,700 |
| Educational Services | $68,840 | 4,740 |
| Support Activities for Transportation | $66,840 | 2,860 |

**BEST-PAYING METROPOLITAN AREAS**

| Metro Area | Median Earnings | Workforce |
|---|---|---|
| Dallas–Fort Worth–Arlington, TX | $84,330 | 1,540 |
| New York–Northern New Jersey–Long Island, NY-NJ-PA | $83,360 | 1,140 |
| Houston–Sugar Land–Baytown, TX | $81,970 | 1,910 |
| Los Angeles–Long Beach–Santa Ana, CA | $80,680 | 1,170 |
| Miami–Fort Lauderdale–Pompano Beach, FL | $77,450 | 1,300 |
| Phoenix-Mesa-Scottsdale, AZ | $63,270 | 1,060 |

needed to train a greater number of student pilots. Job prospects should be best with regional airlines, on low-cost carriers, or in general aviation, because these segments are anticipated to grow faster than the major airlines. In addition, entry-level requirements are lower for regional and commercial jobs. However, pilots with less than 500 flight hours will probably need to accumulate hours as flight instructors or commercial pilots before qualifying for regional airline jobs.

**Major Work Tasks:** Check aircraft prior to flights to ensure that the engines, controls, instruments, and other systems are functioning properly. Contact control towers for takeoff clearances, arrival instructions, and other information, using radio equipment. Start engines, operate controls, and pilot airplanes to transport passengers, mail, or freight according to flight plans, regulations, and procedures. Monitor engine operation, fuel consumption, and functioning of aircraft systems during flights. Consider airport altitudes, outside temperatures, plane weights, and wind speeds and directions to calculate the speed needed to become airborne. Order changes in fuel supplies, loads, routes, or schedules to ensure safety of flights. Obtain and review data such as load weights, fuel supplies, weather conditions, and flight schedules to determine flight plans and identify needed changes. Plan flights according to government and company regulations, using aeronautical charts and navigation instruments. Use instrumentation to pilot aircraft when visibility is poor. Check baggage or cargo to ensure that it has been loaded correctly. Request changes in altitudes or routes as circumstances dictate. Choose routes, altitudes, and speeds that will provide the fastest, safest, and smoothest flights. Coordinate flight activities with ground crews and air traffic control, and inform crew members of flight and test procedures. Write specified information in flight records, such as flight times, altitudes flown, and fuel consumption. Teach company regulations and procedures to other pilots. Instruct other pilots and student pilots in aircraft operations. Co-pilot aircraft or perform captain's duties if required. File instrument flight plans with air traffic control so that flights can be coordinated with other air traffic. Conduct in-flight tests and evaluations at specified altitudes and in all types of weather to determine the receptivity and other characteristics of equipment and systems. Rescue and evacuate injured persons. Supervise other crew members. Perform minor aircraft maintenance and repair work, or arrange for major maintenance.

**Usual Educational Requirement:** Postsecondary vocational training. **Relevant Educational Programs**: Airline/Commercial/Professional Pilot and Flight Crew Training; Flight Instructor Training. **Related Knowledge/Courses:** Transportation; Geography; Mechanical Devices; Physics; Telecommunications; Psychology. **Work Experience Needed:** None. **On-the-Job Training Needed:** None. **Certification/Licensure:** Licensure.

**Personality Types:** Realistic–Investigative–Enterprising. **Key Career Cluster:** 16 Transportation, Distribution, and Logistics. **Key Career Pathway:** 16.1 Transportation Operations.

**Skills:** Operation and control; operation monitoring; science; instructing; troubleshooting; operations analysis; judgment and decision making; management of personnel resources.

**Physical Environment:** Outdoors; sitting; using hands; noise; very hot or cold; contaminants. **Structural Environment:** Freedom to make decisions; frequency of decision making; impact of decisions on co-workers or company results; importance of being exact or accurate; time pressure; structured versus unstructured work.

## Communications Teachers, Postsecondary

*See Teachers, Postsecondary.*

## Compensation and Benefits Managers

**Plan, direct, or coordinate compensation and benefits activities of an organization.**

- Average annual earnings: $95,250
- Middle 50% of earners: $71,000–$130,200
- Earnings growth potential: Medium (43.2%)
- Growth: 2.8%
- Annual job openings: 870
- Self-employed: 2.7%

## BEST-PAYING INDUSTRIES

| Industry | Median Earnings | Workforce |
|---|---|---|
| Insurance Carriers and Related Activities | $107,390 | 1,280 |
| Management of Companies and Enterprises | $105,160 | 4,000 |
| Professional, Scientific, and Technical Services | $99,520 | 2,230 |
| Credit Intermediation and Related Activities | $98,390 | 1,140 |
| Federal, State, and Local Government | $84,940 | 1,790 |

## BEST-PAYING METROPOLITAN AREAS

| Metro Area | Median Earnings | Workforce |
|---|---|---|
| New York–Northern New Jersey–Long Island, NY-NJ-PA | $131,010 | 1,890 |
| San Francisco–Oakland–Fremont, CA | $116,940 | 430 |
| Philadelphia-Camden-Wilmington, PA-NJ-DE-MD | $115,760 | 580 |
| Boston-Cambridge-Quincy, MA-NH | $112,110 | 950 |
| Los Angeles–Long Beach–Santa Ana, CA | $109,780 | 850 |
| Minneapolis–St. Paul–Bloomington, MN-WI | $103,610 | 590 |
| Washington-Arlington-Alexandria, DC-VA-MD-WV | $100,030 | 590 |
| Chicago-Naperville-Joliet, IL-IN-WI | $79,380 | 1,000 |

**Considerations for Job Outlook:** Candidates are expected to face competition for jobs. Those who have a master's degree, certification, or experience working with compensation or benefits plans should have the best job prospects.

**Major Work Tasks:** Direct preparation and distribution of written and verbal information to inform employees of benefits, compensation, and personnel policies. Administer, direct, and review employee benefit programs, including the integration of benefit programs following mergers and acquisitions. Plan, direct, supervise, and coordinate work activities of subordinates and staff relating to employment, compensation, labor relations, and employee relations. Identify and implement benefits to increase the quality of life for employees, by working with brokers and researching benefits issues. Design, evaluate, and modify benefits policies to ensure that programs are current, competitive, and in compliance with legal requirements. Analyze compensation policies, government regulations, and prevailing wage rates to develop competitive compensation plan. Formulate policies, procedures, and programs for recruitment, testing, placement, classification, orientation, benefits and compensation, and labor and industrial relations. Mediate between benefits providers and employees, such as by assisting in handling employees' benefits-related questions or taking suggestions. Fulfill all reporting requirements of all relevant government rules and regulations, including the Employee Retirement Income Security Act (ERISA). Maintain records and compile statistical reports concerning personnel-related data such as hires, transfers, performance appraisals, and absenteeism rates. Develop methods to improve employment policies, processes, and practices, and recommend changes to management. Prepare detailed job descriptions and classification systems and define job levels and families, in partnership with other managers. Manage the design and development of tools to assist employees in benefits selection and to guide managers through compensation decisions. Prepare budgets for personnel operations. Study legislation, arbitration decisions, and collective bargaining contracts to assess industry trends. Advise management on such matters as equal employment opportunity, sexual harassment and discrimination. Plan and conduct new employee orientations to foster positive attitude toward organizational objectives.

**Usual Educational Requirement:** Bachelor's degree. **Relevant Educational Program**: Human Resources Management/Personnel Administration, General. **Related Knowledge/ Courses:** Personnel and Human Resources; Economics and Accounting; Administration and Management; Mathematics; Law and Government; Communications and Media. **Work Experience Needed:** 1 to 5 years. **On-the-Job Training Needed:** None. **Certification/Licensure:** Voluntary certification by association.

**Personality Types:** Enterprising–Conventional–Social. **Key Career Cluster:** 04 Business, Management, and Administration. **Key Career Pathway:** 4.3 Human Resources.

**Skills:** Management of financial resources; operations analysis; systems evaluation; systems analysis; management of personnel resources; time management; negotiation; management of material resources.

**Physical Environment:** Indoors; sitting. **Structural Environment:** structured versus unstructured work; freedom to make decisions; importance of being exact or accurate; time pressure; frequency of decision making; impact of decisions on co-workers or company results.

## Compensation, Benefits, and Job Analysis Specialists

**Conduct programs of compensation and benefits and job analysis for employer.**

- Average annual earnings: $59,090
- Middle 50% of earners: $46,030–$74,040
- Earnings growth potential: Medium (36.4%)
- Growth: 5.0%
- Annual job openings: 2,400
- Self-employed: 2.2%

**Considerations for Job Outlook:** In most industries, a small decrease is expected as compensation and benefits work is outsourced overseas and to the employment services industry; however, this should cause a moderate increase in the employment services industry.

**Major Work Tasks:** Evaluate job positions, determining classification, exempt or non-exempt status, and salary. Ensure company compliance with federal and state laws, including reporting requirements. Advise managers and employees on state and federal employment regulations, collective agreements, benefit and compensation policies, personnel procedures, and classification programs. Plan, develop, evaluate, improve, and communicate methods and techniques for selecting, promoting, compensating, evaluating, and training workers. Provide advice on the resolution of classification and salary complaints. Prepare occupational classifications, job descriptions, and salary scales. Assist in preparing and maintaining personnel records and handbooks. Prepare reports, such as organization and flow charts, and career path reports, to summarize job analysis and evaluation and compensation analysis information. Perform multifactor data and cost analyses that may be used in areas such as support of collective bargaining agreements. Assess need for and develop job analysis instruments and materials. Research job and worker requirements, structural, and functional relationships among jobs and occupations and occupational trends. Observe, interview, and survey employees and conduct focus group meetings to collect job, organiza-

## BEST-PAYING INDUSTRIES

| Industry | Median Earnings | Workforce |
|---|---|---|
| Professional, Scientific, and Technical Services | $63,620 | 10,840 |
| Management of Companies and Enterprises | $60,000 | 10,400 |
| Federal, State, and Local Government | $59,080 | 14,080 |
| Insurance Carriers and Related Activities | $58,610 | 7,500 |
| Educational Services | $54,390 | 5,090 |

## BEST-PAYING METROPOLITAN AREAS

| Metro Area | Median Earnings | Workforce |
|---|---|---|
| Boston-Cambridge-Quincy, MA-NH | $71,500 | 3,090 |
| Washington-Arlington-Alexandria, DC-VA-MD-WV | $69,740 | 2,600 |
| San Francisco–Oakland–Fremont, CA | $68,410 | 2,390 |
| New York–Northern New Jersey–Long Island, NY-NJ-PA | $68,040 | 9,960 |
| Minneapolis–St. Paul–Bloomington, MN-WI | $64,000 | 1,780 |
| Philadelphia-Camden-Wilmington, PA-NJ-DE-MD | $63,640 | 2,040 |
| Los Angeles–Long Beach–Santa Ana, CA | $62,710 | 4,510 |
| Dallas–Fort Worth–Arlington, TX | $60,930 | 2,520 |
| Sacramento–Arden-Arcade–Roseville, CA | $59,080 | 2,180 |
| Chicago-Naperville-Joliet, IL-IN-WI | $58,630 | 1,910 |

tional, and occupational information. Administer employee insurance, pension, and savings plans and working with insurance brokers and plan carriers. Negotiate collective agreements on behalf of employers or workers, and mediate labor disputes and grievances. Develop, implement, administer, and evaluate personnel and labor relations programs, including performance appraisal, affirmative action, and employment equity programs. Research employee benefit and health and safety practices and recommend changes or modifications to existing policies. Analyze organizational, occupational, and industrial data to facilitate organizational functions and provide technical information to business, industry, and government. Advise staff of individuals' qualifications.

**Usual Educational Requirement:** Bachelor's degree. **Relevant Educational Program**: Human Resources Management/Personnel Administration, General. **Related Knowledge/Courses:** Personnel and Human Resources; Economics and Accounting; Law and Government; Administration and Management; Mathematics; English Language. **Work Experience Needed:** None. **On-the-Job Training Needed:** None. **Certification/Licensure:** None.

**Personality Types:** Conventional–Enterprising. **Key Career Cluster:** 04 Business, Management, and Administration. **Key Career Pathway:** 4.3 Human Resources.

**Skills:** Operations analysis; science; systems analysis; mathematics; programming; systems evaluation; management of financial resources; speaking.

**Physical Environment:** Indoors; sitting. **Structural Environment:** Structured versus unstructured work; freedom to make decisions; frequency of decision making; importance of being exact or accurate; impact of decisions on co-workers or company results; time pressure.

195

## Compliance Officers

Examine, evaluate, and investigate eligibility for or conformity with laws and regulations governing contract compliance of licenses and permits.

### BEST-PAYING INDUSTRIES

| Industry | Median Earnings | Workforce |
|---|---|---|
| Professional, Scientific, and Technical Services | $66,790 | 15,970 |
| Management of Companies and Enterprises | $66,000 | 13,300 |
| Federal, State, and Local Government | $59,960 | 112,350 |

### BEST-PAYING METROPOLITAN AREAS

| Metro Area | Median Earnings | Workforce |
|---|---|---|
| San Francisco–Oakland–Fremont, CA | $84,160 | 4,570 |
| Washington-Arlington-Alexandria, DC-VA-MD-WV | $77,360 | 8,060 |
| New York–Northern New Jersey–Long Island, NY-NJ-PA | $76,790 | 16,000 |
| Houston–Sugar Land–Baytown, TX | $72,710 | 4,770 |
| Los Angeles–Long Beach–Santa Ana, CA | $72,220 | 10,390 |
| Philadelphia-Camden-Wilmington, PA-NJ-DE-MD | $69,640 | 4,880 |
| Miami–Fort Lauderdale–Pompano Beach, FL | $69,180 | 5,190 |
| Dallas–Fort Worth–Arlington, TX | $61,260 | 5,540 |

- Average annual earnings: $62,020
- Middle 50% of earners: $46,280–$79,200
- Earnings growth potential: Medium (42.4%)
- Growth: 15.0%
- Annual job openings: 5,860
- Self-employed: 0.0%

**Considerations for Job Outlook:** Much-faster-than-average employment growth is projected.

**Major Work Tasks:** For tasks, see the job specializations.

**Usual Educational Requirement:** Bachelor's degree. **Relevant Educational Program**: Business Administration and Management, General. **Work Experience Needed:** None. **On-the-Job Training Needed:** Moderate-term on-the-job training. **Certification/Licensure:** Licensure for some specializations.

**Key Career Cluster:** 07 Government and Public Administration. **Key Career Pathway:** 7.6 Regulation.

### JOB SPECIALIZATION: CORONERS

**Direct activities such as autopsies, pathological and toxicological analyses, and inquests relating to the investigation of deaths occurring within a legal jurisdiction to determine cause of death or to fix responsibility for accidental, violent, or unexplained deaths.**

**Major Work Tasks:** Perform medicolegal examinations and autopsies, conducting preliminary examinations of the body to identify victims, locate signs of trauma, and identify factors that would indicate time of death. Inquire into the cause, manner, and circumstances of human deaths and establish the identities of deceased persons. Complete death certificates, including the assignment of cause and manner of death. Observe and record the positions and conditions of bodies and related evidence. Collect and document any pertinent medical history information. Observe, record, and preserve any objects or personal property

**196**

related to deaths, including objects such as medication containers and suicide notes. Complete reports and forms required to finalize cases. Remove or supervise removal of bodies from death scenes, using the proper equipment and supplies, and arrange for transportation to morgues. Interview persons present at death scenes to obtain information useful in determining the manner of death. Testify at inquests, hearings, and court trials. Provide information concerning the circumstances of death to relatives of the deceased. Locate and document information regarding the next of kin, including their relationship to the deceased and the status of notification attempts. Confer with officials of public health and law enforcement agencies to coordinate interdepartmental activities. Inventory personal effects recovered from bodies, such as jewelry or wallets. Coordinate the release of personal effects to authorized persons and facilitate the disposition of unclaimed corpses and personal effects. Arrange for the next of kin to be notified of deaths. Collect wills, burial instructions, and other documentation needed for investigations and for handling of the remains. Direct activities of workers conducting autopsies, performing pathological and toxicological analyses, and preparing documents for permanent records. Record the disposition of minor children, as well as details of arrangements made for their care. Witness and certify deaths that are the result of a judicial order.

**Related Knowledge/Courses:** Medicine and Dentistry; Biology; Law and Government; Therapy and Counseling; Psychology; Philosophy and Theology.

**Personality Types:** Investigative–Realistic–Conventional.

**Skills:** Science; social perceptiveness; speaking; writing; active listening; management of personnel resources; active learning; learning strategies.

**Physical Environment:** Indoors; outdoors; standing; very hot or cold; contaminants; exposed to disease or infections. **Structural Environment:** Importance of being exact or accurate; freedom to make decisions; impact of decisions on co-workers or company results; structured versus unstructured work; frequency of decision making; time pressure.

## JOB SPECIALIZATION: ENVIRONMENTAL COMPLIANCE INSPECTORS

**Inspect and investigate sources of pollution to protect the public and environment and ensure conformance with federal, state, and local regulations and ordinances.**

**Major Work Tasks:** Determine the nature of code violations and actions to be taken. Issue written notices of violation; participate in enforcement hearings as necessary. Examine permits, licenses, applications, and records to ensure compliance with licensing requirements. Prepare, organize, and maintain inspection records. Interview individuals to determine the nature of suspected violations and to obtain evidence of violations. Prepare written, oral, tabular, and graphic reports summarizing requirements and regulations, including enforcement and chain of custody documentation. Monitor follow-up actions in cases where violations were found, and review compliance monitoring reports. Investigate complaints and suspected violations regarding illegal dumping, pollution, pesticides, product quality, or labeling laws. Inspect waste pretreatment, treatment, and disposal facilities and systems for conformance to federal, state, or local regulations. Inform individuals and groups of pollution control regulations and inspection findings, and explain how problems can be corrected. Determine sampling locations and methods, and collect water or wastewater samples for analysis, preserving samples with appropriate containers and preservation methods. Verify that hazardous chemicals are handled, stored, and disposed of in accordance with regulations. Research and keep informed of pertinent information and developments in areas such as EPA laws and regulations. Determine which sites and violation reports to investigate, and coordinate compliance and enforcement activities with other government agencies. Observe and record field conditions, gathering, interpreting, and reporting data such as flow meter readings and chemical levels. Learn and observe proper safety precautions, rules, regulations, and practices so that unsafe conditions can be recognized and proper safety protocols implemented. Evaluate label information for accuracy and conformance to regulatory requirements. Inform health professionals, property owners, and the public about harmful properties and related problems of water pollution and contaminated wastewater.

**Related Knowledge/Courses:** Biology; Law and Government; Chemistry; Geography; Physics; Engineering and Technology.

**Personality Types:** Conventional–Investigative–Realistic.

**Skills:** Quality control analysis; science; programming; troubleshooting; reading comprehension; mathematics; writing; active learning.

**Physical Environment:** Indoors; outdoors; sitting; contaminants. **Structural Environment:** Freedom to make decisions; structured versus unstructured work; impact of decisions on co-workers or company results; importance of being exact or accurate; frequency of decision making; time pressure.

## JOB SPECIALIZATION: EQUAL OPPORTUNITY REPRESENTATIVES AND OFFICERS

**Monitor and evaluate compliance with equal opportunity laws, guidelines, and policies to ensure that employment practices and contracting arrangements give equal opportunity without regard to race, religion, color, national origin, sex, age, or disability.**

**Major Work Tasks:** Investigate employment practices or alleged violations of laws to document and correct discriminatory factors. Interpret civil rights laws and equal opportunity regulations for individuals or employers. Study equal opportunity complaints to clarify issues. Meet with persons involved in equal opportunity complaints in order to verify case information and to arbitrate and settle disputes. Coordinate, monitor, or revise complaint procedures to ensure timely processing and review of complaints. Prepare reports of selection, survey, or other statistics and recommendations for corrective action. Conduct surveys and evaluate findings to determine if systematic discrimination exists. Develop guidelines for non-discriminatory employment practices, and monitor their implementation and impact. Review company contracts to determine actions required to meet governmental equal opportunity provisions. Counsel newly hired members of minority or disadvantaged groups, informing them about details of civil rights laws. Provide information, technical assistance, or training to supervisors, managers, or employees on topics such as employee supervision, hiring, grievance procedures, or staff development. Verify that all job descriptions are submitted for review and approval and that descriptions meet regulatory standards. Act as liaisons between minority placement agencies and employers or between job search committees and other equal opportunity administrators. Consult with community representatives to develop technical assistance agreements in accordance with governmental regulations. Meet with job search committees or coordinators to explain the role of the equal opportunity coordinator, to provide resources for advertising, or to explain expectations for future contacts. Participate in the recruitment of employees through job fairs, career days, or advertising plans.

**Related Knowledge/Courses:** Law and Government; Personnel and Human Resources;

Clerical Practices; English Language; Customer and Personal Service.

**Personality Types:** Social–Enterprising–Conventional.

**Skills:** Persuasion; reading comprehension; active listening; programming; active learning; negotiation; writing; speaking.

**Physical Environment:** Indoors; sitting; repetitive motions. **Structural Environment:** Frequency of decision making; importance of being exact or accurate; impact of decisions on co-workers or company results; freedom to make decisions; time pressure; structured versus unstructured work.

### JOB SPECIALIZATION: GOVERNMENT PROPERTY INSPECTORS AND INVESTIGATORS

**Investigate or inspect government property to ensure compliance with contract agreements and government regulations.**

**Major Work Tasks:** Prepare correspondence, reports of inspections or investigations or recommendations for action. Examine records, reports, or other documents to establish facts or detect discrepancies. Monitor investigations of suspected offenders to ensure that they are conducted in accordance with constitutional requirements. Collect, identify, evaluate, or preserve case evidence. Inspect manufactured or processed products to ensure compliance with contract specifications or legal requirements. Coordinate with or assist law enforcement agencies in matters of mutual concern. Testify in court or at administrative proceedings concerning investigation findings. Investigate applications for special licenses or permits, as well as alleged license or permit violations. Inspect government-owned equipment or materials in the possession of private contractors to ensure compliance with contracts or regulations or to prevent misuse. Recommend legal or administrative action to protect government property. Submit samples of products to government laboratories for testing, as required. Locate and interview plaintiffs, witnesses, or

representatives of business or government to gather facts relevant to inspections or alleged violations.

**Related Knowledge/Courses:** Building and Construction; Public Safety and Security; Mechanical Devices; Engineering and Technology; Transportation; Computers and Electronics.

**Personality Types:** Conventional–Enterprising–Realistic.

**Skills:** Quality control analysis; programming; persuasion; operation and control; writing; speaking; systems evaluation; operation monitoring.

**Physical Environment:** Outdoors; indoors; sitting; noise; very hot or cold; contaminants. **Structural Environment:** Freedom to make decisions; impact of decisions on co-workers or company results; importance of being exact or accurate; frequency of decision making; structured versus unstructured work; time pressure.

### JOB SPECIALIZATION: LICENSING EXAMINERS AND INSPECTORS

**Examine, evaluate, and investigate eligibility for, conformity with, or liability under licenses or permits.**

**Major Work Tasks:** Issue licenses to individuals meeting standards. Evaluate applications, records, or documents to gather information about eligibility or liability issues. Administer oral, written, road, or flight tests to license applicants. Score tests and observe equipment operation and control to rate ability of applicants. Advise licensees or other individuals or groups concerning licensing, permit, or passport regulations. Warn violators of infractions or penalties. Prepare reports of activities, evaluations, recommendations, or decisions. Prepare correspondence to inform concerned parties of licensing decisions or appeals processes. Confer with or interview officials, technical or professional specialists, or applicants to obtain information or to clarify facts relevant to licensing decisions. Report law or regulation violations to appropriate boards or agencies. Visit establishments to verify that valid licenses or permits are displayed and that licensing standards are being upheld.

**Related Knowledge/Courses:** Clerical Practices; Customer and Personal Service; Law and Government; Foreign Language; Psychology; Public Safety and Security.

**Personality Types:** Conventional–Enterprising.

**Skills:** Quality control analysis; judgment and decision making; social perceptiveness; speaking; operation monitoring; service orientation; systems evaluation; negotiation.

**Physical Environment:** Indoors; outdoors; sitting; using hands; repetitive motions; contaminants. **Structural Environment:** Frequency of decision making; importance of being exact or accurate; importance of repeating same tasks; impact of decisions on co-workers or company results; time pressure; freedom to make decisions.

## JOB SPECIALIZATION: REGULATORY AFFAIRS SPECIALISTS

**Coordinate and document internal regulatory processes, such as internal audits, inspections, license renewals, or registrations. May compile and prepare materials for submission to regulatory agencies.**

**Major Work Tasks:** Communicate with regulatory agencies regarding pre-submission strategies, potential regulatory pathways, compliance test requirements, or clarification and follow-up of submissions under review. Escort government inspectors during inspections and provide post-inspection follow-up information as requested. Analyze product complaints and make recommendations regarding their reportability. Coordinate, prepare, or review regulatory submissions for domestic or international projects. Interpret regulatory rules or rule changes and ensure that they are communicated through corporate policies and procedures. Provide technical review of data or reports that will be incorporated into regulatory submissions to assure scientific rigor, accuracy, and clarity of presentation. Review product promotional materials, labeling, batch records, specification sheets, or test methods for compliance with applicable regulations and policies. Advise project teams on subjects such as premarket regulatory requirements, export and labeling requirements, or clinical study compliance issues. Compile and maintain regulatory documentation databases or systems. Coordinate efforts associated with the preparation of regulatory documents or submissions. Determine the types of regulatory submissions or internal documentation that are required in situations such as proposed device changes or labeling changes. Develop or conduct employee regulatory training. Identify relevant guidance documents, international standards, or consensus standards and provide interpretive assistance. Maintain current knowledge base of existing and emerging regulations, standards, or guidance documents. Obtain and distribute updated information regarding domestic or international laws, guidelines, or standards. Participate in internal or external audits. Prepare or direct the preparation of additional information or responses as requested by regulatory agencies. Prepare or maintain technical files as necessary to obtain and sustain product approval. Recommend changes to company procedures in response to changes in regulations or standards.

**Related Knowledge/Courses:** Law and Government; Biology; Medicine and Dentistry; Clerical Practices; English Language; Chemistry.

**Personality Types:** Conventional–Enterprising.

**Skills:** Systems analysis; systems evaluation; judgment and decision making; persuasion; writing; speaking; coordination; reading comprehension.

**Physical Environment:** Indoors; sitting. **Structural Environment:** Importance of being exact or accurate; structured versus unstructured work; freedom to make decisions; impact of decisions on co-workers or company results; time pressure; importance of repeating same tasks.

## Computer and Information Research Scientists

**Conduct research into fundamental computer and information science as theorists, designers, or inventors.**

- Average annual earnings: $102,190
- Middle 50% of earners: $79,260–$122,960
- Earnings growth potential: High (44.0%)
- Growth: 18.7%
- Annual job openings: 1,060
- Self-employed: 6.0%

**Considerations for Job Outlook:** Computer and information research scientists are likely to enjoy excellent job prospects. There are a limited number of PhD graduates each year. As a result, many companies report difficulties finding a sufficient supply of these highly skilled workers.

**Major Work Tasks:** Analyze problems to develop solutions involving computer hardware and software. Assign or schedule tasks to meet work priorities and goals. Evaluate project plans and proposals to assess feasibility issues. Apply theoretical expertise and innovation to create or apply new technology, such as adapting principles for applying computers to new uses. Consult with users, management, vendors, and technicians to determine computing needs and system requirements. Meet with managers, vendors, and others to solicit cooperation and resolve problems. Conduct logical analyses of business, scientific, engineering, and other technical problems, formulating mathematical models of problems for solution by computers. Develop and interpret organizational goals, policies, and procedures. Par-

**BEST-PAYING INDUSTRIES**

| Industry | Median Earnings | Workforce |
|---|---|---|
| Publishing Industries (except Internet) | $109,520 | 2,230 |
| Professional, Scientific, and Technical Services | $104,090 | 9,340 |
| Federal, State, and Local Government | $101,420 | 6,560 |
| Educational Services | $91,320 | 2,780 |

**BEST-PAYING METROPOLITAN AREAS**

| Metro Area | Median Earnings | Workforce |
|---|---|---|
| San Francisco–Oakland–Fremont, CA | $120,670 | 1,070 |
| Washington-Arlington-Alexandria, DC-VA-MD-WV | $115,960 | 2,740 |
| San Jose–Sunnyvale–Santa Clara, CA | $114,510 | 1,860 |
| Boston-Cambridge-Quincy, MA-NH | $113,550 | 970 |
| Los Angeles–Long Beach–Santa Ana, CA | $111,010 | 1,460 |
| Chicago-Naperville-Joliet, IL-IN-WI | $104,810 | 670 |
| San Diego–Carlsbad–San Marcos, CA | $100,630 | 930 |
| Baltimore-Towson, MD | $99,620 | 1,520 |
| Dallas–Fort Worth–Arlington, TX | $49,440 | 610 |

ticipate in staffing decisions and direct training of subordinates. Develop performance standards, and evaluate work in light of established standards. Design computers and the software that runs them. Maintain network hardware and software, direct network security measures, and monitor networks to ensure availability to system users. Participate in multidisciplinary projects in areas such as virtual reality, human-computer interaction, or robotics. Approve, prepare, monitor, and adjust operational budgets. Direct daily operations of departments, coordinating project activities with other departments.

**Usual Educational Requirement:** Doctoral or professional degree. **Relevant Educational Programs**: Artificial Intelligence; Bioinformatics; Computer and Information Sciences, Other; Computer and Information Sciences, General; Computer Science; Informatics; Information Science/Studies; Information Technology; Medical Informatics; Modeling, Virtual Environments and Simulation. **Related Knowledge/Courses:** Computers and Electronics; Telecommunications; Engineering and Technology; Mathematics; Design; Education and Training. **Work Experience Needed:** None. **On-the-Job Training Needed:** None. **Certification/Licensure:** None.

**Personality Types:** Investigative–Realistic–Conventional. **Key Career Cluster:** 15 Science, Technology, Engineering, and Mathematics. **Key Career Pathway:** 15.2 Science and Mathematics.

**Skills:** Programming; technology design; systems evaluation; management of financial resources; operations analysis; mathematics; systems analysis; science.

**Physical Environment:** Indoors; sitting; using hands; repetitive motions. **Structural Environment:** Structured versus unstructured work; freedom to make decisions; impact of decisions on co-workers or company results; importance of being exact or accurate; importance of repeating same tasks; time pressure.

## Computer and Information Systems Managers

**Plan, direct, or coordinate activities in such fields as electronic data processing, information systems, systems analysis, and computer programming.**

### BEST-PAYING INDUSTRIES

| Industry | Median Earnings | Workforce |
|---|---|---|
| Professional, Scientific, and Technical Services | $128,130 | 90,380 |
| Management of Companies and Enterprises | $124,260 | 29,860 |
| Insurance Carriers and Related Activities | $119,220 | 15,830 |
| Federal, State, and Local Government | $101,360 | 21,410 |

### BEST-PAYING METROPOLITAN AREAS

| Metro Area | Median Earnings | Workforce |
|---|---|---|
| San Jose–Sunnyvale–Santa Clara, CA | $169,770 | 9,320 |
| San Francisco–Oakland–Fremont, CA | $152,060 | 9,190 |
| New York–Northern New Jersey–Long Island, NY-NJ-PA | $143,800 | 31,130 |
| Washington-Arlington-Alexandria, DC-VA-MD-WV | $141,010 | 19,390 |
| Seattle-Tacoma-Bellevue, WA | $136,820 | 8,260 |
| Boston-Cambridge-Quincy, MA-NH | $133,890 | 14,740 |
| Los Angeles–Long Beach–Santa Ana, CA | $133,180 | 13,290 |
| Dallas–Fort Worth–Arlington, TX | $124,920 | 7,530 |
| Atlanta–Sandy Springs–Marietta, GA | $120,320 | 8,330 |
| Minneapolis–St. Paul–Bloomington, MN-WI | $115,630 | 8,020 |
| Chicago-Naperville-Joliet, IL-IN-WI | $114,990 | 11,050 |

- Average annual earnings: $120,950
- Middle 50% of earners: $94,740–$152,380
- Earnings growth potential: Medium (38.0%)
- Growth: 18.1%
- Annual job openings: 10,280
- Self-employed: 2.7%

**Considerations for Job Outlook:** Prospects should be favorable for this occupation. Many companies note that it is difficult to find qualified applicants for positions. Because innovation is fast paced in IT, opportunities should be best for those who have knowledge of the newest technology.

**Major Work Tasks:** Manage back-up, security, and user help systems. Consult with users, management, vendors, and technicians to assess computing needs and system requirements. Direct daily operations of department, analyzing workflow, establishing priorities, developing standards, and setting deadlines. Assign and review the work of systems analysts, programmers, and other computer-related workers. Stay abreast of advances in technology. Develop computer information resources, providing for data security and control, strategic computing, and disaster recovery. Review and approve all systems charts and programs prior to their implementation. Evaluate the organization's technology use and needs and recommend improvements, such as hardware and software upgrades. Control operational budget and expenditures. Meet with department heads, managers, supervisors, vendors, and others to solicit cooperation and resolve problems. Develop and interpret organizational goals, policies, and procedures. Recruit, hire, train, and supervise staff, or participate in staffing decisions. Review project plans to plan and coordinate project activity. Evaluate data processing proposals to assess project feasibility and requirements. Prepare and review operational reports or project progress reports. Purchase necessary equip-

ment. Provide users with technical support for computer problems.

**Usual Educational Requirement:** Bachelor's degree. **Relevant Educational Programs:** Computer and Information Sciences, General; Computer and Information Systems Security/Information Assurance; Computer Science; Information Resources Management/CIO Training; Information Science/Studies; Information Technology; Information Technology Project Management; Knowledge Management; Management Information Systems, General; Network and System Administration/Administrator; Operations Management and Supervision. **Related Knowledge/Courses:** Telecommunications; Computers and Electronics; Economics and Accounting; Production and Processing; Personnel and Human Resources; Administration and Management. **Work Experience Needed:** More than 5 years. **On-the-Job Training Needed:** None. **Certification/Licensure:** None.

**Personality Types:** Enterprising–Conventional–Investigative. **Key Career Cluster:** 11 Information Technology. **Key Career Pathway:** 11.4 Programming and Software Development.

**Skills:** Management of financial resources; management of material resources; programming; equipment selection; systems evaluation; troubleshooting; repairing; operations analysis.

**Physical Environment:** Indoors; sitting; using hands. **Structural Environment:** Structured versus unstructured work; freedom to make decisions; impact of decisions on co-workers or company results; importance of being exact or accurate; frequency of decision making; time pressure.

## Computer Hardware Engineers

**Research, design, develop, or test computer or computer-related equipment for commercial, industrial, military, or scientific use.**

- Average annual earnings: $100,920
- Middle 50% of earners: $79,600–$125,730
- Earnings growth potential: Medium (36.6%)

## Your Guide to High-Paying Careers

- Growth: 9.0%
- Annual job openings: 2,290
- Self-employed: 1.3%

### BEST-PAYING INDUSTRIES

| Industry | Median Earnings | Workforce |
|---|---|---|
| Federal, State, and Local Government | $103,640 | 4,630 |
| Computer and Electronic Product Manufacturing | $103,560 | 31,280 |
| Professional, Scientific, and Technical Services | $98,810 | 31,540 |

### BEST-PAYING METROPOLITAN AREAS

| Metro Area | Median Earnings | Workforce |
|---|---|---|
| San Jose–Sunnyvale–Santa Clara, CA | $129,640 | 8,840 |
| San Francisco–Oakland–Fremont, CA | $119,400 | 3,030 |
| Los Angeles–Long Beach–Santa Ana, CA | $109,830 | 4,320 |
| Boston-Cambridge-Quincy, MA-NH | $109,200 | 3,690 |
| Washington-Arlington-Alexandria, DC-VA-MD-WV | $106,680 | 5,560 |
| Baltimore-Towson, MD | $105,210 | 1,680 |
| Dallas–Fort Worth–Arlington, TX | $98,990 | 3,940 |
| Austin–Round Rock, TX | $93,050 | 2,860 |
| Phoenix-Mesa-Scottsdale, AZ | $91,890 | 2,480 |
| San Diego–Carlsbad–San Marcos, CA | $88,280 | 3,640 |
| Chicago-Naperville-Joliet, IL-IN-WI | $81,750 | 1,670 |

**Considerations for Job Outlook:** Job applicants with a computer engineering degree from an ABET-accredited program will have better chances of finding a job. Engineers who have a higher-level degree and knowledge or experience with computer software will have the best job prospects.

**Major Work Tasks:** Update knowledge and skills to keep up with rapid advancements in computer technology. Provide technical support to designers, marketing and sales departments, suppliers, engineers, and other team members throughout the product development and implementation process. Test and verify hardware and support peripherals to ensure that they meet specifications and requirements, by recording and analyzing test data. Monitor functioning of equipment and make necessary modifications to ensure system operates in conformance with specifications. Analyze information to determine, recommend, and plan layout, including type of computers and peripheral equipment modifications. Build, test, and modify product prototypes using working models or theoretical models constructed with computer simulation. Analyze user needs and recommend appropriate hardware. Direct technicians, engineering designers, or other technical support personnel as needed. Confer with engineering staff and consult specifications to evaluate interface between hardware and software and operational and performance requirements of overall system. Select hardware and material, assuring compliance with specifications and product requirements. Store, retrieve, and manipulate data for analysis of system capabilities and requirements. Write detailed functional specifications that document the hardware development process and support hardware introduction. Specify power supply requirements and configuration, drawing on system performance expectations and design specifications. Assemble and modify existing pieces of equipment to meet special needs. Evaluate factors, such as reporting formats required, cost constraints, and need for security restrictions to determine hardware configuration. Design and develop computer hardware and support peripherals, including central processing units (CPUs), support logic, microprocessors, custom integrated circuits, and printers and disk drives. Provide training and support to system designers and users. Recommend purchase of equipment to control dust, temperature, and humidity in area of system installation.

**Usual Educational Requirement:** Bachelor's degree. **Relevant Educational Programs**: Computer Engineering, General; Computer Hardware Engineering. **Related Knowledge/ Courses:** Engineering and Technology; Design; Physics; Computers and Electronics; Mathematics; Telecommunications. **Work Experience Needed:** None. **On-the-Job Training Needed:** None. **Certification/Licensure:** None.

**Personality Types:** Investigative–Realistic–Conventional. **Key Career Cluster:** 15 Science, Technology, Engineering, and Mathematics. **Key Career Pathway:** 15.1 Engineering and Technology.

**Skills:** Operations analysis; science; programming; systems evaluation; troubleshooting; equipment selection; technology design; equipment maintenance.

**Physical Environment:** Indoors; sitting. **Structural Environment:** Importance of being exact or accurate; freedom to make decisions; structured versus unstructured work; level of competition; impact of decisions on co-workers or company results; time pressure.

## Computer Programmers

**Create, modify, and test the code, forms, and script that allow computer applications to run.**

- Average annual earnings: $74,280
- Middle 50% of earners: $56,440–$94,130
- Earnings growth potential: Medium (42.3%)

- Growth: 12.0%
- Annual job openings: 12,800
- Self-employed: 5.6%

### BEST-PAYING INDUSTRIES

| Industry | Median Earnings | Workforce |
|---|---|---|
| Publishing Industries (except Internet) | $81,840 | 19,310 |
| Professional, Scientific, and Technical Services | $74,060 | 149,410 |
| Administrative and Support Services | $72,130 | 18,230 |

### BEST-PAYING METROPOLITAN AREAS

| Metro Area | Median Earnings | Workforce |
|---|---|---|
| San Francisco–Oakland–Fremont, CA | $98,790 | 9,080 |
| Seattle-Tacoma-Bellevue, WA | $95,090 | 11,270 |
| San Jose–Sunnyvale–Santa Clara, CA | $88,280 | 7,300 |
| Los Angeles–Long Beach–Santa Ana, CA | $82,700 | 14,030 |
| New York–Northern New Jersey–Long Island, NY-NJ-PA | $82,650 | 24,710 |
| Washington-Arlington-Alexandria, DC-VA-MD-WV | $79,620 | 11,160 |
| Atlanta–Sandy Springs–Marietta, GA | $78,910 | 9,520 |
| Dallas–Fort Worth–Arlington, TX | $77,360 | 10,960 |
| Boston-Cambridge-Quincy, MA-NH | $76,970 | 7,540 |
| Philadelphia-Camden-Wilmington, PA-NJ-DE-MD | $73,710 | 8,460 |
| Chicago-Naperville-Joliet, IL-IN-WI | $72,430 | 17,750 |

**Considerations for Job Outlook:** Job prospects will be best for programmers who have a bachelor's degree or higher and knowledge of a variety of programming languages. Keeping up to date with the newest programming tools will also improve prospects. As employers increasingly contract with outside firms to do programming jobs, more opportunities are expected to arise for experienced programmers who have expertise in a specific area to work as consultants.

**Major Work Tasks:** Correct errors by making appropriate changes and rechecking the program to ensure that the desired results are produced. Conduct trial runs of programs and software applications to be sure they will produce the desired information and that the instructions are correct. Compile and write documentation of program development and subsequent revisions, inserting comments in the coded instructions so others can understand the program. Write, update, and maintain computer programs or software packages to handle specific jobs, such as tracking inventory, storing or retrieving data, or controlling other equipment. Consult with managerial, engineering, and technical personnel to clarify program intent, identify problems, and suggest changes. Perform or direct revision, repair, or expansion of existing programs to increase operating efficiency or adapt to new requirements. Write, analyze, review, and rewrite programs, using workflow charts and diagrams and applying knowledge of computer capabilities, subject matter, and symbolic logic. Investigate whether networks, workstations, the central processing unit of the system, or peripheral equipment are responding to a program's instructions. Prepare detailed workflow charts and diagrams that describe input, output, and logical operation, and convert them into a series of instructions coded in a computer language. Perform systems analysis and programming tasks to maintain and control the use of computer systems software as a systems programmer. Consult with and assist computer operators or system analysts to define and resolve problems in running computer programs. Write or contribute to instructions or manuals to guide end users. Assign, coordinate, and review work and activities of programming personnel. Collaborate with computer manufacturers and other users to develop new programming methods. Train subordinates in programming and program coding.

**Usual Educational Requirement:** Bachelor's degree. **Relevant Educational Programs:** Computer Graphics; Computer Programming, Other; Computer Programming, Specific Applications; Computer Programming, Vendor/Product Certification; Computer Programming/Programmer, General; Computer Science; Computer Software Technology/Technician; Management Information Systems, General; Medical Office Computer Specialist/Assistant Training; Modeling, Virtual Environments and Simulation. **Related Knowledge/Courses:** Computers and Electronics; Mathematics; Design; Administration and Management; English Language; Communications and Media. **Work Experience Needed:** None. **On-the-Job Training Needed:** None. **Certification/Licensure:** Voluntary certification by vendor or association.

**Personality Types:** Investigative–Conventional. **Key Career Cluster:** 11 Information Technology. **Key Career Pathway:** 11.4 Programming and Software Development.

**Skills:** Programming; quality control analysis; operations analysis; technology design; science; systems evaluation; mathematics; systems analysis.

**Physical Environment:** Indoors; sitting; using hands; repetitive motions. **Structural Environment:** Importance of being exact or accurate; importance of repeating same tasks; time pressure; frequency of decision making; structured versus unstructured work; level of competition.

## Computer Science Teachers, Postsecondary

*See Teachers, Postsecondary.*

## Computer Systems Analysts

**Analyze science, engineering, business, and other data processing problems to implement and improve computer systems.**

- Average annual earnings: $79,680
- Middle 50% of earners: $63,030–$100,030
- Earnings growth potential: Medium (37.3%)
- Growth: 22.1%
- Annual job openings: 22,250
- Self-employed: 6.2%

**Considerations for Job Outlook:** Job applicants with a background in business may have better prospects because this occupation often requires knowledge of an organization's business needs. An understanding of the specific field an analyst is working in is also helpful. For example, a hospital may desire an analyst with a background or coursework in health management.

**Major Work Tasks:** Provide staff and users with assistance solving computer-related problems, such as malfunctions and program problems. Test, maintain, and monitor computer

### BEST-PAYING INDUSTRIES

| Industry | Median Earnings | Workforce |
|---|---|---|
| Professional, Scientific, and Technical Services | $83,370 | 175,380 |
| Management of Companies and Enterprises | $81,800 | 41,680 |
| Insurance Carriers and Related Activities | $78,740 | 34,440 |
| Federal, State, and Local Government | $71,570 | 35,370 |

### BEST-PAYING METROPOLITAN AREAS

| Metro Area | Median Earnings | Workforce |
|---|---|---|
| San Francisco–Oakland–Fremont, CA | $96,230 | 14,940 |
| Washington-Arlington-Alexandria, DC-VA-MD-WV | $95,690 | 28,210 |
| Seattle-Tacoma-Bellevue, WA | $91,910 | 10,950 |
| New York–Northern New Jersey–Long Island, NY-NJ-PA | $88,850 | 34,660 |
| Philadelphia-Camden-Wilmington, PA-NJ-DE-MD | $88,180 | 12,640 |
| Los Angeles–Long Beach–Santa Ana, CA | $86,810 | 17,250 |
| Houston–Sugar Land–Baytown, TX | $85,250 | 10,900 |
| Boston-Cambridge-Quincy, MA-NH | $85,020 | 14,680 |
| Dallas–Fort Worth–Arlington, TX | $79,030 | 15,610 |
| Minneapolis–St. Paul–Bloomington, MN-WI | $78,370 | 11,520 |
| Atlanta–Sandy Springs–Marietta, GA | $75,170 | 12,300 |
| Chicago-Naperville-Joliet, IL-IN-WI | $75,130 | 12,160 |

programs and systems, including coordinating the installation of computer programs and systems. Confer with clients regarding the nature of the information processing or computation needs a computer program is to address. Coordinate and link the computer systems within an organization to increase compatibility and so information can be shared. Consult with management to ensure agreement on system principles. Expand or modify system to serve new purposes or improve work flow. Determine computer software or hardware

**207**

needed to set up or alter system. Train staff and users to work with computer systems and programs. Analyze information processing or computation needs and plan and design computer systems, using techniques, such as structured analysis, data modeling, and information engineering. Assess the usefulness of pre-developed application packages and adapt them to a user environment. Define the goals of the system and devise flow charts and diagrams describing logical operational steps of programs. Develop, document, and revise system design procedures, test procedures, and quality standards. Review and analyze computer printouts and performance indicators to locate code problems, and correct errors by correcting codes. Recommend new equipment or software packages. Read manuals, periodicals, and technical reports to learn how to develop programs that meet staff and user requirements. Supervise computer programmers or other systems analysts or serve as project leaders for particular systems projects. Use object-oriented programming languages, as well as client and server applications development processes and multimedia and Internet technology. Interview or survey workers, observe job performance, or perform the job to determine what information is processed and how it is processed. Utilize the computer in the analysis and solution of business problems, such as development of integrated production and inventory control and cost analysis systems.

**Usual Educational Requirement:** Bachelor's degree. **Relevant Educational Programs**: Computer and Information Sciences, General; Computer Systems Analysis/Analyst; Computer Systems Networking and Telecommunications; Information Technology. **Related Knowledge/Courses:** Computers and Electronics; Engineering and Technology; Mathematics; Telecommunications; Clerical Practices; English Language. **Work Experience Needed:** None. **On-the-Job Training Needed:** None. **Certification/Licensure:** None.

**Personality Types:** Investigative–Conventional–Realistic. **Key Career Cluster:** 11 Information Technology. **Key Career Pathway:** 11.4 Programming and Software Development.

**Skills:** Programming; technology design; troubleshooting; quality control analysis; operations analysis; systems evaluation; systems analysis; mathematics.

**Physical Environment:** Indoors; sitting; using hands; repetitive motions; noise. **Structural Environment:** Importance of being exact or accurate; time pressure; freedom to make decisions; structured versus unstructured work; importance of repeating same tasks; impact of decisions on co-workers or company results.

**JOB SPECIALIZATION: INFORMATICS NURSE SPECIALISTS**

**Apply knowledge of nursing and informatics to assist in the design, development, and ongoing modification of computerized health-care systems. May educate staff and assist in problem solving to promote the implementation of the health-care system.**

**Major Work Tasks:** Design, develop, select, test, implement, and evaluate new or modified informatics solutions, data structures, and decision-support mechanisms to support patients, health-care professionals, and their information management and human-computer and human-technology interactions within health-care contexts. Disseminate information about nursing informatics science and practice to the profession, other health-care professions, nursing students, and the public. Translate nursing practice information between nurses and systems engineers, analysts, or designers using object-oriented models or other techniques. Use informatics science to design or implement health information technology applications to resolve clinical or health-care administrative problems. Develop, implement, or evaluate health information technology applications, tools, processes, or structures to assist nurses with data management.

Analyze and interpret patient, nursing, or information systems data to improve nursing services. Analyze computer and information technologies to determine applicability to nursing practice, education, administration, and research. Apply knowledge of computer science, information science, nursing, and informatics theory to nursing practice, education, administration, or research in collaboration with other health informatics specialists. Develop or implement policies or practices to ensure the privacy, confidentiality, or security of patient information. Design, conduct, or provide support to nursing informatics research. Develop or deliver training programs for health information technology, creating operating manuals as needed. Develop strategies, policies, or procedures for introducing, evaluating, or modifying information technology applied to nursing practice, administration, education, or research. Identify, collect, record, or analyze data that are relevant to the nursing care of patients. Read current literature, talk with colleagues, and participate in professional organizations or conferences to keep abreast of developments in informatics. Provide consultation to nurses regarding hardware or software configuration.

**Related Knowledge/Courses:** Medicine and Dentistry; Education and Training; Design; Computers and Electronics; Customer and Personal Service; Administration and Management.

**Personality Types:** Social–Investigative.

**Skills:** Programming; technology design; systems evaluation; systems analysis; equipment selection; active learning; operations analysis; learning strategies.

**Physical Environment:** Indoors; sitting; using hands; repetitive motions. **Structural Environment:** Structured versus unstructured work; freedom to make decisions; importance of being exact or accurate; time pressure; impact of decisions on co-workers or company results; frequency of decision making.

## Construction Managers

**Plan, direct, or coordinate activities concerned with the construction and maintenance of structures, facilities, and systems.**

- Average annual earnings: $82,790
- Middle 50% of earners: $63,790–$109,600
- Earnings growth potential: Medium (40.0%)
- Growth: 16.6%
- Annual job openings: 12,040
- Self-Employed: 63.8%

**Considerations for Job Outlook:** Job opportunities for qualified job seekers are expected to be good. Those with a bachelor's degree in construction science, construction management, or civil engineering, coupled with construction experience, will have the best job prospects. Employment growth will provide many new job openings. A substantial number of construction managers are expected to retire over the next decade, resulting in additional job opportunities. Employment of construction managers, like that of many other construction workers, is sensitive to fluctuations in the economy.

**Major Work Tasks:** Confer with supervisory personnel, owners, contractors, or design professionals to discuss and resolve matters, such as work procedures, complaints, or construc-

### BEST-PAYING INDUSTRIES

| Industry | Median Earnings | Workforce |
|---|---|---|
| Professional, Scientific, and Technical Services | $88,350 | 12,570 |
| Heavy and Civil Engineering Construction | $85,130 | 25,340 |
| Construction of Buildings | $81,830 | 79,360 |
| Specialty Trade Contractors | $79,470 | 61,250 |

**209**

## BEST-PAYING METROPOLITAN AREAS

| Metro Area | Median Earnings | Workforce |
|---|---|---|
| New York–Northern New Jersey–Long Island, NY-NJ-PA | $111,160 | 12,180 |
| Los Angeles–Long Beach–Santa Ana, CA | $99,690 | 7,010 |
| Washington-Arlington-Alexandria, DC-VA-MD-WV | $98,160 | 5,770 |
| Chicago-Naperville-Joliet, IL-IN-WI | $89,270 | 4,930 |
| Miami–Fort Lauderdale–Pompano Beach, FL | $87,700 | 4,420 |
| Houston–Sugar Land–Baytown, TX | $73,860 | 8,710 |
| Dallas–Fort Worth–Arlington, TX | $72,660 | 8,350 |

tion problems. Plan, organize, or direct activities concerned with the construction or maintenance of structures, facilities, or systems. Inspect or review projects to monitor compliance with building and safety codes or other regulations. Study job specifications to determine appropriate construction methods. Prepare and submit budget estimates, progress reports, or cost tracking reports. Develop or implement quality control programs. Develop or implement environmental protection programs. Inspect or review projects to monitor compliance with environmental regulations. Perform or contract others to perform pre-building assessments, such as conceptual cost estimating, rough order of magnitude estimating, feasibility, or energy efficiency, environmental, and sustainability assessments. Plan, schedule, or coordinate construction project activities to meet deadlines. Investigate damage, accidents, or delays at construction sites to ensure that proper construction procedures are being followed. Prepare contracts or negotiate revisions to contractual agreements with ar-

chitects, consultants, clients, suppliers, or subcontractors. Implement new or modified plans in response to delays, bad weather, or construction site emergencies. Interpret and explain plans and contract terms to representatives of the owner or developer, including administrative staff, workers, or clients. Apply for and obtain all necessary permits or licenses. Evaluate construction methods and determine cost-effectiveness of plans, using computer models. Contract or oversee craft work, such as painting or plumbing. Determine labor requirements for dispatching workers to construction sites. Requisition supplies or materials to complete construction projects. Direct acquisition of land for construction projects. Apply green building strategies to reduce energy costs or minimize carbon output or other sources of harm to the environment.

**Usual Educational Requirement:** Associate degree. **Relevant Educational Programs**: Business Administration and Management, General; Business/Commerce, General; Construction Engineering Technology/Technician; Construction Management; Operations Management and Supervision. **Related Knowledge/Courses:** Building and Construction; Design; Engineering and Technology; Mechanical Devices; Economics and Accounting; Administration and Management. **Work Experience Needed:** More than 5 years. **On-the-Job Training Needed:** None. **Certification/ Licensure:** Licensure for some specializations; voluntary certification by association.

**Personality Types:** Enterprising–Realistic– Conventional. **Key Career Cluster:** 02 Architecture and Construction. **Key Career Pathway:** 2.2 Construction.

**Skills:** Management of financial resources; management of material resources; operations analysis; negotiation; management of personnel resources; systems evaluation; systems analysis; mathematics.

**Physical Environment:** Indoors; outdoors; sitting; noise. **Structural Environment:** Freedom

**210**

to make decisions; time pressure; impact of decisions on co-workers or company results; structured versus unstructured work; level of competition; frequency of decision making.

## Cost Estimators

**Prepare cost estimates for product manufacturing, construction projects, or services to aid management in bidding on or determining price of product or service.**

- Average annual earnings: $58,860
- Middle 50% of earners: $44,630–$77,130
- Earnings growth potential: Medium (41.4%)
- Growth: 36.4%
- Annual job openings: 10,300
- Self-employed: 2.2%

**Considerations for Job Outlook:** Job prospects are expected to be good overall. Job seekers with a bachelor's degree and related work experience will have the best job opportunities as employers increasingly seek cost estimators with that background. In manufacturing, those with a strong background in mathematics, statistics, engineering, or accounting and knowledge of cost estimation software, should have the best prospects. In construction, those with knowledge of Building Information Modeling (BIM) software are likely to have the best job prospects. Jobs of cost estimators working in construction, like those of many other trades in the construction industry, are sensitive to changing economic conditions.

**Major Work Tasks:** Analyze blueprints and other documentation to prepare time, cost, materials, and labor estimates. Assess cost effectiveness of products, projects, or services, by tracking actual costs relative to bids as the project develops. Consult with clients, vendors, personnel in other departments or construction foremen to discuss and formulate estimates and resolve issues. Confer with engineers, architects, owners, contractors, and subcontrac-

### BEST-PAYING INDUSTRIES

| Industry | Median Earnings | Workforce |
|---|---|---|
| Heavy and Civil Engineering Construction | $66,830 | 11,760 |
| Construction of Buildings | $61,210 | 31,740 |
| Specialty Trade Contractors | $58,760 | 73,970 |
| Fabricated Metal Product Manufacturing | $56,480 | 10,080 |
| Repair and Maintenance | $51,960 | 12,020 |

### BEST-PAYING METROPOLITAN AREAS

| Metro Area | Median Earnings | Workforce |
|---|---|---|
| New York–Northern New Jersey–Long Island, NY-NJ-PA | $76,070 | 9,400 |
| Washington-Arlington-Alexandria, DC-VA-MD-WV | $66,110 | 4,960 |
| Chicago-Naperville-Joliet, IL-IN-WI | $64,700 | 5,000 |
| Dallas–Fort Worth–Arlington, TX | $64,670 | 4,280 |
| Los Angeles–Long Beach–Santa Ana, CA | $63,900 | 7,140 |
| Houston–Sugar Land–Baytown, TX | $63,860 | 4,050 |
| Philadelphia-Camden-Wilmington, PA-NJ-DE-MD | $61,390 | 5,030 |

tors on changes and adjustments to cost estimates. Prepare estimates used by management for purposes such as planning, organizing, and scheduling work. Prepare estimates for use in selecting vendors or subcontractors. Review material and labor requirements to decide

**211**

whether it is more cost-effective to produce or purchase components. Prepare cost and expenditure statements and other necessary documentation at regular intervals for the duration of the project. Prepare and maintain a directory of suppliers, contractors, and subcontractors. Set up cost monitoring and reporting systems and procedures. Establish and maintain tendering process, and conduct negotiations. Conduct special studies to develop and establish standard hour and related cost data or to effect cost reduction. Visit site and record information about access, drainage and topography, and availability of services such as water and electricity.

**Usual Educational Requirement:** Bachelor's degree. **Relevant Educational Programs**: Business Administration and Management, General; Business/Commerce, General; Construction Engineering; Construction Engineering Technology/Technician; Manufacturing Engineering; Materials Engineering; Mechanical Engineering. **Related Knowledge/Courses:** Engineering and Technology; Mathematics; Building and Construction; Economics and Accounting; Design; Computers and Electronics. **Work Experience Needed:** None. **On-the-Job Training Needed:** None. **Certification/Licensure:** Voluntary certification by association.

**Personality Types:** Conventional–Enterprising. **Key Career Cluster:** 02 Architecture and Construction. **Key Career Pathway:** 2.2 Construction.

**Skills:** Management of financial resources; management of material resources; mathematics; programming; persuasion; systems analysis; active learning; active listening.

**Physical Environment:** Indoors; sitting. **Structural Environment:** Importance of being exact or accurate; freedom to make decisions; time pressure; impact of decisions on co-workers or company results; structured versus unstructured work; level of competition.

## Credit Analysts

**Analyze credit data and financial statements of individuals or firms to determine the degree of risk involved in extending credit or lending money.**

- Average annual earnings: $61,080
- Middle 50% of earners: $46,170–$83,960
- Earnings growth potential: Medium (39.4%)
- Growth: 19.7%
- Annual job openings: 2,590
- Self-employed: 0.0%

**Considerations for Job Outlook:** Efforts to recruit and retain employees, the growing importance of employee training, and new legal standards are expected to increase employment of these workers. College graduates and those with certification should have the best opportunities.

**Major Work Tasks:** Analyze credit data and financial statements to determine the degree of risk involved in extending credit or lending money. Prepare reports that include the degree of risk involved in extending credit or lending money. Confer with credit association and other business representatives to exchange credit information. Generate financial ratios, using computer programs, to evaluate customers' financial status. Review individual or commercial customer files to identify and select delinquent accounts for collection. Compare liquidity, profitability, and credit histories of establishments being evaluated with those of similar establishments in the same industries and geographic locations. Consult with customers to resolve complaints and verify financial and credit transactions. Evaluate customer records and recommend payment plans based on earnings, savings data, payment history, and purchase activity. Complete loan applications, including credit analyses and summaries of loan requests, and submit to loan committees for approval. Analyze financial

## BEST-PAYING INDUSTRIES

| Industry | Median Earnings | Workforce |
|---|---|---|
| Management of Companies and Enterprises | $62,020 | 8,990 |
| Credit Intermediation and Related Activities | $60,520 | 35,020 |

## BEST-PAYING METROPOLITAN AREAS

| Metro Area | Median Earnings | Workforce |
|---|---|---|
| San Francisco–Oakland–Fremont, CA | $89,480 | 1,400 |
| New York–Northern New Jersey–Long Island, NY-NJ-PA | $87,270 | 4,740 |
| Washington-Arlington-Alexandria, DC-VA-MD-WV | $73,790 | 1,580 |
| Charlotte-Gastonia-Concord, NC-SC | $69,890 | 1,590 |
| Los Angeles–Long Beach–Santa Ana, CA | $68,950 | 2,610 |
| Chicago-Naperville-Joliet, IL-IN-WI | $63,120 | 2,970 |
| Minneapolis–St. Paul–Bloomington, MN-WI | $62,370 | 1,350 |
| Dallas–Fort Worth–Arlington, TX | $60,510 | 2,380 |
| Philadelphia-Camden-Wilmington, PA-NJ-DE-MD | $60,300 | 1,840 |
| Atlanta–Sandy Springs–Marietta, GA | $59,340 | 2,000 |
| Boston-Cambridge-Quincy, MA-NH | $58,760 | 1,500 |

data such as income growth, quality of management, and market share to determine expected profitability of loans.

**Usual Educational Requirement:** Bachelor's degree. **Relevant Educational Programs**: Accounting; Credit Management; Finance, General. **Related Knowledge/Courses:** Economics and Accounting; Clerical Practices; Mathematics; Law and Government; English Language. **Work Experience Needed:** None. **On-the-Job Training Needed:** None. **Certification/Licensure:** Voluntary certification by association.

**Personality Types:** Conventional–Enterprising. **Key Career Cluster:** 06 Finance. **Key Career Pathway:** 6.3 Banking and Related Services.

**Skills:** Mathematics; programming; systems evaluation; management of financial resources; operations analysis; critical thinking; active learning; judgment and decision making.

**Physical Environment:** Indoors; sitting; repetitive motions. **Structural Environment:** Frequency of decision making; importance of being exact or accurate; time pressure; structured versus unstructured work; impact of decisions on co-workers or company results; importance of repeating same tasks.

## Criminal Justice and Law Enforcement Teachers, Postsecondary

*See Teachers, Postsecondary.*

## Database Administrators

**Administer, test, and implement computer databases, applying knowledge of database management systems.**

- Average annual earnings: $77,080
- Middle 50% of earners: $57,240–$99,430
- Earnings growth potential: High (44.3%)
- Growth: 30.7%
- Annual job openings: 5,270
- Self-employed: 1.6%

**213**

## Your Guide to High-Paying Careers

### BEST-PAYING INDUSTRIES

| Industry | Median Earnings | Workforce |
|---|---|---|
| Insurance Carriers and Related Activities | $83,690 | 6,290 |
| Management of Companies and Enterprises | $82,290 | 9,210 |
| Professional, Scientific, and Technical Services | $80,990 | 30,120 |
| Administrative and Support Services | $72,680 | 5,820 |
| Federal, State, and Local Government | $68,580 | 6,670 |
| Educational Services | $63,620 | 9,860 |

### BEST-PAYING METROPOLITAN AREAS

| Metro Area | Median Earnings | Workforce |
|---|---|---|
| Washington-Arlington-Alexandria, DC-VA-MD-WV | $97,670 | 6,190 |
| Seattle-Tacoma-Bellevue, WA | $89,370 | 2,250 |
| New York–Northern New Jersey–Long Island, NY-NJ-PA | $86,070 | 8,360 |
| Atlanta–Sandy Springs–Marietta, GA | $84,950 | 3,130 |
| Los Angeles–Long Beach–Santa Ana, CA | $83,310 | 3,450 |
| Chicago-Naperville-Joliet, IL-IN-WI | $82,400 | 4,190 |
| Boston-Cambridge-Quincy, MA-NH | $81,340 | 3,810 |
| Philadelphia-Camden-Wilmington, PA-NJ-DE-MD | $79,380 | 2,480 |
| Dallas–Fort Worth–Arlington, TX | $79,360 | 4,180 |
| Phoenix–Mesa–Scottsdale, AZ | $71,750 | 2,300 |

**Considerations for Job Outlook:** Job prospects should be favorable. Database administrators are in high demand, and firms sometimes have difficulty finding qualified workers. Applicants who have experience with new technology should have the best prospects.

**Major Work Tasks:** Develop standards and guidelines to guide the use and acquisition of software and to protect vulnerable information. Modify existing databases and database management systems or direct programmers and analysts to make changes. Test programs or databases, correct errors, and make necessary modifications. Plan, coordinate, and implement security measures to safeguard information in computer files against accidental or unauthorized damage, modification, or disclosure. Approve, schedule, plan, and supervise the installation and testing of new products and improvements to computer systems such as the installation of new databases. Train users and answer questions. Specify users and user access levels for each segment of database. Develop data model describing data elements and how they are used, following procedures and using pen, template, or computer software. Develop methods for integrating different products so they work properly together, such as customizing commercial databases to fit specific needs. Review project requests describing database user needs to estimate time and cost required to accomplish project. Review procedures in database management system manuals for making changes to database. Work as part of a project team to coordinate database development and determine project scope and limitations. Select and enter codes to monitor database performance and to create production database. Write and code logical and physical database descriptions and specify identifiers of database to management system or direct others in coding descriptions. Establish and calculate optimum values for database parameters, using manuals and calculator. Identify and evaluate industry trends in database systems to serve as a source of information and advice for upper management. Review workflow charts developed by programmer analyst to understand tasks computer will perform, such as updating records. Revise company definition of data as defined in data dictionary.

**Usual Educational Requirement:** Bachelor's degree. **Relevant Educational Programs:** Computer and Information Sciences, General; Computer and Information Systems Security/ Information Assurance; Data Modeling/Warehousing and Database Administration. **Related Knowledge/Courses:** Computers and Electronics; Telecommunications; Clerical Practices; Communications and Media; Engineering and Technology; Mathematics. **Work Experience Needed:** 1 to 5 years. **On-the-Job Training Needed:** None. **Certification/Licensure:** Voluntary certification by vendors or association.

**Personality Types:** Conventional–Investigative. **Key Career Cluster:** 11 Information Technology. **Key Career Pathway:** 11.1 Network Systems.

**Skills:** Programming; technology design; troubleshooting; operations analysis; systems evaluation; management of financial resources; systems analysis; installation.

**Physical Environment:** Indoors; sitting; using hands; repetitive motions; noise. **Structural Environment:** Importance of being exact or accurate; structured versus unstructured work; freedom to make decisions; importance of repeating same tasks; time pressure; consequence of error.

## Dental Hygienists

**Clean teeth and examine oral areas, head, and neck for signs of oral disease.**

- Average annual earnings: $70,210
- Middle 50% of earners: $58,130–$84,570
- Earnings growth potential: Medium (33.7%)
- Growth: 37.7%
- Annual job openings: 10,490
- Self-employed: 1.6%

**Considerations for Job Outlook:** Demand for dental services follows the trends in the economy because patients or private insurance companies pay for these services. As a result, during slow times in the economy, demand for dental services may decrease. During such times, dental hygienists may have difficulty finding employment or, if they are currently employed, they might work fewer hours.

**Major Work Tasks:** Clean calcareous deposits, accretions, and stains from teeth and beneath margins of gums, using dental instruments. Feel and visually examine gums for sores and signs of disease. Chart conditions of decay and disease for diagnosis and treatment by dentist. Feel lymph nodes under

### BEST-PAYING INDUSTRIES

| Industry | Median Earnings | Workforce |
|---|---|---|
| Ambulatory Health-Care Services | $70,430 | 185,490 |

### BEST-PAYING METROPOLITAN AREAS

| Metro Area | Median Earnings | Workforce |
|---|---|---|
| Los Angeles–Long Beach–Santa Ana, CA | $103,070 | 7,050 |
| Boston-Cambridge-Quincy, MA-NH | $81,730 | 4,170 |
| New York–Northern New Jersey–Long Island, NY-NJ-PA | $80,830 | 8,990 |
| Dallas–Fort Worth–Arlington, TX | $74,140 | 4,350 |
| Chicago-Naperville-Joliet, IL-IN-WI | $69,930 | 6,300 |
| Detroit-Warren-Livonia, MI | $64,110 | 4,270 |

patient's chin to detect swelling or tenderness that could indicate presence of oral cancer. Apply fluorides or other cavity preventing agents to arrest dental decay. Examine gums, using probes, to locate periodontal recessed gums and signs of gum disease. Expose and develop X-ray film. Remove excess cement from coronal surfaces of teeth. Administer local anesthetic agents. Record and review patient medical histories. Provide clinical services or health education to improve and maintain the oral health of patients or the general public. Maintain dental equipment and sharpen and sterilize dental instruments. Maintain patient recall system. Make impressions for study casts. Conduct dental health clinics for community groups to augment services of dentist. Remove sutures and dressings. Place and remove rubber dams, matrices, and temporary restorations.

**Usual Educational Requirement:** Associate degree. **Relevant Educational Program:** Dental Hygiene/Hygienist. **Related Knowledge/ Courses:** Medicine and Dentistry; Biology; Psychology; Chemistry; Sales and Marketing; Customer and Personal Service. **Work Experience Needed:** None. **On-the-Job Training Needed:** None. **Certification/Licensure:** Licensure.

**Personality Types:** Social–Realistic–Conventional. **Key Career Cluster:** 08 Health Science. **Key Career Pathway:** 8.1 Therapeutic Services.

**Skills:** Science; service orientation; operation monitoring; operation and control; persuasion; learning strategies; quality control analysis; troubleshooting.

**Physical Environment:** Indoors; sitting; using hands; bending or twisting the body; repetitive motions; noise. **Structural Environment:** Importance of repeating same tasks; importance of being exact or accurate; frequency of decision making; time pressure; structured versus unstructured work; freedom to make decisions.

## Dentists

**Diagnose and treat problems with a patient's teeth, gums, and other parts of the mouth. Provide advice and instruction on taking care of teeth and gums and on diet choices that affect oral health.**

- Average annual earnings: $149,310
- Middle 50% of earners: $105,380–$187,199+
- Earnings growth potential: Very high (50.5%)
- Growth: 20.7%
- Annual job openings: 6,640
- Self-employed: 32.3%

### BEST-PAYING INDUSTRIES

| Industry | Median Earnings | Workforce |
|---|---|---|
| Ambulatory Health-Care Services | $146,990 | 89,150 |

### BEST-PAYING METROPOLITAN AREAS

| Metro Area | Median Earnings | Workforce |
|---|---|---|
| Dallas–Fort Worth–Arlington, TX | $187,199+ | 2,180 |
| Atlanta–Sandy Springs–Marietta, GA | $162,060 | 1,960 |
| Philadelphia–Camden–Wilmington, PA-NJ-DE-MD | $161,380 | 1,950 |
| Boston–Cambridge–Quincy, MA-NH | $144,570 | 2,960 |
| Washington–Arlington–Alexandria, DC-VA-MD-WV | $133,360 | 2,790 |
| New York-Northern New Jersey-Long Island, NY-NJ-PA | $114,720 | 7,690 |
| Los Angeles–Long Beach–Santa Ana, CA | $98,830 | 4,640 |

**Considerations for Job Outlook:** Dentists are likely to hire more hygienists and dental assistants to handle routine services. Productivity increases from new technology should allow dentists to reduce the time needed to see each patient. These factors allow the dentist to see more patients when their practices expand. Dentists will continue to provide care and instruction aimed at promoting good oral hygiene, rather than just providing treatments such as fillings.

**Usual Educational Requirement:** Doctoral or professional degree. **Relevant Educational Programs:** Advanced General Dentistry (Cert., MS, PhD); Dental Public Health Specialty; Dentistry (DDS, DMD); Pediatric Dentistry Residency Program; Pediatric Dentistry/Pedodontics (Cert., MS, PhD). **Related Knowledge/Courses:** Medicine and Dentistry; Biology; Psychology; Chemistry; Economics and Accounting; Customer and Personal Service. **Work Experience Needed:** None. **On-the-Job Training Needed:** Internship/residency. **Certification/Licensure:** Licensure.

**Personality Types:** Investigative–Realistic–Social. **Key Career Cluster:** 08 Health Science. **Key Career Pathway:** 8.1 Therapeutic Services.

**Skills:** Science; management of financial resources; management of material resources; active learning; operation and control; reading comprehension; judgment and decision making; complex problem solving.

**Physical Environment:** Indoors; sitting; using hands; bending or twisting the body; repetitive motions; noise. **Structural Environment:** Frequency of decision making; freedom to make decisions; impact of decisions on co-workers or company results; importance of being exact or accurate; structured versus unstructured work; time pressure.

### JOB SPECIALIZATION: DENTISTS, GENERAL

**Diagnose and treat diseases, injuries, and malformations of teeth and gums and related oral structures. May treat diseases of nerve,** pulp, and other dental tissues affecting vitality of teeth.

- Average annual earnings: $145,240
- Middle 50% of earners: $104,230–$187,200+
- Earnings growth potential: High (49.0%)

#### BEST-PAYING INDUSTRIES

| Industry | Median Earnings | Workforce |
|---|---|---|
| Ambulatory Health-Care Services | $146,990 | 89,150 |

#### BEST-PAYING METROPOLITAN AREAS

| Metro Area | Median Earnings | Workforce |
|---|---|---|
| New York-Northern New Jersey-Long Island, NY-NJ-PA | $133,360 | 7,690 |
| Los Angeles-Long Beach-Santa Ana, CA | $114,720 | 4,640 |

**Major Work Tasks:** Use masks, gloves, and safety glasses to protect themselves and their patients from infectious diseases. Administer anesthetics to limit the amount of pain experienced by patients during procedures. Examine teeth, gums, and related tissues, using dental instruments, X-rays, or other diagnostic equipment, to evaluate dental health, diagnose diseases or abnormalities, and plan appropriate treatments. Formulate plan of treatment for patient's teeth and mouth tissue. Use air turbine and hand instruments, dental appliances, and surgical implements. Advise or instruct patients regarding preventive dental care, the causes and treatment of dental problems, or oral health-care services. Design, make, or fit prosthodontic appliances, such as space maintainers, bridges, or dentures, or write fabrication instructions or prescriptions for denturists or dental technicians. Diagnose and treat diseases, injuries, or malformations of teeth, gums, or related oral structures and provide preventive or corrective services. Fill pulp chamber and canal with endodontic materials. Write prescriptions for antibiotics or other medications. Analyze or evaluate dental needs to determine changes or trends in patterns of dental disease. Treat exposure of pulp-by-pulp capping, removal of pulp from pulp chamber, or root canal, using dental instruments. Eliminate irritating margins of fillings and correct occlusions, using dental instruments. Perform oral or periodontal surgery on the jaw or mouth. Remove diseased tissue, using surgical instruments. Apply fluoride or sealants to teeth. Manage business, employing and supervising staff and handling paperwork and insurance claims. Bleach, clean, or polish teeth to restore natural color. Plan, organize, or maintain dental health programs. Produce or evaluate dental health educational materials.

**Related Knowledge/Courses:** Medicine and Dentistry; Biology; Psychology; Chemistry; Economics and Accounting; Customer and Personal Service.

**Personality Types:** Investigative–Realistic–Social

**Skills:** Science; management of financial resources; management of material resources; active learning; operation and control; reading comprehension; judgment and decision making; complex problem solving.

**Physical Environment:** Indoors; sitting; using hands; bending or twisting the body; repetitive motions; noise. **Structural Environment:** Frequency of decision making; freedom to make decisions; impact of decisions on co-workers or company results; importance of being exact or accurate; structured versus unstructured work; time pressure.

### JOB SPECIALIZATION: ORAL AND MAXILLOFACIAL SURGEONS

**Perform surgery on mouth, jaws, and related head and neck structure to execute difficult and multiple extractions of teeth, to remove tumors and other abnormal growths, to correct abnormal jaw relations by mandibular or maxillary revision, to prepare mouth for insertion of dental prosthesis, or to treat fractured jaws.**

- Average annual earnings: $187,200+
- Middle 50% of earners: $157,430–$187,200+
- Earnings growth potential: (Cannot be calculated)

#### BEST-PAYING INDUSTRIES

| Industry | Median Earnings | Workforce |
|---|---|---|
| Ambulatory Health-Care Services | $187,199+ | 4,630 |

#### BEST-PAYING METROPOLITAN AREAS

| Metro Area | Median Earnings | Workforce |
|---|---|---|
| New York-Northern New Jersey-Long Island, NY-NJ-PA | $187,199+ | 480 |

**Major Work Tasks:** Administer general and local anesthetics. Remove impacted, damaged, and non-restorable teeth. Evaluate the position of the wisdom teeth to determine whether problems exist currently or might occur in the future. Collaborate with other professionals, such as restorative dentists and orthodontists, to plan treatment. Perform surgery to prepare the mouth for dental implants and to aid in the regeneration of deficient bone and gum tissues. Remove tumors and other abnormal growths of the oral and facial regions, using surgical instruments. Treat infections of the oral cavity, salivary glands, jaws, and neck. Treat problems affecting the oral mucosa, such as mouth ulcers and infections. Provide emergency treatment of facial injuries including facial lacerations, intra-oral lacerations, and fractured facial bones. Perform surgery on the mouth and jaws to treat conditions such as cleft lip and palate and jaw growth problems. Restore form and function by moving skin, bone, nerves, and other tissues from other parts of the body to reconstruct the jaws and face. Treat snoring problems, using laser surgery. Perform minor cosmetic procedures, such as chin and cheekbone enhancements. Perform minor facial rejuvenation procedures, including the use of Botox and laser technology.

**Related Knowledge/Courses:** Medicine and Dentistry; Biology; Psychology; Therapy and Counseling; Chemistry; Personnel and Human Resources.

**Personality Types:** Realistic–Social–Investigative

**Skills:** Science; reading comprehension; operations analysis; active learning; complex problem solving; critical thinking; operation and control; service orientation.

**Physical Environment:** Indoors; standing; using hands; bending or twisting the body; repetitive motions; contaminants. **Structural Environment:** Impact of decisions on co-workers or company results; freedom to make decisions; importance of being exact or accurate; frequency of decision making; structured versus unstructured work; consequence of error.

## JOB SPECIALIZATION: ORTHODONTISTS

**Examine, diagnose, and treat dental malocclusions and oral cavity anomalies. Design and fabricate appliances to realign teeth and jaws to produce and maintain normal function and to improve appearance.**

- Average annual earnings: $187,200+
- Middle 50% of earners: $103,070–$187,200+
- Earnings growth potential: (Cannot be calculated)

**Major Work Tasks:** Fit dental appliances in patients' mouths to alter the position and relationship of teeth and jaws or to realign teeth. Study diagnostic records, such as medical or dental histories, plaster models of the teeth,

| Industry | Median Earnings | Workforce |
|---|---|---|
| Ambulatory Health-Care Services | $187,199+ | 5,480 |

| Metro Area | Median Earnings | Workforce |
|---|---|---|
| New York-Northern New Jersey-Long Island, NY-NJ-PA | $187,199+ | 270 |

photos of a patient's face and teeth, and X-rays, to develop patient treatment plans. Diagnose teeth and jaw or other dental-facial abnormalities. Examine patients to assess abnormalities of jaw development, tooth position, and other dental-facial structures. Prepare diagnostic and treatment records. Adjust dental appliances to produce and maintain normal function. Provide patients with proposed treatment plans and cost estimates. Instruct dental officers and technical assistants in orthodontic procedures and techniques. Coordinate orthodontic services with other dental and medical services. Design and fabricate appliances, such as space maintainers, retainers, and labial and lingual arch wires.

**Related Knowledge/Courses:** Medicine and Dentistry; Biology; Sales and Marketing; Physics; Economics and Accounting; Chemistry.

**Personality Types:** Investigative–Realistic–Social

**Skills:** Science; operations analysis; time management; instructing; technology design; writing; active learning; negotiation.

**Physical Environment:** Indoors; sitting; using hands; repetitive motions; exposed to disease or infections. **Structural Environment:** Structured versus unstructured work; freedom to make decisions; frequency of decision making; importance of being exact or accurate; impact of decisions on co-workers or company results; level of competition.

**Construct oral prostheses to replace missing teeth and other oral structures to correct natural and acquired deformation of mouth and jaws; to restore and maintain oral function, such as chewing and speaking; and to improve appearance.**

- Average annual earnings: $169,130

- Middle 50% of earners: $85,560–$187,200+

- Earnings growth potential: Very high (66.8%)

### BEST-PAYING INDUSTRIES

| Industry | Median Earnings | Workforce |
|---|---|---|
| Ambulatory Health-Care Services | $177,240 | 280 |

### BEST-PAYING METROPOLITAN AREAS

| Metro Area | Median Earnings | Workforce |
|---|---|---|

No data available

**Major Work Tasks:** Fit prostheses to patients, making any necessary adjustments and modifications. Design and fabricate dental prostheses, or supervise dental technicians and laboratory bench workers who construct the devices. Measure and take impressions of patients' jaws and teeth to determine the shape and size of dental prostheses, using face bows, dental articulators, recording devices, and other materials. Collaborate with general dentists, specialists, and other health professionals to develop solutions to dental and oral health concerns. Repair, reline, or rebase dentures. Restore function and aesthetics to traumatic injury victims, or to individuals with diseases or birth defects. Use bonding technology on the surface of the teeth to change tooth shape or to close gaps. Treat facial pain and jaw joint problems. Place veneers onto teeth to conceal defects. Bleach discolored teeth to brighten and whiten them. Replace missing teeth and associated oral structures with permanent fixtures, such as implant-supported prostheses, crowns and bridges, or removable fixtures, such as dentures.

**Related Knowledge/Courses:** Medicine and Dentistry; Biology; Chemistry; Psychology; Engineering and Technology; Physics.

**Personality Types:** Investigative–Realistic

**Skills:** Operations analysis; science; technology design; quality control analysis; management of financial resources; social perceptiveness; service orientation; troubleshooting.

**Physical Environment:** Indoors; sitting; using hands; bending or twisting the body; repetitive motions; noise. **Structural Environment:** Freedom to make decisions; importance of being exact or accurate; structured versus unstructured work; impact of decisions on co-workers or company results; frequency of decision making; importance of repeating same tasks.

**All dentists not listed separately.**

- Average annual earnings: $154,990

- Middle 50% of earners: $109,760–$187,200+

- Earnings growth potential: Very high (51.3%)

**Major Work Tasks:** No task data available.

**Related Knowledge/Courses:** No data available

### BEST-PAYING INDUSTRIES

| Industry | Median Earnings | Workforce |
|---|---|---|
| Ambulatory Health-Care Services | $184,520 | 2,650 |
| Federal, State, and Local Government | $147,280 | 2,160 |

## BEST-PAYING METROPOLITAN AREAS

| Metro Area | Median Earnings | Workforce |
|---|---|---|
| Chicago-Joliet-Naperville, IL-IN-WI | $148,600 | 270 |
| New York-Northern New Jersey-Long Island, NY-NJ-PA | $136,930 | 280 |

**Personality Types:** No data available

**Skills:** No data available

**Physical Environment:** No data available.

**Structural Environment:** No data available.

## Detectives and Criminal Investigators

**Conduct investigations related to suspected violations of federal, state, or local laws to prevent or solve crimes.**

- Average annual earnings: $74,300
- Middle 50% of earners: $52,320–$98,940
- Earnings growth potential: High (46.3%)

## BEST-PAYING INDUSTRIES

| Industry | Median Earnings | Workforce |
|---|---|---|
| Federal, State, and Local Government | $74,150 | 108,530 |

## BEST-PAYING METROPOLITAN AREAS

| Metro Area | Median Earnings | Workforce |
|---|---|---|
| Los Angeles–Long Beach–Santa Ana, CA | $102,600 | 3,840 |
| San Diego–Carlsbad–San Marcos, CA | $96,690 | 3,070 |
| Miami–Fort Lauderdale–Pompano Beach, FL | $82,420 | 2,550 |
| Atlanta–Sandy Springs–Marietta, GA | $46,290 | 2,230 |

- Growth: 2.9%
- Annual job openings: 3,010
- Self-employed: 0.8%

**Considerations for Job Outlook:** Continued demand for public safety will lead to new openings for officers in local departments; however, both state and federal jobs may be more competitive. Because they typically offer low salaries, many local departments face high turnover rates, making opportunities more plentiful for qualified applicants. However, some smaller departments may have fewer opportunities as budgets limit the ability to hire additional officers. Jobs in state and federal agencies will remain more competitive as they often offer high pay and more opportunities for both promotions and interagency transfers. Bilingual applicants with a bachelor's degree and law enforcement or military experience, especially investigative experience, should have the best opportunities in federal agencies.

**Major Work Tasks:** For tasks, see the job specializations.

**Usual Educational Requirement:** High school diploma or equivalent. **Relevant Educational Programs**: Criminal Justice/Police Science; Criminalistics and Criminal Science; Cultural/Archaeological Resources Protection; Cyber/Computer Forensics and Counterterrorism; Financial Forensics and Fraud Investigation; Law Enforcement Intelligence Analysis; Law Enforcement Investigation and Interviewing; Law Enforcement Record-Keeping and Evidence Management; Maritime Law Enforcement; Natural Resources Law Enforcement and Protective Services; Suspension and Debarment Investigation. **Work Experience Needed:** 1 to 5 years. **On-the-Job Training Needed:** Moderate-term on-the-job training. **Certification/Licensure:** Licensure in some states.

**Key Career Cluster:** 07 Government and Public Administration. **Key Career Pathway:** 7.6 Regulation.

221

## JOB SPECIALIZATION: CRIMINAL INVESTIGATORS AND SPECIAL AGENTS

**Investigate alleged or suspected criminal violations of federal, state, or local laws to determine if evidence is sufficient to recommend prosecution.**

**Major Work Tasks:** Obtain and verify evidence by interviewing and observing suspects and witnesses or by analyzing records. Record evidence and documents, using equipment such as cameras and photocopy machines. Examine records to locate links in chains of evidence or information. Prepare reports that detail investigation findings. Collaborate with other offices and agencies to exchange information and coordinate activities. Determine scope, timing, and direction of investigations. Testify before grand juries concerning criminal activity investigations. Analyze evidence in laboratories or in the field. Investigate organized crime, public corruption, financial crime, copyright infringement, civil rights violations, bank robbery, extortion, kidnapping, and other violations of federal or state statutes. Identify case issues and evidence needed, based on analysis of charges, complaints, or allegations of law violations. Obtain and use search and arrest warrants. Serve subpoenas or other official papers. Collaborate with other authorities on activities such as surveillance, transcription, and research. Develop relationships with informants to obtain information related to cases. Search for and collect evidence, such as fingerprints, using investigative equipment. Collect and record physical information about arrested suspects, including fingerprints, height and weight measurements, and photographs. Perform undercover assignments and maintain surveillance, including monitoring authorized wiretaps. Compare crime scene fingerprints with those from suspects or fingerprint files to identify perpetrators, using computers. Administer counterterrorism and counternarcotics reward programs. Provide protection for individuals, such as government leaders, political candidates, and visiting foreign dignitaries. Manage security programs designed to protect personnel, facilities, and information. Issue security clearances.

**Related Knowledge/Courses:** Public Safety and Security; Psychology; Law and Government; Customer and Personal Service; Sociology and Anthropology; Therapy and Counseling.

**Personality Types:** Enterprising–Investigative.

**Skills:** Negotiation; science; complex problem solving; persuasion; judgment and decision making; speaking; critical thinking; social perceptiveness.

**Physical Environment:** Outdoors; indoors; sitting; noise; very hot or cold; contaminants.

**Structural Environment:** Freedom to make decisions; impact of decisions on co-workers or company results; structured versus unstructured work; frequency of decision making; importance of being exact or accurate; consequence of error.

## JOB SPECIALIZATION: IMMIGRATION AND CUSTOMS INSPECTORS

**Investigate and inspect persons, common carriers, goods, and merchandise arriving in or departing from the United States or moving between states to detect violations of immigration and customs laws and regulations.**

**Major Work Tasks:** Examine immigration applications, visas, and passports and interview persons to determine eligibility for admission, residence, and travel in the U.S. Detain persons found to be in violation of customs or immigration laws and arrange for legal action, such as deportation. Locate and seize contraband, undeclared merchandise, and vehicles, aircraft, or boats that contain such merchandise. Interpret and explain laws and regulations to travelers, prospective immigrants, shippers, and manufacturers. Inspect cargo, baggage, and personal articles entering or leaving U.S. for compliance with revenue laws and U.S. customs regulations. Record and report job-related activities, findings, transactions, violations, discrepancies, and decisions. Institute civil and criminal prosecutions and cooperate with other law enforcement agencies in the investigation and prosecution of those in violation of immigration or customs laws. Testify regarding decisions at immigration appeals or in federal court. Determine duty and taxes to be paid on goods. Collect samples of merchandise for examination, appraisal, or testing. Investigate applications for duty refunds and petition for remission or mitigation of penalties when warranted.

**Related Knowledge/Courses:** Geography; Law and Government; Public Safety and Security; Foreign Language; Psychology; Sociology and Anthropology.

**Personality Types:** Conventional–Enterprising–Realistic.

**Skills:** Speaking; active listening; writing; negotiation; monitoring; critical thinking; persuasion; judgment and decision making.

**Physical Environment:** Indoors; outdoors; sitting; standing; using hands; repetitive motions.

**Structural Environment:** Frequency of decision making; importance of being exact or accurate; impact of decisions on co-workers or company results; consequence of error; freedom to make decisions; importance of repeating same tasks.

## JOB SPECIALIZATION: INTELLIGENCE ANALYSTS

**Gather, analyze, and evaluate information from a variety of sources, such as law enforcement databases, surveillance, intelligence networks, and geographic information systems. Use data to anticipate and prevent organized crime activities, such as terrorism.**

**Major Work Tasks:** Predict future gang, organized crime, or terrorist activity, using analyses of intelligence data. Study activities relating to narcotics, money laundering, gangs, auto theft rings, terrorism, or other national security threats. Design, use, or maintain databases and software applications, such as geographic information systems (GIS) mapping and artificial intelligence tools. Establish criminal profiles to aid in connecting criminal organizations with their members. Evaluate records of communications, such as telephone calls, to plot activity and determine the size and location of criminal groups and members. Gather and evaluate information, using tools such as aerial photographs, radar equipment, or sensitive radio equipment. Gather intelligence information by field observation, confidential information sources, or public records. Gather, analyze, correlate, or evaluate information from a variety of resources, such as law enforcement databases. Link or chart suspects to criminal organizations or events to determine activities and interrelationships. Prepare comprehensive written reports, presentations, maps, or charts based on research, collection, and analysis of intelligence data. Study the assets of criminal suspects to determine the flow of money from or to targeted groups. Validate known intelligence with data from other sources. Collaborate with representatives from other government and intelligence organizations to share information or coordinate intelligence activities. Interview, interrogate, or interact with witnesses or crime suspects to collect human intelligence. Operate cameras, radios, or other surveillance equipment to intercept communications or document activities. Prepare plans to intercept foreign communications transmissions. Develop defense plans or tactics, using intelligence and other information. Study communication code languages or foreign languages to translate intelligence.

**Related Knowledge/Courses:** Geography; Philosophy and Theology; Sociology and Anthropology; Law and Government; History and Archeology; Foreign Language.

**Personality Types:** Investigative–Conventional–Enterprising.

**Skills:** Programming; reading comprehension; active listening; writing; critical thinking; judgment and decision making; speaking; technology design.

**Physical Environment:** Indoors; sitting; repetitive motions. **Structural Environment:** Importance of being exact or accurate; structured versus unstructured work; freedom to make decisions; impact of decisions on co-workers or company results; time pressure; frequency of decision making.

JOB SPECIALIZATION: POLICE DETECTIVES

**Conduct investigations to prevent crimes or solve criminal cases.**

**Major Work Tasks:** Examine crime scenes to obtain clues and evidence, such as loose hairs, fibers, clothing, or weapons. Secure deceased body and obtain evidence from it, preventing bystanders from tampering with it prior to medical examiner's arrival. Obtain evidence from suspects. Provide testimony as a witness in court. Analyze completed police reports to determine what additional information and investigative work is needed. Prepare charges or responses to charges or information for court cases, according to formalized procedures. Note, mark, and photograph location of objects found, such as footprints, tire tracks, bullets and bloodstains, and take measurements of the scene. Obtain facts or statements from complainants, witnesses, and accused persons and record interviews, using recording device. Obtain summary of incident from officer in charge at crime scene, taking care to avoid disturbing evidence. Examine records and governmental agency files to find identifying data about suspects. Prepare and serve search and arrest warrants. Block or rope off scene and check perimeter to ensure that entire scene is secured. Summon medical help for injured individuals and alert medical personnel to take statements from them. Provide information to lab personnel concerning the source of an item of evidence and tests to be performed. Secure persons at

scene, keeping witnesses from conversing or leaving the scene before investigators arrive. Preserve, process, and analyze items of evidence obtained from crime scenes and suspects, placing them in proper containers and destroying evidence no longer needed. Record progress of investigation, maintain informational files on suspects, and submit reports to commanding officer or magistrate to authorize warrants. Take photographs from all angles of relevant parts of a crime scene, including entrance and exit routes and streets and intersections. Organize scene search, assigning specific tasks and areas of search to individual officers and obtaining adequate lighting as necessary. Question individuals or observe persons and establishments to confirm information given to patrol officers.

**Related Knowledge/Courses:** Public Safety and Security; Law and Government; Psychology; Therapy and Counseling; Customer and Personal Service; Philosophy and Theology.

**Personality Types:** Enterprising–Investigative.

**Skills:** Science; negotiation; operation and control; social perceptiveness; operation monitoring; service orientation; active learning; persuasion.

**Physical Environment:** Outdoors; indoors; sitting; noise; very hot or cold; contaminants. **Structural Environment:** Impact of decisions on co-workers or company results; freedom to make decisions; importance of being exact or accurate; frequency of decision making; structured versus unstructured work; consequence of error.

JOB SPECIALIZATION: POLICE IDENTIFICATION AND RECORDS OFFICERS

**Collect evidence at crime scenes, classify and identify fingerprints, and photograph evidence for use in criminal and civil cases.**

**Major Work Tasks:** Photograph crime or accident scenes for evidence records. Testify in court and present evidence. Dust selected areas of crime scene and lift latent fingerprints, adhering to proper preservation procedures. Look for trace evidence, such as fingerprints, hairs, fibers, or shoe impressions, using alternative light sources when necessary. Analyze and process evidence at crime scenes and in the laboratory, wearing protective equipment and using powders and chemicals. Package, store and retrieve evidence. Maintain records of evidence and write and review reports. Submit evidence to supervisors, crime labs, or court officials for legal proceedings. Identify, compare, classify, and file fingerprints using systems such as Automated Fingerprint Identification System (AFIS) or the Henry Classification System. Serve as technical advisor and coordinate with other law enforcement workers or legal personnel to exchange information on crime scene collection activities. Coordinate or conduct instructional classes or in-services, such as citizen police academy classes and crime scene training for other officers. Perform emergency work during off-hours. Process film and prints from crime or accident scenes. Interview victims, witnesses, suspects, and other law enforcement personnel.

**Related Knowledge/Courses:** Public Safety and Security; Law and Government; Chemistry; Customer and Personal Service; Clerical Practices; Telecommunications.

**Personality Types:** Conventional–Realistic–Investigative.

**Skills:** Operation and control; speaking; operation monitoring; negotiation; critical thinking; active listening; persuasion; service orientation.

**Physical Environment:** Indoors; sitting; using hands; noise; contaminants; exposed to disease or infections. **Structural Environment:** Importance of being exact or accurate; frequency of decision making; impact of decisions on co-workers or company results; freedom to make decisions; structured versus unstructured work; consequence of error.

# Diagnostic Medical Sonographers

**Produce ultrasonic recordings of internal organs for use by physicians.**

- Average annual earnings: $65,860
- Middle 50% of earners: $54,260–$76,890
- Earnings growth potential: Low (31.7%)
- Growth: 43.6%
- Annual job openings: 3,170
- Self-employed: 0.2%

## BEST-PAYING INDUSTRIES

| Industry | Median Earnings | Workforce |
|---|---|---|
| Ambulatory Health-Care Services | $66,100 | 21,280 |
| Hospitals | $65,860 | 34,690 |

## BEST-PAYING METROPOLITAN AREAS

| Metro Area | Median Earnings | Workforce |
|---|---|---|
| Los Angeles–Long Beach–Santa Ana, CA | $76,150 | 1,700 |
| Chicago-Naperville-Joliet, IL-IN-WI | $71,880 | 1,420 |
| Dallas–Fort Worth–Arlington, TX | $67,160 | 1,420 |
| New York–Northern New Jersey–Long Island, NY-NJ-PA | $66,980 | 4,170 |
| Philadelphia-Camden-Wilmington, PA-NJ-DE-MD | $63,270 | 1,610 |
| Miami–Fort Lauderdale–Pompano Beach, FL | $60,490 | 1,600 |

**Considerations for Job Outlook:** Sonographers who are certified in more than one specialty are expected to have better job opportunities.

225

**Major Work Tasks:** Decide which images to include, looking for differences between healthy and pathological areas. Observe screen during scan to ensure that image produced is satisfactory for diagnostic purposes, making adjustments to equipment as required. Observe and care for patients throughout examinations to ensure their safety and comfort. Provide sonogram and oral or written summary of technical findings to physician for use in medical diagnosis. Operate ultrasound equipment to produce and record images of the motion, shape, and composition of blood, organs, tissues, or bodily masses, such as fluid accumulations. Select appropriate equipment settings and adjust patient positions to obtain the best sites and angles. Determine whether scope of exam should be extended, based on findings. Obtain and record accurate patient history, including prior test results or information from physical examinations. Prepare patient for exam by explaining procedure, transferring patient to ultrasound table, scrubbing skin and applying gel, and positioning patient properly. Record and store suitable images, using camera unit connected to the ultrasound equipment. Coordinate work with physicians or other health-care team members, including providing assistance during invasive procedures. Maintain records that include patient information, sonographs and interpretations, files of correspondence, publications and regulations, or quality assurance records, such as pathology, biopsy, or post-operative reports. Perform legal and ethical duties, including preparing safety or accident reports, obtaining written consent from patient to perform invasive procedures, or reporting symptoms of abuse or neglect. Supervise or train students or other medical sonographers. Maintain stock and supplies, preparing supplies for special examinations and ordering supplies when necessary. Clean, check, and maintain sonographic equipment, submitting maintenance requests or performing minor repairs as necessary. Perform clerical duties, such as scheduling exams or special procedures, keeping records, or archiving computerized images.

**Usual Educational Requirement:** Associate degree. **Relevant Educational Program**: Diagnostic Medical Sonography/Sonographer and Ultrasound Technician Training. **Related Knowledge/Courses:** Medicine and Dentistry; Physics; Customer and Personal Service; Biology; Psychology; Therapy and Counseling. **Work Experience Needed:** None. **On-the-Job Training Needed:** None. **Certification/Licensure:** Voluntary certification by association.

**Personality Types:** Investigative–Social–Realistic. **Key Career Cluster:** 08 Health Science. **Key Career Pathway:** 8.2 Diagnostics Services.

**Skills:** Equipment maintenance; science; repairing; operation and control; troubleshooting; equipment selection; operation monitoring; quality control analysis.

**Physical Environment:** Indoors; sitting; standing; using hands; bending or twisting the body; repetitive motions. **Structural Environment:** Importance of being exact or accurate; importance of repeating same tasks; frequency of decision making; freedom to make decisions; impact of decisions on co-workers or company results; time pressure.

## Economics Teachers, Postsecondary

*See Teachers, Postsecondary.*

## Economists

**Conduct research, prepare reports, or formulate plans to address economic problems related to the production and distribution of goods and services or monetary and fiscal policy.**

- Average annual earnings: $91,860
- Middle 50% of earners: $67,150–$123,890
- Earnings growth potential: High (44.0%)
- Growth: 6.1%

- Annual job openings: 580
- Self-employed: 7.7%

### BEST-PAYING INDUSTRIES

| Industry | Median Earnings | Workforce |
|---|---|---|
| Professional, Scientific, and Technical Services | $95,480 | 5,640 |
| Federal, State, and Local Government | $89,710 | 7,070 |
| Religious, Grantmaking, Civic, Professional, and Similar Organizations | $81,010 | 790 |

### BEST-PAYING METROPOLITAN AREAS

| Metro Area | Median Earnings | Workforce |
|---|---|---|
| Washington-Arlington-Alexandria, DC-VA-MD-WV | $112,230 | 5,110 |
| New York–Northern New Jersey–Long Island, NY-NJ-PA | $102,300 | 490 |
| San Francisco–Oakland–Fremont, CA | $99,810 | 900 |
| Los Angeles–Long Beach–Santa Ana, CA | $99,640 | 1,040 |
| Chicago-Naperville-Joliet, IL-IN-WI | $93,290 | 330 |
| Boston-Cambridge-Quincy, MA-NH | $85,090 | 780 |

**Considerations for Job Outlook:** Despite slower-than-average employment growth, job opportunities for individuals with a master's degree or PhD are expected to be good. In particular, those with strong quantitative and analytical skills and related work experience should have the best job prospects. As more companies contract out economics-related work, most job openings for economists will be in consulting services. Applicants with a bachelor's degree are expected to face stiff competition for jobs. Although there will be greater demand for workers with knowledge of economics, many bachelor's degree holders will likely find jobs outside the economist occupation, working instead as research assistants, financial analysts, market analysts, and in similar positions in business and finance. Employment opportunities in government are expected to be highly competitive. Employment of economists is concentrated in large cities.

**Major Work Tasks:** Study economic and statistical data in area of specialization, such as finance, labor, or agriculture. Provide advice and consultation on economic relationships to businesses, public and private agencies, and other employers. Compile, analyze, and report data to explain economic phenomena and forecast market trends, applying mathematical models and statistical techniques. Formulate recommendations, policies, or plans to solve economic problems or to interpret markets. Develop economic guidelines and standards and prepare points of view used in forecasting trends and formulating economic policy. Testify at regulatory or legislative hearings concerning the estimated effects of changes in legislation or public policy and present recommendations based on cost-benefit analyses. Supervise research projects and students' study projects. Forecast production and consumption of renewable resources and supply, consumption and depletion of non-renewable resources. Teach theories, principles, and methods of economics. Study the socioeconomic impacts of new public policies, such as proposed legislation, taxes, services, and regulations. Conduct research on economic issues and disseminate research findings through technical reports or scientific articles in journals. Provide litigation support, such as writing reports for expert testimony or testifying as an expert witness.

**Usual Educational Requirement:** Bachelor's degree. **Relevant Educational Programs**: Agricultural Economics; Applied Economics; Business/Managerial Economics; Development Economics and International Development; Econometrics and Quantitative Economics; Economics, General; Economics, Other; Financial Mathematics; International Economics; Political Economy. **Related Knowledge/Courses:** Economics and Accounting; Mathematics; Geography; Sociology and Anthropology; Law and Government; Education and Training. **Work Experience Needed:** None. **On-the-Job Training Needed:** None. **Certification/Licensure:** None.

**Personality Types:** Investigative–Conventional–Enterprising. **Key Career Cluster:** 07 Government and Public Administration. **Key Career Pathway:** 7.4 Planning.

**Skills:** Mathematics; systems analysis; writing; systems evaluation; programming; judgment and decision making; complex problem solving; speaking.

**Physical Environment:** Indoors; sitting. **Structural Environment:** Freedom to make decisions; structured versus unstructured work; importance of being exact or accurate; level of competition; time pressure; impact of decisions on co-workers or company Results.

### JOB SPECIALIZATION: ENVIRONMENTAL ECONOMISTS

**Assess and quantify the benefits of environmental alternatives, such as use of renewable energy resources.**

**Major Work Tasks:** Prepare and deliver presentations to communicate economic and environmental study results, to present policy recommendations, or to raise awareness of environmental consequences. Demonstrate or promote the economic benefits of sound environmental regulations. Write technical documents or academic articles to communicate study results or economic forecasts. Write social, legal, or economic impact statements to inform decision-makers for natural resource policies, standards, or programs. Write research proposals and grant applications to obtain private or public funding for environmental and economic studies. Examine the exhaustibility of natural resources or the long-term costs of environmental rehabilitation. Develop systems for collecting, analyzing, and interpreting environmental and economic data. Develop environmental research project plans, including information on budgets, goals, deliverables, timelines, and resource requirements. Develop economic models, forecasts, or scenarios to predict future economic and environmental outcomes. Collect and analyze data to compare the environmental implications of economic policy or practice alternatives. Perform complex, dynamic, and integrated mathematical modeling of ecological, environmental, or economic systems. Conduct research to study the relationships among environmental problems and patterns of economic production and consumption. Conduct research on economic and environmental topics, such as alternative fuel use, public and private land use, soil conservation, air and water pollution control, and endangered species protection. Develop programs or policy recommendations to achieve environmental goals in cost-effective ways. Assess the costs and benefits of various activities, policies, or regulations that affect the environment or natural resource stocks. Develop programs or policy recommendations to promote sustainability and sustainable development. Monitor or analyze market and environmental trends. Interpret indicators to ascertain the overall health of an environment. Identify and recommend environmentally-friendly business practices.

**Related Knowledge/Courses:** Economics and Accounting; Mathematics; Geography; Sociology and Anthropology; Law and Government; Biology.

**Personality Types:** Investigative–Enterprising–Conventional.

**Skills:** Mathematics; management of financial resources; systems analysis; programming; systems evaluation; writing; learning strategies; judgment and decision making.

**Physical Environment:** Indoors; sitting. **Structural Environment:** Freedom to make decisions; structured versus unstructured work; importance of being exact or accurate; level of competition; time pressure; impact of decisions on co-workers or company results.

## Education Administrators, All Other

**All education administrators not listed separately.**

- Average annual earnings: $76,860
- Middle 50% of earners: $56,260–$100,830
- Earnings growth potential: High (45.1%)
- Growth: 13.6%
- Annual job openings: 1,360
- Self-employed: 5.7%

**Considerations for Job Outlook:** Increasing student enrollments are expected to drive employment growth for these workers. Prospects are expected to be good.

**Major Work Tasks:** For tasks, see the job specializations.

**Usual Educational Requirement:** Bachelor's degree. **Relevant Educational Programs**: Administration of Special Education; Adult and Continuing Education Administration; Educational Administration and Supervision, Other;

### BEST-PAYING INDUSTRIES

| Industry | Median Earnings | Workforce |
|---|---|---|
| Federal, State, and Local Government | $84,330 | 7,230 |
| Educational Services | $72,660 | 18,060 |

### BEST-PAYING METROPOLITAN AREAS

| Metro Area | Median Earnings | Workforce |
|---|---|---|
| San Diego–Carlsbad–San Marcos, CA | $98,820 | 630 |
| Los Angeles–Long Beach–Santa Ana, CA | $97,050 | 1,320 |
| New York–Northern New Jersey–Long Island, NY-NJ-PA | $89,290 | 1,020 |
| San Francisco–Oakland–Fremont, CA | $73,470 | 640 |
| Minneapolis–St. Paul–Bloomington, MN-WI | $71,720 | 690 |
| Boston-Cambridge-Quincy, MA-NH | $65,810 | 880 |
| Chicago-Naperville-Joliet, IL-IN-WI | $59,710 | 1,420 |

Educational Leadership and Administration, General; Educational, Instructional, and Curriculum Supervision; Higher Education/Higher Education Administration; Superintendency and Educational System Administration; Urban Education and Leadership. **Work Experience Needed:** 1 to 5 years. **On-the-Job Training Needed:** None. **Certification/Licensure:** Licensure in many states.

**Key Career Cluster:** 05 Education and Training. **Key Career Pathway:** 5.1 Administration and Administrative Support.

### JOB SPECIALIZATION: DISTANCE-LEARNING COORDINATORS

**Coordinate day-to-day operations of distance learning programs and schedule courses.**

**Major Work Tasks:** Write and submit grant applications or proposals to secure funding for distance-learning programs. Review distance-learning content to ensure compliance with copyright, licensing, or other requirements. Communicate technical or marketing information about distance learning via podcasts,

**229**

webinars, and other technologies. Train instructors and distance-learning staff in the use or support of distance-learning applications, such as course management software. Troubleshoot and resolve problems with distance-learning equipment or applications. Supervise distance-learning support staff. Purchase equipment or services in accordance with distance-learning plans and budget constraints. Select, direct, and monitor the work of vendors that provide products or services for distance-learning programs. Prepare and manage distance-learning program budgets. Prepare reports summarizing distance-learning statistical data or describing distance-learning program objectives and accomplishments. Negotiate with academic units or instructors and vendors to ensure cost-effective and high-quality distance-learning programs, services, or courses. Monitor technological developments in distance learning for technological means to educational or outreach goals. Evaluate the effectiveness of distance learning programs in promoting knowledge or skill acquisition. Direct and support the technical operation of distance learning classrooms or equipment. Develop distance-learning program goals or plans, including equipment replacement, quality assurance, or course offering plans. Create and maintain websites or databases that support distance learning programs. Assess distance-learning technological or educational needs and goals. Communicate to faculty, students, or other users availability of, or changes to, distance-learning courses or materials, programs, services, or applications. Analyze data to assess distance-learning program status or to inform decisions for distance-learning programs. Provide technical or logistical support to users of distance-learning classrooms, equipment, websites, or services.

**Related Knowledge/Courses:** Education and Training; Communications and Media; Tele-communications; Computers and Electronics; English Language; Sales and Marketing.

**Personality Types:** Enterprising–Conventional.

**Skills:** Management of financial resources; management of material resources; learning strategies; writing; active learning; instructing; negotiation; systems evaluation.

**Physical Environment:** Indoors; sitting; using hands; repetitive motions. **Structural Environment:** Freedom to make decisions; structured versus unstructured work; time pressure; importance of being exact or accurate; importance of repeating same tasks; frequency of decision making.

JOB SPECIALIZATION: FITNESS AND WELLNESS COORDINATORS

**Manage fitness and wellness programs and services. Direct and train staff of health educators, fitness instructors, or recreation workers.**

**Major Work Tasks:** Track attendance, participation, or performance data related to wellness events. Provide individual support or counseling in general wellness or nutrition. Maintain or arrange for maintenance of fitness equipment or facilities. Develop marketing campaigns to promote a healthy lifestyle or participation in fitness or wellness programs. Conduct needs assessments or surveys to determine interest in, or satisfaction with, wellness and fitness programs, events, or services. Teach fitness classes to improve strength, flexibility, cardiovascular conditioning, or general fitness of participants. Select or supervise contractors, such as event hosts or health, fitness, and wellness practitioners. Respond to customer, public, or media requests for information about wellness programs or services. Recommend or approve new program or service offerings to promote wellness and fitness, produce revenues, or minimize costs. Prepare or implement budgets and strategic, operational, purchasing, or maintenance plans. Organize and oversee health screenings or other preventive measures, such as mammography, blood pressure, cholesterol screenings, or flu vaccinations. Organize and oversee events, such as organized runs or walks. Demonstrate proper operation of fitness equipment, such as resistance machines, cardio machines, free weights, or fitness assessment devices. Manage or oversee fitness or recreation facilities, ensuring safe and clean facilities and equipment. Maintain wellness- and fitness-related schedules, records, or reports. Conduct or facilitate training sessions or seminars for wellness and fitness staff. Develop fitness or wellness classes, such as yoga, aerobics, strength training, or aquatics, ensuring a diversity of class offerings. Supervise fitness or wellness specialists, such as fitness instructors, nutritionists, or health educators. Develop or coordinate fitness and wellness programs or services. Interpret insurance data or Health Reimbursement Account (HRA) data to develop programs that address specific needs of target populations.

**Related Knowledge/Courses:** No data available.

**Personality Types:** Enterprising–Social.

**Skills:** No data available.

**Physical Environment:** No data available.
**Structural Environment:** No data available.

## Education Administrators, Elementary and Secondary School

**Plan, direct, or coordinate the academic, administrative, or auxiliary activities of public or private elementary or secondary level schools.**

- Average annual earnings: $87,760
- Middle 50% of earners: $70,920–$108,730
- Earnings growth potential: Medium (33.3%)
- Growth: 9.8%

### BEST-PAYING INDUSTRIES

| Industry | Median Earnings | Workforce |
|---|---|---|
| Educational Services | $87,810 | 222,410 |

### BEST-PAYING METROPOLITAN AREAS

| Metro Area | Median Earnings | Workforce |
|---|---|---|
| New York–Northern New Jersey–Long Island, NY-NJ-PA | $129,120 | 17,600 |
| Washington-Arlington-Alexandria, DC-VA-MD-WV | $106,580 | 5,050 |
| Chicago-Naperville-Joliet, IL-IN-WI | $106,310 | 10,840 |
| Los Angeles–Long Beach–Santa Ana, CA | $106,290 | 6,820 |
| Dallas–Fort Worth–Arlington, TX | $77,650 | 6,060 |
| Houston–Sugar Land–Baytown, TX | $75,040 | 4,560 |

- Annual job openings: 8,970
- Self-employed: 6.1%

**Considerations for Job Outlook:** As student enrollment grows, the number of schools and principals needed to accommodate these students will rise. As a result, demand for principals is expected to grow. Although overall student enrollment is expected to grow, there will be variation by region. Enrollment is projected to grow fastest in the South and West. In the Midwest, enrollment is expected to hold steady, and the Northeast is projected to have declines in enrollment. As a result, employment growth for principals is expected to be faster in the South and West than in the Midwest and Northeast. However, despite expected increases in enrollment, employment growth for public school principals will depend on state and local government budgets.

**Major Work Tasks:** Review and approve new programs, or recommend modifications to existing programs, submitting program proposals for school board approval as necessary. Prepare, maintain, or oversee the preparation and maintenance of attendance, activity, planning, or personnel reports and records. Confer with parents and staff to discuss educational activities, policies, and student behavioral or learning problems. Prepare and submit budget requests and recommendations or grant proposals to solicit program funding. Direct and coordinate school maintenance services and the use of school facilities. Counsel and provide guidance to students regarding personal, academic, vocational, or behavioral issues. Organize and direct committees of specialists, volunteers, and staff to provide technical and advisory assistance for programs. Advocate for new schools to be built or for existing facilities to be repaired or remodeled. Plan and develop instructional methods and content for educational, vocational, or student activity programs. Develop partnerships with businesses, communities, and other organizations to help meet identified educational needs and to provide school-to-work programs. Direct and coordinate activities of teachers, administrators, and support staff at schools, public agencies, and institutions. Evaluate curricula, teaching methods, and programs to determine their effectiveness, efficiency, and utilization and to ensure that school activities comply with federal, state, and local regulations. Set educational standards and goals, and help establish policies and procedures to carry them out. Recruit, hire, train, and evaluate primary and supplemental staff. Enforce discipline and attendance rules. Observe teaching methods and examine learning materials to evaluate and standardize curricula and teaching techniques and to determine areas where improvement is needed. Establish, coordinate, and oversee particular programs across school districts, such as programs to evaluate student academic achievement. Review and interpret government codes and develop programs to ensure adherence to codes and facility safety, security, and maintenance.

**Usual Educational Requirement:** Master's degree. **Relevant Educational Programs**: Educational Leadership and Administration, General; Educational, Instructional, and Curriculum Supervision; Elementary and Middle School Administration/Principalship; Secondary School Administration/Principalship; Superintendency and Educational System Administration. **Related Knowledge/Courses:** Therapy and Counseling; Education and Training; Philosophy and Theology; Sociology and Anthropology; Personnel and Human Resources; History and Archeology. **Work Experience Needed:** 1 to 5 years. **On-the-Job Training Needed:** None. **Certification/Licensure:** Licensure in many states.

**Personality Types:** Enterprising–Social–Conventional. **Key Career Cluster:** 05 Education and Training. **Key Career Pathway:** 5.1 Administration and Administrative Support.

**Skills:** Management of financial resources; management of material resources; learning strategies; management of personnel resources; systems evaluation; systems analysis; persuasion; negotiation.

**Physical Environment:** Indoors; sitting; noise. **Structural Environment:** Freedom to make decisions; structured versus unstructured work; frequency of decision making; impact of decisions on co-workers or company results; time pressure; importance of being exact or accurate.

## Education Administrators, Postsecondary

**Plan, direct, or coordinate research, instructional, student administration and services, and other educational activities at postsecondary institutions.**

- Average annual earnings: $86,490
- Middle 50% of earners: $63,820–$119,890
- Earnings growth potential: Medium (43.4%)
- Growth: 19.0%
- Annual job openings: 6,910
- Self-employed: 4.9%

### BEST-PAYING INDUSTRIES

| Industry | Median Earnings | Workforce |
|---|---|---|
| Educational Services | $86,360 | 121,690 |

### BEST-PAYING METROPOLITAN AREAS

| Metro Area | Median Earnings | Workforce |
|---|---|---|
| Philadelphia-Camden-Wilmington, PA-NJ-DE-MD | $107,450 | 2,690 |
| New York–Northern New Jersey–Long Island, NY-NJ-PA | $102,790 | 7,270 |
| Los Angeles–Long Beach–Santa Ana, CA | $90,530 | 4,460 |
| Boston-Cambridge-Quincy, MA-NH | $88,900 | 5,380 |
| Washington-Arlington-Alexandria, DC-VA-MD-WV | $85,400 | 3,410 |

**Considerations for Job Outlook:** Between 2010 and 2020, a large number of postsecondary education administrators are expected to retire. This should open opportunities for new workers entering the field due to the occupation's need to replace workers who are leaving.

**Major Work Tasks:** Recruit, hire, train, and terminate departmental personnel. Plan, administer, and control budgets, maintain financial records, and produce financial reports. Represent institutions at community and campus events in meetings with other institution personnel and during accreditation processes. Participate in faculty and college committee activities. Establish operational policies and procedures and make any necessary modifications, based on analysis of operations, demographics, and other research information. Participate in student recruitment, selection, and admission, making admissions recommendations when required to do so. Advise students on issues such as course selection, progress toward graduation, and career decisions. Direct, coordinate, and evaluate the activities of personnel, including support staff, engaged in administering academic institutions, departments, or alumni organizations. Formulate strategic plans for the institution. Promote the university by participating in community, state, and national events or meetings and by developing partnerships with industry and secondary education institutions. Provide assistance to faculty and staff in duties, such as teaching classes, conducting orientation programs, issuing transcripts, and scheduling events. Confer with other academic staff to explain and formulate admission requirements and course credit policies. Appoint individuals to faculty positions, and evaluate their performance. Direct activities of administrative departments such as admissions, registration, and career services. Develop curricula, and recommend curricula revisions and additions. Determine course schedules, and coordinate teaching assignments and room assignments to ensure optimum use of buildings and equipment. Consult with government regulatory and licensing agencies to ensure the institution's conformance with applicable standards. Teach courses within their department. Review student misconduct reports requiring disciplinary action, and counsel students regarding such reports. Assess and collect tuition and fees.

**Usual Educational Requirement:** Master's degree. **Relevant Educational Programs:** Com-

233

munity College Education; Educational Leadership and Administration, General; Educational, Instructional, and Curriculum Supervision; Higher Education/Higher Education Administration. **Related Knowledge/ Courses:** Therapy and Counseling; Sociology and Anthropology; Psychology; Personnel and Human Resources; Philosophy and Theology; Education and Training. **Work Experience Needed:** 1 to 5 years. **On-the-Job Training Needed:** None. **Certification/Licensure:** Licensure in many states.

**Personality Types:** Enterprising–Conventional–Social. **Key Career Cluster:** 05 Education and Training. **Key Career Pathway:** 5.1 Administration and Administrative Support.

**Skills:** Management of material resources; management of financial resources; management of personnel resources; negotiation; instructing; time management; systems evaluation; systems analysis.

**Physical Environment:** Indoors; sitting. **Structural Environment:** Freedom to make decisions; structured versus unstructured work; frequency of decision making; impact of decisions on coworkers or company results; importance of being exact or accurate; time pressure.

## Education Teachers, Postsecondary

*See Teachers, Postsecondary.*

## Electrical and Electronic Engineering Technicians

Apply electrical and electronic theory and related knowledge under the direction of engineering staff.

- Average annual earnings: $57,850
- Middle 50% of earners: $44,490–$69,570
- Earnings growth potential: Medium (40.3%)
- Growth: 1.9%

### BEST-PAYING INDUSTRIES

| Industry | Median Earnings | Workforce |
|---|---|---|
| Federal, State, and Local Government | $71,220 | 12,390 |
| Utilities | $65,600 | 7,290 |
| Postal Service | $62,180 | 7,420 |
| Professional, Scientific, and Technical Services | $57,490 | 31,540 |
| Merchant Wholesalers, Durable Goods | $54,100 | 7,530 |
| Computer and Electronic Product Manufacturing | $52,460 | 37,660 |

### BEST-PAYING METROPOLITAN AREAS

| Metro Area | Median Earnings | Workforce |
|---|---|---|
| Washington-Arlington-Alexandria, DC-VA-MD-WV | $68,100 | 3,980 |
| Houston–Sugar Land–Baytown, TX | $63,190 | 3,390 |
| New York–Northern New Jersey–Long Island, NY-NJ-PA | $62,180 | 5,310 |
| Los Angeles–Long Beach–Santa Ana, CA | $59,630 | 6,710 |
| San Jose–Sunnyvale–Santa Clara, CA | $57,900 | 4,260 |
| Phoenix-Mesa-Scottsdale, AZ | $57,220 | 3,150 |
| San Diego–Carlsbad–San Marcos, CA | $57,100 | 3,140 |
| Boston-Cambridge-Quincy, MA-NH | $56,780 | 5,210 |
| Chicago-Naperville-Joliet, IL-IN-WI | $56,010 | 3,590 |
| Dallas–Fort Worth–Arlington, TX | $52,690 | 3,950 |
| Austin–Round Rock, TX | $47,370 | 3,600 |

- Annual job openings: 3,180
- Self-employed: 0.5%

**Considerations for Job Outlook:** Some technicians work in traditional manufacturing industries, many of which are growing slowly or declining. However, employment growth for electrical and electronic engineering technicians will likely occur in engineering services firms as companies seek to contract out these services as a way to lower costs. They also work closely with electrical and electronics and computer hardware engineers in the computer systems design services industry. Demand is expected to be high for technicians in this industry as computer and electronics systems become more integrated. For example, computer, cellular phone, and global positioning systems (GPS) technologies are being included in automobiles and various portable and household electronics systems.

**Major Work Tasks:** For tasks, see the job specializations.

**Usual Educational Requirement:** Associate degree. **Relevant Educational Programs:** Computer Engineering Technology/Technician; Computer Technology/Computer Systems Technology; Electrical and Electronic Engineering Technologies/Technicians, Other; Electrical, Electronic, and Communications Engineering Technology/Technician; Integrated Circuit Design; Semiconductor Manufacturing Technology; Telecommunications Technology/Technician. **Work Experience Needed:** None. **On-the-Job Training Needed:** None. **Certification/Licensure:** None.

**Key Career Cluster:** 15 Science, Technology, Engineering, and Mathematics. **Key Career Pathway:** 15.1 Engineering and Technology.

### JOB SPECIALIZATION: ELECTRICAL ENGINEERING TECHNICIANS

**Apply electrical theory and related knowledge to test and modify developmental or operational electrical machinery and electrical control equipment and circuitry in industrial or commercial plants and laboratories. Usually work under the direction of engineering staff.**

**Major Work Tasks:** Provide technical assistance and resolution when electrical or engineering problems are encountered before, during, and after construction. Assemble electrical and electronic systems and prototypes according to engineering data and knowledge of electrical principles, using hand tools and measuring instruments. Modify electrical prototypes, parts, assemblies, or systems to correct functional deviations. Set up and operate test equipment to evaluate performance of developmental parts, assemblies, or systems under simulated operating conditions, and record results. Collaborate with electrical engineers or other personnel to identify, define, or solve developmental problems. Build, calibrate, maintain, troubleshoot, or repair electrical instruments or testing equipment. Analyze and interpret test information to resolve design-related problems. Draw or modify diagrams and write engineering specifications to clarify design details and functional criteria of experimental electronics units. Conduct inspections for quality control and assurance programs, reporting findings and recommendations. Review existing electrical engineering criteria to identify necessary revisions, deletions, or amendments to outdated material. Plan method or sequence of operations for developing or testing experimental electronic or electrical equipment. Install or maintain electrical control systems or solid state equipment. Write commissioning procedures for electrical installations. Prepare electrical project cost or work-time estimates. Evaluate engineering proposals, shop drawings, and design comments for sound electrical engineering practice and conformance with established safety and design criteria, and recommend approval or disapproval. Prepare contracts and initiate, review, and coordinate modifications to con-

235

tract specifications and plans throughout the construction process. Plan, schedule, and monitor work of support personnel to assist supervisor. Perform supervisory duties, such as recommending work assignments, approving leaves, or completing performance evaluations.

**Related Knowledge/Courses:** Computers and Electronics; Design; Mechanical Devices; Engineering and Technology; Production and Processing; Telecommunications.

**Personality Types:** Realistic–Investigative–Conventional.

**Skills:** Installation; technology design; repairing; equipment maintenance; equipment selection; troubleshooting; quality control analysis; operation monitoring.

**Physical Environment:** Indoors; sitting; using hands; noise. **Structural Environment:** Frequency of decision making; importance of being exact or accurate; freedom to make decisions; time pressure; structured versus unstructured work; impact of decisions on coworkers or company results.

## JOB SPECIALIZATION: ELECTRONICS ENGINEERING TECHNICIANS

**Lay out, build, test, troubleshoot, repair, and modify developmental and production electronic components, parts, equipment, and systems, such as computer equipment, missile control instrumentation, electron tubes, test equipment, and machine tool numerical controls, applying principles and theories of electronics, electrical circuitry, engineering mathematics, electronic and electrical testing, and physics. Usually work under the direction of engineering staff.**

**Major Work Tasks:** Test electronics units, using standard test equipment, and analyze results to evaluate performance and determine need for adjustment. Perform preventative maintenance or calibration of equipment or systems. Read blueprints, wiring diagrams, schematic drawings, or engineering instruc-

tions for assembling electronics units and applying knowledge of electronic theory and components. Identify and resolve equipment malfunctions, working with manufacturers or field representatives as necessary to procure replacement parts. Maintain system logs or manuals to document testing or operation of equipment. Assemble, test, or maintain circuitry or electronic components, according to engineering instructions, technical manuals, or knowledge of electronics, using hand or power tools. Adjust or replace defective or improperly functioning circuitry or electronics components, using hand tools or soldering iron. Procure parts and maintain inventory and related documentation. Maintain working knowledge of state-of-the-art tools or software by reading or attending conferences, workshops, or other training. Provide user applications or engineering support or recommendations for new or existing equipment with regard to installation, upgrades, or enhancements. Write reports or record data on testing techniques, laboratory equipment, or specifications to assist engineers. Provide customer support and education, working with users to identify needs, determine sources of problems, or to provide information on product use. Research equipment or component needs, sources, competitive prices, delivery times, or ongoing operational costs. Design basic circuitry and draft sketches for clarification of details and design documentation under engineers' direction, using drafting instruments or computer-aided design (CAD) equipment. Build prototypes from rough sketches or plans. Develop or upgrade preventative maintenance procedures for components, equipment, parts, or systems. Fabricate parts, such as coils, terminal boards, or chassis, using bench lathes, drills, or other machine tools. Write computer or microprocessor software programs.

**Related Knowledge/Courses:** Engineering and Technology; Design; Mechanical Devices;

Computers and Electronics; Physics; Telecommunications.

**Personality Types:** Realistic–Investigative.

**Skills:** Repairing; equipment maintenance; equipment selection; troubleshooting; science; operations analysis; operation and control; programming.

**Physical Environment:** Indoors; sitting; using hands; noise. **Structural Environment:** Freedom to make decisions; importance of being exact or accurate; structured versus unstructured work; impact of decisions on co-workers or company results; frequency of decision making; time pressure.

## Electrical and Electronics Repairers, Powerhouse, Substation, and Relay

**Inspect, test, repair, or maintain electrical equipment in generating stations, substations, and in-service relays.**

### BEST-PAYING INDUSTRIES

| Industry | Median Earnings | Workforce |
|---|---|---|
| Utilities | $69,150 | 17,020 |
| Federal, State, and Local Government | $69,050 | 3,760 |

### BEST-PAYING METROPOLITAN AREAS

| Metro Area | Median Earnings | Workforce |
|---|---|---|
| Los Angeles–Long Beach–Santa Ana, CA | $85,750 | 570 |
| Philadelphia-Camden-Wilmington, PA-NJ-DE-MD | $71,320 | 520 |
| Chicago-Naperville-Joliet, IL-IN-WI | $69,890 | 700 |
| Washington-Arlington-Alexandria, DC-VA-MD-WV | $69,100 | 880 |

- Average annual earnings: $68,810
- Middle 50% of earners: $58,850–$77,120
- Earnings growth potential: Low (29.8%)
- Growth: 4.9%
- Annual job openings: 690
- Self-employed: 0.0%

**Considerations for Job Outlook:** Overall job opportunities should be best for applicants who have an associate degree in electronics, certification, or related experience. In addition to employment growth, the need to replace workers who transfer to other occupations or leave the labor force will result in some job openings.

**Major Work Tasks:** Construct, test, maintain, and repair substation relay and control systems. Inspect and test equipment and circuits to identify malfunctions or defects, using wiring diagrams and testing devices such as ohmmeters, voltmeters, or ammeters. Consult manuals, schematics, wiring diagrams, and engineering personnel to troubleshoot and solve equipment problems and to determine optimum equipment functioning. Notify facility personnel of equipment shutdowns. Open and close switches to isolate defective relays, performing adjustments or repairs. Prepare and maintain records detailing tests, repairs, and maintenance. Analyze test data to diagnose malfunctions, to determine performance characteristics of systems, or to evaluate effects of system modifications. Test insulators and bushings of equipment by inducing voltage across insulation, testing current, and calculating insulation loss. Repair, replace, and clean equipment and components such as circuit breakers, brushes, and commutators. Disconnect voltage regulators, bolts, and screws, and connect replacement regulators to high-voltage lines. Schedule and supervise the construction and testing of special devices and the implementation of unique monitoring or control systems. Run signal quality and connectivity tests for

**237**

individual cables, and record results. Schedule and supervise splicing or termination of cables in color-code order. Test oil in circuit breakers and transformers for dielectric strength, refilling oil periodically. Maintain inventories of spare parts for all equipment, requisitioning parts as necessary. Set forms and pour concrete footings for installation of heavy equipment.

**Usual Educational Requirement:** Postsecondary vocational training. **Relevant Educational Programs**: Industrial Electronics Technology/Technician; Electrical and Power Transmission Installation/Installer, General; Lineworker Training. **Related Knowledge/ Courses:** Mechanical Devices; Design; Telecommunications; Building and Construction; Physics; Public Safety and Security. **Work Experience Needed:** None. **On-the-Job Training Needed:** Long-term on-the-job training. **Certification/Licensure:** Voluntary certification by association.

**Personality Types:** Realistic–Conventional. **Key Career Cluster:** 02 Architecture and Construction. **Key Career Pathway:** 2.2 Construction.

**Skills:** Equipment maintenance; repairing; troubleshooting; operation and control; quality control analysis; science; operation monitoring; equipment selection.

**Physical Environment:** Outdoors; indoors; standing; using hands; noise; very hot or cold. **Structural Environment:** Importance of being exact or accurate; freedom to make decisions; consequence of error; frequency of decision making; impact of decisions on co-workers or company results; structured versus unstructured work.

## Electrical Engineers

**Research, design, develop, test, or supervise the manufacturing and installation of electrical equipment, components, or systems.**

- Average annual earnings: $87,920
- Middle 50% of earners: $69,690–$110,850
- Earnings growth potential: Medium (35.7%)
- Growth: 7.0%
- Annual job openings: 4,780
- Self-employed: 2.2%

**BEST-PAYING INDUSTRIES**

| Industry | Median Earnings | Workforce |
|---|---|---|
| Transportation Equipment Manufacturing | $96,550 | 9,390 |
| Computer and Electronic Product Manufacturing | $91,970 | 34,550 |
| Federal, State, and Local Government | $91,480 | 8,500 |
| Professional, Scientific, and Technical Services | $88,330 | 50,110 |
| Utilities | $85,970 | 15,900 |
| Machinery Manufacturing | $79,480 | 8,050 |

**Considerations for Job Outlook:** Growth for electrical and electronics engineers will largely occur in engineering services firms, as more companies are expected to cut costs by contracting engineering services rather than directly employing engineers. These engineers will also experience job growth in computer systems design and wireless telecommunications as these industries continue to implement more powerful portable computing devices.

**Major Work Tasks:** Confer with engineers, customers, or others to discuss existing or potential engineering projects or products. Design, implement, maintain, or improve electrical instruments, equipment, facilities, components, products, or systems for commer-

| Metro Area | Median Earnings | Workforce |
|---|---|---|
| San Jose–Sunnyvale–Santa Clara, CA | $113,730 | 6,920 |
| Los Angeles–Long Beach–Santa Ana, CA | $103,090 | 7,610 |
| Boston-Cambridge-Quincy, MA-NH | $100,080 | 7,150 |
| Washington-Arlington-Alexandria, DC-VA-MD-WV | $99,870 | 4,460 |
| Houston–Sugar Land–Baytown, TX | $94,230 | 3,310 |
| New York–Northern New Jersey–Long Island, NY-NJ-PA | $92,060 | 6,950 |
| Philadelphia-Camden-Wilmington, PA-NJ-DE-MD | $90,660 | 3,380 |
| Dallas–Fort Worth–Arlington, TX | $88,540 | 4,450 |
| Minneapolis–St. Paul–Bloomington, MN-WI | $84,970 | 3,270 |
| Chicago-Naperville-Joliet, IL-IN-WI | $84,310 | 3,680 |
| Detroit-Warren-Livonia, MI | $78,920 | 3,400 |

cial, industrial, or domestic purposes. Operate computer-assisted engineering or design software or equipment to perform engineering tasks. Direct or coordinate manufacturing, construction, installation, maintenance, support, documentation, or testing activities to ensure compliance with specifications, codes, or customer requirements. Perform detailed calculations to compute and establish manufacturing, construction, or installation standards or specifications. Plan or implement research methodology or procedures to apply principles of electrical theory to engineering projects. Pre-

pare specifications for purchases of materials or equipment. Supervise or train project team members as necessary. Investigate or test vendors' or competitors' products. Oversee project production efforts to assure projects are completed on time and within budget. Prepare technical drawings, specifications of electrical systems, or topographical maps to ensure that installation and operations conform to standards and customer requirements. Investigate customer or public complaints, determine nature and extent of problem, and recommend remedial measures. Develop budgets, estimating labor, material, and construction costs. Compile data and write reports regarding existing or potential electrical engineering studies or projects. Inspect completed installations and observe operations to ensure conformance to design and equipment specifications and compliance with operational and safety standards. Plan layout of electric power generating plants or distribution lines or stations. Assist in developing capital project programs for new equipment or major repairs. Collect data relating to commercial or residential development, population, or power system interconnection to determine operating efficiency of electrical systems. Conduct field surveys or study maps, graphs, diagrams, or other data to identify and correct power system problems.

**Usual Educational Requirement:** Bachelor's degree. **Relevant Educational Programs**: Electrical and Electronics Engineering; Electrical, Electronics and Communications Engineering, Other. **Related Knowledge/Courses:** Design; Engineering and Technology; Physics; Mechanical Devices; Mathematics; Computers and Electronics. **Work Experience Needed:** None. **On-the-Job Training Needed:** None. **Certification/Licensure:** Licensure for government positions.

**Personality Types:** Investigative–Realistic. **Key Career Cluster:** 15 Science, Technology, Engineering, and Mathematics. **Key Career Pathway:** 15.1 Engineering and Technology.

**239**

**Skills:** Science; troubleshooting; operations analysis; repairing; mathematics; equipment maintenance; operation monitoring; quality control analysis.

**Physical Environment:** Indoors; sitting; noise.
**Structural Environment:** Importance of being exact or accurate; freedom to make decisions; structured versus unstructured work; time pressure; impact of decisions on co-workers or company results; frequency of decision making.

## Electrical Power-Line Installers and Repairers

**Install or repair cables or wires used in electrical power or distribution systems.**

- Average annual earnings: $63,250
- Middle 50% of earners: $48,920–$75,010
- Earnings growth potential: Medium (42.3%)
- Growth: 13.2%
- Annual job openings: 5,270
- Self-employed: 1.1%

### BEST-PAYING INDUSTRIES

| Industry | Median Earnings | Workforce |
|---|---|---|
| Utilities | $66,370 | 61,000 |
| Federal, State, and Local Government | $61,120 | 15,820 |
| Heavy and Civil Engineering Construction | $55,870 | 27,200 |

### BEST-PAYING METROPOLITAN AREAS

| Metro Area | Median Earnings | Workforce |
|---|---|---|
| Chicago-Naperville-Joliet, IL-IN-WI | $81,840 | 2,270 |
| Atlanta–Sandy Springs–Marietta, GA | $46,110 | 2,500 |

**Considerations for Job Outlook:** Good job opportunities are expected overall. Highly skilled workers with apprenticeship training or a two-year associate degree in telecommunications, electronics, or electricity should have the best job opportunities. Employment opportunities should be particularly good for electrical power-line installers and repairers, as many workers in this field are expected to retire. Because of layoffs in the 1990s, more of the electrical power industry is near retirement age than in most industries. This is of special concern for electrical line workers who must be in good physical shape and cannot necessarily put off retirement.

**Major Work Tasks:** Adhere to safety practices and procedures, such as checking equipment regularly and erecting barriers around work areas. Open switches or attach grounding devices to remove electrical hazards from disturbed or fallen lines or to facilitate repairs. Climb poles or use truck-mounted buckets to access equipment. Place insulating or fireproofing materials over conductors and joints. Install, maintain, and repair electrical distribution and transmission systems, including conduits, cables, wires, and related equipment, such as transformers, circuit breakers, and switches. Identify defective sectionalizing devices, circuit breakers, fuses, voltage regulators, transformers, switches, relays, or wiring, using wiring diagrams and electrical-testing instruments. Drive vehicles equipped with tools and materials to job sites. Coordinate work assignment preparation and completion with other workers. Inspect and test power lines and auxiliary equipment to locate and identify problems, using reading and testing instruments. String wire conductors and cables between poles, towers, trenches, pylons, and buildings, setting lines in place and using winches to adjust tension. Test conductors, according to electrical diagrams and specifications, to identify corresponding conductors and to prevent incorrect connections. Replace or straighten damaged poles. Install watt-hour meters and connect service drops between power lines and consumers' facilities. Attach cross-arms, insulators, and auxiliary equipment to poles prior to installing them. Travel in trucks, helicopters, and airplanes to inspect lines for freedom from obstruction and adequacy of insulation. Dig holes, using augers, and set poles, using cranes and power equipment. Trim trees that could be hazardous to the functioning of cables or wires. Splice or solder cables together or to overhead transmission lines, customer service lines, or street light lines, using hand tools, epoxies, or specialized equipment. Clean, tin, and splice corresponding conductors by twisting ends together or by joining ends with metal clamps and soldering connections. Pull up cable by hand from large reels mounted on trucks.

**Usual Educational Requirement:** High school diploma or equivalent. **Relevant Educational Programs**: Electrical and Power Transmission Installation/Installer, General; Electrical and Power Transmission Installers, Other; Lineworker. **Related Knowledge/Courses:** Mechanical Devices; Physics; Telecommunications; Transportation; Customer and Personal Service; Engineering and Technology. **Work Experience Needed:** None. **On-the-Job Training Needed:** Long-term on-the-job training. **Certification/Licensure:** Voluntary certification by association.

**Personality Types:** Realistic–Investigative–Conventional. **Key Career Cluster:** 02 Architecture and Construction. **Key Career Pathway:** 2.2 Construction.

**Skills:** Repairing; equipment maintenance; troubleshooting; installation; operation and control; operation monitoring; equipment selection; quality control analysis.

**Physical Environment:** Outdoors; standing; using hands; noise; very hot or cold; bright or inadequate lighting. **Structural Environment:** Frequency of decision making; importance of being exact or accurate; freedom to make decisions; impact of decisions on co-workers or company results; structured versus unstructured work; time pressure.

## Electronics Engineers, Except Computer

**Research, design, develop, or test electronic components and systems for commercial, industrial, military, or scientific use employing knowledge of electronic theory and materials properties.**

- Average annual earnings: $91,820
- Middle 50% of earners: $72,490–$115,120
- Earnings growth potential: Medium (36.3%)
- Growth: 4.9%
- Annual job openings: 4,060
- Self-employed: 2.1%

**Considerations for Job Outlook:** Growth for electrical and electronics engineers will largely occur in engineering services firms, as more companies are expected to cut costs by contracting engineering services rather than directly employing engineers. These engineers will also experience job growth in computer

### BEST-PAYING INDUSTRIES

| Industry | Median Earnings | Workforce |
| --- | --- | --- |
| Federal, State, and Local Government | $102,410 | 7,760 |
| Professional, Scientific, and Technical Services | $96,040 | 33,750 |
| Computer and Electronic Product Manufacturing | $94,500 | 29,150 |
| Merchant Wholesalers, Durable Goods | $87,590 | 7,620 |
| Telecommunications | $83,020 | 24,810 |

241

## Your Guide to High-Paying Careers

| Metro Area | Median Earnings | Workforce |
|---|---|---|
| San Jose–Sunnyvale–Santa Clara, CA | $124,130 | 8,040 |
| Washington-Arlington-Alexandria, DC-VA-MD-WV | $107,960 | 4,880 |
| Boston-Cambridge-Quincy, MA-NH | $106,380 | 4,800 |
| San Diego–Carlsbad–San Marcos, CA | $103,990 | 3,420 |
| San Francisco–Oakland–Fremont, CA | $100,190 | 3,300 |
| New York–Northern New Jersey–Long Island, NY-NJ-PA | $100,130 | 4,390 |
| Los Angeles–Long Beach–Santa Ana, CA | $96,850 | 9,660 |
| Dallas–Fort Worth–Arlington, TX | $89,710 | 5,230 |
| Phoenix-Mesa-Scottsdale, AZ | $87,690 | 3,300 |
| Denver-Aurora, CO | $83,820 | 2,900 |
| Chicago-Naperville-Joliet, IL-IN-WI | $80,380 | 3,590 |

systems design and wireless telecommunications as these industries continue to implement more powerful portable computing devices.

**Major Work Tasks:** Design electronic components, software, products, or systems for commercial, industrial, medical, military, or scientific applications. Provide technical support and instruction to staff or customers regarding equipment standards, assisting with specific, difficult in-service engineering. Operate computer-assisted engineering and design software and equipment to perform engineering tasks. Analyze system requirements, capacity, cost, and customer needs to determine feasibility of project and develop system plan. Confer with engineers, customers, vendors or others to discuss existing and potential engineering projects or products. Review and evaluate work of others, inside and outside the organization, to ensure effectiveness, technical adequacy, and compatibility in the resolution of complex engineering problems. Determine material and equipment needs and order supplies. Inspect electronic equipment, instruments, products, or systems to ensure conformance to specifications, safety standards, or applicable codes or regulations. Evaluate operational systems, prototypes, and proposals and recommend repair or design modifications, based on factors, such as environment, service, cost, and system capabilities. Prepare documentation containing information such as confidential descriptions or specifications of proprietary hardware or software, product development or introduction schedules, product costs, or information about product performance weaknesses. Direct or coordinate activities concerned with manufacture, construction, installation, maintenance, operation, or modification of electronic equipment, products, or systems. Develop or perform operational, maintenance, or testing procedures for electronic products, components, equipment, or systems. Plan or develop applications or modifications for electronic properties used in components, products, or systems to improve technical performance. Prepare engineering sketches or specifications for construction, relocation, or installation of equipment, facilities, products, or systems. Plan and implement research, methodology, and procedures to apply principles of electronic theory to engineering projects.

**Usual Educational Requirement:** Bachelor's degree. **Relevant Educational Programs**: Electrical and Electronics Engineering; Electrical, Electronics and Communications Engineering, Other; Telecommunications Engineering. **Related Knowledge/Courses:** Design; Engineering and Technology; Physics; Computers and Electronics; Mathematics; Production and Processing. **Work Experience Needed:** None. **On-**

the-Job Training Needed: None. **Certification/ Licensure:** Licensure for government positions.

**Personality Types:** Investigative–Realistic. **Key Career Cluster:** 15 Science, Technology, Engineering, and Mathematics. **Key Career Pathway:** 15.1 Engineering and Technology.

**Skills:** Programming; repairing; technology design; equipment selection; equipment maintenance; troubleshooting; operation and control; quality control analysis.

**Physical Environment:** Indoors; sitting; using hands. **Structural Environment:** Freedom to make decisions; structured versus unstructured work; importance of being exact or accurate; impact of decisions on co-workers or company results; time pressure; level of competition.

### JOB SPECIALIZATION: RADIO FREQUENCY IDENTIFICATION DEVICE SPECIALISTS

**Design and implement radio frequency identification device (RFID) systems used to track shipments or goods.**

**Major Work Tasks:** Verify compliance of developed applications with architectural standards and established practices. Read current literature, attend meetings or conferences, or talk with colleagues to stay abreast of industry research about new technologies. Provide technical support for radio frequency identification device (RFID) technology. Perform systems analysis or programming of RFID technology. Document equipment or process details of RFID technology. Train users in details of system operation. Analyze RFID-related supply chain data. Test tags or labels to ensure readability. Test RFID software to ensure proper functioning. Select appropriate RFID tags and determine placement locations. Perform site analyses to determine system configurations, processes to be impacted, or on-site obstacles to technology implementation. Perform acceptance testing on newly installed or updated systems. Identify operational requirements for new systems to inform selection of technologi-

cal solutions. Determine usefulness of new RFID technologies. Develop process flows, work instructions, or standard operating procedures for RFID systems. Determine means of integrating RFID into other applications. Define and compare possible RFID solutions to inform selection for specific projects. Create simulations or models of RFID systems to provide information for selection and configuration. Install, test, or maintain RFID systems. Integrate tags, readers, or software in RFID designs. Collect data about existing client hardware, software, networking, or key business processes to inform implementation of RFID technology.

**Related Knowledge/Courses:** No data available.

**Personality Types:** Realistic–Investigative–Conventional.

**Skills:** No data available.

**Physical Environment:** No data available. **Structural Environment:** No data available.

## Elevator Installers and Repairers

**Assemble, install, repair, or maintain electric or hydraulic freight or passenger elevators, escalators, or dumbwaiters.**

- Average annual earnings: $76,650
- Middle 50% of earners: $59,800–$90,900
- Earnings growth potential: High (48.4%)
- Growth: 11.3%
- Annual job openings: 820
- Self-employed: 0.0%

### BEST-PAYING INDUSTRIES

| Industry | Median Earnings | Workforce |
|---|---|---|
| Specialty Trade Contractors | $77,500 | 17,620 |

## Your Guide to High-Paying Careers

### BEST-PAYING METROPOLITAN AREAS

| Metro Area | Median Earnings | Workforce |
|---|---|---|
| Los Angeles–Long Beach–Santa Ana, CA | $95,940 | 910 |
| San Francisco–Oakland–Fremont, CA | $90,140 | 540 |
| Philadelphia-Camden-Wilmington, PA-NJ-DE-MD | $85,550 | 640 |
| Washington-Arlington-Alexandria, DC-VA-MD-WV | $84,120 | 890 |
| Baltimore-Towson, MD | $81,060 | 640 |
| New York–Northern New Jersey–Long Island, NY-NJ-PA | $73,930 | 3,350 |
| Chicago-Naperville-Joliet, IL-IN-WI | $73,430 | 620 |
| Dallas–Fort Worth–Arlington, TX | $68,720 | 580 |
| Houston–Sugar Land–Baytown, TX | $67,660 | 1,000 |

**Considerations for Job Outlook:** Overall job opportunities should be excellent because the dangerous and physically challenging aspects of the work reduce the number of qualified applicants. Job prospects for entry-level workers should be best for those who have postsecondary education in electronics or who have experience in the military. Elevators, escalators, moving walkways, and related equipment need to keep working year-round, so employment of elevator repairers is less affected by economic downturns and seasonality than employment in other construction occupations.

**Major Work Tasks:** Assemble, install, repair, and maintain elevators, escalators, moving sidewalks, and dumbwaiters, using hand and power tools, and testing devices such as test lamps, ammeters, and voltmeters. Test newly installed equipment to ensure that it meets specifications, such as stopping at floors for set amounts of time. Locate malfunctions in brakes, motors, switches, and signal and control systems, using test equipment. Check that safety regulations and building codes are met, and complete service reports verifying conformance to standards. Connect electrical wiring to control panels and electric motors. Adjust safety controls, counterweights, door mechanisms, and components such as valves, ratchets, seals, and brake linings. Read and interpret blueprints to determine the layout of system components, frameworks, and foundations and to select installation equipment. Inspect wiring connections, control panel hookups, door installations, and alignments and clearances of cars and hoistways to ensure that equipment will operate properly. Disassemble defective units, and repair or replace parts, such as locks, gears, cables, and electric wiring. Maintain log books that detail all repairs and checks performed. Participate in additional training to keep skills up to date. Attach guide shoes and rollers to minimize the lateral motion of cars as they travel through shafts. Connect car frames to counterweights, using steel cables. Bolt or weld steel rails to the walls of shafts to guide elevators, working from scaffolding or platforms. Assemble elevator cars, installing each car's platform, walls, and doors. Install outer doors and door frames at elevator entrances on each floor of a structure. Install electrical wires and controls by attaching conduit along shaft walls from floor to floor and pulling plastic-covered wires through the conduit. Cut prefabricated sections of framework, rails, and other components to specified dimensions. Operate elevators to determine power demands, and test power consumption to detect overload factors. Assemble electrically powered stairs, steel frameworks, and tracks, and install associated motors and electrical wiring.

**Usual Educational Requirement:** High school diploma or equivalent. **Relevant Educational Program:** Industrial Mechanics and Maintenance Technology. **Related Knowledge/ Courses:** Building and Construction; Mechanical Devices; Physics; Design; Engineering and Technology; Public Safety and Security. **Work Experience Needed:** None. **On-the-Job Training Needed:** Apprenticeship. **Certification/Licensure:** Licensure; voluntary certification by association.

**Personality Types:** Realistic–Investigative–Conventional. **Key Career Cluster:** 02 Architecture and Construction. **Key Career Pathway:** 2.2 Construction.

**Skills:** Repairing; equipment maintenance; installation; troubleshooting; equipment selection; operation and control; quality control analysis; operation monitoring.

**Physical Environment:** Indoors; outdoors; standing; walking and running; using hands; bending or twisting the body. **Structural Environment:** Importance of being exact or accurate; structured versus unstructured work; freedom to make decisions; consequence of error; frequency of decision making; impact of decisions on co-workers or company results.

## Engineering Teachers, Postsecondary

*See Teachers, Postsecondary.*

## Engineering Technicians, Except Drafters, All Other

**All engineering technicians, except drafters, not listed separately.**

- Average annual earnings: $59,440
- Middle 50% of earners: $44,770–$74,620
- Earnings growth potential: High (46.1%)
- Growth: 4.7%
- Annual job openings: 1,680
- Self-employed: 0.5%

**Considerations for Job Outlook:** As network technology becomes more complex and has wider applications, these workers will be

### BEST-PAYING INDUSTRIES

| Industry | Median Earnings | Workforce |
|---|---|---|
| Federal, State, and Local Government | $66,490 | 21,040 |
| Transportation Equipment Manufacturing | $62,000 | 3,360 |
| Professional, Scientific, and Technical Services | $55,320 | 12,690 |

### BEST-PAYING METROPOLITAN AREAS

| Metro Area | Median Earnings | Workforce |
|---|---|---|
| Washington–Arlington-Alexandria, DC-VA-MD-WV | $73,560 | 2,360 |
| Houston–Sugar Land–Baytown, TX | $66,190 | 4,090 |
| San Diego–Carlsbad–San Marcos, CA | $65,380 | 1,600 |
| Baltimore-Towson, MD | $62,870 | 1,570 |
| Los Angeles–Long Beach–Santa Ana, CA | $60,600 | 2,210 |
| New York–Northern New Jersey–Long Island, NY-NJ-PA | $58,530 | 1,330 |
| Chicago-Naperville-Joliet, IL-IN-WI | $57,250 | 2,600 |
| Detroit-Warren-Livonia, MI | $51,060 | 1,750 |
| Dallas–Fort Worth–Arlington, TX | $45,460 | 1,690 |

needed to resolve problems. Prospects should be good; job seekers with a bachelor's degree and relevant work experience should have the best opportunities.

**Major Work Tasks:** For tasks, see the job specializations.

245

**Usual Educational Requirement:** Associate degree. **Relevant Educational Programs**: Architectural Engineering Technology/Technician; Biomedical Technology/Technician; Chemical Engineering Technology/Technician; Computer Hardware Technology/Technician; Energy Management and Systems Technology/Technician; Environmental Control Technologies/Technicians, Other; Heating, Ventilation, Air Conditioning, and Refrigeration Engineering Technology/Technician; Hydraulics and Fluid Power Technology/Technician; Laser and Optical Technology/Technician; Metallurgical Technology/Technician; Mining Technology/Technician; Packaging Science; Plastics and Polymer Engineering Technology/Technician; Solar Energy Technology/Technician; Welding Engineering Technology/Technician. **Work Experience Needed:** None. **On-the-Job Training Needed:** None. **Certification/Licensure:** None.

**Key Career Cluster:** 15 Science, Technology, Engineering, and Mathematics. **Key Career Pathway:** 15.1 Engineering and Technology.

JOB SPECIALIZATION: ELECTRICAL ENGINEERING TECHNOLOGISTS

**Apply engineering theory and technical skills to support electrical engineering activities, such as process control, electrical power distribution, and instrumentation design. Prepare layouts of machinery and equipment, plan the flow of work, conduct statistical studies, and analyze production costs.**

**Major Work Tasks:** Participate in training or continuing education activities to stay abreast of engineering or industry advances. Diagnose, test, or analyze the performance of electrical components, assemblies, or systems. Set up and operate standard or specialized testing equipment. Review installation or quality assurance documentation. Review, develop, and prepare maintenance standards. Compile and maintain records documenting engineering schematics, installed equipment, installation or opera-

tional problems, resources used, repairs, or corrective action performed. Review electrical engineering plans to ensure adherence to design specifications and compliance with applicable electrical codes and standards. Calculate design specifications or cost, material, and resource estimates, and prepare project schedules and budgets. Assist engineers and scientists in conducting applied research in electrical engineering. Supervise the construction or testing of electrical prototypes, according to general instructions and established standards. Install or maintain electrical control systems, industrial automation systems, or electrical equipment, including control circuits, variable speed drives, or programmable logic controllers. Design or modify engineering schematics for electrical transmission and distribution systems or for electrical installation in residential, commercial, or industrial buildings, using computer-aided design (CAD) software. Assemble or test solar photovoltaic products, such as inverters or energy management systems. Build or test electrical components of electric-drive vehicles or prototype vehicles. Conduct statistical studies to analyze or compare production costs for sustainable or nonsustainable designs. Construct and evaluate electrical components for consumer electronics applications such as fuel cells for consumer electronic devices, power saving devices for computers or televisions, and energy efficient power chargers. Create or modify electrical components to be used in renewable energy generation. Evaluate electrical engineering plans to determine whether they comply with applicable environmental standards.

**Related Knowledge/Courses:** Design; Engineering and Technology; Physics; Computers and Electronics; Mechanical Devices; Telecommunications.

**Personality Types:** Realistic–Investigative–Conventional.

246

**Skills:** Installation; management of financial resources; troubleshooting; technology design; science; management of material resources; equipment maintenance; equipment selection.

**Physical Environment:** Indoors; sitting; noise. **Structural Environment:** Freedom to make decisions; structured versus unstructured work; importance of being exact or accurate; impact of decisions on co-workers or company results; frequency of decision making; consequence of error.

### JOB SPECIALIZATION: ELECTROMECHANICAL ENGINEERING TECHNOLOGISTS

**Apply engineering theory and technical skills to support electromechanical engineering activities, such as computer-based process control, instrumentation, and machine design. Prepare layouts of machinery and equipment, plan the flow of work, conduct statistical studies, and analyze production costs.**

**Major Work Tasks:** Modify, maintain, or repair electrical, electronic, or mechanical components, equipment, or systems to ensure proper functioning. Specify, coordinate, or conduct quality-control or quality-assurance programs and procedures. Establish and maintain inventory, records, or documentation systems. Fabricate or assemble mechanical, electrical, or electronic components or assemblies. Select electromechanical equipment, materials, components, or systems to meet functional specifications. Select and use laboratory, operational, or diagnostic techniques or test equipment to assess electromechanical circuits, equipment, processes, systems, or subsystems. Produce electrical, electronic, or mechanical drawings or other related documents or graphics necessary for electromechanical design, using computer-aided design (CAD) software. Install or program computer hardware or machine or instrumentation software in microprocessor-based systems. Consult with machinists or technicians to ensure that electromechanical

equipment or systems meet design specifications. Translate electromechanical drawings into design specifications, applying principles of engineering, thermal or fluid sciences, mathematics, or statistics. Collaborate with engineers to implement electromechanical designs in industrial or other settings. Analyze engineering designs of logic or digital circuitry, motor controls, instrumentation, or data acquisition for implementation into new or existing automated, servomechanical, or other electromechanical systems. Conduct statistical studies to analyze or compare production costs for sustainable and nonsustainable designs. Determine whether selected electromechanical components comply with environmental standards and regulations. Develop or implement programs related to the environmental impact of engineering activities. Identify energy-conserving production or fabrication methods, such as by bending metal rather than cutting and welding or casting metal. Test and analyze thermodynamic systems for renewable energy applications, such as solar or wind, to maximize energy production.

**Related Knowledge/Courses:** Physics; Engineering and Technology; Mechanical Devices; Design; Computers and Electronics; Mathematics.

**Personality Types:** Realistic–Investigative–Conventional.

**Skills:** Installation; repairing; equipment maintenance; troubleshooting; equipment selection; programming; quality control analysis; mathematics.

**Physical Environment:** Sitting; using hands; noise; contaminants; hazardous conditions; hazardous equipment. **Structural Environment:** Freedom to make decisions; structured versus unstructured work; importance of being exact or accurate; time pressure; frequency of decision making; impact of decisions on co-workers or company results.

## JOB SPECIALIZATION: ELECTRONICS ENGINEERING TECHNOLOGISTS

**Apply engineering theory and technical skills to support electronics engineering activities, such as electronics systems and instrumentation design and digital signal processing.**

**Major Work Tasks:** Provide support to technical sales staff regarding product characteristics. Educate equipment operators on the proper use of equipment. Modify, maintain, and repair electronics equipment and systems to ensure that they function properly. Assemble circuitry for electronic systems according to engineering instructions, production specifications, or technical manuals. Specify, coordinate, or conduct quality control or quality assurance programs or procedures. Prepare or maintain design, testing, or operational records and documentation. Troubleshoot microprocessors or electronic instruments, equipment, or systems, using electronic test equipment such as logic analyzers. Set up and operate specialized or standard test equipment to diagnose, test, or analyze the performance of electronic components, assemblies, or systems. Select electronics equipment, components, or systems to meet functional specifications. Replace defective components or parts, using hand tools and precision instruments. Produce electronics drawings or other graphics representing industrial control, instrumentation, sensors, or analog or digital telecommunications networks, using computer-aided design (CAD) software. Inspect newly installed equipment to adjust or correct operating problems. Integrate software or hardware components using computer, microprocessor, or control architecture. Supervise the building or testing of prototypes of electronics circuits, equipment, or systems. Evaluate machine or process control requirements to develop device or controller specifications suited to operating environments. Conduct or supervise the installation and operation of electronic equipment and systems. Analyze and implement engineering designs for producing electronic devices and systems and microprocessor-based control applications, applying principles of mathematics, digital signal processing, network analysis, and computer engineering. Assist scientists and engineers in conducting applied research in electronics engineering. Write software programs for microcontrollers or computers in machine, assembly, or other languages.

**Related Knowledge/Courses:** Engineering and Technology; Telecommunications; Physics; Design; Computers and Electronics; Mechanical.

**Personality Types:** Realistic–Investigative–Conventional.

**Skills:** Repairing; equipment maintenance; equipment selection; troubleshooting; technology design; installation; science; programming.

**Physical Environment:** Indoors; sitting; using hands; noise; hazardous conditions. **Structural Environment:** Importance of being exact or accurate; freedom to make decisions; time pressure; structured versus unstructured work; impact of decisions on co-workers or company results; frequency of decision making.

## JOB SPECIALIZATION: FUEL CELL TECHNICIANS

**Install, operate, and maintain integrated fuel cell systems in transportation, stationary, or portable applications.**

**Major Work Tasks:** Recommend improvements to fuel cell design or performance. Perform routine vehicle maintenance procedures, such as part replacements or tune-ups. Document or analyze fuel cell test data, using spreadsheets or other computer software. Collect or maintain fuel cell test data. Calibrate equipment used for fuel cell testing. Test fuel cells or fuel cell stacks, using complex electronic equipment. Assemble fuel cells or fuel cell stacks according to mechanical or electrical assembly documents or schematics. Troubleshoot fuel cell test equipment. Order fuel cell testing materials. Report results of fuel cell tests. Perform routine or preventive maintenance on fuel cell test equipment. Build fuel cell prototypes, following engineering specifications. Conduct tests or provide technical support for tests of prototype fuel cell engines or thermal management systems. Install or test spark ignition (SI) or compression ignition (CI) engines. Install, calibrate, or operate emissions analyzers, cell assist software, fueling systems, or air conditioning systems in engine testing systems. Perform electrochemical performance or durability testing of solid oxide fuel cells.

**Related Knowledge/Courses:** No data available.

**Personality Types:** Realistic–Conventional–Investigative.

**Skills:** No data available.

**Physical Environment:** No data available. **Structural Environment:** No data available.

## JOB SPECIALIZATION: INDUSTRIAL ENGINEERING TECHNOLOGISTS

**Apply engineering theory and technical skills to support industrial engineering activities, such as quality control, inventory control, and material flow methods. May conduct statistical studies and analyze production costs.**

**Major Work Tasks:** Interpret engineering drawings, sketches, or diagrams. Oversee or inspect production processes. Modify equipment or processes to improve resource or cost efficiency. Compile operational data to develop cost or time estimates, schedules, or specifications. Plan the flow of work or materials to maximize efficiency. Monitor and control inventory. Develop or implement programs to address problems related to production, materials, safety, or quality. Analyze, estimate, or report production costs. Prepare schedules for equipment use or routine maintenance. Request equipment upgrades or purchases. Supervise production workers. Create computer applications for manufacturing processes or operations, using computer-aided design (CAD) or computer-assisted manufacturing (CAM) tools. Prepare reports regarding inventories of raw materials or finished products. Develop or conduct quality control tests to ensure consistent production quality. Collect and analyze data related to quality or industrial health and safety programs. Analyze operational, production, economic, or other data, using statistical procedures. Prepare layouts of machinery or equipment, using drafting equipment or computer-aided design (CAD) software. Conduct time and motion studies to identify opportunities to improve worker efficiency. Design plant or production facility layouts. Analyze material flows or supply chains to identify opportunities to improve efficiency and conserve energy. Conduct statistical studies to analyze or compare production costs for sustainable and nonsustainable designs. Develop computerized diagnostic tools to integrate measurements in real time and reduce production downtime. Integrate high-speed loops and advanced control algorithms with graphical system designs to improve the efficiency of production operations.

**Related Knowledge/Courses:** Production and Processing; Engineering and Technology; Design; Mechanical Devices; Mathematics; Economics and Accounting.

**Personality Types:** Investigative–Realistic–Conventional.

**Skills:** Technology design; operations analysis; mathematics; management of material resources; equipment selection; operation monitoring; management of financial resources; programming.

**Physical Environment:** Indoors; sitting; noise; contaminants. **Structural Environment:** Freedom to make decisions; importance of being exact or accurate; structured versus unstructured work; impact of decisions on co-workers or company results; frequency of decision making; importance of repeating same tasks.

**Apply engineering theory and technical skills to support manufacturing engineering activities. Develop tools; implement designs; and integrate machinery, equipment, and computer technologies to ensure effective manufacturing processes.**

**Major Work Tasks:** Prepare layouts, drawings, or sketches of machinery or equipment, such as shop tooling, scale layouts, or new equipment design, using drafting equipment or computer-aided design (CAD) software. Oversee equipment start-up, characterization, qualification, or release. Create computer applications for manufacturing processes or operations, using computer-aided design (CAD) or computer-assisted manufacturing (CAM) tools. Coordinate equipment purchases, installations, or transfers. Develop manufacturing infrastructure to integrate or deploy new manufacturing processes. Erect manufacturing engineering equipment. Install and evaluate manufacturing equipment, materials, or components. Monitor or measure manufacturing processes to identify ways to reduce losses, decrease time requirements, or improve quality. Design plant layouts or production facilities. Develop or maintain programs associated with automated production equipment. Develop production, inventory, or quality assurance programs. Estimate manufacturing costs. Identify and implement new manufacturing technologies, processes, or equipment. Identify opportunities for improvements in quality, cost, or efficiency of automation equipment. Recommend corrective or preventive actions to assure or improve product quality or reliability. Select material quantities or processing methods needed to achieve efficient production. Verify weights, measurements, counts, or calculations and record results on batch records. Ensure

adherence to safety rules and practices. Operate complex processing equipment. Plan, estimate, or schedule production work. Train manufacturing technicians on topics such as safety, health, fire prevention, or quality. Perform routine equipment maintenance. Analyze manufacturing supply chains to identify opportunities for increased efficiency in the acquisition of raw materials. Design plant or production layouts that minimize environmental impacts. Develop processes to recover, recycle, or reuse waste or scrap materials from manufacturing operations.

**Related Knowledge/Courses:** Engineering and Technology; Design; Mechanical Devices; Physics; Production and Processing; Mathematics.

**Personality Types:** Realistic–Investigative–Conventional.

**Skills:** Equipment selection; installation; technology design; equipment maintenance; programming; management of financial resources; troubleshooting; mathematics.

**Physical Environment:** Indoors; sitting; noise; contaminants. **Structural Environment:** Importance of being exact or accurate; freedom to make decisions; time pressure; impact of decisions on co-workers or company results; structured versus unstructured work; frequency of decision making.

**Apply knowledge of manufacturing engineering systems and tools to set up, test, and adjust manufacturing machinery and equipment, using any combination of electrical, electronic, mechanical, hydraulic, pneumatic, and computer technologies.**

**Major Work Tasks:** Collect hazardous or nonhazardous waste in correctly labeled barrels or other containers and transfer them to collection areas. Monitor and adjust production processes or equipment for quality and productivity. Prepare and assemble materials. Set up and operate production equipment in accordance with current good manufacturing practices and standard operating procedures. Assist engineers in developing, building, or testing prototypes or new products, processes, or procedures. Calibrate or adjust equipment to ensure quality production, using tools such as calipers, micrometers, height gauges, protractors, or ring gauges. Inspect finished products for quality and adherence to customer specifications. Keep production logs. Plan and lay out work to meet production and schedule requirements. Prepare production documents, such as standard operating procedures, manufacturing batch records, inventory reports, or productivity reports. Provide production, progress, or changeover reports to shift supervisors. Set up and verify the functionality of safety equipment. Start up and shut down processing equipment. Test products or subassemblies for functionality or quality. Troubleshoot problems with equipment, devices, or products. Adhere to all applicable regulations, policies, and procedures for health, safety, and environmental compliance. Clean production equipment or work areas. Install new equipment. Measure and record data associated with operating equipment. Provide advice or training to other technicians. Select cleaning materials, tools, or equipment. Build product subassemblies or final assemblies. Build packaging for finished products. Maintain inventory of job materials. Package finished products. Ship packages, following carrier specifications. Clean scrap materials for recycling or reuse, such as preparing aluminum scrap for cold-bonding processes or preparing paper for pulping or ink removal processes. Conduct environmental safety inspections in accordance with standard protocols to ensure production activities comply with environmental regulations or standards. Separate scrap or waste materials for recycling, reuse, or environmentally sound disposal.

**Related Knowledge/Courses:** Mechanical Devices; Design; Engineering and Technology; Production and Processing; Physics; Chemistry.

**Personality Types:** Realistic–Investigative.

**Skills:** Equipment maintenance; repairing; troubleshooting; installation; operation and control; operation monitoring; quality control analysis; equipment selection.

**Physical Environment:** Indoors; standing; using hands; noise; contaminants; hazardous equipment. **Structural Environment:** Importance of being exact or accurate; time pressure; freedom to make decisions; impact of decisions on co-workers or company results; consequence of error; importance of repeating same tasks.

### JOB SPECIALIZATION: MECHANICAL ENGINEERING TECHNOLOGISTS

**Apply engineering theory and technical skills to support mechanical engineering activities, such as generation, transmission, and use of mechanical and fluid energy. Prepare layouts of machinery and equipment and plan the flow of work. May conduct statistical studies and analyze production costs.**

**Major Work Tasks:** Prepare equipment inspection schedules, reliability schedules, work plans, or other records. Prepare cost and materials estimates or project schedules. Provide technical support to other employees regarding mechanical design, fabrication, testing, or documentation. Interpret engineering sketches, specifications, or drawings. Design specialized or customized equipment, machines, or structures. Design molds, tools, dies, jigs, or fixtures for use in manufacturing processes. Conduct failure analyses, document results, and recommend corrective actions. Assist engineers to design, develop, test, or manufacture industrial machinery, consumer products, or other equipment. Analyze or estimate production costs, such as labor, equipment, or plant space. Test machines, components, materials, or products to determine characteristics, such as performance, strength, or response to stress. Prepare specifications, designs, or sketches for machines, components, or systems related to the generation, transmission, or use of mechanical or fluid energy. Prepare layouts of machinery, tools, plants, or equipment. Inspect and test mechanical equipment. Assemble or disassemble complex mechanical systems. Perform routine maintenance on equipment, such as leak detectors, glove boxes, or mechanical pumps. Apply testing or monitoring apparatus to operating equipment. Oversee, monitor, or inspect mechanical installations or construction projects. Assist mechanical engineers in product testing through activities, such as setting up instrumentation for automobile crash tests. Analyze energy requirements and distribution systems to maximize the use of intermittent or inflexible renewable energy sources, such as wind or nuclear. Assist engineers to design or develop electrochemical devices, such as solid oxide membranes or other products for sustainable applications. Conduct statistical studies to analyze or compare production costs for sustainable and nonsustainable designs.

**Related Knowledge/Courses:** Mechanical Devices; Engineering and Technology; Design; Production and Processing; Physics; Mathematics.

**Personality Types:** Realistic–Investigative–Conventional.

**Skills:** Equipment maintenance; repairing; troubleshooting; equipment selection; operation and control; operation monitoring; technology design; quality control analysis.

**Physical Environment:** Indoors; using hands; noise; contaminants; hazardous conditions; hazardous equipment. **Structural Environment:** Freedom to make decisions; structured versus unstructured work; importance of being exact or accurate; impact of decisions on

co-workers or company results; time pressure; consequence of error.

### JOB SPECIALIZATION: NANOTECHNOLOGY ENGINEERING TECHNOLOGISTS

**Implement production processes for nanoscale designs to produce and modify materials, devices, and systems of unique molecular or macromolecular composition. Operate advanced microscopy equipment to manipulate nanoscale objects. Work under the supervision of engineering staff.**

**Major Work Tasks:** Supervise or provide technical direction to technicians engaged in nanotechnology research or production. Install nanotechnology production equipment at customer or manufacturing sites. Contribute written material or data for grant or patent applications. Produce images or measurements, using tools or techniques such as atomic force microscopy, scanning electron microscopy, optical microscopy, particle size analysis, or zeta potential analysis. Prepare detailed verbal or written presentations for scientists, engineers, project managers, or upper management. Prepare capability data, training materials, or other documentation for transfer of processes to production. Develop or modify wet chemical or industrial laboratory experimental techniques for nanoscale use. Collect or compile nanotechnology research or engineering data. Inspect or measure thin films of carbon nanotubes, polymers, or inorganic coatings, using a variety of techniques or analytical tools. Implement new or enhanced methods or processes for the processing, testing, or manufacture of nanotechnology materials or products. Design or conduct experiments, in collaboration with scientists or engineers, supportive of the development of nanotechnology materials, components, devices, or systems. Analyze the life cycle of nanomaterials or nano-enabled products to determine environmental impact. Capture nanoparticle contaminants, using techniques such as electrical fields or electrospinning. Compare the performance or environmental impact of nanomaterials by nanoparticle size, shape, or organization. Mix raw materials or catalysts to manufacture nanoparticles according to specifications, ensuring proper particle size, shape, or organization. Monitor hazardous waste clean-up procedures to ensure proper application of nanocomposites or accomplishment of objectives. Process nanoparticles or nanostructures, using technologies, such as ultraviolet radiation, microwave energy, or catalysis.

**Related Knowledge/Courses:** No data available.

**Personality Types:** Realistic–Investigative–Conventional.

**Skills:** No data available.

**Physical Environment:** No data available.
**Structural Environment:** No data available.

### JOB SPECIALIZATION: NANOTECHNOLOGY ENGINEERING TECHNICIANS

**Operate commercial-scale production equipment to produce, test, and modify materials, devices, and systems of molecular or macromolecular composition. Work under the supervision of engineering staff.**

**Major Work Tasks:** Repair nanotechnology processing or testing equipment or submit work orders for equipment repair. Maintain work area according to cleanroom or other processing standards. Set up or execute nanoparticle experiments according to detailed instructions. Compile information or prepare reports on nanotechnology experiments or applications. Record nanotechnology test results in logs, laboratory notebooks, or spreadsheet software. Produce detailed images or measurement of objects, using tools such as scanning tunneling microscopes or oscilloscopes. Perform functional tests of nano-enhanced assemblies, components, or systems, using equipment, such as torque gauges, or conductivity meters. Monitor equipment during operation to ensure adherence to specifications for characteristics, such as pressure, temperature, or flow. Measure or mix chemicals or compounds in accordance with detailed instructions or formulas. Calibrate nanotechnology equipment, such as weighing, testing, or production equipment. Inspect nanotechnology work products to ensure quality or adherence to specifications. Maintain accurate record or batch-record documentation of nanoproduction. Assist nanoscientists, engineers, or technologists in writing process specifications or documentation. Assist nanoscientists, engineers, or technologists in processing or characterizing materials according to physical or chemical properties. Assemble components, using techniques such as interference fitting, solvent bonding, adhesive bonding, heat sealing, or ultrasonic welding. Operate nanotechnology compounding, testing, processing, or production equipment in accordance with appropriate standard operating procedures, good manufacturing practices, hazardous material restrictions, or health and safety requirements. Measure emission of nanodust or nanoparticles, using systems such as aerosol detection systems, during nanocomposite or other nano-scale production processes. Measure or report toxicity of engineered nanoparticles. Test nano-enabled products to determine amount of shedding or loss of nanoparticles.

**Related Knowledge/Courses:** No data available.

**Personality Types:** Realistic–Conventional–Investigative.

**Skills:** No data available.

**Physical Environment:** No data available.
**Structural Environment:** No data available.

### JOB SPECIALIZATION: NON-DESTRUCTIVE TESTING SPECIALISTS

**Test the safety of structures, vehicles, or vessels using X-ray, ultrasound, fiber-optic or related equipment.**

**Major Work Tasks:** Supervise or direct the work of non-destructive testing (NDT) trainees or staff. Produce images of objects on film using radiographic techniques. Develop or use new NDT methods, such as acoustic emission testing, leak testing, and thermal or infrared testing. Document NDT methods, processes, or results. Map the presence of imperfections within objects using sonic measurements. Make radiographic images to detect flaws in objects while leaving objects intact. Visually examine materials, structures, or components using tools and equipment, such as endoscopes, closed-circuit television systems, and fiber optics for signs of corrosion, metal fatigue, cracks, or other flaws. Interpret or evaluate test results in accordance with applicable codes, standards, specifications, or procedures. Identify defects in solid materials using ultrasonic testing techniques. Select, calibrate, or operate equipment used in the NDT of products or materials. Conduct liquid penetrant tests to locate surface cracks by coating objects with fluorescent dyes, cleaning excess penetrant, and applying developer. Prepare reports on NDT results. Interpret the results of all methods of NDT, such as acoustic emission, electromagnetic, leak, liquid penetrant, magnetic particle, neutron radiographic, radiographic, thermal or infrared, ultrasonic, vibration analysis, and visual testing. Examine structures or vehicles such as aircraft, trains, nuclear reactors, bridges, dams, and pipelines using NDT techniques. Evaluate material properties using radio astronomy, voltage and amperage measurement, or rheometric flow measurement. Identify defects in concrete or other building materials using thermal or infrared testing.

**Related Knowledge/Courses:** Engineering and Technology; Physics; Chemistry; Production and Processing; Mechanical Devices; Design.

**Personality Types:** Realistic–Investigative–Conventional.

**Skills:** Equipment maintenance; troubleshooting; equipment selection; repairing; quality control analysis; operation monitoring; operation and control; programming.

**Physical Environment:** Outdoors; indoors; standing; using hands; noise; very hot or cold.

**Structural Environment:** Time pressure; importance of being exact or accurate; impact of decisions on co-workers or company results; frequency of decision making; freedom to make decisions; consequence of error.

### JOB SPECIALIZATION: PHOTONICS TECHNICIANS

**Build, install, test, and maintain optical and fiber-optic equipment, such as lasers, lenses, and mirrors using spectrometers, interferometers, or related equipment.**

**Major Work Tasks:** Monitor inventory levels and order supplies as necessary. Maintain clean working environments, according to clean room standards. Test or perform failure analysis for optomechanical or optoelectrical products, according to test plans. Assist scientists or engineers in the conduct of photonic experiments. Perform diagnostic analyses of processing steps, using analytical or metrological tools, such as microscopy, profilometry, or ellipsometry devices. Mix, pour, or use processing chemicals or gases according to safety standards or established operating procedures. Assist engineers in the development of new products, fixtures, tools, or processes. Assemble or adjust parts or related electrical units of prototypes to prepare for testing. Set up or operate prototype or test apparatus, such as control consoles, collimators, recording equipment, or cables. Set up or operate assembly or processing equipment, such as lasers, cameras, die bonders, wire bonders, dispensers, reflow ovens, soldering irons, die shears, wire pull testers, temperature or humidity chambers, or optical spectrum analyzers. Assemble fiber optical, optoelectronic, or free-space optics components, subcomponents, assemblies, or sub-

254

assemblies. Adjust or maintain equipment, such as lasers, laser systems, microscopes, oscilloscopes, pulse generators, power meters, beam analyzers, or energy measurement devices. Compute or record photonic test data. Document procedures, such as calibration of optical or fiber optic equipment. Recommend optical or optic equipment design or material changes to reduce costs or processing times. Design, build, or modify fixtures used to assemble parts. Lay out cutting lines for machining, using drafting tools. Splice fibers, using fusion splicing or other techniques. Terminate, cure, polish, or test fiber cables with mechanical connectors. Repair or calibrate products, such as surgical lasers. Perform laser seam welding, heat treatment, or hard facing operations. Fabricate devices, such as optoelectronic or semiconductor devices. Build prototype optomechanical devices for use in equipment, such as aerial cameras, gun sights, or telescopes.

**Related Knowledge/Courses:** Engineering and Technology; Physics; Mechanical Devices; Design; Computers and Electronics; Chemistry.

**Personality Types:** Realistic–Investigative–Conventional.

**Skills:** Installation; equipment selection; equipment maintenance; repairing; troubleshooting; technology design; operation and control; quality control analysis.

**Physical Environment:** Indoors; standing; using hands. **Structural Environment:** Importance of being exact or accurate; time pressure; freedom to make decisions; impact of decisions on co-workers or company results; consequence of error; structured versus unstructured work.

## Engineers, All Other

**All engineers not listed separately.**
- Average annual earnings: $92,030
- Middle 50% of earners: $68,770–$116,660
- Earnings growth potential: High (46.0%)
- Growth: 6.6%
- Annual job openings: 4,480
- Self-employed: 7.7%

**Considerations for Job Outlook:** In aerospace product and parts manufacturing, a small decrease is expected as fewer engineers will be needed because of increasing pressures on costs from competition overseas and increasing use of software to design and test prototypes.

**Major Work Tasks:** For tasks, see the job specializations.

### BEST-PAYING INDUSTRIES

| Industry | Median Earnings | Workforce |
|---|---|---|
| Federal, State, and Local Government | $108,100 | 31,780 |
| Computer and Electronic Product Manufacturing | $91,790 | 7,290 |
| Transportation Equipment Manufacturing | $88,820 | 8,740 |
| Management of Companies and Enterprises | $88,080 | 6,160 |
| Professional, Scientific, and Technical Services | $88,040 | 30,080 |
| Administrative and Support Services | $86,230 | 7,200 |

## Your Guide to High-Paying Careers

### BEST-PAYING METROPOLITAN AREAS

| Metro Area | Median Earnings | Workforce |
|---|---|---|
| Washington–Arlington-Alexandria, DC-VA-MD-WV | $126,240 | 7,400 |
| Houston–Sugar Land–Baytown, TX | $114,450 | 3,810 |
| Los Angeles–Long Beach–Santa Ana, CA | $117,250 | 10,190 |
| Huntsville, AL | $110,790 | 3,070 |
| San Francisco–Oakland–Fremont, CA | $103,160 | 3,060 |
| New York–Northern New Jersey–Long Island, NY-NJ-PA | $100,590 | 4,270 |
| San Diego–Carlsbad–San Marcos, CA | $96,430 | 3,150 |
| Los Angeles–Long Beach–Santa Ana, CA | $95,240 | 4,240 |
| Seattle-Tacoma-Bellevue, WA | $94,360 | 2,520 |
| Chicago-Naperville-Joliet, IL-IN-WI | $84,760 | 7,020 |

**Usual Educational Requirement:** Bachelor's degree. **Relevant Educational Programs**: Architectural Engineering; Assistive/Augmentative Technology and Rehabilitation Engineering; Biochemical Engineering; Biological/Biosystems Engineering; Chemical and Biomolecular Engineering; Construction Engineering; Electromechanical Engineering; Engineering Chemistry; Engineering Design; Engineering Mechanics; Engineering Physics/Applied Physics; Engineering Science; Engineering, General; Engineering, Other; Forest Engineering; Geological/Geophysical Engineering; Geotechnical and Geoenvironmental Engineering; Laser and Optical Engineering; Manufacturing Engineering; Mechatronics, Robotics, and Automation Engineering; Nanotechnology; Ocean Engineering; Paper Science and Engineering; Surveying Engineering; Systems Engineering; Telecommunications Engineering. **Work Experience Needed:** None. **On-the-Job Training Needed:** None. **Certification/Licensure:** Licensure for offering services to public.

**Key Career Cluster:** 15 Science, Technology, Engineering, and Mathematics. **Key Career Pathway:** 15.1 Engineering and Technology.

### JOB SPECIALIZATION: BIOCHEMICAL ENGINEERS

**Apply knowledge of biology, chemistry, and engineering to develop usable, tangible products. Solve problems related to materials, systems, and processes that interact with humans, plants, animals, microorganisms, and biological materials.**

**Major Work Tasks:** Read current scientific or trade literature to stay abreast of scientific, industrial, or technological advances. Prepare technical reports, data summary documents, or research articles for scientific publication, regulatory submissions, or patent applications. Modify or control biological systems to replace, augment, or sustain chemical or mechanical processes. Maintain databases of experiment characteristics or results. Lead studies to examine or recommend changes in process sequences or operation protocols. Direct experimental or developmental activities at contracted laboratories. Consult with chemists or biologists to develop or evaluate novel technologies. Collaborate with manufacturing or quality assurance staff to prepare product specification or safety sheets, standard operating procedures, user manuals, or qualification and validation reports. Devise scalable recovery, purification, or fermentation processes for producing proteins or other biological substances for human or animal therapeutic use, food production or processing, biofuels, or effluent treatment. Develop methodologies for transferring procedures or biological processes from laboratories to commercial-scale manufacturing production. Design or direct bench or pilot production experiments to determine the scale of production methods that optimize product yield and minimize production costs. Design or conduct studies to determine optimal conditions for cell growth, protein production, or protein or virus expression or recovery, using chromatography, separation, or filtration equipment, such as centrifuges or bioreactors. Design or conduct follow-up experimentation, based on generated data, to meet established process objectives. Develop biocatalytic processes to convert biomass to fuels or fine chemicals, using enzymes of bacteria, yeast, or other microorganisms. Confer with research and biomanufacturing personnel to ensure the compatibility of design and production. Develop recovery processes to separate or purify products from fermentation broths or slurries. Advise manufacturing staff regarding problems with fermentation, filtration, or other bioproduction processes.

**Related Knowledge/Courses:** Biology; Chemistry; Engineering and Technology; Physics; Production and Processing; Design.

**Personality Types:** Investigative–Realistic.

**Skills:** Science; operations analysis; mathematics; quality control analysis; systems analysis; technology design; reading comprehension; active learning.

**Physical Environment:** Indoors; sitting; contaminants. **Structural Environment:** Importance of being exact or accurate; freedom to make decisions; structured versus unstructured work; consequence of error; impact of decisions on co-workers or company results; level of competition.

### JOB SPECIALIZATION: ENERGY ENGINEERS

**Design, develop, and evaluate energy-related projects and programs to reduce energy costs or improve energy efficiency during the designing, building, or remodeling stages of construction. May specialize in electrical systems; heating, ventilation, and air-conditioning (HVAC) systems; green buildings; lighting; air quality; or energy procurement.**

**Major Work Tasks:** Conduct jobsite observations, field inspections, or sub-metering to collect data for energy conservation analyses. Perform energy modeling, measurement, verification, commissioning, or retro-commissioning. Consult with construction or renovation clients or other engineers on topics such as Leadership in Energy and Environmental Design (LEED) or Green Buildings. Inspect or monitor energy systems, including heating, ventilating, and air conditioning (HVAC) or daylighting systems to determine energy use or potential energy savings. Manage the development, design, or construction of energy conservation projects to ensure acceptability of budgets and timelines, conformance to federal and state laws, or adherence to approved specifications. Oversee design or construction aspects related to energy, such as energy engineering, energy management, and sustainable design. Direct the work of contractors or staff in the implementation of energy management projects. Evaluate construction design information, such as detail and assembly drawings, design calculations, system layouts and sketches, or specifications. Identify energy savings opportunities and make recommendations to achieve more energy efficient operation. Monitor and analyze energy consumption. Promote awareness or use of alternative or renewable energy sources. Review architectural, mechanical, or electrical plans and specifications to evaluate energy efficiency or determine economic, service, or engineering feasibility. Analyze, interpret, or create graphical representations of energy data, using engineering software. Conduct energy audits to evaluate energy use, costs, or conservation measures. Make recommendations regarding energy fuel selection. Prepare project reports and other program or technical documentation. Provide consultation to clients or other engineers on topics, such as climate control systems, energy modeling, data logging, energy management control systems, lighting or daylighting design, sustainable design, and energy auditing. Review or negotiate energy purchase agreements. Train personnel or clients on topics such as energy management.

**Related Knowledge/Courses:** Engineering and Technology; Building and Construction; Physics; Design; Economics and Accounting; Mechanical.

**Personality Types:** Investigative–Realistic.

**Skills:** Science; operations analysis; systems analysis; mathematics; reading comprehension; complex problem solving; writing; systems evaluation.

**Physical Environment:** Indoors; sitting. **Structural Environment:** Freedom to make decisions; structured versus unstructured work; importance of being exact or accurate; impact of decisions on co-workers or company results; time pressure; level of competition.

### JOB SPECIALIZATION: MANUFACTURING ENGINEERS

**Apply knowledge of materials and engineering theory and methods to design, integrate, and improve manufacturing systems or related processes. May work with commercial or industrial designers to refine product designs to increase producibility and decrease costs.**

**Major Work Tasks:** Apply continuous improvement methods, such as lean manufacturing to enhance manufacturing quality, reliability, or cost-effectiveness. Design layout of equipment or workspaces to achieve maximum efficiency. Identify opportunities or implement changes to improve products or reduce costs using knowledge of fabrication processes, tooling and production equipment, assembly methods, quality control standards, or product design, materials and parts. Communicate manufacturing capabilities, production schedules, or other information to facilitate production processes. Design testing methods and test finished products or process capabilities to establish standards or validate process requirements. Design, install, or troubleshoot manufacturing equipment. Determine root causes of failures using statistical methods and recommend changes in designs, tolerances, or processing methods. Estimate costs, production times, or staffing requirements for new designs. Evaluate manufactured products according to specifications and quality standards. Incorporate new methods and processes to improve existing operations. Investigate or resolve operational problems, such as material use variances or bottlenecks. Prepare documentation for new manufacturing processes or engineering procedures. Purchase equipment, materials, or parts. Review product designs for manufacturability or completeness. Troubleshoot new or existing product problems involving designs, materials, or processes. Prepare reports summarizing information or trends related to manufacturing performance. Provide technical expertise or support related to manufacturing. Read current literature, talk with colleagues, participate in educational programs, attend meetings, attend workshops, or participate in professional organizations or conferences to keep abreast of developments in the manufacturing field. Supervise technicians, technologists, analysts, administrative staff, or other engineers. Train production personnel in new or existing methods. Analyze the financial impacts of sustainable manufacturing, by implementing sustainable manufacturing processes or manufacturing sustainable products.

**Related Knowledge/Courses:** Engineering and Technology; Design; Physics; Production and Processing; Mechanical Devices; Chemistry.

**Personality Types:** Realistic–Investigative.

**Skills:** Technology design; equipment selection; installation; troubleshooting; equipment maintenance; management of financial resources; programming; management of material resources.

**Physical Environment:** Indoors; sitting; noise; contaminants; hazardous equipment. **Structural Environment:** Freedom to make decisions; importance of being exact or accurate; structured versus unstructured work; impact of decisions on co-workers or company results; time pressure; frequency of decision making.

### JOB SPECIALIZATION: MECHATRONICS ENGINEERS

**Apply knowledge of mechanical, electrical, and computer engineering theory and methods to the design of automation, intelligent systems, smart devices, or industrial systems control.**

**Major Work Tasks:** Publish engineering reports, documenting design details or qualification test results. Provide consultation or training on topics, such as mechatronics or automated control. Oversee the work of contractors in accordance with project requirements. Create mechanical design documents for parts, assemblies, or finished products. Maintain technical project files. Analyze existing development or manufacturing procedures and suggest improvements. Implement or test design solutions. Research, select, or apply sensors, communication technologies, or control devices for motion control, position sensing, pressure sensing, or electronic communication. Identify and select materials appropriate for mechatronic system designs. Design engineering systems for the automation of industrial tasks. Create mechanical models and tolerance analyses to simulate mechatronic design concepts. Conduct studies to determine the feasibility, costs, or performance benefits of new mechatronic equipment. Upgrade the design of existing devices by adding mechatronic elements. Design advanced precision equipment for accurate or controlled applications. Apply mechatronic or automated solutions to the transfer of materials, components, or finished goods. Design, develop, or implement control circuits or algorithms for electromechanical or pneumatic devices or systems. Design advanced electronic control systems for mechanical systems. Create embedded software design programs. Develop electronic, mechanical, or computerized processes to perform tasks in dangerous situations, such as underwater exploration or extraterrestrial mining. Design mechatronics components for computer-controlled products, such as cameras, video recorders, automobiles, or airplanes. Design or develop automated control systems for environmental applications, such as waste processing, air quality, or water quality systems. Design self-monitoring mechanical systems, such as gear systems that monitor loading or condition of systems to detect and prevent failures. Monitor or calibrate automated systems, industrial control systems, or system components to maximize efficiency of production.

**Related Knowledge/Courses:** Engineering and Technology; Design; Physics; Mechanical Devices; Production and Processing; Computers and Electronics.

**Personality Types:** Investigative–Realistic–Conventional.

**Skills:** Technology design; operations analysis; mathematics; systems analysis; science; quality control analysis; programming; operation monitoring.

**Physical Environment:** Indoors; sitting; noise. **Structural Environment:** Structured versus unstructured work; freedom to make decisions; importance of being exact or accurate; time pressure; frequency of decision making; impact of decisions on co-workers or company results.

### JOB SPECIALIZATION: MICROSYSTEMS ENGINEERS

**Apply knowledge of electronic and mechanical engineering theory and methods, as well as specialized manufacturing technologies, to**

**design and develop microelectromechanical systems (MEMS) devices.**

**Major Work Tasks:** Manage new product introduction projects to ensure effective deployment of microelectromechanical systems (MEMS) devices or applications. Plan or schedule engineering research or development projects involving MEMS technology. Develop or implement MEMS processing tools, fixtures, gages, dies, molds, or trays. Identify, procure, or develop test equipment, instrumentation, or facilities for characterization of MEMS applications. Develop customer documentation, such as performance specifications, training manuals, or operating instructions. Develop or file intellectual property and patent disclosure or application documents related to MEMS devices, products, or systems. Communicate operating characteristics or performance experience to other engineers or designers for training or new product development purposes. Demonstrate miniaturized systems that contain components, such as microsensors, microactuators, or integrated electronic circuits fabricated on silicon or silicon carbide wafers. Create or maintain formal engineering documents, such as schematics, bills of materials, components or materials specifications, or packaging requirements. Conduct acceptance tests, vendor-qualification protocols, surveys, audits, corrective-action reviews, or performance monitoring of incoming materials or components to ensure conformance to specifications. Refine final MEMS design to optimize design for target dimensions, physical tolerances, or processing constraints. Propose product designs involving MEMS technology, considering market data or customer requirements. Oversee operation of MEMS fabrication or assembly equipment, such as handling, singulation, assembly, wire-bonding, soldering, or package sealing. Investigate characteristics, such as cost, performance, or process capability of potential MEMS device designs, using simulation or modeling software.

**Related Knowledge/Courses:** No data available.

**Personality Types:** Investigative–Realistic–Conventional.

**Skills:** No data available.

**Physical Environment:** No data available.
**Structural Environment:** No data available.

## JOB SPECIALIZATION: NANOSYSTEMS ENGINEERS

**Design, develop, and supervise the production of materials, devices, and systems of unique molecular or macromolecular composition, applying principles of nanoscale physics and electrical, chemical, and biological engineering.**

**Major Work Tasks:** Write proposals to secure external funding or to partner with other companies. Supervise technologists or technicians engaged in nanotechnology research or production. Synthesize, process, or characterize nanomaterials, using advanced tools or techniques. Identify new applications for existing nanotechnologies. Provide technical guidance or support to customers on topics such as nanosystem start-up, maintenance, or use. Generate high-resolution images or measure force-distance curves, using techniques such as atomic force microscopy. Prepare reports, deliver presentations, or participate in program review activities to communicate engineering results or recommendations. Prepare nanotechnology-related invention disclosures or patent applications. Develop processes or identify equipment needed for pilot or commercial nanoscale scale production. Provide scientific or technical guidance or expertise to scientists, engineers, technologists, technicians, or others, using knowledge of chemical, analytical, or biological processes as applied to micro and nanoscale systems. Engineer production processes for specific nanotechnology applications, such as electroplating, nanofabrication, or epoxy. Design or conduct tests of new nanotechnology products, processes, or systems. Coordinate or supervise the work of suppliers or vendors in the designing, building, or testing of nanosystem devices, such as lenses or probes. Design or engineer nanomaterials, nanodevices, nano-enabled products, or nanosystems, using three-dimensional computer-aided design (CAD) software. Create designs or prototypes for nanosystem applications, such as biomedical delivery systems or atomic force microscopes. Conduct research related to a range of nanotechnology topics, such as packaging, heat transfer, fluorescence detection, nanoparticle dispersion, hybrid systems, liquid systems, nanocomposites, nanofabrication, optoelectronics, or nanolithography. Apply nanotechnology to improve the performance or reduce the environmental impact of energy products, such as fuel cells or solar cells.

**Related Knowledge/Courses:** No data available.

**Personality Types:** Investigative–Realistic–Enterprising.

**Skills:** No data available.

**Physical Environment:** No data available.
**Structural Environment:** No data available.

## JOB SPECIALIZATION: PHOTONICS ENGINEERS

**Apply knowledge of engineering and mathematical theory and methods to design technologies specializing in light information and light energy.**

**Major Work Tasks:** Design electro-optical sensing or imaging systems. Determine commercial, industrial, scientific, or other uses for electro-optical applications or devices. Conduct research on new photonics technologies. Design, integrate, or test photonics systems or components. Analyze system performance or operational requirements. Conduct testing to determine functionality or optimization or to establish limits of photonics systems or components. Design gas lasers, solid state lasers, infrared, or other light emitting or light sensitive devices. Determine applications of photonics appropriate to meet product objectives or features. Develop or test photonic prototypes or models. Develop optical or imaging systems, such as optical imaging products, optical components, image processes, signal process technologies, or optical systems. Document design processes including objectives, issues, and outcomes. Assist in the transition of photonic prototypes to production. Oversee or provide expertise on manufacturing, assembly, or fabrication processes. Read current literature, talk with colleagues, continue education, or participate in professional organizations or conferences to keep abreast of developments in the field. Train operators, engineers, or other personnel. Write reports or research proposals. Select, purchase, set up, operate, or troubleshoot state-of-the-art laser cutting equipment. Analyze, fabricate, or test fiber-optic links. Design laser-machining equipment for purposes such as high speed ablation. Develop laser-processed designs, such as laser-cut medical devices. Create or maintain photonic design histories. Design or develop new crystals for photonics applications. Design or redesign optical fibers to minimize energy loss. Design photonics products, such as light sources, displays, or photovoltaics to achieve increased energy efficiency. Design solar energy photonics or other materials or devices to generate energy. Develop photonics sensing or manufacturing technologies to improve the efficiency of manufacturing or related processes.

**Related Knowledge/Courses:** Physics; Engineering and Technology; Design; Mathematics; Mechanical Devices; Computers and Electronics.

**Personality Types:** Investigative–Realistic–Conventional.

**Skills:** Technology design; equipment selection; mathematics; science; repairing; programming; quality control analysis; troubleshooting.

**261**

**Physical Environment:** Indoors; sitting. **Structural Environment:** Structured versus unstructured work; freedom to make decisions; importance of being exact or accurate; impact of decisions on co-workers or company results; consequence of error; time pressure.

**Research, design, develop, and test robotic applications.**

**Major Work Tasks:** Supervise technologists, technicians, or other engineers. Integrate robotics with peripherals, such as welders, controllers, or other equipment. Provide technical support for robotic systems. Review or approve designs, calculations, or cost estimates. Make system device lists or event timing charts. Document robotic application development, maintenance, or changes. Write algorithms or programming code for ad hoc robotic applications. Create back-ups of robot programs or parameters. Process or interpret signals or sensor data. Plan mobile robot paths and teach path plans to robots. Investigate mechanical failures or unexpected maintenance problems. Install, calibrate, operate, or maintain robots. Debug robotics programs. Design end-of-arm tooling. Conduct research on robotic technology to create new robotic systems or system capabilities. Conduct research into the feasibility, design, operation, or performance of robotic mechanisms, components, or systems, such as planetary rovers, multiple mobile robots, reconfigurable robots, or man-machine interactions. Analyze and evaluate robotic systems or prototypes. Design automated robotic systems to increase production volume or precision in high-throughput operations, such as automated ribonucleic acid (RNA) analysis or sorting, moving, or stacking production materials. Design software to control robotic systems for applications, such as military defense or manufacturing. Build, configure, and test robots. Design robotic systems, such as automatic vehicle control, autonomous vehicles,

advanced displays, advanced sensing, robotic platforms, computer vision, or telematics systems. Automate assays on laboratory robotics. Design or program robotics systems for environmental clean-up applications to minimize human exposure to toxic or hazardous materials or to improve the quality or speed of clean-up operations. Design robotics applications for manufacturers of green products, such as wind turbines or solar panels to increase production time, eliminate waste, or reduce costs.

**Related Knowledge/Courses:** Engineering and Technology; Design; Physics; Mechanical Devices; Computers and Electronics; Production and Processing.

**Personality Types:** Investigative–Realistic–Conventional.

**Skills:** Equipment selection; installation; programming; equipment maintenance; technology design; repairing; troubleshooting; mathematics.

**Physical Environment:** Indoors; sitting; using hands; noise; hazardous equipment. **Structural Environment:** Importance of being exact or accurate; freedom to make decisions; structured versus unstructured work; consequence of error; time pressure; degree of automation.

**Perform site-specific engineering analysis or evaluation of energy efficiency and solar projects involving residential, commercial, or industrial customers. Design solar domestic hot water and space heating systems for new and existing structures, applying knowledge of structural energy requirements, local climates, solar technology, and thermodynamics.**

**Major Work Tasks:** Test or evaluate photovoltaic (PV) cells or modules. Review specifications and recommend engineering or manufacturing changes to achieve solar design objectives. Perform thermal, stress, or cost reduction analyses for solar systems. Develop standard operation procedures and quality or safety standards for solar installation work. Design or develop vacuum tube collector systems for solar applications. Provide technical direction or support to installation teams during installation, start-up, testing, system commissioning, or performance monitoring. Perform computer simulation of solar PV generation system performance or energy production to optimize efficiency. Develop design specifications and functional requirements for residential, commercial, or industrial solar energy systems or components. Create plans for solar energy system development, monitoring, and evaluation activities. Create electrical single-line diagrams, panel schedules, or connection diagrams for solar electric systems, using computer-aided design (CAD) software. Create checklists for review or inspection of completed solar installation projects. Design or coordinate design of PV or solar thermal systems, including system components, for residential and commercial buildings. Conduct engineering site audits to collect structural, electrical, and related site information for use in the design of residential or commercial solar power systems.

**Related Knowledge/Courses:** No data available.

**Personality Types:** Realistic–Investigative.

**Skills:** No data available.

**Physical Environment:** No data available.
**Structural Environment:** No data available.

## JOB SPECIALIZATION: VALIDATION ENGINEERS

**Design and plan protocols for equipment and processes to produce products meeting internal and external purity, safety, and quality requirements.**

**Major Work Tasks:** Conduct validation or qualification tests of new or existing processes, equipment, or software in accordance with in-ternal protocols or external standards. Design validation study features, such as sampling, testing, or analytical methodologies. Develop validation master plans, process flow diagrams, test cases, or standard operating procedures. Prepare validation or performance qualification protocols for new or modified manufacturing processes, systems, or equipment for pharmaceutical, electronics, or other types of production. Analyze validation test data to determine whether systems or processes have met validation criteria or to identify root causes of production problems. Conduct audits of validation or performance qualification processes to ensure compliance with internal or regulatory requirements. Create, populate, or maintain databases for tracking validation activities, test results, or validated systems. Direct validation activities, such as protocol creation or testing. Draw samples of raw materials or intermediate and finished products for validation testing. Identify deviations from established product or process standards and provide recommendations for resolving deviations. Prepare detailed reports or design statements based on results of validation and qualification tests or reviews of procedures and protocols. Procure or devise automated lab validation test stations or other test fixtures and equipment. Resolve testing problems by modifying testing methods or revising test objectives and standards. Study product characteristics or customer requirements and confer with management to determine validation objectives and standards. Assist in training equipment operators or other staff on validation protocols and standard operating procedures. Communicate with regulatory agencies regarding compliance documentation or validation results. Coordinate the implementation or scheduling of validation testing with affected departments and personnel. Participate in internal or external training programs to maintain knowledge of validation principles, industry trends, or novel technologies.

**Related Knowledge/Courses:** Engineering and Technology; Design; Production and Processing; Chemistry; Physics; Mathematics.

**Personality Types:** Investigative–Realistic–Conventional.

**Skills:** Science; Operations Analysis; Mathematics; Operation Monitoring; Systems Analysis; Systems Evaluation; Reading Comprehension; Writing.

**Physical Environment:** Indoors; sitting. **Structural Environment:** Importance of being exact or accurate; structured versus unstructured work; time pressure; freedom to make decisions; impact of decisions on co-workers or company results; frequency of decision making.

JOB SPECIALIZATION: WIND ENERGY ENGINEERS

**Design underground or overhead wind farm collector systems and prepare and develop site specifications.**

**Major Work Tasks:** Recommend process or infrastructure changes to improve wind turbine performance, reduce operational costs, or comply with regulations. Create or maintain wind farm layouts, schematics, or other visual documentation for wind farms. Create models to optimize the layout of wind farm access roads, crane pads, crane paths, collection systems, substations, switchyards, or transmission lines. Write reports to document wind farm collector system test results. Oversee the work activities of wind farm consultants or subcontractors. Investigate experimental wind turbines or wind turbine technologies for properties, such as aerodynamics, production, noise, and load. Test wind turbine equipment to determine effects of stress or fatigue. Test wind turbine components, using mechanical or electronic testing equipment. Provide engineering technical support to designers of prototype wind turbines. Perform root cause analysis on wind turbine tower component failures. Monitor wind farm construction to ensure compliance with regulatory standards

or environmental requirements. Direct balance of plant (BOP) construction, generator installation, testing, commissioning, or supervisory control and data acquisition (SCADA) to ensure compliance with specifications. Develop specifications for wind technology components, such as gearboxes, blades, generators, frequency converters, and pad transformers. Develop active control algorithms, electronics, software, electromechanical, or electrohydraulic systems for wind turbines. Design underground or overhead wind farm collector systems. Analyze operation of wind farms or wind farm components to determine reliability, performance, and compliance with specifications.

**Related Knowledge/Courses:** Engineering and Technology; Design; Physics; Building and Construction; Geography; Mathematics.

**Personality Types:** Realistic–Investigative–Enterprising.

**Skills:** Science; mathematics; operations analysis; technology design; systems analysis; programming; systems evaluation; reading comprehension.

**Physical Environment:** Indoors; sitting. **Structural Environment:** Structured versus unstructured work; importance of being exact or accurate; freedom to make decisions; time pressure; impact of decisions on co-workers or company results; frequency of decision making.

## Environmental Engineers

**Research, design, plan, or perform engineering duties in the prevention, control, and remediation of environmental hazards using various engineering disciplines.**

- Average annual earnings: $80,890
- Middle 50% of earners: $62,520–$102,930
- Earnings growth potential: Medium (38.8%)
- Growth: 21.9%
- Annual job openings: 2,260
- Self-employed: 1.1%

264

## BEST-PAYING INDUSTRIES

| Industry | Median Earnings | Workforce |
|---|---|---|
| Professional, Scientific, and Technical Services | $80,720 | 27,340 |
| Federal, State, and Local Government | $77,600 | 13,510 |

## BEST-PAYING METROPOLITAN AREAS

| Metro Area | Median Earnings | Workforce |
|---|---|---|
| Houston–Sugar Land–Baytown, TX | $103,500 | 1,150 |
| Washington-Arlington-Alexandria, DC-VA-MD-WV | $100,820 | 2,120 |
| San Francisco–Oakland–Fremont, CA | $97,790 | 1,500 |
| Seattle-Tacoma-Bellevue, WA | $92,570 | 1,020 |
| Los Angeles–Long Beach–Santa Ana, CA | $91,410 | 1,660 |
| New York–Northern New Jersey–Long Island, NY-NJ-PA | $89,590 | 2,890 |
| Denver-Aurora, CO | $83,900 | 1,040 |
| Chicago-Naperville-Joliet, IL-IN-WI | $79,660 | 1,070 |
| Philadelphia-Camden-Wilmington, PA-NJ-DE-MD | $79,300 | 1,610 |
| Boston-Cambridge-Quincy, MA-NH | $76,810 | 2,340 |
| Atlanta–Sandy Springs–Marietta, GA | $71,680 | 1,270 |

**Considerations for Job Outlook:** All levels of government must comply with environmental regulations, especially federal. Because of this, employment of environmental engineers within the government sector as a whole should remain relatively stable through the year 2020.

**Major Work Tasks:** Prepare, review, or update environmental investigation or recommendation reports. Obtain, update, or maintain plans, permits, or standard operating procedures. Provide technical support for environmental remediation or litigation projects, including remediation system design or determination of regulatory applicability. Monitor progress of environmental improvement programs. Inspect industrial or municipal facilities or programs to evaluate operational effectiveness or ensure compliance with environmental regulations. Provide administrative support for projects by collecting data, providing project documentation, training staff, or performing other general administrative duties. Develop proposed project objectives and targets and report to management on progress in attaining them. Advise corporations or government agencies of procedures to follow in cleaning up contaminated sites to protect people and the environment. Advise industries or government agencies about environmental policies and standards. Inform company employees or other interested parties of environmental issues. Assess the existing or potential environmental impact of land use projects on air, water, or land. Assist in budget implementation, forecasts, or administration. Develop site-specific health and safety protocols, such as spill contingency plans or methods for loading or transporting waste. Coordinate or manage environmental protection programs or projects, assigning or evaluating work. Serve as liaison with federal, state, or local agencies or officials on issues pertaining to solid or hazardous waste program requirements. Prepare hazardous waste manifests or land disposal restriction notifications. Develop or present environmental compliance training or orientation sessions. Provide environmental engineering assistance in network analysis, regulatory analysis, or planning or reviewing database development. Design or supervise the design of systems, processes, or equipment for control, management, or remediation of water, air, or soil quality. Direct installation or operation of environmental monitoring devices or supervise related data collection programs.

**Usual Educational Requirement:** Bachelor's degree. **Relevant Educational Programs**: Environmental/Environmental Health Engineering; Geotechnical and Geoenvironmental Engineering. **Related Knowledge/Courses:** Engineering and Technology; Biology; Chemistry; Design; Physics; Geography. **Work Experience Needed:** None. **On-the-Job Training Needed:** None. **Certification/Licensure:** Licensure for offering services to public.

**Personality Types:** Investigative–Realistic–Conventional. **Key Career Cluster:** 01 Agriculture, Food, and Natural Resources. **Key Career Pathway:** 1.6 Environmental Service Systems.

**Skills:** Science; mathematics; management of financial resources; complex problem solving; writing; systems evaluation; management of material resources; active learning.

**Physical Environment:** Indoors; outdoors; sitting. **Structural Environment:** Importance of being exact or accurate; freedom to make decisions; structured versus unstructured work; impact of decisions on co-workers or company results; time pressure; level of competition.

## JOB SPECIALIZATION: WATER/WASTEWATER ENGINEERS

**Design or oversee projects involving provision of fresh water, disposal of wastewater and sewage, or prevention of flood-related damage. Prepare environmental documentation for water resources, regulatory program compliance, data management and analysis, and fieldwork. Perform hydraulic modeling and pipeline design.**

**Major Work Tasks:** Write technical reports or publications related to water resources development or water use efficiency. Review and critique proposals, plans, or designs related to water or wastewater treatment systems. Provide technical support on water resource or treatment issues to government agencies. Provide technical direction or supervision to junior engineers, engineering or computer-aided design (CAD) technicians, or other technical personnel. Identify design alternatives for the development of new water resources. Develop plans for new water resources or water efficiency programs. Design or select equipment for use in wastewater processing to ensure compliance with government standards. Conduct water quality studies to identify and characterize water pollutant sources. Perform mathematical modeling of underground or surface water resources, such as floodplains, ocean coastlines, streams, rivers, or wetlands. Perform hydrological analyses, using three-dimensional simulation software, to model the movement of water or forecast the dispersion of chemical pollutants in the water supply. Perform hydraulic analyses of water supply systems or water distribution networks to model flow characteristics, test for pressure losses, or to identify opportunities to mitigate risks and improve operational efficiency. Oversee the construction of decentralized or on-site wastewater treatment systems, including reclaimed water facilities. Gather and analyze water use data to forecast water demand. Conduct feasibility studies for the construction of facilities, such as water supply systems, run-off collection networks, water and wastewater treatment plants, or wastewater collection systems. Conduct environmental impact studies related to water and wastewater collection, treatment, or distribution. Conduct cost-benefit analyses for the construction of water supply systems, run-off collection networks, water and wastewater treatment plants, or wastewater collection systems. Analyze the efficiency of water delivery structures, such as dams, tainter gates, canals, pipes, penstocks, or cofferdams.

**Related Knowledge/Courses:** Engineering and Technology; Design; Building and Construction; Biology; Physics; Chemistry.

266

**Personality Types:** Investigative–Realistic–Enterprising.

**Skills:** Science; technology design; mathematics; operations analysis; programming; systems evaluation; systems analysis; complex problem solving.

**Physical Environment:** Indoors; sitting. **Structural Environment:** Importance of being exact or accurate; structured versus unstructured work; impact of decisions on co-workers or company results; level of competition; time pressure; freedom to make decisions.

## Environmental Science Teachers, Postsecondary

*See Teachers, Postsecondary.*

## Environmental Scientists and Specialists, Including Health

**Conduct research or perform investigation for the purpose of identifying, abating, or eliminating sources of pollutants or hazards that affect either the environment or the health of the population.**

- Average annual earnings: $63,570
- Middle 50% of earners: $47,840–$84,690
- Earnings growth potential: Medium (39.3%)
- Growth: 18.7%
- Annual job openings: 4,320
- Self-employed: 5.2%

### BEST-PAYING INDUSTRIES

| Industry | Median Earnings | Workforce |
|---|---|---|
| Professional, Scientific, and Technical Services | $65,660 | 35,610 |
| Federal, State, and Local Government | $61,810 | 36,720 |

### BEST-PAYING METROPOLITAN AREAS

| Metro Area | Median Earnings | Workforce |
|---|---|---|
| Washington-Arlington-Alexandria, DC-VA-MD-WV | $97,580 | 3,700 |
| San Francisco–Oakland–Fremont, CA | $89,610 | 2,120 |
| Seattle-Tacoma-Bellevue, WA | $78,330 | 2,090 |
| Sacramento–Arden-Arcade–Roseville, CA | $78,300 | 2,180 |
| Houston–Sugar Land–Baytown, TX | $75,920 | 2,320 |
| Los Angeles–Long Beach–Santa Ana, CA | $74,530 | 3,270 |
| New York–Northern New Jersey–Long Island, NY-NJ-PA | $65,320 | 2,550 |
| Boston-Cambridge-Quincy, MA-NH | $65,050 | 1,950 |

**Considerations for Job Outlook:** Environmental scientists and specialists should have good job opportunities. In addition to growth, many job openings will be created by scientists who retire, advance to management positions, or change careers.

**Major Work Tasks:** Conduct environmental audits or inspections or investigations of violations. Review and implement environmental technical standards, guidelines, policies, and formal regulations that meet all appropriate requirements. Provide advice on proper standards and regulations or the development of policies, strategies, or codes of practice for environmental management. Prepare charts or graphs from data samples, providing summary information on the environmental relevance of the data. Monitor effects of pollution or land degradation and recommend means of prevention or control. Design or direct studies to obtain technical environmental information about

**267**

planned projects. Collect, synthesize, analyze, manage, and report environmental data, such as pollution emission measurements, atmospheric monitoring measurements, meteorological or mineralogical information, or soil or water samples. Communicate scientific or technical information to the public, organizations, or internal audiences through oral briefings, written documents, workshops, conferences, training sessions, or public hearings. Provide scientific or technical guidance, support, coordination, or oversight to governmental agencies, environmental programs, industry, or the public. Evaluate violations or problems discovered during inspections to determine appropriate regulatory actions or to provide advice on the development and prosecution of regulatory cases. Analyze data to determine validity, quality, and scientific significance and to interpret correlations between human activities and environmental effects. Determine data collection methods to be employed in research projects or surveys. Develop the technical portions of legal documents, administrative orders, or consent decrees. Investigate and report on accidents affecting the environment. Monitor environmental impacts of development activities. Develop programs designed to obtain the most productive, non-damaging use of land. Research sources of pollution to determine their effects on the environment and to develop theories or methods of pollution abatement or control.

**Usual Educational Requirement:** Bachelor's degree. **Relevant Educational Programs**: Environmental Chemistry; Environmental Health; Environmental Science; Environmental Studies; Marine Sciences. **Related Knowledge/Courses:** Biology; Geography; Chemistry; Law and Government; Clerical Practices; Physics. **Work Experience Needed:** None. **On-the-Job Training Needed:** None. **Certification/ Licensure:** None.

**Personality Types:** Investigative–Realistic–Conventional. **Key Career Cluster:** 15 Science, Technology, Engineering, and Mathematics. **Key Career Pathway:** 15.2 Science and Mathematics.

**Skills:** Science; programming; mathematics; operations analysis; reading comprehension; systems analysis; writing; systems evaluation.

**Physical Environment:** Indoors; sitting. **Structural Environment:** Structured versus unstructured work; freedom to make decisions; importance of being exact or accurate; impact of decisions on co-workers or company results; frequency of decision making; time pressure.

## JOB SPECIALIZATION: CLIMATE CHANGE ANALYSTS

**Research and analyze policy developments related to climate change. Make climate-related recommendations for actions, such as legislation, awareness campaigns, or fundraising approaches.**

**Major Work Tasks:** Write reports or academic papers to communicate findings of climate-related studies. Promote initiatives to mitigate climate change with government or environmental groups. Present climate-related information at public interest, governmental, or other meetings. Prepare grant applications to obtain funding for programs related to climate change, environmental management, or sustainability. Gather and review climate-related studies from government agencies, research laboratories, and other organizations. Develop, or contribute to the development of, educational or outreach programs on the environment or climate change. Review existing policies or legislation to identify environmental impacts. Provide analytical support for policy briefs related to renewable energy, energy efficiency, or climate change. Prepare study reports, memoranda, briefs, testimonies, or other written materials to inform government or environmental groups on environmental issues such as climate change. Make legislative recommendations related to climate change or environmental management, based on climate change policies, principles, programs, practices, and processes. Research policies, practices, or procedures for climate or environmental management. Propose new or modified policies involving use of traditional and alternative fuels, transportation of goods, and other factors relating to climate and climate change. Analyze and distill climate-related research findings to inform legislators, regulatory agencies, or other stakeholders. Present and defend proposals for climate change research projects.

**Related Knowledge/Courses:** Geography; Biology; Law and Government; Economics and Accounting; Sociology and Anthropology; Physics.

**Personality Types:** Investigative–Enterprising.

**Skills:** Systems evaluation; systems analysis; writing; active learning; science; complex problem solving; speaking; persuasion.

**Physical Environment:** Indoors; sitting. **Structural Environment:** Structured versus unstructured work; freedom to make decisions; importance of being exact or accurate; level of competition; impact of decisions on co-workers or company results; time pressure.

### JOB SPECIALIZATION: ENVIRONMENTAL RESTORATION PLANNERS

**Collaborate with field and biology staff to oversee the implementation of restoration projects and to develop new products. Process and synthesize complex scientific data into practical strategies for restoration, monitoring or management.**

**Major Work Tasks:** Develop environmental restoration project schedules and budgets. Develop and communicate recommendations for landowners to maintain or restore environmental conditions. Create diagrams to communicate environmental remediation planning using geographic information systems (GIS), computer-aided design (CAD), or other mapping or diagramming software. Apply for permits required for the implementation of environmental remediation projects. Review existing environmental remediation designs. Supervise and provide technical guidance, training, or assistance to employees working in the field to restore habitats. Provide technical direction on environmental planning to energy engineers, biologists, geologists, or other professionals working to develop restoration plans or strategies. Inspect active remediation sites to ensure compliance with environmental or safety policies, standards, or regulations. Plan environmental restoration projects, using biological databases, environmental strategies, and planning software. Identify short- and long-term impacts of environmental remediation activities. Identify environmental mitigation alternatives, ensuring compliance with applicable standards, laws, or regulations. Conduct feasibility and cost-benefit studies for environmental remediation projects. Conduct environmental impact studies to examine the ecological effects of pollutants, disease, human activities, nature, and climate change. Communicate findings of environmental studies or proposals for environmental remediation to other restoration professionals. Collect and analyze data to determine environmental conditions and restoration needs. Develop natural resource management plans, using knowledge of environmental planning or state and federal environmental regulatory requirements. Create habitat management or restoration plans, such as native tree restoration and weed control. Conduct site assessments to certify a habitat or to ascertain environmental damage or restoration needs. Notify regulatory or permitting agencies of deviations from implemented remediation plans.

**Related Knowledge/Courses:** Biology; Geography; Engineering and Technology; Law and Government; Chemistry; Design.

**Personality Types:** Investigative–Realistic–Enterprising.

**Skills:** Science; management of material resources; systems evaluation; management of financial resources; systems analysis; technology design; mathematics; programming.

**Physical Environment:** Indoors; outdoors; sitting. **Structural Environment:** Freedom to make decisions; structured versus unstructured work; impact of decisions on co-workers or company results; level of competition; time pressure.

### JOB SPECIALIZATION: INDUSTRIAL ECOLOGISTS

**Study or investigate industrial production and natural ecosystems to achieve high production, sustainable resources, and environmental safety or protection. May apply principles and activities of natural ecosystems to develop models for industrial systems.**

**Major Work Tasks:** Investigate accidents affecting the environment to assess ecological impact. Investigate the adaptability of various animal and plant species to changed environmental conditions. Review industrial practices, such as the methods and materials used in construction or production, to identify potential liabilities and environmental hazards. Research sources of pollution to determine environmental impact or to develop methods of pollution abatement or control. Provide industrial managers with technical materials on environmental issues, regulatory guidelines, or compliance actions. Plan or conduct studies of the ecological implications of historic or projected changes in industrial processes or development. Plan or conduct field research on topics such as industrial production, industrial ecology, population ecology, and environmental production or sustainability. Monitor the environmental impact of development activities, pollution, or land degradation. Identify or develop strategies or methods to minimize the environmental impact of industrial production processes. Investigate the impact of changed land management or land use practices on ecosystems. Develop or test protocols to monitor ecosystem components and ecological processes. Create complex and dynamic mathematical models of population, community, or ecological systems. Conduct scientific protection, mitigation, or restoration projects to prevent resource damage, maintain the integrity of critical habitats, and minimize the impact of human activities. Carry out environmental assessments in accordance with applicable standards, regulations, or laws. Build and maintain databases of information about energy alternatives, pollutants, natural environments, industrial processes, and other information related to ecological change. Forecast future status or condition of ecosystems, based on changing industrial practices or environmental conditions. Conduct applied research on the effects of industrial processes on the protection, restoration, inventory, monitoring, or reintroduction of species to the natural environment.

**Related Knowledge/Courses:** No data available.

**Personality Types:** Investigative–Enterprising.

**Skills:** No data available.

**Physical Environment:** No data available. **Structural Environment:** No data available.

## Financial Analysts

**Conduct quantitative analyses of information affecting investment programs of public or private institutions.**

- Average annual earnings: $76,950
- Middle 50% of earners: $58,970–$103,410
- Earnings growth potential: Medium (38.8%)
- Growth: 23.0%
- Annual job openings: 10,420
- Self-employed: 4.4%

**Considerations for Job Outlook:** Despite employment growth, competition is expected for

## BEST-PAYING INDUSTRIES

| Industry | Median Earnings | Workforce |
|---|---|---|
| Securities, Commodity Contracts, and Other Financial Investments and Related Activities | $90,560 | 54,210 |
| Professional, Scientific, and Technical Services | $75,920 | 31,340 |
| Credit Intermediation and Related Activities | $75,300 | 32,620 |
| Management of Companies and Enterprises | $75,200 | 30,840 |
| Insurance Carriers and Related Activities | $72,270 | 17,350 |

## BEST-PAYING METROPOLITAN AREAS

| Metro Area | Median Earnings | Workforce |
|---|---|---|
| New York–Northern New Jersey–Long Island, NY-NJ-PA | $97,200 | 35,880 |
| San Francisco–Oakland–Fremont, CA | $94,380 | 8,110 |
| Los Angeles–Long Beach–Santa Ana, CA | $86,060 | 11,740 |
| Washington-Arlington-Alexandria, DC-VA-MD-WV | $85,530 | 12,240 |
| Houston–Sugar Land–Baytown, TX | $80,440 | 5,250 |
| Boston-Cambridge-Quincy, MA-NH | $75,950 | 14,140 |
| Dallas–Fort Worth–Arlington, TX | $73,460 | 7,680 |
| Philadelphia-Camden-Wilmington, PA-NJ-DE-MD | $73,420 | 7,840 |
| Atlanta–Sandy Springs–Marietta, GA | $72,580 | 5,940 |
| Chicago-Naperville-Joliet, IL-IN-WI | $72,540 | 9,510 |
| Minneapolis–St. Paul–Bloomington, MN-WI | $70,560 | 5,090 |

these high-paying jobs. Growth in financial services should create new positions, but there are still far more people who would like to enter the occupation than there are jobs in the occupation. Having certifications and a graduate degree can significantly improve an applicant's prospects.

**Major Work Tasks:** Draw charts and graphs, using computer spreadsheets, to illustrate technical reports. Inform investment decisions by analyzing financial information to forecast business, industry, or economic conditions. Monitor developments in the fields of industrial technology, business, finance, and economic theory. Interpret data on price, yield, stability, future investment-risk trends, economic influences, and other factors affecting investment programs. Monitor fundamental economic, industrial, and corporate developments by analyzing information from financial publications and services, investment banking firms, government agencies, trade publications, company sources, or personal interviews. Recommend investments and investment timing to companies, investment firm staff, or the public. Determine the prices at

which securities should be syndicated and offered to the public. Prepare plans of action for investment, using financial analyses. Evaluate and compare the relative quality of various securities in a given industry. Present oral or written reports on general economic trends, individual corporations, and entire industries. Contact brokers and purchase investments for companies, according to company policy. Collaborate with investment bankers to attract new corporate clients to securities firms. Conduct financial analyses related to investments in green construction or green retrofitting projects. Determine the financial viability of alternative

271

energy generation or fuel production systems, based on power source or feedstock quality, financing costs, potential revenue, and total project costs. Evaluate financial viability and potential environmental benefits of cleantech innovations to secure capital investments from sources such as venture capital firms and government green fund grants. Forecast or analyze financial costs associated with climate change or other environmental factors, such as clean water supply and demand. Identify potential financial investments that are environmentally sound, considering issues such as carbon emissions and biodiversity.

**Usual Educational Requirement:** Bachelor's degree. **Relevant Educational Programs**: Accounting and Business/Management; Accounting and Finance; Finance, General; Financial Mathematics; International Finance; Investments and Securities; Public Finance. **Related Knowledge/Courses:** Economics and Accounting; Mathematics; Law and Government; Clerical Practices; Administration and Management; English Language. **Work Experience Needed:** None. **On-the-Job Training Needed:** None. **Certification/Licensure:** Voluntary certification by association.

**Personality Types:** Conventional–Investigative–Enterprising. **Key Career Cluster:** 06 Finance. **Key Career Pathway:** 6.2 Business Financial Management.

**Skills:** Systems analysis; mathematics; systems evaluation; management of financial resources; operations analysis; writing; active learning; judgment and decision making.

**Physical Environment:** Indoors; sitting. **Structural Environment:** Structured versus unstructured work; freedom to make decisions; importance of being exact or accurate; importance of repeating same tasks; time pressure; impact of decisions on co-workers or company results.

## Financial Examiners

**Enforce or ensure compliance with laws and regulations governing financial and securities institutions and financial and real estate transactions.**

- Average annual earnings: $75,800
- Middle 50% of earners: $56,420–$106,820
- Earnings growth potential: Medium (43.0%)
- Growth: 27.0%
- Annual job openings: 1,410
- Self-employed: 0.0%

**Considerations for Job Outlook:** Implementation of new financial regulations is expected to create a need for more examiners. For example, some large financial institutions that were not previously subject to Federal Deposit Insurance Corporation (FDIC) regulation have now been placed under that agency's supervision. More examiners will be needed to monitor these institutions' available cash levels and risky trading activity. In addition, the creation of the Consumer Financial Protection Bureau (CFPB)

### BEST-PAYING INDUSTRIES

| Industry | Median Earnings | Workforce |
|---|---|---|
| Monetary Authorities-Central Bank | $95,540 | 1,510 |
| Federal, State, and Local Government | $84,630 | 10,140 |
| Securities, Commodity Contracts, and Other Financial Investments and Related Activities | $77,510 | 4,670 |
| Management of Companies and Enterprises | $72,630 | 2,010 |
| Insurance Carriers and Related Activities | $69,200 | 1,490 |
| Credit Intermediation and Related Activities | $63,970 | 6,640 |

**BEST-PAYING METROPOLITAN AREAS**

| Metro Area | Median Earnings | Workforce |
|---|---|---|
| Washington-Arlington-Alexandria, DC-VA-MD-WV | $108,930 | 1,090 |
| San Francisco–Oakland–Fremont, CA | $95,300 | 1,090 |
| New York–Northern New Jersey–Long Island, NY-NJ-PA | $93,490 | 2,360 |
| Dallas–Fort Worth–Arlington, TX | $86,830 | 810 |
| Atlanta–Sandy Springs–Marietta, GA | $83,870 | 870 |
| Boston-Cambridge-Quincy, MA-NH | $82,120 | 1,140 |
| Charlotte-Gastonia-Concord, NC-SC | $81,330 | 620 |
| Chicago-Naperville-Joliet, IL-IN-WI | $78,310 | 1,860 |
| Philadelphia-Camden-Wilmington, PA-NJ-DE-MD | $74,220 | 910 |
| Los Angeles–Long Beach–Santa Ana, CA | $71,640 | 1,410 |
| Richmond, VA | $46,840 | 750 |

will require more financial examiners working on consumer compliance.

**Major Work Tasks:** Investigate activities of institutions to enforce laws and regulations and to ensure legality of transactions and operations or financial solvency. Review and analyze new, proposed, or revised laws, regulations, policies, and procedures to interpret their meaning and determine their impact. Plan, supervise, and review work of assigned subordinates. Recommend actions to ensure compliance with laws and regulations or to protect solvency of institutions. Examine the minutes of meetings of directors, stockholders and committees to investigate the specific authority extended at various levels of management. Prepare reports, exhibits and other supporting schedules that detail an institution's safety and soundness, compliance with laws and regulations, and recommended solutions to questionable financial conditions. Review balance sheets, operating income and expense accounts, and loan documentation to confirm institution assets and liabilities. Review audit reports of internal and external auditors to monitor adequacy of scope of reports or to discover specific weaknesses in internal routines. Train other examiners in the financial examination process. Establish guidelines for procedures and policies that comply with new and revised regulations and direct their implementation. Direct and participate in formal and informal meetings with bank directors, trustees, senior management, counsels, and outside accountants and consultants to gather information and discuss findings. Verify and inspect cash reserves, assigned collateral, and bank-owned securities to check internal control procedures. Review applications for mergers, acquisitions, establishment of new institutions, acceptance in Federal Reserve System, or registration of securities sales to determine their public interest value and conformance to regulations, and recommend acceptance or rejection. Resolve problems concerning the overall financial integrity of banking institutions including loan investment portfolios, capital, earnings, and specific or large troubled accounts.

**Usual Educational Requirement:** Bachelor's degree. **Relevant Educational Programs**: Accounting; Auditing; Financial Forensics and Fraud Investigation; Suspension and Debarment Investigation; Taxation. **Related Knowledge/Courses:** Economics and Accounting; Law and Government; Administration and Management; English Language; Mathematics; Clerical. **Work Experience Needed:** None. **On-**

273

the-Job Training Needed: Moderate-term on-the-job training. Certification/Licensure: Voluntary certification by association.

Personality Types: Enterprising–Conventional. Key Career Cluster: 07 Government and Public Administration. Key Career Pathway: 7.6 Regulation.

Skills: Systems evaluation; systems analysis; operations analysis; management of personnel resources; learning strategies; mathematics; critical thinking; time management.

Physical Environment: Indoors; sitting. Structural Environment: Freedom to make decisions; structured versus unstructured work; impact of decisions on co-workers or company results; importance of being exact or accurate; frequency of decision making; time pressure.

## Financial Managers

**Plan, direct, or coordinate accounting, investing, banking, insurance, securities, and other financial activities of a branch, office, or department of an establishment.**

- Average annual earnings: $109,740
- Middle 50% of earners: $79,930–$149,410
- Earnings growth potential: High (45.7%)
- Growth: 8.8%
- Annual job openings: 14,280
- Self-employed: 5.0%

Considerations for Job Outlook: As with other managerial occupations, job seekers are likely to face competition because the number of job openings is expected to be fewer than the number of applicants. Candidates with expertise in accounting and finance—particularly those with a master's degree or certification—should enjoy the best job prospects. An understanding of international finance and complex financial documents is important.

Major Work Tasks: For tasks, see the job specializations.

### BEST-PAYING INDUSTRIES

| Industry | Median Earnings | Workforce |
|---|---|---|
| Professional, Scientific, and Technical Services | $130,120 | 50,280 |
| Management of Companies and Enterprises | $124,840 | 54,450 |
| Insurance Carriers and Related Activities | $122,410 | 26,230 |
| Federal, State, and Local Government | $102,150 | 39,210 |
| Credit Intermediation and Related Activities | $91,950 | 89,980 |

### BEST-PAYING METROPOLITAN AREAS

| Metro Area | Median Earnings | Workforce |
|---|---|---|
| New York–Northern New Jersey–Long Island, NY-NJ-PA | $155,870 | 44,060 |
| San Francisco–Oakland–Fremont, CA | $142,080 | 12,750 |
| Washington-Arlington-Alexandria, DC-VA-MD-WV | $131,040 | 17,700 |
| Philadelphia-Camden-Wilmington, PA-NJ-DE-MD | $128,930 | 10,930 |
| Los Angeles–Long Beach–Santa Ana, CA | $127,800 | 26,810 |
| Boston-Cambridge-Quincy, MA-NH | $116,410 | 18,090 |
| Chicago-Naperville-Joliet, IL-IN-WI | $112,920 | 21,880 |
| Dallas–Fort Worth–Arlington, TX | $112,430 | 10,330 |
| Minneapolis–St. Paul–Bloomington, MN-WI | $110,400 | 10,950 |

**Usual Educational Requirement:** Bachelor's degree. **Relevant Educational Programs**: Accounting and Business/Management; Accounting and Finance; Credit Management; Finance and Financial Management Services, Other; Finance, General; International Finance; Public Finance. **Work Experience Needed:** More than 5 years. **On-the-Job Training Needed:** None. **Certification/Licensure:** Voluntary certification by association.

**Key Career Cluster:** 04 Business, Management, and Administration. **Key Career Pathway:** 4.2 Business Financial Management and Accounting.

### JOB SPECIALIZATION: FINANCIAL MANAGERS, BRANCH OR DEPARTMENT

**Direct and coordinate financial activities of workers in a branch, office, or department of an establishment, such as branch bank, brokerage firm, risk and insurance department, or credit department.**

**Major Work Tasks:** Establish and maintain relationships with individual or business customers or provide assistance with problems these customers may encounter. Examine, evaluate, or process loan applications. Plan, direct, or coordinate the activities of workers in branches, offices, or departments of establishments, such as branch banks, brokerage firms, risk and insurance departments, or credit departments. Oversee the flow of cash or financial instruments. Recruit staff members and oversee training programs. Network within communities to find and attract new business. Approve, reject, or coordinate the approval or rejection of lines of credit or commercial, real estate, or personal loans. Prepare financial or regulatory reports required by laws, regulations, or boards of directors. Establish procedures for custody or control of assets, records, loan collateral, or securities to ensure safekeeping. Review collection reports to determine the status of collections and the amounts of outstanding balances. Prepare operational or risk reports for management analysis. Evaluate financial reporting systems, accounting or collection procedures, or investment activities and make recommendations for changes to procedures, operating systems, budgets, or other financial control functions. Plan, direct, and coordinate risk and insurance programs of establishments to control risks and losses. Submit delinquent accounts to attorneys or outside agencies for collection. Communicate with stockholders or other investors to provide information or to raise capital. Evaluate data pertaining to costs to plan budgets. Analyze and classify risks and investments to determine their potential impacts on companies. Review reports of securities transactions or price lists to analyze market conditions. Develop or analyze information to assess the current or future financial status of firms. Direct insurance negotiations, select insurance brokers or carriers, and place insurance.

**Related Knowledge/Courses:** Economics and Accounting; Sales and Marketing; Personnel and Human Resources; Customer and Personal Service; Clerical Practices; Mathematics.

**Personality Types:** Enterprising–Conventional.

**Skills:** Management of financial resources; management of personnel resources; persuasion; service orientation; learning strategies; time management; systems evaluation; operations analysis.

**Physical Environment:** Indoors; sitting. **Structural Environment:** Frequency of decision making; importance of being exact or accurate; impact of decisions on co-workers or company results; structured versus unstructured work; freedom to make decisions; level of competition.

### JOB SPECIALIZATION: TREASURERS AND CONTROLLERS

**Direct financial activities, such as planning, procurement, and investments, for all or part of an organization.**

**275**

**Major Work Tasks:** Prepare or direct preparation of financial statements, business activity reports, financial position forecasts, annual budgets, or reports required by regulatory agencies. Supervise employees performing financial reporting, accounting, billing, collections, payroll, and budgeting duties. Delegate authority for the receipt, disbursement, banking, protection, and custody of funds, securities, and financial instruments. Maintain current knowledge of organizational policies and procedures, federal and state policies and directives, and current accounting standards. Conduct or coordinate audits of company accounts and financial transactions to ensure compliance with state and federal requirements and statutes. Receive, record, and authorize requests for disbursements in accordance with company policies and procedures. Monitor and evaluate the performance of accounting and other financial staff, recommending and implementing personnel actions, such as promotions and dismissals. Develop and maintain relationships with banking, insurance, and nonorganizational accounting personnel to facilitate financial activities. Coordinate and direct the financial planning, budgeting, procurement, or investment activities of all or part of an organization. Develop internal control policies, guidelines, and procedures for activities such as budget administration, cash and credit management, and accounting. Analyze the financial details of past, present, and expected operations to identify development opportunities and areas where improvement is needed. Advise management on short-term and long-term financial objectives, policies, and actions. Provide direction and assistance to other organizational units regarding accounting and budgeting policies and procedures and efficient control and utilization of financial resources. Evaluate needs for procurement of funds and investment of surpluses and make appropriate recommendations. Lead staff training and development in budgeting and finan-

cial management areas. Monitor financial activities and details, such as cash flow and reserve levels, to ensure that all legal and regulatory requirements are met.

**Related Knowledge/Courses:** Economics and Accounting; Administration and Management; Personnel and Human Resources; Mathematics; Law and Government; Computers and Electronics.

**Personality Types:** Conventional–Enterprising.

**Skills:** Management of financial resources; systems analysis; mathematics; systems evaluation; management of material resources; operations analysis; judgment and decision making; management of personnel resources.

**Physical Environment:** Indoors; sitting. **Structural Environment:** Importance of being exact or accurate; freedom to make decisions; structured versus unstructured work; impact of decisions on co-workers or company results; frequency of decision making; time pressure.

## Financial Specialists, All Other

**All financial specialists not listed separately.**

- Average annual earnings: $61,160
- Middle 50% of earners: $44,970–$80,980
- Earnings growth potential: Medium (41.7%)
- Growth: 6.1%
- Annual job openings: 4,490
- Self-employed: 1.2%

**Considerations for Job Outlook:** Efforts to recruit and retain employees, the growing importance of employee training, and new legal standards are expected to increase employment of these workers. College graduates and those with certification should have the best opportunities.

**Major Work Tasks:** For tasks, see the job specializations.

## BEST-PAYING INDUSTRIES

| Industry | Median Earnings | Workforce |
|---|---|---|
| Professional, Scientific, and Technical Services | $72,250 | 11,070 |
| Federal, State, and Local Government | $68,410 | 33,260 |
| Securities, Commodity Contracts, and Other Financial Investments and Related Activities | $67,580 | 12,330 |
| Management of Companies and Enterprises | $67,040 | 10,580 |
| Educational Services | $52,890 | 9,560 |
| Credit Intermediation and Related Activities | $49,860 | 41,640 |

## BEST-PAYING METROPOLITAN AREAS

| Metro Area | Median Earnings | Workforce |
|---|---|---|
| San Francisco–Oakland–Fremont, CA | $87,740 | 4,850 |
| New York–Northern New Jersey–Long Island, NY-NJ-PA | $71,080 | 15,430 |
| Chicago-Naperville-Joliet, IL-IN-WI | $65,200 | 8,810 |
| Detroit-Warren-Livonia, MI | $63,460 | 3,600 |
| Dallas–Fort Worth–Arlington, TX | $57,460 | 4,450 |
| Long Beach–Santa Ana, CA | $56,990 | 7,270 |

**Usual Educational Requirement:** Bachelor's degree. **Relevant Educational Programs**: Finance, General; Financial Mathematics. **Work Experience Needed:** None. **On-the-Job Training Needed:** Moderate-term on-the-job training. **Certification/Licensure:** Licensure for some specializations.

**Key Career Cluster:** 06 Finance. **Key Career Pathway:** 6.1 Financial and Investment Planning.

### JOB SPECIALIZATION: FINANCIAL QUANTITATIVE ANALYSTS

**Develop quantitative financial products used to inform individuals and financial institutions engaged in saving, lending, investing, borrowing, or managing risk. Investigate methods for financial analysis to create mathematical models used to develop improved analytical tools and advanced financial investment instruments.**

**Major Work Tasks:** Prepare requirements documentation for use by software developers. Provide application or analytical support to researchers or traders on issues such as valuations or data. Identify, track, or maintain metrics for trading system operations. Collaborate in the development or testing of new analytical software to ensure compliance with user requirements, specifications, or scope. Research new financial products or analytics to determine their usefulness. Maintain or modify all financial analytic models in use. Produce written summary reports of financial research results. Interpret results of financial analysis procedures. Develop core analytical capabilities or model libraries, using advanced statistical, quantitative, or econometric techniques. Define or recommend model specifications or data collection methods. Consult traders or other financial industry personnel to determine the need for new or improved analytical applications. Confer with other financial engineers

**277**

or analysts to understand trading strategies, market dynamics, or trading system performance to inform development of quantitative techniques. Collaborate with product development teams to research, model, validate, or implement quantitative structured solutions for new or expanded markets. Research or develop analytical tools to address issues such as portfolio construction or optimization, performance measurement, attribution, profit and loss measurement, or pricing models. Devise or apply independent models or tools to help verify results of analytical systems. Apply mathematical or statistical techniques to address practical issues in finance, such as derivative valuation, securities trading, risk management, or financial market regulation. Analyze pricing or risks of carbon trading products. Assess the potential impact of climate change on business financial issues, such as damage repairs, insurance costs, or potential disruptions of daily activities. Develop methods of assessing or measuring corporate performance in terms of environmental, social, and governance (ESG) issues. Develop solutions to help clients hedge carbon exposure or risk.

**Related Knowledge/Courses:** No data available.

**Personality Types:** Investigative–Conventional.

**Skills:** No data available.

**Physical Environment:** No data available. **Structural Environment:** No data available.

JOB SPECIALIZATION: FRAUD EXAMINERS, INVESTIGATORS, AND ANALYSTS

**Obtain evidence, take statements, produce reports, and testify to findings regarding resolution of fraud allegations. May coordinate fraud detection and prevention activities.**

**Major Work Tasks:** Maintain knowledge of current events and trends in such areas as money laundering and criminal tools and techniques. Train others in fraud detection and pre-

vention techniques. Research or evaluate new technologies for use in fraud detection systems. Prepare evidence for presentation in court. Negotiate with responsible parties to arrange for recovery of losses due to fraud. Conduct field surveillance to gather case-related information. Testify in court regarding investigation findings. Advise businesses or agencies on ways to improve fraud detection. Review reports of suspected fraud to determine need for further investigation. Prepare written reports of investigation findings. Recommend actions in fraud cases. Lead, or participate in, fraud investigation teams. Interview witnesses or suspects and take statements. Design, implement, or maintain fraud detection tools or procedures. Gather financial documents related to investigations. Evaluate business operations to identify risk areas for fraud. Document all investigative activities. Create and maintain logs, records, or databases of information about fraudulent activity. Coordinate investigative efforts with law enforcement officers and attorneys. Conduct in-depth investigations of suspicious financial activity, such as suspected money-laundering efforts. Analyze financial data to detect irregularities in areas such as billing trends, financial relationships, and regulatory compliance procedures. Obtain and serve subpoenas. Arrest individuals to be charged with fraud.

**Related Knowledge/Courses:** Law and Government; Economics and Accounting; Psychology; Personnel and Human Resources; Sociology and Anthropology; Public Safety and Security.

**Personality Types:** Enterprising–Investigative–Conventional.

**Skills:** Writing; negotiation; active listening; speaking; reading comprehension; persuasion; critical thinking; systems evaluation.

**Physical Environment:** Indoors; sitting. **Structural Environment:** Importance of being exact or accurate; impact of decisions on co-workers or company results; structured versus unstructured work; freedom to make decisions; importance of repeating same tasks; frequency of decision making.

## JOB SPECIALIZATION: INVESTMENT UNDERWRITERS

**Intermediate between corporate issuers of securities and clients regarding private equity investments. Underwrite the issuance of securities to provide capital for client growth. Negotiate and structure the terms of mergers and acquisitions.**

**Major Work Tasks:** Structure marketing campaigns to find buyers for new securities. Supervise, train, or mentor junior team members. Assess companies as investments for clients by examining company facilities. Prepare all materials for transactions or execution of deals. Perform securities valuation or pricing. Employ financial models to develop solutions to financial problems or to assess the financial or capital impact of transactions. Develop and maintain client relationships. Evaluate capital needs of clients and assess market conditions to inform structuring of financial packages. Create client presentations of plan details. Coordinate due diligence processes and the negotiation or execution of purchase or sale agreements. Collaborate on projects with other professionals, such as lawyers, accountants, or public relations experts. Confer with clients to restructure debt, refinance debt, or raise new debt. Analyze financial or operational performance of companies facing financial difficulties to identify or recommend remedies. Advise clients on aspects of capitalization, such as amounts, sources, or timing. Direct communications between corporate issuers of new securities and the general public. Structure or negotiate deals, such as corporate mergers, sales, or acquisitions. Arrange financing of deals from sources such as financial institutions, agencies, or public or private companies. Arrange deals involving green investments in areas such as alternative energy product development, green technologies, or sustainable agriculture. Specialize in green financial instruments, such as socially responsible mutual funds or exchange-traded funds (ETF) that are comprised of green companies.

**Related Knowledge/Courses:** No data available.

**Personality Types:** Conventional–Enterprising.

**Skills:** No data available.

**Physical Environment:** No data available.
**Structural Environment:** No data available.

## JOB SPECIALIZATION: RISK MANAGEMENT SPECIALISTS

**Analyze and make decisions on risk management issues by identifying, measuring, and managing operational and enterprise risks for an organization.**

**Major Work Tasks:** Meet with clients to answer queries on subjects, such as risk exposure, market scenarios, or values-at-risk calculations. Maintain input or data quality of risk management systems. Develop contingency plans to deal with emergencies. Devise scenario analyses reflecting possible severe market events. Analyze new legislation to determine impact on risk exposure. Recommend ways to control or reduce risk. Produce reports or presentations that outline findings, explain risk positions, or recommend changes. Plan, and contribute to development of, risk management systems. Gather risk-related data from internal or external resources. Develop or implement risk-assessment models or methodologies. Document, and ensure communication of, key risks. Devise systems and processes to monitor validity of risk modeling outputs. Conduct statistical analyses to quantify risk using statistical analysis software or econometric models. Identify key risks and mitigating factors of potential investments, such as asset types and values, legal and ownership structures, professional reputations, customer bases, or industry segments. Identify and analyze areas of potential risk to the assets, earning capacity, or success of organizations. Confer with traders to identify and communicate risks associated with specific trading strategies or positions. Provide statistical modeling advice to other departments. Review or draft risk disclosures for offer documents. Consult financial literature to ensure use of the latest models or statistical techniques. Track, measure, or report on aspects of market risk for traded issues. Determine potential environmental impacts of new products or processes on long-term growth and profitability. Determine potential liability related to the use of more sustainable methods of product packaging, such as biodegradable food containers. Evaluate the risks and benefits involved in implementing green building technologies. Evaluate the risks related to green investments, such as renewable energy company stocks.

**Related Knowledge/Courses:** Economics and Accounting; Mathematics; Law and Government; Administration and Management; Computers and Electronics; Personnel and Human Resources.

**Personality Types:** Conventional–Enterprising–Investigative.

**Skills:** Mathematics; programming; systems analysis; management of financial resources; systems evaluation; management of material resources; writing; reading comprehension.

**Physical Environment:** Indoors; sitting. **Structural Environment:** Structured versus unstructured work; importance of being exact or accurate; impact of decisions on co-workers or company results; freedom to make decisions; time pressure; level of competition.

## First-Line Supervisors of Correctional Officers

**Directly supervise and coordinate activities of correctional officers and jailers.**

- Average annual earnings: $57,840
- Middle 50% of earners: $43,950–$75,170
- Earnings growth potential: Medium (34.5%)
- Growth: 5.6%
- Annual job openings: 1,650
- Self-employed: 0.0%

### BEST-PAYING INDUSTRIES

| Industry | Median Earnings | Workforce |
|---|---|---|
| Federal, State, and Local Government | $58,430 | 42,870 |

### BEST-PAYING METROPOLITAN AREAS

| Metro Area | Median Earnings | Workforce |
|---|---|---|
| Baltimore-Towson, MD | $54,440 | 1,250 |
| Houston–Sugar Land–Baytown, TX | $48,850 | 1,180 |

**Considerations for Job Outlook:** Slower-than-average employment growth is expected as slow growth of prisons reduces the ratio of corrections managers.

**Major Work Tasks:** Take, receive, or check periodic inmate counts. Maintain order, discipline, and security within assigned areas in accordance with relevant rules, regulations, policies, and laws. Respond to emergencies, such as escapes. Maintain knowledge of, comply with, and enforce all institutional policies, rules, procedures, and regulations. Supervise and direct the work of correctional officers to ensure the safe custody, discipline, and welfare of inmates. Restrain, secure, or control offenders, using chemical agents, firearms, or other weapons of force as necessary. Supervise or perform searches of inmates or their quarters to locate contraband items. Monitor behavior of subordinates to ensure alert, courteous, and professional behavior toward inmates, parolees, fellow employees, visitors, and the public. Complete administrative paperwork or supervise the preparation or maintenance of records, forms, or reports. Instruct employees or provide on-the-job training. Conduct roll calls of correctional officers. Supervise activities such as searches, shakedowns, riot control, or institutional tours. Carry injured offenders or employees to safety and provide emergency first aid when necessary. Supervise or provide security for offenders performing tasks, such as construction, maintenance, laundry, food service, or other industrial or agricultural operations. Develop work or security procedures. Set up employee work schedules. Resolve problems between inmates. Rate behavior of inmates, promoting acceptable attitudes and behaviors to those with low ratings. Transfer or transport offenders on foot or by driving vehicles, such as trailers, vans, or buses. Convey correctional officers' or inmates' complaints to superiors. Review offender information to identify issues that require special attention. Examine incoming or outgoing mail to ensure conformance with regulations.

**Usual Educational Requirement:** High school diploma or equivalent. **Relevant Educational Programs**: Corrections; Corrections Administration; Criminal Justice/Safety Studies. **Related Knowledge/Courses:** Public Safety and Security; Psychology; Philosophy and Theology; Law and Government; Sociology and Anthropology; Therapy and Counseling. **Work Experience Needed:** 1 to 5 years. **On-the-Job Training Needed:** Moderate-term on-the-job training. **Certification/Licensure:** None.

**Personality Types:** Enterprising–Conventional–Realistic. **Key Career Cluster:** 12 Law, Public Safety, Corrections, and Security. **Key Career Pathway:** 12.1 Correction Services.

**Skills:** Management of personnel resources; time management; coordination; social perceptiveness; monitoring; persuasion; learning strategies; instructing.

**Physical Environment:** Indoors; outdoors; standing; noise; contaminants; exposed to disease or infections. **Structural Environment:** Time pressure; importance of being exact or accurate; importance of repeating same tasks; consequence of error; frequency of decision making; freedom to make decisions.

## First-Line Supervisors of Fire Fighting and Prevention Workers

**Directly supervise and coordinate activities of workers engaged in fire fighting and fire prevention and control.**

- Average annual earnings: $68,210
- Middle 50% of earners: $53,340–$88,040
- Earnings growth potential: Medium (40.3%)
- Growth: 8.2%
- Annual job openings: 3,310
- Self-employed: 0.0%

**Considerations for Job Outlook:** Most job growth will stem from the conversion of volunteer firefighting positions into paid positions. Job seekers are expected to face keen competition. Those who have completed some firefighter education at a community college and have EMT or paramedic certification should have the best prospects.

### BEST-PAYING INDUSTRIES

| Industry | Median Earnings | Workforce |
|---|---|---|
| Federal, State, and Local Government | $68,490 | 58,990 |

Your Guide to High-Paying Careers

## BEST-PAYING METROPOLITAN AREAS

| Metro Area | Median Earnings | Workforce |
|---|---|---|
| New York–Northern New Jersey–Long Island, NY-NJ-PA | $107,630 | 3,570 |
| Chicago-Naperville-Joliet, IL-IN-WI | $97,030 | 2,220 |
| Dallas–Fort Worth–Arlington, TX | $79,230 | 1,400 |
| Boston-Cambridge-Quincy, MA-NH | $73,840 | 2,270 |
| Phoenix-Mesa-Scottsdale, AZ | $66,460 | 1,370 |

**Major Work Tasks:** For tasks, see the job specializations.

**Usual Educational Requirement:** Postsecondary vocational training. **Relevant Educational Programs**: Fire Protection, Other; Fire Services Administration; Natural Resources Law Enforcement and Protective Services. **Work Experience Needed:** 1 to 5 years. **On-the-Job Training Needed:** None. **Certification/Licensure:** Licensure in some states; certification by association; municipal examination.

**Key Career Cluster:** 12 Law, Public Safety, Corrections, and Security. **Key Career Pathway:** 12.2 Emergency and Fire Management Services.

### JOB SPECIALIZATION: FOREST FIRE FIGHTING AND PREVENTION SUPERVISORS

**Supervise fire fighters who control and suppress fires in forests or vacant public land.**

**Major Work Tasks:** Communicate fire details to superiors, subordinates, or interagency dispatch centers, using two-way radios. Serve as a working leader of an engine, hand, helicopter, or prescribed fire crew of three or more firefighters. Maintain fire suppression equipment in good condition, checking equipment periodically to ensure that it is ready for use. Evaluate size, location, and condition of forest fires and request and dispatch crews and position equipment so fires can be contained safely and effectively. Operate wildland fire engines or hoselays. Monitor prescribed burns to ensure that they are conducted safely and effectively. Direct and supervise prescribed burn projects and prepare postburn reports, analyzing burn conditions and results. Identify staff training and development needs to ensure that appropriate training can be arranged. Maintain knowledge of forest fire laws and fire prevention techniques and tactics. Recommend equipment modifications or new equipment purchases. Perform administrative duties, such as compiling and maintaining records, completing forms, preparing reports, or composing correspondence. Recruit or hire forest firefighting personnel. Train workers in skills, such as parachute jumping, fire suppression, aerial observation, or radio communication, in the classroom or on the job. Review and evaluate employee performance. Observe fires or crews from air to determine firefighting force requirements or to note changing conditions that will affect firefighting efforts. Inspect stations, uniforms, equipment, or recreation areas to ensure compliance with safety standards, taking corrective action as necessary. Schedule employee work assignments and set work priorities. Regulate open burning by issuing burning permits, inspecting problem sites, issuing citations for violations of laws and ordinances, or educating the public in proper burning practices. Direct investigations of suspected arson in wildfires, working closely with other investigating agencies. Monitor fire suppression expenditures to ensure that they are necessary and reasonable. Lead work crews in the maintenance of structures or access roads in forest areas.

**Related Knowledge/Courses:** Public Safety and Security; Building and Construction; Mechanical Devices; Customer and Personal Ser-

282

vice; Personnel and Human Resources; Transportation.

**Personality Types:** Enterprising–Realistic–Conventional.

**Skills:** Operations analysis; equipment maintenance; operation and control; management of personnel resources; operation monitoring; coordination; equipment selection; monitoring.

**Physical Environment:** Outdoors; standing; walking and running; using hands; noise; very hot or cold. **Structural Environment:** Freedom to make decisions; frequency of decision making; impact of decisions on co-workers or company results; structured versus unstructured work; importance of being exact or accurate; time pressure.

### JOB SPECIALIZATION: MUNICIPAL FIRE FIGHTING AND PREVENTION SUPERVISORS

**Supervise firefighters who control and extinguish municipal fires, protect life and property, and conduct rescue efforts.**

**Major Work Tasks:** Assign firefighters to jobs at strategic locations to facilitate rescue of persons and maximize application of extinguishing agents. Provide emergency medical services as required, and perform light to heavy rescue functions at emergencies. Assess nature and extent of fire, condition of building, danger to adjacent buildings, and water supply status to determine crew or company requirements. Instruct and drill fire department personnel in assigned duties, including firefighting, medical care, hazardous materials response, fire prevention, and related subjects. Evaluate the performance of assigned firefighting personnel. Direct firefighters' training, assign instructors to training classes, and provide supervisors with reports on training progress and status. Prepare activity reports, listing fire call locations, actions taken, fire types and probable causes, damage estimates, and situation dispositions. Maintain required maps and records. Attend in-service training classes to remain current in knowledge of codes, laws, ordinances, and regulations. Evaluate fire station procedures to ensure efficiency and enforcement of departmental regulations. Direct firefighters in station maintenance duties, and participate in these duties. Recommend personnel actions related to disciplinary procedures, performance, leaves of absence, and grievances. Coordinate the distribution of fire prevention promotional materials. Inspect and test new and existing fire protection systems, fire detection systems, and fire safety equipment to ensure that they are operating properly. Present and interpret fire prevention and fire code information to citizens' groups, organizations, contractors, engineers, and developers. Compile and maintain records on personnel, accidents, equipment, and supplies. Perform maintenance and minor repairs on firefighting equipment, including vehicles, and write and submit proposals to modify, replace, and repair equipment. Direct investigation of cases of suspected arson, hazards, and false alarms and submit reports outlining findings.

**Related Knowledge/Courses:** Building and Construction; Public Safety and Security; Mechanical Devices; Medicine and Dentistry; Chemistry; Personnel and Human Resources.

**Personality Types:** Enterprising–Realistic–Social.

**Skills:** Operation and control; science; equipment selection; repairing; equipment maintenance; quality control analysis; management of personnel resources; operation monitoring.

**Physical Environment:** Outdoors; indoors; standing; using hands; noise; very hot or cold. **Structural Environment:** Impact of decisions on co-workers or company results; freedom to make decisions; frequency of decision making; consequence of error; structured versus unstructured work; importance of being exact or accurate.

## First-Line Supervisors of Mechanics, Installers, and Repairers

**Directly supervise and coordinate the activities of mechanics, installers, and repairers.**

- Average annual earnings: $60,250

- Middle 50% of earners: $46,350–$75,900

- Earnings growth potential: Medium (39.5%)

- Growth: 11.9%

- Annual job openings: 16,490

- Self-employed: 1.2%

### BEST-PAYING INDUSTRIES

| Industry | Median Earnings | Workforce |
|---|---|---|
| Federal, State, and Local Government | $63,850 | 47,870 |
| Merchant Wholesalers, Durable Goods | $59,960 | 23,970 |
| Specialty Trade Contractors | $59,410 | 25,470 |
| Motor Vehicle and Parts Dealers | $55,740 | 45,190 |
| Repair and Maintenance | $53,740 | 48,860 |

### BEST-PAYING METROPOLITAN AREAS

| Metro Area | Median Earnings | Workforce |
|---|---|---|
| New York–Northern New Jersey–Long Island, NY-NJ-PA | $75,350 | 23,600 |
| Los Angeles–Long Beach–Santa Ana, CA | $69,530 | 14,150 |
| Chicago-Naperville-Joliet, IL-IN-WI | $65,720 | 9,860 |
| Dallas–Fort Worth–Arlington, TX | $59,270 | 10,480 |
| Houston–Sugar Land–Baytown, TX | $58,850 | 9,850 |

**Considerations for Job Outlook:** Slower-than-average employment growth is projected.

**Major Work Tasks:** Determine schedules, sequences, and assignments for work activities, based on work priority, quantity of equipment, and skill of personnel. Monitor employees' work levels and review work performance. Examine objects, systems, or facilities and analyze information to determine needed installations, services, or repairs. Participate in budget preparation and administration, coordinating purchasing and documentation and monitoring departmental expenditures. Counsel employees about work-related issues and assist employees to correct job-skill deficiencies. Requisition materials and supplies, such as tools, equipment, or replacement parts. Compute estimates and actual costs of factors such as materials, labor, or outside contractors. Interpret specifications, blueprints, or job orders to construct templates and lay out reference points for workers. Conduct or arrange for worker training in safety, repair, or maintenance techniques, operational procedures, or equipment use. Investigate accidents or injuries and prepare reports of findings. Confer with personnel, such as management, engineering, quality control, customer, or union workers' representatives, to coordinate work activities, resolve employee grievances, or identify and review resource needs. Recommend or initiate personnel actions, such as hires, promotions, transfers, discharges, or disciplinary measures. Perform skilled repair or maintenance operations, using equipment such as hand or power tools, hydraulic presses or shears, or welding equipment. Compile operational or personnel records, such as time and production records, inventory data, repair or maintenance statistics, or test results. Develop, implement, or evaluate maintenance policies and procedures. Inspect, test, and measure completed work, using devices such as hand tools or gauges to verify conformance to standards or repair requirements. Meet with vendors or suppliers to discuss products used in repair work. Develop or implement electronic maintenance programs or computer information management systems. Monitor tool and part inventories and the condition and maintenance of shops to ensure adequate working conditions.

**Usual Educational Requirement:** High school diploma or equivalent. **Relevant Educational Programs**: Electrical and Power Transmission Installation/Installer, General; High Performance and Custom Engine Technician/Mechanic Training; Lineworker Training; Operations Management and Supervision; Recreation Vehicle (RV) Service Technician Training; Vehicle Maintenance and Repair Technologies, General. **Related Knowledge/ Courses:** Mechanical Devices; Building and Construction; Engineering and Technology; Production and Processing; Design; Personnel and Human Resources. **Work Experience Needed:** 1 to 5 years. **On-the-Job Training Needed:** None. **Certification/Licensure:** None.

**Personality Types:** Enterprising–Conventional–Realistic. **Key Career Cluster:** 13 Manufacturing. **Key Career Pathway:** 13.3 Maintenance, Installation, and Repair.

**Skills:** Management of financial resources; repairing; equipment maintenance; management of material resources; troubleshooting; equipment selection; quality control analysis; management of personnel resources.

**Physical Environment:** Indoors; outdoors; standing; using hands; noise; very hot or cold. **Structural Environment:** Freedom to make decisions; structured versus unstructured work; impact of decisions on co-workers or company results; time pressure; frequency of decision making; importance of being exact or accurate.

## First-Line Supervisors of Non-Retail Sales Workers

**Directly supervise and coordinate activities of sales workers other than retail sales workers.**

### BEST-PAYING INDUSTRIES

| Industry | Median Earnings | Workforce |
|---|---|---|
| Professional, Scientific, and Technical Services | $86,800 | 15,840 |
| Wholesale Electronic Markets and Agents and Brokers | $80,760 | 14,670 |
| Insurance Carriers and Related Activities | $76,780 | 13,450 |
| Merchant Wholesalers, Durable Goods | $72,340 | 46,230 |
| Merchant Wholesalers, Nondurable Goods | $70,400 | 28,430 |
| Credit Intermediation and Related Activities | $56,880 | 19,540 |
| Administrative and Support Services | $53,920 | 18,740 |

### BEST-PAYING METROPOLITAN AREAS

| Metro Area | Median Earnings | Workforce |
|---|---|---|
| New York–Northern New Jersey–Long Island, NY-NJ-PA | $101,070 | 20,610 |
| Philadelphia-Camden-Wilmington, PA-NJ-DE-MD | $96,020 | 5,330 |
| Boston-Cambridge-Quincy, MA-NH | $86,350 | 5,220 |
| Miami–Fort Lauderdale–Pompano Beach, FL | $78,210 | 6,930 |
| Dallas–Fort Worth–Arlington, TX | $73,570 | 8,220 |
| Houston–Sugar Land–Baytown, TX | $69,730 | 6,830 |
| Los Angeles–Long Beach–Santa Ana, CA | $63,640 | 9,930 |
| Chicago-Naperville-Joliet, IL-IN-WI | $61,710 | 5,840 |

- Average annual earnings: $70,060
- Middle 50% of earners: $49,680–$100,140
- Earnings growth potential: High (47.9%)
- Growth: 4.0%
- Annual job openings: 12,350
- Self-employed: 41.8%

**Considerations for Job Outlook:** In the U.S. Postal Service, a very large decrease is expected because sales staff will be cut as post offices attempt to cut costs.

**Major Work Tasks:** Listen to and resolve customer complaints regarding services, products, or personnel. Monitor sales staff performance to ensure that goals are met. Hire, train, and evaluate personnel. Confer with company officials to develop methods and procedures to increase sales, expand markets, and promote business. Provide staff with assistance in performing difficult or complicated duties. Plan and prepare work schedules, and assign employees to specific duties. Attend company meetings to exchange product information and coordinate work activities with other departments. Prepare sales and inventory reports for management and budget departments. Formulate pricing policies on merchandise according to profitability requirements. Analyze details of sales territories to assess their growth potential and to set quotas. Visit retailers and sales representatives to promote products and gather information. Direct and supervise employees engaged in sales, inventory-taking, reconciling cash receipts, or performing specific services. Examine merchandise to ensure correct pricing and display, and that it functions as advertised. Keep records pertaining to purchases, sales, and requisitions. Coordinate sales promotion activities, such as preparing merchandise displays and advertising copy. Prepare rental or lease agreements, specifying charges and payment procedures for use of machinery, tools, or other items. Inventory stock and reorder when inventories drop to speci-fied levels. Examine products purchased for resale or received for storage to determine product condition.

**Usual Educational Requirement:** High school diploma or equivalent. **Relevant Educational Programs**: General Merchandising, Sales, and Related Marketing Operations, Other; Selling Skills and Sales Operations; Special Products Marketing Operations. **Related Knowledge/ Courses:** Sales and Marketing; Personnel and Human Resources; Economics and Accounting; Administration and Management; Education and Training; Customer and Personal Service. **Work Experience Needed:** More than 5 years. **On-the-Job Training Needed:** None. **Certification/Licensure:** None.

**Personality Types:** Enterprising–Conventional–Social. **Key Career Cluster:** 14 Marketing, Sales, and Service. **Key Career Pathway:** 14.2 Professional Sales and Marketing.

**Skills:** Management of financial resources; management of material resources; management of personnel resources; negotiation; persuasion; instructing; systems evaluation; social perceptiveness.

**Physical Environment:** Indoors; sitting. **Structural Environment:** Structured versus unstructured work; freedom to make decisions; frequency of decision making; impact of decisions on co-workers or company results; time pressure; importance of being exact or accurate.

## First-Line Supervisors of Police and Detectives

**Directly supervise and coordinate activities of members of police force.**
- Average annual earnings: $78,270
- Middle 50% of earners: $60,250–$101,460
- Earnings growth potential: Medium (39.6%)
- Growth: 2.1%
- Annual job openings: 3,870
- Self-employed: 0.0%

## BEST-PAYING INDUSTRIES

| Industry | Median Earnings | Workforce |
|---|---|---|
| Federal, State, and Local Government | $78,640 | 97,380 |

## BEST-PAYING METROPOLITAN AREAS

| Metro Area | Median Earnings | Workforce |
|---|---|---|
| New York–Northern New Jersey–Long Island, NY-NJ-PA | $110,440 | 11,210 |
| Chicago-Naperville-Joliet, IL-IN-WI | $101,300 | 4,140 |
| Boston-Cambridge-Quincy, MA-NH | $83,160 | 3,160 |
| Atlanta–Sandy Springs–Marietta, GA | $59,250 | 2,030 |
| San Juan–Caguas–Guaynabo, PR | $33,730 | 2,550 |

**Considerations for Job Outlook:** Population growth is the main source of demand for police services. Overall, opportunities in local police departments should be favorable for qualified applicants.

**Major Work Tasks:** Explain police operations to subordinates to assist them in performing their job duties. Inform personnel of changes in regulations and policies, implications of new or amended laws, and new techniques of police work. Supervise and coordinate the investigation of criminal cases, offering guidance and expertise to investigators and ensuring that procedures are conducted in accordance with laws and regulations. Investigate and resolve personnel problems within organization and charges of misconduct against staff. Train staff in proper police work procedures. Maintain logs, prepare reports, and direct the preparation, handling, and maintenance of departmental records. Monitor and evaluate the job performance of subordinates, and authorize promotions and transfers. Direct collection, preparation, and handling of evidence and personal property of prisoners. Develop, implement, and revise departmental policies and procedures. Conduct raids and order detention of witnesses and suspects for questioning. Prepare work schedules and assign duties to subordinates. Discipline staff for violation of department rules and regulations. Cooperate with court personnel and officials from other law enforcement agencies and testify in court as necessary. Review contents of written orders to ensure adherence to legal requirements. Inspect facilities, supplies, vehicles, and equipment to ensure conformance to standards. Prepare news releases and respond to police correspondence. Requisition and issue equipment and supplies. Meet with civic, educational, and community groups to develop community programs and events and to discuss law enforcement subjects. Direct release or transfer of prisoners. Prepare budgets and manage expenditures of department funds.

**Usual Educational Requirement:** High school diploma or equivalent. **Relevant Educational Programs**: Corrections; Criminal Justice/Law Enforcement Administration; Criminal Justice/Safety Studies; Crisis/Emergency/Disaster Management; Critical Incident Response/Special Police Operations; Critical Infrastructure Protection; Cultural/Archaeological Resources Protection; Homeland Security; Law Enforcement Record-Keeping and Evidence Management; Maritime Law Enforcement; Natural Resources Law Enforcement and Protective Services; Protective Services Operations; Terrorism and Counterterrorism Operations. **Related Knowledge/Courses:** Public Safety and Security; Law and Government; Psychology; Sociology and Anthropology; Therapy and Counseling; Personnel and Human Resources. **Work Experience Needed:** 1 to 5 years. **On-the-Job Training Needed:** Moderate-term on-the-job training. **Certification/Licensure:** Licensure in some states.

**Personality Types:** Enterprising–Social–Conventional. **Key Career Cluster:** 12 Law, Public Safety, Corrections, and Security. **Key Career Pathway:** 12.4 Law Enforcement Services.

**Skills:** Management of financial resources; management of personnel resources; persuasion; management of material resources; monitoring; learning strategies; time management; instructing.

**Physical Environment:** Indoors; outdoors; sitting; noise; very hot or cold; bright or inadequate lighting. **Structural Environment:** Frequency of decision making; impact of decisions on co-workers or company results; freedom to make decisions; importance of being exact or accurate; structured versus unstructured work; time pressure.

## Food Scientists and Technologists

**Use chemistry, microbiology, engineering, and other sciences to study the principles underlying the processing and deterioration of foods.**

- Average annual earnings: $58,070
- Middle 50% of earners: $43,170–$79,100
- Earnings growth potential: Medium (41.6%)
- Growth: 8.0%
- Annual job openings: 680
- Self-employed: 10.8%

**Considerations for Job Outlook:** A number of job vacancies will arise as many scientists are expected to retire within the next 10 years.

**Major Work Tasks:** Test new products for flavor, texture, color, nutritional content, and adherence to government and industry standards. Check raw ingredients for maturity or stability for processing and finished products for safety, quality, and nutritional value. Confer with process engineers, plant operators, flavor experts, and packaging and marketing specialists to resolve problems in product development.

### BEST-PAYING INDUSTRIES

| Industry | Median Earnings | Workforce |
|---|---|---|
| Management of Companies and Enterprises | $71,440 | 1,820 |
| Professional, Scientific, and Technical Services | $68,160 | 2,560 |
| Food Manufacturing | $54,890 | 6,430 |
| Educational Services | $47,790 | 1,280 |

### BEST-PAYING METROPOLITAN AREAS

| Metro Area | Median Earnings | Workforce |
|---|---|---|
| San Francisco–Oakland–Fremont, CA | $72,720 | 320 |
| Minneapolis–St. Paul–Bloomington, MN-WI | $69,540 | 1,240 |
| St. Louis, MO-IL | $68,560 | 310 |
| New York–Northern New Jersey–Long Island, NY-NJ-PA | $68,340 | 540 |
| Dallas–Fort Worth–Arlington, TX | $66,020 | 350 |
| Chicago-Naperville-Joliet, IL-IN-WI | $56,770 | 400 |
| San Diego–Carlsbad–San Marcos, CA | $55,200 | 340 |
| Los Angeles–Long Beach–Santa Ana, CA | $52,670 | 640 |
| Atlanta–Sandy Springs–Marietta, GA | $46,710 | 330 |

Evaluate food processing and storage operations and assist in the development of quality assurance programs for such operations. Study methods to improve aspects of foods, such as chemical composition, flavor, color, texture, nutritional value, and convenience. Study the structure and composition of food or the changes foods undergo in storage and processing. Develop new or improved ways of preserving, processing, packaging, storing, and delivering foods, using knowledge of chemistry, microbiology, and other sciences. Develop food standards and production specifications, safety and sanitary regulations, and waste management and water supply specifications. Demonstrate products to clients. Inspect food processing areas to ensure compliance with government regulations and standards for sanitation, safety, quality, and waste management standards. Search for substitutes for harmful or undesirable additives, such as nitrites. Develop new food items for production, based on consumer feedback. Stay up-to-date on new regulations and current events regarding food science by reviewing scientific literature.

**Usual Educational Requirement:** Bachelor's degree. **Relevant Educational Programs:** Agriculture, General; Culinary Science/Culinology; Food Science; Food Technology and Processing; International Agriculture; Viticulture and Enology. **Related Knowledge/Courses:** Food Production; Biology; Chemistry; Production and Processing; Physics; Engineering and Technology. **Work Experience Needed:** None. **On-the-Job Training Needed:** None. **Certification/Licensure:** None.

**Personality Types:** Investigative–Realistic–Conventional. **Key Career Cluster:** 01 Agriculture, Food, and Natural Resources. **Key Career Pathway:** 1.1 Food Products and Processing Systems.

**Skills:** Science; quality control analysis; systems evaluation; systems analysis; negotiation; complex problem solving; writing; active learning.

**Physical Environment:** Indoors; sitting; noise. **Structural Environment:** Importance of being exact or accurate; time pressure; freedom to make decisions; structured versus unstruc-

tured work; level of competition; impact of decisions on co-workers or company results.

## Foreign Language and Literature Teachers, Postsecondary

*See Teachers, Postsecondary.*

## Forestry and Conservation Science Teachers, Postsecondary

*See Teachers, Postsecondary.*

## General and Operations Managers

**Plan, direct, or coordinate the operations of public or private sector organizations.**

- Average annual earnings: $95,440
- Middle 50% of earners: $65,860–$145,210
- Earnings growth potential: Very high (50.9%)
- Growth: 4.6%
- Annual job openings: 41,010
- Self-employed: 1.2%

**Considerations for Job Outlook:** Educational requirements vary by industry, but candidates who can demonstrate strong leadership abilities and experience getting positive results will have better job opportunities.

**Major Work Tasks:** Direct and coordinate activities of businesses or departments concerned with the production, pricing, sales, or distri-

### BEST-PAYING INDUSTRIES

| Industry | Median Earnings | Workforce |
| --- | --- | --- |
| Professional, Scientific, and Technical Services | $132,490 | 197,130 |
| Federal, State, and Local Government | $98,190 | 109,760 |
| Administrative and Support Services | $84,050 | 125,570 |

289

**BEST-PAYING METROPOLITAN AREAS**

| Metro Area | Median Earnings | Workforce |
|---|---|---|
| New York–Northern New Jersey–Long Island, NY-NJ-PA | $138,980 | 115,450 |
| Washington-Arlington-Alexandria, DC-VA-MD-WV | $129,760 | 68,140 |
| Boston-Cambridge-Quincy, MA-NH | $112,880 | 44,600 |
| Los Angeles–Long Beach–Santa Ana, CA | $111,120 | 92,890 |
| Houston–Sugar Land–Baytown, TX | $103,820 | 47,650 |
| Dallas–Fort Worth–Arlington, TX | $100,250 | 51,010 |
| Atlanta–Sandy Springs–Marietta, GA | $97,690 | 48,720 |
| Chicago-Naperville-Joliet, IL-IN-WI | $93,300 | 66,340 |

bution of products. Manage staff, preparing work schedules and assigning specific duties. Review financial statements, sales and activity reports, and other performance data to measure productivity and goal achievement and to determine areas needing cost reduction and program improvement. Establish and implement departmental policies, goals, objectives, and procedures, conferring with board members, organization officials, and staff members as necessary. Determine staffing requirements, and interview, hire and train new employees, or oversee those personnel processes. Oversee activities directly related to making products or providing services. Direct and coordinate organization's financial and budget activities to fund operations, maximize investments, and increase efficiency. Plan and direct activities, such as sales promotions, coordinating with other department heads as required. Monitor businesses and agencies to ensure that they efficiently and effectively provide needed services while staying within budgetary limits. Determine goods and services to be sold, and set prices and credit terms, based on forecasts of customer demand. Manage the movement of goods into and out of production facilities. Locate, select, and procure merchandise for resale, representing management in purchase negotiations. Perform sales floor work, such as greeting or assisting customers, stocking shelves, or taking inventory. Develop or implement product-marketing strategies, including advertising campaigns or sales promotions. Direct non-merchandising departments of businesses, such as advertising or purchasing. Recommend locations for new facilities or oversee the remodeling or renovating of current facilities. Plan store layouts or design displays. Implement or oversee environmental management or sustainability programs addressing issues such as recycling, conservation, or waste management.

**Usual Educational Requirement:** Associate degree. **Relevant Educational Programs**: Business Administration and Management, General; Business/Commerce, General; Entrepreneurship/Entrepreneurial Studies; Finance, General; International Business/Trade/Commerce; Management Science; Parks, Recreation and Leisure Facilities Management, Other; Public Administration; Retail Management. **Related Knowledge/Courses:** Economics and Accounting; Personnel and Human Resources; Administration and Management; Sales and Marketing; Building and Construction; Clerical. **Work Experience Needed:** 1 to 5 years. **On-the-Job Training Needed:** None. **Certification/Licensure:** Licensure for some specializations.

**Personality Types:** Enterprising–Conventional–Social. **Key Career Cluster:** 04 Business, Management, and Administration. **Key Career Pathway:** 4.1 Management.

**Skills:** Management of material resources; management of financial resources; operations analysis; management of personnel resources; negotiation; coordination; systems analysis; persuasion.

**Physical Environment:** Indoors; sitting; standing; noise. **Structural Environment:** Freedom to make decisions; structured versus unstructured work; impact of decisions on co-workers or company results; frequency of decision making; time pressure; importance of being exact or accurate.

## Geography Teachers, Postsecondary

*See Teachers, Postsecondary.*

## Geoscientists, Except Hydrologists and Geographers

**Study the composition, structure, and other physical aspects of the Earth.**

- Average annual earnings: $90,890
- Middle 50% of earners: $63,670–$130,330
- Earnings growth potential: High (46.9%)
- Growth: 21.2%
- Annual job openings: 1,710
- Self-employed: 5.2%

**Considerations for Job Outlook:** Job opportunities should be excellent for geoscientists who graduate with a master's degree. In addition to job growth, many geoscientists are approaching retirement age and a large number of openings are expected as those geoscientists leave the workforce. Geoscientists with a doctoral degree will likely face competition for positions in academia and research. Many openings are expected in consulting firms and the oil and gas industry. Historically, when oil and natural gas prices are low, companies limit exploration and hire fewer geoscientists. When prices are high, however, companies explore and extract more. If oil prices remain high over

### BEST-PAYING INDUSTRIES

| Industry | Median Earnings | Workforce |
|---|---|---|
| Oil and Gas Extraction | $137,750 | 9,640 |
| Educational Services | $80,090 | 1,920 |
| Federal, State, and Local Government | $77,430 | 5,270 |
| Professional, Scientific, and Technical Services | $75,850 | 13,720 |

### BEST-PAYING METROPOLITAN AREAS

| Metro Area | Median Earnings | Workforce |
|---|---|---|
| Houston–Sugar Land–Baytown, TX | $143,710 | 7,720 |
| Dallas–Fort Worth–Arlington, TX | $112,430 | 1,010 |
| Midland, TX | $103,380 | 730 |
| Denver-Aurora, CO | $102,450 | 1,620 |
| Los Angeles–Long Beach–Santa Ana, CA | $96,420 | 1,280 |
| New York–Northern New Jersey–Long Island, NY-NJ-PA | $74,120 | 790 |

the long run, the demand for geoscientists will remain high as well. Fewer opportunities are expected in state and federal government than in the past. Budget constraints are expected to limit hiring by state governments and federal agencies such as the U.S. Geological Survey. Further, more of the work traditionally done by government agencies is expected to be contracted out to consulting firms in the future.

**Major Work Tasks:** Analyze and interpret geological, geochemical, or geophysical information from sources, such as survey data, well logs, bore holes, or aerial photos. Plan or conduct geological, geochemical, or geophysical field studies or surveys, sample collection, or

**291**

drilling and testing programs used to collect data for research or application. Investigate the composition, structure, or history of the Earth's crust through the collection, examination, measurement, or classification of soils, minerals, rocks, or fossil remains. Prepare geological maps, cross-sectional diagrams, charts, or reports concerning mineral extraction, land use, or resource management, using results of field-work or laboratory research. Locate and estimate probable natural gas, oil, or mineral ore deposits or underground water resources, using aerial photographs, charts, or research or survey results. Assess ground or surface water movement to provide advice regarding issues such as waste management, route and site selection, or the restoration of contaminated sites. Conduct geological or geophysical studies to provide information for use in regional development, site selection, or development of public works projects. Communicate geological findings by writing research papers, participating in conferences, or teaching geological science at universities. Measure characteristics of the Earth, such as gravity or magnetic fields, using equipment such as seismographs, gravimeters, torsion balances, or magnetometers. Analyze and interpret geological data, using computer software. Locate and review research articles or environmental, historical, or technical reports. Identify risks for natural disasters, such as mudslides, earthquakes, or volcanic eruptions. Advise construction firms or government agencies on dam or road construction, foundation design, land use, or resource management. Test industrial diamonds or abrasives, soil, or rocks to determine their geological characteristics, using optical, X-ray, heat, acid, or precision instruments. Develop applied software for the analysis and interpretation of geological data.

**Usual Educational Requirement:** Bachelor's degree. **Relevant Educational Programs**: Geochemistry; Geochemistry and Petrology;

Geological and Earth Sciences/Geosciences, Other; Geology/Earth Science, General; Geophysics and Seismology; Marine Sciences; Oceanography, Chemical and Physical; Paleontology. **Related Knowledge/Courses:** Geography; Physics; Chemistry; Biology; History and Archeology; Engineering and Technology. **Work Experience Needed:** None. **On-the-Job Training Needed:** None. **Certification/Licensure:** None.

**Personality Types:** Investigative–Realistic. **Key Career Cluster:** 15 Science, Technology, Engineering, and Mathematics. **Key Career Pathway:** 15.2 Science and Mathematics.

**Skills:** Science; mathematics; reading comprehension; writing; operations analysis; programming; complex problem solving; speaking.

**Physical Environment:** Indoors; outdoors; sitting. **Structural Environment:** Freedom to make decisions; structured versus unstructured work; importance of being exact or accurate; impact of decisions on co-workers or company results; level of competition; frequency of decision making.

## Health and Safety Engineers, Except Mining Safety Engineers and Inspectors

**Promote worksite or product safety by applying knowledge of industrial processes, mechanics, chemistry, psychology, and industrial health and safety laws.**

- Average annual earnings: $76,830
- Middle 50% of earners: $59,570–$98,810
- Earnings growth potential: Medium (40.9%)
- Growth: 13.1%
- Annual job openings: 820
- Self-employed: 0.0%

**Considerations for Job Outlook:** Health and safety engineers can help prevent accidents as biomedical engineers develop advances in their

## BEST-PAYING INDUSTRIES

| Industry | Median Earnings | Workforce |
|---|---|---|
| Chemical Manufacturing | $86,060 | 1,530 |
| Federal, State, and Local Government | $84,820 | 3,040 |
| Professional, Scientific, and Technical Services | $75,870 | 4,310 |
| Heavy and Civil Engineering Construction | $69,910 | 1,890 |

## BEST-PAYING METROPOLITAN AREAS

| Metro Area | Median Earnings | Workforce |
|---|---|---|
| Los Angeles–Long Beach–Santa Ana, CA | $94,250 | 800 |
| Washington-Arlington-Alexandria, DC-VA-MD-WV | $92,760 | 550 |
| San Francisco–Oakland–Fremont, CA | $92,300 | 540 |
| Houston–Sugar Land–Baytown, TX | $91,160 | 730 |
| Dallas–Fort Worth–Arlington, TX | $89,560 | 490 |
| New York–Northern New Jersey–Long Island, NY-NJ-PA | $87,700 | 1,490 |
| Chicago-Naperville-Joliet, IL-IN-WI | $76,980 | 690 |
| Philadelphia-Camden-Wilmington, PA-NJ-DE-MD | $74,260 | 670 |
| Atlanta–Sandy Springs–Marietta, GA | $72,820 | 640 |

field. Accident prevention is likely to become increasingly important for the health-care industry as a way of cutting costs. Another major factor likely to drive employment is the emerging field of software safety engineering. Software must work exactly as intended, especially when it controls, for example, elevators or automobiles, where a glitch in the software could cause serious injury to people and damage to equipment. The number of machines and mechanical devices controlled by software is expected to continue to grow, and the need to apply the principles of systems safety engineering to this software is expected to grow as well.

**Major Work Tasks:** For tasks, see the job specializations.

**Usual Educational Requirement:** Bachelor's degree. **Relevant Educational Program**: Environmental/Environmental Health Engineering. **Work Experience Needed:** None. **On-the-Job Training Needed:** None. **Certification/Licensure:** Licensure for offering services to public.

**Key Career Cluster:** 15 Science, Technology, Engineering, and Mathematics. **Key Career Pathway:** 15.1 Engineering and Technology.

### JOB SPECIALIZATION: INDUSTRIAL SAFETY AND HEALTH ENGINEERS

**Plan, implement, and coordinate safety programs requiring application of engineering principles and technology to prevent or correct unsafe environmental working conditions.**

**Major Work Tasks:** Investigate industrial accidents, injuries, or occupational diseases to determine causes and preventive measures. Report or review findings from accident investigations, facilities inspections, or environmental testing. Maintain and apply knowledge of current policies, regulations, and industrial processes. Inspect facilities, machinery, and safety equipment to identify and correct potential hazards and to ensure safety regulation compliance. Conduct or coordinate worker training in areas, such as safety laws and regulations, hazardous condition monitoring, and use of safety equipment. Review employee safety programs to determine their adequacy.

Interview employers and employees to obtain information about work environments and workplace incidents. Review plans and specifications for construction of new machinery or equipment to determine whether all safety requirements have been met. Compile, analyze, and interpret statistical data related to occupational illnesses and accidents. Interpret safety regulations for others interested in industrial safety, such as safety engineers, labor representatives, and safety inspectors. Recommend process and product safety features that will reduce employees' exposure to chemical, physical, and biological work hazards. Conduct or direct testing of air quality, noise, temperature, or radiation levels to verify compliance with health and safety regulations. Provide technical advice and guidance to organizations on how to handle health-related problems and make needed changes. Confer with medical professionals to assess health risks and to develop ways to manage health issues and concerns. Install safety devices on machinery, or direct device installation. Maintain liaisons with outside organizations such as fire departments, mutual aid societies, and rescue teams so that emergency responses can be facilitated. Evaluate adequacy of actions taken to correct health inspection violations. Write and revise safety regulations and codes. Check floors of plants to ensure that they are strong enough to support heavy machinery. Plan and conduct industrial hygiene research. Design and build safety equipment.

**Related Knowledge/Courses:** Chemistry; Physics; Biology; Engineering and Technology; Design; Building and Construction.

**Personality Types:** Investigative–Conventional–Realistic.

**Skills:** Installation; science; technology design; mathematics; operations analysis; active learning; systems evaluation; systems analysis.

**Physical Environment:** Indoors; outdoors; noise; contaminants; hazardous conditions; hazardous equipment. **Structural Environment:** Impact of decisions on co-workers or company results; structured versus unstructured work; importance of being exact or accurate; freedom to make decisions; time pressure; frequency of decision making.

JOB SPECIALIZATION: FIRE-PREVENTION AND PROTECTION ENGINEERS

**Research causes of fires, determine fire protection methods, and design or recommend materials or equipment, such as structural components or fire-detection equipment to assist organizations in safeguarding life and property against fire, explosion, and related hazards.**

**Major Work Tasks:** Design fire detection equipment, alarm systems, and fire-extinguishing devices and systems. Inspect buildings or building designs to determine fire protection system requirements and potential problems in areas, such as water supplies, exit locations, and construction materials. Advise architects, builders, and other construction personnel on fire-prevention equipment and techniques, and on fire code and standard interpretation and compliance. Determine causes of fires and ways in which they could have been prevented. Direct the purchase, modification, installation, maintenance, and operation of fire-protection systems. Consult with authorities to discuss safety regulations and to recommend changes as necessary. Develop plans for the prevention of destruction by fire, wind, and water. Study the relationships between ignition sources and materials to determine how fires start. Attend workshops, seminars, or conferences to present or obtain information regarding fire prevention and protection. Develop training materials and conduct training sessions on fire protection. Conduct research on fire retardants and the fire safety of materials and devices. Prepare and write reports detailing specific fire prevention and protection issues, such as work performed, revised codes or standards, and proposed re-

294

view schedules. Evaluate fire department performance and the laws and regulations affecting fire prevention or fire safety.

**Related Knowledge/Courses:** Building and Construction; Engineering and Technology; Design; Physics; Chemistry; Mechanical.

**Personality Types:** Investigative–Realistic–Enterprising.

**Skills:** Science; operations analysis; technology design; management of financial resources; management of material resources; systems evaluation; systems analysis; troubleshooting.

**Physical Environment:** Indoors; sitting. **Structural Environment:** Freedom to make decisions; importance of being exact or accurate; structured versus unstructured work; time pressure; impact of decisions on co-workers or company results; frequency of decision making.

**JOB SPECIALIZATION: PRODUCT SAFETY ENGINEERS**

**Develop and conduct tests to evaluate product safety levels and recommend measures to reduce or eliminate hazards.**

**Major Work Tasks:** Investigate causes of accidents, injuries, or illnesses related to product usage in order to develop solutions to minimize or prevent recurrence. Evaluate potential health hazards or damage that could occur from product misuse. Participate in preparation of product usage and precautionary label instructions. Recommend procedures for detection, prevention, and elimination of physical, chemical, or other product hazards. Report accident investigation findings. Conduct research to evaluate safety levels for products.

**Related Knowledge/Courses:** Engineering and Technology; Design; Physics; Mechanical Devices; Chemistry; Public Safety and Security.

**Personality Types:** Investigative–Realistic–Conventional.

**Skills:** Science; operations analysis; quality control analysis; troubleshooting; operation monitoring; writing; reading comprehension; speaking.

**Physical Environment:** Indoors; sitting. **Structural Environment:** Freedom to make decisions; structured versus unstructured work; impact of decisions on co-workers or company results; importance of being exact or accurate; frequency of decision making; time pressure.

## Health Diagnosing and Treating Practitioners, All Other

**All health diagnosing and treating practitioners not listed separately.**

### BEST-PAYING INDUSTRIES

| Industry | Median Earnings | Workforce |
|---|---|---|
| Federal, State, and Local Government | $86,010 | 13,420 |
| Hospitals | $67,510 | 6,620 |
| Ambulatory Health-Care Services | $64,940 | 8,140 |

### BEST-PAYING METROPOLITAN AREAS

| Metro Area | Median Earnings | Workforce |
|---|---|---|
| Washington-Arlington-Alexandria, DC-VA-MD-WV | $122,740 | 4,520 |
| Atlanta–Sandy Springs–Marietta, GA | $96,900 | 1,830 |
| New York–Northern New Jersey–Long Island, NY-NJ-PA | $81,490 | 1,950 |
| San Francisco–Oakland–Fremont, CA | $75,700 | 710 |
| Chicago-Naperville-Joliet, IL-IN-WI | $73,070 | 920 |
| Miami–Fort Lauderdale–Pompano Beach, FL | $66,630 | 1,410 |
| Los Angeles–Long Beach–Santa Ana, CA | $53,290 | 1,130 |

295

- Average annual earnings: $72,710
- Middle 50% of earners: $54,890–$107,370
- Earnings growth potential: High (45.0%)
- Growth: 19.0%
- Annual job openings: 2,120
- Self-employed: 40.0%

**Considerations for Job Outlook:** About-average employment growth is projected.

**Major Work Tasks:** For tasks, see the job specializations.

**Usual Educational Requirement:** Master's degree. **Relevant Educational Programs**: Acupuncture and Oriental Medicine; Alternative and Complementary Medicine and Medical Systems,; Alternative and Complementary Medicine and Medical Systems, Other; Aromatherapy; Ayurvedic Medicine/Ayurveda; Direct Entry Midwifery (LM, CPM); Holistic Health; Homeopathic Medicine/Homeopathy; Naturopathic Medicine/Naturopathy (ND); Polarity Therapy; Reiki. **Work Experience Needed:** None. **On-the-Job Training Needed:** None. **Certification/Licensure:** Licensure or certification in some specializations.

**Key Career Cluster:** 08 Health Science. **Key Career Pathway:** 8.2 Diagnostics Services.

**JOB SPECIALIZATION: ACUPUNCTURISTS**

**Provide treatment of symptoms and disorders using needles and small electrical currents. May provide massage treatment. May also provide preventive treatments.**

**Major Work Tasks:** Formulate herbal preparations to treat conditions, considering herbal properties such as taste, toxicity, effects of preparation, contraindications, and incompatibilities. Maintain and follow standard quality, safety, environmental, and infection control policies and procedures. Maintain detailed and complete records of health-care plans and prognoses. Dispense herbal formulas and inform patients of dosages and frequencies, treatment duration, possible side effects and drug inter-actions. Consider Western medical procedures in health assessment, health-care team communication, and care referrals. Adhere to local, state, and federal laws, regulations, and statutes. Treat patients using tools, such as needles, cups, ear balls, seeds, pellets, and nutritional supplements. Educate patients on topics such as meditation, ergonomics, stretching, exercise, nutrition, the healing process, breathing, and relaxation techniques. Evaluate treatment outcomes and recommend new or altered treatments as necessary to further promote, restore, or maintain health. Assess patients' general physical appearance to make diagnoses. Collect medical histories and general health and lifestyle information from patients. Apply moxibustion directly or indirectly to patients using Chinese, non-scarring, stick, or pole moxa. Apply heat or cold therapy to patients using materials such as heat pads, hydrocollator packs, warm compresses, cold compresses, heat lamps, and vapor coolants. Analyze physical findings and medical histories to make diagnoses according to Oriental medicine traditions. Develop individual treatment plans and strategies. Treat medical conditions using techniques such as acupressure, shiatsu, and tuina. Insert needles to provide acupuncture treatment. Identify correct anatomical and proportional point locations based on patients' anatomy and positions, contraindications, and precautions related to treatments, such as intradermal needles, moxibution, electricity, guasha, and bleeding.

**Related Knowledge/Courses:** Medicine and Dentistry; Therapy and Counseling; Psychology; Philosophy and Theology; Biology; Sociology and Anthropology.

**Personality Types:** Social–Realistic–Investigative.

**Skills:** Social perceptiveness; systems evaluation; science; service orientation; active learning; critical thinking; judgment and decision making; management of material resources.

**Physical Environment:** Indoors; standing; using hands; exposed to disease or infections. **Structural Environment:** freedom to make decisions; structured versus unstructured work; importance of being exact or accurate; frequency of decision making; impact of decisions on co-workers or company results; time pressure.

### JOB SPECIALIZATION: NATUROPATHIC PHYSICIANS

**Diagnose, treat, and help prevent diseases, using a system of practice that is based on the natural healing capacity of individuals. May use physiological, psychological, or mechanical methods. May also use natural medicines, prescription or legend drugs, foods, herbs, or other natural remedies.**

**Major Work Tasks:** Perform mobilizations and high-velocity adjustments to joints or soft tissues, using principles of massage, stretching, or resistance. Maintain professional development through activities such as post-graduate education, continuing education, preceptorships, and residency programs. Order diagnostic imaging procedures such as radiographs (X-rays), ultrasounds, mammograms, and bone densitometry tests, or refer patients to other health professionals for these procedures. Administer treatments or therapies, such as homeopathy, hydrotherapy, Oriental or Ayurvedic medicine, electrotherapy and diathermy, using physical agents including air, heat, cold, water, sound, or ultraviolet light to catalyze the body to heal itself. Administer, dispense, or prescribe natural medicines, such as food or botanical extracts, herbs, dietary supplements, vitamins, nutraceuticals, and amino acids. Conduct physical examinations and physiological function tests for diagnostic purposes. Interview patients to document symptoms and health histories. Educate patients about health-care management. Advise patients about therapeutic exercise and nutritional medicine regimens. Diagnose health conditions based on patients' symptoms and health histories, laboratory and diagnostic radiology test results, or other physiological measurements, such as electrocardiograms and electroencephalographs. Perform venipuncture or skin pricking to collect blood samples. Prescribe synthetic drugs under the supervision of medical doctors or within the allowances of regulatory bodies. Document patients' histories, including identifying data, chief complaints, illnesses, previous medical or family histories, or psychosocial characteristics. Consult with other health professionals to provide optimal patient care, referring patients to traditional health-care professionals as necessary. Monitor updates from public health agencies to keep abreast of health trends. Conduct periodic public health maintenance activities such as immunizations and screenings for diseases and disease risk factors. Obtain medical records from previous physicians or other health-care providers for the purpose of patient evaluation.

**Related Knowledge/Courses:** Medicine and Dentistry; Therapy and Counseling; Biology; Psychology; Philosophy and Theology; Sociology and Anthropology.

**Personality Types:** Investigative–Social.

**Skills:** Science; social perceptiveness; reading comprehension; service orientation; active learning; judgment and decision making; systems evaluation; active listening.

**Physical Environment:** Indoors; sitting; exposed to disease or infections. **Structural Environment:** Frequency of decision making; freedom to make decisions; structured versus unstructured work; impact of decisions on co-workers or company results; importance of being exact or accurate; consequence of error.

### JOB SPECIALIZATION: ORTHOPTISTS

**Diagnose and treat visual system disorders, such as binocular vision and eye movement impairments.**

**Major Work Tasks:** Assist ophthalmologists in diagnostic ophthalmic procedures, such as ultrasonography, fundus photography, and tonometry. Provide non-surgical interventions, including corrective lenses, patches, drops, fusion exercises, or stereograms, to treat conditions such as strabismus, heterophoria, and convergence insufficiency. Develop non-surgical treatment plans for patients with conditions, such as strabismus, nystagmus, and other visual disorders. Perform diagnostic tests or measurements, such as motor testing, visual acuity testing, lensometry, retinoscopy, and color vision testing. Examine patients with problems related to ocular motility, binocular vision, amblyopia, or strabismus. Evaluate, diagnose, or treat disorders of the visual system with an emphasis on binocular vision or abnormal eye movements. Interpret clinical or diagnostic test results. Provide instructions to patients or family members concerning diagnoses or treatment plans. Refer patients to ophthalmic surgeons or other physicians. Develop or use special test and communication techniques to facilitate diagnosis and treatment of children or disabled patients. Collaborate with ophthalmologists, optometrists, or other specialists in the diagnosis, treatment, or management of conditions such as glaucoma, cataracts, and retinal diseases. Prepare diagnostic or treatment reports for other medical practitioners or therapists. Perform vision screening of children in schools or community health centers. Provide training related to clinical methods or orthoptics to students, resident physicians, or other health professionals. Participate in clinical research projects. Present or publish scientific papers.

**Related Knowledge/Courses:** Medicine and Dentistry; Biology; Therapy and Counseling; Psychology; English Language; Customer and Personal Service.

**Personality Types:** Investigative–Social–Realistic.

**Skills:** Science; operations analysis; service orientation; reading comprehension; instructing; active learning; learning strategies; systems evaluation.

**Physical Environment:** Indoors; sitting; using hands; repetitive motions; exposed to disease or infections. **Structural Environment:** Importance of being exact or accurate; freedom to make decisions; frequency of decision making; structured versus unstructured work; impact of decisions on co-workers or company results; time pressure.

## Health Specialties Teachers, Postsecondary

*See Teachers, Postsecondary.*

## History Teachers, Postsecondary

*See Teachers, Postsecondary.*

## Home Economics Teachers, Postsecondary

*See Teachers, Postsecondary.*

## Human Resources Managers

**Plan, direct, or coordinate human resources activities and staff of an organization.**

### BEST-PAYING INDUSTRIES

| Industry | Median Earnings | Workforce |
| --- | --- | --- |
| Management of Companies and Enterprises | $112,550 | 14,780 |
| Professional, Scientific, and Technical Services | $112,210 | 10,530 |
| Educational Services | $95,280 | 6,770 |
| Federal, State, and Local Government | $91,710 | 11,350 |
| Administrative and Support Services | $85,410 | 6,300 |

**298**

## BEST-PAYING METROPOLITAN AREAS

| Metro Area | Median Earnings | Workforce |
|---|---|---|
| Washington-Arlington-Alexandria, DC-VA-MD-WV | $132,020 | 3,800 |
| San Francisco–Oakland–Fremont, CA | $122,320 | 2,320 |
| New York–Northern New Jersey–Long Island, NY-NJ-PA | $120,880 | 8,790 |
| Boston-Cambridge-Quincy, MA-NH | $114,440 | 2,800 |
| Los Angeles–Long Beach–Santa Ana, CA | $110,070 | 4,650 |
| Houston–Sugar Land–Baytown, TX | $107,960 | 2,080 |
| Seattle-Tacoma-Bellevue, WA | $107,720 | 2,110 |
| Atlanta–Sandy Springs–Marietta, GA | $107,530 | 2,260 |
| Dallas–Fort Worth–Arlington, TX | $106,210 | 2,200 |
| Minneapolis–St. Paul–Bloomington, MN-WI | $103,360 | 2,620 |
| Chicago-Naperville-Joliet, IL-IN-WI | $96,220 | 3,970 |

- Average annual earnings: $99,720
- Middle 50% of earners: $76,350–$132,620
- Earnings growth potential: Medium (40.8%)
- Growth: 12.9%
- Annual job openings: 2,690
- Self-employed: 2.7%

**Considerations for Job Outlook:** Job opportunities are expected to vary, depending on the staffing needs of individual companies. Job opportunities should be best in the professional, scientific, and technical consulting industry as organizations continue to contract with outside consulting firms for some of their human resources functions. Candidates with certification or a master's degree—particularly those with a concentration in human resources management or an MBA—should have the best job prospects. Those with a solid background in human resources programs, policies, and employment law should also have better job opportunities.

**Major Work Tasks:** Administer compensation, benefits and performance management systems, and safety and recreation programs. Identify staff vacancies and recruit, interview and select applicants. Allocate human resources, ensuring appropriate matches between personnel. Provide current and prospective employees with information about policies, job duties, working conditions, wages, opportunities for promotion, and employee benefits. Perform difficult staffing duties, including dealing with understaffing, refereeing disputes, firing employees, and administering disciplinary procedures. Advise managers on organizational policy matters, such as equal employment opportunity and sexual harassment, and recommend needed changes. Analyze and modify compensation and benefits policies to establish competitive programs and ensure compliance with legal requirements. Plan and conduct new employee orientation to foster positive attitude toward organizational objectives. Serve as a link between management and employees by handling questions, interpreting and administering contracts, and helping resolve work-related problems. Plan, direct, supervise, and coordinate work activities of subordinates and staff relating to employment, compensation, labor relations, and employee relations. Analyze training needs to design employee development, language training, and health and safety programs. Maintain records and compile statistical reports concerning personnel-related data, such as hires, transfers, performance appraisals, and absenteeism rates. Analyze statistical data and reports to identify and determine causes of personnel problems and develop recommendations for improvement of organization's personnel policies and practices. Plan, organize, direct, control or coordinate the personnel, training, or labor relations activities of an organization. Conduct exit interviews to identify reasons for employee termination. Represent organization at personnel-related hearings and investigations. Prepare personnel forecast to project employment needs. Prepare and follow budgets for personnel operations. Oversee the evaluation, classification and rating of occupations and job positions.

**Usual Educational Requirement:** Bachelor's degree. **Relevant Educational Programs**: Human Resources Management/Personnel Administration, General; Labor and Industrial Relations. **Related Knowledge/Courses:** Personnel and Human Resources; Therapy and Counseling; Sociology and Anthropology; Psychology; Clerical Practices; Administration and Management. **Work Experience Needed:** 1 to 5 years. **On-the-Job Training Needed:** None. **Certification/Licensure:** Voluntary certification by association.

**Personality Types:** Enterprising–Social–Conventional. **Key Career Cluster:** 04 Business, Management, and Administration. **Key Career Pathway:** 4.3 Human Resources.

**Skills:** Management of financial resources; management of personnel resources; management of material resources; systems evaluation; negotiation; persuasion; systems analysis; learning strategies.

**Physical Environment:** Indoors; sitting. **Structural Environment:** Freedom to make decisions; structured versus unstructured work; impact of decisions on co-workers or company results; importance of being exact or accurate; frequency of decision making; time pressure.

## Industrial Engineers

**Design, develop, test, and evaluate integrated systems for managing industrial production processes.**

- Average annual earnings: $78,860
- Middle 50% of earners: $63,640–$96,460
- Earnings growth potential: Medium (35.1%)
- Growth: 6.4%
- Annual job openings: 5,750
- Self-employed: 0.1%

**Considerations for Job Outlook:** This occupation is versatile both in the nature of the work it does and in the industries in which its expertise can be put to use. In addition, because industrial engineers' work can help with cost control by increasing efficiency, these engineers are attractive to employers in most industries, including nonprofits.

### BEST-PAYING INDUSTRIES

| Industry | Median Earnings | Workforce |
|---|---|---|
| Computer and Electronic Product Manufacturing | $86,090 | 29,510 |
| Professional, Scientific, and Technical Services | $84,380 | 28,020 |
| Management of Companies and Enterprises | $82,290 | 12,710 |
| Transportation Equipment Manufacturing | $78,430 | 38,870 |
| Machinery Manufacturing | $72,920 | 17,170 |
| Fabricated Metal Product Manufacturing | $70,950 | 12,440 |

## BEST-PAYING METROPOLITAN AREAS

| Metro Area | Median Earnings | Workforce |
|---|---|---|
| Houston–Sugar Land–Baytown, TX | $104,660 | 5,910 |
| Los Angeles–Long Beach–Santa Ana, CA | $92,600 | 7,860 |
| Boston-Cambridge-Quincy, MA-NH | $88,320 | 5,250 |
| Seattle-Tacoma-Bellevue, WA | $88,280 | 4,580 |
| New York–Northern New Jersey–Long Island, NY-NJ-PA | $85,310 | 4,910 |
| Dallas–Fort Worth–Arlington, TX | $83,740 | 4,950 |
| Detroit-Warren-Livonia, MI | $83,260 | 13,050 |
| Minneapolis–St. Paul–Bloomington, MN-WI | $82,040 | 5,940 |
| Chicago-Naperville-Joliet, IL-IN-WI | $72,070 | 5,020 |

**Major Work Tasks:** Develop manufacturing methods, labor utilization standards, and cost analysis systems to promote efficient staff and facility utilization. Recommend methods for improving utilization of personnel, material, and utilities. Plan and establish sequence of operations to fabricate and assemble parts or products and to promote efficient utilization. Apply statistical methods and perform mathematical calculations to determine manufacturing processes, staff requirements, and production standards. Draft and design layout of equipment, materials, and workspace to illustrate maximum efficiency using drafting tools and computer. Review production schedules, engineering specifications, orders, and related information to obtain knowledge of manufacturing methods, procedures, and activities. Communicate with management and user personnel to develop production and design standards. Record or oversee recording of information to ensure currency of engineering drawings and documentation of production problems. Study operations sequence, material flow, functional statements, organization charts, and project information to determine worker functions and responsibilities. Evaluate precision and accuracy of production and testing equipment and engineering drawings to formulate corrective action plan. Complete production reports, purchase orders, and material, tool, and equipment lists. Estimate production costs, cost saving methods, and the effects of product design changes on expenditures for management review, action, and control. Coordinate and implement quality control objectives, activities, or procedures to resolve production problems, maximize product reliability, or minimize costs. Confer with clients, vendors, staff, and management personnel regarding purchases, product and production specifications, manufacturing capabilities, or project status. Analyze statistical data and product specifications to determine standards and establish quality and reliability objectives of finished product. Formulate sampling procedures and designs and develop forms and instructions for recording, evaluating, and reporting quality and reliability data.

**Usual Educational Requirement:** Bachelor's degree. **Relevant Educational Programs**: Industrial Engineering; Manufacturing Engineering; Packaging Science. **Related Knowledge/Courses:** Engineering and Technology; Design; Production and Processing; Mechanical Devices; Physics; Mathematics. **Work Experience Needed:** None. **On-the-Job Training Needed:** None. **Certification/Licensure:** Licensure for offering services to public.

**Personality Types:** Investigative–Conventional–Enterprising. **Key Career Cluster:** 15 Science, Technology, Engineering, and Mathematics. **Key Career Pathway:** 15.1 Engineering and Technology.

**Skills:** Management of material resources; management of financial resources; mathematics; systems evaluation; systems analysis; reading comprehension; complex problem solving; technology design.

**Physical Environment:** Indoors; sitting; noise; contaminants; hazardous equipment. **Structural Environment:** Structured versus unstructured work; freedom to make decisions; impact of decisions on co-workers or company results; importance of being exact or accurate; frequency of decision making; time pressure.

JOB SPECIALIZATION: HUMAN FACTORS ENGINEERS AND ERGONOMISTS

**Design objects, facilities, and environments to optimize human well-being and overall system performance, applying theory, principles, and data regarding the relationship between humans and respective technology. Investigate and analyze characteristics of human behavior and performance as it relates to the use of technology.**

**Major Work Tasks:** Write, review, or comment on documents, such as proposals, test plans, or procedures. Train users in task techniques or ergonomic principles. Review health, safety, accident, or worker compensation records to evaluate safety program effectiveness or to identify jobs with high incidents of injury. Provide human factors technical expertise on topics, such as advanced user-interface technology development or the role of human users in automated or autonomous sub-systems in advanced vehicle systems. Investigate theoretical or conceptual issues, such as the human design considerations of lunar landers or habitats. Estimate time or resource requirements for ergonomic or human factors research or development projects. Conduct interviews or surveys of users or customers to collect information on topics, such as requirements, needs, fatigue, ergonomics, or interfaces. Recommend workplace changes to improve health and safety,

using knowledge of potentially harmful factors, such as heavy loads or repetitive motions. Provide technical support to clients through activities, such as rearranging workplace fixtures to reduce physical hazards or discomfort or modifying task sequences to reduce cycle time. Prepare reports or presentations summarizing results or conclusions of human factors engineering or ergonomics activities, such as testing, investigation, or validation. Perform statistical analyses, such as social network pattern analysis, network modeling, discrete event simulation, agent-based modeling, statistical natural language processing, computational sociology, mathematical optimization, or systems dynamics. Perform functional, task, or anthropometric analysis, using tools such as checklists, surveys, videotaping, or force measurement. Operate testing equipment, such as heat stress meters, octave band analyzers, motion analysis equipment, inclinometers, light meters, velometers, sling psychrometers, or colormetric detection tubes. Integrate human factors requirements into operational hardware. Establish system operating or training requirements to ensure optimized human-machine interfaces. Inspect work sites to identify physical hazards.

**Related Knowledge/Courses:** Sociology and Anthropology; Engineering and Technology; Psychology; Design; Education and Training; Mathematics.

**Personality Types:** Investigative–Realistic.

**Skills:** Technology design; programming; operations analysis; mathematics; systems evaluation; science; judgment and decision making; reading comprehension.

**Physical Environment:** Indoors; sitting. **Structural Environment:** Structured versus unstructured work; freedom to make decisions; importance of being exact or accurate; impact of decisions on co-workers or company results; time pressure; level of competition.

## Industrial Production Managers

**Plan, direct, or coordinate the work activities and resources necessary for manufacturing products in accordance with cost, quality, and quantity specifications.**

- Average annual earnings: $89,190
- Middle 50% of earners: $69,040–$116,310
- Earnings growth potential: Medium (39.2%)
- Growth: 9.1%
- Annual job openings: 4,900
- Self-employed: 2.8%

**Considerations for Job Outlook:** Despite the projected decline in employment, job openings are expected, due to the need to replace workers who retire. Applicants who have a bachelor's degree in industrial management or business administration should have the best prospects.

### BEST-PAYING INDUSTRIES

| Industry | Median Earnings | Workforce |
|---|---|---|
| Computer and Electronic Product Manufacturing | $100,500 | 11,160 |
| Chemical Manufacturing | $99,250 | 12,860 |
| Transportation Equipment Manufacturing | $91,870 | 15,190 |
| Machinery Manufacturing | $87,270 | 12,480 |
| Fabricated Metal Product Manufacturing | $82,730 | 17,500 |
| Plastics and Rubber Products Manufacturing | $81,480 | 8,100 |
| Food Manufacturing | $80,430 | 11,280 |

### BEST-PAYING METROPOLITAN AREAS

| Metro Area | Median Earnings | Workforce |
|---|---|---|
| New York–Northern New Jersey–Long Island, NY-NJ-PA | $109,860 | 5,690 |
| Houston–Sugar Land–Baytown, TX | $109,620 | 3,930 |
| Detroit-Warren-Livonia, MI | $106,750 | 5,450 |
| Minneapolis–St. Paul–Bloomington, MN-WI | $94,600 | 3,520 |
| Los Angeles–Long Beach–Santa Ana, CA | $93,540 | 7,080 |
| Chicago-Naperville-Joliet, IL-IN-WI | $89,580 | 5,140 |

**Major Work Tasks:** Direct or coordinate production, processing, distribution, or marketing activities of industrial organizations. Develop budgets or approve expenditures for supplies, materials, or human resources, ensuring that materials, labor, or equipment are used efficiently to meet production targets. Review processing schedules or production orders to make decisions concerning inventory requirements, staffing requirements, work procedures, or duty assignments, considering budgetary limitations and time constraints. Review operations and confer with technical or administrative staff to resolve production or processing problems. Hire, train, evaluate, or discharge staff or resolve personnel grievances. Initiate or coordinate inventory or cost control programs. Prepare and maintain production reports or personnel records. Set and monitor product standards, examining samples of raw products or directing testing during processing, to ensure finished products are of prescribed quality. Develop or implement production tracking or quality control systems, analyzing production, quality control, maintenance, or other operational reports to detect production problems.

Review plans and confer with research or support staff to develop new products or processes. Institute employee suggestion or involvement programs. Coordinate or recommend procedures for facility or equipment maintenance or modification, including the replacement of machines. Maintain current knowledge of the quality control field, relying on current literature pertaining to materials use, technological advances, or statistical studies. Negotiate materials prices with suppliers.

**Usual Educational Requirement:** Bachelor's degree. **Relevant Educational Programs:** Business Administration and Management, General; Business/Commerce, General; Engineering/Industrial Management; Industrial Engineering; Logistics, Materials, and Supply Chain Management; Operations Management and Supervision. **Related Knowledge/Courses:** Production and Processing; Personnel and Human Resources; Administration and Management; Engineering and Technology; Mechanical Devices; Education and Training. **Work Experience Needed:** 1 to 5 years. **On-the-Job Training Needed:** None. **Certification/Licensure:** Voluntary certification by association.

**Personality Types:** Enterprising–Conventional. **Key Career Cluster:** 13 Manufacturing. **Key Career Pathway:** 13.1 Production.

**Skills:** Management of financial resources; management of material resources; management of personnel resources; quality control analysis; monitoring; systems analysis; judgment and decision making; coordination.

**Physical Environment:** Indoors; noise. **Structural Environment:** Frequency of decision making; freedom to make decisions; impact of decisions on co-workers or company results; time pressure; structured versus unstructured work; importance of being exact or accurate.

## JOB SPECIALIZATION: BIOFUELS PRODUCTION MANAGERS

**Manage operations at biofuel power-generation facilities. Collect and process information on plant performance, diagnose problems, and design corrective procedures.**

**Major Work Tasks:** Provide training to subordinate or new employees to improve biofuels plant safety or increase the production of biofuels. Provide direction to employees to ensure compliance with biofuels plant safety, environmental, or operational standards and regulations. Monitor transportation and storage of flammable or other potentially dangerous feedstocks or products to ensure adherence to safety guidelines. Draw samples of biofuels products or secondary by-products for quality control testing. Confer with technical and supervisory personnel to report or resolve conditions affecting biofuels plant safety, operational efficiency, and product quality. Supervise production employees in the manufacturing of biofuels, such as biodiesel or ethanol. Shut down and restart biofuels plant or equipment in emergency situations or for equipment maintenance, repairs, or replacements. Review logs, datasheets, or reports to ensure adequate production levels or to identify abnormalities with biofuels production equipment or processes. Prepare and manage biofuels plant or unit budgets. Monitor meters, flow gauges, or other real-time data to ensure proper operation of biofuels production equipment, implementing corrective measures as needed. Conduct cost, material, and efficiency studies for biofuels production plants or operations. Approve proposals for the acquisition, replacement, or repair of biofuels processing equipment or the implementation of new production processes. Adjust temperature, pressure, vacuum, level, flow rate, or transfer of biofuels to maintain processes at required levels. Manage operations at biofuels power generation facilities, including production, shipping, maintenance, or quality assurance activities.

**Related Knowledge/Courses:** No data available.

**Personality Types:** Enterprising–Conventional–Realistic.

**Skills:** No data available.

**Physical Environment:** No data available.
**Structural Environment:** No data available.

JOB SPECIALIZATION: BIOMASS POWER PLANT MANAGERS

**Manage operations at biomass power-generation facilities. Direct work activities at plant, including supervision of operations and maintenance staff.**

**Major Work Tasks:** Manage parts and supply inventories for biomass plants. Monitor and operate communications systems, such as mobile radios. Supervise operations or maintenance employees in the production of power from biomass, such as wood, coal, paper sludge, or other waste or refuse. Review logs, datasheets, or reports to ensure adequate production levels and safe production environments or to identify abnormalities with power production equipment or processes. Review biomass operations performance specifications to ensure compliance with regulatory requirements. Prepare reports on biomass plant operations, status, maintenance, and other information. Prepare and manage biomass plant budgets. Plan and schedule plant activities, such as wood, waste, or refuse fuel deliveries, ash removal, and regular maintenance. Inspect biomass gasification processes, equipment, and facilities for ways to maximize capacity and minimize operating costs. Evaluate power production or demand trends to identify opportunities for improved operations. Supervise biomass plant or substation operations, maintenance, repair, or testing activities. Monitor the operating status of biomass plants by observing control system parameters, distrib-

uted control systems, switchboard gauges, dials, or other indicators. Conduct field inspections of biomass plants, stations, or substations to ensure normal and safe operating conditions. Test, maintain, or repair electrical power distribution machinery or equipment, using hand tools, power tools, and testing devices. Compile and record operational data on forms or in log books. Adjust equipment controls to generate specified amounts of electrical power. Shut down and restart biomass power plants or equipment in emergency situations or for equipment maintenance, repairs, or replacements. Operate controls to start, stop, or regulate biomass-fueled generators, generator units, boilers, engines, or auxiliary systems.

**Related Knowledge/Courses:** Production and Processing; Mechanical Devices; Engineering and Technology; Physics; Building and Construction; Chemistry.

**Personality Types:** Enterprising–Conventional–Realistic.

**Skills:** Management of financial resources; management of material resources; equipment maintenance; repairing; operation monitoring; troubleshooting; management of personnel resources; monitoring.

**Physical Environment:** Indoors; outdoors; sitting; noise; very hot or cold; contaminants.
**Structural Environment:** Frequency of decision making; impact of decisions on co-workers or company results; freedom to make decisions; structured versus unstructured work; consequence of error; importance of being exact or accurate.

JOB SPECIALIZATION: GEOTHERMAL PRODUCTION MANAGERS

**Manage operations at geothermal power generation facilities. Maintain and monitor geothermal plant equipment for efficient and safe plant operations.**

**Major Work Tasks:** Conduct well field site assessments. Select and implement corrosion control or mitigation systems for geothermal plants. Communicate geothermal plant conditions to employees. Record, review, or maintain daily logs, reports, maintenance, and other records associated with geothermal operations. Perform or direct the performance of preventative maintenance on geothermal plant equipment. Monitor geothermal operations, using programmable logic controllers. Identify opportunities to improve plant electrical equipment, controls, or process control methodologies. Identify and evaluate equipment, procedural, or conditional inefficiencies involving geothermal plant systems. Develop operating plans and schedules for geothermal operations. Develop or manage budgets for geothermal operations. Supervise employees in geothermal power plants or well fields. Oversee geothermal plant operations, maintenance, and repairs to ensure compliance with applicable standards or regulations. Inspect geothermal plant or injection well fields to verify proper equipment operations. Troubleshoot and make minor repairs to geothermal plant instrumentation or electrical systems. Prepare environmental permit applications or compliance reports. Obtain permits for constructing, upgrading, or operating geothermal power plants. Negotiate interconnection agreements with other utilities.

**Related Knowledge/Courses:** Mechanical Devices; Building and Construction; Physics; Engineering and Technology; Chemistry; Production and Processing.

**Personality Types:** Enterprising–Conventional.

**Skills:** Management of financial resources; repairing; management of material resources; equipment maintenance; troubleshooting; equipment selection; management of personnel resources; mathematics.

**Physical Environment:** Indoors; outdoors; sitting; noise; very hot or cold; contaminants.
**Structural Environment:** Structured versus unstructured work; freedom to make decisions; impact of decisions on co-workers or company results; importance of being exact or accurate; frequency of decision making; time pressure.

## JOB SPECIALIZATION: HYDROELECTRIC PRODUCTION MANAGERS

**Manage operations at hydroelectric power-generation facilities. Maintain and monitor hydroelectric plant equipment for efficient and safe plant operations.**

**Major Work Tasks:** Develop or implement policy evaluation procedures for hydroelectric generation activities. Provide technical direction in the erection or commissioning of hydroelectric equipment or supporting electrical or mechanical systems. Develop or implement projects to improve efficiency, economy, or effectiveness of hydroelectric plant operations. Supervise hydropower plant equipment installations, upgrades, or maintenance. Respond to problems related to ratepayers, water users, power users, government agencies, educational institutions, or other private or public power resource interests. Plan or manage hydroelectric plant upgrades. Plan or coordinate hydroelectric production operations to meet customer requirements. Perform or direct preventive or corrective containment or clean-up to protect the environment. Operate energized high- or low-voltage hydroelectric power transmission system substations, according to procedures and safety requirements. Negotiate power generation contracts with other public or private utilities. Maintain records of hydroelectric facility operations, maintenance, or repairs. Monitor or inspect hydroelectric equipment, such as hydro-turbines, generators, or control systems. Inspect hydroelectric facilities, including switchyards, control houses, or relay houses, for normal operation or adherence to safety standards. Identify and communicate power system emergencies. Develop or review budgets, annual plans, power contracts, power rates, standing operating procedures, power reviews, or engineering studies. Create or enforce hydrostation voltage schedules. Check hydroelectric operations for compliance with prescribed operating limits, such as loads, voltages, temperatures, lines, or equipment. Supervise or monitor hydroelectric facility operations to ensure that generation or mechanical equipment conform to applicable regulations or standards. Direct operations, maintenance, or repair of hydroelectric power facilities.

**Related Knowledge/Courses:** No data available.

**Personality Types:** Enterprising–Conventional.

**Skills:** No data available.

**Physical Environment:** No data available.
**Structural Environment:** No data available.

### JOB SPECIALIZATION: METHANE/LANDFILL GAS COLLECTION SYSTEM OPERATORS

**Direct daily operations, maintenance, or repair of landfill gas projects, including maintenance of daily logs, determination of service priorities, and compliance with reporting requirements.**

**Major Work Tasks:** Track volume and weight of landfill waste. Recommend or implement practices to reduce turnaround time for trucks in and out of landfill site. Prepare reports on landfill operations and gas collection system productivity or efficiency. Diagnose or troubleshoot gas collection equipment and programmable logic controller (PLC) systems. Coordinate the repair, overhaul, or routine maintenance of diesel engines used in landfill operations. Read meters, gauges, or automatic recording devices at specified intervals to verify gas collection systems operating conditions. Supervise landfill, well field, and other subordinate employees. Prepare and manage landfill gas collection system budgets. Prepare soil reports as required by regulatory or permitting agencies. Oversee landfill gas collection system construction, maintenance, and repair ac-

tivities. Optimize gas collection landfill operational costs and productivity consistent with safety and environmental rules and regulations. Monitor landfill permit requirements for updates. Operate computerized control panels to manage gas compression operations. Monitor gas collection systems emissions data, including biomethane or nitrous oxide levels. Maintain records for landfill gas collection systems to demonstrate compliance with safety and environmental laws, regulations, or policies. Inspect landfill or conduct site audits to ensure adherence to safety and environmental regulations. Implement landfill operational and emergency procedures. Develop or enforce procedures for normal operation, start-up, or shut-down of methane gas collection systems. Evaluate landfill gas collection service requirements to meet operational plans and productivity goals. Oversee gas collection landfill operations, including leachate and gas management or rail operations. Monitor and control liquid or gas landfill extraction systems.

**Related Knowledge/Courses:** No data available.

**Personality Types:** Conventional–Enterprising–Realistic.

**Skills:** No data available.

**Physical Environment:** No data available.
**Structural Environment:** No data available.

### JOB SPECIALIZATION: QUALITY CONTROL SYSTEMS MANAGERS

**Plan, direct, or coordinate quality assurance programs. Formulate quality control policies and control quality of laboratory and production efforts.**

**Major Work Tasks:** Stop production if serious product defects are present. Review statistical studies, technological advances, or regulatory standards and trends to stay abreast of issues in the field of quality control. Generate and maintain quality control operating budgets. Evaluate new testing and sampling methodologies or technologies to determine usefulness. Coordinate the selection and implementation of quality control equipment, such as inspection gauges. Collect and analyze production samples to evaluate quality. Verify that raw materials, purchased parts or components, in-process samples, and finished products meet established testing and inspection standards. Review quality documentation necessary for regulatory submissions and inspections. Review and update standard operating procedures or quality assurance manuals. Produce reports regarding nonconformance of products or processes, daily production quality, root cause analyses, or quality trends. Participate in the development of product specifications. Instruct vendors or contractors on quality guidelines, testing procedures, or ways to eliminate deficiencies. Identify quality problems or areas for improvement and recommend solutions. Instruct staff in quality control and analytical procedures. Identify critical points in the manufacturing process and specify sampling procedures to be used at these points. Document testing procedures, methodologies, or criteria. Direct the tracking of defects, test results, or other regularly reported quality control data. Create and implement inspection and testing criteria or procedures. Communicate quality control information to all relevant organizational departments, outside vendors, or contractors. Analyze quality control test results and provide feedback and interpretation to production management or staff. Oversee workers including supervisors, inspectors, or laboratory workers engaged in testing activities. Monitor performance of quality control systems to ensure effectiveness and efficiency. Direct product testing activities throughout production cycles. Review and approve quality plans submitted by contractors.

**Related Knowledge/Courses:** Chemistry; Biology; Education and Training; Personnel and Human Resources; Clerical Practices; Production and Processing.

**Personality Types:** Enterprising–Conventional–Realistic.

**Skills:** Quality control analysis; management of financial resources; equipment maintenance; troubleshooting; management of material resources; repairing; operation monitoring; judgment and decision making.

**Physical Environment:** Indoors; outdoors; sitting; using hands; noise; contaminants. **Structural Environment:** Importance of being exact or accurate; impact of decisions on co-workers or company Results; frequency of decision making; structured versus unstructured work; time pressure; freedom to make decisions.

## Instructional Coordinators

**Develop instructional material, coordinate educational content, and incorporate current technology in specialized fields that provide guidelines to educators and instructors for developing curricula and conducting courses.**

- Average annual earnings: $60,050
- Middle 50% of earners: $45,220–$76,790
- Earnings growth potential: Medium (42.8%)
- Growth: 19.5%
- Annual job openings: 5,810
- Self-employed: 2.5%

**Considerations for Job Outlook:** Employment growth is anticipated as schools increasingly focus on improving teachers' effectiveness. Many school districts and states are increasingly working to improve teacher effectiveness

### BEST-PAYING INDUSTRIES

| Industry | Median Earnings | Workforce |
|---|---|---|
| Federal, State, and Local Government | $66,970 | 12,890 |
| Educational Services | $61,400 | 101,440 |
| Social Assistance | $39,200 | 8,130 |

## BEST-PAYING METROPOLITAN AREAS

| Metro Area | Median Earnings | Workforce |
|---|---|---|
| Los Angeles–Long Beach–Santa Ana, CA | $76,360 | 6,840 |
| Washington-Arlington-Alexandria, DC-VA-MD-WV | $71,960 | 4,980 |
| Houston–Sugar Land–Baytown, TX | $61,810 | 3,540 |
| Philadelphia-Camden-Wilmington, PA-NJ-DE-MD | $61,130 | 3,110 |
| New York–Northern New Jersey–Long Island, NY-NJ-PA | $58,590 | 7,340 |
| Phoenix-Mesa-Scottsdale, AZ | $52,970 | 3,020 |
| Chicago-Naperville-Joliet, IL-IN-WI | $48,180 | 3,350 |

by focusing on the teacher's role in improving students' learning and test scores. In addition, there is an increased emphasis on holding teachers accountable for student outcomes. Some states and school districts are using students' outcomes and test scores to evaluate teachers. As more schools move toward these techniques, instructional coordinators will be needed to help teachers who are not meeting expectations. Coordinators will work to improve these teachers' skills by offering them professional development, mentoring, and coaching. As schools seek to provide additional training to teachers, demand for instructional coordinators is expected to grow. However, employment growth for instructional coordinators will depend on state and local government budgets. When state and local governments have budget deficits, they may lay off employees, including instructional coordinators. As a result, employment growth may be tempered.

**Major Work Tasks:** Conduct or participate in workshops, committees, and conferences designed to promote the intellectual, social, and physical welfare of students. Plan and conduct teacher training programs and conferences dealing with new classroom procedures, instructional materials and equipment, and teaching aids. Advise teaching and administrative staff in curriculum development, use of materials and equipment, and implementation of state and federal programs and procedures. Recommend, order, or authorize purchase of instructional materials, supplies, equipment, and visual aids designed to meet student educational needs and district standards. Interpret and enforce provisions of state education codes, and rules and regulations of state education boards. Confer with members of educational committees and advisory groups to obtain knowledge of subject areas, and to relate curriculum materials to specific subjects, individual student needs, and occupational areas. Organize production and design of curriculum materials. Research, evaluate, and prepare recommendations on curricula, instructional methods, and materials for school systems. Observe work of teaching staff to evaluate performance and to recommend changes that could strengthen teaching skills. Develop instructional materials to be used by educators and instructors. Prepare grant proposals, budgets, and program policies and goals, or assist in their preparation. Develop tests, questionnaires, and procedures that measure the effectiveness of curricula, and use these tools to determine whether program objectives are being met. Update the content of educational programs to ensure that students are being trained with equipment and processes that are technologically current. Address public audiences to explain program objectives and to elicit support. Advise and teach students. Prepare or approve manuals, guidelines, and reports on state educational policies and practices for distribution to school districts.

**309**

Develop classroom-based and distance learning training courses, using needs assessments and skill level analyses. Inspect instructional equipment to determine if repairs are needed, and authorize necessary repairs.

**Usual Educational Requirement:** Master's degree. **Relevant Educational Programs:** Curriculum and Instruction; Educational/Instructional Technology. **Related Knowledge/Courses:** Education and Training; Therapy and Counseling; Philosophy and Theology; Sociology and Anthropology; Personnel and Human Resources; Psychology. **Work Experience Needed:** More than 5 years. **On-the-Job Training Needed:** None. **Certification/Licensure:** None.

**Personality Types:** Social–Investigative–Enterprising. **Key Career Cluster:** 05 Education and Training. **Key Career Pathway:** 5.1 Administration and Administrative Support.

**Skills:** Learning strategies; instructing; systems evaluation; negotiation; management of material resources; management of personnel resources; writing; time management.

**Physical Environment:** Indoors; standing. **Structural Environment:** Structured versus unstructured work; freedom to make decisions; frequency of decision making; time pressure; importance of being exact or accurate; impact of decisions on co-workers or company results.

## JOB SPECIALIZATION: INSTRUCTIONAL DESIGNERS AND TECHNOLOGISTS

**Develop instructional materials and products and assist in the technology-based redesign of courses. Assist faculty in learning about, becoming proficient in, and applying instructional technology.**

**Major Work Tasks:** Observe and provide feedback on instructional techniques, presentation methods, or instructional aids. Edit instructional materials, such as books, simulation exercises, lesson plans, instructor guides, and tests. Develop measurement tools to evaluate the effectiveness of instruction or training interventions. Develop instructional materials, such as lesson plans, handouts, or examinations. Define instructional, learning, or performance objectives. Assess effectiveness and efficiency of instruction according to ease of instructional technology use and student learning, knowledge transfer, and satisfaction. Analyze performance data to determine effectiveness of instructional systems, courses, or instructional materials. Research and evaluate emerging instructional technologies or methods. Recommend instructional methods, such as individual or group instruction, self-study, lectures, demonstrations, simulation exercises, and role-playing, appropriate for content and learner characteristics. Recommend changes to curricula or delivery methods, based on information such as instructional effectiveness data, current or future performance requirements, feasibility, and costs. Provide technical support to clients in the implementation of designed instruction or in task analyses and instructional systems design. Provide technical advice on the use of current instructional technologies, including computer-based training, desktop videoconferencing, multimedia, and distance learning technologies. Provide analytical support for the design and development of training curricula, learning strategies, educational policies, or courseware standards. Present and make recommendations regarding course design, technology, and instruction delivery options. Interview subject matter experts or conduct other research to develop instructional content. Develop master course documentation or manuals according to applicable accreditation, certification, or other requirements. Develop instruction or training roadmaps for online and blended learning programs. Design learning products, including web-based aids or electronic performance support systems.

**Related Knowledge/Courses:** Education and Training; Communications and Media; Sociology and Anthropology; Computers and Electronics; Design; English Language.

**Personality Types:** Enterprising–Social.

**Skills:** Learning strategies; technology design; instructing; systems evaluation; systems analysis; writing; active learning; negotiation.

**Physical Environment:** Indoors; sitting; repetitive motions. **Structural Environment:** Structured versus unstructured work; freedom to make decisions; time pressure; importance of being exact or accurate; impact of decisions on co-workers or company results; frequency of decision making.

## Insurance Underwriters

**Review individual applications for insurance to evaluate degree of risk involved and determine acceptance of applications.**

- Average annual earnings: $62,870
- Middle 50% of earners: $48,600–$84,600
- Earnings growth potential: Medium (37.9%)
- Growth: 5.9%
- Annual job openings: 3,910
- Self-employed: 0.8%

**Considerations for Job Outlook:** The need to replace workers who retire or transfer to another occupation should create many additional job openings. Job opportunities should be best for those with a background in finance and strong computer and communication skills.

**Major Work Tasks:** Examine documents to determine degree of risk from such factors as applicant financial standing and value and condition of property. Decline excessive risks. Write to field representatives, medical personnel, and others to obtain further information, quote rates, or explain company underwriting policies. Evaluate possibility of losses due to catastrophe or excessive insurance. Decrease value of policy when risk is substandard and

### BEST-PAYING INDUSTRIES

| Industry | Median Earnings | Workforce |
|---|---|---|
| Insurance Carriers and Related Activities | $62,850 | 82,800 |

### BEST-PAYING METROPOLITAN AREAS

| Metro Area | Median Earnings | Workforce |
|---|---|---|
| New York–Northern New Jersey–Long Island, NY-NJ-PA | $80,260 | 7,600 |
| Boston-Cambridge-Quincy, MA-NH | $76,040 | 2,440 |
| Hartford–West Hartford–East Hartford, CT | $75,050 | 2,830 |
| Philadelphia-Camden-Wilmington, PA-NJ-DE-MD | $69,980 | 2,940 |
| Los Angeles–Long Beach–Santa Ana, CA | $69,390 | 3,910 |
| Chicago-Naperville-Joliet, IL-IN-WI | $67,240 | 4,840 |
| Dallas–Fort Worth–Arlington, TX | $65,310 | 2,650 |
| Atlanta–Sandy Springs–Marietta, GA | $63,510 | 3,340 |

specify applicable endorsements or apply rating to ensure safe profitable distribution of risks, using reference materials. Review company records to determine amount of insurance in force on single risk or group of closely related risks. Authorize reinsurance of policy when risk is high.

**Usual Educational Requirement:** Bachelor's degree. **Relevant Educational Programs:** Actuarial Science; Insurance. **Related Knowledge/Courses:** Medicine and Dentistry; Economics and Accounting; Clerical Practices; Therapy and Counseling; Sales and Marketing; Biology. **Work Experience Needed:** None.

**On-the-Job Training Needed:** Moderate-term on-the-job training. **Certification/Licensure:** Voluntary certification by association.

**Personality Types:** Conventional–Enterprising–Investigative. **Key Career Cluster:** 06 Finance. **Key Career Pathway:** 6.4 Insurance Services.

**Skills:** Judgment and decision making; writing; active listening; service orientation; mathematics; speaking; systems evaluation; operations analysis.

**Physical Environment:** Indoors; sitting; repetitive motions. **Structural Environment:** Frequency of decision making; freedom to make decisions; impact of decisions on co-workers or company results; importance of being exact or accurate; time pressure; structured versus unstructured work.

## Judges, Magistrate Judges, and Magistrates

**Arbitrate, advise, adjudicate, or administer justice in a court of law.**

- Average annual earnings: $115,760
- Middle 50% of earners: $54,500–$139,850
- Earnings growth potential: Very high (74.0%)
- Growth: 9.2%
- Annual job openings: 960
- Self-employed: 21.3%

**Considerations for Job Outlook:** The prestige associated with becoming a judge will ensure continued competition for these positions. Most job openings will arise as a result of judges, mediators, and hearing officers leaving the occupation because of retirement, teaching, or expiration of elected term. As with judges, turnover is low for arbitrators, mediators, and conciliators, so opportunities may be limited. Those who specialize in one or more areas of arbitration, mediation, or conciliation should have the best job opportunities.

### BEST-PAYING INDUSTRIES

| Industry | Median Earnings | Workforce |
|---|---|---|
| Federal, State, and Local Government | $115,760 | 27,220 |

### BEST-PAYING METROPOLITAN AREAS

| Metro Area | Median Earnings | Workforce |
|---|---|---|
| Los Angeles–Long Beach–Santa Ana, CA | $171,190 | 560 |
| New York–Northern New Jersey–Long Island, NY-NJ-PA | $138,780 | 1,480 |
| Atlanta–Sandy Springs–Marietta, GA | $85,050 | 650 |

**Major Work Tasks:** Instruct juries on applicable laws, direct juries to deduce the facts from the evidence presented, and hear their verdicts. Rule on admissibility of evidence and methods of conducting testimony. Preside over hearings and listen to allegations made by plaintiffs to determine whether the evidence supports the charges. Read documents on pleadings and motions to ascertain facts and issues. Interpret and enforce rules of procedure or establish new rules in situations where there are no procedures already established by law. Monitor proceedings to ensure that all applicable rules and procedures are followed. Advise attorneys, juries, litigants, and court personnel regarding conduct, issues, and proceedings. Research legal issues and write opinions on the issues. Write decisions on cases. Award compensation for damages to litigants in civil cases in relation to findings by juries or by the court. Settle disputes between opposing attorneys. Impose restrictions upon parties in civil cases until trials can be held. Provide information regarding the judicial system or other legal issues through the media and public speeches. Sentence defendants in criminal cases, on conviction by jury, according to applicable government statutes. Conduct preliminary hearings to decide issues, such as whether there is reasonable and probable cause to hold defendants in felony cases. Supervise other judges, court officers, and the court's administrative staff. Rule on custody and access disputes, and enforce court orders regarding custody and support of children. Grant divorces and divide assets between spouses. Participate in judicial tribunals to help resolve disputes. Perform wedding ceremonies.

**Usual Educational Requirement:** Doctoral or professional degree. **Relevant Educational Program**: Law (LL.B, J.D.). **Related Knowledge/Courses:** Law and Government; Psychology; Therapy and Counseling; Philosophy and Theology; Sociology and Anthropology; English Language. **Work Experience Needed:** More than 5 years. **On-the-Job Training Needed:** Short-term on-the-job training. **Certification/Licensure:** License.

**Personality Types:** Enterprising–Social. **Key Career Cluster:** 12 Law, Public Safety, Corrections, and Security. **Key Career Pathway:** 12.5 Legal Services.

**Skills:** Active listening; critical thinking; speaking; writing; judgment and decision making; active learning; complex problem solving; negotiation.

**Physical Environment:** Indoors; sitting. **Structural Environment:** Freedom to make decisions; impact of decisions on co-workers or company results; frequency of decision making; importance of being exact or accurate; structured versus unstructured work; time pressure.

## Landscape Architects

**Plan and design land areas for projects, such as parks and other recreational facilities, airports, highways, hospitals, schools, land subdivisions, and commercial, industrial, and residential sites.**

### BEST-PAYING INDUSTRIES

| Industry | Median Earnings | Workforce |
|---|---|---|
| Federal, State, and Local Government | $82,570 | 1,710 |
| Professional, Scientific, and Technical Services | $64,350 | 9,470 |
| Administrative and Support Services | $52,930 | 3,200 |

### BEST-PAYING METROPOLITAN AREAS

| Metro Area | Median Earnings | Workforce |
|---|---|---|
| San Francisco–Oakland–Fremont, CA | $95,130 | 530 |
| Los Angeles–Long Beach–Santa Ana, CA | $71,800 | 580 |
| Washington-Arlington-Alexandria, DC-VA-MD-WV | $71,280 | 780 |
| New York–Northern New Jersey–Long Island, NY-NJ-PA | $70,920 | 630 |
| Miami–Fort Lauderdale–Pompano Beach, FL | $70,360 | 350 |
| Denver-Aurora, CO | $70,220 | 340 |
| San Diego–Carlsbad–San Marcos, CA | $69,950 | 380 |
| Boston-Cambridge-Quincy, MA-NH | $68,160 | 500 |
| Dallas–Fort Worth–Arlington, TX | $58,910 | 380 |
| Portland-Vancouver-Beaverton, OR-WA | $58,540 | 330 |
| Seattle-Tacoma-Bellevue, WA | $58,210 | 520 |
| Philadelphia-Camden-Wilmington, PA-NJ-DE-MD | $57,710 | 330 |
| Minneapolis–St. Paul–Bloomington, MN-WI | $54,840 | 580 |

- Average annual earnings: $64,180
- Middle 50% of earners: $48,770–$83,370
- Earnings growth potential: Medium (40.1%)
- Growth: 16.0%
- Annual job openings: 780
- Self-employed: 23.9%

**Considerations for Job Outlook:** Good job opportunities are expected overall. However, competition for jobs in the largest and most prestigious landscape architecture firms should be strong. Many employers prefer to hire entry-level landscape architects who have internship experience, which significantly reduces the amount of on-the-job training required. Job opportunities will be best for landscape architects who develop strong technical and communication skills and an in-depth knowledge of environmental codes and regulations. Those with additional training or experience in urban planning increase their job opportunities for employment in landscape architecture firms that specialize in site planning, as well as in landscape design.

**Major Work Tasks:** Prepare graphic representations or drawings of proposed plans or designs. Collaborate with architects or related professionals on whole building design to maximize the aesthetic features of structures or surrounding land and to improve energy efficiency. Create landscapes that minimize water consumption by incorporating drought-resistant grasses or indigenous plants. Design and integrate rainwater harvesting or gray and reclaimed water systems to conserve water into building or land designs. Identify and select appropriate sustainable materials for use in landscape designs, such as using recycled wood or recycled concrete boards for structural elements or recycled tires for playground bedding. Confer with clients, engineering personnel, or architects on landscape projects. Prepare site plans, specifications, or cost estimates for land development. Analyze data on conditions, such as site location, drainage, or structure location for environmental reports or landscaping plans. Develop marketing materials, proposals, or presentation to generate new work opportunities. Inspect landscape work to ensure compliance with specifications, evaluate quality of materials or work, or advise clients or construction personnel. Present project plans or designs to public stakeholders, such as government agencies or community groups. Integrate existing land features or landscaping into designs. Manage the work completed by subcontractors to ensure quality control. Research latest products, technology, or design trends to stay current in the field. Inspect proposed sites to identify structural elements of land areas or other important site information, such as soil condition, existing landscaping, or the proximity of water management facilities. Develop planting plans for clients to assist them to garden productively or achieve particular aesthetic effects. Collaborate with estimators to cost projects, create project plans, or coordinate bids from landscaping contractors. Prepare conceptual drawings, graphics, or other visual representations of land areas to show predicted growth or development of land areas over time.

**Usual Educational Requirement:** Bachelor's degree. **Relevant Educational Programs**: Environmental Design/Architecture; Landscape Architecture (BS, BSLA, BLA, MSLA, MLA, PhD). **Related Knowledge/Courses:** Design; Building and Construction; Geography; Fine Arts; Biology; History and Archeology. **Work Experience Needed:** None. **On-the-Job Training Needed:** Internship/residency. **Certification/Licensure:** Licensure.

**Personality Types:** Artistic–Investigative–Realistic. **Key Career Cluster:** 02 Architecture and Construction. **Key Career Pathway:** 2.1 Design/Pre-construction.

**Skills:** Operations analysis; science; management of financial resources; management of material resources; systems evaluation; management of personnel resources; persuasion; coordination.

**Physical Environment:** Indoors; outdoors; sitting. **Structural Environment:** Importance of being exact or accurate; structured versus unstructured work; time pressure; freedom to make decisions; level of competition; impact of decisions on co-workers or company results.

## Language and Literature Teachers, Postsecondary

*See Teachers, Postsecondary.*

## Law Teachers, Postsecondary

*See Teachers, Postsecondary.*

## Lawyers

**Represent clients in criminal and civil litigation and other legal proceedings, draw up legal documents, or manage or advise clients on legal transactions.**

- Average annual earnings: $113,530
- Middle 50% of earners: $74,880–$168,010
- Earnings growth potential: Very high (52.2%)
- Growth: 10.1%
- Annual job openings: 21,200
- Self-employed: 21.6%

### BEST-PAYING INDUSTRIES

| Industry | Median Earnings | Workforce |
|---|---|---|
| Professional, Scientific, and Technical Services | $117,040 | 384,000 |
| Federal, State, and Local Government | $96,270 | 122,710 |

### BEST-PAYING METROPOLITAN AREAS

| Metro Area | Median Earnings | Workforce |
|---|---|---|
| San Francisco–Oakland–Fremont, CA | $155,280 | 14,520 |
| Washington-Arlington-Alexandria, DC-VA-MD-WV | $148,510 | 43,200 |
| Los Angeles–Long Beach–Santa Ana, CA | $145,700 | 29,040 |
| New York–Northern New Jersey–Long Island, NY-NJ-PA | $140,470 | 69,200 |
| Chicago-Naperville-Joliet, IL-IN-WI | $132,380 | 25,440 |
| Atlanta–Sandy Springs–Marietta, GA | $131,350 | 12,130 |
| Philadelphia–Camden–Wilmington, PA–NJ–DE–MD | $126,810 | 18,510 |
| Boston-Cambridge-Quincy, MA-NH | $118,090 | 15,920 |
| Dallas–Fort Worth–Arlington, TX | $116,190 | 11,800 |
| Miami–Fort Lauderdale–Pompano Beach, FL | $112,650 | 17,770 |

**Considerations for Job Outlook:** Competition should continue to be strong because more students are graduating from law school each year than there are jobs available. As in the past, some recent law school graduates who have been unable to find permanent positions are turning to the growing number of temporary staffing firms that place attorneys in short-term jobs. This service allows companies to hire lawyers "as needed" and permits beginning lawyers to develop practical skills. Job opportunities are typically affected by cyclical swings in the economy. Because of the strong competition, work experience and a law graduate's

**315**

willingness to relocate are becoming more important. However, to be licensed in another state, a lawyer may have to take an additional state bar examination.

**Major Work Tasks:** Advise clients concerning business transactions, claim liability, advisability of prosecuting or defending lawsuits, or legal rights and obligations. Interpret laws, rulings and regulations for individuals and businesses. Analyze the probable outcomes of cases, using knowledge of legal precedents. Present and summarize cases to judges and juries. Evaluate findings and develop strategies and arguments in preparation for presentation of cases. Gather evidence to formulate defense or to initiate legal actions by such means as interviewing clients and witnesses to ascertain the facts of a case. Represent clients in court or before government agencies. Examine legal data to determine advisability of defending or prosecuting lawsuit. Select jurors, argue motions, meet with judges, and question witnesses during the course of a trial. Present evidence to defend clients or prosecute defendants in criminal or civil litigation. Study Constitution, statutes, decisions, regulations, and ordinances of quasi-judicial bodies to determine ramifications for cases. Prepare and draft legal documents, such as wills, deeds, patent applications, mortgages, leases, and contracts. Prepare legal briefs and opinions, and file appeals in state and federal courts of appeal. Negotiate settlements of civil disputes. Confer with colleagues with specialties in appropriate areas of legal issue to establish and verify bases for legal proceedings. Supervise legal assistants. Perform administrative and management functions related to the practice of law. Search for and examine public and other legal records to write opinions or establish ownership. Act as agent, trustee, guardian, or executor for businesses or individuals. Probate wills and represent and advise executors and administrators of estates. Help develop federal and state programs, draft and interpret laws and legislation, and establish enforcement procedures. Work in environmental law, representing public interest groups, waste disposal companies, or construction firms in their dealings with state and federal agencies.

**Usual Educational Requirement:** Doctoral or professional degree. **Relevant Educational Programs**: Advanced Legal Research/Studies, General (LL.M., M.C.L., M.L.I., M.S.L., J.S.D./ S.J.D.); American/U.S. Law/Legal Studies/Jurisprudence (LL.M., M.C.J., J.S.D./S.J.D.); Banking, Corporate, Finance, and Securities Law (LL.M., J.S.D./S.J.D.); Canadian Law/Legal Studies/Jurisprudence (LL.M., M.C.J., J.S.D./ S.J.D.); Comparative Law (LL.M., M.C.L., J.S.D./ S.J.D.); Energy, Environment, and Natural Resources Law (LL.M., M.S., J.S.D./S.J.D.); Health Law (LL.M., M.J., J.S.D./S.J.D.); Intellectual Property Law; International Business, Trade, and Tax Law (LL.M., J.S.D./S.J.D.); International Law and Legal Studies (LL.M., J.S.D./ S.J.D.); Law (LL.B, J.D.); Legal Research and Advanced Professional Studies, Other; Programs for Foreign Lawyers (LL.M., M.C.L.); Tax Law/Taxation (LL.M., J.S.D./S.J.D.). **Related Knowledge/Courses:** Law and Government; English Language; Personnel and Human Resources; Customer and Personal Service; Economics and Accounting; Administration and Management. **Work Experience Needed:** None. **On-the-Job Training Needed:** None. **Certification/Licensure:** License.

**Personality Types:** Enterprising–Investigative. **Key Career Cluster:** 12 Law, Public Safety, Corrections, and Security. **Key Career Pathway:** 12.5 Legal Services.

**Skills:** Persuasion; negotiation; speaking; writing; critical thinking; judgment and decision making; active learning; operations analysis.

**Physical Environment:** Indoors; sitting. **Structural Environment:** Importance of being exact or accurate; frequency of decision making; impact of decisions on co-workers or company results; structured versus unstructured work; freedom to make decisions; time pressure.

## Library Science Teachers, Postsecondary

*See Teachers, Postsecondary.*

## Loan Officers

**Evaluate, authorize, or recommend approval of commercial, real estate, or credit loans.**

- Average annual earnings: $59,820
- Middle 50% of earners: $43,010–$84,840
- Earnings growth potential: High (45.5%)
- Growth: 14.2%
- Annual job openings: 11,520
- Self-employed: 2.3%

### BEST-PAYING INDUSTRIES

| Industry | Median Earnings | Workforce |
|---|---|---|
| Credit Intermediation and Related Activities | $58,560 | 246,640 |

### BEST-PAYING METROPOLITAN AREAS

| Metro Area | Median Earnings | Workforce |
|---|---|---|
| New York–Northern New Jersey–Long Island, NY-NJ-PA | $102,030 | 17,140 |
| Los Angeles–Long Beach–Santa Ana, CA | $72,800 | 12,040 |
| Chicago-Naperville-Joliet, IL-IN-WI | $68,240 | 9,170 |
| Philadelphia-Camden-Wilmington, PA-NJ-DE-MD | $62,800 | 5,820 |
| Dallas–Fort Worth–Arlington, TX | $56,100 | 10,620 |
| Phoenix-Mesa-Scottsdale, AZ | $53,940 | 8,280 |

**Considerations for Job Outlook:** Prospects for loan officers should improve over the coming decade as lending activity rebounds from the recent recession. Job opportunities should be good for those with a college degree and lending, banking, or sales experience. In addition, some firms require loan officers to find their own clients, so candidates with established contacts and a referral network should have the best job opportunities.

**Major Work Tasks:** Approve loans within specified limits, and refer loan applications outside those limits to management for approval. Meet with applicants to obtain information for loan applications and to answer questions about the process. Analyze applicants' financial status, credit, and property evaluations to determine feasibility of granting loans. Explain to customers the different types of loans and credit options that are available, as well as the terms of those services. Obtain and compile copies of loan applicants' credit histories, corporate financial statements, and other financial information. Review and update credit and loan files. Review loan agreements to ensure that they are complete and accurate according to policy. Compute payment schedules. Stay abreast of new types of loans and other financial services and products to better meet customers' needs. Submit applications to credit analysts for verification and recommendation. Handle customer complaints and take appropriate action to resolve them. Analyze potential loan markets and develop referral networks to locate prospects for loans. Work with clients to identify their financial goals and to find ways of reaching those goals. Confer with underwriters to aid in resolving mortgage application problems. Negotiate payment arrangements with customers who have delinquent loans. Market bank products to individuals and firms, promoting bank services that may meet customers' needs. Supervise loan personnel. Set credit policies, credit lines, procedures, and standards in conjunction with

**317**

senior managers. Provide special services, such as investment banking for clients with more specialized needs. Prepare reports to send to customers whose accounts are delinquent, and forward irreconcilable accounts for collector action. Arrange for maintenance and liquidation of delinquent properties. Interview, hire, and train new employees. Petition courts to transfer titles and deeds of collateral to banks.

**Usual Educational Requirement:** High school diploma or equivalent. **Relevant Educational Programs**: Credit Management; Finance, General. **Related Knowledge/Courses:** Sales and Marketing; Economics and Accounting; Customer and Personal Service; Law and Government; Clerical Practices; Mathematics. **Work Experience Needed:** None. **On-the-Job Training Needed:** Moderate-term on-the-job training. **Certification/Licensure:** Voluntary certification by association.

**Personality Types:** Conventional–Enterprising–Social. **Key Career Cluster:** 06 Finance. **Key Career Pathway:** 6.3 Banking and Related Services.

**Skills:** Service orientation; mathematics; judgment and decision making; speaking; negotiation; active listening; critical thinking; reading comprehension.

**Physical Environment:** Indoors; sitting. **Structural Environment:** Freedom to make decisions; frequency of decision making; importance of being exact or accurate; impact of decisions on co-workers or company results; structured versus unstructured work; importance of repeating same tasks.

## Logisticians

**Analyze and coordinate the logistical functions of a firm or organization.**

- Average annual earnings: $72,780
- Middle 50% of earners: $57,090–$91,210
- Earnings growth potential: Medium (37.9%)
- Growth: 25.5%
- Annual job openings: 4,870
- Self-employed: 0.0%

### BEST-PAYING INDUSTRIES

| Industry | Median Earnings | Workforce |
|---|---|---|
| Federal, State, and Local Government | $77,990 | 27,460 |
| Transportation Equipment Manufacturing | $74,210 | 13,590 |
| Professional, Scientific, and Technical Services | $71,510 | 20,610 |
| Management of Companies and Enterprises | $69,900 | 11,240 |

### BEST-PAYING METROPOLITAN AREAS

| Metro Area | Median Earnings | Workforce |
|---|---|---|
| Washington-Arlington-Alexandria, DC-VA-MD-WV | $88,260 | 5,340 |
| Huntsville, AL | $86,260 | 2,700 |
| Houston–Sugar Land–Baytown, TX | $85,800 | 3,270 |
| Detroit-Warren-Livonia, MI | $84,320 | 3,270 |
| Seattle-Tacoma-Bellevue, WA | $80,150 | 6,080 |
| Los Angeles–Long Beach–Santa Ana, CA | $77,480 | 4,610 |
| Dallas–Fort Worth–Arlington, TX | $75,480 | 4,000 |
| New York–Northern New Jersey–Long Island, NY-NJ-PA | $75,350 | 4,080 |

**Considerations for Job Outlook:** Job prospects should be good for those with a bachelor's degree in supply chain management, industrial engineering, business, or a related field. Prospects should be best for those with a college degree and work experience related to logistics, particularly previous experience using logistical software, or doing logistical work for the military.

**Major Work Tasks:** Maintain and develop positive business relationships with a customer's key personnel involved in or directly relevant to a logistics activity. Develop an understanding of customers' needs and take actions to ensure that such needs are met. Direct availability and allocation of materials, supplies, and finished products. Collaborate with other departments as necessary to meet customer requirements, to take advantage of sales opportunities, or, in the case of shortages, to minimize negative impacts on a business. Protect and control proprietary materials. Review logistics performance with customers against targets, benchmarks, and service agreements. Develop and implement technical project management tools, such as plans, schedules, and responsibility and compliance matrices. Direct team activities, establishing task priorities, scheduling and tracking work assignments, providing guidance, and ensuring the availability of resources. Report project plans, progress, and results. Direct and support the compilation and analysis of technical source data necessary for product development. Explain proposed solutions to customers, management, or other interested parties through written proposals and oral presentations. Develop proposals that include documentation for estimates. Plan, organize, and execute logistics support activities, such as maintenance planning, repair analysis, and test equipment recommendations. Provide project management services, including the provision and analysis of technical data. Participate in the assessment and review of de-

sign alternatives and design change proposal impacts. Support the development of training materials and technical manuals. Stay informed of logistics technology advances and apply appropriate technology to improve logistics processes. Redesign the movement of goods to maximize value and minimize costs. Manage subcontractor activities, reviewing proposals, developing performance specifications, and serving as liaisons between subcontractors and organizations. Manage the logistical aspects of product life cycles, including coordinating or provisioning samples and minimizing obsolescence.

**Usual Educational Requirement:** Bachelor's degree. **Relevant Educational Program**: Operations Management and Supervision. **Related Knowledge/Courses:** Telecommunications; Geography; Economics and Accounting; Computers and Electronics; Administration and Management; Public Safety and Security. **Work Experience Needed:** 1 to 5 years. **On-the-Job Training Needed:** None. **Certification/Licensure:** Licensure for some specializations; voluntary certification by association.

**Personality Types:** Enterprising–Conventional. **Key Career Cluster:** 16 Transportation, Distribution, and Logistics Cluster. **Key Career Pathway:** 16.2 Logistics, Planning, and Management Services.

**Skills:** Operations analysis; management of personnel resources; programming; coordination; monitoring; persuasion; systems evaluation; systems analysis.

**Physical Environment:** Indoors; sitting. **Structural Environment:** Freedom to make decisions; structured versus unstructured work; importance of being exact or accurate; impact of decisions on co-workers or company results; frequency of decision making; level of competition.

### JOB SPECIALIZATION: LOGISTICS ANALYSTS

**Analyze product delivery or supply chain processes to identify or recommend changes.**

**May manage route activity, including invoicing, electronic bills, and shipment tracing.**

**Major Work Tasks:** Identify opportunities for inventory reductions. Monitor industry standards, trends, or practices to identify developments in logistics planning or execution. Enter logistics-related data into databases. Track product flow from origin to final delivery. Write or revise standard operating procedures for logistics processes. Review procedures, such as distribution or inventory management, to ensure maximum efficiency or minimum cost. Recommend improvements to existing or planned logistics processes. Provide ongoing analyses in areas, such as transportation costs, parts procurement, back orders, or delivery processes. Prepare reports on logistics performance measures. Monitor inventory transactions at warehouse facilities to assess receiving, storage, shipping, or inventory integrity. Maintain databases of logistics information. Maintain logistics records in accordance with corporate policies. Develop or maintain models for logistics uses, such as cost estimating or demand forecasting. Confer with logistics management teams to determine ways to optimize service levels, maintain supply-chain efficiency, or minimize cost. Compute reporting metrics, such as on-time delivery rates, order fulfillment rates, or inventory turns. Interpret data on logistics elements, such as availability, maintainability, reliability, supply chain management, strategic sourcing or distribution, supplier management, or transportation. Apply analytic methods or tools to understand, predict, or control logistics operations or processes. Analyze logistics data, using methods such as data mining, data modeling, or cost or benefit analysis. Remotely monitor the flow of vehicles or inventory, using web-based logistics information systems to track vehicles or containers. Develop or maintain payment systems to ensure accuracy of vendor payments. Determine packaging requirements. Develop or maintain freight rate databases for use by supply chain departments to determine the most economical modes of transportation. Contact potential vendors to determine material availability. Contact carriers for rates or schedules.

**Related Knowledge/Courses:** Transportation; Geography; Production and Processing; Computers and Electronics; Mathematics; Telecommunications.

**Personality Types:** Conventional–Enterprising–Investigative.

**Skills:** Mathematics; systems analysis; systems evaluation; management of financial resources; programming; technology design; management of material resources; active learning.

**Physical Environment:** Indoors; sitting. **Structural Environment:** Structured versus unstructured work; freedom to make decisions; importance of being exact or accurate; time pressure; importance of repeating same tasks; impact of decisions on co-workers or company results.

## JOB SPECIALIZATION: LOGISTICS ENGINEERS

**Design and analyze operational solutions for projects, such as transportation optimization, network modeling, process and methods analysis, cost containment, capacity enhancement, routing and shipment optimization, and information management.**

**Major Work Tasks:** Propose logistics solutions for customers. Interview key staff or tour facilities to identify efficiency-improvement, cost-reduction, or service-delivery opportunities. Direct the work of logistics analysts. Develop specifications for equipment, tools, facility layouts, or material-handling systems. Review contractual commitments, customer specifications, or related information to determine logistics or support requirements. Prepare or validate documentation on automated logistics or maintenance-data reporting or management information systems. Identify or develop business rules or standard operating procedures to streamline operating processes. De-

320

velop or maintain cost estimates, forecasts, or cost models. Determine logistics support requirements, such as facility details, staffing needs, or safety or maintenance plans. Conduct logistics studies or analyses, such as time studies, zero-base analyses, rate analyses, network analyses, flow-path analyses, or supply-chain analyses. Analyze or interpret logistics data involving customer service, forecasting, procurement, manufacturing, inventory, transportation, or warehousing. Provide logistics technology or information for effective and efficient support of product, equipment, or system manufacturing or service. Evaluate effectiveness of current or future logistical processes. Apply logistics modeling techniques to address issues such as operational process improvement or facility design or layout. Evaluate the use of inventory tracking technology, web-based warehousing software, or intelligent conveyor systems to maximize plant or distribution center efficiency. Develop logistic metrics, internal analysis tools, or key performance indicators for business units. Identify cost-reduction or process-improvement logistic opportunities. Evaluate the use of technologies, such as global positioning systems (GPS), radio-frequency identification (RFID), route navigation software, or satellite link-up systems, to improve transportation efficiency. Prepare logistic strategies or conceptual designs for production facilities. Design comprehensive supply chains that minimize environmental impacts or costs.

**Related Knowledge/Courses:** Engineering and Technology; Design; Transportation; Telecommunications; Mechanical Devices; Production and Processing.

**Personality Types:** Investigative–Conventional–Realistic.

**Skills:** Equipment selection; operations analysis; programming; systems evaluation; systems analysis; management of material resources; mathematics; management of financial resources.

**Physical Environment:** Indoors; sitting. **Structural Environment:** Freedom to make decisions; structured versus unstructured work; importance of being exact or accurate; time pressure; impact of decisions on co-workers or company results; frequency of decision making.

## Management Analysts

**Conduct organizational studies and evaluations, design systems and procedures, conduct work simplification and measurement studies, and prepare operations and procedures manuals to assist management in operating more efficiently and effectively.**

- Average annual earnings: $78,600
- Middle 50% of earners: $58,620–$104,890
- Earnings growth potential: Medium (43.5%)
- Growth: 21.9%
- Annual job openings: 27,430
- Self-employed: 22.6%

**Considerations for Job Outlook:** Job seekers may face strong competition for management analyst positions because the high earning potential in this occupation makes it attractive to many job seekers. Job opportunities are expected to be best for those who have a graduate degree or a certification, specialized expertise,

### BEST-PAYING INDUSTRIES

| Industry | Median Earnings | Workforce |
|---|---|---|
| Professional, Scientific, and Technical Services | $85,880 | 202,240 |
| Management of Companies and Enterprises | $78,030 | 32,510 |
| Federal, State, and Local Government | $74,870 | 103,070 |
| Insurance Carriers and Related Activities | $72,870 | 35,040 |

## BEST-PAYING METROPOLITAN AREAS

| Metro Area | Median Earnings | Workforce |
| --- | --- | --- |
| San Francisco–Oakland–Fremont, CA | $95,370 | 12,580 |
| Washington-Arlington-Alexandria, DC-VA-MD-WV | $92,010 | 56,540 |
| Boston-Cambridge-Quincy, MA-NH | $90,700 | 19,750 |
| New York–Northern New Jersey–Long Island, NY-NJ-PA | $89,950 | 40,870 |
| Philadelphia-Camden-Wilmington, PA-NJ-DE-MD | $87,460 | 12,090 |
| Chicago-Naperville-Joliet, IL-IN-WI | $82,820 | 21,690 |
| Los Angeles–Long Beach–Santa Ana, CA | $82,430 | 23,500 |
| Dallas–Fort Worth–Arlington, TX | $81,060 | 11,650 |
| Atlanta–Sandy Springs–Marietta, GA | $78,440 | 21,540 |

and a talent for salesmanship and public relations.

**Major Work Tasks:** Gather and organize information on problems or procedures. Analyze data gathered and develop solutions or alternative methods of proceeding. Confer with personnel concerned to ensure successful functioning of newly implemented systems or procedures. Develop and implement records management program for filing, protection, and retrieval of records, and assure compliance with program. Review forms and reports and confer with management and users about format, distribution, and purpose, and to identify problems and improvements. Interview personnel and conduct on-site observation to ascertain unit functions, work performed, and methods, equipment, and personnel used. Document findings of study and prepare recommendations for implementation of new systems, procedures, or organizational changes. Prepare manuals and train workers in use of new forms, reports, procedures or equipment, according to organizational policy. Design, evaluate, recommend, and approve changes of forms and reports. Plan study of work problems and procedures, such as organizational change, communications, information flow, integrated production methods, inventory control, or cost analysis. Recommend purchase of storage equipment and design area layout to locate equipment in space available.

**Usual Educational Requirement:** Bachelor's degree. **Relevant Educational Programs**: Business Administration and Management, General; Business/Commerce, General; Organizational Leadership. **Related Knowledge/Courses:** Personnel and Human Resources; Clerical Practices; Sales and Marketing; Economics and Accounting; Customer and Personal Service; Administration and Management. **Work Experience Needed:** 1 to 5 years. **On-the-Job Training Needed:** None. **Certification/Licensure:** Voluntary certification by association.

**Personality Types:** Investigative–Enterprising–Conventional. **Key Career Cluster:** 04 Business, Management, and Administration. **Key Career Pathway:** 4.1 Management.

**Skills:** Operations analysis; systems evaluation; systems analysis; science; judgment and decision making; management of material resources; management of personnel resources; writing.

**Physical Environment:** Indoors; sitting. **Structural Environment:** Structured versus unstructured work; freedom to make Decisions; impact of decisions on co-workers or company results; frequency of decision making; importance of being exact or accurate; time pressure.

## Managers, All Other

**All managers not listed separately.**

- Average annual Earnings: $100,890
- Middle 50% of earners: $72,620–$129,760
- Earnings growth potential: High (47.9%)
- Growth: 7.9%
- Annual job openings: 24,940
- Self-employed: 55.8%

### BEST-PAYING INDUSTRIES

| Industry | Median Earnings | Workforce |
|---|---|---|
| Management of Companies and Enterprises | $111,100 | 33,270 |
| Professional, Scientific, and Technical Services | $110,670 | 32,390 |
| Federal, State, and Local Government | $103,870 | 105,980 |
| Educational Services | $81,380 | 20,610 |

### BEST-PAYING METROPOLITAN AREAS

| Metro Area | Median Earnings | Workforce |
|---|---|---|
| Washington-Arlington-Alexandria, DC-VA-MD-WV | $126,240 | 33,210 |
| New York–Northern New Jersey–Long Island, NY-NJ-PA | $115,470 | 25,920 |
| Los Angeles–Long Beach–Santa Ana, CA | $113,700 | 12,050 |
| Minneapolis–St. Paul–Bloomington, MN-WI | $103,110 | 10,700 |
| Chicago-Naperville-Joliet, IL-IN-WI | $90,470 | 27,030 |

**Considerations for Job Outlook:** Slower-than-average employment growth is projected.

**Major Work Tasks:** For tasks, see the job specializations.

**Usual Educational Requirement:** High school diploma or equivalent. **Relevant Educational Programs**: American Government and Politics (United States); American History (United States); Anthropology; Anthropology, Other; Applied Behavior Analysis; Applied Economics; Applied Psychology; Archeology; Archives/Archival Administration; Arts, Entertainment, and Media Management, Other; Arts, Entertainment, and Media Management, General; Asian History; Business Administration and Management, General; Business/Commerce, General; Canadian Government and Politics; Canadian History; Clinical Child Psychology; Clinical Psychology; Clinical Research Coordinator; Clinical, Counseling and Applied Psychology, Other; Cognitive Psychology and Psycholinguistics; Community Psychology; Comparative Psychology; Counseling Psychology; Criminal Justice/Law Enforcement Administration; Criminology; Crisis/Emergency/Disaster Management; Critical Infrastructure Protection; Cultural Anthropology; Demography and Population Studies; Development Economics and International Development; others. **Work Experience Needed:** 1 to 5 years. **On-the-Job Training Needed:** None. **Certification/Licensure:** Licensure for some specializations.

**Key Career Cluster:** 04 Business, Management, and Administration. **Key Career Pathway:** 4.1 Management.

### JOB SPECIALIZATION: BROWNFIELD REDEVELOPMENT SPECIALISTS AND SITE MANAGERS

**Participate in planning and directing cleanup and redevelopment of contaminated properties for reuse. Does not include properties sufficiently contaminated to qualify as Superfund sites.**

**Major Work Tasks:** Review or evaluate environmental remediation project proposals. Review or evaluate designs for contaminant treatment or disposal facilities. Provide training on hazardous material or waste clean-up procedures and technologies. Prepare reports or presentations to communicate brownfield redevelopment needs, status, or progress. Negotiate contracts for services or materials needed for environmental remediation. Prepare and submit permit applications for demolition, clean-up, remediation, or construction projects. Maintain records of decisions, actions, and progress related to environmental redevelopment projects. Inspect sites to assess environmental damage or monitor clean-up progress. Plan or implement brownfield redevelopment projects to ensure safety, quality, and compliance with applicable standards or requirements. Identify environmental contamination sources. Estimate costs for environmental clean-up and remediation of land redevelopment projects. Develop or implement plans for revegetation of brownfield sites. Design or implement plans for surface or ground water remediation. Design or implement plans for structural demolition and debris removal. Design or implement measures to improve the water, air, and soil quality of military test sites, abandoned mine land, or other contaminated sites. Design or conduct environmental restoration studies. Coordinate the disposal of hazardous waste. Coordinate on-site activities for environmental clean-up or remediation projects to ensure compliance with environmental laws, standards, regulations, or other requirements. Conduct quantitative risk assessments for human health, environmental, or other risks. Conduct feasibility or cost-benefit studies for environmental remediation projects. Develop or implement plans for the sustainable regeneration of brownfield sites to ensure regeneration of a wider area by providing environmental protection or economic and social benefits. Provide expert witness testimony on issues such as soil, air, or water contamination and associated clean-up measures.

**Related Knowledge/Courses:** Biology; Geography; Building and Construction; Chemistry; Engineering and Technology; Design.

**Personality Types:** Enterprising–Investigative–Conventional.

**Skills:** Management of financial resources; management of material resources; operations analysis; mathematics; coordination; negotiation; science; technology design.

**Physical Environment:** Indoors; outdoors; sitting. **Structural Environment:** Structured versus unstructured work; freedom to make decisions; impact of decisions on co-workers or company results; importance of being exact or accurate; time pressure; frequency of decision making.

JOB SPECIALIZATION: COMPLIANCE MANAGERS

**Plan, direct, or coordinate activities of an organization to ensure compliance with ethical or regulatory standards.**

**Major Work Tasks:** Serve as a confidential point of contact for employees to communicate with management, seek clarification on issues or dilemmas, or report irregularities. Maintain documentation of compliance activities, such as complaints received or investigation outcomes. Consult with corporate attorneys as necessary to address difficult legal compliance issues. Discuss emerging compliance issues with management or employees. Advise internal management or business partners on the implementation or operation of compliance programs. Provide employee training on compliance related topics, policies, or procedures. Report violations of compliance or regulatory standards to duly authorized enforcement agencies as appropriate or required. Provide assistance to internal or external auditors in compliance reviews. Prepare management reports regarding compliance operations and progress. Monitor compliance systems to ensure their effectiveness. Identify compliance issues that require follow-up or investigation.

Keep informed regarding pending industry changes, trends, and best practices and assess the potential impact of these changes on organizational processes. Disseminate written policies and procedures related to compliance activities. File appropriate compliance reports with regulatory agencies. Design or implement improvements in communication, monitoring, or enforcement of compliance standards. Conduct periodic internal reviews or audits to ensure that compliance procedures are followed. Conduct or direct the internal investigation of compliance issues. Assess product, compliance, or operational risks and develop risk management strategies. Verify that all firm and regulatory policies and procedures have been documented, implemented, and communicated. Direct the development or implementation of compliance-related policies and procedures throughout an organization. Verify that software technology is in place to adequately provide oversight and monitoring in all required areas. Collaborate with human resources departments to ensure the implementation of consistent disciplinary action strategies in cases of compliance standard violations.

**Related Knowledge/Courses:** Law and Government; Personnel and Human Resources; Education and Training; Administration and Management; English Language; Computers and Electronics.

**Personality Types:** Conventional–Enterprising–Realistic.

**Skills:** Monitoring; persuasion; writing; coordination; active learning; speaking; critical thinking; learning strategies.

**Physical Environment:** Indoors; sitting; repetitive motions. **Structural Environment:** Freedom to make decisions; importance of being exact or accurate; impact of decisions on co-workers or company results; structured versus unstructured work; frequency of decision making; time pressure.

## JOB SPECIALIZATION: INVESTMENT FUND MANAGERS

**Plan, direct, or coordinate investment strategy or operations for a large pool of liquid assets supplied by institutional investors or individual investors.**

**Major Work Tasks:** Prepare for and respond to regulatory inquiries. Verify regulatory compliance of transaction reporting. Hire or evaluate staff. Direct activities of accounting or operations departments. Develop, implement, or monitor security valuation policies. Attend investment briefings or consult financial media to stay abreast of relevant investment markets. Review offering documents or marketing materials to ensure regulatory compliance. Perform or evaluate research, such as detailed company or industry analyses, to inform financial forecasting, decision making, or valuation. Present investment information, such as product risks, fees, or fund performance statistics. Monitor financial or operational performance of individual investments to ensure portfolios meet risk goals. Monitor regulatory or tax law changes to ensure fund compliance or to capitalize on development opportunities. Meet with investors to determine investment goals or to discuss investment strategies. Identify group or individual target investors for a specific fund. Develop or direct development of offering documents or marketing materials. Evaluate the potential of new product developments or market opportunities, according to factors such as business plans, technologies, or market potential. Develop or implement fund investment policies or strategies. Select or direct the execution of trades. Analyze acquisitions to ensure conformance with strategic goals or regulatory requirements. Manage investment funds to maximize return on client investments. Select specific investments or investment mixes for purchase by an investment fund.

**Related Knowledge/Courses:** No data available.

**Personality Types:** Enterprising–Conventional.

**Skills:** No data available.

**Physical Environment:** No data available.
**Structural Environment:** No data available.

### JOB SPECIALIZATION: LOSS PREVENTION MANAGERS

**Plan and direct policies, procedures, or systems to prevent the loss of assets. Determine risk exposure or potential liability, and develop risk control measures.**

**Major Work Tasks:** Review loss-prevention exception reports and cash discrepancies to ensure adherence to guidelines. Perform cash audits and deposit investigations to fully account for store cash. Provide recommendations and solutions in crisis situations, such as workplace violence, protests, and demonstrations. Monitor and review paperwork procedures and systems to prevent error-related shortages. Maintain databases, such as bad check logs, reports on multiple offenders, and alarm activation lists. Investigate or interview individuals suspected of shoplifting or internal theft. Direct installation of covert surveillance equipment, such as security cameras. Advise retail establishments on development of loss-investigation procedures. Visit stores to ensure compliance with company policies and procedures. Verify correct use and maintenance of physical security systems, such as closed-circuit television, merchandise tags, and burglar alarms. Train loss prevention staff, retail managers, or store employees on loss control and prevention measures. Supervise surveillance, detection, or criminal processing related to theft and criminal cases. Recommend improvements in loss prevention programs, staffing, scheduling, or training. Perform or direct inventory investigations in response to shrink results outside of acceptable ranges. Hire or supervise loss-prevention staff. Maintain documentation of all loss prevention activity. Coordinate theft and fraud investigations involving career criminals or organized group activities. Direct loss prevention audit programs including target store audits, maintenance audits, safety audits, or electronic article surveillance (EAS) audits. Develop and maintain partnerships with federal, state, or local law enforcement agencies or members of the retail loss prevention community. Coordinate or conduct internal investigations of problems, such as employee theft and violations of corporate loss prevention policies. Collaborate with law enforcement to investigate and solve external theft or fraud cases. Assess security needs across locations to ensure proper deployment of loss prevention resources, such as staff and technology.

**Related Knowledge/Courses:** Public Safety and Security; Personnel and Human Resources; Economics and Accounting; Education and Training; Psychology; Administration and Management.

**Personality Types:** Enterprising–Conventional.

**Skills:** Systems evaluation; systems analysis; management of personnel resources; management of material resources; persuasion; management of financial resources; instructing; time management.

**Physical Environment:** Indoors; standing.
**Structural Environment:** Importance of being exact or accurate; impact of decisions on co-workers or company results; freedom to make decisions; frequency of decision making; structured versus unstructured work; time pressure.

### JOB SPECIALIZATION: REGULATORY AFFAIRS MANAGERS

**Plan, direct, or coordinate production activities of an organization to ensure compliance with regulations and standard operating procedures.**

**Major Work Tasks:** Direct the preparation and submission of regulatory agency applications, reports, or correspondence. Formulate or implement regulatory affairs policies and procedures to ensure that regulatory compliance is maintained or enhanced. Provide regulatory guidance to departments or development project teams regarding design, development, evaluation, or marketing of products. Communicate regulatory information to multiple departments and ensure that information is interpreted correctly. Develop regulatory strategies and implementation plans for the preparation and submission of new products. Establish regulatory priorities or budgets and allocate resources and workloads. Implement or monitor complaint processing systems to ensure effective and timely resolution of all complaint investigations. Investigate product complaints and prepare documentation and submissions to appropriate regulatory agencies as necessary. Maintain current knowledge of relevant regulations, including proposed and final rules. Manage activities, such as audits, regulatory agency inspections, or product recalls. Monitor emerging trends regarding industry regulations to determine potential impacts on organizational processes. Oversee documentation efforts to ensure compliance with domestic and international regulations and standards. Participate in the development or implementation of clinical trial protocols. Provide responses to regulatory agencies regarding product information or issues. Represent organizations before domestic or international regulatory agencies on major policy matters or decisions regarding company products. Review all regulatory agency submission materials to ensure timeliness, accuracy, comprehensiveness, or compliance with regulatory standards. Review materials, such as marketing literature or user manuals to ensure that regulatory agency requirements are met. Train staff in regulatory policies or procedures. Contribute to the development or implementa-

tion of business unit strategic and operating plans. Develop and maintain standard operating procedures or local working practices.

**Related Knowledge/Courses:** Biology; Medicine and Dentistry; Law and Government; Chemistry; Clerical Practices; Personnel and Human Resources.

**Personality Types:** Enterprising–Conventional.

**Skills:** Operations analysis; management of personnel resources; systems evaluation; systems analysis; negotiation; coordination; science; writing.

**Physical Environment:** Indoors; sitting. **Structural Environment:** Importance of being exact or accurate; structured versus unstructured work; freedom to make decisions; impact of decisions on co-workers or company results; time pressure; frequency of decision making.

## JOB SPECIALIZATION: SECURITY MANAGERS

**Direct an organization's security functions, including physical security and safety of employees, facilities, and assets.**

**Major Work Tasks:** Write or review security-related documents, such as incident reports, proposals, and tactical or strategic initiatives. Train subordinate security professionals or other organization members in security rules and procedures. Plan security for special and high-risk events. Review financial reports to ensure efficiency and quality of security operations. Develop budgets for security operations. Coordinate security operations or activities with public law enforcement, fire, and other agencies. Attend meetings, professional seminars, or conferences to keep abreast of changes in executive legislative directives or new technologies impacting security operations. Respond to medical emergencies, bomb threats, fire alarms, or intrusion alarms, following emergency response procedures. Prepare reports or make presentations on internal investigations, losses, or violations of regulations, policies, and procedures. Identify, investigate, or resolve security breaches. Monitor security policies, programs or procedures to ensure compliance with internal security policies, licensing requirements, or applicable government security requirements, policies, and directives. Conduct physical examinations of property to ensure compliance with security policies and regulations. Communicate security status, updates, and actual or potential problems, using established protocols. Collect and analyze security data to determine security needs, security program goals, or program accomplishments. Plan, direct, or coordinate security activities to safeguard company assets, employees, guests, or others on company property. Create or implement security standards, policies, and procedures. Monitor and ensure a sound, ethical environment. Develop, implement, manage, or evaluate policies and methods to protect personnel against harassment, threats, or violence. Develop, conduct, support, or assist in governmental reviews, internal corporate evaluations, or assessments of the overall effectiveness of facility and personnel security processes. Assess risks to mitigate potential consequences of incidents and develop a plan to respond to incidents.

**Related Knowledge/Courses:** Public Safety and Security; Geography; Therapy and Counseling; Building and Construction; Psychology; Education and Training.

**Personality Types:** Enterprising–Conventional.

**Skills:** Management of financial resources; management of material resources; systems evaluation; quality control analysis; persuasion; management of personnel resources; coordination; systems analysis.

**Physical Environment:** Indoors; outdoors; sitting. **Structural Environment:** Frequency of decision making; impact of decisions on coworkers or company results; freedom to make decisions; time pressure; importance of being exact or accurate; structured versus unstructured work.

JOB SPECIALIZATION: SUPPLY CHAIN MANAGERS

**Direct or coordinate production, purchasing, warehousing, distribution, or financial forecasting services and activities to limit costs and improve accuracy, customer service, and safety. Examine existing procedures and opportunities for streamlining activities to meet product distribution needs. Direct the movement, storage, and processing of inventory.**

**Major Work Tasks:** Select transportation routes to maximize economy by combining shipments or consolidating warehousing and distribution. Develop material costs forecasts or standard cost lists. Assess appropriate material handling equipment needs and staffing levels to load, unload, move, or store materials. Appraise vendor manufacturing ability through on-site visits and measurements. Negotiate prices and terms with suppliers, vendors, or freight forwarders. Monitor supplier performance to assess ability to meet quality and delivery requirements. Monitor forecasts and quotas to identify changes or to determine their effect on supply chain activities. Meet with suppliers to discuss performance metrics, to provide performance feedback, or to discuss production forecasts or changes. Implement new or improved supply chain processes. Collaborate with other departments, such as procurement, engineering, and quality assurance, to identify or qualify new suppliers. Document physical supply chain processes, such as workflows, cycle times, position responsibilities, or system flows. Develop or implement procedures or systems to evaluate or select suppliers. Design or implement plant warehousing strategies for production materials or finished products. Confer with supply chain planners to forecast demand or create supply plans that ensure availability of materials or products. Define performance metrics for measurement, comparison, or evaluation of supply chain factors, such as product cost or quality. Analyze inventories to determine how to increase inventory turns, reduce waste, or optimize customer service. Analyze information about supplier performance or procurement program success. Participate in the coordination of engineering changes, product line extensions, or new product launches to ensure orderly and timely transitions in material or production flow. Manage activities related to strategic or tactical purchasing, material requirements planning, inventory control, warehousing, or receiving. Develop procedures for coordination of supply chain management with other functional areas, such as sales, marketing, finance, production, or quality assurance.

**Related Knowledge/Courses:** Production and Processing; Transportation; Economics and Accounting; Administration and Management; Geography; Sales and Marketing.

**Personality Types:** Enterprising–Conventional.

**Skills:** Management of material resources; management of financial resources; systems evaluation; negotiation; monitoring; management of personnel resources; systems analysis; complex problem solving.

**Physical Environment:** Indoors; sitting. **Structural Environment:** Freedom to make decisions; structured versus unstructured work; frequency of decision making; impact of decisions on coworkers or company results; time pressure; importance of being exact or accurate.

### JOB SPECIALIZATION: WIND ENERGY OPERATIONS MANAGERS

**Manage wind field operations, including personnel, maintenance activities, financial activities, and planning.**

**Major Work Tasks:** Train or coordinate the training of employees in operations, safety, environmental issues, or technical issues. Track and maintain records for wind operations, such as site performance, downtime events, parts usage, or substation events. Provide technical support to wind field customers, employees, or subcontractors. Manage warranty repair or replacement services. Order parts, tools, or equipment needed to maintain, restore, or improve wind field operations. Maintain operations records, such as work orders, site inspection forms, or other documentation. Review, negotiate, or approve wind farm contracts. Recruit or select wind operations employees, contractors, or subcontractors. Monitor and maintain records of daily facility operations. Estimate costs associated with operations, including repairs or preventive maintenance. Establish goals, objectives, or priorities for wind field operations. Develop relationships and communicate with customers, site managers, developers, land owners, authorities, utility representatives, or residents. Develop processes or procedures for wind operations, including transitioning from construction to commercial operations. Prepare wind field operational budgets. Supervise employees or subcontractors to ensure quality of work or adherence to safety regulations or policies. Oversee the maintenance of wind field equipment or structures, such as towers, transformers, electrical collector systems, roadways, or other site assets.

**Related Knowledge/Courses:** No data available.

**Personality Types:** Enterprising–Conventional–Realistic.

**Skills:** No data available.

**Physical Environment:** No data available. **Structural Environment:** No data available.

### JOB SPECIALIZATION: WIND ENERGY PROJECT MANAGERS

**Lead or manage the development and evaluation of potential wind energy business opportunities, including environmental studies,**

permitting, and proposals. May also manage construction of projects.

**Major Work Tasks:** Supervise the work of subcontractors or consultants to ensure quality and conformance to specifications or budgets. Prepare requests for proposals (RFPs) for wind project construction or equipment acquisition. Manage site assessments or environmental studies for wind fields. Lead or support negotiations involving tax agreements or abatements, power purchase agreements, land use, or interconnection agreements. Update schedules, estimates, forecasts, or budgets for wind projects. Review or evaluate proposals or bids to make recommendations regarding awarding of contracts. Provide verbal or written project status reports to project teams, management, subcontractors, customers, or owners. Review civil design, engineering, or construction technical documentation to ensure compliance with applicable government or industrial codes, standards, requirements, or regulations. Provide technical support for the design, construction, or commissioning of wind farm projects. Prepare wind project documentation, including diagrams or layouts. Manage wind project costs to stay within budget limits. Develop scope of work for wind project functions, such as design, site assessment, environmental studies, surveying, or field support services. Coordinate or direct development, energy assessment, engineering, or construction activities to ensure that wind project needs and objectives are met. Prepare or assist in the preparation of applications for environmental, building, or other required permits. Create wind energy project plans, including project scope, goals, tasks, resources, schedules, costs, contingencies, or other project information.

**Related Knowledge/Courses:** No data available.

**Personality Types:** Enterprising–Conventional–Investigative.

**Skills:** No data available.

**Physical Environment:** No data available.
**Structural Environment:** No data available.

## Market Research Analysts and Marketing Specialists

**Research market conditions in local, regional, or national areas, or gather information to determine potential sales of a product or service, or create a marketing campaign.**

- Average annual earnings: $60,300
- Middle 50% of earners: $43,830–$85,090
- Earnings growth potential: High (44.8%)
- Growth: 41.2%
- Annual job openings: 19,180
- Self-employed: 5.4%

**Considerations for Job Outlook:** Overall job prospects for market research analysts are expected to be good. Rapid employment growth in most industries means good job opportunities should be available throughout the economy. Because many positions require a master's degree, those with a bachelor's degree are expected to face strong competition for jobs. Those with a strong background in statistical and data analysis or related work experience will have better job opportunities. Prospects should be best for job seekers with a master's degree in market research, marketing, statistics, or business administration. Analysts may find more opportunities in consulting and market research firms, as companies without established marketing or research departments often find it easier to hire a person outside the organization to perform market research services.

**Major Work Tasks:** Collect and analyze data on customer demographics, preferences, needs, and buying habits to identify potential markets and factors affecting product demand. Prepare reports of findings, illustrating data graphically and translating complex findings into written text. Measure and assess customer and employee satisfaction. Forecast and track

**330**

## BEST-PAYING INDUSTRIES

| Industry | Median Earnings | Workforce |
|---|---|---|
| Management of Companies and Enterprises | $67,330 | 35,990 |
| Professional, Scientific, and Technical Services | $60,850 | 118,230 |

## BEST-PAYING METROPOLITAN AREAS

| Metro Area | Median Earnings | Workforce |
|---|---|---|
| San Francisco–Oakland–Fremont, CA | $79,900 | 15,250 |
| Seattle-Tacoma-Bellevue, WA | $77,870 | 10,360 |
| New York–Northern New Jersey–Long Island, NY-NJ-PA | $71,120 | 39,940 |
| Washington-Arlington-Alexandria, DC-VA-MD-WV | $66,690 | 19,400 |
| Minneapolis–St. Paul–Bloomington, MN-WI | $64,920 | 9,700 |
| Boston-Cambridge-Quincy, MA-NH | $64,580 | 13,070 |
| Philadelphia-Camden-Wilmington, PA-NJ-DE-MD | $63,750 | 12,850 |
| Dallas–Fort Worth–Arlington, TX | $61,510 | 8,940 |
| Los Angeles–Long Beach–Santa Ana, CA | $60,710 | 24,250 |
| Atlanta–Sandy Springs–Marietta, GA | $59,990 | 8,370 |
| Chicago-Naperville-Joliet, IL-IN-WI | $58,630 | 12,590 |

marketing and sales trends, analyzing collected data. Seek and provide information to help companies determine their position in the marketplace. Measure the effectiveness of marketing, advertising, and communications programs and strategies. Conduct research on consumer opinions and marketing strategies, collaborating with marketing professionals, statisticians, pollsters, and other professionals. Attend staff conferences to provide management with information and proposals concerning the promotion, distribution, design, and pricing of company products or services. Gather data on competitors and analyze their prices, sales, and method of marketing and distribution. Monitor industry statistics and follow trends in trade literature. Devise and evaluate methods and procedures for collecting data, such as surveys, opinion polls, or questionnaires, or arrange to obtain existing data. Develop and implement procedures for identifying advertising needs. Direct trained survey interviewers.

**Usual Educational Requirement:** Bachelor's degree. **Relevant Educational Programs**: Applied Economics; Consumer Merchandising/Retailing Management; International Marketing; Marketing Research; Marketing/Marketing Management, General. **Related Knowledge/Courses:** Sales and Marketing; Clerical Practices; Sociology and Anthropology; Economics and Accounting; Personnel and Human Resources; Computers and Electronics. **Work Experience Needed:** None. **On-the-Job Training Needed:** None. **Certification/Licensure:** Voluntary certification by association.

**Personality Types:** Investigative–Enterprising–Conventional. **Key Career Cluster:** 14 Marketing, Sales, and Service. **Key Career Pathway:** 14.5 Marketing Information Management and Research.

**Skills:** Programming; operations analysis; systems analysis; systems evaluation; reading comprehension; science; management of financial resources; mathematics.

**Physical Environment:** Indoors; sitting. **Structural Environment:** Freedom to make decisions; structured versus unstructured work; importance of being exact or accurate; time pressure; impact of decisions on co-workers or company results; level of competition.

## Marketing Managers

**Plan, direct, or coordinate marketing policies and programs and identify potential customers.**

- Average annual earnings: $119,480
- Middle 50% of earners: $85,740–$160,810
- Earnings growth potential: High (47.6%)
- Growth: 13.6%
- Annual job openings: 7,600
- Self-employed: 5.5%

**Considerations for Job Outlook:** Advertising, promotions, and marketing manager positions are highly desirable and are often sought by other managers and experienced professionals. As a result, strong competition is expected. With Internet-based advertising becoming more important, advertising managers who can navigate the digital world should have the best prospects.

**Major Work Tasks:** Develop pricing strategies, balancing firm objectives and customer satisfaction. Identify, develop, or evaluate marketing strategy, based on knowledge of establishment objectives, market characteristics, and cost and markup factors. Evaluate the financial aspects of product development, such as budgets, expenditures, research and development appropriations, or return-on-investment and profit-loss projections. Formulate, direct, and coordinate marketing activities and policies to promote products and services, working with advertising and promotion managers. Direct the hiring, training, or performance evaluations of marketing or sales staff

### BEST-PAYING INDUSTRIES

| Industry | Median Earnings | Workforce |
|---|---|---|
| Professional, Scientific, and Technical Services | $129,640 | 34,190 |
| Management of Companies and Enterprises | $124,670 | 28,140 |
| Merchant Whole-salers, Durable Goods | $118,940 | 9,100 |

### BEST-PAYING METROPOLITAN AREAS

| Metro Area | Median Earnings | Workforce |
|---|---|---|
| San Jose–Sunnyvale–Santa Clara, CA | $166,840 | 4,330 |
| San Francisco–Oakland–Fremont, CA | $152,370 | 6,100 |
| New York–Northern New Jersey–Long Island, NY-NJ-PA | $151,930 | 16,420 |
| Washington-Arlington-Alexandria, DC-VA-MD-WV | $143,810 | 5,850 |
| Philadelphia-Camden-Wilmington, PA-NJ-DE-MD | $140,220 | 3,990 |
| Boston-Cambridge-Quincy, MA-NH | $132,590 | 6,900 |
| Los Angeles–Long Beach–Santa Ana, CA | $129,600 | 11,010 |
| Seattle-Tacoma-Bellevue, WA | $128,980 | 5,110 |
| Dallas–Fort Worth–Arlington, TX | $122,740 | 4,180 |
| Atlanta–Sandy Springs–Marietta, GA | $118,000 | 4,170 |
| Minneapolis–St. Paul–Bloomington, MN-WI | $117,670 | 6,600 |
| Chicago-Naperville-Joliet, IL-IN-WI | $104,140 | 7,910 |

and oversee their daily activities. Compile lists, describing product or service offerings. Use sales forecasting or strategic planning to ensure the sale and profitability of products, lines, or services, analyzing business developments and monitoring market trends. Select products or accessories to be displayed at trade or special production shows. Coordinate or participate in promotional activities or trade shows, working with developers, advertisers, or production managers, to market products or services. Initiate market research studies or analyze their findings. Consult with buying personnel to gain advice regarding the types of products or services expected to be in demand. Conduct economic or commercial surveys to identify potential markets for products or services. Negotiate contracts with vendors or distributors to manage product distribution, establishing distribution networks or developing distribution strategies. Consult with product development personnel on product specifications such as design, color, or packaging. Confer with legal staff to resolve problems, such as copyright infringement or royalty sharing with outside producers or distributors. Advise business or other groups on local, national, or international factors affecting the buying or selling of products or services. Consult with buying personnel to gain advice regarding environmentally sound or sustainable products. Develop business cases for environmental marketing strategies.

**Usual Educational Requirement:** Bachelor's degree. **Relevant Educational Programs**: Apparel and Textile Marketing Management; Consumer Merchandising/Retailing Management; International Marketing; Marketing Research; Marketing, Other; Marketing/Marketing Management, General; Pharmaceutical Marketing and Management. **Related Knowledge/ Courses:** Sales and Marketing; Customer and Personal Service; Personnel and Human Resources; Communications and Media; Economics and Accounting; Sociology and

Anthropology. **Work Experience Needed:** 1 to 5 years. **On-the-Job Training Needed:** None. **Certification/Licensure:** None.

**Personality Types:** Enterprising–Conventional. **Key Career Cluster:** 04 Business, Management, and Administration. **Key Career Pathway:** 4.5 Marketing.

**Skills:** Management of financial resources; operations analysis; persuasion; negotiation; management of material resources; management of personnel resources; systems evaluation; systems analysis.

**Physical Environment:** Indoors; sitting. **Structural Environment:** Structured versus unstructured work; freedom to make decisions; impact of decisions on co-workers or company results; time pressure; level of competition; frequency of decision making.

## Materials Engineers

**Evaluate materials and develop machinery and processes to manufacture materials for use in products that must meet specialized design and performance specifications.**

- Average annual earnings: $85,150
- Middle 50% of earners: $66,900–$107,510
- Earnings growth potential: Medium (37.9%)
- Growth: 8.7%
- Annual job openings: 810
- Self-employed: 0.0%

**Considerations for Job Outlook:** Despite the relatively lower projected growth rate for this occupation, there should be favorable job prospects as materials engineers are needed to fill positions as more experienced materials engineers get promoted or retire.

**Major Work Tasks:** Analyze product failure data and laboratory test results to determine causes of problems and develop solutions. Monitor material performance and evaluate material deterioration. Supervise the work of

333

## Your Guide to High-Paying Careers

### BEST-PAYING INDUSTRIES

| Industry | Median Earnings | Workforce |
|---|---|---|
| Federal, State, and Local Government | $104,190 | 1,640 |
| Transportation Equipment Manufacturing | $93,690 | 4,950 |
| Computer and Electronic Product Manufacturing | $83,950 | 2,640 |
| Professional, Scientific, and Technical Services | $83,140 | 4,150 |
| Primary Metal Manufacturing | $77,870 | 2,110 |

### BEST-PAYING METROPOLITAN AREAS

| Metro Area | Median Earnings | Workforce |
|---|---|---|
| Washington-Arlington-Alexandria, DC-VA-MD-WV | $112,480 | 470 |
| San Jose–Sunnyvale–Santa Clara, CA | $102,340 | 520 |
| Los Angeles–Long Beach–Santa Ana, CA | $98,400 | 1,600 |
| Boston-Cambridge-Quincy, MA-NH | $87,820 | 1,000 |
| Phoenix-Mesa-Scottsdale, AZ | $87,640 | 500 |
| Chicago-Naperville-Joliet, IL-IN-WI | $87,120 | 850 |
| New York–Northern New Jersey–Long Island, NY-NJ-PA | $85,170 | 550 |
| Houston–Sugar Land–Baytown, TX | $84,900 | 510 |
| Detroit-Warren-Livonia, MI | $82,090 | 820 |
| Dallas–Fort Worth–Arlington, TX | $72,230 | 660 |

technologists, technicians, and other engineers and scientists. Design and direct the testing or control of processing procedures. Evaluate technical specifications and economic factors relating to process or product design objectives. Conduct or supervise tests on raw materials or finished products to ensure their quality. Perform managerial functions, such as preparing proposals and budgets, analyzing labor costs, and writing reports. Solve problems in a number of engineering fields, such as mechanical, chemical, electrical, civil, nuclear, and aerospace. Plan and evaluate new projects, consulting with other engineers and corporate executives as necessary. Review new product plans and make recommendations for material selection based on design objectives, such as strength, weight, heat resistance, electrical conductivity, and cost. Modify properties of metal alloys, using thermal and mechanical treatments. Guide technical staff engaged in developing materials for specific uses in projected products or devices. Plan and implement laboratory operations for the purpose of developing material and fabrication procedures that meet cost, product specification, and performance standards. Determine appropriate methods for fabricating and joining materials. Supervise production and testing processes in industrial settings, such as metal refining facilities, smelting or foundry operations, or nonmetallic materials production operations. Replicate the characteristics of materials and their components with computers. Teach in colleges and universities. Design processing plants and equipment. Conduct training sessions on new material products, applications, or manufacturing methods for customers and their employees. Write for technical magazines, journals, and trade association publications.

**Usual Educational Requirement:** Bachelor's degree. **Relevant Educational Programs**: Ceramic Sciences and Engineering; Materials Engineering; Metallurgical Engineering; Polymer/Plastics Engineering; Textile Sciences and

Engineering. **Related Knowledge/Courses:** Engineering and Technology; Chemistry; Physics; Production and Processing; Design; Mechanical. **Work Experience Needed:** None. **On-the-Job Training Needed:** None. **Certification/Licensure:** Licensure beyond entry level in some states.

**Personality Types:** Investigative–Realistic–Enterprising. **Key Career Cluster:** 15 Science, Technology, Engineering, and Mathematics. **Key Career Pathway:** 15.1 Engineering and Technology.

**Skills:** Science; operations analysis; technology design; mathematics; management of financial resources; quality control analysis; active learning; management of material resources.

**Physical Environment:** Indoors; sitting. **Structural Environment:** Freedom to make decisions; importance of being exact or accurate; structured versus unstructured work; impact of decisions on co-workers or company results; time pressure; consequence of error.

## Mathematical Science Teachers, Postsecondary

*See Teachers, Postsecondary.*

## Mechanical Engineers

**Perform engineering duties in planning and designing tools, engines, machines, and other mechanically functioning equipment.**

- Average annual earnings: $80,580
- Middle 50% of earners: $64,530–$100,620
- Earnings growth potential: Medium (35.4%)
- Growth: 8.8%
- Annual job openings: 9,960
- Self-employed: 2.3%

### BEST-PAYING INDUSTRIES

| Industry | Median Earnings | Workforce |
|---|---|---|
| Federal, State, and Local Government | $90,550 | 13,340 |
| Professional, Scientific, and Technical Services | $85,180 | 73,670 |
| Computer and Electronic Product Manufacturing | $84,860 | 19,730 |
| Transportation Equipment Manufacturing | $83,540 | 32,660 |
| Machinery Manufacturing | $72,270 | 35,290 |
| Fabricated Metal Product Manufacturing | $69,890 | 15,820 |

### BEST-PAYING METROPOLITAN AREAS

| Metro Area | Median Earnings | Workforce |
|---|---|---|
| Washington-Arlington-Alexandria, DC-VA-MD-WV | $95,700 | 5,350 |
| Houston–Sugar Land–Baytown, TX | $93,900 | 7,570 |
| Boston-Cambridge-Quincy, MA-NH | $89,810 | 7,500 |
| Los Angeles–Long Beach–Santa Ana, CA | $88,110 | 8,660 |
| New York–Northern New Jersey–Long Island, NY-NJ-PA | $86,470 | 8,640 |
| Dallas–Fort Worth–Arlington, TX | $83,280 | 5,220 |
| Chicago-Naperville-Joliet, IL-IN-WI | $76,550 | 6,980 |

**Considerations for Job Outlook:** Although prospects for mechanical engineers overall are expected to be good, they will be best for those with training in the latest software tools, such as Advanced Visualization Process (AVP). AVP allows engineers and designers to take a project from the conceptual phase directly to a finished product, eliminating the need for prototypes.

**Major Work Tasks:** Read and interpret blueprints, technical drawings, schematics, or computer-generated reports. Confer with engineers or other personnel to implement operating procedures, resolve system malfunctions, or provide technical information. Research and analyze customer design proposals, specifications, manuals, or other data to evaluate the feasibility, cost, or maintenance requirements of designs or applications. Specify system components or direct modification of products to ensure conformance with engineering design and performance specifications. Research, design, evaluate, install, operate, and maintain mechanical products, equipment, systems and processes to meet requirements, applying knowledge of engineering principles. Investigate equipment failures and difficulties to diagnose faulty operation and to make recommendations to maintenance crew. Assist drafters in developing the structural design of products using drafting tools or computer-assisted design (CAD) or drafting equipment and software. Conduct research that tests or analyzes the feasibility, design, operation, or performance of equipment, components, or systems. Recommend design modifications to eliminate machine or system malfunctions. Develop and test models of alternate designs and processing methods to assess feasibility, operating condition effects, possible new applications, and necessity of modification. Develop, coordinate, or monitor all aspects of production, including selection of manufacturing methods, fabrication, or operation of product designs. Write performance requirements for product development or engineering projects. Provide feedback to design engineers on customer problems or needs. Oversee installation, operation, maintenance, or repair to ensure that machines or equipment are installed and functioning according to specifications. Estimate costs and submit bids for engineering, construction, or extraction projects, and prepare contract documents. Perform personnel functions such as supervision of production workers, technicians, technologists and other engineers, or design of evaluation programs. Solicit new business and provide technical customer service.

**Usual Educational Requirement:** Bachelor's degree. **Relevant Educational Programs**: Electromechanical Engineering; Mechanical Engineering. **Related Knowledge/Courses:** Design; Engineering and Technology; Physics; Mechanical Devices; Production and Processing; Mathematics. **Work Experience Needed:** None. **On-the-Job Training Needed:** None. **Certification/Licensure:** Licensure for offering services to public.

**Personality Types:** Investigative–Realistic–Conventional. **Key Career Cluster:** 15 Science, Technology, Engineering, and Mathematics. **Key Career Pathway:** 15.1 Engineering and Technology.

**Skills:** Science; technology design; operations analysis; installation; mathematics; programming; quality control analysis; troubleshooting.

**Physical Environment:** Indoors; sitting; noise. **Structural Environment:** Importance of being exact or accurate; structured versus unstructured work; freedom to make decisions; impact of decisions on co-workers or company results; time pressure; level of competition.

## JOB SPECIALIZATION: AUTOMOTIVE ENGINEERS

**Develop new or improved designs for vehicle structural members, engines, transmissions and other vehicle systems, using computer-**

assisted design technology. Direct building, modification, and testing of vehicle and components.

**Major Work Tasks:** Read current literature, attend meetings or conferences, or talk with colleagues to stay abreast of new automotive technology or competitive products. Establish production or quality control standards. Prepare or present technical or project status reports. Develop or implement operating methods or procedures. Write, review, or maintain engineering documentation. Conduct research studies to develop new concepts in the field of automotive engineering. Coordinate production activities with other functional units, such as procurement, maintenance, or quality control. Provide technical direction to other engineers or engineering support personnel. Perform failure, variation, or root cause analyses. Develop or integrate control feature requirements. Develop engineering specifications or cost estimates for automotive design concepts. Develop calibration methodologies, test methodologies, or tools. Conduct automotive design reviews. Calibrate vehicle systems, including control algorithms or other software systems. Build models for algorithm or control feature verification testing. Alter or modify designs to obtain specified functional or operational performance. Design or analyze automobile systems in areas such as aerodynamics, alternate fuels, ergonomics, hybrid power, brakes, transmissions, steering, calibration, safety, or diagnostics. Conduct or direct system-level automotive testing. Design control systems or algorithms for purposes such as automotive energy management, emissions management, or increased operational safety or performance. Create design alternatives for vehicle components, such as camless or dual-clutch engines or alternative air-conditioning systems, to increase fuel efficiency. Design vehicles for increased recyclability or use of natural, renewable, or recycled materials in vehicle construction. Design vehicles that use lighter materials, such as aluminum, magnesium alloy, or plastic, to improve fuel efficiency. Develop specifications for vehicles powered by alternative fuels or alternative power methods.

**Related Knowledge/Courses:** No data available.

**Personality Types:** Realistic–Investigative.

**Skills:** No data available.

**Physical Environment:** No data available.

**Structural Environment:** No data available.

## JOB SPECIALIZATION: FUEL CELL ENGINEERS

**Design, evaluate, modify, and construct fuel cell components and systems for transportation, stationary, or portable applications.**

**Major Work Tasks:** Write technical reports or proposals related to engineering projects. Read current literature, attend meetings or conferences, or talk with colleagues to stay abreast of new technology or competitive products. Validate design of fuel cells, fuel cell components, or fuel cell systems. Simulate or model fuel cell, motor, or other system information, using simulation software programs. Recommend or implement changes to fuel cell system designs. Provide technical consultation or direction related to the development or production of fuel cell systems. Plan or conduct experiments to validate new materials, optimize start-up protocols, reduce conditioning time, or examine contaminant tolerance. Integrate electric drive subsystems with other vehicle systems to optimize performance or mitigate faults. Identify or define vehicle and system integration challenges for fuel cell vehicles. Fabricate prototypes of fuel cell components, assemblies, stacks, or systems. Develop fuel cell materials or fuel cell test equipment. Conduct post-service or failure analyses, using electromechanical diagnostic principles or procedures. Design or implement fuel cell testing or development programs. Characterize component or fuel cell performances by generating operating maps, defining operating conditions, identifying design refinements, or executing durability assessments. Calculate the efficiency or power output of a fuel cell system or process. Analyze fuel cell or related test data, using statistical software. Design fuel cell systems, subsystems, stacks, assemblies, or components, such as electric traction motors or power electronics. Prepare test stations, instrumentation, or data acquisition systems for use in specific tests of fuel cell components or systems. Plan or implement fuel cell cost reduction or product improvement projects in collaboration with other engineers, suppliers, support personnel, or customers. Coordinate fuel cell engineering or test schedules with departments outside engineering, such as manufacturing. Authorize release of fuel cell parts, components, or subsystems for production.

**Related Knowledge/Courses:** No data available.

**Personality Types:** Realistic–Investigative.

**Skills:** No data available.

**Physical Environment:** No data available.
**Structural Environment:** No data available.

## Medical and Clinical Laboratory Technologists

**Perform complex medical laboratory tests for diagnosis, treatment, and prevention of disease. May train or supervise staff.**

- Average annual earnings: $57,580
- Middle 50% of earners: $48,610–$68,930
- Earnings growth potential: Low (31.3%)
- Growth: 11.3%
- Annual job openings: 5,210
- Self-employed: 0.8%

**Considerations for Job Outlook:** An increase in the aging population will lead to a greater need to diagnose medical conditions, such as cancer or type 2 diabetes, through laboratory procedures. Medical laboratory technologists and technicians will be needed to use and

### BEST-PAYING INDUSTRIES

| Industry | Median Earnings | Workforce |
|---|---|---|
| Hospitals | $58,260 | 96,780 |
| Ambulatory Health-Care Services | $55,510 | 46,700 |

### BEST-PAYING METROPOLITAN AREAS

| Metro Area | Median Earnings | Workforce |
|---|---|---|
| Los Angeles–Long Beach–Santa Ana, CA | $77,700 | 4,280 |
| New York–Northern New Jersey–Long Island, NY-NJ-PA | $66,160 | 10,400 |
| Washington-Arlington-Alexandria, DC-VA-MD-WV | $62,250 | 3,360 |
| Philadelphia-Camden-Wilmington, PA-NJ-DE-MD | $61,100 | 3,720 |
| Dallas–Fort Worth–Arlington, TX | $57,520 | 3,930 |
| Houston–Sugar Land–Baytown, TX | $56,910 | 3,640 |
| Chicago-Naperville-Joliet, IL-IN-WI | $55,790 | 4,180 |

maintain the equipment needed for diagnosis and treatment.

**Major Work Tasks:** Analyze laboratory findings to check the accuracy of the results. Conduct chemical analysis of body fluids, including blood, urine, or spinal fluid, to determine presence of normal or abnormal components. Operate, calibrate, or maintain equipment used in quantitative or qualitative analysis, such as spectrophotometers, calorimeters, flame photometers, or computer-controlled analyzers. Enter data from analysis of medical tests or clinical results into computer for storage. Analyze samples of biological material for chemical content or reaction. Set up, clean, and maintain laboratory equipment. Provide technical information about test results to physicians, family members, or researchers. Supervise, train, or direct lab assistants, medical and clinical laboratory technicians or technologists, or other medical laboratory workers engaged in laboratory testing. Develop, standardize, evaluate, or modify procedures, techniques, or tests used in the analysis of specimens or in medical laboratory experiments. Cultivate, isolate, or assist in identifying microbial organisms or perform various tests on these microorganisms. Establish or monitor quality assurance programs or activities to ensure the accuracy of laboratory results. Collect and study blood samples to determine the number of cells, their morphology, or their blood group, blood type, or compatibility for transfusion purposes, using microscopic techniques. Obtain, cut, stain, and mount biological material on slides for microscopic study and diagnosis, following standard laboratory procedures. Select and prepare specimens and media for cell cultures, using aseptic technique and knowledge of medium components and cell requirements. Conduct medical research under direction of microbiologist or biochemist. Harvest cell cultures at optimum time, based on knowledge of cell cycle differences and culture conditions.

**Usual Educational Requirement:** Bachelor's degree. **Relevant Educational Programs**: Clinical Laboratory Science/Medical Technology/Technologist Training; Clinical/Medical Laboratory Science and Allied Professions, Other; Cytogenetics/Genetics/Clinical Genetics Technology/Technologist; Cytotechnology/Cytotechnologist; Histologic Technology/Histotechnologist Training. **Related Knowledge/Courses:** Biology; Medicine and Dentistry; Chemistry; Mechanical Devices; Customer and Personal Service; Clerical. **Work Experience Needed:** None. **On-the-Job Training Needed:** None. **Certification/Licensure:** Licensure.

**Personality Types:** Investigative–Realistic–Conventional. **Key Career Cluster:** 08 Health Science. **Key Career Pathway:** 8.2 Diagnostics Services.

**Skills:** Science; equipment selection; equipment maintenance; operation monitoring; quality control analysis; operation and control; troubleshooting; repairing.

**Physical Environment:** Indoors; standing; using hands; repetitive motions; contaminants; exposed to disease or infections. **Structural Environment:** Importance of being exact or accurate; frequency of decision making; time pressure; impact of decisions on co-workers or company results; freedom to make decisions; importance of repeating same tasks.

### JOB SPECIALIZATION: CYTOGENETIC TECHNOLOGISTS

**Analyze chromosomes found in biological specimens, such as amniotic fluids, bone marrow, and blood to aid in the study, diagnosis, or treatment of genetic diseases.**

**Major Work Tasks:** Develop and implement training programs for trainees, medical students, resident physicians or post-doctoral fellows. Stain slides to make chromosomes visible for microscopy. Summarize test results and report to appropriate authorities. Select or prepare specimens and media for cell cultures, using aseptic techniques, knowledge of medium components, or cell nutritional requirements. Select banding methods to permit identification of chromosome pairs. Identify appropriate methods of specimen collection, preservation, or transport. Prepare slides of cell cultures following standard procedures. Select appropriate methods of preparation and storage of media to maintain potential of hydrogen (pH), sterility, or ability to support growth. Harvest cell cultures, using substances such as mitotic arrestants, cell releasing agents, and cell fixatives. Create chromosome images using computer imaging systems. Determine optimal time sequences and methods for manual or robotic cell harvests. Examine chromosomes found in biological specimens to detect abnormalities. Recognize and report abnormalities in the color, size, shape, composition, or pattern of cells. Communicate test results or technical information to patients, physicians, family members, or researchers. Prepare biological specimens, such as amniotic fluids, bone marrow, tumors, chorionic villi, and blood, for chromosome examinations. Count numbers of chromosomes and identify the structural abnormalities by viewing culture slides through microscopes, light microscopes, or photomicroscopes. Arrange and attach chromosomes in numbered pairs on karyotype charts, using standard genetics laboratory practices and nomenclature, to identify normal or abnormal chromosomes. Analyze chromosomes found in biological specimens to aid diagnoses and treatments for genetic diseases, such as congenital birth defects, fertility problems, and hematological disorders. Input details of specimens into logs or computer systems. Maintain laboratory equipment, such as photomicroscopes, inverted microscopes, and standard darkroom equipment. Supervise subordinate laboratory staff.

**Related Knowledge/Courses:** Biology; Chemistry; Medicine and Dentistry; Education and Training.

**Personality Types:** Investigative–Realistic–Conventional.

**Skills:** Science; reading comprehension; writing; active learning; speaking; mathematics; instructing; active listening.

**Physical Environment:** Indoors; sitting; using hands; repetitive motions; contaminants; exposed to disease or infections. **Structural Environment:** Importance of being exact or accurate; importance of repeating same tasks; time pressure; consequence of error; frequency of decision making; impact of decisions on co-workers or company results.

## JOB SPECIALIZATION: CYTOTECHNOLOGISTS

**Stain, mount, and study cells to detect evidence of cancer, hormonal abnormalities, and other pathological conditions following established standards and practices.**

**Major Work Tasks:** Examine cell samples to detect abnormalities in the color, shape, or size of cellular components and patterns. Examine specimens using microscopes to evaluate specimen quality. Prepare and analyze samples, such as Papanicolaou (PAP) smear body fluids and fine needle aspirations (FNAs), to detect abnormal conditions. Provide patient clinical data or microscopic findings to assist pathologists in the preparation of pathology reports. Assist pathologists or other physicians to collect cell samples by FNA biopsies. Document specimens by verifying patients' and specimens' information. Maintain effective laboratory operations by adhering to standards of specimen collection, preparation, or laboratory safety. Submit slides with abnormal cell structures to pathologists for further examination. Adjust, maintain, or repair laboratory equipment, such as microscopes. Assign tasks or coordinate task assignments to ensure adequate performance of laboratory activities. Attend continuing education programs that address laboratory issues. Examine specimens to detect abnormal hormone conditions. Prepare cell samples by applying special staining techniques, such as chromosomal staining, to differentiate cells or cell components.

**Related Knowledge/Courses:** Biology; Medicine and Dentistry; Chemistry; Clerical.

**Personality Types:** Investigative–Realistic.

**Skills:** Science; reading comprehension; writing; mathematics; operation monitoring; judgment and decision making; instructing; learning strategies.

**Physical Environment:** Indoors; sitting; using hands; repetitive motions; contaminants; exposed to disease or infections. **Structural Envi-**

340

ronment: Importance of being exact or accurate; importance of repeating same tasks; frequency of decision making; impact of decisions on co-workers or company results; consequence of error; time pressure.

## JOB SPECIALIZATION: HISTOTECHNOLOGISTS AND HISTOLOGIC TECHNICIANS

**Prepare histologic slides from tissue sections for microscopic examination and diagnosis by pathologists. May assist in research studies.**

**Major Work Tasks:** Cut sections of body tissues for microscopic examination using microtomes. Embed tissue specimens into paraffin wax blocks or infiltrate tissue specimens with wax. Freeze tissue specimens. Mount tissue specimens on glass slides. Stain tissue specimens with dyes or other chemicals to make cell details visible under microscopes. Examine slides under microscopes to ensure tissue preparation meets laboratory requirements. Identify tissue structures or cell components to be used in the diagnosis, prevention, or treatment of diseases. Operate computerized laboratory equipment to dehydrate, decalcify, or microincinerate tissue samples. Perform procedures associated with histochemistry to prepare specimens for immunofluorescence or microscopy. Maintain laboratory equipment, such as microscopes, mass spectrometers, microtomes, immunostainers, tissue processors, embedding centers, and water baths. Prepare or use prepared tissue specimens for teaching, research, or diagnostic purposes. Supervise histology laboratory activities. Teach students or other staff. Perform electron microscopy or mass spectrometry to analyze specimens.

**Related Knowledge/Courses:** Biology; Chemistry; Medicine and Dentistry; Production and Processing; Mechanical Devices; Education and Training.

**Personality Types:** Realistic–Investigative–Conventional.

**Skills:** Science; equipment maintenance; equipment selection; repairing; operation and con-trol; troubleshooting; mathematics; operation monitoring.

**Physical Environment:** Indoors; sitting; using hands; repetitive motions; contaminants; exposed to disease or infections. **Structural Environment:** Time pressure; importance of being exact or accurate; importance of repeating same tasks; consequence of error; frequency of decision making; freedom to make decisions.

# Medical and Health Services Managers

**Plan, direct, or coordinate medical and health services in hospitals, clinics, managed care organizations, public health agencies, or similar organizations.**

- Average annual earnings: $88,580
- Middle 50% of earners: $69,160–$114,920
- Earnings growth potential: Medium (39.1%)
- Growth: 22.4%
- Annual job openings: 14,190
- Self-employed: 4.2%

**Considerations for Job Outlook:** As the large baby-boom population ages and people remain active later in life, the health-care industry as a whole will see an increase in the demand for medical services. This increase will in turn result in an increase in the number of

### BEST-PAYING INDUSTRIES

| Industry | Median Earnings | Workforce |
|---|---|---|
| Hospitals | $95,030 | 121,070 |
| Federal, State, and Local Government | $93,640 | 24,970 |
| Ambulatory Health-Care Services | $81,610 | 80,720 |
| Nursing and Residential Care Facilities | $73,460 | 33,790 |

**341**

## Your Guide to High-Paying Careers

### BEST-PAYING METROPOLITAN AREAS

| Metro Area | Median Earnings | Workforce |
|---|---|---|
| New York–Northern New Jersey–Long Island, NY-NJ-PA | $108,150 | 24,510 |
| Los Angeles–Long Beach–Santa Ana, CA | $104,570 | 9,300 |
| Washington-Arlington-Alexandria, DC-VA-MD-WV | $99,420 | 7,470 |
| Boston-Cambridge-Quincy, MA-NH | $99,320 | 7,630 |
| Philadelphia-Camden-Wilmington, PA-NJ-DE-MD | $91,760 | 7,080 |
| Chicago-Naperville-Joliet, IL-IN-WI | $90,500 | 8,750 |

physicians, patients, and procedures, as well as in the number of facilities. Managers will be needed to organize and manage medical information and staffs in the health-care industry. There will likely be increased demand for nursing care facility administrators as well as baby boomers age. Employment is expected to grow in offices of health practitioners. Many services previously provided in hospitals will shift to these settings, especially as medical technologies improve. Demand in medical group practice management is expected to grow as medical group practices become larger and more complex.

**Major Work Tasks:** Direct, supervise, and evaluate work activities of medical, nursing, technical, clerical, service, maintenance, and other personnel. Establish objectives and evaluative or operational criteria for units they manage. Direct or conduct recruitment, hiring, and training of personnel. Develop and maintain computerized record management systems to store and process data, such as personnel activities and information, and to produce reports. Develop and implement organizational policies and procedures for the facility or medical unit. Conduct and administer fiscal operations, including accounting, planning budgets, authorizing expenditures, establishing rates for services, and coordinating financial reporting. Establish work schedules and assignments for staff, according to workload, space and equipment availability. Maintain communication between governing boards, medical staff, and department heads by attending board meetings and coordinating interdepartmental functioning. Monitor the use of diagnostic services, inpatient beds, facilities, and staff to ensure effective use of resources and assess the need for additional staff, equipment, and services. Maintain awareness of advances in medicine, computerized diagnostic and treatment equipment, data processing technology, government regulations, health insurance changes, and financing options. Manage change in integrated health-care delivery systems, such as work restructuring, technological innovations, and shifts in the focus of care. Prepare activity reports to inform management of the status and implementation plans of programs, services, and quality initiatives. Plan, implement, and administer programs and services in a health-care or medical facility, including personnel administration, training, and coordination of medical, nursing, and physical plant staff. Consult with medical, business, and community groups to discuss service problems, respond to community needs, enhance public relations, coordinate activities and plans, and promote health programs. Inspect facilities and recommend building or equipment modifications to ensure emergency readiness and compliance to access, safety, and sanitation regulations.

**Usual Educational Requirement:** Bachelor's degree. **Relevant Educational Programs:** Clinical Research Coordinator; Community Health and Preventive Medicine; Health Information/Medical Records Administration/Administrator; Health Policy Analysis; Health Services Ad-

342

ministration; Health Unit Manager/Ward Supervisor Training; Health/Health-Care Administration/Management; Hospital and Health-Care Facilities Administration/Management; Long-Term Care Administration/ Management; Nursing Administration; Nursing Practice; Public Health, General. **Related Knowledge/Courses:** Economics and Accounting; Personnel and Human Resources; Administration and Management; Sales and Marketing; Medicine and Dentistry; Law and Government. **Work Experience Needed:** None. **On-the-Job Training Needed:** None. **Certification/Licensure:** Licensure for some specializations.

**Personality Types:** Enterprising–Conventional–Social. **Key Career Cluster:** 04 Business, Management, and Administration. **Key Career Pathway:** 4.1 Management.

**Skills:** Management of financial resources; operations analysis; management of material resources; science; management of personnel resources; systems evaluation; coordination; time management.

**Physical Environment:** Indoors; sitting; exposed to disease or infections. **Structural Environment:** Impact of decisions on co-workers or company results; frequency of decision making; structured versus unstructured work; freedom to make decisions; importance of being exact or accurate; time pressure.

## Medical Scientists, Except Epidemiologists

**Conduct research dealing with the understanding of human diseases and the improvement of human health.**

- Average annual earnings: $76,980
- Middle 50% of earners: $53,380–$107,250
- Earnings growth potential: High (46.3%)
- Growth: 36.4%
- Annual job openings: 4,260
- Self-employed: 0.6%

### BEST-PAYING INDUSTRIES

| Industry | Median Earnings | Workforce |
|---|---|---|
| Professional, Scientific, and Technical Services | $87,450 | 37,310 |
| Ambulatory Health-Care Services | $76,940 | 8,410 |
| Hospitals | $70,020 | 14,360 |
| Educational Services | $54,800 | 21,210 |

### BEST-PAYING METROPOLITAN AREAS

| Metro Area | Median Earnings | Workforce |
|---|---|---|
| San Jose–Sunnyvale–Santa Clara, CA | $106,140 | 2,110 |
| Washington-Arlington-Alexandria, DC-VA-MD-WV | $100,130 | 3,020 |
| Philadelphia-Camden-Wilmington, PA-NJ-DE-MD | $98,400 | 3,680 |
| San Francisco–Oakland–Fremont, CA | $93,800 | 7,080 |
| Boston-Cambridge-Quincy, MA-NH | $91,750 | 8,560 |
| Chicago-Naperville-Joliet, IL-IN-WI | $85,850 | 2,460 |
| Durham, NC | $85,080 | 2,020 |
| Los Angeles–Long Beach–Santa Ana, CA | $83,030 | 7,460 |
| San Diego–Carlsbad–San Marcos, CA | $82,420 | 5,310 |
| New York–Northern New Jersey–Long Island, NY-NJ-PA | $79,880 | 5,440 |
| Baltimore-Towson, MD | $76,790 | 2,030 |
| Seattle-Tacoma-Bellevue, WA | $59,930 | 3,900 |
| Dallas–Fort Worth–Arlington, TX | $55,730 | 2,450 |

343

**Considerations for Job Outlook:** Ongoing medical research, as well as an increased reliance on pharmaceuticals, will likely maintain current levels of demand for medical scientists. A growing and aging population also is expected to increase demand for these scientists. Most employment growth for medical scientists over the next 10 years will likely be in private industry. Medical scientists will continue to be needed because they contribute to the development of treatments and medicines that improve human health.

**Major Work Tasks:** Plan and direct studies to investigate human or animal disease, preventive methods, and treatments for disease. Follow strict safety procedures when handling toxic materials to avoid contamination. Evaluate effects of drugs, gases, pesticides, parasites, and microorganisms at various levels. Study animal and human health and physiological processes. Conduct research to develop methodologies, instrumentation, and procedures for medical application, analyzing data and presenting findings to the scientific audience and general public. Write and publish articles in scientific journals. Teach principles of medicine and medical and laboratory procedures to physicians, residents, students, and technicians. Prepare and analyze organ, tissue, and cell samples to identify toxicity, bacteria, or microorganisms or to study cell structure. Standardize drug dosages, methods of immunization, and procedures for manufacture of drugs and medicinal compounds. Investigate cause, progress, life cycle, or mode of transmission of diseases or parasites. Confer with health departments, industry personnel, physicians, and others to develop health safety standards and public health improvement programs. Consult with and advise physicians, educators, researchers, and others regarding medical applications of physics, biology, and chemistry. Use equipment, such as atomic absorption spectrometers, electron microscopes, flow cytometers, and chromatography systems.

**Usual Educational Requirement:** Doctoral or professional degree. **Relevant Educational Programs**: Aerospace Physiology and Medicine; Anatomy; Biochemistry; Biomedical Sciences, General; Biophysics; Biostatistics; Cardiovascular Science; Cell Physiology; Cell/Cellular Biology and Histology; Endocrinology; Environmental Toxicology; Epidemiology; Exercise Physiology; Gerontology; Human/Medical Genetics; Immunology; Medical Microbiology and Bacteriology; Medical Science; Molecular Biology; Molecular Medicine; Molecular Pharmacology; Molecular Physiology; Molecular Toxicology; Neuroanatomy; Neurobiology and Anatomy; Neurobiology and Behavior; Neurobiology and Neurosciences, Other; Neuropharmacology; Oncology and Cancer Biology; Pathology/Experimental Pathology; Pharmaceutical Sciences; Pharmacology; Pharmacology and Toxicology; Pharmacology and Toxicology, Other; Physiology, General; Physiology, Pathology, and Related Sciences, Other; Reproductive Biology; Toxicology; Vision Science/Physiological Optics. **Related Knowledge/Courses:** Biology; Chemistry; Medicine and Dentistry; Physics; Mathematics; English Language. **Work Experience Needed:** None. **On-the-Job Training Needed:** None. **Certification/Licensure:** None.

**Personality Types:** Investigative–Realistic–Artistic. **Key Career Cluster:** 08 Health Science. **Key Career Pathway:** 8.5 Biotechnology Research and Development.

**Skills:** Science; operations analysis; reading comprehension; mathematics; systems evaluation; systems analysis; complex problem solving; writing.

**Physical Environment:** Indoors; sitting. **Structural Environment:** Importance of being exact or accurate; structured versus unstructured work; freedom to make decisions; impact of decisions on co-workers or company results; time pressure; frequency of decision making.

## Microbiologists

**Investigate the growth, structure, development, and other characteristics of microscopic organisms, such as bacteria, algae, or fungi.**

- Average annual earnings: $66,260
- Middle 50% of earners: $48,900–$92,730
- Earnings growth potential: Medium (40.1%)
- Growth: 13.3%

### BEST-PAYING INDUSTRIES

| Industry | Median Earnings | Workforce |
|---|---|---|
| Federal, State, and Local Government | $74,860 | 4,670 |
| Chemical Manufacturing | $67,090 | 4,850 |
| Professional, Scientific, and Technical Services | $62,500 | 5,430 |
| Educational Services | $52,960 | 1,630 |

### BEST-PAYING METROPOLITAN AREAS

| Metro Area | Median Earnings | Workforce |
|---|---|---|
| Washington-Arlington-Alexandria, DC-VA-MD-WV | $98,280 | 1,320 |
| Atlanta–Sandy Springs–Marietta, GA | $81,480 | 600 |
| Los Angeles–Long Beach–Santa Ana, CA | $79,410 | 720 |
| New York–Northern New Jersey–Long Island, NY-NJ-PA | $70,640 | 1,220 |
| Boston-Cambridge-Quincy, MA-NH | $68,790 | 1,330 |
| Philadelphia-Camden-Wilmington, PA-NJ-DE-MD | $61,880 | 640 |
| San Diego–Carlsbad–San Marcos, CA | $58,850 | 600 |

- Annual job openings: 720
- Self-employed: 4.7%

**Considerations for Job Outlook:** Most of the applied research projects that microbiologists are involved in require the expertise of scientists in multiple fields such as biochemistry, chemistry, and medicine. Microbiologists who have a broad understanding of microbiology and its relationship to other disciplines should have the best opportunities. A large portion of basic research in microbiology depends on funding from the federal government through the National Institutes of Health and the National Science Foundation. Therefore, federal budgetary decisions will affect job prospects in basic research from year to year. Typically, there is strong competition among microbiologists for research funding.

**Major Work Tasks:** Examine physiological, morphological, and cultural characteristics, using microscope, to identify and classify microorganisms in human, water, and food specimens. Provide laboratory services for health departments, for community environmental health programs and for physicians needing information for diagnosis and treatment. Observe action of microorganisms upon living tissues of plants, higher animals, and other microorganisms, and on dead organic matter. Investigate the relationship between organisms and disease, including the control of epidemics and the effects of antibiotics on microorganisms. Supervise biological technologists and technicians and other scientists. Study growth, structure, development, and general characteristics of bacteria and other microorganisms to understand their relationship to human, plant, and animal health. Prepare technical reports and recommendations based upon research outcomes. Study the structure and function of human, animal and plant tissues, cells, pathogens, and toxins. Use a variety of specialized equipment, such as electron microscopes, gas chromatographs and high pressure liquid chromatographs, electrophoresis units, thermocyclers, fluorescence activated cell sorters and phosphoimagers. Conduct chemical analyses of substances, such as acids, alcohols, and enzymes. Isolate and maintain cultures of bacteria or other microorganisms in prescribed or developed media, controlling moisture, aeration, temperature, and nutrition. Research use of bacteria and microorganisms to develop vitamins, antibiotics, amino acids, grain alcohol, sugars, and polymers. Monitor and perform tests on water, food, and the environment to detect harmful microorganisms or to obtain information about sources of pollution, contamination, or infection. Develop new products and procedures for sterilization, food and pharmaceutical supply preservation, or microbial contamination detection.

**Usual Educational Requirement:** Bachelor's degree. **Relevant Educational Programs:** Cell/Cellular Biology and Anatomical Sciences, Other; Microbiology and Immunology; Microbiology, General; Soil Microbiology; Structural Biology. **Related Knowledge/Courses:** Biology; Chemistry; Medicine and Dentistry; English Language; Education and Training; Mathematics. **Work Experience Needed:** None. **On-the-Job Training Needed:** None. **Certification/Licensure:** None.

**Personality Types:** Investigative–Realistic. **Key Career Cluster:** 15 Science, Technology, Engineering, and Mathematics. **Key Career Pathway:** 15.2 Science and Mathematics.

**Skills:** Science; active learning; mathematics; programming; operations analysis; reading comprehension; learning strategies; writing.

**Physical Environment:** Indoors; sitting; using hands; exposed to disease or infections; hazardous conditions. **Structural Environment:** Importance of being exact or accurate; freedom to make decisions; structured versus unstructured work; time pressure; level of competition; impact of decisions on co-workers or company results.

## Multimedia Artists and Animators

**Create special effects, animation, or other visual images using film, video, computers, or other electronic tools and media for use in products or creations.**

- Average annual earnings: $61,370
- Middle 50% of earners: $45,640–$85,410

### BEST-PAYING INDUSTRIES

| Industry | Median Earnings | Workforce |
|---|---|---|
| Motion Picture and Sound Recording Industries | $72,510 | 9,170 |
| Publishing Industries (except Internet) | $60,250 | 4,570 |
| Professional, Scientific, and Technical Services | $59,060 | 9,050 |

### BEST-PAYING METROPOLITAN AREAS

| Metro Area | Median Earnings | Workforce |
|---|---|---|
| Los Angeles–Long Beach–Santa Ana, CA | $80,340 | 5,990 |
| San Francisco–Oakland–Fremont, CA | $72,520 | 1,800 |
| New York–Northern New Jersey–Long Island, NY-NJ-PA | $66,730 | 2,670 |
| Boston-Cambridge-Quincy, MA-NH | $64,470 | 590 |
| Seattle-Tacoma-Bellevue, WA | $63,780 | 2,360 |
| Chicago-Naperville-Joliet, IL-IN-WI | $59,010 | 850 |
| Raleigh-Cary, NC | $56,070 | 700 |
| Dallas–Fort Worth–Arlington, TX | $55,110 | 790 |
| Atlanta–Sandy Springs–Marietta, GA | $52,470 | 790 |

- Earnings growth potential: Medium (43.2%)
- Growth: 8.3%
- Annual job openings: 2,140
- Self-employed: 58.8%

**Considerations for Job Outlook:** Despite job growth, there will be competition for job openings because many people are interested in entering the occupation. Opportunities should be best for those who have artistic talent or who are highly skilled in creating computer graphics.

**Major Work Tasks:** Design complex graphics and animation, using independent judgment, creativity, and computer equipment. Create two-dimensional and three-dimensional images depicting objects in motion or illustrating a process, using computer animation or modeling programs. Make objects or characters appear lifelike by manipulating light, color, texture, shadow, and transparency, or manipulating static images to give the illusion of motion. Apply story development, directing, cinematography, and editing to animation to create storyboards that show the flow of the animation and map out key scenes and characters. Create basic designs, drawings, and illustrations for product labels, cartons, direct mail, or television. Develop briefings, brochures, multimedia presentations, webpages, promotional products, technical illustrations, and computer artwork for use in products, technical manuals, literature, newsletters and slide shows. Participate in design and production of multimedia campaigns, handling budgeting and scheduling, and assisting with such responsibilities as production coordination, background design, and progress tracking. Assemble, typeset, scan, and produce digital camera-ready art or film negatives and printer's proofs. Script, plan, and create animated narrative sequences under tight deadlines, using computer software and hand-drawing techniques. Create pen-and-paper images to be scanned, edited, colored, textured or animated by computer. Use models to simulate the behavior of animated objects in the finished sequence. Create and install special effects as required by the script, mixing chemicals and fabricating needed parts from wood, metal, plaster, and clay. Convert real objects to animated objects through modeling, using techniques such as optical scanning. Implement and maintain configuration control systems.

**Usual Educational Requirement:** Bachelor's degree. **Relevant Educational Programs**: Animation, Interactive Technology, Video Graphics and Special Effects; Digital Arts; Drawing; Game and Interactive Media Design; Graphic Design; Intermedia/Multimedia; Modeling, Virtual Environments and Simulation; Painting; Webpage, Digital/Multimedia, and Information Resources Design. **Related Knowledge/Courses:** Fine Arts; Communications and Media; Design; Computers and Electronics; Sales and Marketing; English Language. **Work Experience Needed:** None. **On-the-Job Training Needed:** Moderate-term on-the-job training. **Certification/Licensure:** None.

**Personality Types:** Artistic–Investigative. **Key Career Cluster:** 03 Arts, Audiovisual Technology, and Communications. **Key Career Pathway:** 3.3 Visual Arts.

**Skills:** Technology design; programming; coordination; management of financial resources; negotiation; management of material resources; active listening; systems evaluation.

**Physical Environment:** Indoors; sitting; using hands; repetitive motions. **Structural Environment:** Freedom to make decisions; importance of being exact or accurate; time pressure; structured versus unstructured work; frequency of decision making; level of competition.

## Natural Sciences Managers

Plan, direct, or coordinate activities in such fields as life sciences, physical sciences, mathematics, statistics, and research and development in these fields.

### BEST-PAYING INDUSTRIES

| Industry | Median Earnings | Workforce |
|---|---|---|
| Professional, Scientific, and Technical Services | $143,690 | 17,390 |
| Management of Companies and Enterprises | $140,090 | 2,840 |
| Chemical Manufacturing | $116,300 | 5,480 |
| Federal, State, and Local Government | $100,690 | 14,880 |
| Educational Services | $82,200 | 3,180 |

### BEST-PAYING METROPOLITAN AREAS

| Metro Area | Median Earnings | Workforce |
|---|---|---|
| San Diego–Carlsbad–San Marcos, CA | $174,050 | 1,540 |
| Boston-Cambridge-Quincy, MA-NH | $167,290 | 2,380 |
| San Francisco–Oakland–Fremont, CA | $166,500 | 2,490 |
| Philadelphia-Camden-Wilmington, PA-NJ-DE-MD | $161,470 | 1,720 |
| New York–Northern New Jersey–Long Island, NY-NJ-PA | $151,640 | 3,510 |
| Los Angeles–Long Beach–Santa Ana, CA | $141,080 | 1,460 |
| Durham, NC | $139,730 | 1,140 |
| Washington-Arlington-Alexandria, DC-VA-MD-WV | $129,540 | 3,570 |

- Average annual earnings: $115,730
- Middle 50% of earners: $88,750–$156,720
- Earnings growth potential: Medium (43.8%)
- Growth: 7.7%
- Annual job openings: 3,350
- Self-employed: 2.4%

**Considerations for Job Outlook:** In addition to job openings resulting from employment growth, openings will result from the need to replace managers who retire or move into other occupations. Competition for job openings will likely be strong because of the high salaries that natural sciences managers command and the greater resources and control over projects that scientists can gain from becoming managers.

**Major Work Tasks:** Confer with scientists, engineers, regulators, or others to plan or review projects or to provide technical assistance. Develop client relationships and communicate with clients to explain proposals, present research findings, establish specifications, or discuss project status. Plan or direct research, development, or production activities. Prepare project proposals. Design or coordinate successive phases of problem analysis, solution proposals, or testing. Review project activities and prepare and review research, testing, or operational reports. Hire, supervise, or evaluate engineers, technicians, researchers, or other staff. Determine scientific or technical goals within broad outlines provided by top management and make detailed plans to accomplish these goals. Develop or implement policies, standards, or procedures for the architectural, scientific, or technical work performed to ensure regulatory compliance or operations enhancement. Develop innovative technology or train staff for its implementation. Provide for stewardship of plant or animal resources or habitats, studying land use, monitoring animal populations, or providing shelter, resources, or medical treatment for ani-

348

mals. Conduct own research in field of expertise. Recruit personnel or oversee the development or maintenance of staff competence. Advise or assist in obtaining patents or meeting other legal requirements. Prepare and administer budgets, approve and review expenditures, and prepare financial reports. Make presentations at professional meetings to further knowledge in the field.

**Usual Educational Requirement:** Bachelor's degree. **Relevant Educational Programs**: Acoustics; Aerospace Physiology and Medicine; Algebra and Number Theory; Analysis and Functional Analysis; Analytical Chemistry; Anatomy; Animal Genetics; Animal Physiology; Applied Mathematics, General; Applied Mathematics, Other; Astronomy; Astronomy and Astrophysics, Other; Astrophysics; Atmospheric Chemistry and Climatology; Atmospheric Physics and Dynamics; Atmospheric Sciences and Meteorology, General; Atmospheric Sciences and Meteorology, Other; Atomic/Molecular Physics; Biochemistry; Biochemistry and Molecular Biology; Biochemistry, Biophysics and Molecular Biology, Other; Biological and Biomedical Sciences, Other; Biological and Physical Sciences; Biology/Biological Sciences, General; Biomathematics, Bioinformatics, and Computational Biology, Other; Biometry/Biometrics; Biophysics; Biopsychology; Biostatistics; Biotechnology; Botany/Plant Biology; Botany/Plant Biology, Other; Cell/Cellular Biology and Anatomical Sciences, Other; Cell/Cellular Biology and Histology; others. **Related Knowledge/Courses:** Biology; Chemistry; Engineering and Technology; Law and Government; Administration and Management; Production and Processing. **Work Experience Needed:** More than 5 years. **On-the-Job Training Needed:** None. **Certification/Licensure:** None.

**Personality Types:** Enterprising–Investigative. **Key Career Cluster:** 01 Agriculture, Food, and Natural Resources. **Key Career Pathway:** 1.5 Natural Resources Systems.

**Skills:** Science; operations analysis; management of financial resources; technology design; management of personnel resources; mathematics; time management; reading comprehension.

**Physical Environment:** Indoors; sitting; noise. **Structural Environment:** Freedom to make decisions; structured versus unstructured work; impact of decisions on co-workers or company results; frequency of decision making; importance of being exact or accurate; time pressure.

## JOB SPECIALIZATION: CLINICAL RESEARCH COORDINATORS

**Plan, direct, or coordinate clinical research projects. Direct the activities of workers engaged in clinical research projects to ensure compliance with protocols and overall clinical objectives. May evaluate and analyze clinical data.**

**Major Work Tasks:** Review scientific literature, participate in continuing education activities, or attend conferences and seminars to maintain current knowledge of clinical studies affairs and issues. Prepare for or participate in quality assurance audits conducted by study sponsors, federal agencies, or specially designated review groups. Participate in preparation and management of research budgets and monetary disbursements. Confer with healthcare professionals to determine the best recruitment practices for studies. Track enrollment status of subjects and document dropout information, such as dropout causes and subject contact efforts. Review proposed study protocols to evaluate factors, such as sample collection processes, data management plans, and potential subject risks. Record adverse event and side effect data and confer with investigators regarding the reporting of events to oversight agencies. Prepare study-related documentation such as protocol worksheets, procedural manuals, adverse event reports, institutional review board documents, and progress reports. Participate in the development of study protocols including guidelines for administration or data collection procedures. Oversee subject enrollment to ensure that informed consent is properly obtained and documented. Order drugs or devices necessary for study completion. Instruct research staff in scientific and procedural aspects of studies including standards of care, informed consent procedures, or documentation procedures. Identify protocol problems, inform investigators of problems, or assist in problem resolution efforts, such as protocol revisions. Communicate with laboratories or investigators regarding laboratory findings. Collaborate with investigators to prepare presentations or reports of clinical study procedures, results, and conclusions. Code, evaluate, or interpret collected study data. Assess eligibility of potential subjects through methods, such as screening interviews, reviews of medical records, and discussions with physicians and nurses. Monitor study activities to ensure compliance with protocols and with all relevant local, federal, and state regulatory and institutional polices.

**Related Knowledge/Courses:** Medicine and Dentistry; Biology; Administration and Management; Clerical Practices; Law and Government; English Language.

**Personality Types:** Enterprising–Investigative–Conventional.

**Skills:** Science; management of material resources; management of financial resources; management of personnel resources; coordination; active learning; systems evaluation; negotiation.

**Physical Environment:** Indoors; sitting. **Structural Environment:** Importance of being exact or accurate; freedom to make decisions; structured versus unstructured work; time pressure; frequency of decision making; impact of decisions on co-workers or company results.

## JOB SPECIALIZATION: WATER RESOURCE SPECIALISTS

**Design or implement programs and strategies related to water resource issues, such as supply, quality, and regulatory compliance issues.**

**Major Work Tasks:** Review or evaluate designs for water detention facilities, storm drains, flood control facilities, or other hydraulic structures. Negotiate for water rights with communities or water facilities to meet water supply demands. Perform hydrologic, hydraulic, or water quality modeling. Compile water resource data, using geographic information systems (GIS) or global position systems (GPS) software. Compile and maintain documentation on the health of a body of water. Write proposals, project reports, informational brochures, or other documents on wastewater purification, water supply and demand, or other water resource subjects. Recommend new or revised policies, procedures, or regulations to support water resource or conservation goals. Provide technical expertise to assist communities in the development or implementation of storm water monitoring or other water programs. Present water resource proposals to government, public interest groups, or community groups. Monitor water use, demand, or quality in a particular geographic area. Identify and characterize specific causes or sources of water pollution. Develop plans to protect watershed health or rehabilitate watersheds. Develop or implement standardized water monitoring and assessment methods. Conduct technical studies for water resources on topics such as pollutants and water treatment options. Conduct, or oversee the conduct of, investigations on matters, such as water storage, wastewater discharge, pollutants, permits, or other compliance and regulatory issues. Conduct cost-benefit studies for watershed improvement projects or water management alternatives. Analyze storm water systems to identify opportunities for water resource improvements.

Develop strategies for watershed operations to meet water supply and conservation goals or to ensure regulatory compliance with clean water laws or regulations. Conduct, or oversee the conduct of, chemical, physical, and biological water quality monitoring or sampling to ensure compliance with water quality standards. Supervise teams of workers who capture water from wells and rivers. Identify methods for distributing purified wastewater into rivers, streams, or oceans.

**Related Knowledge/Courses:** Engineering and Technology; Geography; Biology; Design; Physics; Chemistry.

**Personality Types:** Investigative–Enterprising–Conventional.

**Skills:** Systems evaluation; systems analysis; science; management of financial resources; mathematics; management of material resources; technology design; quality control analysis.

**Physical Environment:** Indoors; outdoors; sitting. **Structural Environment:** Importance of being exact or accurate; structured versus unstructured work; impact of decisions on coworkers or company results; freedom to make decisions; frequency of decision making; time pressure.

## Network and Computer Systems Administrators

**Install, configure, and support an organization's local area network (LAN), wide area network (WAN), and Internet systems or a segment of a network system.**

- Average annual earnings: $72,560
- Middle 50% of earners: $56,470–$92,370
- Earnings growth potential: Medium (38.9%)
- Growth: 27.8%
- Annual job openings: 15,530
- Self-employed: 0.8%

### BEST-PAYING INDUSTRIES

| Industry | Median Earnings | Workforce |
|---|---|---|
| Telecommunications | $79,810 | 17,910 |
| Professional, Scientific, and Technical Services | $76,820 | 91,410 |
| Management of Companies and Enterprises | $74,960 | 22,970 |
| Federal, State, and Local Government | $69,130 | 18,460 |
| Educational Services | $61,830 | 36,400 |

### BEST-PAYING METROPOLITAN AREAS

| Metro Area | Median Earnings | Workforce |
|---|---|---|
| San Francisco–Oakland–Fremont, CA | $91,540 | 8,920 |
| Washington-Arlington-Alexandria, DC-VA-MD-WV | $90,100 | 20,400 |
| Houston–Sugar Land–Baytown, TX | $85,360 | 8,150 |
| New York–Northern New Jersey–Long Island, NY-NJ-PA | $84,670 | 23,280 |
| Philadelphia-Camden-Wilmington, PA-NJ-DE-MD | $83,330 | 9,670 |
| Boston-Cambridge-Quincy, MA-NH | $80,750 | 8,640 |
| Los Angeles–Long Beach–Santa Ana, CA | $77,910 | 14,270 |
| Atlanta–Sandy Springs–Marietta, GA | $76,790 | 8,300 |
| Dallas–Fort Worth–Arlington, TX | $76,210 | 10,910 |
| Chicago-Naperville-Joliet, IL-IN-WI | $74,180 | 10,010 |

**Considerations for Job Outlook:** Job opportunities should be favorable for this occupation. Prospects should be best for applicants who have a bachelor's degree in computer science and who are up to date on the latest technology.

**Major Work Tasks:** Perform data back-ups and disaster recovery operations. Maintain and administer computer networks and related computing environments, including computer hardware, systems software, applications software, and all configurations. Plan, coordinate, and implement network security measures to protect data, software, and hardware. Operate master consoles to monitor the performance of computer systems and networks and to coordinate computer network access and use. Design, configure, and test computer hardware, networking software and operating system software. Recommend changes to improve systems and network configurations, and determine hardware or software requirements related to such changes. Confer with network users about how to solve existing system problems. Monitor network performance to determine whether adjustments need to be made and to determine where changes will need to be made in the future. Train people in computer system use. Load computer tapes and disks, and install software and printer paper or forms. Gather data pertaining to customer needs, and use the information to identify, predict, interpret, and evaluate system and network requirements. Analyze equipment performance records to determine the need for repair or replacement. Maintain an inventory of parts for emergency repairs. Coordinate with vendors and with company personnel to facilitate purchases. Diagnose, troubleshoot, and resolve hardware, software, or other network and system problems, and replace defective components when necessary. Configure, monitor, and maintain email applications or virus protection software. Research new technologies by attending seminars, reading trade articles, or taking classes, and implement or recommend the implementation of new technologies. Implement and provide technical support for voice services and equipment, such as private branch exchange, voicemail system, and telecom system. Perform routine network startup and shutdown procedures, and maintain control records. Maintain logs related to network functions, as well as maintenance and repair records.

**Usual Educational Requirement:** Bachelor's degree. **Relevant Educational Programs:** Computer and Information Sciences, General; Computer and Information Systems Security/Information Assurance; Network and System Administration/Administrator. **Related Knowledge/Courses:** Telecommunications; Computers and Electronics; Clerical Practices; Administration and Management; Engineering and Technology. **Work Experience Needed:** None. **On-the-Job Training Needed:** None. **Certification/Licensure:** Voluntary certification by vendor or association.

**Personality Types:** Investigative–Realistic–Conventional. **Key Career Cluster:** 11 Information Technology. **Key Career Pathway:** 11.1 Network Systems.

**Skills:** Programming; equipment maintenance; troubleshooting; equipment selection; technology design; repairing; installation; operation and control.

**Physical Environment:** Indoors; sitting; using hands; repetitive motions; noise. **Structural Environment:** Importance of being exact or accurate; structured versus unstructured work; freedom to make decisions; importance of repeating same tasks; impact of decisions on coworkers or company results; time pressure.

## Nuclear Engineers

**Conduct research on nuclear engineering projects or apply principles and theory of nuclear science.**

- Average annual earnings: $104,270
- Middle 50% of earners: $85,290–$122,760
- Earnings growth potential: Medium (33.9%)
- Growth: 10.2%
- Annual job openings: 620
- Self-employed: 0.0%

### BEST-PAYING INDUSTRIES

| Industry | Median Earnings | Workforce |
|---|---|---|
| Professional, Scientific, and Technical Services | $115,530 | 8,050 |
| Utilities | $99,080 | 6,640 |

### BEST-PAYING METROPOLITAN AREAS

| Metro Area | Median Earnings | Workforce |
|---|---|---|
| Memphis, TN-MS-AR | $115,740 | 680 |
| Chicago-Naperville-Joliet, IL-IN-WI | $115,710 | 520 |
| San Diego–Carlsbad–San Marcos, CA | $104,410 | 450 |
| Richmond, VA | $103,900 | 720 |
| Cleveland-Elyria-Mentor, OH | $91,810 | 590 |
| Augusta–Richmond County, GA-SC | $90,440 | 470 |

**Considerations for Job Outlook:** Job prospects are expected to be relatively favorable for this occupation because many in the aging workforce will retire. The small number of nuclear engineering graduates is likely to be in rough balance with the number of job openings. In addition, training in new fields, such as nuclear medicine, should help to improve a person's chances of finding a job.

**Major Work Tasks:** Examine accidents to obtain data that can be used to design preventive measures. Monitor nuclear facility operations to identify any design, construction, or operation practices that violate safety regulations and laws or that could jeopardize the safety of operations. Keep abreast of developments and changes in the nuclear field by reading technical journals or by independent study and research. Perform experiments that will provide information about acceptable methods of nuclear material usage, nuclear fuel reclamation, or waste disposal. Design or oversee construction or operation of nuclear reactors or power plants or nuclear fuels reprocessing and reclamation systems. Design or develop nuclear equipment, such as reactor cores, radiation shielding, or associated instrumentation or control mechanisms. Initiate corrective actions or order plant shutdowns in emergency situations. Recommend preventive measures to be taken in the handling of nuclear technology, based on data obtained from operations monitoring or from evaluation of test results. Write operational instructions to be used in nuclear plant operation or nuclear fuel or waste handling and disposal. Conduct tests of nuclear fuel behavior and cycles or performance of nuclear machinery and equipment to optimize performance of existing plants. Direct operating or maintenance activities of operational nuclear power plants to ensure efficiency and conformity to safety standards. Synthesize analyses of test results, and use the results to prepare technical reports of findings and recommendations. Prepare construction project proposals that include cost estimates, and discuss proposals with interested parties such as vendors, contractors, and nuclear facility review boards. Analyze available data and consult with other scientists to determine parameters of experimentation and suitability of analytical models. Design and direct nuclear research projects to discover facts, to test or modify theoretical models, or to develop new theoretical models or new uses for current models. Conduct environmental studies related to topics such as nuclear power generation, nuclear waste disposal, or nuclear weapon deployment.

**Usual Educational Requirement:** Bachelor's degree. **Relevant Educational Program**: Nuclear Engineering. **Related Knowledge/ Courses:** Engineering and Technology; Physics; Design; Chemistry; Mathematics; Mechanical. **Work Experience Needed:** None. **On-the-Job Training Needed:** None. **Certification/Licensure:** Licensure beyond entry level.

**Personality Types:** Investigative–Realistic–Conventional. **Key Career Cluster:** 15 Science, Technology, Engineering, and Mathematics. **Key Career Pathway:** 15.1 Engineering and Technology.

**Skills:** Operations analysis; science; technology design; operation monitoring; troubleshooting; mathematics; quality control analysis; systems evaluation.

**Physical Environment:** Indoors; sitting; exposed to radiation. **Structural Environment:** Importance of being exact or accurate; freedom to make decisions; structured versus unstructured work; impact of decisions on co-workers or company results; time pressure; consequence of error.

## Nuclear Medicine Technologists

**Prepare, administer, and measure radioactive isotopes in therapeutic, diagnostic, and tracer studies using a variety of radioisotope equipment.**

- Average annual earnings: $70,180
- Middle 50% of earners: $59,980–$82,690
- Earnings growth potential: Low (28.0%)
- Growth: 18.9%
- Annual job openings: 750
- Self-employed: 0.0%

**Considerations for Job Outlook:** Nuclear medicine technologists can improve their job pros-

**BEST-PAYING INDUSTRIES**

| Industry | Median Earnings | Workforce |
|---|---|---|
| Ambulatory Health-Care Services | $71,160 | 6,190 |
| Hospitals | $69,870 | 13,670 |

**BEST-PAYING METROPOLITAN AREAS**

| Metro Area | Median Earnings | Workforce |
|---|---|---|
| Los Angeles–Long Beach–Santa Ana, CA | $91,060 | 590 |
| New York–Northern New Jersey–Long Island, NY-NJ-PA | $80,800 | 1,160 |
| Boston-Cambridge-Quincy, MA-NH | $78,990 | 420 |
| Chicago-Naperville-Joliet, IL-IN-WI | $73,170 | 560 |
| Orlando-Kissimmee, FL | $72,850 | 450 |
| Philadelphia-Camden-Wilmington, PA-NJ-DE-MD | $72,490 | 490 |
| Miami–Fort Lauderdale–Pompano Beach, FL | $67,350 | 630 |
| Dallas–Fort Worth–Arlington, TX | $65,230 | 520 |

pects by getting a specialty certification. A technologist can earn a certification in positron emission tomography (PET), nuclear cardiology (NCT), magnetic resonance imaging (MRI), or computed tomography (CT). The Nuclear Medicine Technology Certification Board (NMTCB) offers NCT and PET certification exams. The American Registry of Radiologic Technologists (ARRT) offers the CT and MRI certification exams.

**Major Work Tasks:** Calculate, measure, and record radiation dosage or radiopharmaceuticals received, used, and disposed, using computer and following physician's prescription. Detect and map radiopharmaceuticals in patients' bodies, using a camera to produce photographic or computer images. Explain test procedures and safety precautions to patients and provide them with assistance during test procedures. Produce a computer-generated or film image for interpretation by a physician. Process cardiac function studies, using computer. Dispose of radioactive materials and store radiopharmaceuticals, following radiation safety procedures. Record and process results of procedures. Prepare stock radiopharmaceuticals, adhering to safety standards that minimize radiation exposure to workers and patients. Maintain and calibrate radioisotope and laboratory equipment. Gather information on patients' illnesses and medical history to guide the choice of diagnostic procedures for therapy. Measure glandular activity, blood volume, red cell survival, or radioactivity of patient, using scanners, Geiger counters, scintillometers, or other laboratory equipment. Train or supervise student or subordinate nuclear medicine technologists. Administer radiopharmaceuticals or radiation intravenously to detect or treat diseases, using radioisotope equipment, under direction of a physician. Perform quality control checks on laboratory equipment or cameras. Position radiation fields, radiation beams, and patient to allow for most effective treatment of patient's disease, using computer. Add radioactive substances to biological specimens, such as blood, urine, or feces, to determine therapeutic drug or hormone levels. Develop treatment procedures for nuclear medicine treatment programs.

**Usual Educational Requirement:** Associate degree. **Relevant Educational Program:** Nuclear Medical Technology/Technologist. **Related Knowledge/Courses:** Biology; Medicine and Dentistry; Chemistry; Physics; Customer and Personal Service; Psychology. **Work**

**Experience Needed:** None. **On-the-Job Training Needed:** None. **Certification/Licensure:** Voluntary certification by association.

**Personality Types:** Investigative–Realistic–Social. **Key Career Cluster:** 08 Health Science. **Key Career Pathway:** 8.2 Diagnostics Services.

**Skills:** Science; equipment maintenance; repairing; operation and control; quality control analysis; equipment selection; troubleshooting; operation monitoring.

**Physical Environment:** Indoors; standing; using hands; exposed to radiation; exposed to disease or infections. **Structural Environment:** Importance of being exact or accurate; frequency of decision making; freedom to make decisions; consequence of error; structured versus unstructured work; impact of decisions on co-workers or company results.

## Nursing Instructors and Teachers, Postsecondary

*See Teachers, Postsecondary.*

## Occupational Health and Safety Specialists

**Review, evaluate, and analyze work environments and design programs and procedures to control, eliminate, and prevent disease or injury.**

- Average annual earnings: $66,790
- Middle 50% of earners: $51,320–$82,880
- Earnings growth potential: Medium (40.0%)
- Growth: 8.5%
- Annual job openings: 2,570
- Self-employed: 3.1%

**Considerations for Job Outlook:** New environmental regulations and laws will require specialists to create and enforce procedures in the workplace. The increased adoption of nuclear power as a source of energy may be a major factor for job growth for specialists in that field.

## Your Guide to High-Paying Careers

### BEST-PAYING INDUSTRIES

| Industry | Median Earnings | Workforce |
|---|---|---|
| Professional, Scientific, and Technical Services | $66,400 | 6,560 |
| Federal, State, and Local Government | $65,050 | 18,770 |

### BEST-PAYING METROPOLITAN AREAS

| Metro Area | Median Earnings | Workforce |
|---|---|---|
| New York–Northern New Jersey–Long Island, NY-NJ-PA | $74,770 | 2,700 |
| Houston–Sugar Land–Baytown, TX | $71,800 | 2,570 |
| Los Angeles–Long Beach–Santa Ana, CA | $68,550 | 2,260 |
| Dallas–Fort Worth–Arlington, TX | $66,300 | 1,260 |

These specialists will be needed to create and carry out programs to maintain the safety of both the workers and the environment. Insurance and workers' compensation costs have become a concern for many employers and insurance companies, especially with an aging population remaining in the workforce longer.

**Major Work Tasks:** Order suspension of activities that pose threats to workers' health or safety. Recommend measures to help protect workers from potentially hazardous work methods, processes, or materials. Investigate accidents to identify causes or to determine how such accidents might be prevented in the future. Investigate the adequacy of ventilation, exhaust equipment, lighting, or other conditions that could affect employee health, comfort, or performance. Develop or maintain hygiene programs, such as noise surveys, continuous atmosphere monitoring, ventilation surveys, or asbestos management plans. Inspect or evaluate workplace environments, equipment, or practices to ensure compliance with safety standards and government regulations. Collaborate with engineers or physicians to institute control or remedial measures for hazardous or potentially hazardous conditions or equipment. Conduct safety training or education programs and demonstrate the use of safety equipment. Provide new-employee health and safety orientations and develop materials for these presentations. Collect samples of dust, gases, vapors, or other potentially toxic materials for analysis. Investigate health-related complaints and inspect facilities to ensure that they comply with public health legislation and regulations. Coordinate "right-to-know" programs regarding hazardous chemicals or other substances. Maintain or update emergency response plans or procedures. Develop or maintain medical monitoring programs for employees. Inspect specified areas to ensure the presence of fire prevention equipment, safety equipment, or first-aid supplies. Conduct audits at hazardous waste sites or industrial sites or participate in hazardous waste site investigations. Collect samples of hazardous materials or arrange for sample collection. Maintain inventories of hazardous materials or hazardous wastes, using waste tracking systems to ensure that materials are handled properly. Prepare hazardous, radioactive, or mixed waste samples for transportation or storage by treating, compacting, packaging, and labeling them.

**Usual Educational Requirement:** Bachelor's degree. **Relevant Educational Programs**: Environmental Health; Industrial Safety Technology/Technician; Occupational Health and Industrial Hygiene; Occupational Safety and Health Technology/Technician. **Related Knowledge/Courses:** Biology; Chemistry; Building and Construction; Physics; Engineering and Technology; Education and Training. **Work Experience Needed:** None. **On-the-Job Training Needed:** Moderate-term on-the-job training. **Certification/Licensure:** Licensure for some specializations; voluntary certification by association.

**Personality Types:** Investigative–Conventional. **Key Career Cluster:** 01 Agriculture, Food, and Natural Resources. **Key Career Pathway:** 1.6 Environmental Service Systems.

**Skills:** Science; operations analysis; operation monitoring; quality control analysis; persuasion; systems evaluation; systems analysis; technology design.

**Physical Environment:** Indoors; outdoors; noise; contaminants; hazardous conditions; hazardous equipment. **Structural Environment:** Freedom to make decisions; importance of being exact or accurate; impact of decisions on co-workers or company results; structured versus unstructured work; frequency of decision making; time pressure.

## Occupational Therapists

**Assess, plan, organize, and participate in rehabilitative programs that help build or restore vocational, homemaking, and daily living skills.**

- Average annual earnings: $75,400
- Middle 50% of earners: $62,510–$90,270
- Earnings growth potential: Medium (33.0%)
- Growth: 33.5%
- Annual job openings: 5,710
- Self-employed: 6.0%

**Considerations for Job Outlook:** Job opportunities should be good for licensed occupational therapists in all setting, particularly in acute hospital, rehabilitation, and orthopedic settings because the elderly receive most of their treatment in these settings. Occupational therapists with specialized knowledge in a treatment area also will have increased job prospects.

**BEST-PAYING INDUSTRIES**

| Industry | Median Earnings | Workforce |
|---|---|---|
| Nursing and Residential Care Facilities | $82,270 | 11,620 |
| Ambulatory Health-Care Services | $78,120 | 39,030 |
| Hospitals | $75,140 | 29,760 |
| Educational Services | $66,580 | 14,970 |

**BEST-PAYING METROPOLITAN AREAS**

| Metro Area | Median Earnings | Workforce |
|---|---|---|
| Los Angeles–Long Beach–Santa Ana, CA | $89,000 | 3,790 |
| Dallas–Fort Worth–Arlington, TX | $86,820 | 2,380 |
| New York–Northern New Jersey–Long Island, NY-NJ-PA | $78,880 | 7,220 |
| Chicago-Naperville-Joliet, IL-IN-WI | $77,140 | 3,500 |
| Boston-Cambridge-Quincy, MA-NH | $75,210 | 3,440 |
| Philadelphia-Camden-Wilmington, PA-NJ-DE-MD | $73,310 | 2,550 |

**Major Work Tasks:** Complete and maintain necessary records. Evaluate patients' progress and prepare reports that detail progress. Test and evaluate patients' physical and mental abilities and analyze medical data to determine realistic rehabilitation goals for patients. Select activities that will help individuals learn work and life-management skills within limits of their mental or physical capabilities. Plan, organize, and conduct occupational therapy programs in hospital, institutional, or community settings to help rehabilitate those impaired because of illness, injury, or psychological or developmental problems. Recommend

**357**

changes in patients' work or living environments, consistent with their needs and capabilities. Consult with rehabilitation team to select activity programs or coordinate occupational therapy with other therapeutic activities. Help clients improve decision making, abstract reasoning, memory, sequencing, coordination, and perceptual skills, using computer programs. Develop and participate in health promotion programs, group activities, or discussions to promote client health, facilitate social adjustment, alleviate stress, and prevent physical or mental disability. Provide training and supervision in therapy techniques and objectives for students or nurses and other medical staff. Design and create, or requisition, special supplies and equipment, such as splints, braces, and computer-aided adaptive equipment. Plan and implement programs and social activities to help patients learn work or school skills and adjust to handicaps. Lay out materials, such as puzzles, scissors and eating utensils for use in therapy, and clean and repair these tools after therapy sessions. Advise on health risks in the workplace or on health-related transition to retirement. Conduct research in occupational therapy. Provide patients with assistance in locating or holding jobs. Train caregivers how to provide for the needs of a patient during and after therapy.

**Usual Educational Requirement:** Master's degree. **Relevant Educational Program**: Occupational Therapy/Therapist Training. **Related Knowledge/Courses:** Therapy and Counseling; Psychology; Sociology and Anthropology; Medicine and Dentistry; Biology; Philosophy and Theology. **Work Experience Needed:** None. **On-the-Job Training Needed:** None. **Certification/Licensure:** Licensure; also voluntary certification by association.

**Personality Types:** Social–Investigative. **Key Career Cluster:** 08 Health Science. **Key Career Pathway:** 8.1 Therapeutic Services.

**Skills:** Operations analysis; science; service orientation; social perceptiveness; active listening; writing; persuasion; learning strategies.

**Physical Environment:** Indoors; standing; using hands; bending or twisting the body; exposed to disease or infections. **Structural Environment:** Structured versus unstructured work; freedom to make decisions; frequency of decision making; time pressure; impact of decisions on co-workers or company results; importance of being exact or accurate.

## JOB SPECIALIZATION: LOW VISION THERAPISTS, ORIENTATION AND MOBILITY SPECIALISTS, AND VISION REHABILITATION THERAPISTS

**Provide therapy to patients with visual impairments to improve their functioning in daily life activities. May train patients in activities, such as computer use, communication skills, or home management skills.**

**Major Work Tasks:** Teach cane skills, including cane use with a guide, diagonal techniques, and two-point touches. Refer clients to services, such as eye care, health care, rehabilitation, and counseling, to enhance visual and life functioning or when condition exceeds scope of practice. Provide consultation, support, or education to groups such as parents and teachers. Participate in professional development activities, such as reading literature, continuing education, attending conferences, and collaborating with colleagues. Obtain, distribute, or maintain low vision devices. Design instructional programs to improve communication using devices, such as slates and styluses, braillers, keyboards, adaptive handwriting devices, talking book machines, digital books, and optical character readers (OCRs). Collaborate with specialists, such as rehabilitation counselors, speech pathologists, and occupational therapists, to provide client solutions. Administer tests and interpret test results to develop rehabilitation plans for clients. Teach clients to travel independently using a variety of actual or simulated travel situations or exercises. Train clients to use tactile, auditory, kinesthetic, olfactory, and propioceptive information. Train clients to use adaptive equipment, such as large print, reading stands, lamps, writing implements, software, and electronic devices. Monitor clients' progress to determine whether changes in rehabilitation plans are needed. Write reports or complete forms to document assessments, training, progress, or follow-up outcomes. Develop rehabilitation or instructional plans collaboratively with clients, based on results of assessments, needs, and goals. Assess clients' functioning in areas, such as vision, orientation and mobility skills, social and emotional issues, cognition, physical abilities, and personal goals. Train clients with visual impairments to use mobility devices or systems such as human guides, dog guides, electronic travel aids (ETAs), and other adaptive mobility devices (AMDs). Identify visual impairments related to basic life skills in areas such as self-care, literacy, communication, health management, home management, and meal preparation.

**Related Knowledge/Courses:** Therapy and Counseling; Psychology; Sociology and Anthropology; Education and Training; Transportation; Medicine and Dentistry.

**Personality Types:** Social–Investigative–Realistic.

**Skills:** Technology design; learning strategies; writing; negotiation; social perceptiveness; service orientation; reading comprehension; active learning.

**Physical Environment:** Outdoors; indoors; standing. **Structural Environment:** Freedom to make decisions; structured versus unstructured work; frequency of decision making; impact of decisions on co-workers or company results; importance of being exact or accurate; time pressure.

## Operations Research Analysts

**Formulate and apply mathematical modeling and other optimizing methods to develop and interpret information that assists management.**

- Average annual earnings: $72,100
- Middle 50% of earners: $53,120–$97,170
- Earnings growth potential: Medium (43.8%)
- Growth: 14.6%
- Annual job openings: 3,000
- Self-employed: 0.1%

**Considerations for Job Outlook:** Analysts who are able to communicate their recommendations to managers and to workers outside of operations research should have the best job prospects. Opportunities should be better for those who have a master's or doctorate degree in operations research, management science, or a related field.

### BEST-PAYING INDUSTRIES

| Industry | Median Earnings | Workforce |
|---|---|---|
| Securities, Commodity Contracts, and Other Financial Investments and Related Activities | $91,470 | 3,460 |
| Professional, Scientific, and Technical Services | $76,860 | 16,880 |
| Management of Companies and Enterprises | $72,630 | 5,530 |
| Federal, State, and Local Government | $72,560 | 9,940 |
| Insurance Carriers and Related Activities | $66,920 | 5,780 |
| Credit Intermediation and Related Activities | $60,430 | 7,530 |

**359**

## Your Guide to High-Paying Careers

| Metro Area | Median Earnings | Workforce |
|---|---|---|
| New York–Northern New Jersey–Long Island, NY-NJ-PA | $110,840 | 4,580 |
| Washington-Arlington-Alexandria, DC-VA-MD-WV | $94,230 | 6,230 |
| San Francisco–Oakland–Fremont, CA | $89,690 | 1,590 |
| Seattle-Tacoma-Bellevue, WA | $83,620 | 1,810 |
| Minneapolis–St. Paul–Bloomington, MN-WI | $83,130 | 1,410 |
| Los Angeles–Long Beach–Santa Ana, CA | $80,520 | 1,800 |
| Houston–Sugar Land–Baytown, TX | $73,990 | 1,390 |
| Chicago-Naperville-Joliet, IL-IN-WI | $69,680 | 1,410 |
| Dallas–Fort Worth–Arlington, TX | $68,940 | 2,290 |
| Boston-Cambridge-Quincy, MA-NH | $66,600 | 2,460 |
| Miami–Fort Lauderdale–Pompano Beach, FL | $55,020 | 1,520 |

**Major Work Tasks:** Formulate mathematical or simulation models of problems, relating constants and variables, restrictions, alternatives, conflicting objectives, and their numerical parameters. Collaborate with others in the organization to ensure successful implementation of chosen problem solutions. Analyze information obtained from management to conceptualize and define operational problems. Perform validation and testing of models to ensure adequacy and reformulate models as necessary. Collaborate with senior managers and decision makers to identify and solve a variety of problems and to clarify management objectives. Define data requirements and gather and validate information, applying judgment and statistical tests. Study and analyze information about alternative courses of action to determine which plan will offer the best outcomes. Prepare management reports defining and evaluating problems and recommending solutions. Break systems into their component parts, assign numerical values to each component, and examine the mathematical relationships between them. Specify manipulative or computational methods to be applied to models. Observe the current system in operation and gather and analyze information about each of the parts of component problems, using a variety of sources. Design, conduct, and evaluate experimental operational models in cases where models cannot be developed from existing data. Develop and apply time and cost networks to plan, control, and review large projects. Develop business methods and procedures, including accounting systems, file systems, office systems, logistics systems, and production schedules.

**Usual Educational Requirement:** Bachelor's degree. **Relevant Educational Programs**: Management Science; Operations Research. **Related Knowledge/Courses:** Mathematics; Computers and Electronics; Engineering and Technology; Production and Processing; Economics and Accounting; Transportation. **Work Experience Needed:** None. **On-the-Job Training Needed:** None. **Certification/Licensure:** None.

**Personality Types:** Investigative–Conventional–Enterprising. **Key Career Cluster:** 04 Business, Management, and Administration. **Key Career Pathway:** 4.4 Business Analysis.

**Skills:** Operations analysis; mathematics; science; systems evaluation; programming; systems analysis; complex problem solving; active learning.

**Physical Environment:** Indoors; sitting. **Structural Environment:** Freedom to make decisions;

structured versus unstructured work; importance of being exact or accurate; impact of decisions on co-workers or company results; level of competition; time pressure.

## Optometrists

**Diagnose, manage, and treat conditions and diseases of the human eye and visual system.**

- Average annual earnings: $97,820
- Middle 50% of earners: $75,100–$128,480
- Earnings growth potential: High (46.2%)
- Growth: 33.1%
- Annual job openings: 2,340
- Self-employed: 21.6%

### BEST-PAYING INDUSTRIES

| Industry | Median Earnings | Workforce |
|---|---|---|
| Health- and Personal-Care Stores | $102,890 | 3,550 |
| Ambulatory Health-Care Services | $97,850 | 24,010 |

### BEST-PAYING METROPOLITAN AREAS

| Metro Area | Median Earnings | Workforce |
|---|---|---|
| Washington-Arlington-Alexandria, DC-VA-MD-WV | $117,540 | 760 |
| Chicago-Naperville-Joliet, IL-IN-WI | $110,010 | 1,080 |
| New York–Northern New Jersey–Long Island, NY-NJ-PA | $106,280 | 1,710 |
| Los Angeles–Long Beach–Santa Ana, CA | $89,250 | 1,270 |
| Houston–Sugar Land–Baytown, TX | $72,540 | 860 |

**Considerations for Job Outlook:** Because the number of optometrists is limited by the number of accredited optometry schools, licensed optometrists should expect good job prospects. Admission to Doctor of Optometry programs is competitive, however, as it is for professional degree programs in other fields. In addition, a large number of currently practicing optometrists is expected to retire over the coming decade, creating opportunities for new optometrists.

**Major Work Tasks:** Examine eyes, using observation, instruments, and pharmaceutical agents, to determine visual acuity and perception, focus and coordination and to diagnose diseases and other abnormalities such as glaucoma or color blindness. Analyze test results and develop a treatment plan. Prescribe, supply, fit and adjust eyeglasses, contact lenses and other vision aids. Prescribe medications to treat eye diseases if state laws permit. Educate and counsel patients on contact lens care, visual hygiene, lighting arrangements, and safety factors. Consult with and refer patients to ophthalmologist or other health-care practitioner if additional medical treatment is determined necessary. Remove foreign bodies from the eye. Provide patients undergoing eye surgeries, such as cataract and laser vision correction, with pre- and post-operative care. Prescribe therapeutic procedures to correct or conserve vision. Provide vision therapy and low vision rehabilitation.

**Usual Educational Requirement:** Doctoral or professional degree. **Relevant Educational Program**: Optometry (OD). **Related Knowledge/Courses:** Medicine and Dentistry; Biology; Therapy and Counseling; Physics; Sales and Marketing; Economics and Accounting. **Work Experience Needed:** None. **On-the-Job Training Needed:** None. **Certification/Licensure:** Licensure.

**Personality Types:** Investigative–Social–Realistic. **Key Career Cluster:** 08 Health Science. **Key Career Pathway:** 8.1 Therapeutic Services.

**Skills:** Science; operations analysis; reading comprehension; management of financial resources; quality control analysis; operation and control; management of material resources; service orientation.

**Physical Environment:** Indoors; sitting; using hands; exposed to disease or infections. **Structural Environment:** Importance of being exact or accurate; frequency of decision making; structured versus unstructured work; freedom to make decisions; time pressure; impact of decisions on co-workers or company results.

## Personal Financial Advisors

**Advise clients on financial plans, using knowledge of tax and investment strategies, securities, insurance, pension plans, and real estate.**

- Average annual earnings: $67,520
- Middle 50% of earners: $44,140–$111,450
- Earnings growth potential: Very high (52.2%)
- Growth: 32.1%
- Annual job openings: 9,020
- Self-employed: 23.9%

**Considerations for Job Outlook:** Personal financial advisors are expected to face competition as the combination of relatively high wages

### BEST-PAYING INDUSTRIES

| Industry | Median Earnings | Workforce |
|---|---|---|
| Securities, Commodity Contracts, and Other Financial Investments and Related Activities | $78,350 | 103,360 |
| Credit Intermediation and Related Activities | $47,780 | 46,890 |

### BEST-PAYING METROPOLITAN AREAS

| Metro Area | Median Earnings | Workforce |
|---|---|---|
| New York–Northern New Jersey–Long Island, NY-NJ-PA | $97,890 | 24,720 |
| San Francisco–Oakland–Fremont, CA | $82,240 | 5,890 |
| Boston-Cambridge-Quincy, MA-NH | $79,930 | 6,660 |
| Philadelphia-Camden-Wilmington, PA-NJ-DE-MD | $79,730 | 4,170 |
| Atlanta–Sandy Springs–Marietta, GA | $72,570 | 3,700 |
| Chicago-Naperville-Joliet, IL-IN-WI | $69,800 | 8,640 |
| Miami–Fort Lauderdale–Pompano Beach, FL | $68,500 | 4,710 |
| Los Angeles–Long Beach–Santa Ana, CA | $64,610 | 9,240 |
| Dallas–Fort Worth–Arlington, TX | $64,540 | 4,310 |

and few formal educational requirements attracts many applicants for each opening.

**Major Work Tasks:** Analyze financial information obtained from clients to determine strategies for meeting clients' financial objectives. Answer clients' questions about the purposes and details of financial plans and strategies. Interview clients to determine their current income, expenses, insurance coverage, tax status, financial objectives, risk tolerance, or other information needed to develop a financial plan. Implement financial planning recommendations or refer clients to someone who can assist them with plan implementation. Prepare or interpret for clients information, such as investment performance reports, financial document summaries, or income projections. Guide clients in the gathering of information, such as bank account records, income tax returns, life and disability insurance records, pension plans, or wills. Contact clients periodically to determine any changes in their financial status. Meet with clients' other advisors, such as attorneys, accountants, trust officers, or investment bankers, to fully understand clients' financial goals and circumstances. Devise debt liquidation plans that include payoff priorities and timelines. Recommend to clients strategies in cash management, insurance coverage, investment planning, or other areas to help them achieve their financial goals. Review clients' accounts and plans regularly to determine whether life changes, economic changes, environmental concerns, or financial performance indicate a need for plan reassessment. Manage client portfolios, keeping client plans up-to-date. Recruit and maintain client bases. Explain to clients the personal financial advisor's responsibilities and the types of services to be provided. Investigate available investment opportunities to determine compatibility with client financial plans. Monitor financial market trends to ensure that client plans are responsive. Recommend financial products, such as stocks, bonds, mutual funds, or insurance. Open accounts for clients and disburse funds from accounts to creditors as agent for clients. Conduct seminars or workshops on financial planning topics, such as retirement planning, estate planning, or the evaluation of severance packages.

**Usual Educational Requirement:** Bachelor's degree. **Relevant Educational Programs**: Finance, General; Financial Planning and Services. **Related Knowledge/Courses:** Economics and Accounting; Sales and Marketing; Therapy and Counseling; Law and Government; Clerical Practices; Mathematics. **Work Experience Needed:** None. **On-the-Job Training Needed:** None. **Certification/Licensure:** None.

**Personality Types:** Enterprising–Conventional–Social. **Key Career Cluster:** 06 Finance. **Key Career Pathway:** 6.1 Financial and Investment Planning.

**Skills:** Management of financial resources; operations analysis; mathematics; service orientation; persuasion; systems evaluation; systems analysis; speaking.

**Physical Environment:** Indoors; sitting. **Structural Environment:** Importance of being exact or accurate; frequency of decision making; impact of decisions on c-workers or company results; level of competition; time pressure; structured versus unstructured work.

## Petroleum Engineers

**Devise methods to improve oil and gas extraction and production and determine the need for new or modified tool designs.**

- Average annual earnings: $130,280
- Middle 50% of earners: $97,860–$183,520
- Earnings growth potential: Medium (42.4%)
- Growth: 17.0%
- Annual job openings: 1,180
- Self-employed: 3.6%

### BEST-PAYING INDUSTRIES

| Industry | Median Earnings | Workforce |
|---|---|---|
| Oil and Gas Extraction | $144,810 | 19,880 |
| Management of Companies and Enterprises | $143,240 | 2,120 |
| Petroleum and Coal Products Manufacturing | $120,440 | 2,120 |
| Professional, Scientific, and Technical Services | $119,550 | 4,360 |
| Support Activities for Mining | $101,800 | 5,120 |

**363**

## Your Guide to High-Paying Careers

### BEST-PAYING METROPOLITAN AREAS

| Metro Area | Median Earnings | Workforce |
|---|---|---|
| Oklahoma City, OK | $170,130 | 1,970 |
| Dallas–Fort Worth–Arlington, TX | $156,820 | 2,360 |
| Midland, TX | $147,080 | 1,000 |
| Houston–Sugar Land–Baytown, TX | $140,730 | 14,160 |
| Washington-Arlington-Alexandria, DC-VA-MD-WV | $139,610 | 980 |
| Tulsa, OK | $136,940 | 910 |
| Denver-Aurora, CO | $133,520 | 1,090 |
| New Orleans–Metairie–Kenner, LA | $123,160 | 1,130 |

**Considerations for Job Outlook:** Job prospects are expected to be highly favorable because of projected growth and because many petroleum engineers retire or leave the occupation for other reasons.

**Major Work Tasks:** Assess costs and estimate the production capabilities and economic value of oil and gas wells to evaluate the economic viability of potential drilling sites. Monitor production rates, and plan rework processes to improve production. Analyze data to recommend placement of wells and supplementary processes to enhance production. Specify and supervise well modification and stimulation programs to maximize oil and gas recovery. Direct and monitor the completion and evaluation of wells, well testing, or well surveys. Assist engineering and other personnel to solve operating problems. Develop plans for oil and gas field drilling and for product recovery and treatment. Maintain records of drilling and production operations. Confer with scientific, engineering, and technical personnel to resolve design, research, and testing problems. Write technical reports for engineering and management personnel. Evaluate findings to develop, design, or test equipment or processes. Assign work to staff to obtain maximum utilization of personnel. Interpret drilling and testing information for personnel. Coordinate the installation, maintenance, and operation of mining and oil field equipment. Design and implement environmental controls on oil and gas operations. Supervise the removal of drilling equipment, the removal of any waste, and the safe return of land to structural stability when wells or pockets are exhausted. Inspect oil and gas wells to determine that installations are completed. Simulate reservoir performance for different recovery techniques, using computer models. Take samples to assess the amount and quality of oil, the depth at which resources lie, and the equipment needed to properly extract them. Coordinate activities of workers engaged in research, planning, and development. Design or modify mining and oil field machinery and tools, applying engineering principles. Test machinery and equipment to ensure that it is safe and conforms to performance specifications. Conduct engineering research experiments to improve or modify mining and oil machinery and operations.

**Usual Educational Requirement:** Bachelor's degree. **Relevant Educational Programs**: Geotechnical and Geoenvironmental Engineering; Petroleum Engineering. **Related Knowledge/Courses:** Engineering and Technology; Physics; Geography; Chemistry; Economics and Accounting; Design. **Work Experience Needed:** None. **On-the-Job Training Needed:** None. **Certification/Licensure:** Licensure for offering services to public.

**Personality Types:** Investigative–Realistic–Conventional. **Key Career Cluster:** 15 Science, Technology, Engineering, and Mathematics. **Key Career Pathway:** 15.1 Engineering and Technology.

**Skills:** Science; systems evaluation; management of financial resources; management of

**364**

material resources; mathematics; operation monitoring; technology design; systems analysis.

**Physical Environment:** Indoors; sitting. **Structural Environment:** Structured versus unstructured work; freedom to make decisions; impact of decisions on co-workers or company results; importance of being exact or accurate; frequency of decision making; time pressure.

## Pharmacists

**Dispense drugs prescribed by physicians and other health practitioners and provide information to patients about medications and their use.**

### BEST-PAYING INDUSTRIES

| Industry | Median Earnings | Workforce |
|---|---|---|
| General Merchandise Stores | $125,100 | 31,870 |
| Health and Personal Care Stores | $117,840 | 123,020 |
| Food and Beverage Stores | $116,000 | 22,590 |
| Hospitals | $114,100 | 65,200 |

### BEST-PAYING METROPOLITAN AREAS

| Metro Area | Median Earnings | Workforce |
|---|---|---|
| Los Angeles–Long Beach–Santa Ana, CA | $129,810 | 8,880 |
| Miami–Fort Lauderdale–Pompano Beach, FL | $113,440 | 5,670 |
| Chicago-Naperville-Joliet, IL-IN-WI | $113,310 | 7,570 |
| New York–Northern New Jersey–Long Island, NY-NJ-PA | $112,260 | 18,330 |
| Philadelphia-Camden-Wilmington, PA-NJ-DE-MD | $111,930 | 6,300 |

- Average annual earnings: $116,670
- Middle 50% of earners: $103,350–$133,700
- Earnings growth potential: Very low (23.5%)
- Growth: 25.4%
- Annual job openings: 13,960
- Self-employed: 2.0%

**Considerations for Job Outlook:** Because a significant number of pharmacists are expected to retire in the coming decade, new pharmacists should expect good job prospects.

**Major Work Tasks:** Review prescriptions to assure accuracy, to ascertain the needed ingredients, and to evaluate their suitability. Provide information and advice regarding drug interactions, side effects, dosage, and proper medication storage. Analyze prescribing trends to monitor patient compliance and to prevent excessive usage or harmful interactions. Order and purchase pharmaceutical supplies, medical supplies, or drugs, maintaining stock and storing and handling it properly. Maintain records, such as pharmacy files, patient profiles, charge system files, inventories, control records for radioactive nuclei, or registries of poisons, narcotics, or controlled drugs. Provide specialized services to help patients manage conditions, such as diabetes, asthma, smoking cessation, or high blood pressure. Advise customers on the selection of medication brands, medical equipment, or health-care supplies. Collaborate with other health-care professionals to plan, monitor, review, or evaluate the quality or effectiveness of drugs or drug regimens, providing advice on drug applications or characteristics. Compound and dispense medications as prescribed by doctors and dentists, by calculating, weighing, measuring, and mixing ingredients, or oversee these activities. Refer patients to other health professionals or agencies when appropriate. Plan, implement, or maintain procedures for mixing, packaging, or labeling pharmaceuticals, according to policy and legal requirements, to ensure quality, security, and proper disposal. Manage pharmacy operations, hiring or supervising staff, performing administrative duties, or buying or selling non-pharmaceutical merchandise. Assess the identity, strength, or purity of medications. Teach pharmacy students serving as interns in preparation for their graduation or licensure. Offer health promotion or prevention activities, such as training people to use blood pressure devices or diabetes monitors. Contact insurance companies to resolve billing issues. Prepare sterile solutions or infusions for use in surgical procedures, emergency rooms, or patients' homes.

**Usual Educational Requirement:** Doctoral or professional degree. **Relevant Educational Programs**: Clinical and Industrial Drug Development (MS, PhD); Clinical, Hospital, and Managed Care Pharmacy (MS, PhD); Industrial and Physical Pharmacy and Cosmetic Sciences (MS, PhD); Medicinal and Pharmaceutical Chemistry (MS, PhD); Natural Products Chemistry and Pharmacognosy (MS, PhD); Pharmaceutical Sciences; Pharmaceutics and Drug Design (MS, PhD); Pharmacoeconomics/Pharmaceutical Economics (MS, PhD); Pharmacy (PharmD [USA], PharmD or BS/BPharm [Canada]); Pharmacy Administration and Pharmacy Policy and Regulatory Affairs (MS, PhD). **Related Knowledge/Courses:** Medicine and Dentistry; Chemistry; Biology; Therapy and Counseling; Psychology; Customer and Personal Service. **Work Experience Needed:** None. **On-the-Job Training Needed:** None. **Certification/Licensure:** Licensure.

**Personality Types:** Investigative–Conventional–Social. **Key Career Cluster:** 08 Health Science. **Key Career Pathway:** 8.1 Therapeutic Services.

**Skills:** Science; management of material resources; reading comprehension; operations analysis; instructing; service orientation; management of personnel resources; monitoring.

**Physical Environment:** Indoors; standing; using hands; repetitive motions; noise; exposed to disease or infections. **Structural Environment:** Importance of being exact or accurate; consequence of error; impact of decisions on co-workers or company results; frequency of decision making; freedom to make decisions; importance of repeating same tasks.

## Philosophy and Religion Teachers, Postsecondary

*See Teachers, Postsecondary.*

## Physical Scientists, All Other

**All physical scientists not listed separately.**

- Average annual earnings: $91,640
- Middle 50% of earners: $59,000–$122,470
- Earnings growth potential: Very high (53.9%)
- Growth: 8.5%
- Annual job openings: 1,330
- Self-employed: 11.9%

**Considerations for Job Outlook:** In federal government, a small increase is expected as funding for scientific research programs is expected to fare better than other areas of government in future budgets.

**Major Work Tasks:** For tasks, see the job specializations.

**Usual Educational Requirement:** Bachelor's degree. **Relevant Educational Programs**: Ma-

### BEST-PAYING INDUSTRIES

| Industry | Median Earnings | Workforce |
|---|---|---|
| Professional, Scientific, and Technical Services | $107,590 | 6,490 |
| Federal, State, and Local Government | $100,850 | 10,350 |
| Educational Services | $52,460 | 5,920 |

**366**

## BEST-PAYING METROPOLITAN AREAS

| Metro Area | Median Earnings | Workforce |
|---|---|---|
| Washington-Arlington-Alexandria, DC-VA-MD-WV | $115,730 | 3,220 |
| Baltimore-Towson, MD | $109,810 | 520 |
| New York–Northern New Jersey–Long Island, NY-NJ-PA | $99,430 | 870 |
| Albany-Schenectady-Troy, NY | $86,250 | 540 |
| Chicago-Naperville-Joliet, IL-IN-WI | $60,060 | 1,970 |
| Durham, NC | $59,480 | 710 |
| Indianapolis-Carmel, IN | $52,830 | 520 |

rine Sciences; Natural Sciences; Physical Sciences, Other. **Work Experience Needed:** None. **On-the-Job Training Needed:** None. **Certification/Licensure:** None.

**Key Career Cluster:** 15 Science, Technology, Engineering, and Mathematics. **Key Career Pathway:** 15.2 Science and Mathematics.

### JOB SPECIALIZATION: REMOTE SENSING SCIENTISTS AND TECHNOLOGISTS

**Apply remote sensing principles and methods to analyze data and solve problems in areas, such as natural resource management, urban planning, and homeland security. May develop new analytical techniques and sensor systems or develop new applications for existing systems.**

**Major Work Tasks:** Analyze data acquired from aircraft, satellites, or ground-based platforms, using statistical analysis software, image analysis software, or Geographic Information Systems (GIS). Develop or build databases for remote sensing or related geospatial project information. Integrate other geospatial data sources into projects. Prepare or deliver reports or presentations of geospatial project information. Organize and maintain geospatial data and associated documentation. Process aerial or satellite imagery to create products, such as landcover maps. Design or implement strategies for collection, analysis, or display of geographic data. Direct all activity associated with implementation, operation, or enhancement of remote sensing hardware or software. Collect supporting data, such as climatic or field survey data to corroborate remote sensing data analyses. Compile and format image data to increase its usefulness. Conduct research into the application or enhancement of remote sensing technology. Discuss project goals, equipment requirements, or methodologies with colleagues or team members. Develop automated routines to correct for the presence of image distorting artifacts, such as ground vegetation. Develop new analytical techniques or sensor systems. Manage or analyze data obtained from remote sensing systems to obtain meaningful results. Monitor quality of remote sensing data collection operations to determine if procedural or equipment changes are necessary. Direct installation or testing of new remote sensing hardware or software. Attend meetings or seminars or read current literature to maintain knowledge of developments in the field of remote sensing. Participate in fieldwork. Recommend new remote sensing hardware or software acquisitions. Set up or maintain remote sensing data collection systems. Train technicians in the use of remote sensing technology. Apply remote sensing data or techniques to address environmental issues, such as surface water modeling or dust cloud detection. Use remote sensing data for forest or carbon tracking activities involved in assessing the impact of environmental change.

**Related Knowledge/Courses:** Geography; Biology; Physics; Computers and Electronics; Engineering and Technology; Mathematics.

**Personality Types:** Realistic–Investigative.

**Skills:** Science; operations analysis; mathematics; writing; systems evaluation; systems analysis; reading comprehension; complex problem solving.

**Physical Environment:** Indoors; sitting. **Structural Environment:** Importance of being exact or accurate; freedom to make decisions; structured versus unstructured work; impact of decisions on co-workers or company results; level of competition; time pressure.

## Physical Therapists

**Assess, plan, organize, and participate in rehabilitative programs that improve mobility, relieve pain, increase strength, and improve or correct disabling conditions.**

### BEST-PAYING INDUSTRIES

| Industry | Median Earnings | Workforce |
|---|---|---|
| Nursing and Residential Care Facilities | $85,950 | 14,300 |
| Hospitals | $80,260 | 55,770 |
| Ambulatory Health-Care Services | $79,210 | 103,380 |

### BEST-PAYING METROPOLITAN AREAS

| Metro Area | Median Earnings | Workforce |
|---|---|---|
| Los Angeles–Long Beach–Santa Ana, CA | $88,090 | 6,900 |
| Dallas–Fort Worth–Arlington, TX | $87,960 | 3,960 |
| New York–Northern New Jersey–Long Island, NY-NJ-PA | $85,050 | 13,710 |
| Boston-Cambridge-Quincy, MA-NH | $78,940 | 5,080 |
| Chicago-Naperville-Joliet, IL-IN-WI | $78,580 | 7,870 |
| Philadelphia-Camden-Wilmington, PA-NJ-DE-MD | $77,970 | 4,370 |

- Average annual earnings: $79,860
- Middle 50% of earners: $66,950–$92,860
- Earnings growth potential: Low (30.4%)
- Growth: 39.0%
- Annual job openings: 10,060
- Self-employed: 7.5%

**Considerations for Job Outlook:** Job opportunities will likely be good for licensed physical therapists in all settings. Job opportunities should be particularly good in acute hospital, skilled nursing, and orthopedic settings, where the elderly are most often treated. Job prospects should be especially favorable in rural areas because many physical therapists live in highly populated urban and suburban areas.

**Major Work Tasks:** Plan, prepare, or carry out individually designed programs of physical treatment to maintain, improve, or restore physical functioning, alleviate pain, or prevent physical dysfunction in patients. Perform and document an initial exam, evaluating data to identify problems and determine a diagnosis prior to intervention. Evaluate effects of treatment at various stages and adjust treatments to achieve maximum benefit. Administer manual exercises, massage, or traction to help relieve pain, increase patient strength, or decrease or prevent deformity or crippling. Instruct patient and family in treatment procedures to be continued at home. Confer with the patient, medical practitioners, or appropriate others to plan, implement, or assess the intervention program. Review physician's referral and patient's medical records to help determine diagnosis and physical therapy treatment required. Record prognosis, treatment, response, and progress in patient's chart or enter information into computer. Obtain patients' informed consent to proposed interventions. Discharge patient from physical therapy when goals or projected outcomes have been attained and provide for appropriate follow-up care or referrals. Test and measure patient's strength, motor development and function, sensory perception, functional capacity, or respiratory or circulatory efficiency and record data. Identify and document goals, anticipated progress, and plans for reevaluation. Provide information to the patient about the proposed intervention, its material risks and expected benefits, and any reasonable alternatives. Direct, supervise, assess, and communicate with supportive personnel. Administer treatment involving application of physical agents, using equipment, moist packs, ultraviolet or infrared lamps, or ultrasound machines. Teach physical therapy students or those in other health professions. Evaluate, fit, or adjust prosthetic or orthotic devices or recommend modification to orthotist. Provide educational information about physical therapy or physical therapists, injury prevention, ergonomics, or ways to promote health. Refer clients to community resources or services.

**Usual Educational Requirement:** Doctoral or professional degree. **Relevant Educational Programs**: Kinesiotherapy/Kinesiotherapist; Physical Therapy/Therapist Training. **Related Knowledge/Courses:** Therapy and Counseling; Medicine and Dentistry; Biology; Psychology; Sociology and Anthropology; Education and Training. **Work Experience Needed:** None. **On-the-Job Training Needed:** None. **Certification/Licensure:** Licensure in most states; also voluntary certification by association.

**Personality Types:** Social–Investigative–Realistic. **Key Career Cluster:** 08 Health Science. **Key Career Pathway:** 8.1 Therapeutic Services.

**Skills:** Science; operations analysis; social perceptiveness; service orientation; reading comprehension; writing; speaking; instructing.

**Physical Environment:** Indoors; standing; using hands; exposed to disease or infections. **Structural Environment:** Freedom to make decisions; structured versus unstructured work; frequency of decision making; time pressure;

impact of decisions on co-workers or company results; importance of being exact or accurate.

## Physician Assistants

**Provide health-care services typically performed by a physician, under the supervision of a physician.**

- Average annual earnings: $90,930
- Middle 50% of earners: $78,640–$108,580
- Earnings growth potential: Low (31.3%)
- Growth: 29.5%
- Annual job openings: 4,060
- Self-employed: 0.8%

**Considerations for Job Outlook:** Good job prospects are expected. This should be particularly true for physician assistants working in rural

### BEST-PAYING INDUSTRIES

| Industry | Median Earnings | Workforce |
|---|---|---|
| Hospitals | $93,660 | 19,350 |
| Ambulatory Health-Care Services | $90,450 | 56,470 |

### BEST-PAYING METROPOLITAN AREAS

| Metro Area | Median Earnings | Workforce |
|---|---|---|
| Los Angeles–Long Beach–Santa Ana, CA | $108,220 | 2,000 |
| New York–Northern New Jersey–Long Island, NY-NJ-PA | $97,870 | 7,230 |
| Boston-Cambridge-Quincy, MA-NH | $91,200 | 1,900 |
| Washington-Arlington-Alexandria, DC-VA-MD-WV | $84,010 | 1,960 |
| Philadelphia-Camden-Wilmington, PA-NJ-DE-MD | $80,430 | 1,950 |

and medically underserved areas, as well as physician assistants working in primary care.

**Major Work Tasks:** Examine patients to obtain information about their physical condition. Interpret diagnostic test results for deviations from normal. Make tentative diagnoses and decisions about management and treatment of patients. Obtain, compile, and record patient medical data, including health history, progress notes, and results of physical examination. Administer or order diagnostic tests, such as X-ray, electrocardiogram, and laboratory tests. Prescribe therapy or medication with physician approval. Perform therapeutic procedures, such as injections, immunizations, suturing and wound care, and infection management. Instruct and counsel patients about prescribed therapeutic regimens, normal growth and development, family planning, emotional problems of daily living, and health maintenance. Provide physicians with assistance during surgery or complicated medical procedures. Supervise and coordinate activities of technicians and technical assistants. Visit and observe patients on hospital rounds or house calls, updating charts, ordering therapy, and reporting back to physician. Order medical and laboratory supplies and equipment.

**Usual Educational Requirement:** Master's degree. **Relevant Educational Program**: Physician Assistant Training. **Related Knowledge/Courses:** Medicine and Dentistry; Biology; Therapy and Counseling; Psychology; Chemistry; Sociology and Anthropology. **Work Experience Needed:** None. **On-the-Job Training Needed:** None. **Certification/Licensure:** Licensure.

**Personality Types:** Social–Investigative–Realistic. **Key Career Cluster:** 08 Health Science. **Key Career Pathway:** 8.1 Therapeutic Services.

**Skills:** Science; instructing; service orientation; judgment and decision making; social percep-

tiveness; operations analysis; reading comprehension; persuasion.

**Physical Environment:** Indoors; standing; using hands; exposed to disease or infections. **Structural Environment:** Frequency of decision making; impact of decisions on co-workers or company results; freedom to make decisions; importance of being exact or accurate; consequence of error; structured versus unstructured work.

### JOB SPECIALIZATION: ANESTHESIOLOGIST ASSISTANTS

**Assist anesthesiologists in the administration of anesthesia for surgical and non-surgical procedures. Monitor patient status and provide patient care during surgical treatment.**

**Major Work Tasks:** Verify availability of operating room supplies, medications, and gases. Participate in seminars, workshops, or other professional activities to keep abreast of developments in anesthesiology. Provide airway management interventions, including tracheal intubation, fiber optics, or ventilary support. Respond to emergency situations by providing cardiopulmonary resuscitation (CPR), basic cardiac life support (BLS), advanced cardiac life support (ACLS), or pediatric advanced life support (PALS). Pretest and calibrate anesthesia delivery systems and monitors. Provide clinical instruction, supervision, or training to staff in areas, such as anesthesia practices. Collect samples or specimens for diagnostic testing. Collect and document patients' preanesthetic health histories. Monitor and document patients' progress during post-anesthesia period. Assist anesthesiologists in monitoring of patients including electrocardiogram (EKG), direct arterial pressure, central venous pressure, arterial blood gas, hematocrit, or routine measurement of temperature, respiration, blood pressure, and heart rate. Assist in the provision of advanced life-support techniques, including those procedures using high frequency ventilation or intra-arterial cardiovascular assistance devices. Assist anesthesiologists in performing anesthetic procedures, such as epidural and spinal injections. Assist in the application of monitoring techniques, such as pulmonary artery catheterization, electroencephalographic spectral analysis, echocardiography, and evoked potentials. Administer blood, blood products, or supportive fluids. Control anesthesia levels during procedures. Administer anesthetic, adjuvant, or accessory drugs under the direction of an anesthesiologist.

**Related Knowledge/Courses:** Medicine and Dentistry; Biology; Chemistry; Therapy and Counseling; Psychology; Physics.

**Personality Types:** Realistic–Social–Investigative.

**Skills:** Operation and control; science; operation monitoring; equipment selection; troubleshooting; repairing; equipment maintenance; quality control analysis.

**Physical Environment:** Indoors; standing; walking and running; using hands; repetitive motions; noise. **Structural Environment:** Importance of being exact or accurate; structured versus unstructured work; freedom to make decisions; importance of repeating same tasks; consequence of error; time pressure.

## Physicians and Surgeons

**Diagnose illnesses and prescribe and administer treatment for people suffering from injury or disease.**

- Average annual earnings: $187,200+
- Middle 50% of earners: $129,130–$187,200+
- Earnings growth potential: (Cannot be calculated)
- Growth: 24.4%
- Annual job openings: 30,510
- Self-employed: 12.4%

### BEST-PAYING INDUSTRIES

| Industry | Median Earnings | Workforce |
|---|---|---|
| Ambulatory Health-Care Services | $187,199+ | 392,780 |
| Federal, State, and Local Government | $179,760 | 39,900 |
| Hospitals | $154,430 | 145,960 |

### BEST-PAYING METROPOLITAN AREAS

| Metro Area | Median Earnings | Workforce |
|---|---|---|
| New York-Northern New Jersey-Long Island, NY-NJ-PA | $165,344 | 56,030 |

**Considerations for Job Outlook:** Job prospects should be good for physicians who are willing to practice in rural and low-income areas, because these areas tend to have difficulty attracting physicians. Job prospects also should be good for physicians in specialties dealing with health issues that largely affect aging baby boomers. For example, physicians specializing in cardiology and radiology will be needed because the risks for heart disease and cancer increase as people age.

**Major Work Tasks:** For tasks, see the job specializations.

**Usual Educational Requirement:** Doctoral or professional degree. **Relevant Educational Program**: See specialized occupations. **Related Knowledge/Courses:** No data available. **Work Experience Needed:** None. **On-the-Job Training Needed:** Internship/residency. **Certification/Licensure:** Licensure.

**Personality Types:** Investigative–Social–Realistic. **Key Career Cluster:** 08 Health Science. **Key Career Pathway:** 8.1 Therapeutic Services.

**Skills:** No data available.

**Physical Environment:** No data available. **Structural Environment:** Freedom to make decisions; importance of being exact or accurate; frequency of decision making; impact of decisions on co-workers or company results; structured versus unstructured work; consequence of error.

## JOB SPECIALIZATION: ANESTHESIOLOGISTS

**Administer anesthetics during surgery or other medical procedures.**

- Average annual earnings: $187,200+
- Middle 50% of earners: $187,200+–$187,200+
- Earnings growth potential: (Cannot be calculated)

### BEST-PAYING INDUSTRIES

| Industry | Median Earnings | Workforce |
|---|---|---|
| Ambulatory Health-Care Services | $187,199+ | 25,440 |
| Hospitals | $187,199+ | 3,730 |

### BEST-PAYING METROPOLITAN AREAS

| Metro Area | Median Earnings | Workforce |
|---|---|---|
| New York-Northern New Jersey-Long Island, NY-NJ-PA | $187,199+ | 2,470 |

**Major Work Tasks:** Administer anesthetic or sedation during medical procedures, using local, intravenous, spinal, or caudal methods. Monitor patient before, during, and after anesthesia and counteract adverse reactions or complications. Provide and maintain life support and airway management and help prepare patients for emergency surgery. Record type and amount of anesthesia and patient condition throughout procedure. Examine patient, obtain medical history, and use diagnostic tests to determine risk during surgical, obstetrical, and other medical procedures. Position patient on operating table to maximize patient comfort and surgical accessibility. Decide when patients have recovered or stabilized enough to be sent to another room or ward or to be sent home following outpatient surgery. Coordinate administration of anesthetics with surgeons during operation. Confer with other medical professionals to determine type and method of anesthetic or sedation to render patient insensible to pain. Coordinate and direct work of nurses, medical technicians, and other healthcare providers. Order laboratory tests, X-rays, and other diagnostic procedures. Diagnose illnesses, using examinations, tests, and reports. Manage anesthesiological services, coordinating them with other medical activities and formulating plans and procedures. Provide medical care and consultation in many settings, prescribing medication and treatment and referring patients for surgery. Inform students and staff of types and methods of anesthesia administration, signs of complications, and emergency methods to counteract reactions. Instruct individuals and groups on ways to preserve health and prevent disease. Schedule and maintain use of surgical suite, including operating, wash-up, waiting rooms, and anesthetic and sterilizing equipment. Conduct medical research to aid in controlling and curing disease, to investigate new medications, and to develop and test new medical techniques.

**Related Knowledge/Courses:** Medicine and Dentistry; Biology; Chemistry; Psychology; Physics; Therapy and Counseling.

**Personality Types:** Investigative–Realistic–Social

**Skills:** Science; operation monitoring; operation and control; reading comprehension; judgment and decision making; monitoring; active learning; time management.

**Physical Environment:** Indoors; sitting; standing; using hands; noise; contaminants. **Structural Environment:** Importance of being exact or accurate; freedom to make decisions; impact of decisions on co-workers or company results; frequency of decision making; consequence of error; structured versus unstructured work.

**Diagnose, treat, and help prevent diseases and injuries that commonly occur in the general population.**

- Average annual earnings: $172,020
- Middle 50% of earners: $129,440–$187,200+
- Earnings growth potential: Very high (50.7%)

### BEST-PAYING INDUSTRIES

| Industry | Median Earnings | Workforce |
|---|---|---|
| Ambulatory Health-Care Services | $173,900 | 82,940 |
| Hospitals | $171,830 | 19,190 |

### BEST-PAYING METROPOLITAN AREAS

| Metro Area | Median Earnings | Workforce |
|---|---|---|

No data available

**Major Work Tasks:** Prescribe or administer treatment, therapy, medication, vaccination, and other specialized medical care to treat or prevent illness, disease, or injury. Order, perform, and interpret tests and analyze records, reports, and examination information to diagnose patients' condition. Monitor patients' conditions and progress and reevaluate treatments as necessary. Collect, record, and maintain patient information, such as medical history, reports, and examination results. Explain procedures and discuss test results or prescribed treatments with patients. Advise patients and community members concerning diet, activity, hygiene, and disease prevention. Refer patients to medical specialists or other practitioners when necessary. Direct and coordinate activities of nurses, students, assistants, specialists, therapists, and other medical staff. Coordinate work with nurses, social workers, rehabilitation therapists, pharmacists, psychologists, and other health-care providers. Plan, implement, or administer health programs or standards in hospitals, businesses, or communities for prevention or treatment of injury or illness. Deliver babies. Operate on patients to remove, repair, or improve functioning of diseased or injured body parts and systems. Conduct research to study anatomy and develop or test medications, treatments, or procedures to prevent or control disease or injury. Train residents, medical students, and other health-care professionals. Prepare government or organizational reports which include birth, death, and disease statistics, workforce evaluations, or medical status of individuals.

**Related Knowledge/Courses:** Medicine and Dentistry; Therapy and Counseling; Psychology; Biology; Customer and Personal Service; Sociology and Anthropology.

**Personality Types:** Investigative–Social

**Skills:** Science; judgment and decision making; active listening; social perceptiveness; reading comprehension; operations analysis; management of personnel resources; complex problem solving.

**Physical Environment:** Indoors; sitting; exposed to disease or infections. **Structural Environment:** Freedom to make decisions; impact of decisions on co-workers or company results; importance of being exact or accurate; consequence of error; structured versus unstructured work; frequency of decision making.

**Diagnose and provide non-surgical treatment of diseases and injuries of internal organ systems. Provide care mainly for adults who have a wide range of problems associated with the internal organs.**

## Your Guide to High-Paying Careers

- Average annual earnings: $187,200+
- Middle 50% of earners: $137,310–$187,200+
- Earnings growth potential: (Cannot be calculated)

### BEST-PAYING INDUSTRIES

| Industry | Median Earnings | Workforce |
|---|---|---|
| Ambulatory Health-Care Services | $187,199+ | 33,470 |
| Hospitals | $161,920 | 9,910 |

### BEST-PAYING METROPOLITAN AREAS

| Metro Area | Median Earnings | Workforce |
|---|---|---|
| New York-Northern New Jersey-Long Island, NY-NJ-PA | $161,580 | 3,300 |

**Major Work Tasks:** Treat internal disorders, such as hypertension, heart disease, diabetes, and problems of the lung, brain, kidney, and gastrointestinal tract. Analyze records, reports, test results, or examination information to diagnose medical condition of patient. Prescribe or administer medication, therapy, and other specialized medical care to treat or prevent illness, disease, or injury. Provide and manage long-term, comprehensive medical care, including diagnosis and non-surgical treatment of diseases, for adult patients in an office or hospital. Manage and treat common health problems, such as infections, influenza, and pneumonia, as well as serious, chronic, and complex illnesses, in adolescents, adults, and the elderly. Monitor patients' conditions and progress and reevaluate treatments as necessary. Collect, record, and maintain patient information, such as medical history, reports, and examination results. Make diagnoses when different illnesses occur together or in situations where the diagnosis may be obscure. Explain procedures and discuss test results or prescribed treatments with patients. Advise patients and community members, concerning diet, activity, hygiene, and disease prevention. Refer patient to medical specialist or other practitioner when necessary. Immunize patients to protect them from preventable diseases. Advise surgeon of a patient's risk status and recommend appropriate intervention to minimize risk. Direct and coordinate activities of nurses, students, assistants, specialists, therapists, and other medical staff. Provide consulting services to other doctors caring for patients with special or difficult problems. Prepare government or organizational reports on birth, death, and disease statistics, workforce evaluations, or the medical status of individuals. Operate on patients to remove, repair, or improve functioning of diseased or injured body parts and systems. Plan, implement, or administer health programs in hospitals, businesses, or communities for prevention and treatment of injuries or illnesses. Conduct research to develop or test medications, treatments, or procedures to prevent or control disease or injury.

**Related Knowledge/Courses:** Medicine and Dentistry; Therapy and Counseling; Psychology; Sociology and Anthropology; Biology; Customer and Personal Service.

**Personality Types:** Investigative–Social–Realistic

**Skills:** Science; operations analysis; reading comprehension; active learning; writing; critical thinking; judgment and decision making; social perceptiveness.

**Physical Environment:** Indoors; standing; walking and running; using hands; exposed to disease or infections. **Structural Environment:** Freedom to make decisions; structured versus unstructured work; importance of being exact or accurate; frequency of decision making; impact of decisions on co-workers or company results; time pressure.

374

## JOB SPECIALIZATION: OBSTETRICIANS AND GYNECOLOGISTS

**Diagnose, treat, and help prevent diseases of women, especially those affecting the reproductive system and the process of childbirth.**

- Average annual earnings: $187,200+
- Middle 50% of earners: $165,830–$187,200+
- Earnings growth potential: (Cannot be calculated)

### BEST-PAYING INDUSTRIES

| Industry | Median Earnings | Workforce |
|---|---|---|
| Ambulatory Health-Care Services | $187,199+ | 16,770 |
| Hospitals | $187,199+ | 3,680 |

### BEST-PAYING METROPOLITAN AREAS

| Metro Area | Median Earnings | Workforce |
|---|---|---|
| Houston-Sugar Land-Baytown, TX | $187,199+ | 1,020 |

**Major Work Tasks:** Care for and treat women during prenatal, natal, and postnatal periods. Explain procedures and discuss test results or prescribed treatments with patients. Treat diseases of female organs. Monitor patients' conditions and progress and reevaluate treatments as necessary. Perform cesarean sections or other surgical procedures as needed to preserve patients' health and deliver babies safely. Prescribe or administer therapy, medication, and other specialized medical care to treat or prevent illness, disease, or injury. Analyze records, reports, test results, or examination information to diagnose medical condition of patient. Collect, record, and maintain patient information, such as medical histories, reports, and examination results. Advise patients and community members concerning diet, activity, hygiene, and disease prevention. Refer patient to medical specialist or other practitioner when necessary. Consult with or provide consulting services to other physicians. Direct and coordinate activities of nurses, students, assistants, specialists, therapists, and other medical staff. Plan, implement, or administer health programs in hospitals, businesses, or communities for prevention and treatment of injuries or illnesses. Prepare government and organizational reports on birth, death, and disease statistics, workforce evaluations, or the medical status of individuals. Conduct research to develop or test medications, treatments, or procedures to prevent or control disease or injury.

**Related Knowledge/Courses:** Medicine and Dentistry; Biology; Therapy and Counseling; Psychology; Customer and Personal Service; Chemistry.

**Personality Types:** Investigative–Social–Realistic

**Skills:** Science; operations analysis; reading comprehension; active listening; judgment and decision making; active learning; instructing; critical thinking.

**Physical Environment:** Indoors; standing; using hands; exposed to disease or infections. **Structural Environment:** Importance of being exact or accurate; freedom to make decisions; structured versus unstructured work; impact of decisions on co-workers or company results; frequency of decision making; consequence of error.

## JOB SPECIALIZATION: PEDIATRICIANS, GENERAL

**Diagnose, treat, and help prevent children's diseases and injuries.**

- Average annual earnings: $154,650
- Middle 50% of earners: $123,090–$187,200+
- Earnings growth potential: High (43.8%)

375

## Your Guide to High-Paying Careers

| Industry | Median Earnings | Workforce |
|---|---|---|
| Ambulatory Health-Care Services | $158,370 | 24,730 |
| Hospitals | $147,400 | 4,500 |

| Metro Area | Median Earnings | Workforce |
|---|---|---|
| New York-Northern New Jersey-Long Island, NY-NJ-PA | $156,940 | 2,830 |
| Los Angeles-Long Beach-Santa Ana, CA | $147,580 | 2,080 |

**Major Work Tasks:** Examine patients or order, perform, and interpret diagnostic tests to obtain information on medical condition and determine diagnosis. Examine children regularly to assess their growth and development. Prescribe or administer treatment, therapy, medication, vaccination, and other specialized medical care to treat or prevent illness, disease, or injury in infants and children. Collect, record, and maintain patient information, such as medical history, reports, and examination results. Advise patients, parents or guardians, and community members concerning diet, activity, hygiene, and disease prevention. Treat children who have minor illnesses, acute and chronic health problems, and growth and development concerns. Explain procedures and discuss test results or prescribed treatments with patients and parents or guardians. Monitor patients' conditions and progress and re-evaluate treatments as necessary. Plan and execute medical care programs to aid in the mental and physical growth and development of children and adolescents. Refer patient to medical specialist or other practitioner when necessary. Direct and coordinate activities of nurses, students, assistants, specialists, thera-

pists, and other medical staff. Provide consulting services to other physicians. Plan, implement, or administer health programs or standards in hospitals, businesses, or communities for prevention or treatment of injury or illness. Operate on patients to remove, repair, or improve functioning of diseased or injured body parts and systems. Conduct research to study anatomy and develop or test medications, treatments, or procedures to prevent or control disease or injury. Prepare government or organizational reports of birth, death, and disease statistics, workforce evaluations, or medical status of individuals.

**Related Knowledge/Courses:** Medicine and Dentistry; Therapy and Counseling; Biology; Psychology; Sociology and Anthropology; Chemistry.

**Personality Types:** Investigative–Social

**Skills:** Science; operations analysis; reading comprehension; judgment and Decision Making; Systems Evaluation; Service Orientation; Active Learning; Instructing.

**Physical Environment:** Indoors; standing; exposed to disease or infections. **Structural Environment:** Frequency of decision making; freedom to make decisions; importance of being exact or accurate; structured versus unstructured work; consequence of error; impact of decisions on co-workers or company results.

### JOB SPECIALIZATION: PSYCHIATRISTS

**Diagnose, treat, and help prevent disorders of the mind.**

- Average annual earnings: $173,330
- Middle 50% of earners: $120,480–$187,200+
- Earnings growth potential: Very high (59.1%)

**Major Work Tasks:** Analyze and evaluate patient data or test findings to diagnose nature or extent of mental disorder. Prescribe, direct, or administer psychotherapeutic treatments or medications to treat mental, emotional, or be-

BEST-PAYING INDUSTRIES

| Industry | Median Earnings | Workforce |
|---|---|---|
| Federal, State, and Local Government | $178,810 | 2,600 |
| Ambulatory Health-Care Services | $175,510 | 11,250 |
| Hospitals | $170,940 | 6,760 |
| Educational Services | $122,790 | 1,760 |

BEST-PAYING METROPOLITAN AREAS

| Metro Area | Median Earnings | Workforce |
|---|---|---|
| New York-Northern New Jersey-Long Island, NY-NJ-PA | $168,390 | 3,260 |
| Los Angeles-Long Beach-Santa Ana, CA | $170,780 | 2,170 |

havioral disorders. Collaborate with physicians, psychologists, social workers, psychiatric nurses, or other professionals to discuss treatment plans and progress. Gather and maintain patient information and records, including social or medical history obtained from patients, relatives, or other professionals. Counsel outpatients or other patients during office visits. Design individualized care plans, using a variety of treatments. Examine or conduct laboratory or diagnostic tests on patients to provide information on general physical condition or mental disorder. Advise or inform guardians, relatives, or significant others of patients' conditions or treatment. Review and evaluate treatment procedures and outcomes of other psychiatrists or medical professionals. Prepare and submit case reports or summaries to government or mental health agencies. Serve on committees to promote or maintain community mental health services or delivery systems. Teach, take continuing education classes, attend conferences or seminars, or conduct research and publish findings to increase understanding of mental, emotional, or behavioral states or disorders.

**Related Knowledge/Courses:** Therapy and Counseling; Medicine and Dentistry; Psychology; Biology; Sociology and Anthropology; Philosophy and Theology.

**Personality Types:** Investigative–Social–Artistic

**Skills:** Science; social perceptiveness; operations analysis; persuasion; negotiation; service orientation; instructing; judgment and decision making.

**Physical Environment:** Indoors; sitting; exposed to disease or infections. **Structural Environment:** Freedom to make decisions; structured versus unstructured work; impact of decisions on co-workers or company results; importance of being exact or accurate; frequency of decision making; time pressure.

**JOB SPECIALIZATION: SURGEONS**

**Treat diseases, injuries, and deformities by invasive methods, such as manual manipulation, or by using instruments and appliances.**

- Average annual earnings: $187,200+
- Middle 50% of earners: $187,200+–$187,200+
- Earnings growth potential: (Cannot be calculated)

BEST-PAYING INDUSTRIES

| Industry | Median Earnings | Workforce |
|---|---|---|
| Ambulatory Health-Care Services | $187,199+ | 33,160 |
| Hospitals | $187,199+ | 7,540 |

BEST-PAYING METROPOLITAN AREAS

| Metro Area | Median Earnings | Workforce |
|---|---|---|
| New York-Northern New Jersey-Long Island, NY-NJ-PA | $187,199+ | 3,140 |

377

**Major Work Tasks:** Analyze patient's medical history, medication allergies, physical condition, and examination results to verify operation's necessity and to determine best procedure. Operate on patients to correct deformities, repair injuries, prevent and treat diseases, or improve or restore patients' functions. Follow established surgical techniques during the operation. Prescribe preoperative and postoperative treatments and procedures, such as sedatives, diets, antibiotics, and preparation and treatment of the patient's operative area. Examine patient to obtain information on medical condition and surgical risk. Diagnose bodily disorders and orthopedic conditions and provide treatments, such as medicines and surgeries, in clinics, hospital wards, and operating rooms. Direct and coordinate activities of nurses, assistants, specialists, residents, and other medical staff. Provide consultation and surgical assistance to other physicians and surgeons. Refer patient to medical specialist or other practitioners when necessary. Examine instruments, equipment, and operating room to ensure sterility. Prepare case histories. Manage surgery services, including planning, scheduling and coordination, determination of procedures, and procurement of supplies and equipment. Conduct research to develop and test surgical techniques that can improve operating procedures and outcomes.

**Related Knowledge/Courses:** Medicine and Dentistry; Biology; Therapy and Counseling; Psychology; Customer and Personal Service; English Language.

**Personality Types:** Investigative–Realistic–Social

**Skills:** Science; reading comprehension; active learning; instructing; judgment and decision making; complex problem solving; social perceptiveness; active listening.

**Physical Environment:** Indoors; standing; using hands; repetitive motions; exposed to disease or infections. **Structural Environment:** Importance of being exact or accurate; freedom to make decisions; frequency of decision making; impact of decisions on co-workers or company results; consequence of error; structured versus unstructured work.

### JOB SPECIALIZATION: PHYSICIANS AND SURGEONS, ALL OTHER

**All physicians and surgeons not listed separately.**

- Average annual earnings: $187,200+
- Middle 50% of earners: $109,790–$187,200+
- Earnings growth potential: (Cannot be calculated)

#### BEST-PAYING INDUSTRIES

| Industry | Median Earnings | Workforce |
|---|---|---|
| Ambulatory Health-Care Services | $187,199+ | 165,030 |
| Federal, State, and Local Government | $180,770 | 33,080 |
| Hospitals | $113,600 | 90,650 |
| Educational Services | $60,210 | 14,110 |

#### BEST-PAYING METROPOLITAN AREAS

| Metro Area | Median Earnings | Workforce |
|---|---|---|
| New York-Northern New Jersey-Long Island, NY-NJ-PA | $163,010 | 37,960 |
| Chicago-Joliet-Naperville, IL-IN-WI | $161,430 | 14,290 |

**Major Work Tasks:** No task data available.

**Related Knowledge/Courses:** No data available.

**Personality Types:** No data available.

**Skills:** No data available.

**Physical Environment:** No data available.
**Structural Environment:** No data available.

## Physicists

Conduct research into physical phenomena, develop theories on the basis of observation and experiments, and devise methods to apply physical laws and theories.

- Average annual earnings: $106,840
- Middle 50% of earners: $79,830–$140,550
- Earnings growth potential: High (46.1%)
- Growth: 14.2%
- Annual job openings: 800
- Self-employed: 1.4%

**Considerations for Job Outlook:** Competition for permanent research appointments, such as those at colleges and universities, is expected to be strong. Increasingly, those with a PhD need to work through multiple postdoctoral appointments before finding a permanent position. In addition, the number of research proposals submitted for funding has been growing faster than the amount of funds available, causing more competition for research grants. Despite competition for traditional research jobs, prospects should be good for physicists in applied research, development, and related technical fields. Graduates with any academic degree in physics or astronomy, from bachelor's degree to doctorate, will find their knowledge of science and mathematics useful for entry into many other occupations. A large part of physics and astronomy research depends on federal funds, so federal budgets have a large impact on job prospects from year to year.

**Major Work Tasks:** Perform complex calculations as part of the analysis and evaluation of data, using computers. Describe and express observations and conclusions in mathematical terms. Analyze data from research conducted to detect and measure physical phenomena. Report experimental results by writing papers for scientific journals or by presenting information at scientific conferences. Design computer simulations to model physi-

### BEST-PAYING INDUSTRIES

| Industry | Median Earnings | Workforce |
|---|---|---|
| Hospitals | $152,280 | 1,080 |
| Professional, Scientific, and Technical Services | $108,950 | 8,210 |
| Federal, State, and Local Government | $106,370 | 3,550 |
| Educational Services | $81,180 | 3,010 |

### BEST-PAYING METROPOLITAN AREAS

| Metro Area | Median Earnings | Workforce |
|---|---|---|
| Houston–Sugar Land–Baytown, TX | $137,840 | 620 |
| Seattle-Tacoma-Bellevue, WA | $129,670 | 400 |
| San Jose–Sunnyvale–Santa Clara, CA | $129,240 | 610 |
| Washington-Arlington-Alexandria, DC-VA-MD-WV | $123,390 | 2,210 |
| Albuquerque, NM | $123,130 | 360 |
| New York–Northern New Jersey–Long Island, NY-NJ-PA | $111,690 | 1,410 |
| Boston-Cambridge-Quincy, MA-NH | $110,260 | 440 |
| Chicago-Naperville-Joliet, IL-IN-WI | $107,310 | 960 |
| San Francisco–Oakland–Fremont, CA | $104,370 | 990 |
| San Diego–Carlsbad–San Marcos, CA | $95,740 | 450 |
| Los Angeles–Long Beach–Santa Ana, CA | $94,070 | 1,110 |

**379**

cal data so that it can be better understood. Collaborate with other scientists in the design, development, and testing of experimental, industrial, or medical equipment, instrumentation, and procedures. Direct testing and monitoring of contamination of radioactive equipment and recording of personnel and plant area radiation exposure data. Observe the structure and properties of matter and the transformation and propagation of energy, using equipment, such as masers, lasers, and telescopes to explore and identify the basic principles governing these phenomena. Develop theories and laws on the basis of observation and experiments, and apply these theories and laws to problems in areas, such as nuclear energy, optics, and aerospace technology. Teach physics to students. Develop manufacturing, assembly, and fabrication processes of lasers, masers, infrared, and other light-emitting and light-sensitive devices. Conduct application evaluations and analyze results to determine commercial, industrial, scientific, medical, military, or other uses for electro-optical devices. Develop standards of permissible concentrations of radioisotopes in liquids and gases. Conduct research pertaining to potential environmental impacts of atomic energy-related industrial development to determine licensing qualifications. Advise authorities of procedures to be followed in radiation incidents or hazards, and assist in civil defense planning.

**Usual Educational Requirement:** Doctoral or professional degree. **Relevant Educational Programs**: Acoustics; Astrophysics; Atomic/Molecular Physics; Condensed Matter and Materials Physics; Elementary Particle Physics; Engineering Physics/Applied Physics; Health/Medical Physics; Nuclear Physics; Optics/Optical Sciences; Physics, General; Physics, Other; Plasma and High-Temperature Physics; Theoretical and Mathematical Physics. **Related Knowledge/Courses:** Physics; Mathematics; Engineering and Technology; Computers and Electronics; Telecommunica-

tions; English Language. **Work Experience Needed:** None. **On-the-Job Training Needed:** None. **Certification/Licensure:** None.

**Personality Types:** Investigative–Realistic. **Key Career Cluster:** 15 Science, Technology, Engineering, and Mathematics. **Key Career Pathway:** 15.2 Science and Mathematics.

**Skills:** Science; programming; mathematics; technology design; active learning; reading comprehension; learning strategies; writing.

**Physical Environment:** Indoors; sitting. **Structural Environment:** Structured versus unstructured work; freedom to make decisions; importance of being exact or accurate; impact of decisions on co-workers or company results; time pressure; level of competition.

## Physics Teachers, Postsecondary

*See Teachers, Postsecondary.*

## Podiatrists

**Diagnose and treat diseases and deformities of the human foot.**

- Average annual earnings: $116,440
- Middle 50% of earners: $81,880–$167,500
- Earnings growth potential: Very high (54.9%)
- Growth: 20.0%
- Annual job openings: 510
- Self-employed: 26.1%

**Considerations for Job Outlook:** Job prospects for trained podiatrists should be good, given that there are a limited number of colleges of podiatry. In addition, the retirement of cur-

### BEST-PAYING INDUSTRIES

| Industry | Median Earnings | Workforce |
|---|---|---|
| Ambulatory Health-Care Services | $117,000 | 7,930 |
| Federal, State, and Local Government | $112,820 | 720 |

## BEST-PAYING METROPOLITAN AREAS

| Metro Area | Median Earnings | Workforce |
|---|---|---|
| Washington-Arlington-Alexandria, DC-VA-MD-WV | $153,870 | 280 |
| Miami–Fort Lauderdale–Pompano Beach, FL | $141,950 | 250 |
| Chicago-Naperville-Joliet, IL-IN-WI | $129,240 | 410 |
| Phoenix-Mesa-Scottsdale, AZ | $129,000 | 230 |
| Detroit-Warren-Livonia, MI | $121,150 | 190 |
| Boston-Cambridge-Quincy, MA-NH | $116,730 | 210 |
| Cleveland-Elyria-Mentor, OH | $112,570 | 250 |
| New York–Northern New Jersey–Long Island, NY-NJ-PA | $110,270 | 1,080 |
| Philadelphia-Camden-Wilmington, PA-NJ-DE-MD | $108,460 | 310 |
| Baltimore-Towson, MD | $106,000 | 210 |
| Los Angeles–Long Beach–Santa Ana, CA | $82,700 | 330 |

rently practicing podiatrists in the coming years is expected to increase the number of job openings for podiatrists.

**Major Work Tasks:** Diagnose diseases and deformities of the foot using medical histories, physical examinations, X-rays, and laboratory test results. Prescribe medications, corrective devices, physical therapy, or surgery. Surgically treat conditions, such as corns, calluses, ingrown nails, tumors, shortened tendons, bunions, cysts, and abscesses. Advise patients about treatments and foot care techniques necessary for prevention of future problems. Refer patients to physicians when symptoms indicative of systemic disorders, such as arthritis or diabetes, are observed in feet and legs. Correct deformities by means of plaster casts and strapping. Make and fit prosthetic appliances. Perform administrative duties, such as hiring employees, ordering supplies, and keeping records. Educate the public about the benefits of foot care through techniques, such as speaking engagements, advertising, and other forums. Treat deformities, using mechanical methods, such as whirlpool or paraffin baths, and electrical methods, such as short-wave and low-voltage currents. Treat bone, muscle, and joint disorders affecting the feet and ankles.

**Usual Educational Requirement:** Doctoral or professional degree. **Relevant Educational Programs:** Podiatric Medicine and Surgery—24 Residency Program; Podiatric Medicine and Surgery—36 Residency Program; Podiatric Medicine/Podiatry (DPM). **Related Knowledge/Courses:** Medicine and Dentistry; Therapy and Counseling; Biology; Personnel and Human Resources; Clerical Practices; Customer and Personal Service. **Work Experience Needed:** None. **On-the-Job Training Needed:** Internship/residency. **Certification/Licensure:** Licensure; also voluntary certification by association.

**Personality Types:** Investigative–Social–Realistic. **Key Career Cluster:** 08 Health Science. **Key Career Pathway:** 8.1 Therapeutic Services.

**Skills:** Science; reading comprehension; active learning; management of financial resources; management of material resources; technology design; active listening; judgment and decision making.

**Physical Environment:** Indoors; sitting; using hands; contaminants; exposed to radiation; exposed to disease or infections. **Structural Environment:** Freedom to make decisions; frequency of decision making; importance of being exact or accurate; structured versus unstructured work; impact of decisions on co-workers or company results; consequence of error.

## Political Science Teachers, Postsecondary

*See Teachers, Postsecondary.*

## Producers and Directors

**Produce or direct stage, television, radio, video, or motion picture productions for entertainment, information, or instruction.**

- Average annual earnings: $71,350
- Middle 50% of earners: $46,100–$115,150
- Earnings growth potential: Very high (55.0%)
- Growth: 11.0%
- Annual job openings: 4,970
- Self-employed: 28.7%

**Considerations for Job Outlook:** Producers and directors face intense competition for jobs because there are many more people who want to work in this field than there are jobs available. In film, directors who have experience on movies sets should have the best job prospects. Producers who have good business skills will likely have the best prospects.

### BEST-PAYING INDUSTRIES

| Industry | Median Earnings | Workforce |
|---|---|---|
| Motion Picture and Sound Recording Industries | $93,050 | 35,410 |
| Professional, Scientific, and Technical Services | $82,380 | 6,600 |
| Performing Arts, Spectator Sports, and Related Industries | $60,320 | 9,990 |
| Broadcasting (except Internet) | $56,890 | 23,060 |

### BEST-PAYING METROPOLITAN AREAS

| Metro Area | Median Earnings | Workforce |
|---|---|---|
| Los Angeles–Long Beach–Santa Ana, CA | $113,940 | 20,110 |
| New York–Northern New Jersey–Long Island, NY-NJ-PA | $94,940 | 15,330 |
| Washington-Arlington-Alexandria, DC-VA-MD-WV | $84,850 | 2,740 |
| Philadelphia-Camden-Wilmington, PA-NJ-DE-MD | $76,190 | 1,800 |
| Atlanta–Sandy Springs–Marietta, GA | $66,080 | 1,770 |
| Miami–Fort Lauderdale–Pompano Beach, FL | $63,580 | 1,990 |
| Boston-Cambridge-Quincy, MA-NH | $61,580 | 1,890 |
| Chicago-Naperville-Joliet, IL-IN-WI | $60,680 | 1,900 |

**Major Work Tasks:** For tasks, see the job specializations.

**Usual Educational Requirement:** Bachelor's degree. **Relevant Educational Programs**: Cinematography and Film/Video Production; Directing and Theatrical Production; Documentary Production; Drama and Dramatics/Theatre Arts, General; Dramatic/Theatre Arts and Stagecraft, Other; Film/Cinema/Video Studies; Musical Theatre; Radio and Television; Theatre/Theatre Arts Management. **Work Experience Needed:** 1 to 5 years. **On-the-Job Training Needed:** None. **Certification/Licensure:** None.

**Key Career Cluster:** 03 Arts, Audiovisual Technology, and Communications. **Key Career Pathway:** 3.4 Performing Arts.

## JOB SPECIALIZATION: DIRECTORS—STAGE, MOTION PICTURES, TELEVISION, AND RADIO

Interpret script, conduct rehearsals, and direct activities of cast and technical crew for stage, motion pictures, television, or radio programs.

**Major Work Tasks:** Direct live broadcasts, films and recordings, or non-broadcast programming for public entertainment or education. Supervise and coordinate the work of camera, lighting, design, and sound crew members. Confer with technical directors, managers, crew members, and writers to discuss details of production, such as photography, script, music, sets, and costumes. Plan details, such as framing, composition, camera movement, sound, and actor movement for each shot or scene. Establish pace of programs and sequences of scenes according to time requirements and cast and set accessibility. Identify and approve equipment and elements required for productions, such as scenery, lights, props, costumes, choreography, and music. Select plays or scripts for production, and determine how material should be interpreted and performed. Compile cue words and phrases, and cue announcers, cast members, and technicians during performances. Consult with writers, producers, or actors about script changes, or "workshop" scripts, through rehearsal with writers and actors to create final drafts. Study and research scripts to determine how they should be directed. Cut and edit film or tape to integrate component parts into desired sequences. Collaborate with film and sound editors during the post-production process as films are edited and soundtracks are added. Communicate to actors the approach, characterization, and movement needed for each scene in such a way that rehearsals and takes are minimized. Choose settings and locations for films and determine how scenes will be shot in these settings. Compile scripts, program notes, and other material related to productions. Perform producers' duties, such as securing financial backing, establishing and administering budgets, and recruiting cast and crew. Review film daily to check on work in progress and to plan for future filming. Collaborate with producers to hire crew members, such as art directors, cinematographers, and costumer designers. Interpret stage-set diagrams to determine stage layouts, and supervise placement of equipment and scenery.

**Related Knowledge/Courses:** Communications and Media; Fine Arts; Telecommunications; Production and Processing; Computers and Electronics; Engineering and Technology.

**Personality Types:** Enterprising–Artistic.

**Skills:** Management of personnel resources; negotiation; management of material resources; persuasion; coordination; speaking; instructing; time management.

**Physical Environment:** Indoors; sitting; using hands; repetitive motions; noise. **Structural Environment:** Frequency of decision making; importance of being exact or accurate; time pressure; freedom to make decisions; impact of decisions on co-workers or company results; importance of repeating same tasks.

## JOB SPECIALIZATION: PRODUCERS

**Plan and coordinate various aspects of radio, television, stage, or motion picture production, such as selecting script; coordinating writing, directing, and editing; and arranging financing.**

**Major Work Tasks:** Coordinate the activities of writers, directors, managers, and other personnel throughout the production process. Monitor postproduction processes to ensure accurate completion of details. Conduct meetings with staff to discuss production progress and to ensure production objectives are attained. Resolve personnel problems that arise during the production process by acting as liaisons between dissenting parties when necessary. Review film, recordings, or rehearsals to ensure conformance to production and broadcast standards. Perform administrative duties, such as preparing operational reports,

383

distributing rehearsal call sheets and script copies, and arranging for rehearsal quarters. Write and edit news stories from information collected by reporters and other sources. Research production topics using the Internet, video archives, and other informational sources. Perform management activities, such as budgeting, scheduling, planning, and marketing. Determine production size, content, and budget, establishing details, such as production schedules and management policies. Compose and edit scripts or provide screenwriters with story outlines from which scripts can be written. Produce shows for special occasions, such as holidays or testimonials. Write and submit proposals to bid on contracts for projects. Hire directors, principal cast members, and key production staff members. Arrange financing for productions. Select plays, scripts, books, or ideas to be produced. Obtain and distribute costumes, props, music, and studio equipment needed to complete productions. Negotiate contracts with artistic personnel, often in accordance with collective bargaining agreements. Maintain knowledge of minimum wages and working conditions established by unions or associations of actors and technicians. Plan and coordinate the production of musical recordings, selecting music and directing performers. Negotiate with parties, including independent producers and the distributors and broadcasters who will be handling completed productions. Develop marketing plans for finished products, collaborating with sales associates to supervise product distribution.

**Related Knowledge/Courses:** Communications and Media; Fine Arts; Philosophy and Theology; Sociology and Anthropology; History and Archeology; Geography.

**Personality Types:** Enterprising–Artistic.

**Skills:** Management of financial resources; management of material resources; coordination; management of personnel resources; time management; persuasion; negotiation; monitoring.

**Physical Environment:** Indoors; sitting. **Structural Environment:** Time pressure; importance of being exact or accurate; frequency of decision making; freedom to make decisions; impact of decisions on co-workers or company results; structured versus unstructured work.

## JOB SPECIALIZATION: PROGRAM DIRECTORS

**Direct and coordinate activities of personnel engaged in preparation of radio or television station program schedules and programs, such as sports or news.**

**Major Work Tasks:** Plan and schedule programming and event coverage, based on broadcast length, time availability, and other factors, such as community needs, ratings data, and viewer demographics. Monitor and review programming to ensure that schedules are met, guidelines are adhered to, and performances are of adequate quality. Direct and coordinate activities of personnel engaged in broadcast news, sports, or programming. Check completed program logs for accuracy and conformance with Federal Communications Commission (FCC) rules and regulations and resolve program log inaccuracies. Establish work schedules and assign work to staff members. Coordinate activities between departments, such as news and programming. Perform personnel duties, such as hiring staff and evaluating work performance. Evaluate new and existing programming to assess suitability and the need for changes, using information, such as audience surveys and feedback. Confer with directors and production staff to discuss issues, such as production and casting problems, budgets, policies, and news coverage. Select, acquire, and maintain programs, music, films, and other needed materials and obtain legal clearances for their use as necessary. Monitor network transmissions for advisories concerning daily program schedules, program content, special feeds, or program changes. Develop promotions for current programs and specials. Prepare copy and edit tape so that material is ready for broadcasting. Develop ideas for programs and features that a station could produce. Review information about programs and schedules to ensure accuracy and provide such information to local media outlets. Act as a liaison between talent and directors, providing information that performers or guests need to prepare for appearances and communicating relevant information from guests, performers, or staff to directors. Develop budgets for programming and broadcasting activities and monitor expenditures to ensure that they remain within budgetary limits. Participate in the planning and execution of fundraising activities. Read news, read or record public service and promotional announcements, or perform other on-air duties.

**Related Knowledge/Courses:** Communications and Media; Telecommunications; Personnel and Human Resources; Clerical Practices; Computers and Electronics; English Language.

**Personality Types:** Enterprising–Conventional–Artistic.

**Skills:** Management of financial resources; management of material resources; operations analysis; management of personnel resources; systems evaluation; systems analysis; time management; coordination.

**Physical Environment:** Indoors; sitting; using hands. **Structural Environment:** Time pressure; freedom to make decisions; structured versus unstructured work; frequency of decision making; importance of being exact or accurate; level of competition.

## JOB SPECIALIZATION: TALENT DIRECTORS

**Audition and interview performers to select most appropriate talent for parts in stage, television, radio, or motion picture productions.**

**Major Work Tasks:** Review performer information, such as photos, résumés, voice tapes, videos, and union membership, to decide whom to audition for parts. Read scripts and confer with producers to determine the types and numbers of performers required for a given production. Select performers for roles or submit lists of suitable performers to producers or directors for final selection. Audition and interview performers to match their attributes to specific roles or to increase the pool of available acting talent. Maintain talent files that include information such as performers' specialties, past performances, and availability. Prepare actors for auditions by providing scripts and information about roles and casting requirements. Serve as liaisons between directors, actors, and agents. Attend or view productions to maintain knowledge of available actors. Negotiate contract agreements with performers, with agents, or between performers and agents or production companies. Contact agents and actors to provide notification of audition and performance opportunities and to set up audition times. Hire and supervise workers who help locate people with specified attributes and talents. Arrange for or design screen tests or auditions for prospective performers. Locate performers or extras for crowd and background scenes, and stand-ins or photo doubles for actors, by direct contact or through agents.

**Related Knowledge/Courses:** Fine Arts; Communications and Media; Clerical Practices; Sales and Marketing; Computers and Electronics; Telecommunications.

**Personality Types:** Enterprising–Artistic.

**Skills:** Negotiation; persuasion; management of personnel resources; speaking; social perceptiveness; reading comprehension; monitoring; coordination.

**Physical Environment:** Indoors; sitting; noise. **Structural Environment:** Time pressure; structured versus unstructured work; impact of decisions on co-workers or company results; freedom to make decisions; importance of being exact or accurate; level of competition.

## JOB SPECIALIZATION: TECHNICAL DIRECTORS/MANAGERS

**Coordinate activities of technical departments, such as taping, editing, engineering, and maintenance, to produce radio or television programs.**

**Major Work Tasks:** Test equipment to ensure proper operation. Monitor broadcasts to ensure that programs conform to station or network policies and regulations. Observe pictures through monitors, and direct camera and video staff concerning shading and composition. Act as liaisons between engineering and production departments. Supervise and assign duties to workers engaged in technical control and production of radio and television programs. Schedule use of studio and editing facilities for producers and engineering and maintenance staff. Confer with operations directors to formulate and maintain fair and attainable technical policies for programs. Train workers in use of equipment such as switchers, cameras, monitors, microphones, and lights. Discuss filter options, lens choices, and the visual effects of objects being filmed with photography directors and video operators. Direct technical aspects of newscasts and other productions, checking and switching between video sources and taking responsibility for the on-air product, including camera shots and graphics. Operate equipment to produce programs or broadcast live programs from remote locations. Switch between video sources in a studio or on multi-camera remotes, using equipment such as switchers, video slide projectors, and video effects generators. Set up and execute video transitions and special effects such as fades, dissolves, cuts, keys, and supers, using computers to manipulate pictures as necessary. Collaborate with promotions directors to produce on-air station promotions. Follow instructions from production managers and directors during productions, such as commands for camera cuts, effects, graphics, and takes.

**Related Knowledge/Courses:** Communications and Media; Telecommunications; Fine Arts; Engineering and Technology; Production and Processing; Computers and Electronics.

**Personality Types:** Enterprising–Realistic–Conventional.

**Skills:** Equipment selection; management of personnel resources; monitoring; coordination; operation and control; systems analysis; instructing; operation monitoring.

**Physical Environment:** Indoors; sitting; using hands. **Structural Environment:** Importance of being exact or accurate; freedom to make decisions; structured versus unstructured work; frequency of decision making; time pressure; impact of decisions on co-workers or company results.

## Psychologists, All Other

**All psychologists not listed separately.**

- Average annual earnings: $90,020
- Middle 50% of earners: $65,560–$104,540
- Earnings growth potential: Very high (53.1%)
- Growth: 18.2%
- Annual job openings: 870
- Self-employed: 32.1%

### BEST-PAYING INDUSTRIES

| Industry | Median Earnings | Workforce |
|---|---|---|
| Federal, State, and Local Government | $92,740 | 6,710 |
| Hospitals | $83,650 | 530 |
| Ambulatory Health-Care Services | $76,590 | 1,660 |
| Educational Services | $74,350 | 880 |

| Metro Area | Median Earnings | Workforce |
|---|---|---|
| New York–Northern New Jersey–Long Island, NY-NJ-PA | $104,550 | 420 |
| Baltimore-Towson, MD | $97,930 | 210 |
| Seattle-Tacoma-Bellevue, WA | $90,230 | 290 |
| Boston-Cambridge-Quincy, MA-NH | $89,460 | 300 |
| Tampa–St. Petersburg–Clearwater, FL | $87,280 | 280 |
| Miami–Fort Lauderdale–Pompano Beach, FL | $66,410 | 390 |

**Considerations for Job Outlook:** Job prospects should be best for those who have a doctoral degree in an applied specialty and those with a specialist or doctoral degree in school psychology. Because admission to psychology graduate programs is so selective, job opportunities for doctoral graduates are expected to be fair.

**Major Work Tasks:** For tasks, see the job specializations.

**Usual Educational Requirement:** Master's degree. **Relevant Educational Programs**: Applied Behavior Analysis; Applied Psychology; Behavioral Sciences; Clinical, Counseling and Applied Psychology, Other; Cognitive Psychology and Psycholinguistics; Community Psychology; Comparative Psychology; Educational Psychology; Environmental Psychology; Experimental Psychology; Family Psychology; Forensic Psychology; Personality Psychology; Physiological Psychology/Psychobiology; Psychology, General; Psychology, Other; Psychometrics and Quantitative Psychology; Psychopharmacology; Research and Experimental Psychology, Other; Social Psy-

chology. **Work Experience Needed:** None. **On-the-Job Training Needed:** Internship/residency. **Certification/Licensure:** Voluntary certification by association.

**Key Career Cluster:** 10 Human Services. **Key Career Pathway:** 10.2 Counseling and Mental Health Services.

**JOB SPECIALIZATION: NEUROPSYCHOLOGISTS AND CLINICAL NEUROPSYCHOLOGISTS**

**Apply theories and principles of neuropsychology to diagnose and treat disorders of higher cerebral functioning.**

**Major Work Tasks:** Write or prepare detailed clinical neuropsychological reports using data from psychological or neuropsychological tests, self-report measures, rating scales, direct observations, or interviews. Provide psychotherapy, behavior therapy, or other counseling interventions to patients with neurological disorders. Provide education or counseling to individuals and families. Participate in educational programs, in-service training, or workshops to remain current in methods and techniques. Read current literature, talk with colleagues, and participate in professional organizations or conferences to keep abreast of developments in neuropsychology. Interview patients to obtain comprehensive medical histories. Identify and communicate risks associated with specific neurological surgical procedures, such as epilepsy surgery. Educate and supervise practicum students, psychology interns, or hospital staff. Diagnose and treat conditions, such as chemical dependency, alcohol dependency, Acquired Immune Deficiency Syndrome (AIDS), dementia, and environmental toxin exposure. Distinguish between psychogenic and neurogenic syndromes, two or more suspected etiologies of cerebral dysfunction, or between disorders involving complex seizures. Diagnose and treat neural and psychological conditions in medical and surgical populations, such as patients with early dementing illness or chronic pain with a neurological basis. Design or implement rehabilitation plans for patients with cognitive dysfunction. Establish neurobehavioral baseline measures for monitoring progressive cerebral disease or recovery. Compare patients' progress before and after pharmacologic, surgical, or behavioral interventions. Diagnose and treat psychiatric populations for conditions, such as somatoform disorder, dementias, and psychoses. Diagnose and treat conditions involving injury to the central nervous system, such as cerebrovascular accidents, neoplasms, infectious or inflammatory diseases, degenerative diseases, head traumas, demyelinating diseases, and various forms of dementing illnesses. Diagnose and treat pediatric populations for conditions, such as learning disabilities with developmental or organic bases.

**Related Knowledge/Courses:** Therapy and Counseling; Psychology; Medicine and Dentistry; Biology; Sociology and Anthropology; Philosophy and Theology.

**Personality Types:** Investigative–Social–Artistic.

**Skills:** Science; social perceptiveness; reading comprehension; active learning; writing; learning strategies; critical thinking; instructing.

**Physical Environment:** Indoors; sitting; using hands; exposed to disease or infections. **Structural Environment:** Importance of being exact or accurate; freedom to make decisions; structured versus unstructured work; impact of decisions on co-workers or company results; time pressure; frequency of decision making.

## Psychology Teachers, Postsecondary

*See Teachers, Postsecondary.*

## Public Relations and Fundraising Managers

Plan, direct, or coordinate activities designed to create or maintain a favorable public image or raise issue awareness.

- Average annual earnings: $95,450
- Middle 50% of earners: $69,520–$134,690
- Earnings growth potential: High (45.9%)
- Growth: 16.4%
- Annual job openings: 2,790
- Self-employed: 0.9%

**Considerations for Job Outlook:** In addition to job growth for other reasons, opportunities should come from the need to replace public relations managers and specialists who retire or leave the occupation. Competition for entry-level jobs will likely be strong.

**Major Work Tasks:** Write interesting and effective press releases, prepare information for media kits, and develop and maintain company Internet or webpages. Develop and maintain the company's corporate image and identity, which includes the use of logos and

### BEST-PAYING INDUSTRIES

| Industry | Median Earnings | Workforce |
| --- | --- | --- |
| Professional, Scientific, and Technical Services | $120,610 | 7,860 |
| Management of Companies and Enterprises | $111,030 | 5,120 |
| Religious, Grantmaking, Civic, Professional, and Similar Organizations | $93,580 | 10,520 |
| Educational Services | $87,730 | 8,550 |
| Federal, State, and Local Government | $85,060 | 4,010 |
| Social Assistance | $67,270 | 2,800 |

**BEST-PAYING METROPOLITAN AREAS**

| Metro Area | Median Earnings | Workforce |
|---|---|---|
| New York–Northern New Jersey–Long Island, NY-NJ-PA | $134,340 | 5,920 |
| Washington-Arlington-Alexandria, DC-VA-MD-WV | $126,310 | 3,970 |
| San Francisco–Oakland–Fremont, CA | $118,470 | 1,560 |
| Boston-Cambridge-Quincy, MA-NH | $116,750 | 2,170 |
| Seattle-Tacoma-Bellevue, WA | $101,230 | 1,390 |
| Minneapolis–St. Paul–Bloomington, MN-WI | $98,290 | 1,240 |
| Los Angeles–Long Beach–Santa Ana, CA | $94,410 | 2,480 |
| Atlanta–Sandy Springs–Marietta, GA | $92,730 | 1,080 |
| Chicago-Naperville-Joliet, IL-IN-WI | $91,130 | 2,370 |

signage. Manage communications budgets. Manage special events, such as sponsorship of races, parties introducing new products, or other activities the firm supports to gain public attention through the media without advertising directly. Draft speeches for company executives, and arrange interviews and other forms of contact for them. Assign, supervise and review the activities of public relations staff. Evaluate advertising and promotion programs for compatibility with public relations efforts. Direct activities of external agencies, establishments, and departments that develop and implement communication strategies and information programs. Formulate policies and procedures related to public information programs, working with public relations executives. Respond to requests for information about employers' activities or status. Facilitate consumer relations, or the relationship between parts of the company, such as the managers and employees, or different branch offices. Establish and maintain effective working relationships with clients, government officials, and media representatives and use these relationships to develop new business opportunities. Identify main client groups and audiences, determine the best way to communicate publicity information to them, and develop and implement a communication plan. Confer with labor relations managers to develop internal communications that keep employees informed of company activities. Establish goals for soliciting funds, develop policies for collection and safeguarding of contributions, and coordinate disbursement of funds. Maintain company archives. Manage in-house communication courses. Produce films and other video products, regulate their distribution, and operate film library. Observe and report on social, economic, and political trends that might affect employers.

**Usual Educational Requirement:** Bachelor's degree. **Relevant Educational Programs**: Public Relations, Advertising, and Applied Communication; Public Relations/Image Management. **Related Knowledge/Courses:** Sales and Marketing; Communications and Media; Customer and Personal Service; Personnel and Human Resources; English Language; Administration and Management. **Work Experience Needed:** 1 to 5 years. **On-the-Job Training Needed:** None. **Certification/Licensure:** Voluntary certification by association.

**Personality Types:** Enterprising–Artistic. **Key Career Cluster:** 04 Business, Management, and Administration. **Key Career Pathway:** 4.1 Management.

**Skills:** Management of financial resources; persuasion; negotiation; management of material resources; management of personnel resources; coordination; systems evaluation; systems analysis.

**Physical Environment:** Indoors; sitting. **Structural Environment:** Importance of being exact or accurate; impact of decisions on co-workers or company results; frequency of decision making; structured versus unstructured work; freedom to make decisions; time pressure.

## Purchasing Agents, Except Wholesale, Retail, and Farm Products

**Purchase machinery, equipment, tools, parts, supplies, or services necessary for the operation of an establishment.**

- Average annual earnings: $58,760
- Middle 50% of earners: $45,160–$76,040
- Earnings growth potential: Medium (38.5%)
- Growth: 5.3%
- Annual job openings: 9,120
- Self-employed: 1.3%
  Best-Paying Industries

**Considerations for Job Outlook:** Growth will be driven largely by the performance of the wholesale and retail industries. Continued employment decreases in manufacturing, as well as decreases in the federal government which includes defense purchasing, are expected. However, growth is expected for this occupation in firms that provide health-care and computer systems design and related services.

**Major Work Tasks:** Purchase the highest quality merchandise at the lowest possible price and in correct amounts. Prepare purchase orders, solicit bid proposals, and review requisitions for goods and services. Research and evaluate suppliers based on price, quality, selection, service, support, availability, reliability, production and distribution capabilities, and the supplier's reputation and history. Analyze price proposals, financial reports, and other data and information to determine rea-

### BEST-PAYING INDUSTRIES

| Industry | Median Earnings | Workforce |
|---|---|---|
| Federal, State, and Local Government | $69,080 | 49,410 |
| Professional, Scientific, and Technical Services | $63,640 | 26,750 |
| Transportation Equipment Manufacturing | $63,570 | 19,250 |
| Management of Companies and Enterprises | $62,270 | 17,310 |
| Computer and Electronic Product Manufacturing | $61,400 | 16,060 |

### BEST-PAYING METROPOLITAN AREAS

| Metro Area | Median Earnings | Workforce |
|---|---|---|
| Washington-Arlington-Alexandria, DC-VA-MD-WV | $77,370 | 10,580 |
| Seattle-Tacoma-Bellevue, WA | $71,670 | 6,330 |
| Philadelphia-Camden-Wilmington, PA-NJ-DE-MD | $65,920 | 7,520 |
| New York–Northern New Jersey–Long Island, NY-NJ-PA | $64,710 | 14,750 |
| Boston-Cambridge-Quincy, MA-NH | $64,680 | 5,960 |
| Detroit-Warren-Livonia, MI | $64,490 | 6,240 |
| Los Angeles–Long Beach–Santa Ana, CA | $61,390 | 12,820 |
| Dallas–Fort Worth–Arlington, TX | $61,170 | 7,340 |
| Houston–Sugar Land–Baytown, TX | $60,100 | 6,970 |
| Chicago-Naperville-Joliet, IL-IN-WI | $58,240 | 6,100 |

sonable prices. Monitor and follow applicable laws and regulations. Negotiate, renegotiate, and administer contracts with suppliers, vendors, and other representatives. Monitor shipments to ensure that goods come in on time and resolve problems related to undelivered goods. Confer with staff, users, and vendors to discuss defective or unacceptable goods or services and determine corrective action. Evaluate and monitor contract performance to ensure compliance with contractual obligations and to determine need for changes. Maintain and review computerized or manual records of items purchased, costs, deliveries, product performance, and inventories. Review catalogs, industry periodicals, directories, trade journals, and Internet sites and consult with other department personnel to locate necessary goods and services. Study sales records and inventory levels of current stock to develop strategic purchasing programs that facilitate employee access to supplies. Interview vendors and visit suppliers' plants and distribution centers to examine and learn about products, services, and prices. Arrange the payment of duty and freight charges. Hire, train, or supervise purchasing clerks, buyers, and expediters. Write and review product specifications, maintaining a working technical knowledge of the goods or services to be purchased. Monitor changes affecting supply and demand, tracking market conditions, price trends, or futures markets. Formulate policies and procedures for bid proposals and procurement of goods and services. Attend meetings, trade shows, conferences, conventions, and seminars to network with people in other purchasing departments.

**Usual Educational Requirement:** High school diploma or equivalent. **Relevant Educational Programs**: General Merchandising, Sales, and Related Marketing Operations, Other; Sales, Distribution, and Marketing Operations, General. **Related Knowledge/Courses:** Economics and Accounting; Transportation; Law and Government; Production and Processing; Clerical Practices; Administration and Management. **Work Experience Needed:** None. **On-the-Job Training Needed:** Long-term on-the-job training. **Certification/Licensure:** Voluntary certification by association.

**Personality Types:** Conventional–Enterprising. **Key Career Cluster:** 13 Manufacturing. **Key Career Pathway:** 13.1 Production.

**Skills:** Management of financial resources; management of material resources; negotiation; persuasion; operations analysis; active learning; judgment and decision making; complex problem solving.

**Physical Environment:** Indoors; sitting. **Structural Environment:** Frequency of decision making; importance of being exact or accurate; time pressure; freedom to make decisions; structured versus unstructured work; impact of decisions on co-workers or company results.

## Purchasing Managers

**Plan, direct, or coordinate the activities of buyers, purchasing officers, and related workers involved in purchasing materials, products, and services.**

- Average annual earnings: $100,170
- Middle 50% of earners: $74,750–$129,760
- Earnings growth potential: Medium (42.7%)
- Growth: 7.2%
- Annual job openings: 2,560
- Self-employed: 1.1%

**Considerations for Job Outlook:** Growth will be driven largely by the performance of the wholesale and retail industries. Continued employment decreases in manufacturing, as well as decreases in federal government which includes defense purchasing, are expected. However, growth is expected for this occupation in firms that provide health-care and computer systems design and related services. The

## Your Guide to High-Paying Careers

### BEST-PAYING INDUSTRIES

| Industry | Median Earnings | Workforce |
| --- | --- | --- |
| Professional, Scientific, and Technical Services | $117,770 | 4,920 |
| Federal, State, and Local Government | $115,710 | 7,630 |
| Management of Companies and Enterprises | $112,430 | 11,420 |
| Computer and Electronic Product Manufacturing | $105,970 | 4,280 |
| Transportation Equipment Manufacturing | $97,860 | 4,320 |
| Merchant Wholesalers, Durable Goods | $90,890 | 4,090 |

### BEST-PAYING METROPOLITAN AREAS

| Metro Area | Median Earnings | Workforce |
| --- | --- | --- |
| New York–Northern New Jersey–Long Island, NY-NJ-PA | $127,430 | 4,450 |
| Washington-Arlington-Alexandria, DC-VA-MD-WV | $126,250 | 4,040 |
| Houston–Sugar Land–Baytown, TX | $119,660 | 1,540 |
| Atlanta–Sandy Springs–Marietta, GA | $110,890 | 1,480 |
| Los Angeles–Long Beach–Santa Ana, CA | $106,210 | 3,090 |
| Dallas–Fort Worth–Arlington, TX | $104,530 | 1,510 |
| Boston-Cambridge-Quincy, MA-NH | $103,150 | 1,970 |
| Minneapolis–St. Paul–Bloomington, MN-WI | $102,340 | 2,050 |
| Chicago-Naperville-Joliet, IL-IN-WI | $85,240 | 3,150 |

trends affecting growth for agents and buyers will also affect purchasing managers, although there should still be a need for purchasing managers to plan and direct buying activities for organizations and to supervise purchasing agents and buyers.

**Major Work Tasks:** Maintain records of goods ordered and received. Locate vendors of materials, equipment or supplies, and interview them to determine product availability and terms of sales. Prepare and process requisitions and purchase orders for supplies and equipment. Control purchasing department budgets. Interview and hire staff, and oversee staff training. Review purchase order claims and contracts for conformance to company policy. Analyze market and delivery systems to assess present and future material availability. Develop and implement purchasing and contract management instructions, policies, and procedures. Participate in the development of specifications for equipment, products, or substitute materials. Resolve vendor or contractor grievances and claims against suppliers. Represent companies in negotiating contracts and formulating policies with suppliers. Review, evaluate, and approve specifications for issuing and awarding bids. Direct and coordinate activities of personnel engaged in buying, selling, and distributing materials, equipment, machinery, and supplies. Prepare reports regarding market conditions and merchandise costs. Administer online purchasing systems. Prepare bid awards requiring board approval. Arrange for disposal of surplus materials.

**Usual Educational Requirement:** Bachelor's degree. **Relevant Educational Program**: Purchasing, Procurement/Acquisitions and Contracts Management. **Related Knowledge/ Courses:** Production and Processing; Economics and Accounting; Transportation; Administration and Management; Personnel and Human Resources; Sales and Marketing. **Work Experience Needed:** More than 5 years. **On-the-Job Training Needed:** None. **Certification/**

**Licensure:** Voluntary certification by association.

**Personality Types:** Enterprising–Conventional. **Key Career Cluster:** 04 Business, Management, and Administration. **Key Career Pathway:** 4.1 Management.

**Skills:** Management of financial resources; management of material resources; negotiation; management of personnel resources; persuasion; systems evaluation; systems analysis; coordination.

**Physical Environment:** Indoors; sitting. **Structural Environment:** Impact of decisions on coworkers or company results; freedom to make decisions; frequency of decision making; structured versus unstructured work; time pressure; importance of being exact or accurate.

## Radiation Therapists

**Provide radiation therapy to patients as prescribed by a radiologist according to established practices and standards.**

- Average annual earnings: $77,560
- Middle 50% of earners: $63,340–$94,790
- Earnings growth potential: Medium (33.3%)
- Growth: 20.3%
- Annual job openings: 670
- Self-employed: 0.0%

**Considerations for Job Outlook:** The risk of cancer increases as people age, so an aging population will increase demand for radiation therapists. Early diagnosis and the development of more sophisticated treatment techniques will also increase employment.

### BEST-PAYING INDUSTRIES

| Industry | Median Earnings | Workforce |
|---|---|---|
| Ambulatory Health-Care Services | $81,530 | 6,120 |
| Hospitals | $75,210 | 11,010 |

### BEST-PAYING METROPOLITAN AREAS

| Metro Area | Median Earnings | Workforce |
|---|---|---|
| Los Angeles–Long Beach–Santa Ana, CA | $90,960 | 460 |
| Houston–Sugar Land–Baytown, TX | $77,020 | 370 |
| Phoenix-Mesa-Scottsdale, AZ | $72,890 | 410 |

**Major Work Tasks:** Administer prescribed doses of radiation to specific body parts, using radiation therapy equipment according to established practices and standards. Position patients for treatment with accuracy, according to prescription. Enter data into computer and set controls to operate or adjust equipment or regulate dosage. Follow principles of radiation protection for patient, self, and others. Maintain records, reports, or files as required, including such information as radiation dosages, equipment settings, or patients' reactions. Review prescription, diagnosis, patient chart, and identification. Conduct most treatment sessions independently in accordance with the long-term treatment plan and under the general direction of the patient's physician. Check radiation therapy equipment to ensure proper operation. Observe and reassure patients during treatment and report unusual reactions to physician or turn equipment off if unexpected adverse reactions occur. Check for side effects, such as skin irritation, nausea, or hair loss to assess patients' reaction to treatment. Educate, prepare, and reassure patients and their families by answering questions, providing physical assistance, and reinforcing physicians' advice regarding treatment reactions or post-treatment care. Calculate actual treatment dosages delivered during each session. Prepare or construct equipment, such as immobilization, treatment, or protection devices. Photograph treated area of patient and process film. Help physicians, radiation oncologists, or clinical

393

physicists to prepare physical or technical aspects of radiation treatment plans, using information about patient condition and anatomy. Train or supervise student or subordinate radiotherapy technologists. Act as liaison with physicist and supportive care personnel. Provide assistance to other health-care personnel during dosimetry procedures and tumor localization. Schedule patients for treatment times. Implement appropriate follow-up care plans. Store, sterilize, or prepare the special applicators containing the radioactive substance implanted by the physician.

**Usual Educational Requirement:** Associate degree. **Relevant Educational Program**: Medical Radiologic Technology/Science—Radiation Therapist. **Related Knowledge/Courses:** Medicine and Dentistry; Therapy and Counseling; Biology; Physics; Psychology; Customer and Personal Service. **Work Experience Needed:** None. **On-the-Job Training Needed:** None. **Certification/Licensure:** Licensure or certification.

**Personality Types:** Social–Realistic–Conventional. **Key Career Cluster:** 08 Health Science. **Key Career Pathway:** 8.1 Therapeutic Services.

**Skills:** Equipment maintenance; operation and control; equipment selection; science; quality control analysis; troubleshooting; repairing; operation monitoring.

**Physical Environment:** Indoors; standing; walking and running; using hands; bending or twisting the body; repetitive motions. **Structural Environment:** Importance of being exact or accurate; importance of repeating same tasks; consequence of error; time pressure; impact of decisions on co-workers or company results; frequency of decision making.

## Real Estate Brokers

**Operate real estate offices, or work for commercial real estate firms, overseeing real estate transactions.**

- Average annual earnings: $58,350
- Middle 50% of earners: $35,970–$99,350
- Earnings growth potential: Very high (56.1%)
- Growth: 7.6%
- Annual job openings: 2,970
- Self-employed: 57.3%

### BEST-PAYING INDUSTRIES

| Industry | Median Earnings | Workforce |
|---|---|---|
| Real Estate | $57,760 | 32,780 |

### BEST-PAYING METROPOLITAN AREAS

| Metro Area | Median Earnings | Workforce |
|---|---|---|
| Philadelphia-Camden-Wilmington, PA-NJ-DE-MD | $107,510 | 1,010 |
| New York–Northern New Jersey–Long Island, NY-NJ-PA | $101,880 | 1,880 |
| Los Angeles–Long Beach–Santa Ana, CA | $96,730 | 2,530 |
| Atlanta–Sandy Springs–Marietta, GA | $66,100 | 1,730 |
| Washington-Arlington-Alexandria, DC-VA-MD-WV | $59,910 | 1,270 |
| Chicago-Naperville-Joliet, IL-IN-WI | $53,520 | 1,410 |
| Charlotte-Gastonia-Concord, NC-SC | $50,270 | 1,320 |
| Phoenix-Mesa-Scottsdale, AZ | $46,020 | 990 |
| Denver-Aurora, CO | $45,560 | 960 |
| Miami–Fort Lauderdale–Pompano Beach, FL | $45,420 | 1,340 |

**Considerations for Job Outlook:** Although the real estate market depends on economic conditions, it is relatively easy to enter the occupation. In times of economic growth, brokers and sales agents will have good job opportunities. In an economic downturn, there tend to be fewer job opportunities, and brokers and agents often have a lower income due to fewer sales and purchases.

**Major Work Tasks:** Sell, for a fee, real estate owned by others. Obtain agreements from property owners to place properties for sale with real estate firms. Monitor fulfillment of purchase contract terms to ensure that they are handled in a timely manner. Compare a property with similar properties that have recently sold to determine its competitive market price. Act as an intermediary in negotiations between buyers and sellers over property prices and settlement details and during the closing of sales. Generate lists of properties for sale, their locations, descriptions, and available financing options, using computers. Maintain knowledge of real estate law, local economies, fair housing laws, types of available mortgages, financing options, and government programs. Check work completed by loan officers, attorneys, or other professionals to ensure that it is performed properly. Arrange for financing of property purchases. Appraise property values, assessing income potential when relevant. Maintain awareness of current income tax regulations, local zoning, building and tax laws, and growth possibilities of the area where a property is located. Manage or operate real estate offices, handling associated business details. Supervise agents who handle real estate transactions. Rent properties or manage rental properties. Arrange for title searches of properties being sold. Give buyers virtual tours of properties in which they are interested, using computers. Review property details to ensure that environmental regulations are met. Develop, sell, or lease property used for industry or manufacturing. Maintain working knowledge of various factors that determine a farm's capacity to produce, such as agricultural variables and proximity to market centers and transportation facilities.

**Usual Educational Requirement:** High school diploma or equivalent. **Relevant Educational Programs**: Real Estate; Real Estate Development. **Related Knowledge/Courses:** Sales and Marketing; Building and Construction; Law and Government; Customer and Personal Service; Personnel and Human Resources; Economics and Accounting. **Work Experience Needed:** 1 to 5 years. **On-the-Job Training Needed:** None. **Certification/Licensure:** Licensure.

**Personality Types:** Enterprising–Conventional. **Key Career Cluster:** 14 Marketing, Sales, and Service. **Key Career Pathway:** 14.2 Professional Sales and Marketing.

**Skills:** Negotiation; persuasion; judgment and decision making; active learning; speaking; management of financial resources; service orientation; active listening.

**Physical Environment:** Indoors; outdoors; sitting. **Structural Environment:** Structured versus unstructured work; freedom to make decisions; frequency of decision making; impact of decisions on co-workers or company results; level of competition; importance of being exact or accurate.

## Recreation and Fitness Studies Teachers, Postsecondary

*See Teachers, Postsecondary.*

## Registered Nurses

**Assess patient health problems and needs, develop and implement nursing care plans, and maintain medical records.**

- Average annual earnings: $65,470
- Middle 50% of earners: $53,670–$78,700
- Earnings growth potential: Low (31.2%)
- Growth: 26.0%

- Annual job openings: 120,740
- Self-employed: 0.9%

### BEST-PAYING INDUSTRIES

| Industry | Median Earnings | Workforce |
|---|---|---|
| Federal, State, and Local Government | $68,550 | 145,840 |
| Hospitals | $67,210 | 1,632,290 |
| Ambulatory Health-Care Services | $61,600 | 457,060 |
| Nursing and Residential Care Facilities | $58,830 | 183,760 |

### BEST-PAYING METROPOLITAN AREAS

| Metro Area | Median Earnings | Workforce |
|---|---|---|
| Los Angeles–Long Beach–Santa Ana, CA | $86,370 | 89,140 |
| Boston-Cambridge-Quincy, MA-NH | $80,850 | 59,260 |
| New York–Northern New Jersey–Long Island, NY-NJ-PA | $80,690 | 153,620 |
| Philadelphia-Camden-Wilmington, PA-NJ-DE-MD | $71,680 | 62,640 |
| Chicago-Naperville-Joliet, IL-IN-WI | $69,110 | 85,380 |
| Dallas–Fort Worth–Arlington, TX | $68,400 | 54,780 |

**Considerations for Job Outlook:** Overall, job opportunities for registered nurses are expected to be excellent. Employers in some parts of the country and in some employment settings report difficulty in attracting and keeping enough registered nurses. Job opportunities should be excellent, even in hospitals, because of the relatively high turnover of hospital nurses. To attract and keep qualified nurses, hospitals may offer signing bonuses, family-friendly work schedules, or subsidized training. In physicians' offices and outpatient care centers, registered nurses may face greater competition for positions because these jobs generally offer regular working hours and provide more comfortable working conditions than hospitals. Generally, registered nurses with at least a bachelor's degree in nursing (BSN) will have better job prospects than those without one.

**Major Work Tasks:** Maintain accurate, detailed reports and records. Monitor, record, and report symptoms or changes in patients' conditions. Record patients' medical information and vital signs. Modify patient treatment plans as indicated by patients' responses and conditions. Consult and coordinate with health-care team members to assess, plan, implement, or evaluate patient care plans. Monitor all aspects of patient care, including diet and physical activity. Direct or supervise less-skilled nursing or health-care personnel or supervise a particular unit. Prepare patients for and assist with examinations or treatments. Assess the needs of individuals, families, or communities, including assessment of individuals' home or work environments, to identify potential health or safety problems. Instruct individuals, families, or other groups on topics such as health education, disease prevention, or childbirth and develop health improvement programs. Prepare rooms, sterile instruments, equipment, or supplies and ensure that stock of supplies is maintained. Refer students or patients to specialized health resources or community agencies furnishing assistance. Consult with institutions or associations regarding issues or concerns relevant to the practice and profession of nursing. Administer medications to patients and monitor patients for reactions or side effects. Order, interpret, and evaluate diagnostic tests to identify and assess patient's condition. Observe nurses and visit patients to ensure proper nursing care. Inform physician of patient's condition during anesthesia. Administer local, inhalation, intravenous, or other anesthetics. Provide health care, first aid, immunizations, or assistance in convalescence or rehabilitation in locations, such as schools, hospitals, or industry. Perform physical examinations, make tentative diagnoses, and treat patients en route to hospitals or at disaster site triage centers. Conduct specified laboratory tests. Hand items to surgeons during operations. Prescribe or recommend drugs, medical devices, or other forms of treatment, such as physical therapy, inhalation therapy, or related therapeutic procedures.

**Usual Educational Requirement:** Associate degree. **Relevant Educational Programs**: Adult Health Nurse/Nursing; Clinical Nurse Leader; Clinical Nurse Specialist Training; Critical Care Nursing; Emergency Room/Trauma Nursing; Family Practice Nurse/Nursing; Geriatric Nurse/Nursing; Maternal/Child Health and Neonatal Nurse/Nursing; Nursing Administration; Nursing Practice; Nursing Science; Occupational and Environmental Health Nursing; Palliative Care Nursing; Pediatric Nurse/Nursing; Perioperative/Operating Room and Surgical Nurse/Nursing; Psychiatric/Mental Health Nurse/Nursing; Public Health/Community Nurse/Nursing; Registered Nursing, Nursing Administration, Nursing Research; Registered Nursing/Registered Nurse Training; Women's Health Nurse/Nursing. **Related Knowledge/Courses:** Psychology; Therapy and Counseling; Medicine and Dentistry; Biology; Philosophy and Theology; Sociology and Anthropology. **Work Experience Needed:** None. **On-the-Job Training Needed:** None. **Certification/Licensure:** Licensure.

**Personality Types:** Social–Investigative–Conventional. **Key Career Cluster:** 08 Health Science. **Key Career Pathway:** 8.1 Therapeutic Services.

**Skills:** Social perceptiveness; service orientation; science; quality control analysis; learning strategies; coordination; instructing; management of material resources.

**Physical Environment:** Indoors; standing; walking and running; using hands; bending or twisting the body; exposed to disease or infections. **Structural Environment:** Importance of being exact or accurate; frequency of decision making; impact of decisions on co-workers or company results; structured versus unstructured work; freedom to make decisions; time pressure.

## JOB SPECIALIZATION: ACUTE CARE NURSES

**Provide advanced nursing care for patients with acute conditions, such as heart attacks, respiratory distress syndrome, or shock. May care for pre- and post-operative patients or perform advanced, invasive diagnostic, or therapeutic procedures.**

**Major Work Tasks:** Analyze the indications, contraindications, risk complications, and cost-benefit trade-offs of therapeutic interventions. Diagnose acute or chronic conditions that could result in rapid physiological deterioration or life-threatening instability. Distinguish between normal and abnormal developmental and age-related physiological and behavioral changes in acute, critical, and chronic illness. Manage patients' pain relief and sedation by providing pharmacologic and non-pharmacologic interventions, monitoring patients' responses, and changing care plans accordingly. Interpret information obtained from electrocardiograms (EKGs) or radiographs (X-rays). Perform emergency medical procedures, such as basic cardiac life support (BLS), advanced cardiac life support (ACLS), and other condition stabilizing interventions. Assess urgent and emergent health conditions using both physiologically and technologically derived data. Assess the impact of illnesses or injuries on patients' health, function, growth, development, nutrition, sleep, rest, quality of life, or family, social and educational relationships. Collaborate with members of multidisciplinary health-care teams to plan, manage, or assess patient treatments. Discuss

**397**

illnesses and treatments with patients and family members. Document data related to patients' care, including assessment results, interventions, medications, patient responses, or treatment changes. Treat wounds or superficial lacerations. Set up, operate, or monitor invasive equipment and devices, such as colostomy or tracheotomy equipment, mechanical ventilators, catheters, gastrointestinal tubes, and central lines. Obtain specimens or samples for laboratory work. Order, perform, or interpret the results of diagnostic tests and screening procedures based on assessment results, differential diagnoses, and knowledge about age, gender and health status of clients. Participate in patients' care meetings and conferences. Refer patients for specialty consultations or treatments. Administer blood and blood product transfusions or intravenous infusions, monitoring patients for adverse reactions. Assist patients in organizing their health-care system activities.

**Related Knowledge/Courses:** Therapy and Counseling; Medicine and Dentistry; Psychology; Biology; Philosophy and Theology; Sociology and Anthropology.

**Personality Types:** Social–Investigative–Realistic.

**Skills:** Science; social perceptiveness; reading comprehension; operation monitoring; service orientation; systems evaluation; operation and control; operations analysis.

**Physical Environment:** Indoors; standing; walking and running; using hands; noise; contaminants. **Structural Environment:** Consequence of error; importance of being exact or accurate; frequency of decision making; time pressure; impact of decisions on co-workers or company results; freedom to make decisions.

### JOB SPECIALIZATION: ADVANCED PRACTICE PSYCHIATRIC NURSES

**Provide advanced nursing care for patients with psychiatric disorders. May provide psychotherapy under the direction of psychiatrists.**

**Major Work Tasks:** Teach classes in mental health topics, such as stress reduction. Participate in activities aimed at professional growth and development, including conferences or continuing education activities. Direct or provide home health services. Monitor the use and status of medical and pharmaceutical supplies. Develop practice protocols for mental health problems based on review and evaluation of published research. Develop, implement, or evaluate programs, such as outreach activities, community mental health programs, and crisis situation response activities. Write prescriptions for psychotropic medications as allowed by state regulations and collaborative practice agreements. Refer patients requiring more specialized or complex treatment to psychiatrists, primary care physicians, or other medical specialists. Participate in treatment team conferences regarding diagnosis or treatment of difficult cases. Interpret diagnostic or laboratory tests, such as electrocardiograms (EKGs) and renal functioning tests. Evaluate patients' behavior to formulate diagnoses or assess treatments. Develop and implement treatment plans. Monitor patients' medication usage and results. Educate patients and family members about mental health and medical conditions, preventive health measures, medications, or treatment plans. Distinguish between physiologically and psychologically based disorders and diagnose appropriately. Document patients' medical and psychological histories, physical assessment results, diagnoses, treatment plans, prescriptions, or outcomes. Consult with psychiatrists or other professionals when unusual or complex cases are encountered. Assess patients' mental and physical status based on the presenting symptoms and complaints. Collaborate with interdisciplinary team members, including psychiatrists, psychologists, or nursing staff, to develop, implement, or evaluate treatment plans. Administer

398

medications including those administered by injection. Diagnose psychiatric disorders and mental health conditions. Conduct individual, group, or family psychotherapy for those with chronic or acute mental disorders. Treat patients for routine physical health problems.

**Related Knowledge/Courses:** Therapy and Counseling; Psychology; Medicine and Dentistry; Sociology and Anthropology; Philosophy and Theology; Biology.

**Personality Types:** Social–Investigative.

**Skills:** Social perceptiveness; science; negotiation; service orientation; persuasion; systems evaluation; learning strategies; reading comprehension.

**Physical Environment:** Indoors; sitting; exposed to disease or infections. **Structural Environment:** Freedom to make decisions; structured versus unstructured work; importance of being exact or accurate; frequency of decision making; impact of decisions on coworkers or company results; consequence of error.

### JOB SPECIALIZATION: CLINICAL NURSE SPECIALISTS

**Plan, direct, or coordinate daily patient care activities in a clinical practice. Ensure adherence to established clinical policies, protocols, regulations, and standards.**

**Major Work Tasks:** Coordinate or conduct educational programs or in-service training sessions on topics, such as clinical procedures. Observe, interview, and assess patients to identify care needs. Evaluate the quality and effectiveness of nursing practice or organizational systems. Provide specialized direct and indirect care to inpatients and outpatients within a designated specialty, such as obstetrics, neurology, oncology, or neonatal care. Maintain departmental policies, procedures, objectives, or infection control standards. Collaborate with other health-care professionals and service providers to ensure optimal patient care.

Develop nursing service philosophies, goals, policies, priorities, or procedures. Develop, implement, or evaluate standards of nursing practice in specialty areas, such as pediatrics, acute care, and geriatrics. Develop or assist others in development of care and treatment plans. Make clinical recommendations to physicians, other health-care providers, insurance companies, patients, or health-care organizations. Plan, evaluate, or modify treatment programs based on information gathered by observing and interviewing patients or by analyzing patient records. Present clients with information required to make informed health-care and treatment decisions. Instruct nursing staff in areas, such as the assessment, development, implementation, and evaluation of disability, illness, management, technology, or resources. Direct or supervise nursing care staff in the provision of patient therapy. Identify training needs or conduct training sessions for nursing students or medical staff. Read current literature, talk with colleagues, or participate in professional organizations or conferences to keep abreast of developments in nursing. Monitor or evaluate medical conditions of patients in collaboration with other health-care professionals. Participate in clinical research projects by reviewing protocols, reviewing patient records, monitoring compliance, and meeting with regulatory authorities. Perform discharge planning for patients. Prepare reports to document patients' care activities. Write nursing orders.

**Related Knowledge/Courses:** Medicine and Dentistry; Therapy and Counseling; Biology; Psychology; Sociology and Anthropology; Philosophy and Theology.

**Personality Types:** Enterprising–Social–Conventional.

**Skills:** Science; operations analysis; service orientation; instructing; social perceptiveness; active listening; active learning; persuasion.

**Physical Environment:** Indoors; noise; contaminants; exposed to disease or infections.

**Structural Environment:** Freedom to make decisions; structured versus unstructured work; frequency of decision making; importance of being exact or accurate; impact of decisions on co-workers or company results; consequence of error.

### JOB SPECIALIZATION: CRITICAL CARE NURSES

**Provide advanced nursing care for patients in critical or coronary care units.**

**Major Work Tasks:** Identify patients' age-specific needs and alter care plans as necessary to meet those needs. Provide post-mortem care. Evaluate patients' vital signs or laboratory data to determine emergency intervention needs. Perform approved therapeutic or diagnostic procedures based upon patients' clinical status. Administer blood and blood products, monitoring patients for signs and symptoms related to transfusion reactions. Administer medications intravenously, by injection, orally, through gastric tubes, or by other methods. Advocate for patients' and families' needs, or provide emotional support for patients and their families. Set up and monitor medical equipment and devices such as cardiac monitors, mechanical ventilators and alarms, oxygen delivery devices, transducers, or pressure lines. Monitor patients' fluid intake and output to detect emerging problems, such as fluid and electrolyte imbalances. Monitor patients for changes in status and indications of conditions, such as sepsis or shock and institute appropriate interventions. Assess patients' pain levels or sedation requirements. Assess patients' psychosocial status and needs, including areas such as sleep patterns, anxiety, grief, anger, and support systems. Collaborate with other health-care professionals to develop and revise treatment plans based on identified needs and assessment data. Collect specimens for laboratory tests. Compile and analyze data obtained from monitoring or diagnostic tests. Conduct pulmonary assessments to identify abnormal respiratory patterns or breathing sounds that indicate problems. Document patients' medical histories and assessment findings. Document patients' treatment plans, interventions, outcomes, or plan revisions. Identify patients who are at risk of complications due to nutritional status. Prioritize nursing care for assigned critically ill patients, based on assessment data or identified needs. Assist physicians with procedures, such as bronchoscopy, endoscopy, endotracheal intubation, or elective cardioversion. Ensure that equipment or devices are properly stored after use. Identify malfunctioning equipment or devices.

**Related Knowledge/Courses:** Medicine and Dentistry; Biology; Psychology; Therapy and Counseling; Sociology and Anthropology; Philosophy and Theology.

**Personality Types:** Social–Investigative–Realistic.

**Skills:** Science; social perceptiveness; operation and control; operation monitoring; quality control analysis; service orientation; operations analysis; monitoring.

**Physical Environment:** Indoors; standing; walking and running; using hands; bending or twisting the body; noise. **Structural Environment:** Importance of being exact or accurate; consequence of error; frequency of decision making; impact of decisions on co-workers or company results; structured versus unstructured Work; freedom to make decisions.

## Sales Engineers

**Sell business goods or services, the selling of which requires a technical background equivalent to a bachelor's degree in engineering.**

- Average annual earnings: $91,830
- Middle 50% of earners: $70,530–$119,480
- Earnings growth potential: Medium (39.4%)

**400**

- Growth: 14.4%
- Annual job openings: 3,210
- Self-employed: 0.0%

**Considerations for Job Outlook:** Successful sales engineers must have strong technical knowledge of the products they are selling, in addition to having interpersonal skills and the ability to persuade. Job prospects should be good for candidates with these abilities.

**Major Work Tasks:** Plan and modify product configurations to meet customer needs. Confer with customers and engineers to assess equipment needs and to determine system requirements. Collaborate with sales teams to understand customer requirements, to promote the sale of company products, and to provide sales support. Develop, present, or respond to proposals for specific customer requirements, including request for proposal responses and industry-specific solutions. Sell products requiring extensive technical expertise and support for installation and use, such as material handling equipment, numerical-control machinery, and computer systems. Diagnose problems with installed equipment. Recommend

### BEST-PAYING INDUSTRIES

| Industry | Median Earnings | Workforce |
|---|---|---|
| Professional, Scientific, and Technical Services | $105,760 | 14,460 |
| Telecommunications | $97,130 | 6,040 |
| Wholesale Electronic Markets and Agents and Brokers | $95,500 | 6,880 |
| Computer and Electronic Product Manufacturing | $90,380 | 6,430 |
| Merchant Wholesalers, Durable Goods | $85,020 | 15,720 |
| Machinery Manufacturing | $75,740 | 5,270 |

### BEST-PAYING METROPOLITAN AREAS

| Metro Area | Median Earnings | Workforce |
|---|---|---|
| San Jose–Sunnyvale–Santa Clara, CA | $125,340 | 3,480 |
| Washington-Arlington-Alexandria, DC-VA-MD-WV | $114,080 | 1,570 |
| San Francisco–Oakland–Fremont, CA | $108,690 | 2,760 |
| New York–Northern New Jersey–Long Island, NY-NJ-PA | $105,850 | 3,720 |
| Dallas–Fort Worth–Arlington, TX | $101,000 | 2,240 |
| Boston-Cambridge-Quincy, MA-NH | $97,840 | 3,450 |
| Philadelphia-Camden-Wilmington, PA-NJ-DE-MD | $94,200 | 2,030 |
| Houston–Sugar Land–Baytown, TX | $92,190 | 2,030 |
| Los Angeles–Long Beach–Santa Ana, CA | $91,880 | 3,810 |
| Chicago-Naperville-Joliet, IL-IN-WI | $87,020 | 2,870 |
| Atlanta–Sandy Springs–Marietta, GA | $86,960 | 1,630 |
| Minneapolis–St. Paul–Bloomington, MN-WI | $83,420 | 1,640 |
| Detroit-Warren-Livonia, MI | $76,820 | 1,510 |

improved materials or machinery to customers, documenting how such changes will lower costs or increase production. Prepare and deliver technical presentations that explain products or services to customers and prospective customers. Provide technical and non-technical support and services to clients or other staff members regarding the use, operation, and maintenance of equipment. Research and identify potential customers for products or services. Visit prospective buyers at commercial, industrial, or other establishments to show samples or catalogs and to inform them about product pricing, availability, and advantages. Create sales or service contracts for products or services. Arrange for demonstrations or trial installations of equipment. Keep informed on industry news and trends, products, services, competitors, relevant information about legacy, existing, and emerging technologies, and the latest product-line developments. Provide information needed for the development of custom-made machinery. Develop sales plans to introduce products in new markets. Identify resale opportunities and support them to achieve sales plans. Document account activities, generate reports, and keep records of business transactions with customers and suppliers. Maintain sales forecasting reports. Secure and renew orders and arrange delivery. Attend company training seminars to become familiar with product lines. Write technical documentation for products.

**Usual Educational Requirement:** Bachelor's degree. **Relevant Educational Programs**: Aerospace, Aeronautical, and Astronautical/Space Engineering; Agricultural Engineering; Architectural Engineering; Biochemical Engineering; Bioengineering and Biomedical Engineering; Chemical Engineering; Civil Engineering; Computer Engineering; Construction Engineering; Electrical and Electronics Engineering; Electromechanical Engineering; Engineering Design; Engineering Science; Engineering, General; Environmental/Environmental Health Engineering; Geological/Geophysical Engineering; Industrial Engineering; Laser and Optical Engineering; Manufacturing Engineering; Materials Engineering; Mechanical Engineering; Mechatronics, Robotics, and Automation Engineering; Metallurgical Engineering; Mining and Mineral Engineering; Nanotechnology; Naval Architecture and Marine Engineering; Nuclear Engineering; Ocean Engineering; Petroleum Engineering; Structural Engineering; Surveying Engineering; Systems Engineering; Telecommunications Engineering; Transportation and Highway Engineering; Water Resources Engineering; others. **Related Knowledge/Courses:** Sales and Marketing; Engineering and Technology; Computers and Electronics; Customer and Personal Service; Mathematics; Production and Processing. **Work Experience Needed:** None. **On-the-Job Training Needed:** Moderate-term on-the-job training. **Certification/Licensure:** None.

**Personality Types:** Enterprising–Realistic–Investigative. **Key Career Cluster:** 14 Marketing, Sales, and Service. **Key Career Pathway:** 14.2 Professional Sales and Marketing.

**Skills:** Technology design; persuasion; negotiation; mathematics; systems evaluation; systems analysis; management of material resources; reading comprehension.

**Physical Environment:** Indoors; sitting; using hands. **Structural Environment:** Impact of decisions on co-workers or company results; structured versus unstructured work; frequency of decision making; freedom to make decisions; time pressure; importance of being exact or accurate.

## Sales Managers

**Plan, direct, or coordinate the actual distribution or movement of a product or service to the customer.**

- Average annual earnings: $105,260
- Middle 50% of earners: $72,210–$150,610
- Earnings growth potential: High (49.7%)
- Growth: 11.7%
- Annual job openings: 13,970
- Self-employed: 5.6%

**Considerations for Job Outlook:** Strong competition is expected for jobs because other managers and highly experienced professionals often seek these jobs.

## BEST-PAYING INDUSTRIES

| Industry | Median Earnings | Workforce |
|---|---|---|
| Professional, Scientific, and Technical Services | $132,780 | 25,540 |
| Merchant Wholesalers, Durable Goods | $116,700 | 31,050 |
| Management of Companies and Enterprises | $115,000 | 28,350 |
| Merchant Wholesalers, Nondurable Goods | $105,130 | 22,830 |
| Motor Vehicle and Parts Dealers | $96,110 | 25,420 |

## BEST-PAYING METROPOLITAN AREAS

| Metro Area | Median Earnings | Workforce |
|---|---|---|
| New York–Northern New Jersey–Long Island, NY-NJ-PA | $153,770 | 23,570 |
| San Francisco–Oakland–Fremont, CA | $131,480 | 9,010 |
| Boston-Cambridge-Quincy, MA-NH | $131,050 | 10,230 |
| Dallas–Fort Worth–Arlington, TX | $118,430 | 9,260 |
| Atlanta–Sandy Springs–Marietta, GA | $117,400 | 9,400 |
| Los Angeles–Long Beach–Santa Ana, CA | $114,370 | 23,270 |
| Houston–Sugar Land–Baytown, TX | $114,120 | 7,340 |
| Minneapolis–St. Paul–Bloomington, MN-WI | $108,650 | 9,670 |
| Chicago-Naperville-Joliet, IL-IN-WI | $98,790 | 17,380 |
| Phoenix-Mesa-Scottsdale, AZ | $93,190 | 7,310 |

**Major Work Tasks:** Resolve customer complaints regarding sales and service. Monitor customer preferences to determine focus of sales efforts. Determine price schedules and discount rates. Review operational records and reports to project sales and determine profitability. Confer or consult with department heads to plan advertising services and to secure information on equipment and customer specifications. Prepare budgets and approve budget expenditures. Plan and direct staffing, training, and performance evaluations to develop and control sales and service programs. Oversee regional and local sales managers and their staffs. Direct and coordinate activities involving sales of manufactured products, services, commodities, real estate or other subjects of sale. Direct, coordinate, and review activities in sales and service accounting and recordkeeping and in receiving and shipping operations. Advise dealers and distributors on policies and operating procedures to ensure functional effectiveness of business. Represent company at trade association meetings to promote products. Visit franchised dealers to stimulate interest in establishment or expansion of leasing programs. Confer with potential customers regarding equipment needs and advise customers on types of equipment to purchase. Direct clerical staff to keep records of export correspondence, bid requests, and credit collections and to maintain current information on tariffs, licenses, and restrictions. Direct foreign sales and service outlets of an organization. Assess marketing potential of new and existing store locations, considering statistics and expenditures.

**Usual Educational Requirement:** Bachelor's degree. **Relevant Educational Programs**: Business Administration and Management, General; Business/Commerce, General; Consumer Merchandising/Retailing Management; Marketing/Marketing Management, General; Pharmaceutical Marketing and Management. **Related Knowledge/Courses:** Sales and Mar-

**403**

keting; Personnel and Human Resources; Economics and Accounting; Administration and Management; Customer and Personal Service; Psychology. **Work Experience Needed:** 1 to 5 years. **On-the-Job Training Needed:** None. **Certification/Licensure:** None.

**Personality Types:** Enterprising–Conventional. **Key Career Cluster:** 04 Business, Management, and Administration. **Key Career Pathway:** 4.5 Marketing.

**Skills:** Management of financial resources; management of personnel resources; management of material resources; persuasion; systems evaluation; monitoring; negotiation; operations analysis.

**Physical Environment:** Indoors; sitting. **Structural Environment:** Freedom to make decisions; level of competition; structured versus unstructured work; impact of decisions on co-workers or company results; time pressure; importance of being exact or accurate.

## Sales Representatives, Wholesale and Manufacturing, Technical and Scientific Products

**Sell goods for wholesalers or manufacturers where technical or scientific knowledge is required.**

- Average annual earnings: $74,970
- Middle 50% of earners: $51,780–$106,480
- Earnings growth potential: Very high (50.3%)
- Growth: 16.4%
- Annual job openings: 15,970
- Self-employed: 3.8%

**Considerations for Job Outlook:** Job candidates should see very good opportunities. Because workers frequently leave this occupation, there are usually a relatively large number of openings.

**Major Work Tasks:** Contact new and existing customers to discuss their needs and to explain

### BEST-PAYING INDUSTRIES

| Industry | Median Earnings | Workforce |
|---|---|---|
| Wholesale Electronic Markets and Agents and Brokers | $84,220 | 60,990 |
| Computer and Electronic Product Manufacturing | $80,460 | 19,370 |
| Professional, Scientific, and Technical Services | $74,750 | 43,800 |
| Merchant Wholesalers, Durable Goods | $68,250 | 108,890 |

### BEST-PAYING METROPOLITAN AREAS

| Metro Area | Median Earnings | Workforce |
|---|---|---|
| San Jose–Sunnyvale–Santa Clara, CA | $101,860 | 8,130 |
| Philadelphia-Camden-Wilmington, PA-NJ-DE-MD | $95,650 | 9,210 |
| Boston-Cambridge-Quincy, MA-NH | $88,340 | 14,090 |
| New York–Northern New Jersey–Long Island, NY-NJ-PA | $87,860 | 16,250 |
| Houston–Sugar Land–Baytown, TX | $87,310 | 11,930 |
| San Francisco–Oakland–Fremont, CA | $84,420 | 7,930 |
| Phoenix-Mesa-Scottsdale, AZ | $76,150 | 7,360 |
| Los Angeles–Long Beach–Santa Ana, CA | $75,980 | 16,890 |
| Atlanta–Sandy Springs–Marietta, GA | $74,270 | 8,440 |
| Dallas–Fort Worth–Arlington, TX | $72,780 | 9,090 |
| Miami–Ft. Lauderdale–Pompano Beach, FL | $71,970 | 10,640 |
| Chicago-Naperville-Joliet, IL-IN-WI | $71,590 | 17,920 |

how these needs could be met by specific products and services. Answer customers' questions about products, prices, availability, or credit terms. Quote prices, credit terms, or other bid specifications. Emphasize product features based on analyses of customers' needs and on technical knowledge of product capabilities and limitations. Negotiate prices or terms of sales or service agreements. Maintain customer records, using automated systems. Identify prospective customers by using business directories, following leads from existing clients, participating in organizations and clubs, and attending trade shows and conferences. Prepare sales contracts for orders obtained, and submit orders for processing. Select the correct products or assist customers in making product selections based on customers' needs, product specifications, and applicable regulations. Collaborate with colleagues to exchange information, such as selling strategies or marketing information. Prepare sales presentations or proposals to explain product specifications or applications. Demonstrate and explain the operation and use of products. Provide customers with ongoing technical support. Inform customers of estimated delivery schedules, service contracts, warranties, or other information pertaining to purchased products. Attend sales and trade meetings, and read related publications in order to obtain information about market conditions, business trends, and industry developments. Visit establishments to evaluate needs or to promote product or service sales. Complete expense reports, sales reports, or other paperwork. Initiate sales campaigns and follow marketing plan guidelines in order to meet sales and production expectations. Recommend ways for customers to alter product usage in order to improve production. Complete product and development training as required. Provide feedback to product design teams so that products can be tailored to clients' needs. Arrange for installation and testing of products or machinery. Verify that materials lists are accurate and that delivery schedules meet project deadlines.

**Usual Educational Requirement:** Bachelor's degree. **Relevant Educational Program**: Selling Skills and Sales Operations. **Related Knowledge/Courses:** Sales and Marketing; Customer and Personal Service; Production and Processing; Administration and Management; Transportation; Computers and Electronics. **Work Experience Needed:** None. **On-the-Job Training Needed:** Moderate-term on-the-job training. **Certification/Licensure:** Licensure for some specializations; voluntary certification by association.

**Personality Types:** Enterprising–Conventional. **Key Career Cluster:** 14 Marketing, Sales, and Service. **Key Career Pathway:** 14.2 Professional Sales and Marketing.

**Skills:** Persuasion; negotiation; management of financial resources; management of material resources; active listening; speaking; operations analysis; reading comprehension.

**Physical Environment:** Indoors; sitting. **Structural Environment:** Freedom to make decisions; structured versus unstructured work; impact of decisions on co-workers or company results; level of competition; importance of being exact or accurate; time pressure.

## JOB SPECIALIZATION: SOLAR SALES REPRESENTATIVES AND ASSESSORS

**Contact new or existing customers to determine their solar equipment needs, suggest systems or equipment, or estimate costs.**

**Major Work Tasks:** Generate solar energy customer leads to develop new accounts. Prepare proposals, quotes, contracts, or presentations for potential solar customers. Select solar energy products, systems, or services for customers based on electrical energy requirements, site conditions, price, or other factors. Assess sites to determine suitability for solar equipment, using equipment such as tape measures, compasses, and computer software. Calculate potential solar resources or solar array production for a particular site, considering issues such as climate, shading, and roof orientation. Create customized energy management packages to satisfy customer needs. Develop marketing or strategic plans for sales territories. Gather information from prospective customers to identify their solar energy needs. Prepare or review detailed design drawings, specifications, or lists related to solar installations. Provide customers with information, such as quotes, orders, sales, shipping, warranties, credit, funding options, incentives, or tax rebates. Provide technical information about solar power, solar systems, equipment, and services to potential customers or dealers. Take quote requests or orders from dealers or customers. Demonstrate use of solar and related equipment to customers or dealers.

**Related Knowledge/Courses:** Sales and Marketing; Engineering and Technology; Building and Construction; Design; Economics and Accounting; Customer and Personal Service.

**Personality Types:** Enterprising–Conventional–Realistic.

**Skills:** Persuasion; negotiation; service orientation; mathematics; management of financial resources; technology design; speaking; systems evaluation.

**Physical Environment:** Indoors; outdoors; sitting. **Structural Environment:** Structured versus unstructured work; freedom to make decisions; frequency of decision making; impact of decisions on co-workers or company results; importance of being exact or accurate; level of competition.

## Securities, Commodities, and Financial Services Sales Agents

**Buy and sell securities or commodities in investment and trading firms, or provide financial services to businesses and individuals.**

- Average annual earnings: $71,720
- Middle 50% of earners: $40,890–$138,930

- Earnings growth potential: Very high (55.3%)
- Growth: 15.2%
- Annual job openings: 13,370
- Self-employed: 10.8%

**Considerations for Job Outlook:** The high pay associated with securities, commodities, and financial services sales agents draws many more applicants than there are openings. Therefore, competition for jobs is intense. Certification and a graduate degree, such as a Chartered Financial Analyst (CFA) certification and a master's degree in business or finance, can significantly improve an applicant's prospects. For entry-level jobs, having an excellent grade-point average (GPA) in college is important.

**Major Work Tasks:** For tasks, see the job specializations.

**Usual Educational Requirement:** Bachelor's degree. **Relevant Educational Programs**: Business and Personal/Financial Services Marketing Operations; Financial Planning and Services; Investments and Securities. **Work Experience Needed:** None. **On-the-Job Training Needed:** Moderate-term on-the-job training. **Certification/Licensure:** Licensure; voluntary certification by association.

**Key Career Cluster:** 06 Finance. **Key Career Pathway:** 6.1 Financial and Investment Planning.

### BEST-PAYING INDUSTRIES

| Industry | Median Earnings | Workforce |
|---|---|---|
| Securities, Commodity Contracts, and Other Financial Investments and Related Activities | $101,590 | 178,410 |
| Credit Intermediation and Related Activities | $44,780 | 126,390 |

## BEST-PAYING METROPOLITAN AREAS

| Metro Area | Median Earnings | Workforce |
|---|---|---|
| New York–Northern New Jersey–Long Island, NY-NJ-PA | $126,680 | 66,580 |
| Boston-Cambridge-Quincy, MA-NH | $103,870 | 8,050 |
| San Francisco–Oakland–Fremont, CA | $96,020 | 9,110 |
| Philadelphia-Camden-Wilmington, PA-NJ-DE-MD | $79,650 | 8,530 |
| Chicago-Naperville-Joliet, IL-IN-WI | $76,270 | 19,450 |
| Miami–Fort Lauderdale–Pompano Beach, FL | $75,620 | 7,420 |
| Los Angeles–Long Beach–Santa Ana, CA | $74,730 | 14,900 |
| Minneapolis–St. Paul–Bloomington, MN-WI | $60,760 | 7,000 |
| Dallas–Fort Worth–Arlington, TX | $59,030 | 10,310 |
| Houston–Sugar Land–Baytown, TX | $53,730 | 8,880 |
| Phoenix-Mesa-Scottsdale, AZ | $44,710 | 7,180 |

## JOB SPECIALIZATION: SALES AGENTS, SECURITIES, AND COMMODITIES

Buy and sell securities in investment and trading firms and develop and implement financial plans for individuals, businesses, and organizations.

**Major Work Tasks:** Complete sales order tickets and submit for processing of client-requested transactions. Interview clients to determine clients' assets, liabilities, cash flow, insurance coverage, tax status, or financial objectives. Record transactions accurately, and keep clients informed about transactions. Develop financial plans based on analysis of clients' financial status, and discuss financial options with clients. Review all securities transactions to ensure accuracy of information and conformance to governing agency regulations. Offer advice on the purchase or sale of particular securities. Relay buy or sell orders to securities exchanges or to firm trading departments. Identify potential clients, using advertising campaigns, mailing lists, or personal contacts. Review financial periodicals, stock and bond reports, business publications, or other material to identify potential investments for clients or to keep abreast of trends affecting market conditions. Contact prospective customers to determine customer needs, present information, or explain available services. Prepare documents needed to implement plans selected by clients. Analyze market conditions to determine optimum times to execute securities transactions. Explain stock market terms or trading practices to clients. Inform and advise concerned parties regarding fluctuations or securities transactions affecting plans or accounts. Calculate costs for billings or commissions. Supply the latest price quotes on any security, as well as information on the activities or financial positions of the corporations issuing these securities. Prepare financial reports to monitor client or corporate finances. Read corporate reports and calculate ratios to determine best prospects for profit on stock purchases and to monitor client accounts.

**Related Knowledge/Courses:** Economics and Accounting; Customer and Personal Service; Sales and Marketing; Clerical Practices; Law and Government; Mathematics.

**Personality Types:** Enterprising–Conventional.

**Skills:** Systems analysis; persuasion; systems evaluation; management of financial resources; reading comprehension; judgment and decision making; negotiation; service orientation.

**407**

**Physical Environment:** Indoors; sitting. **Structural Environment:** Importance of being exact or accurate; impact of decisions on co-workers or company results; level of competition; structured versus unstructured work; frequency of decision making; time pressure.

### JOB SPECIALIZATION: SALES AGENTS, FINANCIAL SERVICES

**Sell financial services, such as loan, tax, and securities counseling to customers of financial institutions and business establishments.**

**Major Work Tasks:** Determine customers' financial services needs and prepare proposals to sell services that address these needs. Contact prospective customers to present information and explain available services. Sell services or equipment, such as trusts, investments, or check processing services. Prepare forms or agreements to complete sales. Develop prospects from current commercial customers, referral leads, or sales or trade meetings. Review business trends to advise customers regarding expected fluctuations. Make presentations on financial services to groups to attract new clients. Evaluate costs and revenue of agreements to determine continued profitability.

**Related Knowledge/Courses:** Sales and Marketing; Economics and Accounting; Customer and Personal Service; Clerical Practices; Mathematics; Law and Government.

**Personality Types:** Enterprising–Conventional.

**Skills:** Persuasion; management of financial resources; mathematics; speaking; systems evaluation; service orientation; active listening; writing.

**Physical Environment:** Indoors; sitting. **Structural Environment:** Importance of being exact or accurate; structured versus unstructured work; freedom to make decisions; level of competition; frequency of decision making; impact of decisions on co-workers or company results.

### JOB SPECIALIZATION: SECURITIES AND COMMODITIES TRADERS

**Buy and sell securities and commodities to transfer debt, capital, or risk. Establish and negotiate unit prices and terms of sale.**

**Major Work Tasks:** Agree on buying or selling prices at optimal levels for clients. Buy or sell stocks, bonds, commodity futures, foreign currencies, or other securities on behalf of investment dealers. Make bids or offers to buy or sell securities. Analyze target companies or investment opportunities to inform investment decisions. Develop or maintain supplier or customer relationships. Devise trading, option, or hedge strategies. Identify opportunities or develop channels for purchase or sale of securities or commodities. Inform other traders, managers, or customers of market conditions, including volume, price, competition, or dynamics. Monitor markets or positions. Process paperwork for special orders, including margin or option purchases. Receive sales order tickets and inspect forms to determine accuracy of information. Report all positions or trading results. Review securities transactions to ensure conformance to regulations. Track and analyze factors that affect price movement, such as trade policies, weather conditions, political developments, or supply and demand changes. Write or sign sales order confirmation forms to record or approve security transactions. Make transportation arrangements for sold or purchased commodities. Prepare financial reports, such as reviews of portfolio positions. Reconcile account-related statements, such as quarterly or annual statements or confirmations. Report deficiencies in account payments, securities deliveries, or documentation requirements to avoid rule violations. Supervise support staff and ensure proper execution of contracts. Buy, sell, or trade carbon emissions permits. Identify or pursue investment strategies related to the green economy, including green hedge funds, renewable energy markets, or clean technology investment opportunities.

**Related Knowledge/Courses:** No data available.

**Personality Types:** Enterprising–Conventional.

**Skills:** No data available.

**Physical Environment:** No data available.
**Structural Environment:** No data available.

## Ship Engineers

Supervise and coordinate activities of crew engaged in operating and maintaining engines, boilers, deck machinery, and electrical, sanitary, and refrigeration equipment aboard ship.

- Average annual earnings: $70,890
- Middle 50% of earners: $51,380–$93,470
- Earnings growth potential: Medium (43.1%)
- Growth: 18.0%
- Annual job openings: 620
- Self-employed: 0.0%

**Considerations for Job Outlook:** Job prospects should be favorable. Many workers leave water transportation occupations, especially sailors and marine oilers, because recently hired workers often decide they do not enjoy spending a lot of time away at sea. In addition, a number of officers and engineers are approaching retirement, creating job openings. The number of applicants for all types of jobs may be limited by high regulatory and security requirements.

### BEST-PAYING INDUSTRIES

| Industry | Median Earnings | Workforce |
|---|---|---|
| Support Activities for Transportation | $75,470 | 1,970 |
| Water Transportation | $74,080 | 5,990 |
| Federal, State, and Local Government | $62,690 | 1,830 |

### BEST-PAYING METROPOLITAN AREAS

| Metro Area | Median Earnings | Workforce |
|---|---|---|
| New Orleans–Metairie–Kenner, LA | $85,580 | 460 |
| Miami–Fort Lauderdale–Pompano Beach, FL | $82,770 | 1,240 |
| Houma–Bayou Cane–Thibodaux, LA | $80,600 | 690 |
| New York–Northern New Jersey–Long Island, NY-NJ-PA | $79,880 | 770 |
| Seattle-Tacoma-Bellevue, WA | $72,290 | 770 |
| Tampa–St. Petersburg–Clearwater, FL | $62,510 | 260 |
| Virginia Beach–Norfolk–Newport News, VA-NC | $57,220 | 1,460 |
| Mobile, AL | $54,900 | 340 |

**Major Work Tasks:** Monitor the availability, use, or condition of lifesaving equipment or pollution preventatives to ensure that international regulations are followed. Monitor engine, machinery, or equipment indicators when vessels are underway and report abnormalities to appropriate shipboard staff. Maintain electrical power, heating, ventilation, refrigeration, water, or sewerage systems. Record orders for changes in ship speed or direction and note gauge readings or test data, such as revolutions per minute or voltage output, in engineering logs or bellbooks. Perform or participate in emergency drills, as required. Maintain complete records of engineering department activities, including machine operations. Start engines to propel ships and regulate engines and power transmissions to control speeds of ships, according to directions from captains or bridge computers. Monitor and test operations of engines or other equipment so that malfunctions and their causes can be identified. Maintain or repair engines, electric motors, pumps, winches, or other mechanical or electrical equipment or assist other crew members with maintenance or repair duties. Perform general marine vessel maintenance or repair work, such as repairing leaks, finishing interiors, refueling, or maintaining decks. Operate or maintain off-loading liquid pumps or valves. Clean engine parts and keep engine rooms clean. Supervise the activities of marine engine technicians engaged in the maintenance or repair of mechanical or electrical marine vessels and inspect their work to ensure that it is performed properly. Order and receive engine room stores, such as oil or spare parts, maintain inventories, and record usage of supplies. Act as a liaison between a ship's captain and shore personnel to ensure that schedules and budgets are maintained and that the ship is operated safely and efficiently. Install engine controls, propeller shafts, or propellers. Fabricate engine replacement parts, such as valves, stay rods, or bolts, using metalworking machinery.

**Usual Educational Requirement:** Bachelor's degree. **Relevant Educational Program**: Marine Science/Merchant Marine Officer. **Related Knowledge/Courses:** Mechanical Devices; Building and Construction; Transportation; Engineering and Technology; Public Safety and Security; Chemistry. **Work Experience Needed:** None. **On-the-Job Training Needed:** None. **Certification/Licensure:** Licensure.

**Personality Types:** Realistic–Conventional–Enterprising. **Key Career Cluster:** 16 Transportation, Distribution, and Logistics. **Key Career Pathway:** 16.1 Transportation Operations.

**Skills:** Repairing; equipment maintenance; troubleshooting; equipment selection; operation and control; operation monitoring; quality control analysis; science.

**Physical Environment:** Outdoors; standing; using hands; noise; very hot or cold; bright or inadequate lighting. **Structural Environment:** Frequency of decision making; impact of decisions on co-workers or company results; importance of being exact or accurate; freedom to make decisions; structured versus unstructured work; importance of repeating same tasks.

## Social and Community Service Managers

Plan, direct, or coordinate the activities of a social service program or community outreach organization.

- Average annual earnings: $59,970
- Middle 50% of earners: $45,640–$77,650
- Earnings growth potential: Medium (39.6%)
- Growth: 26.7%
- Annual job openings: 6,480
- Self-employed: 4.9%

**Considerations for Job Outlook:** Growth is due to the needs of an aging population. An increase in the number of older adults will result in growth in demand for social services. Elderly people often need services, such as adult day care and meal delivery. Social and community service managers, who administer programs that provide these services, will likely be needed to meet this increased demand. As a

### BEST-PAYING INDUSTRIES

| Industry | Median Earnings | Workforce |
|---|---|---|
| Federal, State, and Local Government | $70,340 | 24,780 |
| Religious, Grantmaking, Civic, Professional, and Similar Organizations | $61,500 | 14,340 |
| Social Assistance | $55,100 | 45,670 |
| Nursing and Residential Care Facilities | $53,090 | 13,540 |

| Metro Area | Median Earnings | Workforce |
|---|---|---|
| New York–Northern New Jersey–Long Island, NY-NJ-PA | $76,620 | 9,600 |
| Los Angeles–Long Beach–Santa Ana, CA | $69,410 | 4,620 |
| San Francisco–Oakland–Fremont, CA | $66,660 | 2,650 |
| Philadelphia-Camden-Wilmington, PA-NJ-DE-MD | $65,190 | 3,250 |
| Boston-Cambridge-Quincy, MA-NH | $60,300 | 3,680 |
| Chicago-Naperville-Joliet, IL-IN-WI | $58,730 | 3,860 |

result, employment of social and community service managers is expected to grow fastest in industries serving the elderly, such as home health-care services and services for the elderly and persons with disabilities. Services for the elderly and persons with disabilities are included in the individual and family services industry.

**Major Work Tasks:** Establish and maintain relationships with other agencies and organizations in community to meet community needs and to ensure that services are not duplicated. Prepare and maintain records and reports, such as budgets, personnel records, or training manuals. Direct activities of professional and technical staff members and volunteers. Evaluate the work of staff and volunteers to ensure that programs are of appropriate quality and that resources are used effectively. Establish and oversee administrative procedures to meet objectives set by boards of directors or senior management. Participate in the determination of organizational policies regarding such issues as participant eligibility, program requirements, and program benefits. Research and analyze member or community needs to determine program directions and goals. Speak to community groups to explain and interpret agency purposes, programs, and policies. Recruit, interview, and hire or sign up volunteers and staff. Represent organizations in relations with governmental and media institutions. Plan and administer budgets for programs, equipment, and support services. Act as consultants to agency staff and other community programs regarding the interpretation of program-related federal, state, and county regulations and policies. Provide direct service and support to individuals or clients, such as handling a referral for child advocacy issues, conducting a needs evaluation, or resolving complaints. Implement and evaluate staff, volunteer, or community training programs. Analyze proposed legislation, regulations, or rule changes to determine how agency services could be impacted. Direct fundraising activities and the preparation of public relations materials.

**Usual Educational Requirement:** Bachelor's degree. **Relevant Educational Programs**: Business Administration and Management, General; Business/Commerce, General; Community Organization and Advocacy; Human Services, General; Non-Profit/Public/Organizational Management; Public Administration; Social Work; Social Work, Other; Youth Services/Administration. **Related Knowledge/Courses:** Therapy and Counseling; Psychology; Sociology and Anthropology; Philosophy and Theology; Personnel and Human Resources; Customer and Personal Service. **Work Experience Needed:** 1 to 5 years. **On-the-Job Training Needed:** None. **Certification/Licensure:** None.

**Personality Types:** Enterprising–Social. **Key Career Cluster:** 10 Human Services. **Key Career Pathway:** 10.2 Counseling and Mental Health Services.

**Skills:** Management of financial resources; management of personnel resources; opera-

411

tions analysis; management of material resources; systems evaluation; social perceptiveness; systems analysis; time management.

**Physical Environment:** Indoors; sitting. **Structural Environment:** Impact of decisions on coworkers or company results; frequency of decision making; freedom to make decisions; structured versus unstructured work; time pressure; consequence of error.

## Social Scientists and Related Workers, All Other

**All social scientists and related workers not listed separately.**

- Average annual earnings: $76,540
- Middle 50% of earners: $60,110–$95,580
- Earnings growth potential: Medium (38.8%)
- Growth: 8.1%
- Annual job openings: 1,760
- Self-employed: 11.5%

**Considerations for Job Outlook:** In federal government, a small increase is expected as the federal government increasingly uses demographers, ethnographers, and other social scientists to understand its citizens and their needs.

**Major Work Tasks:** For tasks, see the job specializations.

**Usual Educational Requirement:** Bachelor's degree. **Relevant Educational Programs**: Be-

### BEST-PAYING INDUSTRIES

| Industry | Median Earnings | Workforce |
|---|---|---|
| Professional, Scientific, and Technical Services | $83,210 | 7,460 |
| Federal, State, and Local Government | $76,920 | 19,220 |
| Educational Services | $62,210 | 2,780 |

### BEST-PAYING METROPOLITAN AREAS

| Metro Area | Median Earnings | Workforce |
|---|---|---|
| Baltimore-Towson, MD | $97,940 | 690 |
| Washington-Arlington-Alexandria, DC-VA-MD-WV | $94,960 | 6,110 |
| Los Angeles–Long Beach–Santa Ana, CA | $89,380 | 1,350 |
| San Francisco–Oakland–Fremont, CA | $86,850 | 790 |
| Chicago-Naperville-Joliet, IL-IN-WI | $77,910 | 720 |

havioral Sciences; Demography and Population Studies; Education Policy Analysis; Gerontology; Health Policy Analysis; Learning Sciences; Linguistic, Comparative, and Related Language Studies and Services, Other; Research Methodology and Quantitative Methods; Social Sciences, General; Social Sciences, Other. **Work Experience Needed:** None. **On-the-Job Training Needed:** None. **Certification/Licensure:** None.

**Key Career Cluster:** 10 Human Services. **Key Career Pathway:** 10.3 Family and Community Services.

### JOB SPECIALIZATION: TRANSPORTATION PLANNERS

**Prepare studies for proposed transportation projects. Gather, compile, and analyze data. Study the use and operation of transportation systems. Develop transportation models or simulations.**

**Major Work Tasks:** Prepare or review engineering studies or specifications. Represent jurisdictions in the legislative or administrative approval of land development projects. Prepare necessary documents to obtain project approvals or permits. Direct urban traffic counting programs. Develop or test new methods or models of transportation analysis. Analyze transportation-related consequences of federal and state legislative proposals. Analyze information from traffic counting programs. Review development plans for transportation system effects, infrastructure requirements, or compliance with applicable transportation regulations. Prepare reports or recommendations on transportation planning. Produce environmental documents, such as environmental assessments or environmental impact statements. Participate in public meetings or hearings to explain planning proposals, to gather feedback from those affected by projects, or to achieve consensus on project designs. Document and evaluate transportation project needs and costs. Develop design ideas for new or improved transport infrastructure, such as junction improvements, pedestrian projects, bus facilities, and car parking areas. Develop computer models to address transportation planning issues. Design transportation surveys to identify areas of public concern. Analyze and interpret data from traffic modeling software, geographic information systems, or associated databases. Collaborate with engineers to research, analyze, or resolve complex transportation design issues. Recommend transportation system improvements or projects, based on economic, population, land-use or traffic projections. Define regional or local transportation planning problems or priorities. Analyze information related to transportation, such as land use policies, environmental impact of projects, or long-range planning needs. Define or update information such as urban boundaries or classification of roadways. Collaborate with other professionals to develop sustainable transportation strategies at the local, regional, or national levels.

**Related Knowledge/Courses:** Geography; Transportation; Law and Government; History and Archeology; Design; Sociology and Anthropology.

**Personality Types:** Investigative–Conventional–Realistic.

**Skills:** Systems evaluation; management of material resources; operations analysis; mathematics; systems analysis; management of financial resources; technology design; complex problem solving.

**Physical Environment:** Indoors; sitting. **Structural Environment:** Freedom to make decisions; structured versus unstructured work; impact of decisions on co-workers or company results; importance of being exact or accurate; time pressure; frequency of decision making.

## Social Work Teachers, Postsecondary

*See Teachers, Postsecondary.*

## Sociology Teachers, Postsecondary

*See Teachers, Postsecondary.*

## Software Developers, Applications

**Develop, create, and modify general computer applications software or specialized utility programs.**

- Average annual earnings: $90,060
- Middle 50% of earners: $70,850–$113,280
- Earnings growth potential: Medium (38.7%)
- Growth: 27.6%
- Annual job openings: 19,790
- Self-employed: 2.3%

**Considerations for Job Outlook:** Job prospects will be best for applicants with knowledge of the most up-to-date programming tools and languages. Consulting opportunities for software developers also should be good as businesses seek help to manage, upgrade, and customize their increasingly complicated computer systems.

**Major Work Tasks:** Confer with systems analysts, engineers, programmers, and others to

**413**

## Your Guide to High-Paying Careers

### BEST-PAYING INDUSTRIES

| Industry | Median Earnings | Workforce |
|---|---|---|
| Computer and Electronic Product Manufacturing | $97,960 | 32,050 |
| Publishing Industries (except Internet) | $96,450 | 49,940 |
| Management of Companies and Enterprises | $89,280 | 31,730 |
| Professional, Scientific, and Technical Services | $89,180 | 252,710 |

### BEST-PAYING METROPOLITAN AREAS

| Metro Area | Median Earnings | Workforce |
|---|---|---|
| San Jose–Sunnyvale–Santa Clara, CA | $116,070 | 24,160 |
| San Francisco–Oakland–Fremont, CA | $106,250 | 21,670 |
| Washington-Arlington-Alexandria, DC-VA-MD-WV | $104,840 | 32,150 |
| Seattle-Tacoma-Bellevue, WA | $102,020 | 36,300 |
| New York–Northern New Jersey–Long Island, NY-NJ-PA | $99,310 | 52,620 |
| Boston-Cambridge-Quincy, MA-NH | $97,210 | 26,710 |
| Los Angeles–Long Beach–Santa Ana, CA | $94,590 | 23,740 |
| Denver-Aurora, CO | $91,620 | 12,460 |
| Dallas–Fort Worth–Arlington, TX | $90,090 | 17,170 |
| Chicago-Naperville-Joliet, IL-IN-WI | $86,590 | 22,000 |

design system and to obtain information on project limitations and capabilities, performance requirements, and interfaces. Modify existing software to correct errors, allow it to adapt to new hardware, or to improve its performance. Analyze user needs and software requirements to determine feasibility of design within time and cost constraints. Consult with customers about software system design and maintenance. Coordinate software system installation and monitor equipment functioning to ensure specifications are met. Design, develop, and modify software systems, using scientific analysis and mathematical models to predict and measure outcome and consequences of design. Develop and direct software system testing and validation procedures, programming, and documentation. Supervise the work of programmers, technologists and technicians, and other engineering and scientific personnel. Obtain and evaluate information on factors, such as reporting formats required, costs, and security needs to determine hardware configuration. Determine system performance standards. Store, retrieve, and manipulate data for analysis of system capabilities and requirements. Analyze information to determine, recommend, and plan computer specifications and layouts, and peripheral equipment modifications. Train users to use new or modified equipment. Specify power supply requirements and configuration. Recommend purchase of equipment to control dust, temperature, and humidity in area of system installation.

**Usual Educational Requirement:** Bachelor's degree. **Relevant Educational Programs**: Artificial Intelligence; Bioinformatics; Computer Engineering, General; Computer Programming, Specific Applications; Computer Programming/Programmer, General; Computer Science; Computer Software Engineering; Computer Software Technology/Technician; Informatics; Information Technology; Medical Informatics; Modeling, Virtual Environments

**414**

and Simulation. **Related Knowledge/Courses:** Computers and Electronics; Mathematics; Engineering and Technology; Design; English Language. **Work Experience Needed:** None. **On-the-Job Training Needed:** None. **Certification/Licensure:** Voluntary certification by vendor or association.

**Personality Types:** Investigative–Realistic–Conventional. **Key Career Cluster:** 11 Information Technology. **Key Career Pathway:** 11.4 Programming and Software Development.

**Skills:** Programming; troubleshooting; technology design; systems evaluation; operations analysis; mathematics; systems analysis; science.

**Physical Environment:** Indoors; sitting; repetitive motions. **Structural Environment:** Importance of being exact or accurate; freedom to make decisions; structured versus unstructured work; impact of decisions on co-workers or company results; importance of repeating same tasks; frequency of decision making.

## Software Developers, Systems Software

**Research, design, develop, and test operating systems-level software, compilers, and network distribution software.**

- Average annual earnings: $99,000
- Middle 50% of earners: $78,930–$123,560
- Earnings growth potential: Medium (36.6%)
- Growth: 32.4%
- Annual job openings: 16,800
- Self-employed: 2.3%

**Considerations for Job Outlook:** Job prospects will be best for applicants with knowledge of the most up-to-date programming tools and languages. Consulting opportunities for software developers also should be good as businesses seek help to manage, upgrade, and customize their increasingly complicated computer systems.

### BEST-PAYING INDUSTRIES

| Industry | Median Earnings | Workforce |
|---|---|---|
| Computer and Electronic Product Manufacturing | $105,030 | 58,410 |
| Professional, Scientific, and Technical Services | $99,860 | 176,980 |
| Publishing Industries (except Internet) | $99,370 | 27,700 |

### BEST-PAYING METROPOLITAN AREAS

| Metro Area | Median Earnings | Workforce |
|---|---|---|
| San Jose–Sunnyvale–Santa Clara, CA | $127,660 | 24,790 |
| Washington-Arlington-Alexandria, DC-VA-MD-WV | $111,450 | 32,710 |
| Los Angeles–Long Beach–Santa Ana, CA | $110,040 | 21,330 |
| San Francisco–Oakland–Fremont, CA | $109,890 | 15,440 |
| Boston-Cambridge-Quincy, MA-NH | $108,910 | 27,890 |
| New York–Northern New Jersey–Long Island, NY-NJ-PA | $101,930 | 18,540 |
| Philadelphia-Camden-Wilmington, PA-NJ-DE-MD | $98,140 | 10,850 |
| Dallas–Fort Worth–Arlington, TX | $97,070 | 13,940 |
| Atlanta–Sandy Springs–Marietta, GA | $94,520 | 9,300 |
| Chicago-Naperville-Joliet, IL-IN-WI | $91,830 | 13,580 |
| Houston–Sugar Land–Baytown, TX | $88,780 | 8,370 |

**415**

**Major Work Tasks:** Modify existing software to correct errors, to adapt it to new hardware, or to upgrade interfaces and improve performance. Design or develop software systems, using scientific analysis and mathematical models to predict and measure outcome and consequences of design. Consult with engineering staff to evaluate interface between hardware and software, develop specifications and performance requirements, or resolve customer problems. Analyze information to determine, recommend, and plan installation of a new system or modification of an existing system. Develop or direct software system testing or validation procedures. Direct software programming and development of documentation. Consult with customers or other departments on project status, proposals, or technical issues, such as software system design or maintenance. Coordinate installation of software system. Store, retrieve, and manipulate data for analysis of system capabilities and requirements. Confer with data processing or project managers to obtain information on limitations or capabilities for data processing projects. Prepare reports or correspondence concerning project specifications, activities, or status. Advise customer about or perform maintenance of software system. Monitor functioning of equipment to ensure system operates in conformance with specifications. Evaluate factors, such as reporting formats required, cost constraints, or need for security restrictions to determine hardware configuration. Supervise and assign work to programmers, designers, technologists, technicians, or other engineering or scientific personnel. Train users to use new or modified equipment. Use microcontrollers to develop control signals, implement control algorithms, or measure process variables, such as temperatures, pressures, or positions. Recommend purchase of equipment to control dust, temperature, or humidity in area of system installation. Specify power supply requirements and configuration.

**Usual Educational Requirement:** Bachelor's degree. **Relevant Educational Programs**: Artificial Intelligence; Computer Engineering, General; Computer Programming, Specific Applications; Computer Programming/Programmer, General; Computer Science; Computer Software Engineering; Computer Software Technology/Technician; Informatics; Information Science/Studies; Information Technology. **Related Knowledge/Courses:** Computers and Electronics; Telecommunications; Engineering and Technology; Design; Mathematics; Physics. **Work Experience Needed:** None. **On-the-Job Training Needed:** None. **Certification/Licensure:** Voluntary certification by vendor or association.

**Personality Types:** Investigative–Conventional–Realistic. **Key Career Cluster:** 11 Information Technology. **Key Career Pathway:** 11.4 Programming and Software Development.

**Skills:** Programming; operations analysis; mathematics; active listening; reading comprehension; complex problem solving; critical thinking; speaking.

**Physical Environment:** Indoors; sitting. **Structural Environment:** Importance of being exact or accurate; freedom to make decisions; structured versus unstructured work; level of competition; time pressure; importance of repeating same tasks.

## Soil and Plant Scientists

**Conduct research in breeding, physiology, production, yield, and management of crops and agricultural plants or trees, shrubs, and nursery stock, their growth in soils, and control of pests.**

- Average annual earnings: $58,740
- Middle 50% of earners: $45,720–$75,270
- Earnings growth potential: Medium (38.7%)
- Growth: 12.1%
- Annual job openings: 860
- Self-employed: 10.5%

## BEST-PAYING INDUSTRIES

| Industry | Median Earnings | Workforce |
| --- | --- | --- |
| Federal, State, and Local Government | $64,110 | 2,830 |
| Merchant Wholesalers, Nondurable Goods | $63,280 | 1,550 |
| Professional, Scientific, and Technical Services | $58,740 | 4,520 |
| Educational Services | $46,620 | 1,880 |

## BEST-PAYING METROPOLITAN AREAS

| Metro Area | Median Earnings | Workforce |
| --- | --- | --- |
| Des Moines–West Des Moines, IA | $67,400 | 1,200 |
| San Francisco–Oakland–Fremont, CA | $66,780 | 460 |
| Portland-Vancouver-Beaverton, OR-WA | $55,810 | 260 |
| Chicago-Naperville-Joliet, IL-IN-WI | $54,890 | 330 |

**Considerations for Job Outlook:** A number of job vacancies will arise as many scientists are expected to retire within the next 10 years.

**Major Work Tasks:** Communicate research or project results to other professionals or the public or teach related courses, seminars, or workshops. Provide information or recommendations to farmers or other landowners regarding ways in which they can best use land, promote plant growth, or avoid or correct problems, such as erosion. Investigate responses of soils to specific management practices to determine the use capabilities of soils and the effects of alternative practices on soil productivity. Develop methods of conserving or managing soil that can be applied by farmers or forestry companies. Conduct experiments to develop new or improved varieties of field crops, focusing on characteristics, such as yield, quality, disease resistance, nutritional value, or adaptation to specific soils or climates. Investigate soil problems or poor water quality to determine sources and effects. Study soil characteristics to classify soils on the basis of factors, such as geographic location, landscape position, or soil properties. Develop improved measurement techniques, soil conservation methods, soil sampling devices, or related technology. Conduct experiments investigating how soil forms, changes, or interacts with land-based ecosystems or living organisms. Identify degraded or contaminated soils and develop plans to improve their chemical, biological, or physical characteristics. Survey undisturbed or disturbed lands for classification, inventory, mapping, environmental impact assessments, environmental protection planning, conservation planning, or reclamation planning. Perform chemical analyses of the microorganism content of soils to determine microbial reactions or chemical mineralogical relationships to plant growth. Provide advice regarding the development of regulatory standards for land reclamation or soil conservation. Develop new or improved methods or products for controlling or eliminating weeds, crop diseases, or insect pests. Conduct research to determine best methods of planting, spraying, cultivating, harvesting, storing, processing, or transporting horticultural products.

**Usual Educational Requirement:** Bachelor's degree. **Relevant Educational Programs**: Agricultural and Horticultural Plant Breeding; Agriculture, General; Agroecology and Sustainable Agriculture; Agronomy and Crop Science; Horticultural Science; Plant Protection and Integrated Pest Management; Plant Sciences, General; Plant Sciences, Other; Range Science and Management; Soil Chemistry and Physics; Soil Microbiology; Soil Science and Agronomy, General; Soil Sciences, Other; Viticulture and Enology. **Related Knowledge/**

**Courses:** Biology; Food Production; Geography; Chemistry; Physics; Education and Training. **Work Experience Needed:** None. **On-the-Job Training Needed:** None. **Certification/Licensure:** Voluntary certification by association.

**Personality Types:** Investigative–Realistic. **Key Career Cluster:** 01 Agriculture, Food, and Natural Resources. **Key Career Pathway:** 1.2 Plant Systems.

**Skills:** Science; operations analysis; mathematics; reading comprehension; speaking; systems evaluation; systems analysis; writing.

**Physical Environment:** Indoors; outdoors; sitting. **Structural Environment:** Freedom to make decisions; importance of being exact or accurate; structured versus unstructured work; level of competition; impact of decisions on co-workers or company results; time pressure.

## Special Education Teachers, Secondary School

**Teach secondary school subjects to educationally and physically handicapped students.**

- Average annual earnings: $56,830
- Middle 50% of earners: $45,450–$72,010
- Earnings growth potential: Medium (32.4%)
- Growth: 7.3%
- Annual job openings: 5,110
- Self-employed: 0.4%

**Considerations for Job Outlook:** From 2010 to 2020, a significant number of older special education teachers are expected to reach retirement age. Their retirement will create job openings for new teachers. In addition, many schools, particularly those in urban and rural areas, have difficulties recruiting and keeping special education teachers. As a result, special education teachers should have little difficulty finding employment. Job opportunities may be

### BEST-PAYING INDUSTRIES

| Industry | Median Earnings | Workforce |
|---|---|---|
| Educational Services | $56,910 | 130,490 |

### BEST-PAYING METROPOLITAN AREAS

| Metro Area | Median Earnings | Workforce |
|---|---|---|
| New York–Northern New Jersey–Long Island, NY-NJ-PA | $78,390 | 14,150 |
| Chicago-Naperville-Joliet, IL-IN-WI | $70,450 | 5,750 |
| Los Angeles–Long Beach–Santa Ana, CA | $67,780 | 4,860 |
| Washington-Arlington-Alexandria, DC-VA-MD-WV | $65,700 | 3,020 |
| Boston-Cambridge-Quincy, MA-NH | $62,280 | 3,030 |
| Philadelphia-Camden-Wilmington, PA-NJ-DE-MD | $61,910 | 4,200 |

upon a variety of instructional techniques and technologies. Meet with other professionals to discuss individual students' needs and progress. Confer with parents or guardians, other teachers, counselors, and administrators to resolve students' behavioral and academic problems. Meet with parents and guardians to discuss their children's progress and to determine priorities for their children and their resource needs. Guide and counsel students with adjustment or academic problems, or special academic interests.

**Usual Educational Requirement:** Bachelor's degree. **Relevant Educational Programs**: Education/Teaching of Individuals in Secondary Special Education Programs; Education/Teaching of Individuals Who are Developmentally Delayed; Education/Teaching of Individuals with Autism; Education/Teaching of Individuals with Emotional Disturbances;

Education/Teaching of Individuals with Hearing Impairments, Including Deafness; Education/Teaching of Individuals with Mental Retardation; Education/Teaching of Individuals with Multiple Disabilities; Education/Teaching of Individuals with Orthopedic and Other Physical Health Impairments; Education/Teaching of Individuals with Specific Learning Disabilities; Education/Teaching of Individuals with Speech or Language Impairments; Education/Teaching of Individuals with Traumatic Brain Injuries; Education/Teaching of Individuals with Vision Impairments Including Blindness; Special Education and Teaching, General. **Related Knowledge/Courses:** Therapy and Counseling; History and Archeology; Psychology; Geography; Philosophy and Theology; Sociology and Anthropology. **Work Experience Needed:** None. **On-the-Job Training Needed:** Internship/residency. **Certification/Licensure:** License in public schools.

**Personality Types:** Social–Investigative. **Key Career Cluster:** 05 Education and Training. **Key Career Pathway:** 5.3 Teaching/Training.

**Skills:** Learning strategies; social perceptiveness; service orientation; instructing; operations analysis; monitoring; active learning; reading comprehension.

**Physical Environment:** Indoors; standing; noise. **Structural Environment:** Freedom to make decisions; structured versus unstructured work; time pressure; frequency of decision making; impact of decisions on co-workers or company results; importance of being exact or accurate.

## Speech-Language Pathologists

**Assess and treat persons with speech, language, voice, and fluency disorders.**
- Average annual earnings: $69,870
- Middle 50% of earners: $55,170–$87,630
- Earnings growth potential: Medium (36.5%)

- Growth: 23.4%
- Annual job openings: 5,230
- Self-employed: 8.9%

### BEST-PAYING INDUSTRIES

| Industry | Median Earnings | Workforce |
|---|---|---|
| Nursing and Residential Care Facilities | $84,680 | 6,350 |
| Ambulatory Health-Care Services | $76,340 | 29,130 |
| Hospitals | $74,180 | 16,660 |
| Educational Services | $63,190 | 59,480 |

### BEST-PAYING METROPOLITAN AREAS

| Metro Area | Median Earnings | Workforce |
|---|---|---|
| Los Angeles–Long Beach–Santa Ana, CA | $86,170 | 3,720 |
| New York–Northern New Jersey–Long Island, NY-NJ-PA | $81,280 | 8,490 |
| Boston-Cambridge-Quincy, MA-NH | $72,020 | 2,710 |
| Chicago-Naperville-Joliet, IL-IN-WI | $70,470 | 6,290 |
| Dallas–Fort Worth–Arlington, TX | $65,630 | 3,300 |

**Considerations for Job Outlook:** As the large baby-boom population grows older, there will be more instances of health conditions that cause speech or language impairments, such as strokes and hearing loss. These increases are expected to add to the number of speech and language disorders in the population and require more speech-language pathologists to treat these patients. Increased awareness of speech and language disorders, such as stuttering, in younger children should also lead to

**419**

a need for more speech-language pathologists who specialize in treating that age group.

**Major Work Tasks:** Monitor patients' progress and adjust treatments accordingly. Administer hearing or speech and language evaluations, tests, or examinations to patients to collect information on type and degree of impairments, using written or oral tests or special instruments. Develop or implement treatment plans for problems, such as stuttering, delayed language, swallowing disorders, or inappropriate pitch or harsh voice problems, based on own assessments and recommendations of physicians, psychologists, or social workers. Instruct clients in techniques for more effective communication, such as sign language, lip reading, or voice improvement. Teach clients to control or strengthen tongue, jaw, face muscles, or breathing mechanisms. Develop speech exercise programs to reduce disabilities. Consult with and advise educators or medical staff on speech or hearing topics, such as communication strategies or speech and language stimulation. Design, develop, or employ alternative diagnostic or communication devices or strategies. Conduct lessons or direct educational or therapeutic games to assist teachers dealing with speech problems. Communicate with non-speaking students, using sign language or computer technology. Use computer applications to identify or assist with communication disabilities. Evaluate hearing or speech and language test results, barium swallow results, or medical or background information to diagnose and plan treatment for speech, language, fluency, voice, or swallowing disorders. Write reports and maintain proper documentation of information, such as client Medicaid or billing records or caseload activities, including the initial evaluation, treatment, progress, and discharge of clients. Develop individual or group activities or programs in schools to deal with behavior, speech, language, or swallowing problems. Participate in and write reports for meetings regarding patients' progress, such as individualized educational planning (IEP) meetings, in-service meetings, or intervention assistance team meetings. Complete administrative responsibilities, such as coordinating paperwork, scheduling case management activities, or writing lesson plans.

**Usual Educational Requirement:** Master's degree. **Relevant Educational Programs**: Audiology/Audiologist and Speech-Language Pathology/Pathologist; Communication Disorders Sciences and Services, Other; Communication Disorders, General; Communication Sciences and Disorders, General; Speech-Language Pathology/Pathologist. **Related Knowledge/Courses:** Therapy and Counseling; Psychology; English Language; Medicine and Dentistry; Sociology and Anthropology; Foreign Language. **Work Experience Needed:** None. **On-the-Job Training Needed:** None. **Certification/Licensure:** Licensure in most states; also voluntary certification by association.

**Personality Types:** Social–Investigative–Artistic. **Key Career Cluster:** 08 Health Science. **Key Career Pathway:** 8.1 Therapeutic Services.

**Skills:** Science; learning strategies; operations analysis; systems evaluation; social perceptiveness; writing; instructing; technology design.

**Physical Environment:** Indoors; sitting; exposed to disease or infections. **Structural Environment:** Freedom to make decisions; structured versus unstructured work; importance of being exact or accurate; impact of decisions on co-workers or company results; frequency of decision making; time pressure.

## Statisticians

**Develop or apply mathematical or statistical theory and methods to collect, organize, interpret, and summarize numerical data to provide usable information.**

- Average annual earnings: $75,560
- Middle 50% of earners: $55,360–$99,340

- Earnings growth potential: High (44.1%)
- Growth: 14.1%
- Annual job openings: 1,870
- Self-employed: 2.8%

### BEST-PAYING INDUSTRIES

| Industry | Median Earnings | Workforce |
|---|---|---|
| Federal, State, and Local Government | $79,870 | 6,790 |
| Professional, Scientific, and Technical Services | $77,840 | 7,240 |
| Insurance Carriers and Related Activities | $69,720 | 2,240 |
| Educational Services | $66,210 | 2,460 |
| Hospitals | $56,800 | 1,480 |

### BEST-PAYING METROPOLITAN AREAS

| Metro Area | Median Earnings | Workforce |
|---|---|---|
| San Francisco–Oakland–Fremont, CA | $103,890 | 640 |
| Washington-Arlington-Alexandria, DC-VA-MD-WV | $97,340 | 3,820 |
| San Jose–Sunnyvale–Santa Clara, CA | $94,000 | 590 |
| Boston-Cambridge-Quincy, MA-NH | $91,060 | 1,480 |
| Los Angeles–Long Beach–Santa Ana, CA | $83,550 | 870 |
| Minneapolis–St. Paul–Bloomington, MN-WI | $79,830 | 570 |
| Philadelphia-Camden-Wilmington, PA-NJ-DE-MD | $74,060 | 890 |
| Seattle-Tacoma-Bellevue, WA | $65,080 | 720 |

**Considerations for Job Outlook:** Job prospects for statisticians will be very good. Graduates with a master's degree in statistics and with a strong background in an allied related field, such as finance, biology, engineering, or computer science, should have the best prospects of finding jobs related to their field of study.

**Major Work Tasks:** Report results of statistical analyses, including information in the form of graphs, charts, and tables. Process large amounts of data for statistical modeling and graphic analysis, using computers. Identify relationships and trends in data, as well as any factors that could affect the results of research. Analyze and interpret statistical data to identify significant differences in relationships among sources of information. Prepare data for processing by organizing information, checking for any inaccuracies, and adjusting and weighting the raw data. Evaluate the statistical methods and procedures used to obtain data to ensure validity, applicability, efficiency, and accuracy. Evaluate sources of information to determine any limitations in terms of reliability or usability. Plan data collection methods for specific projects and determine the types and sizes of sample groups to be used. Design research projects that apply valid scientific techniques and use information obtained from baselines or historical data to structure uncompromised and efficient analyses. Develop an understanding of fields to which statistical methods are to be applied to determine whether methods and results are appropriate. Supervise and provide instructions for workers collecting and tabulating data. Apply sampling techniques or use complete enumeration bases to determine and define groups to be surveyed. Adapt statistical methods to solve specific problems in many fields, such as economics, biology, and engineering. Develop and test experimental designs, sampling techniques, and analytical methods. Examine theories, such as those of probability and inference, to discover mathematical bases for new or improved methods of obtaining and evaluating numerical data. Report results of statistical analyses in peer-reviewed papers and technical manuals. Develop software applications or programming to use for statistical modeling and graphic analysis. Present statistical and non-statistical results using charts, bullets, and graphs in meetings or conferences to audiences, such as clients, peers, and students.

**Usual Educational Requirement:** Master's degree. **Relevant Educational Programs**: Applied Mathematics, General; Biostatistics; Business Statistics; Computational and Applied Mathematics; Mathematical Statistics and Probability; Mathematics and Statistics; Mathematics, General; Research Methodology and Quantitative Methods; Statistics, General; Statistics, Other. **Related Knowledge/Courses:** Mathematics; Computers and Electronics; English Language; Administration and Management; Education and Training. **Work Experience Needed:** None. **On-the-Job Training Needed:** None. **Certification/Licensure:** None.

**Personality Types:** Conventional–Investigative. **Key Career Cluster:** 15 Science, Technology, Engineering, and Mathematics. **Key Career Pathway:** 15.2 Science and Mathematics.

**Skills:** Programming; mathematics; science; operations analysis; active learning; reading comprehension; writing; critical thinking.

**Physical Environment:** Indoors; sitting. **Structural Environment:** Importance of being exact or accurate; freedom to make decisions; structured versus unstructured work; impact of decisions on co-workers or company results; level of competition; time pressure.

## JOB SPECIALIZATION: BIOSTATISTICIANS

**Develop and apply biostatistical theory and methods to the study of life sciences.**

**Major Work Tasks:** Write research proposals or grant applications for submission to external bodies. Teach graduate or continuing education courses or seminars in biostatistics. Read current literature, attend meetings or conferences, and talk with colleagues to keep abreast of methodological or conceptual developments in fields, such as biostatistics, pharmacology, life sciences, and social sciences. Prepare statistical data for inclusion in reports to data monitoring committees, federal regulatory agencies, managers, or clients. Prepare articles for publication or presentation at professional conferences. Calculate sample size requirements for clinical studies. Determine project plans, timelines, or technical objectives for statistical aspects of biological research studies. Assign work to biostatistical assistants or programmers. Write program code to analyze data using statistical analysis software. Write detailed analysis plans and descriptions of analyses and findings for research protocols or reports. Plan or direct research studies related to life sciences. Prepare tables and graphs to present clinical data or results. Monitor clinical trials or experiments to ensure adherence to established procedures or to verify the quality of data collected. Draw conclusions or make predictions based on data summaries or statistical analyses. Develop or use mathematical models to track changes in biological phenomena, such as the spread of infectious diseases. Design surveys to assess health issues. Develop or implement data analysis algorithms. Design research studies in collaboration with physicians, life scientists, or other professionals. Design or maintain databases of biological data. Collect data through surveys or experimentation. Review clinical or other medical research protocols and recommend appropriate statistical analyses. Provide biostatistical consultation to clients or colleagues. Apply research or simulation results to extend biological theory or recommend new research projects. Analyze clinical or survey data using statistical approaches such as longitudinal analysis, mixed effect modeling, logistic regression analyses, and model building techniques.

**Related Knowledge/Courses:** Mathematics; Biology; Computers and Electronics; Medicine and Dentistry; English Language; Education and Training.

**Personality Types:** Investigative–Conventional.

**Skills:** Programming; science; mathematics; writing; reading comprehension; operations analysis; active learning; instructing.

**Physical Environment:** Indoors; sitting. **Structural Environment:** Importance of being exact or accurate; freedom to make decisions; structured versus unstructured work; impact of decisions on co-workers or company results; time pressure; level of competition.

### JOB SPECIALIZATION: CLINICAL DATA MANAGERS

**Apply knowledge of health-care and database management to analyze clinical data and to identify and report trends.**

**Major Work Tasks:** Provide support and information to functional areas, such as marketing, clinical monitoring, and medical affairs. Evaluate processes and technologies, and suggest revisions to increase productivity and efficiency. Develop technical specifications for data management programming and communicate needs to information technology staff. Contribute to the compilation, organization, and production of protocols, clinical study reports, regulatory submissions, or other controlled documentation. Write work instruction manuals, data capture guidelines, or standard operating procedures. Track the flow of work forms, including in-house data flow or electronic forms transfer. Train staff on technical procedures or software program usage. Supervise the work of data management project staff. Prepare data analysis listings and activity, performance, or progress reports. Perform quality control audits to ensure accuracy, completeness, or proper usage of clinical systems and data. Monitor work productivity or quality to ensure compliance with standard operating procedures. Generate data queries based on validation checks or errors and omissions identified during data entry to resolve identified problems. Design and validate clinical databases, including designing or testing logic checks. Confer with end users to define or implement clinical system requirements, such as data release formats, delivery schedules, and testing protocols. Process clinical data, including receipt, entry, verification, or filing of information. Develop project-specific data management plans that address areas, such as data coding, reporting, or transfer, database locks, and work flow processes. Design forms for receiving, processing, or tracking data. Read technical literature and participate in continuing education or professional associations to maintain awareness of current database technology and best practices. Prepare appropriate formatting to datasets as requested. Develop or select specific software programs for various research scenarios. Analyze clinical data using appropriate statistical tools.

**Related Knowledge/Courses:** Medicine and Dentistry; Biology; Clerical Practices; Administration and Management; Computers and Electronics.

**Personality Types:** Conventional–Investigative.

**Skills:** Programming; operations analysis; mathematics; technology design; instructing; systems evaluation; systems analysis; management of personnel resources.

**Physical Environment:** Indoors; sitting; repetitive motions. **Structural Environment:** Importance of being exact or accurate; importance of

423

repeating same tasks; time pressure; freedom to make decisions; structured versus unstructured work.

## Supervisors of Construction and Extraction Workers

**Directly supervise and coordinate activities of construction or extraction workers.**

- Average annual earnings: $59,700
- Middle 50% of earners: $46,510–$76,030
- Earnings growth potential: Medium (38.2%)
- Growth: 23.5%
- Annual job openings: 25,970
- Self-employed: 15.9%

### BEST-PAYING INDUSTRIES

| Industry | Median Earnings | Workforce |
|---|---|---|
| Construction of Buildings | $60,040 | 116,120 |
| Heavy and Civil Engineering Construction | $59,860 | 60,410 |
| Specialty Trade Contractors | $58,440 | 157,910 |
| Federal, State, and Local Government | $57,030 | 41,570 |

### BEST-PAYING METROPOLITAN AREAS

| Metro Area | Median Earnings | Workforce |
|---|---|---|
| New York–Northern New Jersey–Long Island, NY-NJ-PA | $81,380 | 20,620 |
| Los Angeles–Long Beach–Santa Ana, CA | $74,820 | 12,190 |
| Washington-Arlington-Alexandria, DC-VA-MD-WV | $67,470 | 11,760 |
| Houston–Sugar Land–Baytown, TX | $59,120 | 16,310 |
| Dallas–Fort Worth–Arlington, TX | $54,610 | 12,990 |

**Considerations for Job Outlook:** A faster-than-average increase is expected as the streamlining of employment, such as reducing administrative staff, will reduce these non-craft workers relative to supervisors.

**Major Work Tasks:** Read specifications, such as blueprints, to determine construction requirements or to plan procedures. Estimate material or worker requirements to complete jobs. Supervise, coordinate, or schedule the activities of construction or extractive workers. Confer with managerial or technical personnel, other departments, or contractors to resolve problems or to coordinate activities. Coordinate work activities with other construction project activities. Order or requisition materials or supplies. Locate, measure, and mark site locations or placement of structures or equipment, using measuring and marking equipment. Record information, such as personnel, production, or operational data on specified forms or reports. Assign work to employees, based on material or worker requirements of specific jobs. Provide assistance to workers engaged in construction or extraction activities, using hand tools or other equipment. Train workers in construction methods, operation of equipment, safety procedures, or company policies. Analyze worker or production problems and recommend solutions, such as improving production methods or implementing motivational plans. Arrange for repairs of equipment or machinery. Suggest or initiate personnel actions, such as promotions, transfers, or hires. Inspect work progress, equipment, or construction sites to verify safety or to ensure that specifications are met.

**Usual Educational Requirement:** High school diploma or equivalent. **Relevant Educational Programs**: Blasting/Blaster; Building Construction Technology; Building/Construction Site Management/Manager; Building/Home/Construction Inspection/Inspector; Building/Property Maintenance; Carpentry/Carpenter; Carpet, Floor, and Tile Worker; Concrete Finishing/Concrete Finisher; Construction

Trades, General; Drywall Installation/ Drywaller; Electrician; Glazier Training; Insulator Training; Masonry/Mason Training; Painting/Painter and Wall Coverer Training; Pipefitting/Pipefitter and Sprinkler Fitter; Plumbing Technology/Plumber; Roofer Training; Well Drilling/Driller. **Related Knowledge/Courses:** Building and Construction; Production and Processing; Mechanical Devices; Transportation; Public Safety and Security; Design. **Work Experience Needed:** More than 5 years. **On-the-Job Training Needed:** None. **Certification/Licensure:** None.

**Personality Types:** Enterprising–Realistic–Conventional. **Key Career Cluster:** 02 Architecture and Construction. **Key Career Pathway:** 2.2 Construction.

**Skills:** Equipment selection; equipment maintenance; operation and control; management of personnel resources; operations analysis; management of material resources; repairing; operation monitoring.

**Physical Environment:** Outdoors; standing; walking and running; using hands; noise; very hot or cold. **Structural Environment:** Freedom to make decisions; impact of decisions on coworkers or company results; structured versus unstructured work; frequency of decision making; importance of being exact or accurate; time pressure.

### JOB SPECIALIZATION: SOLAR ENERGY INSTALLATION MANAGERS

**Direct work crews installing residential or commercial solar photovoltaic or thermal systems.**

**Major Work Tasks:** Plan and coordinate installations of photovoltaic (PV) solar and solar thermal systems to ensure conformance to codes. Supervise solar installers, technicians, and subcontractors for solar installation projects to ensure compliance with safety standards. Assess potential solar installation sites to determine feasibility and design requirements. Assess system performance or function-

ality at the system, subsystem, and component levels. Coordinate or schedule building inspections for solar installation projects. Monitor work of contractors and subcontractors to ensure projects conform to plans, specifications, schedules, or budgets. Perform start-up of systems for testing or customer implementation. Provide technical assistance to installers, technicians, or other solar professionals in areas such as solar electric systems, solar thermal systems, electrical systems, and mechanical systems. Visit customer sites to determine solar system needs, requirements, or specifications. Develop and maintain system architecture, including all piping, instrumentation, or process flow diagrams. Estimate materials, equipment, and personnel needed for residential or commercial solar installation projects. Evaluate subcontractors or subcontractor bids for quality, cost, and reliability. Identify means to reduce costs, minimize risks, or increase efficiency of solar installation projects. Prepare solar installation project proposals, quotes, budgets, or schedules. Purchase or rent equipment for solar energy system installation.

**Related Knowledge/Courses:** No data available.

**Personality Types:** Enterprising–Realistic.

**Skills:** No data available.

**Physical Environment:** No data available. **Structural Environment:** No data available.

## Surveyors

**Make exact measurements and determine property boundaries.**

- Average annual earnings: $56,230
- Middle 50% of earners: $41,780–$73,800
- Earnings growth potential: Medium (42.8%)
- Growth: 25.4%
- Annual job openings: 2,420
- Self-employed: 13.8%

## Your Guide to High-Paying Careers

### BEST-PAYING INDUSTRIES

| Industry | Median Earnings | Workforce |
|---|---|---|
| Federal, State, and Local Government | $65,860 | 4,880 |
| Heavy and Civil Engineering Construction | $57,250 | 2,010 |
| Professional, Scientific, and Technical Services | $54,490 | 29,190 |

### BEST-PAYING METROPOLITAN AREAS

| Metro Area | Median Earnings | Workforce |
|---|---|---|
| Los Angeles–Long Beach–Santa Ana, CA | $85,710 | 1,080 |
| New York–Northern New Jersey–Long Island, NY-NJ-PA | $70,900 | 1,480 |
| Chicago-Naperville-Joliet, IL-IN-WI | $65,640 | 810 |
| Washington-Arlington-Alexandria, DC-VA-MD-WV | $58,020 | 880 |
| Houston–Sugar Land–Baytown, TX | $53,450 | 2,020 |

**Considerations for Job Outlook:** Although surveyors have traditionally relied on construction projects for many of their opportunities, increased demand for geographic data should mean better opportunities for professionals who are involved in developing and using GIS technology and digital mapmaking. Other opportunities should result from the many surveyors who are expected to retire or permanently leave the occupation for other reasons.

**Major Work Tasks:** Prepare and maintain sketches, maps, reports, and legal descriptions of surveys to describe, certify, and assume liability for work performed. Verify the accuracy of survey data, including measurements and calculations conducted at survey sites. Direct or conduct surveys to establish legal boundaries for properties, based on legal deeds and titles. Record the results of surveys, including the shape, contour, location, elevation, and dimensions of land or land features. Calculate heights, depths, relative positions, property lines, and other characteristics of terrain. Prepare or supervise preparation of all data, charts, plots, maps, records, and documents related to surveys. Write descriptions of property boundary surveys for use in deeds, leases, or other legal documents. Plan and conduct ground surveys designed to establish baselines, elevations, and other geodetic measurements. Search legal records, survey records, and land titles to obtain information about property boundaries in areas to be surveyed. Coordinate findings with the work of engineering and architectural personnel, clients, and others concerned with projects. Adjust surveying instruments to maintain their accuracy. Establish fixed points for use in making maps using geodetic and engineering instruments. Determine longitudes and latitudes of important features and boundaries in survey areas using theodolites, transits, levels, and satellite-based global positioning systems (GPS). Train assistants and helpers, and direct their work in such activities as performing surveys or drafting maps. Analyze survey objectives and specifications to prepare survey proposals or to direct others in survey proposal preparation. Compute geodetic measurements and interpret survey data to determine positions, shapes, and elevations of geomorphic and topographic features. Develop criteria for survey methods and procedures. Conduct research in surveying and mapping methods using knowledge of techniques of photogrammetric map compilation and electronic data processing. Survey bodies of water to determine navigable channels and to secure data for construction of breakwaters, piers, and other marine structures.

426

**Usual Educational Requirement:** Bachelor's degree. **Relevant Educational Program**: Surveying Technology/Surveying. **Related Knowledge/Courses:** Geography; Design; Building and Construction; History and Archeology; Engineering and Technology; Law and Government. **Work Experience Needed:** None. **On-the-Job Training Needed:** None. **Certification/Licensure:** Licensure.

**Personality Types:** Realistic–Conventional–Investigative. **Key Career Cluster:** 02 Architecture and Construction. **Key Career Pathway:** 2.1 Design/Pre-Construction.

**Skills:** Science; equipment selection; mathematics; repairing; equipment maintenance; management of personnel resources; operation monitoring; operation and control.

**Physical Environment:** Outdoors; indoors; standing; walking and running; using hands; noise. **Structural Environment:** Importance of being exact or accurate; impact of decisions on co-workers or company results; frequency of decision making; freedom to make decisions; importance of repeating same tasks; time pressure.

### JOB SPECIALIZATION: GEODETIC SURVEYORS

**Measure large areas of Earth's surface, using satellite observations, global navigation satellite systems (GNSS), light detection and ranging (LIDAR), or related sources.**

**Major Work Tasks:** Review existing standards, controls, or equipment used, recommending changes or upgrades as needed. Provide training and interpretation in the use of methods or procedures for observing and checking controls for geodetic and plane coordinates. Plan or direct the work of geodetic surveying staff, providing technical consultation as needed. Distribute compiled geodetic data to government agencies or the general public. Read current literature, talk with colleagues, continue education, or participate in professional organizations or conferences to keep abreast of developments in technology, equipment, or systems. Verify the mathematical correctness of newly collected survey data. Request additional survey data when field collection errors occur or engineering surveying specifications are not maintained. Prepare progress or technical reports. Maintain databases of geodetic and related information including coordinate, descriptive, or quality assurance data. Compute, retrace, or adjust existing surveys of features, such as highway alignments, property boundaries, utilities, control, and other surveys to match the ground elevation dependent grids, geodetic grids, or property boundaries and to ensure accuracy and continuity of data used in engineering, surveying, or construction projects. Compute horizontal and vertical coordinates of control networks using direct leveling or other geodetic survey techniques, such as triangulation, trilateration, and traversing to establish features of the earth's surface. Calculate the exact horizontal and vertical position of points on the earth's surface. Analyze control or survey data to ensure adherence to project specifications or land survey standards. Assess the quality of control data to determine the need for additional survey data for engineering, construction, or other projects. Determine orientation of tracts of land, including position, boundaries, size, and shape using theodolites, electronic distance measuring equipment, satellite-based positioning equipment, land information systems, or other geodetic survey equipment.

**Related Knowledge/Courses:** Geography; Physics; Mathematics; Engineering and Technology; Computers and Electronics; Design.

**Personality Types:** Investigative–Conventional–Realistic.

**Skills:** Mathematics; programming; science; equipment selection; quality control analysis; operation and control; management of personnel resources; writing.

**Physical Environment:** Outdoors; indoors; standing; using hands; very hot or cold. **Struc-**

tural Environment: Importance of being exact or accurate; freedom to make decisions; impact of decisions on co-workers or company results; structured versus unstructured work; frequency of decision making; importance of repeating same tasks.

## Teachers, Postsecondary

**Teach courses at a level beyond high school.**

- Average annual earnings: $64,409
- Middle 50% of earners: $45,477–$91,548
- Earnings growth potential: Medium (41.6%)
- Growth: 17.4%
- Annual job openings: 58,610
- Self-employed: 0.5%

**Considerations for Job Outlook:** Enrollments in postsecondary institutions are expected to continue rising as more people attend college and as workers return to school to update their skills. Opportunities for part-time or temporary positions should be favorable, but significant competition exists for tenure-track positions.

**Major Work Tasks:** Evaluate and grade students' class work, assignments, and papers. Compile, administer, and grade examinations or assign this work to others. Prepare course materials, such as syllabi, homework assignments, and handouts. Maintain student attendance records, grades, and other required records. Initiate, facilitate, and moderate class discussions. Plan, evaluate, and revise curriculums, course content, and course materials and methods of instruction. Maintain regularly scheduled office hours to advise and assist students. Keep abreast of developments in the field by reading current literature, talking with colleagues, and participating in professional conferences. Select and obtain materials and supplies, such as textbooks and laboratory equipment. Collaborate with colleagues to address teaching and research issues. Participate in student recruitment, registration, and place-ment activities. Compile bibliographies of specialized materials for outside reading assignments. Supervise undergraduate or graduate teaching, internship, and research work. Conduct research in a particular field of knowledge and present findings in professional journals, books, electronic media, or at professional conferences. Serve on academic or administrative committees that deal with institutional policies, departmental matters, and academic issues. Act as advisers to student organizations. Perform administrative duties such as serving as department head. Provide professional consulting services to government or industry. Participate in campus and community events. Write grant proposals to procure external research funding.

**Major Work Tasks:** For additional tasks, see the job specializations.

**Usual Educational Requirement:** Doctoral or professional degree. **Work Experience Needed:** None. **On-the-Job Training Needed:** None.

**Key Career Cluster:** 05 Education and Training. **Key Career Pathway:** 5.3 Teaching/Training.

### JOB SPECIALIZATION: ANTHROPOLOGY AND ARCHEOLOGY TEACHERS, POSTSECONDARY

**Teach courses in anthropology or archeology.**

- Average annual earnings: $76,020
- Middle 50% of earners: $56,760–$100,560
- Earnings growth potential: High (45.0%)

**Major Work Tasks:** Prepare and deliver lectures to undergraduate or graduate students on topics, such as research methods, urban anthropology, and language and culture. Advise students on laboratory and field research.

### BEST-PAYING INDUSTRIES

| Industry | Median Earnings | Workforce |
|---|---|---|
| Educational Services | $76,000 | 5,680 |

BEST-PAYING METROPOLITAN AREAS

| Metro Area | Median Earnings | Workforce |
|---|---|---|
| New York–Northern New Jersey–Long Island, NY-NJ-PA | $106,350 | 510 |
| Los Angeles–Long Beach–Santa Ana, CA | $93,000 | 200 |
| Philadelphia-Camden-Wilmington, PA-NJ-DE-MD | $90,590 | 150 |
| Washington-Arlington-Alexandria, DC-VA-MD-WV | $78,310 | 160 |

Supervise students' laboratory or field work. Review manuscripts for publication in books and professional journals. (Also, perform the same tasks listed for Teachers, Postsecondary.)

**Relevant Educational Programs**: Anthropology; Anthropology, Other; Archeology; Cultural Anthropology; Medical Anthropology; Physical and Biological Anthropology; Social Science Teacher Education; Sociology and Anthropology. **Related Knowledge/Courses**: History and Archeology; Sociology and Anthropology; Geography; Philosophy and Theology; Foreign Language; Education and Training. **Certification/Licensure**: None.

**Personality Types**: Social–Investigative.

**Skills**: Science; writing; speaking; reading comprehension; learning strategies; instructing; systems evaluation; active learning.

**Physical Environment**: Indoors; sitting. **Structural Environment**: Freedom to make decisions; structured versus unstructured work; importance of being exact or accurate; level of competition; time pressure; impact of decisions on co-workers or company results.

## JOB SPECIALIZATION: ARCHITECTURE TEACHERS, POSTSECONDARY

**Teach courses in architecture and architectural design, such as architectural environmental design, interior architecture/design, and landscape architecture.**

- Average annual earnings: $71,610
- Middle 50% of earners: $54,210–$93,320
- Earnings growth potential: Medium (41.4%)

### BEST-PAYING INDUSTRIES

| Industry | Median Earnings | Workforce |
|---|---|---|
| Educational Services | $71,620 | 7,280 |

### BEST-PAYING METROPOLITAN AREAS

| Metro Area | Median Earnings | Workforce |
|---|---|---|
| Lansing–East Lansing, MI | $81,420 | 160 |
| Providence–Fall River–Warwick, RI-MA | $80,950 | 170 |
| Miami–Fort Lauderdale–Pompano Beach, FL | $77,970 | 150 |
| Los Angeles–Long Beach–Santa Ana, CA | $76,070 | 150 |
| Denver-Aurora, CO | $75,840 | 180 |
| New York–Northern New Jersey–Long Island, NY-NJ-PA | $75,420 | 490 |

**Major Work Tasks**: Evaluate and grade students' work performed in design studios. Prepare and deliver lectures to undergraduate or graduate students on topics, such as architectural design methods, aesthetics and design, and structures and materials. (Also, perform the tasks listed for Teachers, Postsecondary.)

**Relevant Educational Programs**: Architectural and Building Sciences/Technology; Architectural Engineering; Architectural Sciences and Technology, Other; Architecture (BArch, BA/BS, MArch, MA/MS, PhD); City/Urban, Community and Regional Planning; Environmental Design/Architecture; Interior Architecture; Interior Design; Landscape Architecture (BS, BSLA, BLA, MSLA, MLA, PhD). **Related Knowledge/Courses**: Fine Arts; Design; Building and Construction; History and Archeology; Engineering and Technology; Philosophy and Theology. **Certification/Licensure**: License.

**Personality Types**: Social–Artistic.

**Skills**: Writing; instructing; learning strategies; reading comprehension; speaking; mathematics; active learning; operations analysis.

**Physical Environment**: Indoors; sitting. **Structural Environment**: Freedom to make decisions; structured versus Unstructured Work; Level of Competition; Importance of being exact or accurate; time pressure; impact of decisions on co-workers or company results.

### JOB SPECIALIZATION: AREA, ETHNIC, AND CULTURAL STUDIES TEACHERS, POSTSECONDARY

**Teach courses pertaining to the culture and development of an area, an ethnic group, or any other group, such as Latin American studies, women's studies, or urban affairs.**

- Average annual earnings: $67,360
- Middle 50% of earners: $49,970–$93,360
- Earnings growth potential: Very high (51.4%)

**Major Work Tasks**: Prepare and deliver lectures to undergraduate or graduate students on topics, such as race and ethnic relations,

#### BEST-PAYING INDUSTRIES

| Industry | Median Earnings | Workforce |
|---|---|---|
| Educational Services | $67,340 | 9,700 |

#### BEST-PAYING METROPOLITAN AREAS

| Metro Area | Median Earnings | Workforce |
|---|---|---|
| New York–Northern New Jersey–Long Island, NY-NJ-PA | $95,680 | 1,060 |
| Boston-Cambridge-Quincy, MA-NH | $81,760 | 360 |
| Los Angeles–Long Beach–Santa Ana, CA | $79,390 | 320 |
| Austin–Round Rock, TX | $64,840 | 230 |
| Phoenix-Mesa-Scottsdale, AZ | $58,490 | 360 |
| Washington-Arlington-Alexandria, DC-VA-MD-WV | $49,840 | 590 |

gender studies, and cross-cultural perspectives. Incorporate experiential or site visit components into courses. (Also, perform the tasks listed for Teachers, Postsecondary.)

**Relevant Educational Programs**: African Studies; African-American/Black Studies; American Indian/Native American Studies; American/United States Studies/Civilization; Area Studies, Other; Asian Studies/Civilization; Asian-American Studies; Balkans Studies; Baltic Studies; Canadian Studies; Caribbean Studies; Chinese Studies; Commonwealth Studies; Deaf Studies; Disability Studies; East Asian Studies; Ethnic Studies; Ethnic, Cultural Minority, Gender, and Group Studies, Other; European Studies/Civilization; Folklore Studies; French Studies; Gay/Lesbian Studies; German Studies; Hispanic-American, Puerto Rican, and Mexican-American/Chicano Studies; Intercultural/Multicultural and Diversity Studies; Irish Studies; Islamic Studies; Italian Studies; Japanese Studies; Jewish/Judaic Studies; Korean Studies; Latin American and Caribbean Studies; Latin American Studies; Near and Middle Eastern Studies; Pacific Area/Pacific Rim Studies; Polish Studies; Regional Studies (U.S., Canadian, Foreign); Russian Studies; others. **Related Knowledge/ Courses:** Foreign Language; Sociology and Anthropology; History and Archeology; Geography; Philosophy and Theology; Education and Training. **Certification/Licensure:** None.

**Personality Types:** Social–Investigative–Artistic.

**Skills:** Science; writing; reading comprehension; speaking; learning strategies; instructing; active listening; active learning.

**Physical Environment:** Indoors; sitting. **Structural Environment:** Freedom to make decisions; structured versus unstructured work; importance of being exact or accurate; level of competition; impact of decisions on co-workers or company results; time pressure.

### JOB SPECIALIZATION: ART, DRAMA, AND MUSIC TEACHERS, POSTSECONDARY

**Teach courses in drama, music, and the arts, including fine and applied art, such as painting and sculpture or design and crafts.**

#### BEST-PAYING INDUSTRIES

| Industry | Median Earnings | Workforce |
|---|---|---|
| Educational Services | $62,160 | 92,440 |

#### BEST-PAYING METROPOLITAN AREAS

| Metro Area | Median Earnings | Workforce |
|---|---|---|
| New York–Northern New Jersey–Long Island, NY-NJ-PA | $98,670 | 9,510 |
| Los Angeles–Long Beach–Santa Ana, CA | $78,210 | 5,590 |
| San Francisco–Oakland–Fremont, CA | $71,670 | 2,880 |
| Boston-Cambridge-Quincy, MA-NH | $68,730 | 4,120 |
| Chicago-Naperville-Joliet, IL-IN-WI | $54,630 | 1,980 |

- Average annual earnings: $62,160
- Middle 50% of earners: $45,300–$87,490
- Earnings growth potential: High (46.7%)

**Major Work Tasks:** Prepare and deliver lectures to undergraduate or graduate students on topics, such as acting techniques, fundamentals of music, and art history. Explain and demonstrate artistic techniques. Prepare students for performances, exams, or assessments. Display students' work in schools, galleries, and exhibitions. Organize performance groups and direct their rehearsals. (Also, perform the tasks listed for Teachers, Postsecondary.)

**Relevant Educational Programs**: Art History, Criticism and Conservation; Art Teacher Education; Art/Art Studies, General; Arts, Entertainment, and Media Management, Other; Arts, Entertainment, and Media Management, General; Ballet; Brass Instruments; Ceramic Arts and Ceramics; Cinematography and Film/Video Production; Commercial Photography; Conducting; Costume Design; Crafts/Craft Design, Folk Art and Artisanry; Dance, General; Dance, Other; Design and Visual Communications, General; Digital Arts; Directing and Theatrical Production; Documentary Production; Drama and Dance Teacher Education; Drama and Dramatics/Theatre Arts, General; Dramatic/Theatre Arts and Stagecraft, Other; Fashion/Apparel Design; Fiber, Textile, and Weaving Arts; Film/Cinema/Video Studies; Film/Video and Photographic Arts, Other; Fine and Studio Arts Management; Fine Arts and Art Studies, Other; Fine/Studio Arts, General; Graphic Design; Industrial and Product Design; Intermedia/Multimedia; Jazz/Jazz Studies; Keyboard Instruments; others. **Related Knowledge/Courses:** Fine Arts; Philosophy and Theology; History and Archeology; Education and Training; Communications and Media; Sociology and Anthropology. **Certification/Licensure:** None.

**Personality Types:** Social–Artistic.

**Skills:** Instructing; learning strategies; speaking; reading comprehension; time management; writing; active learning; operations analysis.

**Physical Environment:** Indoors; standing; using hands. **Structural Environment:** Freedom to make decisions; structured versus unstructured work; time pressure; impact of decisions on co-workers or company results; frequency of decision making; importance of being exact or accurate.

### JOB SPECIALIZATION: ATMOSPHERIC, EARTH, MARINE, AND SPACE SCIENCES TEACHERS, POSTSECONDARY

**Teach courses in the physical sciences, except chemistry and physics.**

- Average annual earnings: $82,180
- Middle 50% of earners: $57,390–$117,040
- Earnings growth potential: High (48.8%)

#### BEST-PAYING INDUSTRIES

| Industry | Median Earnings | Workforce |
|---|---|---|
| Educational Services | $82,190 | 10,930 |

#### BEST-PAYING METROPOLITAN AREAS

| Metro Area | Median Earnings | Workforce |
|---|---|---|
| Los Angeles–Long Beach–Santa Ana, CA | $114,430 | 760 |
| New York–Northern New Jersey–Long Island, NY-NJ-PA | $106,770 | 600 |
| Chicago-Naperville-Joliet, IL-IN-WI | $73,150 | 220 |

**Major Work Tasks:** Prepare and deliver lectures to undergraduate or graduate students on topics, such as structural geology, micrometeorology, and atmospheric thermodynamics. Answer questions from the public and media. Purchase and maintain equipment to support research projects. Supervise laboratory work

and field work. (Also, perform the tasks listed for Teachers, Postsecondary.)

**Relevant Educational Programs**: Astronomy; Astrophysics; Atmospheric Chemistry and Climatology; Atmospheric Physics and Dynamics; Atmospheric Sciences and Meteorology, General; Atmospheric Sciences and Meteorology, Other; Earth Science Teacher Education; Geochemistry; Geochemistry and Petrology; Geological and Earth Sciences/Geosciences, Other; Geology/Earth Science, General; Geophysics and Seismology; Hydrology and Water Resources Science; Meteorology; Oceanography, Chemical and Physical; Paleontology; Planetary Astronomy and Science; Science Teacher Education/General Science Teacher Education. **Related Knowledge/Courses:** Chemistry; Physics; Geography; Education and Training; Biology; Mathematics. **Certification/Licensure:** None.

**Personality Types:** Social–Investigative.

**Skills:** Science; writing; mathematics; learning strategies; reading comprehension; speaking; operations analysis; active listening.

**Physical Environment:** Indoors; sitting. **Structural Environment:** Freedom to make decisions; structured versus unstructured work; level of competition; importance of being exact or accurate; time pressure; impact of decisions on co-workers or company results.

### JOB SPECIALIZATION: BIOLOGICAL SCIENCE TEACHERS, POSTSECONDARY

**Teach courses in biological sciences.**

- Average annual earnings: $74,180
- Middle 50% of earners: $53,060–$106,300
- Earnings growth potential: High (46.2%)

**Major Work Tasks:** Prepare and deliver lectures to undergraduate or graduate students on topics, such as molecular biology, marine biology, and botany. Assist students who need extra help with their coursework outside of class. Evaluate and grade students' laboratory work. Prepare materials for laboratory activi-

## BEST-PAYING INDUSTRIES

| Industry | Median Earnings | Workforce |
|---|---|---|
| Educational Services | $73,310 | 48,540 |

## BEST-PAYING METROPOLITAN AREAS

| Metro Area | Median Earnings | Workforce |
|---|---|---|
| Boston-Cambridge-Quincy, MA-NH | $95,520 | 1,640 |
| Los Angeles–Long Beach–Santa Ana, CA | $92,350 | 1,120 |
| Washington-Arlington-Alexandria, DC-VA-MD-WV | $91,390 | 1,180 |
| New York–Northern New Jersey–Long Island, NY-NJ-PA | $87,330 | 2,460 |
| Chicago-Naperville-Joliet, IL-IN-WI | $48,360 | 1,240 |

ties. Review papers for publication in journals. (Also, perform the tasks listed for Teachers, Postsecondary.)

**Relevant Educational Programs**: Aerospace Physiology and Medicine; Anatomy; Animal Physiology; Biochemistry; Biochemistry and Molecular Biology; Biochemistry, Biophysics and Molecular Biology, Other; Biological and Biomedical Sciences, Other; Biology Teacher Education; Biology/Biological Sciences, General; Biomathematics, Bioinformatics, and Computational Biology, Other; Biometry/Biometrics; Biophysics; Biotechnology; Botany/Plant Biology; Botany/Plant Biology, Other; Cell/Cellular Biology and Anatomical Sciences, Other; Cell/Cellular Biology and Histology; Computational Biology; Ecology; Ecology and Evolutionary Biology; Ecology, Evolution, Systematics and Population Biology, Other; Entomology; Evolutionary Biology; Genetics, Other; Genome Sciences/Genomics;

Human Biology; Immunology; Marine Biology and Biological Oceanography; Microbiological Sciences and Immunology, Other; Microbiology and Immunology; Microbiology, General; Molecular Biology; Molecular Genetics; Molecular Medicine; Neuroanatomy; others. **Related Knowledge/Courses:** Biology; Chemistry; Education and Training; Geography; Physics; English Language. **Certification/Licensure:** None.

**Personality Types:** Social–Investigative.

**Skills:** Science; writing; reading comprehension; instructing; speaking; learning strategies; active learning; operations analysis.

**Physical Environment:** Indoors; sitting. **Structural Environment:** Structured versus unstructured work; freedom to make decisions; importance of being exact or accurate; impact of decisions on co-workers or company results; time pressure; frequency of decision making.

### JOB SPECIALIZATION: BUSINESS TEACHERS, POSTSECONDARY

**Teach courses in business administration and management, such as accounting, finance, human resources, labor and industrial relations, marketing, and operations research.**

### BEST-PAYING INDUSTRIES

| Industry | Median Earnings | Workforce |
|---|---|---|
| Educational Services | $73,640 | 82,400 |

### BEST-PAYING METROPOLITAN AREAS

| Metro Area | Median Earnings | Workforce |
|---|---|---|
| Los Angeles–Long Beach–Santa Ana, CA | $92,900 | 2,480 |
| New York–Northern New Jersey–Long Island, NY-NJ-PA | $81,670 | 5,470 |
| Chicago-Naperville-Joliet, IL-IN-WI | $48,370 | 2,450 |

433

- Average annual earnings: $73,660
- Middle 50% of earners: $48,850–$109,050
- Earnings growth potential: Very high (53.1%)

**Major Work Tasks:** Collaborate with members of the business community to improve programs, to develop new programs, and to provide student access to learning opportunities, such as internships. Prepare and deliver lectures to undergraduate or graduate students on topics, such as financial accounting, principles of marketing, and operations management. (Also, perform the tasks listed for Teachers, Postsecondary.)

**Relevant Educational Programs**: Accounting; Actuarial Science; Business Administration and Management, General; Business Statistics; Business Teacher Education; Business/Commerce, General; Business/Corporate Communications; Entrepreneurship/Entrepreneurial Studies; Finance, General; Financial Planning and Services; Franchising and Franchise Operations; Hotel, Motel, and Restaurant Management; Human Resources Management/Personnel Administration, General; Insurance; International Business/Trade/Commerce; International Finance; International Marketing; Investments and Securities; Labor and Industrial Relations; Logistics, Materials, and Supply Chain Management; Management Science; Marketing Research; Marketing/Marketing Management, General; Operations Management and Supervision; Organizational Behavior Studies; Organizational Leadership; Project Management; Public Finance; Purchasing, Procurement/Acquisitions and Contracts Management; Research and Development Management; Retail Management; others. **Related Knowledge/Courses:** Sociology and Anthropology; Education and Training; Communications and Media; Sales and Marketing; Economics and Accounting; English Language. **Certification/Licensure:** Certification if appropriate in specialty.

**Personality Types:** Social–Enterprising–Investigative.

**Skills:** Writing; learning strategies; instructing; speaking; reading comprehension; active learning; mathematics; critical thinking.

**Physical Environment:** Indoors; sitting. **Structural Environment:** Freedom to make decisions; structured versus unstructured work; importance of being exact or accurate; time pressure; frequency of decision making; impact of decisions on co-workers or company results.

## JOB SPECIALIZATION: CHEMISTRY TEACHERS, POSTSECONDARY

**Teach courses pertaining to the chemical and physical properties and compositional changes of substances.**

- Average annual earnings: $71,140
- Middle 50% of earners: $53,290–$97,080
- Earnings growth potential: Medium (42.5%)

### BEST-PAYING INDUSTRIES

| Industry | Median Earnings | Workforce |
|---|---|---|
| Educational Services | $71,140 | 20,430 |

### BEST-PAYING METROPOLITAN AREAS

| Metro Area | Median Earnings | Workforce |
|---|---|---|
| Boston-Cambridge-Quincy, MA-NH | $101,340 | 450 |
| Los Angeles–Long Beach–Santa Ana, CA | $97,950 | 500 |
| New York–Northern New Jersey–Long Island, NY-NJ-PA | $91,480 | 1,600 |

**Major Work Tasks:** Prepare and deliver lectures to undergraduate or graduate students on topics, such as organic chemistry, analytical chemistry, and chemical separation. Evaluate and grade students' laboratory work. Establish, teach, and monitor students' compliance with safety rules for handling chemicals, equipment, and other hazardous materials. Prepare and submit required reports related to instruction. Serve on committees or in professional societies. Supervise students' laboratory work. (Also, perform the tasks listed for Teachers, Postsecondary.)

**Relevant Educational Programs**: Analytical Chemistry; Chemical Physics; Chemistry Teacher Education; Chemistry, General; Chemistry, Other; Environmental Chemistry; Forensic Chemistry; Geochemistry; Inorganic Chemistry; Materials Chemistry; Organic Chemistry; Physical Chemistry; Polymer Chemistry; Science Teacher Education/General Science Teacher Education; Theoretical Chemistry. **Related Knowledge/Courses:** Chemistry; Physics; Biology; Education and Training; Mathematics; Engineering and Technology. **Certification/Licensure:** None.

**Personality Types:** Social–Investigative–Realistic.

**Skills:** Science; writing; speaking; instructing; reading comprehension; learning strategies; active learning; operations analysis.

**Physical Environment:** Indoors; sitting; contaminants; hazardous conditions. **Structural Environment:** Freedom to make decisions; structured versus unstructured work; importance of being exact or accurate; frequency of decision making; impact of decisions on co-workers or company results; level of competition.

## JOB SPECIALIZATION: COMMUNICATIONS TEACHERS, POSTSECONDARY

**Teach courses in communications, such as organizational communications, public relations, radio or television broadcasting, and journalism.**

- Average annual earnings: $62,180
- Middle 50% of earners: $45,810–$85,000
- Earnings growth potential: High (45.9%)

### BEST-PAYING INDUSTRIES

| Industry | Median Earnings | Workforce |
|---|---|---|
| Educational Services | $62,170 | 30,020 |

### BEST-PAYING METROPOLITAN AREAS

| Metro Area | Median Earnings | Workforce |
|---|---|---|
| Los Angeles–Long Beach–Santa Ana, CA | $101,350 | 1,120 |
| Washington-Arlington-Alexandria, DC-VA-MD-WV | $72,110 | 680 |

**Major Work Tasks:** Prepare and deliver lectures to undergraduate or graduate students on topics, such as public speaking, media criticism, and oral traditions. (Also, perform the tasks listed for Teachers, Postsecondary.)

**Relevant Educational Programs**: Advertising; Broadcast Journalism; Communication, General; Communication, Journalism, and Related Programs, Other; Digital Communication and Media/Multimedia; Documentary Production; Health Communication; International and Intercultural Communication; Journalism; Journalism, Other; Mass Communication/Media Studies; Political Communication; Public Relations, Advertising, and Applied Communication; Public Relations/Image Management; Radio and Television; Speech Communication and Rhetoric; Sports Communication; Technical and Scientific Communication. **Related Knowledge/Courses:** Communications and Media; English Language; Sociology and Anthropology; Philosophy and Theology; Education and Training; History and Archeology. **Certification/Licensure:** None.

**Personality Types:** Social–Artistic.

**Skills:** Learning strategies; instructing; speaking; writing; reading comprehension; active learning; active listening; critical thinking.

**Physical Environment:** Indoors; sitting. **Structural Environment:** Freedom to make decisions; structured versus unstructured work; frequency of decision making; time pressure; impact of decisions on co-workers or company results; importance of being exact or accurate.

### JOB SPECIALIZATION: COMPUTER SCIENCE TEACHERS, POSTSECONDARY

**Teach courses in computer science.**

#### BEST-PAYING INDUSTRIES

| Industry | Median Earnings | Workforce |
|---|---|---|
| Educational Services | $72,200 | 34,310 |

#### BEST-PAYING METROPOLITAN AREAS

| Metro Area | Median Earnings | Workforce |
|---|---|---|
| Ann Arbor, MI | $118,490 | 890 |
| Los Angeles–Long Beach–Santa Ana, CA | $98,530 | 1,280 |
| New York–Northern New Jersey–Long Island, NY-NJ-PA | $88,200 | 1,860 |
| Washington-Arlington-Alexandria, DC-VA-MD-WV | $85,830 | 800 |
| Philadelphia-Camden-Wilmington, PA-NJ-DE-MD | $71,620 | 870 |
| Chicago-Naperville-Joliet, IL-IN-WI | $66,320 | 1,280 |

- Average annual earnings: $72,200
- Middle 50% of earners: $51,450–$101,800
- Earnings growth potential: High (49.7%)

**Major Work Tasks:** Direct research of other teachers or of graduate students working for advanced academic degrees. Evaluate and grade students' laboratory work. Prepare and deliver lectures to undergraduate or graduate students on topics, such as programming, data structures, and software design. Supervise students' laboratory work. (Also, perform the tasks listed for Teachers, Postsecondary.)

**Relevant Educational Programs**: Computer and Information Sciences, General; Computer Programming/Programmer, General; Computer Science; Computer Systems Analysis/Analyst; Computer Teacher Education; Information Science/Studies. **Related Knowledge/Courses:** Computers and Electronics; Engineering and Technology; Education and Training; Telecommunications; Design; English Language. **Certification/Licensure:** None.

**Personality Types:** Social–Investigative–Conventional.

**Skills:** Programming; learning strategies; instructing; writing; speaking; reading comprehension; active learning; mathematics.

**Physical Environment:** Indoors; sitting; repetitive motions. **Structural Environment:** Structured versus unstructured work; freedom to make decisions; importance of being exact or accurate; frequency of decision making; time pressure; impact of decisions on co-workers or company results.

### JOB SPECIALIZATION: CRIMINAL JUSTICE AND LAW ENFORCEMENT TEACHERS, POSTSECONDARY

**Teach courses in criminal justice, corrections, and law enforcement administration.**

- Average annual earnings: $58,040
- Middle 50% of earners: $43,440–$74,900
- Earnings growth potential: High (44.2%)

| Industry | Median Earnings | Workforce |
|---|---|---|
| Educational Services | $58,130 | 13,940 |

**BEST-PAYING METROPOLITAN AREAS**

| Metro Area | Median Earnings | Workforce |
|---|---|---|
| Los Angeles–Long Beach–Santa Ana, CA | $73,570 | 350 |
| New York–Northern New Jersey–Long Island, NY-NJ-PA | $70,320 | 810 |
| Miami–Fort Lauderdale–Pompano Beach, FL | $69,270 | 360 |
| Cleveland-Elyria-Mentor, OH | $67,200 | 300 |

**Major Work Tasks:** Prepare and deliver lectures to undergraduate or graduate students on topics, such as criminal law, defensive policing, and investigation techniques. (Also, perform the tasks listed for Teachers, Postsecondary.)

**Relevant Educational Programs:** Corrections; Corrections Administration; Corrections and Criminal Justice, Other; Criminal Justice/Law Enforcement Administration; Criminal Justice/Police Science; Criminal Justice/Safety Studies; Criminalistics and Criminal Science; Critical Incident Response/Special Police Operations; Cultural/Archaeological Resources Protection; Cyber/Computer Forensics and Counterterrorism; Financial Forensics and Fraud Investigation; Forensic Science and Technology; Juvenile Corrections; Law Enforcement Intelligence Analysis; Law Enforcement Investigation and Interviewing; Law Enforcement Record-Keeping and Evidence Management; Maritime Law Enforcement; Protective Services Operations; Security and Loss Prevention Services; Suspension and Debarment Investigation; Terrorism and Counterterrorism Operations. **Related Knowledge/Courses:** Sociology and Anthropology; Law and Government; History and Archeology; Public Safety and Security; Therapy and Counseling; Philosophy and Theology. **Certification/Licensure:** None.

**Personality Types:** Social–Investigative.

**Skills:** Speaking; learning strategies; instructing; reading comprehension; writing; active listening; active learning; monitoring.

**Physical Environment:** Indoors; sitting; standing; noise. **Structural Environment:** Freedom to make decisions; structured versus unstructured Work; impact of decisions on co-workers or company results; frequency of decision making; time pressure; importance of being exact or accurate.

**JOB SPECIALIZATION: ECONOMICS TEACHERS, POSTSECONDARY**

**Teach courses in economics.**

- Average annual earnings: $87,950
- Middle 50% of earners: $63,470–$118,810
- Earnings growth potential: High (49.9%)

**BEST-PAYING INDUSTRIES**

| Industry | Median Earnings | Workforce |
|---|---|---|
| Educational Services | $87,950 | 13,390 |

**BEST-PAYING METROPOLITAN AREAS**

| Metro Area | Median Earnings | Workforce |
|---|---|---|
| Los Angeles–Long Beach–Santa Ana, CA | $110,130 | 280 |
| Boston-Cambridge-Quincy, MA-NH | $101,730 | 460 |
| Washington-Arlington-Alexandria, DC-VA-MD-WV | $96,950 | 390 |
| Chicago-Naperville-Joliet, IL-IN-WI | $64,520 | 270 |

**Major Work Tasks:** Prepare and deliver lectures to undergraduate or graduate students on topics, such as econometrics, price theory, and macroeconomics. (Also, perform the tasks listed for Teachers, Postsecondary.)

**Relevant Educational Programs:** Applied Economics; Business/Managerial Economics; Development Economics and International Development; Econometrics and Quantitative Economics; Economics, General; Economics, Other; International Economics; Political Economy; Social Science Teacher Education. **Related Knowledge/Courses:** Economics and Accounting; History and Archeology; Mathematics; Geography; English Language; Law and Government. **Certification/Licensure:** None.

**Personality Types:** Social–Investigative.

**Skills:** Science; operations analysis; learning strategies; instructing; mathematics; active learning; writing; speaking.

**Physical Environment:** Indoors; sitting. **Structural Environment:** Freedom to make decisions; structured versus unstructured work; frequency of decision making; importance of being exact or accurate; time pressure; impact of decisions on co-workers or company results.

### JOB SPECIALIZATION: EDUCATION TEACHERS, POSTSECONDARY

**Teach courses pertaining to education, such as counseling, curriculum, guidance, instruction, teacher education, and teaching English as a second language.**

- Average annual earnings: $59,350
- Middle 50% of earners: $44,160–$78,190
- Earnings growth potential: High (46.0%)

### BEST-PAYING INDUSTRIES

| Industry | Median Earnings | Workforce |
|---|---|---|
| Educational Services | $87,950 | 13,390 |

### BEST-PAYING METROPOLITAN AREAS

| Metro Area | Median Earnings | Workforce |
|---|---|---|
| Philadelphia-Camden-Wilmington, PA-NJ-DE-MD | $68,360 | 1,480 |
| Los Angeles–Long Beach–Santa Ana, CA | $67,390 | 1,540 |
| Phoenix-Mesa-Scottsdale, AZ | $66,890 | 2,150 |
| Chicago-Naperville-Joliet, IL-IN-WI | $44,680 | 2,470 |

**Major Work Tasks:** Prepare and deliver lectures to undergraduate or graduate students on topics, such as children's literature, learning and development, and reading instruction. Supervise students' fieldwork, internship, and research work. Advise and instruct teachers employed in school systems by providing activities, such as in-service seminars. Serve as a liaison between the university and other governmental and educational agencies. (Also, perform the tasks listed for Teachers, Postsecondary.)

**Relevant Educational Programs:** Agricultural Teacher Education; Art Teacher Education; Biology Teacher Education; Business Teacher Education; Chemistry Teacher Education; Computer Teacher Education; Drama and Dance Teacher Education; Driver and Safety Teacher Education; Earth Science Teacher Education; Education Policy Analysis; Education, General; English/Language Arts Teacher Education; Family and Consumer Sciences/Home Economics Teacher Education; Foreign Language Teacher Education; French Language Teacher Education; Geography Teacher Education; German Language Teacher Education; Health Teacher Education; History Teacher Education; Learning Sciences; Mathematics Teacher Education; Music Teacher Education; Physical Education Teaching and Coaching; Physics Teacher Education; Reading Teacher

Education; Sales and Marketing Operations/ Marketing and Distribution Teacher Education; Science Teacher Education/General Science Teacher Education; Social Science Teacher Education; Social Studies Teacher Education; others. **Related Knowledge/Courses:** Sociology and Anthropology; Education and Training; Psychology; Therapy and Counseling; English Language; Philosophy and Theology. **Certification/Licensure:** None.

**Personality Types:** Social–Artistic–Investigative.

**Skills:** Writing; speaking; learning strategies; reading comprehension; instructing; active listening; science; operations analysis.

**Physical Environment:** Indoors; sitting. **Structural Environment:** Freedom to make decisions; structured versus unstructured work; frequency of decision making; importance of being exact or accurate; time pressure; impact of decisions on co-workers or company results.

### JOB SPECIALIZATION: ENGINEERING TEACHERS, POSTSECONDARY

**Teach courses pertaining to the application of physical laws and principles of engineering for the development of machines, materials, instruments, processes, and services.**

- Average annual earnings: $92,670
- Middle 50% of earners: $69,400–$122,800
- Earnings growth potential: High (45.2%)

**Major Work Tasks:** Prepare and deliver lectures to undergraduate or graduate students on topics, such as mechanics, hydraulics, and robotics. Supervise students' laboratory work. (Also, perform the tasks listed for Teachers, Postsecondary.)

**Relevant Educational Programs**: Aerospace, Aeronautical and Astronautical/Space Engineering; Agricultural Engineering; Architectural Engineering; Biochemical Engineering; Bioengineering and Biomedical Engineering; Biological/Biosystems Engineering; Ceramic Sciences and Engineering; Chemical and

### BEST-PAYING INDUSTRIES

| Industry | Median Earnings | Workforce |
|---|---|---|
| Educational Services | $92,670 | 33,970 |

### BEST-PAYING METROPOLITAN AREAS

| Metro Area | Median Earnings | Workforce |
|---|---|---|
| Los Angeles–Long Beach–Santa Ana, CA | $117,800 | 970 |
| Philadelphia-Camden-Wilmington, PA-NJ-DE-MD | $115,330 | 1,020 |
| Boston-Cambridge-Quincy, MA-NH | $106,880 | 840 |
| Austin–Round Rock, TX | $102,470 | 980 |
| Atlanta–Sandy Springs–Marietta, GA | $93,720 | 860 |
| New York–Northern New Jersey–Long Island, NY-NJ-PA | $88,920 | 2,310 |

Biomolecular Engineering; Chemical Engineering; Chemical Engineering, Other; Civil Engineering, General; Civil Engineering, Other; Computer Engineering, General; Computer Engineering, Other; Computer Hardware Engineering; Computer Software Engineering; Construction Engineering; Electrical and Electronics Engineering; Electrical, Electronics and Communications Engineering, Other; Electromechanical Engineering; Engineering Chemistry; Engineering Design; Engineering Mechanics; Engineering Physics/Applied Physics; Engineering Science; Engineering, General; Engineering, Other; Environmental/ Environmental Health Engineering; Forest Engineering; Geological/Geophysical Engineering; Geotechnical and Geoenvironmental Engineering; others. **Related Knowledge/ Courses:** Physics; Engineering and Technology; Design; Mathematics; Chemistry; Educa-

**439**

tion and Training. **Certification/Licensure:** License if required in specialty.

**Personality Types:** Social–Investigative–Realistic.

**Skills:** Mathematics; science; instructing; reading comprehension; writing; learning strategies; speaking; operations analysis.

**Physical Environment:** Indoors; sitting. **Structural Environment:** Structured versus unstructured work; freedom to make decisions; importance of being exact or accurate; time pressure; frequency of decision making; impact of decisions on co-workers or company results.

### JOB SPECIALIZATION: ENGLISH LANGUAGE AND LITERATURE TEACHERS, POSTSECONDARY

**Teach courses in English language and literature, including linguistics and comparative literature.**

- Average annual earnings: $60,040
- Middle 50% of earners: $43,540–$83,310
- Earnings growth potential: High (46.5%)

**Major Work Tasks:** Prepare and deliver lectures to undergraduate or graduate students on topics, such as poetry, novel structure, and translation and adaptation. Teach writing classes. Participate in cultural and literary activities, such as traveling abroad and attending performing arts events. (Also, perform the tasks listed for Teachers, Postsecondary.)

**Relevant Educational Programs**: American Literature (Canadian); American Literature (United States); Children's and Adolescent Literature; Comparative Literature; Creative Writing; English Language and Literature, General; English Language and Literature/Letters, Other; English Literature (British and Commonwealth); English/Language Arts Teacher Education; General Literature; Literature, Other; Professional, Technical, Business, and Scientific Writing; Rhetoric and Composition;

### BEST-PAYING INDUSTRIES

| Industry | Median Earnings | Workforce |
| --- | --- | --- |
| Educational Services | $60,040 | 72,670 |

### BEST-PAYING METROPOLITAN AREAS

| Metro Area | Median Earnings | Workforce |
| --- | --- | --- |
| Los Angeles–Long Beach–Santa Ana, CA | $96,690 | 2,290 |
| New York–Northern New Jersey–Long Island, NY-NJ-PA | $79,270 | 5,530 |
| Washington-Arlington-Alexandria, DC-VA-MD-WV | $67,300 | 1,680 |
| Philadelphia-Camden-Wilmington, PA-NJ-DE-MD | $67,240 | 2,040 |
| Chicago-Naperville-Joliet, IL-IN-WI | $45,510 | 2,020 |

Rhetoric and Composition/Writing Studies, Other; Writing, General. **Related Knowledge/Courses:** Philosophy and Theology; Fine Arts; Communications and Media; English Language; History and Archeology; Sociology and Anthropology. **Certification/Licensure:** None.

**Personality Types:** Social–Artistic–Investigative.

**Skills:** Learning strategies; writing; instructing; reading comprehension; speaking; judgment and decision making; active listening; active learning.

**Physical Environment:** Indoors; sitting. **Structural Environment:** Freedom to make decisions; structured versus unstructured work; impact of decisions on co-workers or company results; importance of being exact or accurate; time pressure; level of competition.

**440**

## JOB SPECIALIZATION: ENVIRONMENTAL SCIENCE TEACHERS, POSTSECONDARY

### Teach courses in environmental science.

- Average annual earnings: $77,320
- Middle 50% of earners: $55,930–$107,670
- Earnings growth potential: High (46.4%)

#### BEST-PAYING INDUSTRIES

| Industry | Median Earnings | Workforce |
|---|---|---|
| Educational Services | $77,430 | 4,980 |

#### BEST-PAYING METROPOLITAN AREAS

| Metro Area | Median Earnings | Workforce |
|---|---|---|
| Philadelphia-Camden-Wilmington, PA-NJ-DE-MD | $109,810 | 140 |
| Baltimore-Towson, MD | $98,700 | 130 |
| Boston-Cambridge-Quincy, MA-NH | $94,930 | 130 |
| New York–Northern New Jersey–Long Island, NY-NJ-PA | $81,080 | 560 |
| Chicago-Naperville-Joliet, IL-IN-WI | $66,180 | 120 |

**Major Work Tasks:** Prepare and deliver lectures to undergraduate or graduate students on topics, such as hazardous waste management, industrial safety, and environmental toxicology. Supervise, evaluate, and grade students' laboratory work. Review papers or serve on editorial boards for scientific journals, and review grant proposals for various agencies. (Also, perform the tasks listed for Teachers, Postsecondary.)

**Relevant Educational Programs:** Environmental Chemistry; Environmental Science; Environmental Studies; Science Teacher Education/General Science Teacher Education. **Related**

**Knowledge/Courses:** Geography; Biology; Education and Training; Communications and Media; History and Archeology; Sociology and Anthropology. **Certification/Licensure:** None.

**Personality Types:** Social–Investigative–Artistic.

**Skills:** Science; writing; reading comprehension; instructing; learning strategies; operations analysis; complex problem solving; active learning.

**Physical Environment:** Indoors; sitting. **Structural Environment:** Freedom to make decisions; structured versus unstructured work; importance of being exact or accurate; level of competition; time pressure; frequency of decision making.

## JOB SPECIALIZATION: FOREIGN LANGUAGE AND LITERATURE TEACHERS, POSTSECONDARY

### Teach languages and literature courses in languages other than English. Includes teachers of American Sign Language (ASL).

- Average annual earnings: $58,670
- Middle 50% of earners: $44,620–$78,980
- Earnings growth potential: Medium (43.3%)

**Major Work Tasks:** Prepare and deliver lectures to undergraduate or graduate students on topics, such as how to speak and write a foreign language and the cultural aspects of areas where a particular language is used. Organize and direct study abroad programs. (Also, perform the tasks listed for Teachers, Postsecondary.)

**Relevant Educational Programs:** African Languages, Literatures, and Linguistics; Albanian Language and Literature; American Indian/Native American Languages, Literatures, and Linguistics; Ancient Near Eastern and Biblical Languages, Literatures, and Linguistics; Ancient/Classical Greek Language and Litera-

**441**

### BEST-PAYING INDUSTRIES

| Industry | Median Earnings | Workforce |
|---|---|---|
| Educational Services | $58,670 | 29,790 |

### BEST-PAYING METROPOLITAN AREAS

| Metro Area | Median Earnings | Workforce |
|---|---|---|
| New York–Northern New Jersey–Long Island, NY-NJ-PA | $74,030 | 2,190 |
| Los Angeles–Long Beach–Santa Ana, CA | $66,590 | 1,460 |
| Washington-Arlington-Alexandria, DC-VA-MD-WV | $53,940 | 1,630 |
| Chicago-Naperville-Joliet, IL-IN-WI | $30,710 | 690 |

ture; Applied Linguistics; Arabic Language and Literature; Australian/Oceanic/Pacific Languages, Literatures, and Linguistics; Baltic Languages, Literatures, and Linguistics; Bengali Language and Literature; Bosnian, Serbian, and Croatian Languages and Literatures; Bulgarian Language and Literature; Burmese Language and Literature; Catalan Language and Literature; Celtic Languages, Literatures, and Linguistics; Chinese Language and Literature; Classics and Classical Languages, Literatures, and Linguistics, General; Classics and Classical Languages, Literatures, and Linguistics, Other; Czech Language and Literature; Danish Language and Literature; Dutch/Flemish Language and Literature; others. **Related Knowledge/Courses:** Foreign Language; History and Archeology; Philosophy and Theology; Sociology and Anthropology; English Language; Education and Training. **Certification/Licensure:** None.

**Personality Types:** Social–Artistic–Investigative.

**Skills:** Writing; learning strategies; speaking; instructing; reading comprehension; active listening; active learning; operations analysis.

**Physical Environment:** Indoors; sitting. **Structural Environment:** Freedom to make decisions; structured versus unstructured work; frequency of decision making; importance of being exact or accurate; impact of decisions on co-workers or company results; time pressure.

## JOB SPECIALIZATION: FORESTRY AND CONSERVATION SCIENCE TEACHERS, POSTSECONDARY

**Teach courses in forestry and conservation science.**

- Average annual earnings: $81,930
- Middle 50% of earners: $57,800–$101,860
- Earnings growth potential: High (48.8%)

**Major Work Tasks:** Prepare and deliver lectures to undergraduate or graduate students on topics, such as forest resource policy, forest pathology, and mapping. Provide information to the public by leading workshops and training programs and by developing educational materials. Review papers for colleagues and scientific journals. Supervise students' laboratory or field work. (Also, perform the tasks listed for Teachers, Postsecondary.)

### BEST-PAYING INDUSTRIES

| Industry | Median Earnings | Workforce |
|---|---|---|
| Educational Services | $81,950 | 2,480 |

### BEST-PAYING METROPOLITAN AREAS

| Metro Area | Median Earnings | Workforce |
|---|---|---|
| Philadelphia-Camden-Wilmington, PA-NJ-DE-MD | $104,490 | 90 |
| New York–Northern New Jersey–Long Island, NY-NJ-PA | $82,330 | 160 |

442

**Relevant Educational Programs**: Agroecology and Sustainable Agriculture; Forest Management/Forest Resources Management; Forest Resources Production and Management; Forest Sciences and Biology; Forestry, General; Forestry, Other; Land Use Planning and Management/Development; Natural Resources and Conservation, Other; Natural Resources Management and Policy; Natural Resources Management and Policy, Other; Natural Resources/Conservation, General; Range Science and Management; Science Teacher Education/General Science Teacher Education; Urban Forestry; Water, Wetlands, and Marine Resources Management; Wildlife, Fish, and Wildlands Science and Management; Wood Science and Wood Products/Pulp and Paper Technology. **Related Knowledge/Courses:** Biology; Geography; Education and Training; Chemistry; Communications and Media; Philosophy and Theology. **Certification/Licensure:** None.

**Personality Types:** Social–Investigative–Realistic.

**Skills:** Instructing; science; writing; speaking; learning strategies; reading comprehension; active learning; active listening.

**Physical Environment:** Indoors; sitting. **Structural Environment:** Structured versus unstructured work; freedom to make decisions; importance of being exact or accurate; level of competition; time pressure; impact of decisions on co-workers or company results.

### JOB SPECIALIZATION: GEOGRAPHY TEACHERS, POSTSECONDARY

### Teach courses in geography.

- Average annual earnings: $67,820
- Middle 50% of earners: $50,290–$88,700
- Earnings growth potential: High (45.5%)

**Major Work Tasks:** Prepare and deliver lectures to undergraduate or graduate students on topics, such as urbanization, environmental systems, and cultural geography. Maintain geographic information systems laboratories,

### BEST-PAYING INDUSTRIES

| Industry | Median Earnings | Workforce |
|---|---|---|
| Educational Services | $67,820 | 4,460 |

### BEST-PAYING METROPOLITAN AREAS

| Metro Area | Median Earnings | Workforce |
|---|---|---|
| Philadelphia-Camden-Wilmington, PA-NJ-DE-MD | $79,410 | 120 |
| New York–Northern New Jersey–Long Island, NY-NJ-PA | $70,740 | 110 |
| Chicago-Naperville-Joliet, IL-IN-WI | $52,180 | 130 |

performing duties such as updating software. Perform spatial analysis and modeling using geographic information system techniques. Supervise students' laboratory and field work. (Also, perform the tasks listed for Teachers, Postsecondary.)

**Relevant Educational Programs**: Geographic Information Science and Cartography; Geography; Geography Teacher Education; Geography, Other. **Related Knowledge/Courses:** Geography; History and Archeology; Biology; Sociology and Anthropology; English Language; Education and Training. **Certification/Licensure:** None.

**Personality Types:** Social–Investigative.

**Skills:** Science; writing; instructing; speaking; reading comprehension; learning strategies; active learning; operations analysis.

**Physical Environment:** Indoors; sitting; noise. **Structural Environment:** Freedom to make decisions; structured versus unstructured work; importance of being exact or accurate; level of competition; frequency of decision making; impact of decisions on co-workers or company results.

443

## JOB SPECIALIZATION: HEALTH SPECIALTIES TEACHERS, POSTSECONDARY

**Teach courses in health specialties in fields, such as dentistry, laboratory technology, medicine, pharmacy, public health, therapy, and veterinary medicine.**

- Average annual earnings: $81,140
- Middle 50% of earners: $53,170–$130,100
- Earnings growth potential: Very high (53.1%)

### BEST-PAYING INDUSTRIES

| Industry | Median Earnings | Workforce |
|---|---|---|
| Educational Services | $80,200 | 145,370 |

### BEST-PAYING METROPOLITAN AREAS

| Metro Area | Median Earnings | Workforce |
|---|---|---|
| Denver-Aurora, CO | $123,110 | 3,090 |
| New York–Northern New Jersey–Long Island, NY-NJ-PA | $113,090 | 8,250 |
| San Francisco–Oakland–Fremont, CA | $100,480 | 4,410 |
| Los Angeles–Long Beach–Santa Ana, CA | $85,280 | 3,900 |
| Dallas–Fort Worth–Arlington, TX | $71,360 | 3,850 |
| Baltimore-Towson, MD | $47,220 | 3,390 |

**Major Work Tasks:** Prepare and deliver lectures to undergraduate or graduate students on topics, such as public health, stress management, and worksite health promotion. Supervise laboratory sessions. (Also, perform the tasks listed for Teachers, Postsecondary.)

**Relevant Educational Programs**: Animal-Assisted Therapy; Art Therapy/Therapist Training; Asian Bodywork Therapy; Audiology/Audiologist; Audiology/Audiologist and Speech-Language Pathology/Pathologist; Behavioral Aspects of Health; Biostatistics; Blood Bank Technology Specialist Training; Cardiovascular Technology/Technologist; Chiropractic (DC); Clinical Laboratory Science/Medical Technology/Technologist Training; Clinical/Medical Laboratory Assistant Training; Clinical/Medical Laboratory Technician; Communication Disorders, General; Communication Sciences and Disorders, General; Cytotechnology/Cytotechnologist; Dance Therapy/Therapist Training; Dental Assisting/Assistant; Dental Clinical Sciences, General (MS, PhD); Dental Hygiene/Hygienist; Dental Laboratory Technology/Technician; Dentistry (DDS, DMD); Diagnostic Medical Sonography/Sonographer and Ultrasound Technician Training; Electrocardiograph Technology/Technician; Electroneurodiagnostic/Electroencephalographic Technology/Technologist; others. **Related Knowledge/Courses:** Medicine and Dentistry; Biology; Education and Training; Therapy and Counseling; Sociology and Anthropology; Psychology. **Certification/Licensure:** License or certification in specialty.

**Personality Types:** Social–Investigative.

**Skills:** Science; writing; instructing; active listening; reading comprehension; speaking; learning strategies; active learning.

**Physical Environment:** Indoors; sitting; exposed to disease or infections. **Structural Environment:** Freedom to make decisions; importance of being exact or accurate; structured versus unstructured work; impact of decisions on co-workers or company results; time pressure; frequency of decision making.

**444**

## JOB SPECIALIZATION: HISTORY TEACHERS, POSTSECONDARY

**Teach courses in human history and historiography.**

- Average Annual Earnings: $65,870
- Middle 50% of Earners: $48,420–$88,740
- Earnings Growth Potential: High (49.0%)

### BEST-PAYING INDUSTRIES

| Industry | Median Earnings | Workforce |
|---|---|---|
| Educational Services | $65,870 | 23,580 |

### BEST-PAYING METROPOLITAN AREAS

| Metro Area | Median Earnings | Workforce |
|---|---|---|
| Los Angeles–Long Beach–Santa Ana, CA | $94,480 | 510 |
| New York–Northern New Jersey–Long Island, NY-NJ-PA | $82,090 | 1,440 |
| Boston-Cambridge-Quincy, MA-NH | $80,200 | 480 |
| Washington-Arlington-Alexandria, DC-VA-MD-WV | $79,800 | 590 |
| Philadelphia-Camden-Wilmington, PA-NJ-DE-MD | $76,970 | 560 |
| Baltimore-Towson, MD | $73,160 | 590 |

**Major Work Tasks:** Prepare and deliver lectures to undergraduate or graduate students on topics, such as ancient history, postwar civilizations, and the history of third-world countries. (Also, perform the tasks listed for Teachers, Postsecondary.)

**Relevant Educational Programs**: American History (United States); Asian History; Canadian History; European History; History and Philosophy of Science and Technology; History Teacher Education; History, General; History, Other; Military History; Public/Applied History. **Related Knowledge/Courses:** History and Archeology; Philosophy and Theology; Geography; Sociology and Anthropology; Foreign Language; English Language. **Certification/Licensure:** None.

**Personality Types:** Social–Investigative–Artistic.

**Skills:** Writing; learning strategies; speaking; reading comprehension; instructing; active learning; operations analysis; judgment and decision making.

**Physical Environment:** Indoors; sitting. **Structural Environment:** Freedom to make decisions; structured versus unstructured work; importance of being exact or accurate; time pressure; level of competition; frequency of decision making.

## JOB SPECIALIZATION: HOME ECONOMICS TEACHERS, POSTSECONDARY

**Teach courses in child care, family relations, finance, nutrition, and related subjects pertaining to home management.**

- Average annual earnings: $64,040
- Middle 50% of earners: $45,810–$87,470
- Earnings growth potential: High (47.5%)

### BEST-PAYING INDUSTRIES

| Industry | Median Earnings | Workforce |
|---|---|---|
| Educational Services | $64,040 | 4,700 |

### BEST-PAYING METROPOLITAN AREAS

| Metro Area | Median Earnings | Workforce |
|---|---|---|
| Los Angeles–Long Beach–Santa Ana, CA | $93,400 | 140 |
| Philadelphia-Camden-Wilmington, PA-NJ-DE-MD | $73,250 | 190 |

**Major Work Tasks:** Prepare and deliver lectures to undergraduate or graduate students on topics, such as food science, nutrition, and child care. (Also, perform the tasks listed for Teachers, Postsecondary.)

**Relevant Educational Programs**: Business Family and Consumer Sciences/Human Sciences; Child Care and Support Services Management; Family and Consumer Sciences/Home Economics Teacher Education; Family and Consumer Sciences/Human Sciences, General; Foodservice Systems Administration/Management; Human Development and Family Studies, General. **Related Knowledge/Courses:** Sociology and Anthropology; Education and Training; Philosophy and Theology; Therapy and Counseling; Psychology; History and Archeology. **Certification/Licensure:** None.

**Personality Types:** Social–Investigative–Artistic.

**Skills:** Learning strategies; instructing; speaking; writing; active learning; science; active listening; reading comprehension.

**Physical Environment:** Indoors; standing; noise. **Structural Environment:** Structured versus unstructured work; freedom to make decisions; time pressure; importance of being exact or accurate; frequency of decision making; impact of decisions on co-workers or company results.

### JOB SPECIALIZATION: LAW TEACHERS, POSTSECONDARY

### Teach courses in law.

- Average annual earnings: $99,950
- Middle 50% of earners: $60,760–$158,450
- Earnings growth potential: Very high (68.4%)

**Major Work Tasks:** Prepare and deliver lectures to undergraduate or graduate students on topics, such as civil procedure, contracts, and torts. Assign cases for students to hear and

### BEST-PAYING INDUSTRIES

| Industry | Median Earnings | Workforce |
|---|---|---|
| Educational Services | $99,980 | 15,250 |

### BEST-PAYING METROPOLITAN AREAS

| Metro Area | Median Earnings | Workforce |
|---|---|---|
| Los Angeles–Long Beach–Santa Ana, CA | $132,250 | 310 |
| Boston-Cambridge-Quincy, MA-NH | $122,830 | 1,000 |
| Minneapolis–St. Paul–Bloomington, MN-WI | $121,670 | 350 |
| New York–Northern New Jersey–Long Island, NY-NJ-PA | $110,260 | 1,260 |
| Miami–Fort Lauderdale–Pompano Beach, FL | $108,400 | 430 |
| Philadelphia-Camden-Wilmington, PA-NJ-DE-MD | $92,770 | 370 |
| Washington-Arlington-Alexandria, DC-VA-MD-WV | $73,650 | 1,200 |

try. (Also, perform the tasks listed for Teachers, Postsecondary.)

**Relevant Educational Programs**: Intellectual Property Law; Law (LL.B, J.D.); Legal Studies, General. **Related Knowledge/Courses:** Law and Government; Education and Training; History and Archeology; English Language; Communications and Media; Philosophy and Theology. **Certification/Licensure:** License.

**Personality Types:** Social–Investigative–Enterprising.

**Skills:** Speaking; Writing; Active Learning; Reading Comprehension; Instructing; Learning Strategies; Active Listening; Critical Thinking.

**446**

**Physical Environment:** Indoors; sitting. **Structural Environment:** Freedom to make decisions; structured versus unstructured work; impact of decisions on co-workers or company results; importance of being exact or accurate; frequency of decision making; time pressure.

JOB SPECIALIZATION: LIBRARY SCIENCE TEACHERS, POSTSECONDARY

**Teach courses in library science.**

- Average annual earnings: $65,780
- Middle 50% of earners: $52,440–$84,240
- Earnings growth potential: Medium (34.3%)

BEST-PAYING INDUSTRIES

| Industry | Median Earnings | Workforce |
|---|---|---|
| Educational Services | $65,780 | 4,510 |

BEST-PAYING METROPOLITAN AREAS

| Metro Area | Median Earnings | Workforce |
|---|---|---|
| Dallas–Fort Worth–Arlington, TX | $62,530 | 100 |

**Major Work Tasks:** Prepare and deliver lectures to undergraduate or graduate students on topics, such as collection development, archival methods, and indexing and abstracting. Edit manuscripts for professional journals. (Also, perform the tasks listed for Teachers, Postsecondary.)

**Relevant Educational Programs:** Children and Youth Library Services; Library and Information Science. **Related Knowledge/Courses:** Education and Training; Sociology and Anthropology; Communications and Media; English Language; History and Archeology; Telecommunications. **Certification/Licensure:** None.

**Personality Types:** Social–Investigative–Conventional.

**Skills:** Writing; learning strategies; speaking; reading comprehension; instructing; active listening; active learning; monitoring.

**Physical Environment:** Indoors; sitting; repetitive motions. **Structural Environment:** Freedom to make decisions; structured versus unstructured work; importance of being exact or accurate; time pressure; impact of decisions on co-workers or company results; level of competition.

JOB SPECIALIZATION: MATHEMATICAL SCIENCE TEACHERS, POSTSECONDARY

**Teach courses pertaining to mathematical concepts, statistics, and actuarial science and to the application of original and standardized mathematical techniques in solving specific problems and situations.**

- Average annual earnings: $64,990
- Middle 50% of earners: $46,770–$90,090
- Earnings growth potential: High (47.9%)

BEST-PAYING INDUSTRIES

| Industry | Median Earnings | Workforce |
|---|---|---|
| Educational Services | $64,970 | 53,490 |

BEST-PAYING METROPOLITAN AREAS

| Metro Area | Median Earnings | Workforce |
|---|---|---|
| Los Angeles–Long Beach–Santa Ana, CA | $95,240 | 1,990 |
| New York–Northern New Jersey–Long Island, NY-NJ-PA | $86,150 | 3,120 |
| Philadelphia-Camden-Wilmington, PA-NJ-DE-MD | $70,640 | 1,290 |

**Major Work Tasks:** Prepare and deliver lectures to undergraduate or graduate students on topics, such as linear algebra, differential equations, and discrete mathematics. (Also,

447

perform the tasks listed for Teachers, Postsecondary.)

**Relevant Educational Programs**: Algebra and Number Theory; Analysis and Functional Analysis; Applied Mathematics, General; Applied Mathematics, Other; Business Statistics; Computational and Applied Mathematics; Financial Mathematics; Geometry/Geometric Analysis; Logic; Mathematical Biology; Mathematical Statistics and Probability; Mathematics and Statistics; Mathematics and Statistics, Other; Mathematics Teacher Education; Mathematics, General; Mathematics, Other; Statistics, General; Statistics, Other; Topology and Foundations. **Related Knowledge/Courses:** Mathematics; Education and Training; Physics; Computers and Electronics; English Language; Sociology and Anthropology. **Certification/Licensure:** None.

**Personality Types:** Social–Investigative–Artistic.

**Skills:** Mathematics; writing; instructing; learning strategies; reading comprehension; active learning; speaking; critical thinking.

**Physical Environment:** Indoors; sitting; using hands. **Structural Environment:** Freedom to make decisions; structured versus unstructured work; importance of being exact or accurate; time pressure; impact of decisions on co-workers or company results; frequency of decision making.

### JOB SPECIALIZATION: NURSING INSTRUCTORS AND TEACHERS, POSTSECONDARY

**Demonstrate and teach patient care in classroom and clinical units to nursing students.**

- Average annual earnings: $64,850
- Middle 50% of earners: $51,370–$82,250
- Earnings growth potential: Medium (38.4%)

**Major Work Tasks:** Prepare and deliver lectures to undergraduate or graduate students on topics, such as pharmacology, mental health nursing, and community health-care practices.

### BEST-PAYING INDUSTRIES

| Industry | Median Earnings | Workforce |
|---|---|---|
| Educational Services | $63,980 | 53,140 |

### BEST-PAYING METROPOLITAN AREAS

| Metro Area | Median Earnings | Workforce |
|---|---|---|
| Los Angeles–Long Beach–Santa Ana, CA | $89,230 | 1,200 |
| New York–Northern New Jersey–Long Island, NY-NJ-PA | $80,110 | 2,690 |
| Chicago-Naperville-Joliet, IL-IN-WI | $69,630 | 1,210 |

Supervise, evaluate, and grade students' laboratory and clinical work. Assess clinical education needs and patient and client teaching needs using a variety of methods. Coordinate training programs with area universities, clinics, hospitals, health agencies, or vocational schools. Demonstrate patient care in clinical units of hospitals. Maintain a clinical practice. Mentor junior and adjunct faculty members. (Also, perform the tasks listed for Teachers, Postsecondary.)

**Relevant Educational Programs**: Adult Health Nurse/Nursing; Clinical Nurse Specialist Training; Emergency Room/Trauma Nursing; Family Practice Nurse/Nursing; Geriatric Nurse/Nursing; Maternal/Child Health and Neonatal Nurse/Nursing; Nurse Anesthetist Training; Nurse Midwife/Nursing Midwifery; Nursing Education; Nursing Science; Palliative Care Nursing; Pediatric Nurse/Nursing; Perioperative/Operating Room and Surgical Nurse/Nursing; Psychiatric/Mental Health Nurse/Nursing; Public Health/Community Nurse/Nursing; Registered Nursing, Nursing Administration, Nursing Research; Registered Nursing/Registered Nurse Training; Women's Health Nurse/Nursing. **Related Knowledge/**

**Courses:** Therapy and Counseling; Biology; Sociology and Anthropology; Medicine and Dentistry; Education and Training; Psychology. **Certification/Licensure:** License.

**Personality Types:** Social–Investigative.

**Skills:** Instructing; science; learning strategies; reading comprehension; writing; speaking; active learning; social perceptiveness.

**Physical Environment:** Indoors; sitting; exposed to disease or infections. **Structural Environment:** Freedom to make decisions; structured versus unstructured work; impact of decisions on co-workers or company results; importance of being exact or accurate; frequency of decision making; consequence of error.

### JOB SPECIALIZATION: PHILOSOPHY AND RELIGION TEACHERS, POSTSECONDARY

### Teach courses in philosophy, religion, and theology.

- Average annual earnings: $64,990
- Middle 50% of earners: $48,760–$87,680
- Earnings growth potential: High (48.2%)

**Major Work Tasks:** Prepare and deliver lectures to undergraduate or graduate students and the community on topics, such as ethics, logic, and contemporary religious thought. (Also, perform the tasks listed for Teachers, Postsecondary.)

**Relevant Educational Programs:** Applied and Professional Ethics; Bible/Biblical Studies; Buddhist Studies; Christian Studies; Divinity/Ministry (BD, MDiv.); Ethics; Hindu Studies; Missions/Missionary Studies and Missiology; Pastoral Studies/Counseling; Philosophy; Philosophy and Religious Studies, General; Philosophy and Religious Studies, Other; Philosophy, Other; Pre-Theology/Pre-Ministerial Studies; Rabbinical Studies (M.H.L./Rav); Religion/Religious Studies; Religious Education; Religious/Sacred Music; Talmudic Stud-

ies; Theological and Ministerial Studies, Other; Theology/Theological Studies. **Related Knowledge/Courses:** Philosophy and Theology; History and Archeology; Foreign Language; English Language; Communications and Media; Education and Training. **Certification/Licensure:** None.

**Personality Types:** Social–Artistic–Investigative.

**Skills:** Writing; learning strategies; reading comprehension; speaking; instructing; active learning; active listening; critical thinking.

**Physical Environment:** Indoors; sitting. **Structural Environment:** Structured versus unstructured work; freedom to make decisions; impact of decisions on co-workers or company results; importance of being exact or accurate; time pressure; frequency of decision making.

### BEST-PAYING INDUSTRIES

| Industry | Median Earnings | Workforce |
| --- | --- | --- |
| Educational Services | $65,110 | 22,780 |

### BEST-PAYING METROPOLITAN AREAS

| Metro Area | Median Earnings | Workforce |
| --- | --- | --- |
| Boston-Cambridge-Quincy, MA-NH | $86,570 | 530 |
| Los Angeles–Long Beach–Santa Ana, CA | $82,440 | 640 |
| New York–Northern New Jersey–Long Island, NY-NJ-PA | $78,990 | 1,620 |
| Philadelphia-Camden-Wilmington, PA-NJ-DE-MD | $64,410 | 600 |
| Minneapolis–St. Paul–Bloomington, MN-WI | $59,030 | 670 |

449

JOB SPECIALIZATION: PHYSICS TEACHERS, POSTSECONDARY

## JOB SPECIALIZATION: PHYSICS TEACHERS, POSTSECONDARY

### Teach courses pertaining to the laws of matter and energy.

- Average annual earnings: $78,540
- Middle 50% of earners: $57,350–$109,030
- Earnings growth potential: High (44.9%)

### BEST-PAYING INDUSTRIES

| Industry | Median Earnings | Workforce |
|---|---|---|
| Educational Services | $78,270 | 13,770 |

### BEST-PAYING METROPOLITAN AREAS

| Metro Area | Median Earnings | Workforce |
|---|---|---|
| Los Angeles–Long Beach–Santa Ana, CA | $102,640 | 390 |
| Boston-Cambridge-Quincy, MA-NH | $99,190 | 370 |
| New York–Northern New Jersey–Long Island, NY-NJ-PA | $93,700 | 900 |
| Washington-Arlington-Alexandria, DC-VA-MD-WV | $93,030 | 320 |
| Chicago-Naperville-Joliet, IL-IN-WI | $58,940 | 320 |

**Major Work Tasks:** Prepare and deliver lectures to undergraduate or graduate students on topics, such as quantum mechanics, particle physics, and optics. Supervise, evaluate, and grade students' laboratory work. Maintain and repair laboratory equipment. (Also, perform the tasks listed for Teachers, Postsecondary.)

**Relevant Educational Programs:** Acoustics; Astronomy and Astrophysics, Other; Atomic/Molecular Physics; Chemical Physics; Condensed Matter and Materials Physics; Elementary Particle Physics; Nuclear Physics; Optics/Optical Sciences; Physics Teacher Education; Physics, General; Physics, Other; Plasma and High-Temperature Physics; Science Teacher Education/General Science Teacher Education; Theoretical and Mathematical Physics. **Related Knowledge/Courses:** Physics; Mathematics; Engineering and Technology; Geography; Computers and Electronics; Design. **Certification/Licensure:** None.

**Personality Types:** Social–Investigative.

**Skills:** Science; writing; reading comprehension; speaking; mathematics; learning strategies; instructing; active learning.

**Physical Environment:** Indoors; sitting. **Structural Environment:** Freedom to make decisions; structured versus unstructured work; importance of being exact or accurate; level of competition; impact of decisions on co-workers or company results; time pressure.

## JOB SPECIALIZATION: POLITICAL SCIENCE TEACHERS, POSTSECONDARY

### Teach courses in political science, international affairs, and international relations.

- Average annual earnings: $72,170
- Middle 50% of earners: $52,660–$101,780
- Earnings growth potential: High (48.5%)

**Major Work Tasks:** Prepare and deliver lectures to undergraduate or graduate students on topics, such as classical political thought, international relations, and democracy and citizenship. (Also, perform the tasks listed for Teachers, Postsecondary.)

**Relevant Educational Programs:** American Government and Politics (United States); Education Policy Analysis; International Policy Analysis; International Relations and Affairs; International Relations and National Security Studies, Other; National Security Policy Studies; Political Economy; Political Science and Government, General; Political Science and Government, Other; Public Policy Analysis, General; Social Science Teacher Education. **Related Knowledge/Courses:** Philosophy and Theology; History and Archeology; Sociology

| Industry | Median Earnings | Workforce |
|---|---|---|
| Educational Services | $72,160 | 16,760 |

BEST-PAYING METROPOLITAN AREAS

| Metro Area | Median Earnings | Workforce |
|---|---|---|
| Boston-Cambridge-Quincy, MA-NH | $95,660 | 410 |
| Philadelphia-Camden-Wilmington, PA-NJ-DE-MD | $84,400 | 400 |
| Washington-Arlington-Alexandria, DC-VA-MD-WV | $64,700 | 1,370 |
| Dallas–Fort Worth–Arlington, TX | $54,270 | 360 |

and Anthropology; Law and Government; Geography; Communications and Media. **Certification/Licensure:** None.

**Personality Types:** Social–Enterprising–Artistic.

**Skills:** Science; writing; speaking; instructing; learning strategies; operations analysis; reading comprehension; active learning.

**Physical Environment:** Indoors; sitting. **Structural Environment:** Freedom to make decisions; structured versus unstructured work; importance of being exact or accurate; frequency of decision making; impact of decisions on coworkers or company results; level of competition.

JOB SPECIALIZATION: PSYCHOLOGY TEACHERS, POSTSECONDARY

**Teach courses in psychology, such as child, clinical, and developmental psychology, and psychological counseling.**

- Average annual earnings: $68,020
- Middle 50% of earners: $50,340–$90,190
- Earnings growth potential: High (47.4%)

BEST-PAYING INDUSTRIES

| Industry | Median Earnings | Workforce |
|---|---|---|
| Educational Services | $68,000 | 38,040 |

BEST-PAYING METROPOLITAN AREAS

| Metro Area | Median Earnings | Workforce |
|---|---|---|
| Los Angeles–Long Beach–Santa Ana, CA | $83,130 | 1,410 |
| Boston-Cambridge-Quincy, MA-NH | $77,480 | 800 |
| New York–Northern New Jersey–Long Island, NY-NJ-PA | $77,240 | 2,640 |
| San Francisco–Oakland–Fremont, CA | $72,510 | 940 |
| Philadelphia-Camden-Wilmington, PA-NJ-DE-MD | $72,050 | 830 |
| Chicago-Naperville-Joliet, IL-IN-WI | $62,390 | 810 |

**Major Work Tasks:** Prepare and deliver lectures to undergraduate or graduate students on topics, such as abnormal psychology, cognitive processes, and work motivation. Develop and use multimedia course materials and other current technology, such as online courses. Provide clinical services to clients, such as assessing psychological problems and conducting psychotherapy. Review books and journal articles for potential publication. Supervise students' laboratory work. Supervise the clinical work of practicum students. (Also, perform the tasks listed for Teachers, Postsecondary.)

**Relevant Educational Programs:** Applied Behavior Analysis; Applied Psychology; Clinical Psychology; Clinical, Counseling and Applied Psychology, Other; Cognitive Psychology and Psycholinguistics; Community Psychology; Comparative Psychology; Counseling Psychology; Developmental and Child Psychology; Educational Psychology; Experimental Psychology; Industrial and Organizational Psychology; Marriage and Family Therapy/Counseling; Personality Psychology; Physiological Psychology/Psychobiology; Psychology, General; Psychology, Other; Psychometrics and Quantitative Psychology; Research and Experimental Psychology, Other; School Psychology; Social Psychology; Social Science Teacher Education. **Related Knowledge/Courses:** Psychology; Therapy and Counseling; Philosophy and Theology; Sociology and Anthropology; Education and Training; Biology. **Certification/Licensure:** None.

**Personality Types:** Social–Investigative–Artistic.

**Skills:** Science; learning strategies; writing; social perceptiveness; speaking; instructing; reading comprehension; active learning.

**Physical Environment:** Indoors; sitting. **Structural Environment:** Freedom to make decisions; structured versus unstructured work; importance of being exact or accurate; level of competition; impact of decisions on co-workers or company results; frequency of decision making.

### JOB SPECIALIZATION: RECREATION AND FITNESS STUDIES TEACHERS, POSTSECONDARY

**Teach courses pertaining to recreation, leisure, and fitness studies, including exercise physiology and facilities management.**

- Average annual earnings: $57,920
- Middle 50% of earners: $40,760–$79,940
- Earnings growth potential: Very high (52.8%)

**Major Work Tasks:** Prepare and deliver lectures to undergraduate or graduate students on topics, such as anatomy, therapeutic recreation, and conditioning theory. Prepare stu-

### BEST-PAYING INDUSTRIES

| Industry | Median Earnings | Workforce |
|---|---|---|
| Educational Services | $68,080 | 19,240 |

### BEST-PAYING METROPOLITAN AREAS

| Metro Area | Median Earnings | Workforce |
|---|---|---|
| Los Angeles–Long Beach–Santa Ana, CA | $90,800 | 890 |
| New York–Northern New Jersey–Long Island, NY-NJ-PA | $67,140 | 860 |
| Philadelphia-Camden-Wilmington, PA-NJ-DE-MD | $60,760 | 410 |
| Phoenix-Mesa-Scottsdale, AZ | $32,010 | 670 |

dents to act as sports coaches. (Also, perform the tasks listed for Teachers, Postsecondary.)

**Relevant Educational Programs**: Health and Physical Education, General; Parks, Recreation, and Leisure Studies; Physical Education Teaching and Coaching; Sport and Fitness Administration/Management; Sports Studies. **Related Knowledge/Courses:** Education and Training; Therapy and Counseling; Biology; Sociology and Anthropology; Medicine and Dentistry; Psychology. **Certification/Licensure:** Certification if appropriate in specialty.

**Personality Types:** Social.

**Skills:** Learning strategies; science; instructing; writing; operations analysis; active learning; reading comprehension; speaking.

**Physical Environment:** Indoors; standing. **Structural Environment:** Freedom to make decisions; structured versus unstructured work; importance of being exact or accurate; impact of decisions on co-workers or company results; frequency of decision making; time pressure.

## JOB SPECIALIZATION: SOCIAL WORK TEACHERS, POSTSECONDARY

### Teach courses in social work.

- Average annual earnings: $63,250
- Middle 50% of earners: $49,670–$86,620
- Earnings growth potential: High (44.5%)

#### BEST-PAYING INDUSTRIES

| Industry | Median Earnings | Workforce |
|---|---|---|
| Educational Services | $63,250 | 9,810 |

#### BEST-PAYING METROPOLITAN AREAS

| Metro Area | Median Earnings | Workforce |
|---|---|---|
| Philadelphia-Camden-Wilmington, PA-NJ-DE-MD | $74,340 | 230 |
| Pittsburgh, PA | $70,740 | 300 |
| New York–Northern New Jersey–Long Island, NY-NJ-PA | $57,350 | 850 |
| Dallas–Fort Worth–Arlington, TX | $51,940 | 210 |

**Major Work Tasks:** Prepare and deliver lectures to undergraduate or graduate students on topics, such as family behavior, child and adolescent mental health, and social intervention evaluation. Supervise students' laboratory and field work. (Also, perform the tasks listed for Teachers, Postsecondary.)

**Relevant Educational Programs**: Clinical/Medical Social Work; Social Work; Social Work, Other. **Related Knowledge/Courses:** Therapy and Counseling; Sociology and Anthropology; Psychology; Philosophy and Theology; Education and Training; English Language. **Certification/Licensure:** License.

**Personality Types:** Social–Investigative.

**Skills:** Instructing; writing; active learning; speaking; learning strategies; reading comprehension; active listening; critical thinking.

**Physical Environment:** Indoors; sitting. **Structural Environment:** Freedom to make decisions; structured versus unstructured work; time pressure; frequency of decision making; impact of decisions on co-workers or company results; importance of being exact or accurate.

## JOB SPECIALIZATION: SOCIOLOGY TEACHERS, POSTSECONDARY

### Teach courses in sociology.

- Average annual earnings: $66,150
- Middle 50% of earners: $49,210–$89,330
- Earnings growth potential: High (46.5%)

#### BEST-PAYING INDUSTRIES

| Industry | Median Earnings | Workforce |
|---|---|---|
| Educational Services | $66,140 | 16,880 |

#### BEST-PAYING METROPOLITAN AREAS

| Metro Area | Median Earnings | Workforce |
|---|---|---|
| Boston-Cambridge-Quincy, MA-NH | $85,690 | 450 |
| Philadelphia-Camden-Wilmington, PA-NJ-DE-MD | $72,100 | 560 |
| Baltimore-Towson, MD | $68,060 | 340 |

**Major Work Tasks:** Prepare and deliver lectures to undergraduate or graduate students on topics, such as race and ethnic relations, measurement and data collection, and workplace social relations. Supervise students' laboratory and field work. (Also, perform the tasks listed for Teachers, Postsecondary.)

**Relevant Educational Programs**: Rural Sociology; Social Science Teacher Education; Sociology; Sociology and Anthropology. **Related Knowledge/Courses:** Sociology and Anthropology; Philosophy and Theology; History and Archeology; Education and Training; English

Language; Geography. **Certification/Licensure:** None.

**Personality Types:** Social–Investigative–Artistic.

**Skills:** Science; learning strategies; writing; instructing; speaking; reading comprehension; active learning; operations analysis.

**Physical Environment:** Indoors; sitting. **Structural Environment:** Freedom to make decisions; structured versus unstructured work; frequency of decision making; time pressure; level of competition; importance of being exact or accurate.

## Technical Writers

**Write technical materials, such as equipment manuals, appendices, or operating and maintenance instructions.**

- Average annual earnings: $65,500
- Middle 50% of earners: $49,910–$83,190
- Earnings growth potential: Medium (40.9%)
- Growth: 17.2%
- Annual job openings: 1,830
- Self-employed: 9.3%

**Considerations for Job Outlook:** Job opportunities, especially for applicants with technical skills, are expected to be good. The growing

### BEST-PAYING INDUSTRIES

| Industry | Median Earnings | Workforce |
|---|---|---|
| Publishing Industries (except Internet) | $72,250 | 3,670 |
| Computer and Electronic Product Manufacturing | $69,190 | 3,140 |
| Administrative and Support Services | $67,320 | 2,870 |
| Professional, Scientific, and Technical Services | $66,440 | 18,570 |

### BEST-PAYING METROPOLITAN AREAS

| Metro Area | Median Earnings | Workforce |
|---|---|---|
| San Jose–Sunnyvale–Santa Clara, CA | $99,690 | 1,200 |
| Seattle-Tacoma-Bellevue, WA | $88,030 | 1,300 |
| San Francisco–Oakland–Fremont, CA | $86,280 | 1,170 |
| Boston-Cambridge-Quincy, MA-NH | $79,670 | 1,810 |
| Washington-Arlington-Alexandria, DC-VA-MD-WV | $74,210 | 4,020 |
| Los Angeles–Long Beach–Santa Ana, CA | $70,850 | 1,500 |
| San Diego–Carlsbad–San Marcos, CA | $70,720 | 930 |
| New York–Northern New Jersey–Long Island, NY-NJ-PA | $70,630 | 2,700 |
| Philadelphia-Camden-Wilmington, PA-NJ-DE-MD | $70,550 | 1,130 |
| Chicago-Naperville-Joliet, IL-IN-WI | $64,380 | 1,000 |
| Dallas–Fort Worth–Arlington, TX | $63,590 | 1,220 |
| Detroit-Warren-Livonia, MI | $60,190 | 930 |

reliance on technologically sophisticated products in the home and the workplace and the increasing complexity of medical and scientific information needed for daily living will create many new job opportunities for technical writers. In addition to job openings stemming from employment growth, some openings will arise as experienced workers retire, transfer to other occupations, or leave the labor force. However, there will be competition among freelance technical writers.

**Major Work Tasks:** Organize material and complete writing assignment according to set standards regarding order, clarity, conciseness, style, and terminology. Maintain records and files of work and revisions. Edit, standardize, or make changes to material prepared by other writers or establishment personnel. Confer with customer representatives, vendors, plant executives, or publisher to establish technical specifications and to determine subject material to be developed for publication. Review published materials and recommend revisions or changes in scope, format, content, and methods of reproduction and binding. Select photographs, drawings, sketches, diagrams, and charts to illustrate material. Study drawings, specifications, mockups, and product samples to integrate and delineate technology, operating procedure, and production sequence and detail. Interview production and engineering personnel and read journals and other material to become familiar with product technologies and production methods. Observe production, developmental, and experimental activities to determine operating procedure and detail. Arrange for typing, duplication, and distribution of material. Assist in laying out material for publication. Analyze developments in specific field to determine need for revisions in previously published materials and development of new material. Review manufacturer's and trade catalogs, drawings and other data relative to operation, maintenance, and service of equipment. Draw sketches to illustrate specified materials or assembly sequence. Develop or maintain online help documentation.

**Usual Educational Requirement:** Bachelor's degree. **Relevant Educational Programs**: Business/Corporate Communications; Family and Consumer Sciences/Human Sciences Communication; Professional, Technical, Business, and Scientific Writing; Technical and Scientific Communication; Writing, General. **Related Knowledge/Courses:** Clerical Practices; Communications and Media; English Language; Computers and Electronics; Public

Safety and Security; Telecommunications. **Work Experience Needed:** 1 to 5 years. **On-the-Job Training Needed:** Short-term on-the-job training. **Certification/Licensure:** None.

**Personality Types:** Artistic–Investigative–Conventional. **Key Career Cluster:** 15 Science, Technology, Engineering, and Mathematics. **Key Career Pathway:** 15.1 Engineering and Technology.

**Skills:** Writing; reading comprehension; operations analysis; active learning; active listening; speaking; critical thinking; persuasion.

**Physical Environment:** Indoors; sitting; using hands; repetitive motions; noise. **Structural Environment:** Importance of being exact or accurate; importance of repeating same tasks; freedom to make decisions; time pressure; frequency of decision making; structured versus unstructured work.

## Training and Development Managers

**Plan, direct, or coordinate the training and development activities and staff of an organization.**

- Average annual earnings: $95,400
- Middle 50% of earners: $72,020–$126,720
- Earnings growth potential: Medium (43.3%)
- Growth: 14.6%
- Annual job openings: 1,160
- Self-employed: 2.7%

**Considerations for Job Outlook:** Across most industries, employment of training and development managers is expected to grow as companies develop and introduce new media and technology into their training programs. Job prospects will vary by organization, but opportunities for training and development managers should be best in the management, scientific, and technical consulting services industry. Training and development contracting firms are often better equipped with the technology and technical expertise to produce new training initiatives, so some organizations will likely contract out portions of their training or program development work to these companies. Those who have a master's degree, certification, or work experience in training and development, another human resource field, management, or teaching should have the best job prospects.

**Major Work Tasks:** Conduct orientation sessions and arrange on-the-job training for new hires. Evaluate instructor performance and the effectiveness of training programs, providing recommendations for improvement. Develop testing and evaluation procedures. Conduct or arrange for ongoing technical training and personal development classes for staff members. Confer with management and conduct surveys to identify training needs based on projected production processes, changes, and other factors. Develop and organize training manuals, multimedia visual aids, and other

### BEST-PAYING INDUSTRIES

| Industry | Median Earnings | Workforce |
|---|---|---|
| Professional, Scientific, and Technical Services | $109,090 | 2,760 |
| Management of Companies and Enterprises | $102,350 | 4,400 |
| Insurance Carriers and Related Activities | $98,780 | 1,590 |
| Hospitals | $96,260 | 1,670 |
| Credit Intermediation and Related Activities | $94,940 | 1,380 |
| Educational Services | $86,620 | 2,780 |
| Administrative and Support Services | $83,090 | 2,290 |
| Federal, State, and Local Government | $78,080 | 1,810 |

### BEST-PAYING METROPOLITAN AREAS

| Metro Area | Median Earnings | Workforce |
|---|---|---|
| New York–Northern New Jersey–Long Island, NY-NJ-PA | $122,390 | 2,610 |
| Philadelphia-Camden-Wilmington, PA-NJ-DE-MD | $120,940 | 620 |
| Boston-Cambridge-Quincy, MA-NH | $112,520 | 1,020 |
| Los Angeles–Long Beach–Santa Ana, CA | $110,630 | 1,010 |
| Washington-Arlington-Alexandria, DC-VA-MD-WV | $108,130 | 1,280 |
| Dallas–Fort Worth–Arlington, TX | $103,550 | 620 |
| Atlanta–Sandy Springs–Marietta, GA | $98,310 | 750 |
| Minneapolis–St. Paul–Bloomington, MN-WI | $92,940 | 740 |
| Chicago-Naperville-Joliet, IL-IN-WI | $91,050 | 1,340 |

educational materials. Plan, develop, and provide training and staff development programs using knowledge of the effectiveness of methods, such as classroom training, demonstrations, on-the-job training, meetings, conferences, and workshops. Analyze training needs to develop new training programs or modify and improve existing programs. Train instructors and supervisors in techniques and skills for training and dealing with employees. Prepare training budget for department or organization. Review and evaluate training and apprenticeship programs for compliance with government standards. Coordinate established courses with technical and professional courses provided by community schools and designate training procedures.

**Usual Educational Requirement:** Bachelor's degree. **Relevant Educational Program**: Hu-

456

man Resources Management/Personnel Administration, General. **Related Knowledge/ Courses:** Personnel and Human Resources; Education and Training; Sociology and Anthropology; Sales and Marketing; Therapy and Counseling; English Language. **Work Experience Needed:** 1 to 5 years. **On-the-Job Training Needed:** None. **Certification/Licensure:** Voluntary certification by association.

**Personality Types:** Enterprising–Social. **Key Career Cluster:** 04 Business, Management, and Administration. **Key Career Pathway:** 4.3 Human Resources.

**Skills:** Management of financial resources; learning strategies; management of personnel resources; instructing; systems evaluation; management of material resources; speaking; persuasion.

**Physical Environment:** Indoors; sitting. **Structural Environment:** Freedom to make decisions; structured versus unstructured work; time pressure; impact of decisions on co-workers or company results; frequency of decision making; importance of being exact or accurate.

## Transportation Inspectors

**Inspect equipment or goods in connection with the safe transport of cargo or people.**

- Average annual earnings: $63,680
- Middle 50% of earners: $43,510–$86,930
- Earnings growth potential: Very high (50.1%)
- Growth: 14.4%
- Annual job openings: 1,070
- Self-employed: 9.1%

**Considerations for Job Outlook:** About-average employment growth is projected.

**Major Work Tasks:** For tasks, see the job specializations.

**Usual Educational Requirement:** Some college, no degree. **Relevant Educational Program:** No

### BEST-PAYING INDUSTRIES

| Industry | Median Earnings | Workforce |
|---|---|---|
| Air Transportation | $69,240 | 1,520 |
| Rail Transportation | $58,700 | 4,290 |
| Support Activities for Transportation | $49,940 | 2,230 |
| Repair and Maintenance | $28,560 | 1,590 |

### BEST-PAYING METROPOLITAN AREAS

| Metro Area | Median Earnings | Workforce |
|---|---|---|
| Dallas–Fort Worth–Arlington, TX | $84,220 | 820 |
| Phoenix-Mesa-Scottsdale, AZ | $78,310 | 620 |
| New York–Northern New Jersey–Long Island, NY-NJ-PA | $68,300 | 3,470 |
| Los Angeles–Long Beach–Santa Ana, CA | $68,150 | 560 |
| Atlanta–Sandy Springs–Marietta, GA | $63,370 | 1,120 |
| Houston–Sugar Land–Baytown, TX | $57,910 | 570 |
| Chicago-Naperville-Joliet, IL-IN-WI | $55,290 | 740 |
| Seattle-Tacoma-Bellevue, WA | $28,750 | 670 |

related CIP programs; this job is learned through work experience in a related occupation. **Work Experience Needed:** None. **On-the-Job Training Needed:** Short-term on-the-job training. **Certification/Licensure:** Voluntary certification for some specializations.

**Key Career Cluster:** 07 Government and Public Administration. **Key Career Pathway:** 7.6 Regulation.

## JOB SPECIALIZATION: AVIATION INSPECTORS

**Inspect aircraft, maintenance procedures, air navigational aids, air traffic controls, and communications equipment to ensure conformance with federal safety regulations.**

**Major Work Tasks:** Inspect work of aircraft mechanics, performing maintenance, modification, or repair and overhaul of aircraft and aircraft mechanical systems to ensure adherence to standards and procedures. Examine aircraft access plates and doors for security. Examine landing gear, tires, and exteriors of fuselage, wings, and engines for evidence of damage or corrosion and the need for repairs. Prepare and maintain detailed repair, inspection, investigation, and certification records and reports. Inspect new, repaired, or modified aircraft to identify damage or defects and to assess airworthiness and conformance to standards, using checklists, hand tools, and test instruments. Examine maintenance records and flight logs to determine if service and maintenance checks and overhauls were performed at prescribed intervals. Start aircraft and observe gauges, meters, and other instruments to detect evidence of malfunctions. Recommend replacement, repair, or modification of aircraft equipment. Recommend changes in rules, policies, standards, and regulations, based on knowledge of operating conditions, aircraft improvements, and other factors. Investigate air accidents and complaints to determine causes. Observe flight activities of pilots to assess flying skills and to ensure conformance to flight and safety regulations. Conduct flight test programs to test equipment, instruments, and systems under a variety of conditions, using both manual and automatic controls. Approve or deny issuance of certificates of airworthiness. Analyze training programs and conduct oral and written examinations to ensure the competency of persons operating, installing, and repairing aircraft equipment. Schedule and coordinate in-flight testing programs with ground crews and air traffic control to ensure availability of ground tracking, equipment monitoring, and related services.

**Related Knowledge/Courses:** Mechanical Devices; Production and Processing; Transportation; Chemistry; Engineering and Technology; Physics.

**Personality Types:** Realistic–Conventional–Investigative.

**Skills:** Equipment maintenance; science; troubleshooting; repairing; equipment selection; operation monitoring; quality control analysis; operation and control.

**Physical Environment:** Indoors; sitting; noise; contaminants. **Structural Environment:** Importance of being exact or accurate; frequency of decision making; time pressure; freedom to make decisions; impact of decisions on co-workers or company results; importance of repeating same tasks.

## JOB SPECIALIZATION: FREIGHT AND CARGO INSPECTORS

**Inspect the handling, storage, and stowing of freight and cargoes.**

**Major Work Tasks:** Prepare and submit reports after completion of freight shipments. Inspect shipments to ensure that freight is securely braced and blocked. Record details about freight conditions, handling of freight, and any problems encountered. Advise crews in techniques of stowing dangerous and heavy cargo. Observe loading of freight to ensure that crews comply with procedures. Recommend remedial procedures to correct any violations found during inspections. Inspect loaded cargo, cargo lashed to decks or in storage facilities, and cargo handling devices to determine compliance with health and safety regulations and need for maintenance. Measure ships' holds and depths of fuel and water in tanks, using sounding lines and tape measures. Notify workers of any special treatment required for shipments. Direct crews to reload freight or to

458

insert additional bracing or packing as necessary. Check temperatures and humidities of shipping and storage areas to ensure that they are at appropriate levels to protect cargo. Determine cargo transportation capabilities by reading documents that set forth cargo loading and securing procedures, capacities, and stability factors. Read draft markings to determine depths of vessels in water. Issue certificates of compliance for vessels without violations. Write certificates of admeasurement that list details, such as designs, lengths, depths, and breadths of vessels, and methods of propulsion. Calculate gross and net tonnage, hold capacities, volumes of stored fuel and water, cargo weights, and ship stability factors, using mathematical formulas. Post warning signs on vehicles containing explosives or flammable or radioactive materials. Measure heights and widths of loads to ensure they will pass over bridges or through tunnels on scheduled routes. Time rolls of ships, using stopwatches. Determine types of licenses and safety equipment required, and compute applicable fees such as tolls and wharfage fees.

**Related Knowledge/Courses:** Transportation; Public Safety and Security; Engineering and Technology; Physics; Geography; Mechanical.

**Personality Types:** Realistic–Conventional.

**Skills:** Operation and control; quality control analysis; operation monitoring; science; management of personnel resources; troubleshooting; writing; time management.

**Physical Environment:** Outdoors; indoors; standing; noise; very hot or cold; bright or inadequate lighting. **Structural Environment:** Importance of being exact or accurate; structured versus unstructured work; freedom to make decisions; impact of decisions on coworkers or company results; frequency of decision making; time pressure.

## JOB SPECIALIZATION: TRANSPORTATION VEHICLE, EQUIPMENT AND SYSTEMS INSPECTORS, EXCEPT AVIATION

**Inspect and monitor transportation equipment, vehicles, or systems to ensure compliance with regulations and safety standards.**

**Major Work Tasks:** Inspect vehicles or other equipment for evidence of abuse, damage, or mechanical malfunction. Inspect vehicles or equipment to ensure compliance with rules, standards, or regulations. Examine transportation vehicles, equipment, or systems to detect damage, wear, or malfunction. Conduct vehicle or transportation equipment tests, using diagnostic equipment. Inspect repairs to transportation vehicles or equipment to ensure that repair work was performed properly. Prepare reports on investigations or inspections and actions taken. Issue notices and recommend corrective actions when infractions or problems are found. Investigate complaints regarding safety violations. Examine carrier operating rules, employee qualification guidelines, or carrier training and testing programs for compliance with regulations or safety standards. Investigate and make recommendations on carrier requests for waiver of federal standards. Review commercial vehicle logs, shipping papers, or driver and equipment records to detect any problems or to ensure compliance with regulations. Investigate incidents or violations, such as delays, accidents, and equipment failures. Negotiate with authorities, such as local government officials, to eliminate hazards along transportation routes. Evaluate new methods of packaging, testing, shipping, or transporting hazardous materials to ensure adequate public safety protection. Attach onboard diagnostics (OBD) scanner cables to vehicles to conduct emissions inspections. Compare emissions findings with applicable emissions standards. Conduct remote inspections of motor vehicles, using handheld controllers and remotely directed vehicle inspection devices. Conduct visual inspections of emission control equipment and smoke emitted from gasoline or diesel vehicles. Identify emissions testing procedures and standards appropriate for the age and technology of vehicles. Identify modifications to engines, fuel systems, emissions control equipment, or other vehicle systems to determine the impact of modifications on inspection procedures or conclusions.

**Related Knowledge/Courses:** Mechanical Devices; Transportation; Public Safety and Security; Engineering and Technology; Administration and Management; Physics.

**Personality Types:** Realistic–Conventional–Investigative.

**Skills:** Equipment maintenance; repairing; troubleshooting; science; operation and control; quality control analysis; operation monitoring; equipment selection.

**Physical Environment:** Outdoors; standing; walking and running; using hands; bending or twisting the body; repetitive motions. **Structural Environment:** Time pressure; impact of decisions on co-workers or company results; importance of being exact or accurate; freedom to make decisions; frequency of decision making; structured versus unstructured work.

## Transportation, Storage, and Distribution Managers

**Plan, direct, or coordinate transportation, storage, or distribution activities in accordance with organizational policies and applicable government laws or regulations.**

- Average annual earnings: $81,830
- Middle 50% of earners: $62,590–$107,540
- Earnings growth potential: Medium (41.3%)
- Growth: 10.0%

- Annual job openings: 3,370
- Self-employed: 6.2%

### BEST-PAYING INDUSTRIES

| Industry | Median Earnings | Workforce |
|---|---|---|
| Management of Companies and Enterprises | $96,740 | 6,780 |
| Federal, State, and Local Government | $92,250 | 12,700 |
| Merchant Wholesalers, Nondurable Goods | $75,610 | 8,820 |
| Truck Transportation | $75,390 | 9,990 |
| Warehousing and Storage | $75,260 | 8,230 |
| Merchant Wholesalers, Durable Goods | $74,950 | 6,550 |

### BEST-PAYING METROPOLITAN AREAS

| Metro Area | Median Earnings | Workforce |
|---|---|---|
| New York–Northern New Jersey–Long Island, NY-NJ-PA | $100,150 | 5,630 |
| Seattle-Tacoma-Bellevue, WA | $96,990 | 2,200 |
| Houston–Sugar Land–Baytown, TX | $94,440 | 2,750 |
| Dallas–Fort Worth–Arlington, TX | $87,180 | 2,800 |
| Los Angeles–Long Beach–Santa Ana, CA | $83,050 | 4,630 |
| Atlanta–Sandy Springs–Marietta, GA | $79,390 | 2,690 |
| Chicago-Naperville-Joliet, IL-IN-WI | $76,440 | 3,830 |

**Considerations for Job Outlook:** In courier services, a small decrease is expected as better technology and routing increase efficiency and decrease the demand for transportation workers and managers in this industry.

**Major Work Tasks:** For tasks, see the job specializations.

**Usual Educational Requirement:** High school diploma or equivalent. **Relevant Educational Programs**: Aeronautics/Aviation/Aerospace Science and Technology, General; Aviation/Airway Management and Operations; Business Administration and Management, General; Business/Commerce, General; Logistics, Materials, and Supply Chain Management; Public Administration; Transportation/Mobility Management. **Work Experience Needed:** More than 5 years. **On-the-Job Training Needed:** None. **Certification/Licensure:** None.

**Key Career Cluster:** 04 Business, Management, and Administration. **Key Career Pathway:** 4.1 Management.

### JOB SPECIALIZATION: LOGISTICS MANAGERS

**Plan, direct, or coordinate purchasing, warehousing, distribution, forecasting, customer service, or planning services. Manage logistics personnel and logistics systems and direct daily operations.**

**Major Work Tasks:** Train shipping department personnel in roles or responsibilities regarding global logistics strategies. Maintain metrics, reports, process documentation, customer service logs, or training or safety records. Implement specific customer requirements, such as internal reporting or customized transportation metrics. Resolve problems concerning transportation, logistics systems, imports or exports, or customer issues. Develop risk management programs to ensure continuity of supply in emergency scenarios. Plan or implement improvements to internal or external logistics systems or processes. Recommend optimal transportation modes, routing, equipment, or frequency. Participate in carrier management processes, such as selection, qualification, or performance evaluation. Negotiate transportation rates or services. Monitor product import or export processes to ensure compliance with regulatory or legal requirements. Establish or monitor specific supply chain-based performance measurement systems. Ensure carrier compliance with company policies or procedures for product transit or delivery. Direct distribution center operation to ensure achievement of cost, productivity, accuracy, or timeliness objectives. Create policies or procedures for logistics activities. Collaborate with other departments to integrate logistics with business systems or processes, such as customer sales, order management, accounting, or shipping. Analyze the financial impact of proposed logistics changes, such as routing, shipping modes, product volumes or mixes, or carriers. Supervise the work of logistics specialists, planners, or schedulers. Plan or implement material flow management systems to meet production requirements. Direct inbound or outbound logistics operations, such as transportation or warehouse activities, safety performance, or logistics quality management. Analyze all aspects of corporate logistics to determine the most cost-effective or efficient means of transporting products or supplies.

**Related Knowledge/Courses:** Transportation; Production and Processing; Geography; Administration and Management; Economics and Accounting; Personnel and Human Resources.

**Personality Types:** Enterprising–Conventional.

**Skills:** Management of financial resources; management of material resources; management of personnel resources; negotiation; time management; systems evaluation; monitoring; operations analysis.

**Physical Environment:** Indoors; sitting. **Structural Environment:** Freedom to make decisions; time pressure; importance of being exact or ac-

461

curate; structured versus unstructured work; impact of decisions on co-workers or company results; frequency of decision making.

**JOB SPECIALIZATION: STORAGE AND DISTRIBUTION MANAGERS**

**Plan, direct, and coordinate the storage and distribution operations within organizations or the activities of organizations that are engaged in storing and distributing materials and products.**

**Major Work Tasks:** Supervise the activities of workers engaged in receiving, storing, testing, and shipping products or materials. Plan, develop, or implement warehouse safety and security programs and activities. Review invoices, work orders, consumption reports, or demand forecasts to estimate peak delivery periods and to issue work assignments. Schedule or monitor air or surface pickup, delivery, or distribution of products or materials. Interview, select, and train warehouse and supervisory personnel. Confer with department heads to coordinate warehouse activities, such as production, sales, records control, or purchasing. Respond to customers' or shippers' questions and complaints regarding storage and distribution services. Inspect physical conditions of warehouses, vehicle fleets, or equipment and order testing, maintenance, repairs, or replacements. Develop and document standard and emergency operating procedures for receiving, handling, storing, shipping, or salvaging products or materials. Issue shipping instructions and provide routing information to ensure that delivery times and locations are coordinated. Prepare and manage departmental budgets. Prepare or direct preparation of correspondence, reports, and operations, maintenance, and safety manuals. Track and trace goods while they are en route to their destinations, expediting orders when necessary. Develop or implement plans for facility modification or expansion, such as equipment purchase or changes in space allocation

or structural design. Examine products or materials to estimate quantities or weight and type of container required for storage or transport. Negotiate with carriers, warehouse operators, or insurance company representatives for services and preferential rates. Examine invoices and shipping manifests for conformity to tariff and customs regulations. Arrange for necessary shipping documentation and contact customs officials to effect release of shipments. Advise sales and billing departments of transportation charges for customers' accounts. Evaluate freight or inventory costs associated with transit times to ensure that costs are appropriate. Participate in setting transportation and service rates.

**Related Knowledge/Courses:** Transportation; Personnel and Human Resources; Production and Processing; Administration and Management; Economics and Accounting; Public Safety and Security.

**Personality Types:** Enterprising–Conventional.

**Skills:** Management of financial resources; management of material resources; operations analysis; management of personnel resources; negotiation; coordination; operation and control; persuasion.

**Physical Environment:** Indoors; standing.
**Structural Environment:** Time pressure; importance of being exact or accurate; freedom to make decisions; frequency of decision making; structured versus unstructured work; impact of decisions on co-workers or company results.

**JOB SPECIALIZATION: TRANSPORTATION MANAGERS**

**Plan, direct, and coordinate the transportation operations within an organization or the activities of organizations that provide transportation services.**

**Major Work Tasks:** Direct activities related to dispatching, routing, or tracking transportation vehicles, such as aircraft or railroad cars.

Plan, organize, or manage the work of subordinate staff to ensure that the work is accomplished in a manner consistent with organizational requirements. Direct investigations to verify and resolve customer or shipper complaints. Serve as contact persons for all workers within assigned territories. Implement schedule and policy changes. Collaborate with other managers or staff members to formulate and implement policies, procedures, goals, or objectives. Monitor operations to ensure that staff members comply with administrative policies and procedures, safety rules, union contracts, and government regulations. Promote safe work activities by conducting safety audits, attending company safety meetings, or meeting with individual staff members. Monitor spending to ensure that expenses are consistent with approved budgets. Direct and coordinate, through subordinates, activities of operations department to obtain use of equipment, facilities, and human resources. Analyze expenditures and other financial information to develop plans, policies, or budgets for increasing profits or improving services. Negotiate and authorize contracts with equipment and materials suppliers, and monitor contract fulfillment. Supervise workers assigning tariff classifications and preparing billing. Set operations policies and standards, including determining safety procedures for the handling of dangerous goods. Recommend or authorize capital expenditures for acquisition of new equipment or property to increase efficiency and services of operations department. Prepare management recommendations, such as proposed fee and tariff increases or schedule changes. Conduct employee training sessions on subjects such as hazardous material handling, employee orientation, quality improvement, or computer use. Direct procurement processes, including equipment research and testing, vendor contracts, or requisitions approval. Develop criteria, application instructions, procedural manuals, or contracts for federal or state public transportation programs.

**Related Knowledge/Courses:** Transportation; Geography; Production and Processing; Personnel and Human Resources; Administration and Management; Economics and Accounting.

**Personality Types:** Enterprising–Conventional.

**Skills:** Management of financial resources; systems evaluation; negotiation; systems analysis; social perceptiveness; operations analysis; management of material resources; management of personnel resources.

**Physical Environment:** Indoors; sitting. **Structural Environment:** Freedom to make decisions; frequency of decision making; structured versus unstructured work; time pressure; impact of decisions on co-workers or company results; importance of being exact or accurate.

## Urban and Regional Planners

**Develop comprehensive plans and programs for use of land and physical facilities of jurisdictions, such as towns, cities, counties, and metropolitan areas.**

- Average annual earnings: $65,230
- Middle 50% of earners: $51,740–$81,630
- Earnings growth potential: Medium (36.4%)
- Growth: 16.2%
- Annual job openings: 1,680
- Self-employed: 1.7%

**Considerations for Job Outlook:** Job opportunities for planners often depend on economic conditions. When municipalities and developers have funds for development projects, planners are in higher demand. However, planners may face strong competition for jobs in an economic downturn, when there is less funding for development work. Although government funding issues will affect employment of planners in the short term, job prospects should im-

**BEST-PAYING INDUSTRIES**

| Industry | Median Earnings | Workforce |
|---|---|---|
| Professional, Scientific, and Technical Services | $69,860 | 8,280 |
| Federal, State, and Local Government | $64,100 | 28,800 |

**BEST-PAYING METROPOLITAN AREAS**

| Metro Area | Median Earnings | Workforce |
|---|---|---|
| Sacramento–Arden-Arcade–Roseville, CA | $81,620 | 790 |
| San Francisco–Oakland–Fremont, CA | $80,970 | 2,120 |
| Seattle-Tacoma-Bellevue, WA | $76,310 | 1,610 |
| Los Angeles–Long Beach–Santa Ana, CA | $75,770 | 2,700 |
| Boston-Cambridge-Quincy, MA-NH | $67,030 | 1,130 |

prove over the 2010–2020 decade. Planners will be needed to help plan, oversee, and carry out development projects that were deferred because of poor economic conditions. Combined with the increasing demands of a growing population, long-term prospects for qualified planners should be good. Job prospects will be best for those with a master's degree from an accredited planning program and relevant work experience. Planners who are willing to relocate for work also will have more job opportunities.

**Major Work Tasks:** Design, promote, or administer government plans or policies affecting land use, zoning, public utilities, community facilities, housing, or transportation. Recommend approval, denial, or conditional approval of proposals. Determine the effects of regulatory limitations on projects. Assess the feasibility of proposals and iden-

tify necessary changes. Create, prepare, or requisition graphic or narrative reports on land use data, including land area maps overlaid with geographic variables, such as population density. Advise planning officials on project feasibility, cost-effectiveness, regulatory conformance, or possible alternatives. Conduct field investigations, surveys, impact studies, or other research to compile and analyze data on economic, social, regulatory, or physical factors affecting land use. Discuss with planning officials the purpose of land use projects, such as transportation, conservation, residential, commercial, industrial, or community use. Keep informed about economic or legal issues involved in zoning codes, building codes, or environmental regulations. Mediate community disputes or assist in developing alternative plans or recommendations for programs or projects. Coordinate work with economic consultants or architects during the formulation of plans or the design of large pieces of infrastructure. Review and evaluate environmental impact reports pertaining to private or public planning projects or programs. Hold public meetings with government officials, social scientists, lawyers, developers, the public, or special interest groups to formulate, develop, or address issues regarding land use or community plans. Supervise or coordinate the work of urban planning technicians or technologists. Investigate property availability. Advocate for sustainability to community groups, government agencies, the general public, or special interest groups. Develop plans for public or alternative transportation systems for urban or regional locations to reduce carbon output associated with transportation. Evaluate proposals for infrastructure projects or other development for environmental impact or sustainability.

**Usual Educational Requirement:** Master's degree. **Relevant Educational Programs:** City/Urban, Community and Regional Planning; Real Estate Development; Urban Studies/Affairs. **Related Knowledge/Courses:** Geography; History and Archeology; Transportation; Design; Law and Government; Building and Construction. **Work Experience Needed:** None. **On-the-Job Training Needed:** None. **Certification/Licensure:** Voluntary certification by association.

**Personality Types:** Investigative–Enterprising–Artistic. **Key Career Cluster:** 07 Government and Public Administration. **Key Career Pathway:** 7.4 Planning.

**Skills:** Systems analysis; operations analysis; management of financial resources; science; systems evaluation; judgment and decision making; mathematics; programming.

**Physical Environment:** Indoors; sitting; noise. **Structural Environment:** Structured versus unstructured work; time pressure; freedom to make decisions; frequency of decision making; impact of decisions on co-workers or company results; importance of being exact or accurate.

## Veterinarians

Diagnose, treat, or research diseases and injuries of animals.

- Average annual earnings: $84,460
- Middle 50% of earners: $67,040–$108,640
- Earnings growth potential: Medium (39.0%)
- Growth: 35.9%
- Annual job openings: 3,420
- Self-employed: 9.3%

**Considerations for Job Outlook:** Overall job opportunities for veterinarians are expected to be good. Although veterinary medicine is growing quickly, there are only 28 accredited veterinary programs in the United States, which produce a limited number of graduates—about 2,500—each year. However, most veterinary graduates are attracted to companion animal care, so job opportunities in that field will be fewer than in other areas. Job opportunities in

### BEST-PAYING INDUSTRIES

| Industry | Median Earnings | Workforce |
|---|---|---|
| Professional, Scientific, and Technical Services | $84,560 | 51,910 |

### BEST-PAYING METROPOLITAN AREAS

| Metro Area | Median Earnings | Workforce |
|---|---|---|
| New York–Northern New Jersey–Long Island, NY-NJ-PA | $113,600 | 2,260 |
| Los Angeles–Long Beach–Santa Ana, CA | $106,260 | 1,410 |
| Washington-Arlington-Alexandria, DC-VA-MD-WV | $98,670 | 1,260 |
| Chicago-Naperville-Joliet, IL-IN-WI | $74,430 | 1,540 |

large animal practice, public health, and government should be best. Although jobs in farm animal care are not growing as quickly as those in companion animal care, opportunities will be better because fewer veterinarians compete to work with large animals. There also will be excellent job opportunities for government veterinarians in food safety, animal health, and public health.

**Major Work Tasks:** Examine animals to detect and determine the nature of diseases or injuries. Treat sick or injured animals by prescribing medication, setting bones, dressing wounds, or performing surgery. Inoculate animals against various diseases, such as rabies or distemper. Collect body tissue, feces, blood, urine, or other body fluids for examination and analysis. Operate diagnostic equipment, such as radiographic or ultrasound equipment, and interpret the resulting images. Educate the public about diseases that can be spread from animals to humans. Train or supervise workers who handle or care for animals. Euthanize animals. Establish or conduct quarantine or testing procedures that prevent the spread of diseases to other animals or to humans and that comply with applicable government regulations. Conduct postmortem studies and analyses to determine the causes of animals' deaths. Plan or execute animal nutrition or reproduction programs. Research diseases to which animals could be susceptible. Advise animal owners regarding sanitary measures, feeding, general care, medical conditions, or treatment options. Attend lectures, conferences, or continuing education courses. Perform administrative or business management tasks, such as scheduling appointments, accepting payments from clients, budgeting, or maintaining business records. Counsel clients about the deaths of their pets or about euthanasia decisions for their pets. Provide care to a wide range of animals or specialize in a particular species, such as horses or exotic birds. Direct the overall operations of animal hospitals, clinics, or mobile services to farms. Drive mobile clinic vans to farms so that health problems can be treated or prevented. Specialize in a particular type of treatment, such as dentistry, pathology, nutrition, surgery, microbiology, or internal medicine. Inspect and test horses, sheep, poultry, or other animals to detect the presence of communicable diseases. Inspect animal housing facilities to determine their cleanliness and adequacy. Determine the effects of drug therapies, antibiotics, or new surgical techniques by testing them on animals.

**Usual Educational Requirement:** Doctoral or professional degree. **Relevant Educational Programs**: Comparative and Laboratory Animal Medicine (Cert., MS, PhD); Laboratory Animal Medicine; Large Animal/Food Animal and Equine Surgery and Medicine (Cert., MS, PhD); Poultry Veterinarian Residency Program;

Small/Companion Animal Surgery and Medicine (Cert., MS, PhD); Theriogenology; Veterinary Anatomy (Cert., MS, PhD); Veterinary Anesthesiology; Veterinary Behaviorist Residency Program; Veterinary Biomedical and Clinical Sciences, Other (Cert., MS, PhD); Veterinary Clinical Pharmacology Residency Program; Veterinary Dentistry; Veterinary Dermatology; Veterinary Emergency and Critical Care Medicine; Veterinary Infectious Diseases (Cert., MS, PhD); Veterinary Internal Medicine; Veterinary Medicine (DVM); Veterinary Microbiology; Veterinary Microbiology and Immunobiology (Cert., MS, PhD); Veterinary Nutrition; Veterinary Ophthalmology; Veterinary Pathology; Veterinary Pathology and Pathobiology (Cert., MS, PhD); Veterinary Physiology (Cert., MS, PhD); Veterinary Practice; others. **Related Knowledge/Courses:** Medicine and Dentistry; Biology; Chemistry; Sales and Marketing; Therapy and Counseling; Customer and Personal Service. **Work Experience Needed:** None. **On-the-Job Training Needed:** None. **Certification/Licensure:** Licensure; also certification in some specializations.

**Personality Types:** Investigative–Realistic. **Key Career Cluster:** 01 Agriculture, Food, and Natural Resources. **Key Career Pathway:** 1.3 Animal Systems.

**Skills:** Science; reading comprehension; operations analysis; instructing; service orientation; writing; active learning; judgment and decision making.

**Physical Environment:** Indoors; standing; using hands; noise; contaminants; exposed to radiation. **Structural Environment:** Frequency of decision making; freedom to make decisions; impact of decisions on co-workers or company results; consequence of error; structured versus unstructured work; importance of being exact or accurate.

## Zoologists and Wildlife Biologists

**Study the origins, behavior, diseases, genetics, and life processes of animals and wildlife.**

- Average annual earnings: $57,710
- Middle 50% of earners: $45,790–$73,010
- Earnings growth potential: Medium (35.7%)
- Growth: 7.4%
- Annual job openings: 590
- Self-employed: 4.6%

### BEST-PAYING INDUSTRIES

| Industry | Median Earnings | Workforce |
|---|---|---|
| Federal, State, and Local Government | $58,590 | 11,760 |
| Professional, Scientific, and Technical Services | $58,430 | 4,060 |
| Educational Services | $54,520 | 1,130 |

### BEST-PAYING METROPOLITAN AREAS

| Metro Area | Median Earnings | Workforce |
|---|---|---|
| Seattle-Tacoma-Bellevue, WA | $68,600 | 950 |
| Los Angeles–Long Beach–Santa Ana, CA | $68,560 | 510 |
| Portland-Vancouver-Beaverton, OR-WA | $67,520 | 660 |
| San Diego–Carlsbad–San Marcos, CA | $56,760 | 430 |

**Considerations for Job Outlook:** Zoologists and wildlife biologists should have good job opportunities. In addition to job growth, many job openings will be created by zoologists and wildlife biologists who retire, advance to management positions, or change careers. Year to year, the number of job openings available in local, state, and federal government agencies, such as the United States Fish and Wildlife Service, will vary based on the budgets for these agencies.

**Major Work Tasks:** Study animals in their natural habitats, assessing effects of environment and industry on animals, interpreting findings, and recommending alternative operating conditions for industry. Inventory or estimate plant and wildlife populations. Make recommendations on management systems and planning for wildlife populations and habitat, consulting with stakeholders and the public at large to explore options. Disseminate information by writing reports and scientific papers or journal articles and by making presentations and giving talks for schools, clubs, interest groups, and park interpretive programs. Study characteristics of animals, such as origin, interrelationships, classification, life histories and diseases, development, genetics, and distribution. Organize and conduct experimental studies with live animals in controlled or natural surroundings. Inform and respond to public regarding wildlife and conservation issues, such as plant identification, hunting ordinances, and nuisance wildlife. Analyze characteristics of animals to identify and classify them. Perform administrative duties, such as fundraising, public relations, budgeting, and supervision of zoo staff. Oversee the care and distribution of zoo animals, working with curators and zoo directors to determine the best way to contain animals, maintain their habitats, and manage facilities. Coordinate preventive programs to control the outbreak of wildlife diseases. Prepare collections of preserved specimens or microscopic slides for species identification and study of development or disease. Raise specimens for study and observation or for use in experiments. Collect and dissect animal specimens and examine specimens under microscope. Check for, and ensure compliance with, environmental laws and notify law enforcement when violations are identified.

**Usual Educational Requirement:** Bachelor's degree. **Relevant Educational Programs**: Animal Behavior and Ethology; Animal Physiology; Ecology; Entomology; Marine Sciences; Wildlife Biology; Wildlife, Fish, and Wildlands Science and Management; Zoology/Animal Biology; Zoology/Animal Biology, Other. **Related Knowledge/Courses:** Biology; Geography; Clerical Practices; Chemistry; Computers and Electronics; Education and Training. **Work Experience Needed:** None. **On-the-Job Training Needed:** None. **Certification/Licensure:** None.

**Personality Types:** Investigative–Realistic. **Key Career Cluster:** 01 Agriculture, Food, and Natural Resources. **Key Career Pathway:** 1.3 Animal Systems.

**Skills:** Science; writing; reading comprehension; systems evaluation; systems analysis; time management; operation and control; mathematics.

**Physical Environment:** Indoors; outdoors; sitting. **Structural Environment:** Structured versus unstructured work; impact of decisions on co-workers or company results; importance of being exact or accurate; freedom to make decisions; frequency of decision making; time pressure.

# Definitions of Key Terms in the Part II Descriptions

The terms used for skills and knowledge/courses in the part II descriptions are taken directly from the O*NET database. Because these terms may not be completely clear to you, here are definitions.

## Skills

**Active learning:** Understanding the implications of new information for both current and future problem solving and decision making.

**Active listening:** Giving full attention to what other people are saying, taking time to understand the points being made, asking questions as appropriate, and not interrupting at inappropriate times.

**Complex problem solving:** Identifying complex problems and reviewing related information to develop and evaluate options and implement solutions.

**Coordination:** Adjusting actions in relation to others' actions.

**Critical thinking:** Using logic and reasoning to identify the strengths and weaknesses of alternative solutions, conclusions, or approaches to problems.

**Equipment maintenance:** Performing routine maintenance on equipment and determining when and what kind of maintenance is needed.

**Equipment selection:** Determining the kind of tools and equipment needed to do a job.

**Installation:** Installing equipment, machines, wiring, or programs to meet specifications.

**Instructing:** Teaching others how to do something.

**Judgment and decision making:** Considering the relative costs and benefits of potential actions to choose the most appropriate one.

**Learning strategies:** Selecting and using training or instructional methods and procedures appropriate for the situation when learning or teaching new things.

**Management of financial resources:** Determining how money will be spent to get the work done and accounting for these expenditures.

**Management of material resources:** Obtaining and seeing to the appropriate use of equipment, facilities, and materials needed to do certain work.

**Management of personnel resources:** Motivating, developing, and directing people as they work, identifying the best people for the job.

**Mathematics:** Using mathematics to solve problems.

469

**Monitoring:** Monitoring and assessing performance of yourself, other individuals, or organizations to make improvements or take corrective action.

**Negotiation:** Bringing others together and trying to reconcile differences.

**Operation and control:** Controlling operations of equipment or systems.

**Operation monitoring:** Watching gauges, dials, or other indicators to make sure a machine is working properly.

**Operations analysis:** Analyzing needs and product requirements to create a design.

**Persuasion:** Persuading others to change their minds or behavior.

**Programming:** Writing computer programs for various purposes.

**Quality control analysis:** Conducting tests and inspections of products, services, or processes to evaluate quality or performance.

**Reading comprehension:** Understanding written sentences and paragraphs in work related documents.

**Repairing:** Repairing machines or systems using the needed tools.

**Science:** Using scientific rules and methods to solve problems.

**Service orientation:** Actively looking for ways to help people.

**Social perceptiveness:** Being aware of others' reactions and understanding why they react as they do.

**Speaking:** Talking to others to convey information effectively.

**Systems analysis:** Determining how a system should work and how changes in conditions, operations, and the environment will affect outcomes.

**Systems evaluation:** Identifying measures or indicators of system performance and the actions needed to improve or correct performance relative to the goals of the system.

**Technology design:** Generating or adapting equipment and technology to serve user needs.

**Time management:** Managing one's own time and the time of others.

**Troubleshooting:** Determining causes of operating errors and deciding what to do about it.

**Writing:** Communicating effectively in writing as appropriate for the needs of the audience.

## Knowledge/Courses

**Administration and Management:** Business and management principles involved in strategic planning, resource allocation, human resources modeling, leadership technique, production methods, and coordination of people and resources.

**Biology:** Plant and animal organisms, their tissues, cells, functions, interdependencies, and interactions with each other and the environment.

**Building and Construction:** Materials, methods, and the tools involved in the construction or repair of houses, buildings, or other structures such as highways and roads.

**Chemistry:** The chemical composition, structure, and properties of substances and of the chemical processes and transformations that they undergo. This includes uses of chemicals and their interactions, danger signs, production techniques, and disposal methods.

**Clerical Practices:** Administrative and clerical procedures and systems, such as word processing, managing files and records, stenography and transcription,

470

designing forms, and other office procedures and terminology.

**Communications and Media:** Media production, communication, and dissemination techniques and methods. This includes alternative ways to inform and entertain via written, oral, and visual media.

**Computers and Electronics:** Circuit boards, processors, chips, electronic equipment, and computer hardware and software, including applications and programming.

**Customer and Personal Service:** Principles and processes for providing customer and personal services. This includes customer needs assessment, meeting quality standards for services, and evaluation of customer satisfaction.

**Design:** Design techniques, tools, and principles involved in production of precision technical plans, blueprints, drawings, and models.

**Economics and Accounting:** Economic and accounting principles and practices, the financial markets, banking, and the analysis and reporting of financial data.

**Education and Training:** Principles and methods for curriculum and training design, teaching and instruction for individuals and groups, and the measurement of training effects.

**Engineering and Technology:** The practical application of engineering science and technology, including how to apply principles, techniques, procedures, and equipment to the design and production of various goods and services.

**English Language:** The structure and content of the English language including the meaning and spelling of words, rules of composition, and grammar.

**Fine Arts:** The theory and techniques required to compose, produce, and perform works of music, dance, visual arts, drama, and sculpture.

**Food Production:** Techniques and equipment for planting, growing, and harvesting food products (both plant and animal) for consumption, including storage and handling techniques.

**Foreign Language:** The structure and content of a foreign (non-English) language, including the meaning and spelling of words, rules of composition and grammar, and pronunciation.

**Geography:** Principles and methods for describing the features of land, sea, and air masses, including their physical characteristics, locations, interrelationships, and distribution of plant, animal, and human life.

**History and Archeology:** Historical events and their causes, indicators, and effects on civilizations and cultures.

**Law and Government:** Laws, legal codes, court procedures, precedents, government regulations, executive orders, agency rules, and the democratic political process.

**Mathematics:** Arithmetic, algebra, geometry, calculus, statistics, and their applications.

**Mechanical Devices:** Machines and tools, including their designs, uses, repair, and maintenance.

**Medicine and Dentistry:** The information and techniques needed to diagnose and treat human injuries, diseases, and deformities. This includes symptoms, treatment alternatives, drug properties and interactions, and preventive healthcare measures.

**Personnel and Human Resources:** Principles and procedures for personnel recruitment, selection, training, compensation and benefits, labor relations and negotiation, and personnel information systems.

471

**Philosophy and Theology:** Different philosophical systems and religions. This includes their basic principles, values, ethics, ways of thinking, customs, practices, and their impact on human culture.

**Physics:** Physical principles, laws, their interrelationships, and applications to understanding fluid, material, and atmospheric dynamics, and mechanical, electrical, atomic and sub-atomic structures and processes.

**Production and Processing:** Raw materials, production processes, quality control, costs, and other techniques for maximizing the effective manufacture and distribution of goods.

**Psychology:** Human behavior and performance; individual differences in ability, personality, and interests; learning and motivation; psychological research methods; and the assessment and treatment of behavioral and affective disorders.

**Public Safety and Security:** Relevant equipment, policies, procedures, and strategies to promote effective local, state, or national security operations for the protection of people, data, property, and institutions.

**Sales and Marketing:** Principles and methods for showing, promoting, and selling products or services. This includes marketing strategy and tactics, product demonstration, sales techniques, and sales control systems.

**Sociology and Anthropology:** Group behavior and dynamics, societal trends and influences, human migrations, ethnicity, and cultures and their history and origins.

**Telecommunications:** Transmission, broadcasting, switching, control, and operation of telecommunications systems.

**Therapy and Counseling:** Principles, methods, and procedures for diagnosis, treatment, and rehabilitation of physical and mental dysfunctions and for career counseling and guidance.

**Transportation:** Principles and methods for moving people or goods by air, rail, sea, or road, including the relative costs and benefits.

# CREDITS

Cover design: Sabine Groten
Cover photo: Thinkstock/iStock/Sergiy Palamarchuk
Layout and typesetting: Wish Publishing
Copy editing: Elizabeth Evans